Fodor's

ESSENTIAL
ISRAEL

WELCOME TO ISRAEL

Within its small perimeter Israel packs in abundant riches, from cherished religious sites and well-preserved archaeological treasures to spectacular natural wonders. Holy land to Jews, Christians, and Muslims, this is where biblical place-names like Jerusalem and the Galilee come vibrantly alive. Here, too, you can party by the Mediterranean in Tel Aviv, float in the super-salty Dead Sea, and explore cool mountain waterfalls or sweeping desert landscapes. Whether you're in a shrine or on a hiking trail, Israel is a place to renew the spirit.

TOP REASONS TO GO

★ **Jerusalem:** This unique, golden-stone city is the crossroads of three faiths.

★ **Ancient Sites:** Masada, Megiddo, Caesarea, and others reveal millennia of history.

★ **Open-Air Markets:** Bustling crowds, fragrant foods, and colorful artisan gifts beckon.

★ **Desert Adventures:** Memorable camel treks, jeep rides, and hikes await in the Negev.

★ **Local Food:** Falafel, hummus, grilled fish, and Israeli wine tempt the palate.

★ **Biblical Landscapes:** Around the Galilee, scenes evoke New Testament scriptures.

Fodor's ESSENTIAL ISRAEL

Design: Tina Malaney, *Associate Art Director*

Photography: Jennifer Arnow, *Senior Photo Editor*

Maps: Rebecca Baer, *Senior Map Editor*; David Lindroth, Mark Stroud and Harry Colomb (Moon Street Cartography), *Cartographers*

Production: Angela L. McLean, *Senior Production Manager*; Jennifer DePrima, *Editorial Production Manager*

Sales: Jacqueline Lebow, *Sales Director*

Business & Operations: Chuck Hoover, *Chief Marketing Officer*; Joy Lai, *Vice President and General Manager*; Stephen Horowitz, *Head of Business Development and Partnerships*

Writers: Inbal Baum, Shari Giddens Helmer, Mike Rogoff, Shira Rubin

Editor: Linda Cabasin

Production Editor: Carrie Parker

1st Edition

ISBN 978-0-14-754676-0

ISSN 2475–1251

All details in this book are based on information supplied to us at press time. Always confirm information when it matters, especially if you're making a detour to visit a specific place. Fodor's expressly disclaims any liability, loss, or risk, personal or otherwise, that is incurred as a consequence of the use of any of the contents of this book.

SPECIAL SALES

This book is available at special discounts for bulk purchases for sales promotions or premiums. For more information, e-mail specialmarkets@penguinrandomhouse.com.

PRINTED IN THE UNITED STATES OF AMERICA

10 9 8 7 6 5 4 3 2 1

CONTENTS

Fodor's Features

CONTENTS

MAPS

ABOUT THIS GUIDE

Fodor's Recommendations

Everything in this guide is worth doing—we don't cover what isn't—but exceptional sights, hotels, and restaurants are recognized with additional accolades. **Fodor's**Choice ★ indicates our top recommendations. Care to nominate a new place? Visit Fodors.com/contact-us.

Trip Costs

We list prices wherever possible to help you budget well. Hotel and restaurant price categories from $ to $$$$ are noted alongside each recommendation. For hotels, we include the lowest cost of a standard double room in high season. For restaurants, we cite the average price of a main course at dinner or, if dinner isn't served, at lunch. For attractions, we always list adult admission fees; discounts are usually available for children, students, and senior citizens.

Hotels

Our local writers vet every hotel to recommend the best overnights in each price category, from budget to expensive. Unless otherwise specified, you can expect private bath, phone, and TV in your room. For expanded hotel reviews, facilities, and deals visit Fodors.com.

Top Picks		Hotels &
★ **Fodor's**Choice		**Restaurants**
	🏨	Hotel
Listings		Number of
✉ Address		rooms
🖂 Branch address	🍽	Meal plans
☎ Telephone	W	Restaurant
🖷 Fax	⤸	Reservations
⊕ Website	🏛	Dress code
✍ E-mail	⊟	No credit cards
✑ Admission fee	💲	Price
⊙ Open/closed		
times	**Other**	
Ⓜ Subway	⇨	See also
⊹ Directions or	☞	Take note
Map coordinates	🏌	Golf facilities

Restaurants

Unless we state otherwise, restaurants are open for lunch and dinner daily. We mention dress code only when there's a specific requirement and reservations only when they're essential or not accepted. To make restaurant reservations, visit Fodors.com.

Credit Cards

The hotels and restaurants in this guide typically accept credit cards. If not, we'll say so.

EUGENE FODOR

Hungarian-born Eugene Fodor (1905–91) began his travel career as an interpreter on a French cruise ship. The experience inspired him to write *On the Continent* (1936), the first guidebook to receive annual updates and discuss a country's way of life as well as its sights. Fodor later joined the U.S. Army and worked for the OSS in World War II. After the war, he kept up his intelligence work while expanding his guidebook series. During the Cold War, many guides were written by fellow agents who understood the value of insider information. Today's guides continue Fodor's legacy by providing travelers with timely coverage, insider tips, and cultural context.

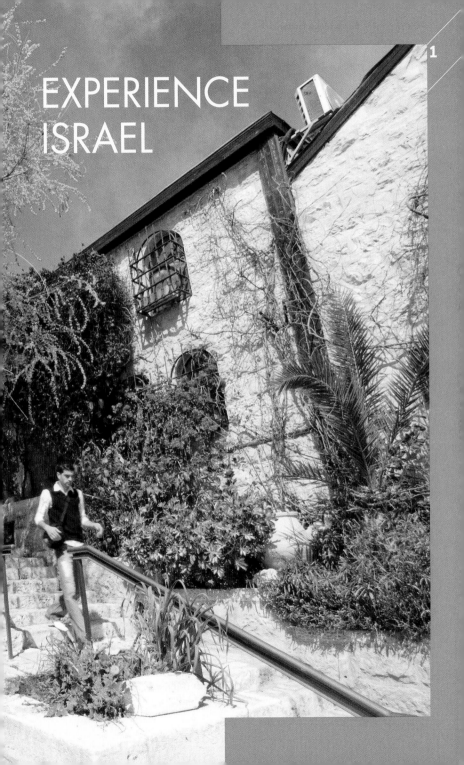

EXPERIENCE
ISRAEL

ISRAEL TODAY

Israelis are at once warmly hospitable and feisty. The country's ethnic, religious, and political mix, endlessly fascinating, can be exasperating as well. But, with legendary resilience, Israelis thrive on complexity, and life between the headlines is astonishingly normal.

A Vibrant Economy

Israel's founding fathers were socialists and its early economy largely agrarian. That's history, though. Agriculture today is sophisticated and technology-based, but its share of the country's exports is less than 3%, as the economy has burgeoned and reinvented itself.

With few natural resources—beyond newly discovered natural gas—the human factor was always crucial. Diamond cutting, an early initiative of Jewish refugees from wartime Holland and Belgium, supplies some 40% of the world's cut and polished stones and 20% of all Israel's exports. Tourism is big, of course, with 3.5 million visitors a year, mostly Holy Land pilgrims and Jewish "roots" travelers. The discovery of underwater gas fields off the coast of Haifa has Israel poised to become an energy exporter to Egypt and Jordan.

The real story of the last quarter century is high-tech. Israel is second only to the United States in the number of start-ups; computer systems, imaging, medical research, and biotech are leading specialties; and Israeli companies with attractive expertise are constantly being snapped up by big foreign corporations.

The country's financial environment, including vigilant bank regulation, has helped it weather global crises better than most. In 2010, Israel was accepted into the Organisation for Economic Cooperation and Development (OECD), yet the gap between the haves and have-nots is high, and one out of every five Israeli families lives below the poverty line.

The Palestine Conundrum

Relations between Israel and the Palestinians have always been fraught. There is mounting concern that time is running out for a "two-state solution," which envisages Israel and a viable sovereign Palestine state existing alongside each other. No other options have gotten widespread support on either side.

In 2012 the Palestinian Authority's president, Mahmoud Abbas, requested and received a status upgrade at the United Nations. The status changed from "nonmember observer entity" to "nonmember observer state," which seems to indicate that the U.N. might eventually consider recognizing Palestinian statehood. The Palestinian Authority controls the West Bank, one of two Palestinian territories. It has virtually no sway in Gaza, which is run by Hamas, Fatah's Islamist rivals who were locked in conflict with Israel in July and August of 2014.

The 2014 bout of fighting between Israel and Palestine has highlighted the rift in Palestinian society: Hamas-controlled Gaza continues to have conflicts with Israel while the Palestinian Authority–controlled West Bank makes tiny steps at the grassroots level of cooperation between Israeli and Palestinian entrepreneurs, artists, and teachers.

Beyond the Headlines

Israel is so often a source of breaking news that its life beyond the headlines seems like a well-kept secret. The big cities are very cosmopolitan; a vigorous Israeli film industry has won kudos and awards at international festivals; and the nationwide Book Week is a major cultural event. Classical orchestras, ensembles, and solo artists perform in Israel and abroad. Athletes have enjoyed occasional bright moments on the Olympic podium—though Israeli Paralympians are always among the medalists—and in European club basketball. Israel is a world-class chess nation, as Israelis proudly discovered when grandmaster Boris Gelfand challenged the world champion in 2012: the Israeli was just edged out in a sudden-death tiebreaker.

Academia is strong. Eight Israelis have been awarded Nobel Prizes since 2002—six in chemistry and two in economics. Innovative research groups continue to make important biological and medical breakthroughs, at the conceptual, technological, and pharmacological levels, for the treatment of cancer and many other diseases, in fields like nanotechnology and stem-cell treatment.

In the important business of Arab–Jewish relations (within Israel), much needs to be done; but there are joint business ventures, bilingual theater groups and bands, and interschool dialogue and collaborative projects.

Greening Israel

Israel's chronic water shortage has spurred the search for creative solutions. Drip irrigation is a clear winner; seawater desalination and wastewater treatment (an extraordinary 75% reclaimed) top up the reserves. Rooftop solar panels for domestic water heaters punctuate city skylines, and small solar-energy plants operate in the Negev Desert. Israel has embraced green concepts, developing and often exporting homegrown environmental products and technologies. Cities are widening their recycling programs, encouraging bikers, and improving public transportation. Organic produce is easier than ever to come by.

Judaism in Israel Today

There's no firm separation of religion and state in Israel. Matters of personal status—marriage, divorce, adoption, and conversion—are the preserve of the religious authorities of the community concerned. For this reason there's no civil marriage; if one partner doesn't convert to the faith of the other, the couple must marry abroad. Within the Jewish community, such functions fall under the supervision of the Orthodox chief rabbinate, much to the dismay of members of the tiny but growing Conservative and Reform movements and of the large number of nonobservant Jews.

Almost half of all Israeli Jews call themselves secular. The religiously observant—strict adherence to Sabbath laws and dietary laws, regular attendance at worship services, and so on—account for about 20%. At least another one-third of the Jewish population identify themselves as "traditional," meaning they observe some Jewish customs to some extent, often as a nod to Jewish heritage or a sense of family duty. Ultra-Orthodox (*haredi* in Hebrew) is the smaller of the two mainstreams that make up the Orthodox Jewish community; you can easily recognize the men by their black hats and garb. Their parallel universe embraces religion as a 24/7 lifestyle. Their independent school system, 80% government-funded, teaches only religious subjects. While some haredi men do go out to work, many have committed themselves to full-time study.

WHAT'S WHERE

Numbers refer to chapter numbers.

2 Jerusalem. The walls of the Old City embrace sites sacred to Judaism, Christianity, and Islam. Rub shoulders in the vibrant markets, sip coffee in a stone courtyard, and poke around the modern museums and tempting malls of a city that contains enough parallel universes to deserve to be called unique.

3 Around Jerusalem and the Dead Sea. Explore King Herod's mountaintop palace-citadel of Masada, float in the super-saline Dead Sea, or frolic under waterfalls in the Ein Gedi canyon. Bethlehem is another memorable option.

4 Tel Aviv. The "city that never sleeps" is Israel's cultural and entertainment center. Don't miss its beautiful beaches, lively seaside promenade, Bauhaus architecture, charming old neighborhoods, and first-class restaurants and nightlife.

5 Haifa and the Northern Coast. Although you're never far from a Mediterranean beach, take time to see the sights in Haifa, like the Baha'i Shrine and Gardens, and Akko's medieval Old City. South of Haifa are the impressive ruins of Roman Caesarea and the forested hills of Mount Carmel wine country.

6 Lower Galilee. Verdant valleys, rolling hills, and the freshwater Sea of Galilee are counterpoints to the historical riches in this region. Hike the Arbel cliffs, explore archaeology at Beit She'an and Zippori, and visit Nazareth and the famed sites of Jesus's ministry.

7 Upper Galilee and the Golan. Historical treasures, quaint B&Bs, and the great outdoors draw visitors to Israel's northeast corner. The mountaintop city of Tzfat (Safed), cradle of Jewish mysticism, and Rosh Pina, a delightful restored village, are major draws, as well as Tel Dan Nature Reserve.

8 Eilat and the Negev. Visiting the Negev is about experiencing the desert's quiet vistas and remarkable geological treasures, and enjoying Eilat's gorgeous beaches and Red Sea coral reefs. The massive Makhtesh Ramon (Ramon Crater) and the developing city of Beersheva present different views of this diverse area.

9 Petra. Take a side trip across the border to the remains of ancient Petra, in nearby Jordan, to see the magnificent temples and tombs carved out of red sandstone cliffs by the Nabatean people.

NEED TO KNOW

ISRAEL
Jerusalem
West Bank
Gaza
Mediterranean Sea

AT A GLANCE

Capital: Jerusalem

Population: 8,580,000

Currency: Israeli new shekel

Money: ATMs are common; credit cards widely accepted

Language: Hebrew

Country Code: 972

Emergencies: 100, 101, 102

Driving: On the right

Electricity: 220v/50 cycles; plugs have 3 round or flat prongs in a Y-shape

Time: Seven hours ahead of New York

Documents: Valid passport for stays up to 90 days

Mobile Phones: GSM (900 and 1800 bands), CDMA

Major Mobile Companies: Cellcom, Partner, Pelephone

WEBSITES

Ministry of Tourism:
⊕ www.goisrael.com

Nature and Parks Authority:
⊕ www.touristisrael.com

GETTING AROUND

✈ **Air Travel:** Israel's main airport, Ben Gurion International Airport, is a few miles southeast of Tel Aviv.

🚌 **Bus Travel:** Buses in Israel are comfortable and air-conditioned. Many have Wi-Fi. They run Sunday to Thursday from 5:30 am to 12:30 am.

🚗 **Car Travel:** Car rental rates are reasonable and roads well maintained, but Israelis can be aggressive drivers. You can hire a driver.

🚆 **Train Travel:** Many cities are easily accessible by train, although it's often faster to take the bus.

PLAN YOUR BUDGET

	HOTEL ROOM	MEAL	ATTRACTIONS
Low Budget	$150	NIS 30	Western Wall, Free
Mid Budget	$300	NIS 70	Israel Museum ticket, NIS 54
High Budget	$500	NIS 150	The Relaxation Pools at Dolphin Reef admission, NIS 195

WAYS TO SAVE

Avoid restaurants. Try the excellent prepared food from supermarkets and eat cheap local favorites, such as falafel and hummus.

Buy a park pass. Israel Nature and Parks Authority (⊕ www.parks.org.il) sells discounted passes to historic sites and nature reserves.

Take the bus. Whether you're going from city to city or simply getting around town, traveling by public transport is the cheapest way to go.

Take a walking tour. Some cities offer both self-guided and guided walking tours at no cost to visitors.

PLAN YOUR TIME

Hassle Factor	Medium. Flying time from New York is around 11 hours; from L.A., it's about 18 hours. International passengers must arrive at the airport three hours prior to departure to allow for security checks.
3 days	With only three days in Israel, you might find it easiest to base yourself in Jerusalem, stopping in Tel Aviv either on your way in or your way out of the country.
1 week	A week is enough time to explore the museums and experience the great nightlife in Tel Aviv, spend a few days in Jerusalem, Bethlehem, and the Galilee.
2 weeks	Two weeks is enough time to get a feel for Jerusalem, the Dead Sea, the Galilee, the Mediterranean Coast (including Tel Aviv and Akko), and either Eliat or the Negev.

WHEN TO GO

High Season: Israel has several high seasons, but each attracts different types of visitors. Tourism is high during Jewish and Christian holidays.

Low Season: July and August are the hottest months, and travelers are often put off by the sweltering temperatures, especially in areas of lower-lying elevation.

Value Season: May and June are in between high seasons, and prices are more affordable. The weather is still splendid, and historical sites and other attractions are yet to be filled with tourists.

BIG EVENTS

February and August: Eilat hosts some of the world's most-acclaimed jazz artists during the biannual Red Sea Jazz Festival ⊕ en.redseajazz.co.il.

March and April: Passover is a great time to visit Israel (though hotel prices rise), and many of the museums offer free admission during the Jewish holiday.

May and December: You'll hear folk music from around the world at the biannual Jacob's Ladder Festival. ⊕ www.jlfestival.com.

December: Christmas in Bethlehem is celebrated with numerous processions and special church services. Nazareth also hosts Christmas festivities.

READ THIS

■ **The Holy Land: An Oxford Archaeological Guide,** Jerome Murphy-O'Connor. A scholarly guide to the archaeological sites of Israel.

■ **How to Understand Israel in 60 Days or Less,** Sarah Glidden. A travelogue in graphic novel form.

■ **A Tale of Love and Darkness,** Amos Oz. An account of growing up in Jerusalem in the 1940s–50s.

WATCH THIS

■ **Ben Hur.** A classic film set in the Holy Land.

■ **Jellyfish.** An award-winning film about the lives of three women in Jerusalem.

■ **Ajami.** Stories of life in a mixed Muslim-Jewish neighborhood.

EAT THIS

■ **Falafel:** These deep-fried balls of chickpea flour are the nation's most-loved street food

■ **Matzoh balls:** Dumplings, often served in soup and popular during Passover

■ **Israeli salad:** A salad of diced cucumber and tomato, usually topped with onions, lemon, and olive oil

■ **Hummus:** A chickpea-and-tahini (sesame-seed paste) dip, commonly served with pita bread

ISRAEL MADE EASY

Customs of the Country

Western-style social graces aren't the strong suit of the average Israeli. But, despite the country's legendary informality, the traditions and customs of its many ethnic and religious communities form an entire corpus of social norms. Sensitivity to those norms can open doors; ignoring them may cause offense. The best example is the modest dress code required (especially for women) in conservative religious environments—Muslim holy places, some churches and monasteries, and (strictest of all) ultra-Orthodox Jewish shrines and neighborhoods. Covered shoulders, modest necklines, and either full-length pants or (safest) skirts below the knees are de rigueur.

Eating Out

Restaurants that abide by kosher dietary regulations, to satisfy a particular clientele, close for Friday dinner and Saturday lunch (Sabbath ends after dark). Kosher hotel eateries remain open, but do not serve menu items that require cooking on the spot. "Kosher" has nothing to do with particular cuisines but with certain restrictions (no pork or shellfish, no dairy and meat products on the same menu, and more). Kosher restaurants today not only have to compete with nonkosher rivals but also must satisfy an increasingly demanding kosher clientele, so the variety of kosher food is growing. Tipping is 12% minimum. Mostly, tips are expected in cash, but adding it to the bill is becoming more common, especially in Tel Aviv.

There's great coffee all over Israel. Latte is called *hafuch*; and if you want black coffee, ask for "filter" coffee or *Americano*. Tap water is safe throughout Israel.

Greetings

Israelis don't stand on ceremony and greet each other warmly with either a slap on the back (for men) or an air kiss on both cheeks (for women). Tourists are usually greeted with a handshake. Ultra-Orthodox Jewish men don't acknowledge women, and very religious Jews of either gender don't shake hands or mingle socially with members of the opposite sex.

Israelis are known for their bluntness. That openness extends to discussions on religion and politics, too, so don't be afraid to speak your mind (but expect candor in return).

The Jewish Sabbath

The Sabbath extends from sundown Friday until nightfall on Saturday. Most shops and restaurants in Jewish neighborhoods close, but Arab areas in Jerusalem's Old City, and towns like Nazareth and Akko still bustle. While Jerusalem quiets down by Friday afternoon, Tel Aviv remains lively, although bus services are suspended in both cities. Sunday is the first day of the regular work- and school week.

Language

Hebrew is the national language of Israel, but travelers can get by with English. Virtually every hotel has English-speaking staff, as do most restaurants and many shops in the major cities. In smaller towns and rural areas it might be more challenging. A few words of Hebrew, such as *toda* (thank you), *bevakasha* (please), and *shalom* (hello or goodbye) are warmly appreciated.

Arabic is Israel's other official language, spoken by Arabs, Druze, and a dwindling number of Jews with family roots in Arab lands. Because Israel is a nation of immigrants, mistakes and various accents are tolerated cheerfully.

Israelis use a lot of hand gestures when they talk. A common gesture is to turn the palm upwards and press the thumb and two fingers together to mean "wait a minute"; this has no negative connotations. Just as harmless is the Israeli who says "I don't believe you" to express that something is unbelievably wonderful.

Money and Shopping

The Israeli shekel (designated NIS) is the currency, but the U.S. dollar is accepted in places accustomed to dealing with tourists. At this writing, US$1 is equal to NIS 3.84. Rates for hotels, guiding services, and car rentals are always quoted and paid for in foreign currency, thus avoiding the 17% local V.A.T. Many better stores give a government V.A.T. refund on purchases above NIS 400, claimable at the airport duty-free or Jordanian border. Licensed exchange booths on busy streets or in shopping malls are convenient places to change money; banks have lines, unhelpful hours, and unattractive rates. Although ATM transaction fees may be higher abroad than at home, ATM rates are good because they're based on wholesale rates given by major banks. Avoid buying gold, silver, gemstones, and antiquities in bazaars (like Jerusalem's Old City souk), where things aren't always what they seem and prices fluctuate wildly.

Safety

Israel is news, it seems—for better or for worse. To be sure, there have been several major security situations over the last decade or so, but intense media coverage has sometimes exaggerated the scope and significance of a localized incident. Yet much of the populace seems unmoved. At this writing, the country is entirely calm, though there continue to be security concerns about the Palestinian Territories and some bordering countries. In Jerusalem, the Old City can be thronged during the day and virtually empty at night. Spend your evenings elsewhere. The Arab neighborhoods of East Jerusalem are perhaps not as welcoming as they were once, but unless there's some general security issue at the time, the daytime wanderer shouldn't encounter anything more serious than pickpockets.

At the time of this writing, Israeli authorities were barring their citizens from visiting Palestinian autonomous areas such as Bethlehem and Jericho, but tourists can take an Arab cab. Your concierge or Israeli tour guide may be able to set up a Palestinian guide on the other side. There are standard security checks along the roads to the West Bank, and car-rental companies generally don't allow their vehicles to cross into those areas.

Expect to have your handbags searched as a matter of course when you enter bus and train terminals, department stores, places of entertainment, museums, and public buildings. These checks are usually quick and courteous.

Visiting Sacred Sites

Muslim sites are generally closed for tourists on Friday, the Muslim holy day. Avoid the Muslim Quarter of Jerusalem's Old City between noon and 2 pm on Friday, when the flow of worshippers in the streets can be uncomfortable or even rowdy. Some Christian sites close on Sunday; others open after morning worship. Many Jewish religious sites, museums, and historical sites close early on Friday: some remain closed through Saturday (the Jewish Sabbath).

ISRAEL
TOP ATTRACTIONS

Old City of Jerusalem

(A) Its golden stones are saturated with history, sanctified by pilgrim prayers, and scarred by war. Explore the exotic medieval Church of the Holy Sepulcher, mingle with Jewish worshippers at the venerated Western Wall, and stroll the Haram esh-Sharif—the Temple Mount plaza—to view the golden Dome of the Rock. Pick your way through the alleyways and markets for great photo ops and a lesson in the challenges of coexistence.

Masada, the Dead Sea, and Ein Gedi

(B) Panoramic views and the ruins of King Herod's mountaintop palace-fortress are reason enough to climb Masada, as a predawn hike or by swift cable car, but the echoes of the Jewish rebellion against Rome make Masada what it is. Float in the hyperbrine of the nearby Dead Sea, and frolic in the oasis of Ein Gedi, with its waterfalls.

Israel Museum, Jerusalem

(C) This sprawling world-class museum boasts permanent exhibitions of the Dead Sea Scrolls, a quarter-acre model of ancient Jerusalem, and wings dedicated to archaeology, fine art, and Jewish life and art.

Jordan River Sources

(D) Rushing water and wild vegetation make the Upper Galilee panhandle one of Israel's most beautiful regions. The 3,000-year-old ruins of biblical Tel Dan overlook the Jordan River's largest tributary; and nearby Banias, with hiking trails alongside spectacular rapids, is Caesarea Philippi of the New Testament.

Tel Aviv

(E) Cosmopolitan and bustling, the city conveys the energy of modern Israel. There's the beach and promenade, a reinvented seaport, culture, great restaurants and nightlife, gentrified old 'hoods, and 1930s Bauhaus architecture.

Sea of Galilee

(F) This shimmering freshwater lake, known in Hebrew as the *Kinneret,* is linked to many events in the life of Jesus. Pilgrims flock to its shores, sail the waters, and gather for baptism at the River Jordan, where it leaves the lake.

Negev Desert Highlands

(G) The Negev highlands are full of surprises. The enormous Makhtesh Ramon (Ramon Crater) and two smaller ones are unique geological phenomena. The ruined town of Avdat pioneered desert water conservation 2,000 years ago. Ein Avdat is an exquisite spring-fed chalk canyon where ibex are often seen. Modern Israeli history, boutique wineries, and Jeeps and camels complete the picture.

Baha'i Shrine and Gardens

(H) Haifa is the world center for the Baha'i faith, and the magnificent landmark gold-domed Shrine of the Bab caps the tomb of its 19th-century prophet-herald. Free walking tours give the best appreciation of the manicured gardens that cascade down Mount Carmel.

Caesarea

(I) King Herod built the great port city more than 2,000 years ago. The renovated Roman theater is back in business; scuba enthusiasts can see elements of the Herodian port; and an ancient aqueduct slices across a beach. Crusader fortifications mix with latter-day restaurants and galleries to create a serene getaway.

Akko

(J) The picturesque port city has seen it all: Canaanites and Greeks, Crusaders and Napoléon, Turks and Brits. Visit the excellently preserved medieval quarters; browse the copperware shops; eat hummus and seafood; and explore the small port, the Turkish bathhouse, and the British prison from which Jewish resistance fighters broke out in the 1940s.

QUINTESSENTIAL ISRAEL

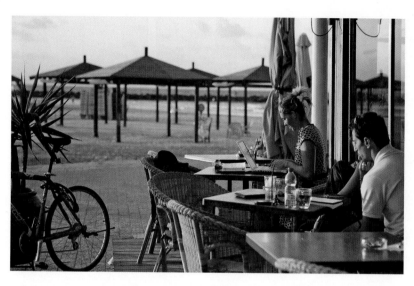

Falafel and Shawarma

Falafel sandwiches are a fast-food staple in Israel, and stands are everywhere, from the busy streets of downtown Tel Aviv to the ultra-Orthodox areas of Jerusalem and the Eilat beach promenade.

It starts with a scoop of seasoned chickpeas ground and formed into small spheres that are quickly fried in oil and then thrust—six or so—into a pita or wrap. Patrons give a nod or a "no thanks" to some hummus or *harif* (hot sauce) and to each of the colorful accompaniments: finely chopped cucumbers and tomatoes, shredded cabbage (white or red), parsley, pickles, and even french fries stuffed on top. Many customers drizzle their creation with self-serve sauces like *amba* (spicy pickled mango) and tahini.

Be sure to have a few extra napkins ready, and assume the falafel position before taking your first bite: leaning forward well away from clothing and shoes.

Equally wonderful is shawarma, similar to the Greek gyro (minus the pork). Slices of grilled turkey or chicken meat (or, rarely, the more traditional lamb) are sliced off a vertical rotating rotisserie spit and served with the same accompaniments as falafel.

The Sabra Personality

The local mythos is that Israelis have prickly personalities. Although you hear the word *savlanut* (patience) bandied about, natives don't seem to be blessed with an overabundance of that quality.

The character of Israelis was once compared to a local cactus that produces a "prickly pear" known as the *sabra*. The term "Sabra" has become a sobriquet for the native Israeli: prickly on the outside but sweet on the inside! Fortunately, this national tendency toward abruptness is tempered with a generous dose of Mediterranean warmth.

Israel is more than holy sites and turbulent politics; to get a sense of the country, familiarize yourself with some of the features of daily life.

Markets and Bargaining

Israel's open-air markets are just the place to soak up local culture while shopping for snacks to stock your hotel room. Machaneh Yehuda in Jerusalem and Tel Aviv's Carmel Market are famous. For markets that sell decorative brass, ceramic and glass items, beads, embroidered dresses, and jackets or secondhand funky clothes, head to Jerusalem's Old City (the souk) or the Jaffa Flea Market.

Bargaining can be fun, but there are some useful pointers. Never answer the question "How much do you want to pay?" When the seller names a price, come back with about half. If the seller balks, be prepared to walk out; if you're called back, they want to make a sale. If you're in a hurry, vendors know it and don't drop the price. Not every vendor is in the mood for the bargaining game: don't begin the process unless your intentions are serious.

Café Culture

Café sitting is an integral part of Israeli life, especially in the major cities where it seems as if there's a café on every corner. The locals love their *café hafuch* (latte: literally, "upside-down coffee"). In many cafés, a request for cappuccino gets you the same beverage, perhaps with more froth and a shake of cinnamon. Rival Israeli coffee chains have multiplied like crazy across the country since the late '90s. The coffee, invariably made in Italian machines, is usually excellent. Unlike European cafés where the waiters get antsy if you stay too long, in Israel you can sit unhassled for long periods. And free Wi-Fi, while not yet universal, is commonplace. Pastries range from old-fashioned strudels to flaky brioches. Most cafés offer reasonably priced full breakfasts, sandwiches, salads, pizza, quiches, and soups.

IF YOU LIKE

Archaeology

For an earlier generation, archaeology was something of an Israeli national pastime; but it's still exciting to walk, Bible in hand, in the footsteps of the ancients. Thousands of years of civilization are often directly underfoot and remain remarkably intact. The region's dry air has helped preserve entire ancient cities, many of which are easily accessible from Jerusalem or Tel Aviv. Here are a few of the top archaeology sites.

Caesarea, Haifa and the Northern Coast. The remains of this Mediterranean port city, an ancient capital of the region, include a Roman-era theater, a hippodrome, a sunken harbor, and Crusader ruins.

City of David, Jerusalem. The birthplace of the city, dripping with mystery, is a maze of excavated passageways deep underground. Here you'll find King Hezekiah's 2,700-year-old water tunnel.

Jerusalem Archaeological Park, Jerusalem. This area encompasses the Temple Mount, Mount of Olives, the Kidron Valley, and the Hinnom Valley. The air-conditioned Davidson Center holds interesting artifacts.

Masada, Around Jerusalem and the Dead Sea. This winter retreat of King Herod also served as a formidable defensive bulwark against invaders. It's the site of a siege by Roman troops that ended in mass suicide.

Tel Dan Nature Reserve, Upper Galilee and the Golan. This huge biblical-era city is home to the world's oldest known gated archway, built by Bronze Age inhabitants.

Tel Megiddo, Lower Galilee. The remains of more than 25 levels of civilization are being excavated in the Jezreel Valley, along with an ancient water system.

The Great Outdoors

Israel's bounty includes its impressive nature reserves, home to an astonishing array of wildlife. The country is a major stop on bird migration routes from Europe to Africa: an estimated 500 million "frequent flyers" rest awhile in the autumn and spring. The vast desert of the Negev has its own subtle beauty. Respect its power: never hike desert trails alone, avoid intensely hot days, wear a hat and other protective clothing, and drink copiously. Here are some of the best places to explore the wild side of Israel.

Ein Gedi Nature Reserve, Around Jerusalem and the Dead Sea. This desert oasis on the western shore of the Dead Sea is perhaps Israel's best, in part because of its nature reserve, which can be explored on multiple trails. It's home to ibex (wild goats) and hyrax (small furry creatures).

Hermon Stream (Banias) Nature Reserve, Upper Galilee and the Golan. Israel's most impressive waterfall is fed from the spring at the foot of Mount Hermon, which flows powerfully through a canyon before cascading over the rocks. An easy trail leads to great views of waterfalls and cataracts.

Makhtesh Ramon, Eilat and the Negev. One of three massive craters in the Negev, this is the most popular for its intriguing geological formations, unusual fossils, panoramic views, and desert wildlife. Together with the surrounding area, it forms the Ramon Nature Reserve, the largest in Israel.

Tel Dan Nature Reserve, Upper Galilee and the Golan. Full of biblical-era ruins, Tel Dan has three trails running through about 120 protected acres dotted with laurel trees.

Sacred Spaces

Faith has many voices in the Holy Land, and sanctity wears many different robes. For the uninitiated, it can be a bewildering multisensory experience. Some pilgrims find the hubbub at many sites disconcerting, but keep in mind that most places were not pristine in their day either.

Jerusalem remains the epicenter and a focal point for the three major religions of the region. Find religious enlightenment, or a good deal of biblical history, at these favorite sites.

Baha'i Shrine and Gardens, Haifa and the Northern Coast. The gold-domed landmark on the slopes of Mount Carmel covers the tomb of the Bab, the forerunner of the Baha'i religion. Its gardens provide a serene environment for this gentle faith.

Basilica of the Annunciation, Around Jerusalem and the Dead Sea. The Angel Gabriel is believed to have delivered Mary the news that she would give birth to Jesus in this cave in Nazareth, now part of a Roman Catholic church.

Capernaum National Park, Lower Galilee. Jesus's home during the years of his ministry is the location of many biblical stories, from the conversion of fishermen Peter, Andrew, James, and John into Apostles to the synagogue where Jesus gave the sermon about the bread of life.

Jerusalem. Here you'll find sacred sites for three major religions, including the Garden of Gethsemane, the Via Dolorosa, and the Church of the Holy Sepulcher for Christians; the tomb of King David and the Western Wall for Jews; and, for Muslims, the al-Aqsa Mosque and the golden-topped Dome of the Rock, where the Prophet Muhammad is believed to have ascended to heaven.

Museums

With so much rich history underfoot, Israel stocks its many impressive museums with a quality of artifacts rarely matched in the world. In fact, the country has more museums per capita than anywhere else in the world. More than 200 cover art, science, history, design, architecture, and technology. Many take innovative approaches using multimedia exhibits. Begin with these favorites.

Herzl Museum, Jerusalem. This museum near Mount Herzl National Memorial Park re-creates the life and times of the founder of the Zionist movement.

Holocaust History Museum, Jerusalem. At the must-see Yad Vashem, this museum provides a powerful and thought-provoking documentation of a dark period.

Israel Museum, Jerusalem. Regarded as the country's leading cultural institution, this museum is perhaps best known for its archaeology collection, home of the Dead Sea Scrolls.

L.A. Mayer Museum for Islamic Art, Jerusalem. This undervisited museum has an impressive collection and an unrelated but stunning display of period timepieces.

Tel Aviv Museum of Art, Tel Aviv. One of the leading art institutions in the country, the museum is especially attractive for aficionados of modern art and architecture, with both Israeli and international work.

Tikotin Museum of Japanese Art, Haifa and the Northern Coast. The only museum dedicated to Japanese art in the Middle East, this favorite sits atop Mount Carmel.

Underwater Observatory and Marine Park, Eilat and the Negev. The exceptional coral reef in Eilat provides the setting for this popular place, where creatures from the deep surround you.

ISRAEL: PEOPLE, RELIGION, AND STATE

"I could not conceive of a small country having so large a history," wrote Mark Twain after his visit to the Holy Land in 1867. The rich history certainly fascinates, as does the complex political situation despite, or because of, its constant sense of urgency. But beyond that are the people, a varied population of 8.5 million, representing a startlingly wide array of ethnicities, nationalities, religious beliefs, and lifestyles. The diversity of Israel's population is one of the country's greatest strengths—and one of its essential challenges. It may explain, for example, why defining a national identity is still a work in progress, even after more than 60 years.

Creating a Nation

Israel's founding generation saw the country as a modern reincarnation of the ancient Jewish nation-state. Israel was the "Promised Land" of Abraham and Moses, the Israelite kingdom of David and Solomon, and the home of Jesus of Nazareth and the Jewish Talmudic sages. Although the Jewish presence in the country has been unbroken for more than 3,000 years, several massive exiles—first by the Babylonians in 586 BC and then by the Romans in AD 70—created a Diaspora, a dispersion of the Jewish people throughout the world. The sense of historical roots still resonates for many, probably most, Jewish Israelis; and bringing their brethren home has been a national priority from the beginning.

The attachment to the ancient homeland, and a yearning for the restoration of "Zion and Jerusalem," weaves through the entire fabric of Jewish history and religious tradition. Over the centuries, many Jews trickled back to Eretz Yisrael (the Land of Israel), while others looked forward to fulfilling their dream of return in some future—many felt imminent—messianic age. Not all were prepared to wait for divine intervention, however, and in the late 19th century, a variety of Jewish nationalist organizations emerged, bent on creating a home for their people in Israel (then the district of Palestine in the Ottoman Empire). Zionism was created as a political movement to give structure and impetus to that idea.

Some early Zionist leaders, like founding father Theodor Herzl, believed that the urgent priority was simply a Jewish haven that would be safe from persecution, wherever that haven might be. Argentina was suggested, and Great Britain offered Uganda. In light of Jewish historical and emotional links to the land of Israel, most Zionists rejected these "territorialist" proposals.

Differing Views

The establishment of the State of Israel did not, of course, meet with universal rejoicing. To the Arab world, it was anathema, an alien implant in a Muslim Middle East. Palestinian Arabs today mark Israel's independence as the *Nakba*, the Catastrophe, a moment in time when their own national aspirations were thwarted. For many ultra-Orthodox Jews, the founding of Israel was an arrogant preempting of God's divine plan; and to make matters worse, the newly minted state was blatantly secular, despite its many concessions to religious interests. This internal battle over the character of the Jewish state, and the implacable hostility of Israel's neighbors—which has resulted in more than six decades of unremitting conflict—have been the two main issues engaging the country since its birth.

The Israeli People

Roughly 6 million of Israel's citizens—a little more than 75%—are Jewish. Some trace their family roots back many generations on local soil; others are first- to fourth-generation *olim* (immigrants) from dozens of different countries. The first modern pioneers arrived from Russia in 1882, purchased land, and set about developing it with romantic zeal. A couple of decades later, inspired by the socialist ideas then current in Eastern Europe, a much larger wave founded the first kibbutzim—collective villages or communes. In time, these fiercely idealistic farmers became something of a moral elite, having little financial power but providing a greatly disproportionate percentage of the country's political leadership, military officer cadre, and intelligentsia.

Most of the immigrants before Israel's independence in 1948 were Ashkenazi Jews (of Central or Eastern European descent), but the biggest wave in the first decade of statehood came from the Arab lands of North Africa and the Middle East. Israel's Jewish population—600,000 at the time of independence—doubled within 3½ years and tripled within 10.

In the late 1980s and early '90s, a wave of about three-quarters of a million Jews moved to Israel from the former Soviet Union. The Russian influence is felt everywhere in Israel today, not least in the fields of technology and classical music. In the early 1980s, a smaller group of Jews from the long-isolated Ethiopian community trekked across Sudan, on their odyssey to the dreamed-of "Jerusalem." Many perished en route. Another 14,500 were airlifted into Israel over one weekend in 1991. Their challenge—and that of Israeli society—has been their integration into a modern technological society. Since 2013, Jews from France have moved to Israel in significant numbers: more than 7,500 arrived in 2015.

The vast majority of Israel's 1.7 million Arabic-speaking citizens are Muslims (among them about 200,000 Bedouin), followed by 130,000 Druze (a separate religious group), and about 125,000 Christian Arabs. Most Israeli Arabs live in the mixed Jewish-Arab towns of Jaffa, Ramla, Lod, Haifa, and Akko; a number of good-sized towns and villages on the eastern edge of the coastal plain; in Nazareth and throughout the Lower Galilee; and, in the case of the Bedouin, in the Negev Desert. The extent to which they're integrated with Israeli Jews often depends on location. In Haifa, for example, there's little tension between the two ethnic groups. On the other hand, Jerusalem's quarter-million Arab residents are Palestinian not Israeli, and the situation is more fraught. All Israeli Arabs are equal under the law and vote for and serve in the *Knesset,* the Israeli parliament.

However, social and economic gaps between the Arab and Jewish sectors do exist, and Arab complaints of government neglect and unequal allocation of resources have sometimes spilled into angry street demonstrations and other antiestablishment activity. The Muslims in Israel are mainstream Sunnis and regarded as both politically and religiously moderate by the standards of the region. Nevertheless, in recent years there has been some radicalization of the community's youth, who identify politically with the Palestinian liberation movement and/or religiously with the Islamic revival that has swept the Middle East.

FLAVORS OF ISRAEL

Many Israelis divide the day into at least six excuses to eat. There's breakfast, a 10 am snack, a quick lunch, a 5 pm coffee break (around the time that the Western world is calling for a cocktail), a full dinner, and a snack before bed, just for good measure. Satisfying this appetite is made easier by the great grab-and-go food with soul, including crispy falafel, sold on Israel's streets and in small food joints.

A good number of Israel's restaurants are kosher, and conform to Jewish dietary laws: menus may contain meat or dairy but not both, and pork products and shellfish are out (fish is neutral). Strictly kosher restaurants are closed on the Jewish Sabbath and religious holidays. The majority of hotels countrywide serve kosher food. Bon appétit or, as they say here, *betayavon!*

Israeli Breakfast

The classic Israeli breakfast is legendary, but fewer busy Israelis have time to make this extravaganza at home these days. You mostly find it at hotels, B&Bs, and cafés. Hotel buffets include bowls of brightly colored "Israeli" salads, platters of cheeses, piles of fresh fruit, granola, hot and cold cereals, baskets of various breads and baked goods ranging from cinnamon or chocolate twists to quiche, smoked fish, fresh fruit juices, made-to-order eggs (*betza ayin*, or "egg like an eye," means a fried egg, *chavitah* is omelet, and *mekushkash* is scrambled), and pancakes (locals pour on maple syrup or chocolate sauce). Country lodgings such as B&Bs serve homemade versions, and city coffeehouses specialize in the Israeli breakfast, accompanied by croissants and cappuccino, often served until 1 pm—and sometimes all day.

The Essential Cup of Coffee

Gone are the days when the only coffee available was instant, tiny cups of Turkish coffee (*café Turki*), or its lazy counterpart, *botz* ("mud": powdered grounds stirred into boiling water). Israel today has a coffee culture on a par with Europe's. Most places use Italian machines; the past decade has seen the advent of Western-style coffee-shop chains, the biggest being Aroma, Café Hillel, Café Joe, Arcaffe, and Café Café. You can have a robust and flavorful latte (known as *hafuch*, or "upside-down"); an *Americano* should you be homesick; espresso; and in the summer, iced coffee known as *barad*, a slushy chilled confection made with crushed ice. Soy milk is often available, as is decaf (*natoul* in Hebrew). In the Old City of Jerusalem and Arab establishments, coffee is made with the addition of a pinch of cardamom, or *hel*.

Israeli Salad

There are several different kinds of chopped salads in Israel, but there's one classic, which is no question a trademark dish, with origins in Arab cuisine. Basically, it's a combination of fresh cucumbers, tomatoes, and onion, and the secret's in the chopping—each ingredient must be chopped small and evenly. Cooks who fly in the face of tradition might add chopped parsley and mint, and bits of chopped lemon. Then the salad is dashed with quality olive oil and fresh lemon juice and a sprinkle of salt and pepper or *za'atar*, a Middle Eastern herb of hyssop with a sprinkle of sesame seeds. It can be eaten on its own with white cheese and bread before work, spooned into a pita with falafel and hummus at any time of day, and with the main dish at most every meal.

Grilled Meats and Steaks

Virtually every town has at least one Middle Eastern grill restaurant, where you can find kebab, skewered grilled chicken (dark-meat baby chicken, or *pargit*, is a favorite), lamb, beef, mixed grill, or spit-grilled shawarma, generally prepared with turkey seasoned with lamb fat, cumin, coriander, and other spices. If you want a good steak, don't worry: order entrecôte and see for yourself. You can even get a good hamburger these days. In Jerusalem, around the open fruit and vegetable market, are grilled-meat eateries famous for chicken and beef on skewers, called *shipudim*, and their *me'orav Yerushalmi* (Jerusalem mixed grill): chicken hearts, livers, and spleen.

Seafood

There are fish restaurants all over the country, but locals say the best ones are in cities and towns that border the Mediterranean (like Tel Aviv, Jaffa, Haifa, and Akko), around the Kinneret (Sea of Galilee), and in Eilat. In nonkosher restaurants, the chance of finding shrimp, squid, and other nonkosher seafood on the menu has increased substantially.

Salatim

The word *salat* in Hebrew means salad. But many small dishes, served cold, as an appetizer, are called *salatim*. It's basically a mezze. In less fancy restaurants, and often in fish and grilled-meat places, these are slung onto the table along with a basket of pita before you've even managed to get comfortable. They're usually free, but ask. Dig into selections such as two or three types of eggplant, cumin-flecked carrot salad, tahini-enriched hummus, fried cauliflower, pickled vegetables, and cracked-wheat salad (tabbouleh), but leave room for the main course, too.

Cheeses

Holy Land cows are hard at work providing milk for cheeses, and these top the list, followed by goat- and sheep-milk cheese and, last but not least, the healthy buffalo cheese—mostly mozzarella. Soft, white cheeses reign supreme. An Israeli favorite is *gvina levana,* a spreadable white cheese available in a variety of fat percentages. A few famous cheeses are Bulgarit ("Bulgarian"), a firmer, tangier version of feta (sheep or goat); Brinza (half goat, half sheep); Tzfatit, originally made in the northern city of Tzfat, not too salty; the ubiquitous goat cheese, feta; and Tomme (goat), a zingy white cheese. Hard, yellow cheeses have always been around, but the variety and the quality have soared.

Wines

The excellent wine in Israel is made from major international grape varieties in five main wine regions from north to south. Many labels have developed reputations as being among the best in the region.

World Cuisine

The last decade or so has brought fusion cuisines to Israel—a superb blend of local flavors and ingredients with French-Italian-Asian or Californian influences—designed by young Israeli chefs, many of whom have studied or cooked abroad.

Although fine-dining restaurants dot the Galilee, the Golan, Jerusalem, and other parts of the country, it's worth saving up to eat at one of Tel Aviv's top establishments. These restaurants are most often pricey, and though dressing up is never necessary, feel free. The locals also adore sushi, and Japanese restaurants and fast-food sushi joints abound. Culinary explorers can also try home-cooked ethnic foods—like Moroccan, Persian, Bukharian, or Tripolitan (Libyan) fare.

ISRAEL WITH KIDS

Your choices for keeping the kids busy in Israel are both abundant and varied. Let them expend energy exploring Crusader castles or caves in nature reserves. For fun on the water, try rafting on the Jordan River—and there are the beaches, of course. Check the Friday papers' entertainment guides (they have a children's section) or websites for up-to-date information on special activities.

Eating Out

Restaurants are often happy to accommodate those seeking simple fare like pasta or chicken schnitzel and fries. Fast food is easily accessible and doesn't have to be junk. Falafel or shawarma, kebabs, and cheese- or potato-filled pastries called *bourekas* are very common, and pizza parlors abound.

Nature (and Old Stuff, Too)

Israel's nature reserves and national parks (⊕ *www.parks.org.il*) have plenty for the whole family to do. In the north, you can cycle around a part of the restored Hula Lake (at the site called Agmon Ha'Hula); laugh and learn at the fun 3-D movie about bird migrations at the **Hula Lake Nature Reserve**; kayak or raft the placid waters of the **Jordan River**; and bounce around some awesome landscapes in a Jeep or a 4x4 dune buggy. (In the south, the Negev Desert and Eilat Mountains have comparable off-road experiences.) Explore the medieval **Nimrod's Fortress** on the slopes of Mount Hermon, or the remains of mighty **Belvoir** overlooking the Upper Jordan Valley.

Standouts in the south are the oases and walking trails of **Ein Gedi Nature Reserve** (with a bonus of bathing under fresh waterfalls) and **Ein Avdat**. The wondrous **Masada**, Herod's mountaintop palace-fortress, is a real treat and can be reached by foot along the steep Snake Path (recommended for older kids), but there's always the cable car.

Walking is a lively and easy activity to do anywhere. Top in Jerusalem is the Old Testament–period **City of David**, south of the Old City. It's a maze of rock-hewn corridors, ending with a 30-minute wade in the spring water of Hezekiah's Tunnel. (There's a dry exit, too.) The **Ramparts Walk** on part of the city walls offers views of the Old City's residential quarters as well as of new Jerusalem outside the walls. Smaller kids can do part of it (with strict adult supervision).

In Tel Aviv, the **Tel Aviv Port** is great for coffee and a stroll—and even little kids can run around (with a bit of adult attention) while you enjoy iced drinks and the balmy weather. The city's beaches and beachfront promenade are also good for walking and using up energy.

Museums

A dirty word among kids? Maybe so, but the following museums might change some minds.

In West Jerusalem, the **Israel Museum's Youth Wing** has outdoor play areas as well as exhibitions, often interactive, and a "recycling room" where children can use their creative energy freely. Great rainy-day options include the **Bloomfield Science Museum** in Givat Ram.

The **Eretz Israel Museum** in Tel Aviv has a series of pavilions on its campus, each with a different theme: pottery, coins, glass, folklore, anthropology, and more. It also has a planetarium—complete with moon rocks. Nearby is the engaging **Museum of the Jewish People**, which tells the story of Jewish life outside Israel over the centuries.

Haifa's **National Museum of Science, Technology, and Space (MadaTech)** and the **National Maritime Museum** are geared to young and curious minds—of any age.

The **Israel Air Force Museum,** at the Hatzerim Air Force base (west of Beersheva), houses a huge collection of IAF airplanes and helicopters—from World War II Spitfires and Mustangs to contemporary F-16s and Cobras. Each exhibit has a story to tell. Guided tours in English can be arranged. This could be a stop on the way to or from Eilat, or a doable day trip from Jerusalem or Tel Aviv.

At One with the Animals

In addition to the wonderful **Tisch Family Zoological Gardens** in Jerusalem, with its emphasis on fauna that feature in the Bible or are native to Israel, the small but delightful **Haifa Zoo** offers numerous options for time out with animals.

In the high Negev Desert, near Mitzpe Ramon, about as far as you can get from their native Andes mountains, gentle alpacas wait for you to hand-feed them. At the **Alpaca Farm** you can learn as well about the whole process of raising them and spinning their marvelously soft wool.

Horseback riding is an option pretty much throughout the country. In the Galilee, end a trail—of a few hours or a couple of days—with hot apple pie at **Vered Hagalil** or with a chunky steak at **Bat Ya'ar,** in the Biriya Forest near Tzfat (Safed). There are numerous outfits that do camel-hump trails in the Negev (near Beersheva and Arad) and near **Eilat.**

In the Upper Hula Valley, **Tel Dan Nature Reserve** is both beautiful and home to unusual wildlife; trails let you access different areas. Bird-watching isn't a casual activity, but if you have budding birders in the family, Israel provides excellent opportunities because it is on major migration routes. The **Hula Lake Nature Reserve** provides excellent viewing in season.

In Eilat the **Underwater Observatory and Marine Park,** with a large aquarium complex, gives visitors of all ages an excellent opportunity to observe colorful, rare fish and more.

Beaches

You're never too far from a beach in Israel—but check for a lifeguard. This is a given at city beaches, but not at those off the beaten track.

For such a tiny country, the range of different beach experiences is amazing, from the Mediterranean to the Red Sea to the freshwater Sea of Galilee. **Tel Aviv** is right on the Mediterranean and has an enjoyable promenade and plenty of public beaches.

The **Dead Sea,** actually a hypersalty lake, draws people from all over the world to luxuriate in its waters, hot springs, and black medicinal mud. Kids (and adults) can float but not swim here. The southern shores—the lowest point on the surface of the planet—are filled with hotels that offer beach access.

And More ...

The whole family enjoys getting their hands dirty at the three-hour **Dig for a Day** (⊕ *www.archesem.com*)—a chance to dig, sift, and examine artifacts.

Off the Tel Aviv–Jerusalem highway at Latrun is **Mini Israel**—hundreds of exact-replica models of the main sites around the country, historical, archaeological, and modern. It's great for an all-of-Israel orientation.

ISRAEL AND THE PERFORMING ARTS

Israel has a wealth of cultural activity that reflects both its ethnic diversity and its cosmopolitanism. Innovation and experimentation cross-pollinate traditional forms, creating an exciting Israeli performing-arts scene infused by West and East. Look for listings in sections of the Friday *Haaretz* ("The Guide") and *The Jerusalem Post* ("Billboard"), available in many hotels. Online, ⊕ *www.timeout.com/israel* will give you the latest updates on things to do.

Music

Israel's traditionally strong classical and opera scene was enhanced a generation ago by a wave of immigrant musicians from the former Soviet Union. Apart from the deep reservoir of local talent, a steady stream of visiting artists, ensembles, and even full operatic companies enrich the scene every year. The world-renowned **Israel Philharmonic Orchestra** (⊕ *www.ipo.co.il*) is based in Tel Aviv but plays concert series in Haifa and Jerusalem as well. Look for the **Jerusalem Symphony** (⊕ *www.jso.co.il*) and **Haifa Symphony** orchestras (⊕ *www.haifasymphony.co.il*) in their respective cities, but smaller orchestras and ensembles appear in other, often remote, venues, too. Chamber music listings are full and varied: check out intimate auditoriums like the **Felicja Blumental Center**, the **Israel Music Conservatory** (Stricker), and the **Tel Aviv Museum of Art** in Tel Aviv; the **Jerusalem Music Center** (Mishkenot), the **Eden-Tamir Center (Ein Kerem)**, and various churches in the holy city; and the **Rappaport Hall** and **Tikotin (Japanese) Museum** in Haifa.

The **Israeli Opera** (⊕ *www.israel-opera.co.il*) stages up to 10 productions per season (November to July), including a crowd-pleasing extravaganza at the foot of Masada (near the Dead Sea) toward season's end. Its home base, the **Tel Aviv Performing Arts Center (TAPAC)**, hosts smaller operatic and musical events as well.

Noteworthy annual festivals include the multidisciplinary **Israel Festival** (Jerusalem ⊕ *www.israel-festival.org.il*), the **Abu Gosh Vocal Festival** (near Jerusalem ⊕ *www.agfestival.co.il*), and three chamber music festivals: **Upper Galilee Voice of Music** (Kibbutz Kfar Blum), **Eilat** (Eilat ⊕ *www.eilat-festival.co.il*), and **Jerusalem International Chamber Music Festival** (Jerusalem ⊕ *www.jcmf.org.il*). Check websites for accurate dates for these events.

Popular Music: Israeli rock bands and balladeers fill radio playlists and venues around the country. Popular watering holes are Tel Aviv's **Zappa Club** and an ever-changing list of places in the Tel Aviv Port, a nightlife center. Big foreign acts like Elton John, Madonna, and The Rolling Stones take over the **Tel Aviv Performing Arts Center** or the outdoor **Yarkon Park**.

Jerusalem doesn't rock nearly as much as Tel Aviv, but look for cool gigs at **Zappa at the Lab** and **Yellow Submarine**. The week-long midsummer Hutzot Hayotzer Arts and Crafts Festival in **Sultan's Pool**, just outside Jaffa Gate, has good Israeli acts nightly for no extra charge.

Jazz, Ethnic, and World Music have come of age at Eilat's **Red Sea Jazz Festival** (⊕ *en.redseajazz.co.il*), a twice-yearly jazz summit. The summer festival is a fixture on the international calendar, when local artists like trumpeter Avishai Cohen and his siblings return from the New York scene. The winter festival shines a light on home-grown talent. Tel Aviv's **Shablul Jazz** is the premier club, but pubs like **Mike's Place** can be hot as well. Middle Eastern influences are common in Israeli pop songs—that's a given—but even the quintessentially New World genre of jazz hasn't escaped fusion with Yemenite or Ethiopian sounds.

The **Jerusalem International Oud Festival** celebrates a musical tradition that extends from Spain to India (⊕ *www.confederationhouse.org*).

The Upper Galilee mountain town of Tzfat (Safed), home of 16th-century Jewish mysticism, is the setting for the annual **Klezmer Festival** (⊕ *www.safed.co.il*). Expect three summer days of fiddles, clarinets, and Eastern European schmaltz.

The veteran **Ein Gev Festival** in April, on the eastern shore of the Sea of Galilee, is devoted to Hebrew songs, many of them in a choral format.

Dance

Israel owes its visibility on the world dance radar to modern, not ballet. Still, if tradition speaks to you, check the listings for the Tel Aviv–based **Israel Ballet** (⊕ *www.iballet.co.il*) or the more contemporary **Jerusalem Dance Theater** (⊕ *www.jdtcom.com*).

The center of Israeli modern dance is the finely restored **Suzanne Dellal Centre for Dance and Theatre** in Tel Aviv's historic Neve Tzedek neighborhood. Its four performance halls are home ground for the veteran and world-renowned **Batsheva Dance Company** (⊕ *www.batsheva.co.il*)—with legendary artistic director Ohad Naharin—and the **Inbal Pinto & Avshalom Pollak Dance Company** (⊕ *www.inbalpinto.com*). The center's season peaks with **Summer Dance**, a two-month feast of top local and international talent. **Tel Aviv Dance** is an autumn festival, while December brings the more intimate yet more intense **International Exposure.**

The field is much wider, however. The **Kibbutz Contemporary Dance Company** (⊕ *www.kcdc.co.il*)) has a fine reputation, and the Jerusalem-based **Vertigo Dance Company** (⊕ *www.vertigo.org.il*) takes the audience into new territory. (Ensembles are constantly on the road: regardless of their home base, they might be performing near you.) The **Israel Festival** brings top-class acts to Jerusalem, and the capital now enjoys its own dance festival, **Machol Shalem**, in winter.

Theater

Theater in Israel is almost exclusively staged in Hebrew, with the exception of Tel Aviv's **Cameri Theatre**, which presents some of its popular productions with English subtitles.

The **Israel Festival** in Jerusalem is the place to take in an array of the best of the performing arts.

Language may not matter at Jerusalem's annual **International Festival of Puppet Theater** (⊕ *www.traintheater.co.il*) in summer.

Film

Israel has a thriving film industry. The best movie meccas are the **Cinematheques** in Tel Aviv, Haifa, and Jerusalem. Most Israeli films have English subtitles. Real film buffs note the summer dates of the **Jerusalem International Film Festival.** The Haifa Cinematheque has a similar festival in fall (⊕ *www.haifaff.co.il*).

Tel Aviv celebrates **White Nights** in June—an all-night bash when most major museums, theaters, and clubs stay open.

ISRAEL'S MAJOR HOLIDAYS

Time is figured in different ways in Israel. The Western Gregorian calendar—the solar year from January to December—is the basis of day-to-day life and commerce, but the school year, for example, which runs from September through June, follows the Hebrew lunar calendar. Jewish religious festivals are observed as national public holidays, when businesses and some museums are closed (on Yom Kippur, the Day of Atonement, *all* sites are closed).

The Muslim calendar is also lunar but without the compensatory leap-year mechanism of its Hebrew counterpart. Muslim holidays thus drift through the seasons and can fall at any time of the year.

Even the Christian calendar isn't uniform: Christmas is celebrated on different days by the Roman Catholic (Latin) community, the Greek Orthodox Church, and the Armenian Orthodox Church.

Major Jewish Holidays

The phrase "Not religious" in the text indicates that the holiday might be part of the religious tradition, but few or no public restrictions apply. On holy days, when the text indicates "Religious," most of the Sabbath restrictions apply.

In Israel the three festivals of Passover, Shavuot, and Sukkot/Simhat Torah are observed as prescribed in the Bible: for seven, one, and eight days, respectively. Historically, communities outside Israel have added a day to each festival (though many modern liberal communities have adopted the Israeli model). All Jewish holidays begin at sundown the evening before the day of the holiday.

Shabbat (Sabbath). Religious. The Day of Rest in Israel is Saturday, the Jewish Sabbath, which begins at sundown Friday and ends at nightfall Saturday.

Torah-observant Jews don't cook, travel, answer the telephone, or use money or writing materials during the Shabbat, hence the Sabbath ban on photography at Jewish holy sites like the Western Wall. In Jerusalem, where religious influence is strong, the Downtown area clears out on Friday afternoon, and some religious neighborhoods are even closed to traffic.

Kosher restaurants close on the Sabbath, except for the main hotel restaurants, where some menu restrictions apply. In the holy city itself, your dining choices are considerably reduced, but there are more nonkosher eateries than there used to be. Outside Jerusalem, however, you are scarcely affected; in fact, many restaurants do their best business of the week on the Sabbath because nonreligious Israelis take to the roads.

In Arab areas, such as East Jerusalem and Nazareth, Muslims take time off for the week's most important devotions at midday Friday, but much less than on Sunday, when most Christian shopkeepers in those towns close their doors. Saturday is market day, and these towns buzz with activity.

There's no public intercity transportation on the Sabbath, although the private sherut taxis drive between the main cities. Urban buses operate only in Nazareth and, on a reduced schedule, in Haifa. Shabbat is also the busiest day for nature reserves and national parks—indeed, anywhere the city folk can get away for a day. Keep this in mind if you fancy a long drive; the highways toward the main cities can be choked with returning weekend traffic on Saturday afternoon.

Rosh Hashanah (Jewish New Year), September 21–22, 2017; September 10–11, 2018. Religious. This two-day holiday and Yom Kippur are collectively known as the High Holy Days. Rosh Hashanah traditionally begins a 10-day period of introspection and repentance. Observant Jews attend relatively long synagogue services and eat festive meals, including apples and honey to symbolize the hoped-for sweetness of the new year. Nonobservant Jews often use this holiday to picnic and go to the beach.

Yom Kippur (Day of Atonement), September 30, 2017; September 19, 2018. Religious. Yom Kippur is the most solemn day of the Jewish year. Observant Jews fast, wear white clothing, avoid leather footwear, and abstain from pleasures of the flesh. Israeli radio and television stations shut down. By law, all sites, entertainment venues, and most restaurants must close. Much of the country comes to a halt, and in Jerusalem and other cities the roads are almost completely empty, aside from emergency vehicles. It's considered a privilege to be invited to someone's house to "break the fast" as the holiday ends, at nightfall.

Sukkot (Feast of Tabernacles), October 5–11, 2017; September 24–30, 2018. Religious. Jews build open-roof huts or shelters called *sukkot* (singular *sukkah*) on porches and in backyards to remember the makeshift lodgings of the biblical Israelites as they wandered in the desert. The more observant eat as many of their meals as possible in their sukkah.

Simhat Torah, October 13, 2017; October 2, 2018. Religious. The last day of the Sukkot festival season, this holiday marks the end—and the immediate recommencement—of the annual cycle of the reading of the Torah, the Five Books of Moses. Joyful singing and dancing (often in the street) as people carry the Torah scrolls characterize the services.

Hanukkah, December 13–20, 2017; December 3–10, 2018. Not religious. A Jewish rebellion in the 2nd century BC renewed Jewish control of Jerusalem. In the rededicated Temple, the tradition tells, a vessel was found with enough oil to burn for a day. It miraculously burned for eight days, hence the eight-day holiday marked by the lighting of an increasing number of candles (on a candelabrum called a *hanukkiah*) from night to night. Schools take a winter break. Shops, businesses, and services all remain open.

Purim, March 12, 2017; March 1, 2018 (celebrated one day later in Jerusalem). Not religious. Children dress up in costumes on the days leading up to Purim. In synagogues and on public television, devout Jews read the Scroll of Esther, the story of the valiant Jewish queen who prevented the massacre of her people in ancient Persia. On Purim day, it's customary to exchange gifts of foods with friends. Many towns hold street festivals.

Pesach (Passover), April 11–18, 2017; March 31–April 7, 2018. First and last days religious. Dietary restrictions in force throughout. Passover is preceded by spring-cleaning to remove all traces of leavened bread and related products from the household. During the seven-day holiday itself, no bread is sold in Jewish stores. On the first evening of the holiday, Jewish families gather to retell the ancient story of their people's exodus from Egyptian bondage and to eat a festive and highly symbolic meal called the seder (Hebrew for "order"). Hotels have communal seders.

Yom Ha'atzma'ut (Independence Day), May 2, 2017; April 19, 2018. Not religious. Israel declared independence on May 14, 1948, but the exact date of Yom Ha'atzma'ut every year follows the Hebrew calendar. Although there are gala events, fireworks, and military parades all over the country, most Israelis go picnicking or swimming. Stores are closed, but public transportation runs, and most tourist sites are open.

Shavuot (Feast of Weeks), May 31–June 1, 2017; May 20–21, 2018. Religious. This holiday, seven weeks after Passover, marks the harvest of the first fruits and, according to tradition, the day on which Moses received the Torah ("the Law") on Mount Sinai. It's customary to eat dairy products.

Christian Holidays

Easter, April 16, 2017; April 1, 2018. This major festival celebrates the resurrection of Jesus. The nature and timing of its ceremonies and services are colorfully different in each Christian tradition represented in the Holy Land—Roman Catholic (Latin), Protestant, Greek Orthodox, Armenian Orthodox, Ethiopian, and so on. The Western churches—Roman Catholic and Protestant—observe the date above. Check the dates for different groups such as the Armenian Orthodox, Greek Orthodox, and Russian Orthodox churches, who base their holidays on the older Julian calendar.

Christmas. Except in towns with a large indigenous Christian population, such as Nazareth and Bethlehem, Christmas isn't a high-visibility holiday in Israel. The Christmas of the Catholic and Protestant traditions is, of course, celebrated on December 25, but the Greek Orthodox calendar observes it on January 7, while the Armenian Orthodox wait until January 19. Christmas Eve (December 24) is the time for the international choir assembly in Bethlehem's Manger Square, followed by the Roman Catholic midnight mass in the adjacent church. Take a cab to the border crossing (don't forget your passport), and pick up a shared cab to Manger Square on the Palestinian side. Check first with the Israeli Ministry of Tourism information office that the choral event is on schedule.

Muslim Holidays

Muslims observe Friday as their holy day, but it's accompanied by none of the restrictions and far less of the solemnity of the Jewish Shabbat and the Christian Sabbath (in their strictest forms). The noontime prayer on Friday is the most important of the week and is typically preceded by a sermon, often broadcast from mosques' loudspeakers. The dates of Muslim holidays shift each year because of the lunar calendar. Holidays begin at sundown the evening before the day of the holiday.

Ramadan, May 27–June 25, 2017; May 16–June 14, 2018. This monthlong fast commemorates the month in which the Koran was first revealed to Muhammad. Devout Muslims must abstain from food, drink, tobacco, and sex during daylight hours; the three-day festival of Eid el-Fitr marks the conclusion of the period. The dates are affected by the sighting of the new moon and can change slightly at the very last moment. The Muslim holy sites on Jerusalem's Haram esh-Sharif (the Temple Mount) are only open a few morning hours during this time and closed to tourists.

Eid al-Adha, September 1–4, 2017; August 21–24, 2018. This festival commemorating Abraham's willingness to sacrifice his son marks the end of the annual Haj, or pilgrimage to Mecca.

GREAT ITINERARIES

JERUSALEM, THE DEAD SEA, AND THE GALILEE, 9 DAYS

Israel is a small but varied country. This itinerary lets you see the high points of Jerusalem and the northern half of the country in nine days; linger in Tel Aviv at its conclusion and the desert if you have another two to nine days.

Jerusalem, Days 1 and 2

You could spend a lifetime in Jerusalem, but two days is probably a good minimum to get a feel for the city. First, spend a day getting an overview of the holy sites of Judaism, Christianity, and Islam in the Old City. Start with the Western Wall, then go up to the Temple Mount (morning hours) to view the Muslim shrines. Follow the Via Dolorosa to the Church of the Holy Sepulcher. Stop for a Middle Eastern–style lunch in the Christian Quarter before walking down into the Jewish Quarter. (Note: The Temple Mount is closed Friday and Saturday, and some Jewish Quarter sites close early Friday and don't reopen until Sunday.) Explore the remarkable underworld of biblical (Old Testament) Jerusalem, at the City of David, or, if you have a car, pick up one or two of the panoramic views.

On your second day, venture farther afield in West Jerusalem. Many consider the Israel Museum and Yad Vashem, home to the Holocaust History Museum, essential if you're visiting Jerusalem. Mount Herzl National Memorial Park is also a meaningful excursion. A good plan is to avoid burnout by doing one of the big museums on Day 2, the other on Day 3. (Note: Yad Vashem and Mount Herzl are closed Saturday.) Add the Machaneh Yehuda produce market (closed Saturday) and the Knesset menorah.

Around the Dead Sea, Days 3 and 4

After getting an early start in your rental car, head east through the stark Judean Desert to Qumran, where the Dead Sea Scrolls were discovered. You can spend an hour (max) touring the ruins and seeing the audiovisual presentation. About 45 minutes south of Qumran along the Dead Sea shore is Ein Gedi, where a leisurely hike to the waterfall and back should take about 1½ hours, including a dip in a freshwater pool. End the day with a float in the Dead Sea, and spend the night in one of the fine hotels at Ein Bokek, at the southern end of the lake. The spa treatments featuring the famously curative Dead Sea mud are a highlight for many.

In the morning, hike the Snake Path—or take the cable car—up Masada, site of Herod's winter palace. The gate to the trail opens before dawn so you can catch the sunrise at the top. Later, head back to Jerusalem to spend the night.

Note: If you don't have a car, one-day bus tours from Jerusalem let you see Masada and the Dead Sea. Or you can also drive to Qumran, Ein Gedi, the Dead Sea, and Masada for the day and return to Jerusalem: that's a full day, and you'd need to plan your time carefully.

The Galilee, Days 5–7

From Jerusalem, where you've spent the night, make an early start for a busy day. Retrace your steps down Route 1 East, stopping just north of the Dead Sea–Jerusalem highway at the oasis town of Jericho, the world's oldest city. It's almost worth a trip through this lush town—with its date palms, orange groves, banana plantations, bougainvillea, and papaya trees—just to be able to say "I was there," but Tel Jericho is also a significant archaeological site. Sample the baklava and orange juice. Jericho is in the Palestinian Authority, so check ahead of time for any entry restrictions. Most car-rental agencies don't allow their cars into Palestinian areas. You must show your passport at the checkpoint.

Take the Jordan Valley route (Route 90) to the Galilee, stopping at the extensive Roman-Byzantine ruins at Beit She'an, where you can have lunch in town or take a sandwich to the site. The Crusader castle of Belvoir rounds out the day, and you can enjoy a lakeside fish dinner in Tiberias, where you spend the night.

The next day, spend an hour or two in the far north at the Tel Dan Nature Reserve, with its rushing water and biblical archaeology. Nearby Banias has Roman shrines, a fine walk, and the Suspended Trail overlooking a cauldron of seething white water. Depending on how you spend your day, you can also visit one of the many fine wineries on the Golan Heights, or do some hiking or bird-watching at Gamla. Stay overnight in Tiberias again, or better yet, farther north in a Hula Valley B&B.

On your third day, explore the treasures of Tzfat, with its beautiful vistas, old synagogues, and art and Judaica galleries. Spend the afternoon hiking or horseback riding at Bat Ya'ar (reserve if you want to go trail riding) or kayaking at Hagoshrim or Kfar Blum (seasonal, but no need to reserve). Stay overnight in Tiberias or at your Hula Valley B&B.

The Mediterranean Coast, Days 8 and 9

From Tiberias or your Hula Valley B&B, head west to the coast. Your first stop can be the cable-car ride to the sea grottoes of Rosh Hanikra. Then travel to Akko, with its Crusader halls and picturesque harbor. Akko is also an excellent place for a fish lunch. Then drive to Haifa for a view from the Dan Panorama Hotel at the top of Mount Carmel. Spend the night in Haifa.

The following day, visit Haifa's Baha'i Shrine and its magnificent gardens, then continue down the coast to visit the village of Zichron Ya'akov, home of the Carmel Winery and the Beit Aaronson Museum. Have lunch and then head to Tel Aviv, stopping at the Roman ruins of Caesarea on the way. In Tel Aviv, you can enjoy a night on the town, perhaps in Neve Tzedek or Jaffa. From Tel Aviv you can head to the airport if it's time to go home.

TEL AVIV, EILAT, AND PETRA, 9 DAYS

Tel Aviv, Days 1 and 2

There's a wealth of options for your time and attention in Tel Aviv, where you can wander through lively markets, explore the twisting streets of Jaffa, or enjoy a dip in the Mediterranean Sea. Learn a little more about military history at the Palmach Museum, stroll along more than 3 miles of oceanfront boardwalk, or explore the White City, the UNESCO World Heritage Site famous for the cream-colored walls of its Bauhaus architecture. Spend at least two days here to balance museum time with beach time.

The Negev, Days 3 and 4

From Tel Aviv, head south toward Beersheva and Route 40. Beersheva is less than a two-hour drive from Tel Aviv. Driving south, stop at Sde Boker, where you can have lunch and see David Ben-Gurion's house and grave site overlooking the biblical Wilderness of Zin. Near Sde Boker is Ein Avdat, a wilderness oasis that has a trail with stone steps and ladders leading up the magnificent white chalk canyon. This part of the trail is one-way up, so the driver needs to go back to the car and drive around to meet the others. Drive on to Mitzpe Ramon, on the edge of the immense Makhtesh Ramon (Ramon Crater). Spend the night here, then enjoy the natural wonders of the Ramon Crater the next day. Spend a second night here as well.

Eilat and Petra, Days 5–9

Eilat is less than a three-hour drive from Mitzpe Ramon. Drive south on Route 40 to where it joins Route 90 and continue south on the Arava Road, which runs parallel to the border with Jordan.

Stop at Yotvata Hai-Bar Nature Reserve, and then at Timna Park for a short walk and view of Solomon's Pillars, arriving in Eilat in the late afternoon. A minimum of two days here allows you to see all the highlights; in three to five days you can add some serious beach or diving time and take a side trip to Petra, in Jordan, to see the magnificent remains of this ancient city of the Nabatean people, You probably want to pick one hotel in Eilat as a base.

GREAT ITINERARIES

IN THE FOOTSTEPS OF JESUS, 6 DAYS

Visit the Holy Land, they say, and you'll never read the Bible the same way again; the landscapes and shrines that you'll see, and your encounters with local members of Christian communities at the landmarks of Jesus's life, will have a profound and lasting impact.

Jerusalem and Bethlehem, Days 1 and 2

Spend your first day retracing the climax of the story of Jesus in Jerusalem, starting at the Mount of Olives. This is where Jesus taught and wept over the city (Luke 19:41), and the tear-shaped Dominus Flevit church commemorates it. The walk down the Mount of Olives road, also known as the Palm Sunday road, leads to the ancient olive trees in the Garden of Gethsemane, where you can contemplate Jesus's "passion" and arrest.

Follow the Via Dolorosa, stopping at each Station of the Cross, to the Church of the Holy Sepulcher, where most Christians believe Jesus was crucified, buried, and resurrected. The Garden Tomb—the site of Calvary for many Protestants—offers an island of tranquility. Take your time contemplating the sites; this won't be a rushed day.

The next day, you can explore the Southern Wall excavations at the Jerusalem Archaeological Park and Davidson Center, adjacent to the Old City's Dung Gate. Scholars believe Jesus could have walked the stones of the ancient street here, and climbed the Southern Steps to the Temple. Down the hill is the City of David, the Old Testament heart of Jerusalem, including the excavated Area G and Warren's Shaft, and King Hezekiah's water tunnel. The steps of the pool of Siloam, where a blind man had his sight restored (John 9:7–11), were discovered only a few years ago. Add a visit to the Room of the Last Supper on Mount Zion, near Zion Gate, and then have lunch.

In the afternoon, you can visit Bethlehem, the birthplace of Jesus, to see the Church of the Nativity, one of the oldest churches in the world. Bethlehem is in the Palestinian Authority, so bring your passport. Most car-rental agencies don't allow their cars into Palestinian areas. It's best to take a taxi to the border crossing east of Jerusalem's Gilo neighborhood. The crossing for tourists is usually uncomplicated, and there are Palestinian taxis waiting on the other side to take you to the church. Or you can opt to spend the afternoon in Jerusalem.

On the way to the Galilee, Day 3

Making an early start, head east through the barren Judean Desert to Qumran, where the Dead Sea Scrolls were found. Some scholars believe John the Baptist may have passed through here, and a visit to the site—you can spend an hour here—is an opportunity to learn about the desert in which Jesus sought solitude, purity, and inspiration.

Then head up the Jordan Valley (Route 90), passing through or near Jericho (depending on political conditions). Jesus also healed a blind man here (Mark 10:46), and had a meal with the tax collector Zacchaeus (Luke 19:1–5). If the security situation isn't favorable, the Israeli soldiers at the checkpoint at Jericho don't allow you in (again, read a newspaper and use common sense). If you skip Jericho, Route 90 swings past it to the east. In Jericho, though, a visit to Tel Jericho, the first conquest of the Israelites in the Holy Land (Joshua 6),

TIPS

First and foremost, bring along your Bible; it gets a lot of use.

You don't need a car in Jerusalem, but you do need one for the rest of this itinerary. Your best bet is to pick up a car on the afternoon of the day before you head out of Jerusalem, so that you can make an early start the next day (remember that rental agencies are normally not open on Saturday). The agency provides you with a basic road map and advice.

Gas stations are numerous, many with convenience stores to stock up on snacks.

is a must. You can have lunch at the restaurant next to the tell or at a truck stop on the way north from Jericho.

Then it's on to the ruins at Beit She'an, including the ancient main street, a bathhouse, and mosaics. Not only is this an important Old Testament site, it was also the capital of the Decapolis, a league of 10 Roman cities, among which Jesus taught and healed (Mark 7:31).

Farther north, pilgrims go to Yardenit to be baptized in the Jordan River and remember the baptism of Jesus in these waters. Spend the night in Tiberias on the Sea of Galilee; enjoy a fish dinner.

Sea of Galilee, Day 4

Start the day heading north to see the ancient wooden boat at Ginosar, which evokes Gospel descriptions of life on the lake—see, for example, Matthew 9:1. Then, after meditating on Jesus's famous sermon (Matthew 5) in the gardens of the

Mount of Beatitudes and its chapel (off Route 90 north of the Sea of Galilee), descend to Tabgha to see the mosaics of the Church of the Multiplication of Loaves and Fishes. From a lakeshore perch at the nearby Church of the Primacy of St. Peter, where Jesus appeared to the disciples after the Resurrection (John 21), you can marvel at how Scripture and landscape blend before your eyes.

Farther east, the ruins of ancient Capernaum—the center of Jesus's local ministry—include a magnificent pillared synagogue (partially restored) and Peter's house.

An archaeological mound across the Jordan River, north of the Sea of Galilee, is ancient Bethsaida, where the Gospels say Jesus healed and taught (Luke 9:10, 10:13). To get there, continue east of Capernaum, cross the Jordan River north of the Sea of Galilee, turn left onto Route 888, and a short distance thereafter turn left to Bethsaida in the Jordan River Park. From there, head back down to the lake and continue around its eastern shore to Kursi National Park and the ruins of a Byzantine church where, it's said, Jesus cast out demons into a herd of swine that stampeded into the water (Matthew 8:28–30).

A good idea for lunch is the fish restaurant at Kibbutz Ein Gev. Ask about a cruise on the lake after lunch (the kibbutz also has a boat company). Spend the night in Tiberias or at one of the kibbutz guesthouses or B&Bs in the Hula Valley.

The Hula Valley and Banias (Caesarea Philippi), Day 5

The next day, drive through the Hula Valley; it's especially remarkable in the spring when the flowers bloom and bring alive Jesus's famous teaching from the Sermon on the Mount: "Consider the lilies of the field, how they grow" (Matthew 6:28). At the base of Mount Hermon (which some scholars see as an alternative candidate for the site of the Transfiguration, as described in Mark 9:2–8), northeast of the Hula Valley, is Banias (Caesarea Philippi), where Jesus asked the disciples, "Who do people say I am?" (Matthew 16:13–20); it's in the Hermon Stream (Banias) Nature Reserve. The remains of a pagan Roman shrine are a powerful backdrop for contemplation of that message. Tel Dan, an important city in the biblical Kingdom of Israel, has a beautiful nature reserve. Stay overnight at your B&B or kibbutz hotel in the Hula Valley.

The Galilee Hills and the Coast, Day 6

Head for the hills, connecting to Route 77 and turning south onto Route 754 to Cana to see the church that commemorates Jesus's first miracle: changing water into wine (John 2:1–11). Continue to Nazareth, Jesus's childhood town. The massive modern Basilica of the Annunciation is built over a rock dwelling where Catholics believe the angel Gabriel appeared to Mary (Luke 1:26–38). The Greek Orthodox tradition is that the event took place at the village well, and their church is built over that site, some distance away. Nazareth's restaurants make tasty lunch stops.

A drive through the lush Jezreel Valley, via Route 60 and then north on Route 65 (the New Testament Valley of Armageddon), brings you to Mount Tabor, long identified as the Mount of Transfiguration. The valley is named Armageddon (Revelation 16:16), after the archaeological site of Tel Megiddo, now a national park south of Afula on Route 65. The drive back to Jerusalem from Tel Megiddo takes 1½ hours, using the Route 6 toll road, or you can spend the night in Haifa and return to Jerusalem the next day.

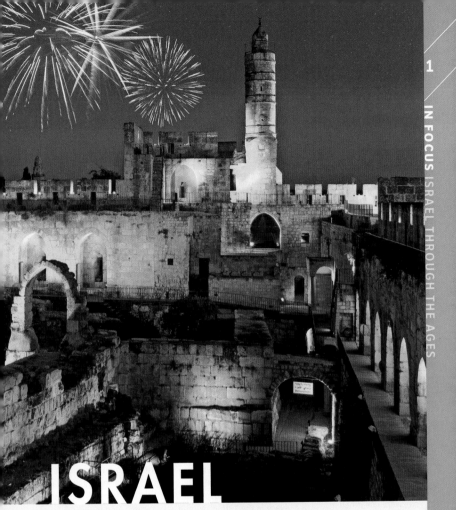

ISRAEL
THROUGH THE AGES

Where else in the world can you find the living history of three major religions that have been intertwined for more than 1,000 years? Israel is the crossroads for Christianity, Islam, and Judaism, and many of the remarkable sites here help to tell this country's unique story. One of the best examples can be found in Jerusalem's Old City, where you can visit the Church of the Holy Sepulcher, the Dome of the Rock, and the Western Wall all within a short walk of each other.

(top left) The Bible—David playing the harp while bringing the Ark of the Covenant from Kirjath-Jearim with other musicians. (bottom) The goddess Asherah was worshipped by some in ancient Israel as the consort of El and in Judah as the consort of Yahweh (some Hebrews baked small cakes for her festival). (right) Artist's depiction of Solomon's court (Ingobertus, c. 880).

1.2 million BC

Prehistory

The land that is now Israel served as a land bridge for Homo Erectus on his epic journey out of Africa. The oldest human remains found outside that continent, 1.4 million years old, were unearthed at Ubediya near Lake Kinneret (Sea of Galilee). It was in the Carmel Caves in northern Israel that the only indication of direct contact between Neanderthal Man and Homo Sapiens, 40,000 years ago, has been found, lending credence to the theory that they lived contemporaneously.

2000–1000 BC

Early Biblical Period

The arrival of Abraham, Isaac, and Jacob marked the beginning of the Patriarchal Age, dated to around 1800 BC. The Israelite exodus from Egypt took place in the 13th century BC. It was at this time that Israel was divided into Canaanite city-kingdoms. As the Israelites established themselves in the hill country, the Philistines, originating in the Aegean, were landing on the coastal plain. Around 1150, the Philistines invaded. A place name deriving from their presence endures to this day—Palestine.

1000–928 BC

United Monarchy

David conquered Jerusalem around 1000 BC, united the Israelite tribes into one kingdom, and established his capital here. David's son, Solomon, became king in 968 BC. Around 950 BC, Solomon built the First Temple in Jerusalem, the religious center. Shortly after Solomon's death in 928 BC, the kingdom split in two—the northern tribes, which seceded and formed the Kingdom of Israel, and the southern tribes, now known as the Kingdom of Judah.

(top left) Hexagonal cylinder of King Sennacherib of Assyria inscribed with an account of his invasion of Palestine and the siege of Jerusalem in the reign of Hezekiah, King of Judah, dated 686 BC. (top center) 1860 engraving of the Western Wall. (top right) Masada. (bottom left) Mosaic in the Church of the Holy Sepulcher, Jerusalem.

928–587 BC

For 200 years, the Kingdom of Israel and the Kingdom of Judah co-existed, though relations were sometimes hostile. But in 721 BC, the Assyrian army, which dominated the region, conquered Israel and took its residents eastward into captivity. The fate of these "ten lost tribes" would be a subject of speculation by scholars thereafter. In 586 BC, the Assyrians were defeated by a new power, the Babylonians. Their king, Nebuchadnezzar, conquered Judah and destroyed Jerusalem and the temple. Those who survived were exiled to the "rivers of Babylon."

538 BC–AD 73

Second Temple Period

This exile ended after only 50 years when Cyrus the Great of Persia conquered Babylonia and permitted the exiles to return to Judah. Jerusalem was rebuilt and a new temple erected. The vast Persian Empire was defeated by Alexander the Great in 333 BC. Judah the Maccabee claimed victory over Hellenistic armies in 165 BC and rededicated the defiled Jewish temple. Judean independence brought the Hasmonean dynasty to power in 142 BC, which the Romans ended when they annexed the country in 63 BC.

Jesus was born in Bethlehem, and 26 years later began his ministry, teaching mostly around the Sea of Galilee. In AD 29, Jesus and his disciples celebrated Passover in Jerusalem; he was arrested, put on trial, and crucified by the Romans soon after.

In AD 66, the Jews rose up against Roman rule. Their fierce revolt failed and Jerusalem and the temple were destroyed in the process, in AD 70. A vestige of the temple compound, the Western Wall, is venerated by Jews to this day. The last Jewish stronghold, Masada, fell three years later.

325 Constantine
makes Christianity
the imperial religion

622 Muhammad's
hejira and the
beginning of Islam

1099 Crusaders
conquer Jerusalem

500   700   900   1100

(immediate left) Bar Kochba's coin: top, the Jewish Temple facade with the rising star; reverse: A lulav, the text that reads: "to the freedom of Jerusalem." (top left) Saladin, commander of Muslim forces, battles Christians in the 3rd Crusade. (top right) Richard the Lionheart In battle during the Crusades.

Late Roman & Byzantine Period

AD 73–640

In 132, the Roman emperor Hadrian threatened to rebuild Jerusalem as a pagan city and another Jewish revolt broke out, led by Bar-Kochba. In retribution, Hadrian leveled Jerusalem in 135 and changed the name of the country to Syria Palestina. Many of the remaining Jews were killed, enslaved, or exiled.

It wasn't until the 4th century AD that the Roman emperor Constantine made Christianity the imperial religion. This revived life in the Holy Land, making it a focus of pilgrimage and church construction that included the Church of the Nativity in Bethlehem. In spite of persecution, a vibrant Jewish community still existed.

Muhammad's *hejira* (flight) from Mecca to Medina in Arabia took place in 622, marking the beginning of Islam. This became Year One on the Muslim calendar. When Muhammad died in 632, his followers burst out of Arabia and created a Muslim empire that within a century would extend from India to Spain.

Medieval Period

640–1516

The Dome of the Rock was constructed in Jerusalem in 691 by Caliph Abd al-Malik. In 1099, the Crusaders conquered the city and massacred Jews and Muslims there. Cities like Akko (also called Acre) and castles like Belvoir were developed around 1100. Muslim reconquest of the land under the Mamluks began in 1265. In 1291 Akko fell, marking the end of the Crusades. An outstanding period of architecture followed, especially in Jerusalem's Temple Mount (Haram esh-Sharif) and in the Muslim Quarter.

1265 Muslim reconquest begins	Akko falls in 1291, marking the end of the Crusader kingdom	1516 Mamluks defeated in Syria by the Ottoman Turks	1897 First World Zionist Conference
1300	**1500**	**1700**	**1900**

1

IN FOCUS ISRAEL THROUGH THE AGES

(top left) Jewish settlers known as Biluim, in Palestine, 1880s. The 38th Zionist congress, 1933. (bottom left) *Palestine Post* headline announcing declaration of independence in 1948.

Modern Period

1516–1917

In 1516, the Mamluks were defeated in Syria by the Ottoman Turks. Egyptian nationalists took control of Israel in 1832, but were expelled in 1840 with help from European nations. The country's population shifted in the 19th century, when the steamship made access easy.

The first World Zionist Conference, organized by Theodor Herzl, took place in 1897, fueling the idea of a Jewish homeland. In 1909, Tel Aviv was founded, and Degania, the first kibbutz, was established on the southern shore of the Sea of Galilee.

Creation of a Jewish State

1917–1948

The conquest of Palestine by the British in the First World War ushered in many critical changes. In 1917, the British government expressed support in the Balfour Declaration for creation of a Jewish homeland. Arab nationalism began to rise around 1920 in the post-Ottoman Middle East after Ottoman Turkey, which sided with Germany during the first World War, abandoned Palestine. This marked the point at which tension between Jews and Arabs began to increase, peaking in the massacre of Jews in 1920, 1929, and again in 1936. Various Jewish militias formed to counter the violence.

The British "White Paper" of 1939 restricted Jewish immigration and land purchase in Palestine. Tensions with Britain, and clashes between Arabs and Jews, peaked after World War II. The United Nations Partition Plan of 1947 envisioned two states in Palestine, one Jewish and one Arab. With the end of the British mandate in May 1948, David Ben-Gurion, the Palestinian Jewish leader who would later become Israel's first prime minister, declared Israel a Jewish state. In the following months, Israel survived invasions by the armies of several Arab nations.

(left) David Ben-Gurion in 1918. (top right) Knesset, Israeli parliament, Jerusalem. (bottom right) Israeli flag.

The First 50 Years

1948–1998

Fighting ended January, 1949, and a U.N.-supervised cease-fire agreement was signed. Transjordan annexed the West Bank and East Jerusalem; Egypt annexed the Gaza Strip. Palestinian Arabs who fled or were expelled settled in neighboring countries; those who stayed became Israeli citizens. The first elections to the Knesset took place, and David Ben-Gurion was elected prime minister. In 1950, the Knesset enacted the Law of Return, giving any Jew the right to Israeli citizenship.

Around 1964, the Palestine Liberation Organization (PLO) was founded, which sought an independent state for Palestinians and refused to recognize Israel as a state. In 1967, the Six-Day War broke out; Israel occupied territory including the Golan Heights. Egypt and Syria attacked Israel on Yom Kippur in 1973. The Lebanon War in 1982 met with unprecedented Israeli opposition. In 1987, the *intifada* (uprising) brought sustained Palestinian Arab unrest. The Oslo Accords, signed in 1994, involved mutual recognition of Israel and the PLO, as well as Palestinian autonomy in the Gaza Strip and parts of the West Bank.

Israel Today

1998–Present

After Ehud Barak was elected prime minister in 1999, Israel withdrew from Lebanon. The second *intifada* began in 2000 and subsided in 2005, costing more than 3,000 Israeli and Palestinian lives. When Israel withdrew from the Gaza Strip (2005), the Islamist Hamas took over and made it a base for rocket attacks against Israel. In November 2012, the Palestinian Authority won United Nations recognition of Palestine as a sovereign (but non-member) state. Despite this, tensions continue to flare periodically.

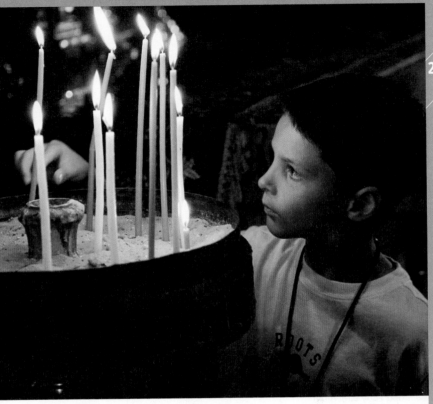

JERUSALEM

WELCOME TO JERUSALEM

TOP REASONS TO GO

★ **The Old City:** For an astonishing montage of religions and cultures, the heart of Jerusalem—with the Holy Sepulcher, Arab bazaar, and Western Wall—has few equals anywhere in the world.

★ **Mount of Olives:** This classic panorama puts the entire Old City, with the golden Dome of the Rock, squarely within your lens. The view is best with the morning sun behind you.

★ **Machaneh Yehuda:** You can munch a falafel as you watch shoppers swirl and eddy through West Jerusalem's outstanding produce market.

★ **Israel Museum:** Renewed and revitalized, this museum is a winner, with the Dead Sea Scrolls, a huge outdoor model, and a stunning collection of fine art, archaeology, and Judaica.

★ **City of David:** Plunge underground to explore Jerusalem's most ancient remains, and wade the 2,700-year-old water tunnel that once saved the besieged city—or exit dry.

ROMEMA

KEREM AVRAHAM

Central Bus Station

MEKOR BARUKH

Machaneh Yehuda Market

MACHANEH YEHUDA

Bezal'el

Bezal'el

Sacher Park

SHA'AREI HESED

GIVAT RAM

Knesset

KIRYAT WOLFSON

CENTER CITY

Yad Veshem Holocaust Museum

← NEVE GRANOT

Ruppin

Ramban

REHAVIA

3

Israel Museum

NAYOT

1 **The Old City.** With its narrow streets and hidden alleys, Jerusalem's legendary Old City is a labyrinth of memories and a bewitching kaleidoscope of colors and cultures best epitomized by the *souk*, or bazaar. Its headline sights are the Church of the Holy Sepulcher, the Western Wall, and the Dome of the Rock, redolent with religion and full of history.

2 **East Jerusalem.** Most visitors, particularly Christians, will identify with two or three particular sites—Mount of Olives, Gethsemane, and the Garden Tomb are the obvious ones. Just outside the Old City, the Rockefeller Archaeological Museum is a little-known gem.

3 **West Jerusalem.** Within this extensive side of Jerusalem are several great

**Map labels:**

University Garden

Yehezkel

GE'ULA

BEIT ISRAEL

Me'a She'arim

Khalid Ibn-Al-Walid

Ikhwan A-Safa

EAST JERUSALEM

El-Muqadasi

WADI AL-JOZ

2

M'EA SHE'ARIM

Strauss

Nablus Rd.

Shmu'el Ben Adaya

Saladin St.

Boat #1

U.S. Consulate

Rockefeller Archaeological Museum

Garden Tomb

Sultan Suleiman

Orson Hyde Garden

Hanevi'im

Jaffa Rd.

RUSSIAN COMPOUND

MORASHA

Herod's Gate

MUSLIM QUARTER

Shivtei Israel

Hanevi'm

Damascus Gate

Damascus Gate

2

NAHALAT SHIVA

Shlomzion Hamalka

Hatzanchanim

Arab Bazaar

Via Dolorosa

Lions' Gate

MOUNT OF OLIVES

uda

4

New Gate

CHRISTIAN QUARTER

Church of the Holy Sepulcher

TEMPLE MOUNT

Gethsemane

Ophel Rd.

Jericho Rd.

Independence Park

Yitzhak Kariv (Mamilla)

OLD CITY 1

Dome of the Rock

Jewish Cemetery

Agron

King David St.

Jaffa Gate

Western Wall

JEWISH QUARTER

al-Aqsa Mosque

CITY OF DAVID

KEY

Light rail

YEMIN MOSHE

Keren Hayesod

Dung Gate

Ma'ale Ha-Shalom

SILWAN

Hativat Yerushalayim

ARMENIAN QUARTER

Zion Gate

Jabotinsky

Hebron Rd.

MOUNT ZION

5

GERMAN COLONY

Hativat Yerushalayim

---

but unrelated sights, some a few miles apart. Savor the extraordinary Israel Museum and the Yad Vashem Holocaust Museum.

4 Center City. West Jerusalem's Downtown areas have more subtle attractions than the 'postcard snapshots' suggest. Check out the Yemin Moshe and Nahalat Shiva neighborhoods, Ben-Yehuda Street, and the Machaneh Yehuda market.

5 German Colony and Baka. Stone architecture, trendy restaurants, and great coffee shops offer a refreshing change of pace from the holy and historical.

GETTING ORIENTED

Hilly Jerusalem has two centers of gravity—the Old City, on the east side; and the modern Center City, on the west. Jerusalem is Israel's capital and home to its national institutions, most in Jewish West Jerusalem. East Jerusalem, including the Old City, is largely (but not entirely) Arab. Coexistence is sometimes fragile, and the two communities tend to keep to themselves.

Updated by
Mike Rogoff
and Shira
Rubin

Jerusalem is a city suspended between heaven and earth, East and West, past and present—parallel universes of flowing caftans and trendy coffee shops. For some people, Jerusalem is a condition, like being in love; for others, it is a state of mind, a constant tension between rival flags and faiths, or members of the same faith. You may feel moved, energized, or swept into the maelstrom of contemporary issues—but the city will not leave you unaffected.

The word *unique* is easy to throw around, but Jerusalem has a real claim on it. The city is sacred to half the human race, and its iconic Old City walls embrace primary sites of the three great monotheistic religions. For Jews, Jerusalem has always been their spiritual focus and historical national center; the imposing Western Wall is the last remnant of the ancient Second Temple complex. For almost 2,000 years, Christians have venerated Jerusalem as the place where their faith was shaped—through the death, burial, and resurrection of Jesus of Nazareth—and the candlelit Church of the Holy Sepulcher is where the greater part of Christendom recognizes those events. Islamic tradition identifies Jerusalem as the *masjid al-aqsa,* the "farthermost place," from which Muhammad ascended to Heaven for his portentous meeting with God: the dazzling, gold-top Dome of the Rock marks the spot.

The Old City is far more than shrines, however. Its arches, hidden courtyards, and narrow cobblestone alleyways beckon you back in time. The streets are crowded with travelers, pilgrims, and vendors of everything from tourist trinkets and leather sandals to fresh produce and embroidered fabrics. Your senses are assaulted by intense colors and by the aromas of turmeric, fresh mint, wild sage, and cardamom-spiced coffee. The blare of Arabic music and the burble of languages fill the air.

Step outside the Old City and you'll be transported into the 21st century—well, at least the 20th: quaint neighborhoods, some restored, embody an earlier simplicity. West Jerusalem forms the bulk of a modern metropolis of 850,000, Israel's largest city. It's not as cosmopolitan as

Tel Aviv, but it does have good restaurants, fine hotels, vibrant markets, and upscale neighborhoods. The Downtown triangle of Jaffa Street, King George Street, and Ben-Yehuda Street, the elegant Mamilla Mall outside Jaffa Gate, and the restored First Station are natural gathering places.

The city prides itself on its historical continuity. A municipal bylaw dating back to 1918 makes it mandatory to face even high-rise commercial buildings with the honey-colored "Jerusalem stone," the local limestone that has served Jerusalem's builders since, well, forever. Watch the stone walls glow at sunset—the source of the by-now clichéd but still compelling phrase "Jerusalem of Gold"—and understand the mystical hold Jerusalem has had on so many minds and hearts for so many thousands of years.

JERUSALEM PLANNER

WHEN TO GO

Jerusalem, like Israel in general, is a year-round destination, but the very best months are late March through April, and October through November, when prices are lower and the weather is good, even warm. Winter is colder than in Tel Aviv, but sunny days often follow gloomy ones. Jerusalem gets its own back in the hot, rainless summer months; the inland capital is dry and cools off toward evening. Avoid the main Jewish holidays, when hotels charge peak prices, and some tourist attractions are more crowded than usual.

PLANNING YOUR TIME

Israel itineraries tend to favor Jerusalem. The Old City alone offers an absorbing two days. Beyond its religious shrines are ancient sites, panoramic walks, and museums. Allow time for poking around the Arab market and the stores of the Jewish Quarter. The immediate environs—the City of David, Mount of Olives, Mount Zion, and a few sites north of the Old City walls—can add another day. West Jerusalem's spread-out attractions take patience to explore. Add time for shopping and you're quickly up to a five- to six-day stay. Jerusalem is also a convenient base for day trips to Masada and the Dead Sea, and even Tel Aviv.

A few tips for maximizing your time: Make a list of must-see sights. Pay attention to opening times and plot out your day's destinations to minimize backtracking. Mix experiences each day, to avoid overdosing on museums, shrines, or archaeology. Above all, take time to let your senses absorb the city. Take time to walk around and sip a coffee at a sidewalk café. Jerusalem is as much about atmosphere as it is a checklist of world-class sights.

TRAVEL PRECAUTIONS

Violence against individuals is rare and tourists aren't specific targets. Nevertheless, avoid Muslim Quarter backstreets, and be cautious walking around the Old City at night (when almost everything is closed anyway). The important weekly Muslim prayers around midday Friday sometimes get passionate if there's a hot Palestinian-Israeli issue in the news. Emotions can spill into the streets of the Muslim Quarter as the crowds leave the al-Aqsa Mosque.

As in any major tourist destination, pickpockets can be a problem: keep purses closed and close to you, and wallets in less accessible pockets. Don't leave valuables in parked cars, and use hotel safes.

GETTING HERE AND AROUND

AIR TRAVEL

A 40-minute drive from Jerusalem, Ben Gurion International Airport is the region's largest gateway and the point of entry for most travelers entering Israel. *For more information on air travel to Israel and airport transfer, see Getting Here and Around in Travel Smart.*

BUS TRAVEL

Taking the bus from Ben Gurion Airport to Jerusalem Central Station (or vice versa) is cheap but slow. The Egged shuttle bus, Lines 5 and 5a (fare NIS 5, Israel shekels only), takes 10 minutes to the El Al Junction on Route 40, just outside the airport. Connect to Egged bus, Line 947 (fare NIS 21.50) to Jerusalem's Central Bus Station. Afkim Bus 485 connects the airport with the Central Bus Station and several other stops, offering hourly service for NIS 16. A much easier, but sometimes tedious, alternative is a 10-seat *sherut* taxi (limo-van), run by Nesher. They depart from Ben Gurion Airport (outside Terminal 3) as soon as they fill up, and drop you at any Jerusalem address for NIS 64.

Intercity buses travel all over the country from the Central Bus Station, with frequent departures on more popular routes. A few (like Eilat) require prebooking, which can be done online at ⊕ *www.egged.co.il.* *See Getting Here and Around in Travel Smart for more information.*

Egged also operates the extensive bus service within Jerusalem. The fare is NIS 5.90, and you don't need exact change. If you have several days in Jerusalem, consider a Rav Kav card, available at the Central Bus Station, which is good for travel on buses and the light-rail, and allows for transfers between them within a 90-minute period. Extra credit on the card can be bought from bus drivers but not on the train.

CAR TRAVEL

By car, Route 1 is the chief route to Jerusalem. Route 443 is often quicker, although it passes through a quiet part of the West Bank and, though unlikely, you may be stopped very briefly at an Israeli army checkpoint.

In the city, walking and hailing or ordering a taxi or van as needed is a better idea than a rental car: traffic, navigation, and parking may be more than your schedule and disposition can bear.

LIGHT-RAIL TRAVEL

Jerusalem's single light-rail line is useful (if it's going your way) and pleasant (if it's not rush hour). It runs from Pisgat Ze'ev in the far northeast of the city, via French Hill, Damascus Gate, Jaffa Street, the Central Bus Station, over the Bridge of Strings, to Mount Herzl in the southwest. The trains operate Sunday to Thursday between 5:30 am and midnight. On Friday and Jewish holiday eves, the last train leaves from either terminus about two hours before sunset, and service resumes on Saturday about an hour after dark. Route details and updated schedules are available online in English. Single tickets (NIS 5.90) can be purchased from machines at each station platform

CLOSE UP

Jerusalem Through the Ages

2

The first known mention of Jerusalem is in Egyptian "hate texts" of the 20th century BC, but many archaeologists give the city a considerably earlier founding date. Abraham and the biblical Joshua may have been here, but it was King David, circa 1004 BC, who captured the city and made it his capital, thus propelling it onto the center stage of history.

FIRST AND SECOND TEMPLES

King David's son Solomon built the "First" Temple, giving the city a preeminence it enjoyed until its destruction by the Babylonians, and the exile of its population, in 586 BC. Jews returned 50 years later, rebuilt the Temple (the "Second"), and began the slow process of revival. By the 2nd century BC, Jerusalem was again a vibrant Jewish capital, albeit one with a good dose of Hellenistic cultural influence. Herod the Great (who reigned 37 BC–4 BC) revamped the Temple on a magnificent scale and expanded the city into a cosmopolis of world renown.

This was the Jerusalem Jesus knew, a city of monumental architecture, teeming—especially during the Jewish pilgrim festivals—with tens of thousands of visitors. It was here that the Romans crucified Jesus (circa AD 29), and here, too, that the Great Jewish Revolt against Rome erupted, ending in AD 70 with the destruction (once again) of the city and the Temple.

FROM THE ROMANS TO THE BRITISH

The Roman emperor Hadrian built a redesigned Jerusalem as the pagan polis of Aelia Capitolina (AD 135), an urban plan that became the basis for the Old City of today. The Byzantines made it a Christian center, with a massive wave of church building (4th–6th centuries AD), until the Arab conquest of AD 638 brought the holy city under Muslim sway. Except during the golden age of the Ummayad Dynasty, in the late 7th and early 8th centuries, Jerusalem was no more than a provincial town under the Muslim regimes of the early Middle Ages. The Crusaders stormed it in 1099 and made it the capital of their Latin Kingdom. With the reconquest of Jerusalem by the Muslims, the city again lapsed into a languid provincialism for 700 years under the Mamluk and Ottoman empires. The British conquest in 1917 thrust the city back into the world limelight as rising Jewish and Arab nationalisms vied to possess it.

DIVIDED AND REUNITED

Jerusalem was divided by the 1948 war: the larger Jewish western sector became the capital of the new State of Israel, while Jordan annexed the smaller, predominantly Arab eastern sector, which included the Old City. The Six-Day War of 1967 reunited the city under Israeli rule, but the concept of an Arab "East" Jerusalem and a Jewish "West" Jerusalem remains, even though new Jewish neighborhoods in the northeastern and southeastern parts of town have made the distinction oversimplified.

The holy city continues to engage the attention of devotees of Christianity, Judaism, and Islam. Between Jews and Arabs it remains a source of hot dispute and occasional violence as rival visions clash for possession of the city's past and control of its future.

using cash shekels or a credit card, but the process is a bit cumbersome. Validation in the train of the ticket or Rav Kav card *(see Bus Travel, above)* must be done immediately on boarding.

Information Jerusalem Light Rail. ☎ *073/210–0601* ⊕ *www.citypass.co.il/english.*

TAXI TRAVEL

The fare for taxis to and from the airport is NIS 280 during the day and NIS 320 after 9 pm.

Taxis can be flagged on the street, reserved by phone, or picked up at major hotels. The law requires taxi drivers to use their meters.

TRAIN TRAVEL

Trains run from Jerusalem's Malcha Train Station to Tel Aviv. There is no service on the Sabbath or Jewish religious holidays. The last train on Friday or holiday eves departs from either city about two hours before sunset. Service resumes late Saturday night (⊕ *www.rail.co.il* for updated schedules). The trip takes 85 minutes and costs NIS 20 one way, NIS 32 return. It's a fun family excursion.

TOURS

BIKE TOURS

Bike Jerusalem. You should be fairly skilled to join Bike Jerusalem's day tours through the city, but the night tours can accommodate less-experienced bikers (cost from NIS 230). The price includes bike and helmet rentals. If you want, you can also just rent a bike and set out on your own (cost from NIS 60). The company prides itself on its broad range of biking excursions throughout the country and its English-speaking guides. ⊠ *Jaffa Gate* ☎ *02/579–6353, 052/320–1273* ⊕ *www.bikejerusalem.com* ☒ *NIS 230.*

Jerusalem Midnight Biking. This company offers its nighttime rides through the alleyways of the Old City, as well as daytime rides through other parts of Jerusalem (cost from NIS 230). Private tours allow you more flexibility about what you do and see. The cost includes bike and helmet rentals. Tours are led by English-speaking guides and are limited to riders age 12 and over. Tours meet on Kariv Street, just outside Jaffa Gate. ⊠ *Jerusalem* ☎ *02/566–1441, 050/979–1035* ⊕ *www.jerusalem-biking.com* ☒ *NIS 115–NIS 230.*

ORIENTATION TOURS

Bein Harim Tours. Half-day Jerusalem orientation tours include a panoramic view of the Old City and a close-up view of the highlights. Except for Saturday, full-day tours usually add the Holocaust museum at Yad Vashem (although many visitors prefer to do this museum on their own so they can see it at their own pace). The price includes pickup from major Jerusalem hotels (additional charge for pickup in Tel Aviv and coast). ⊠ *Tel Aviv* ☎ *03/542–2000* ⊕ *www.beinharimtours.com* ☒ *$48–$89.*

PRIVATE GUIDES

The daily rate for a guide-driven car or limo-van, up to seven passengers, is in the range of $700; tourists paying in foreign currency are exempt from V.A.T. (Value-Added Tax). Entrance fees are not included and over-mileage charges apply. Many guides will offer their services without a car for $250 to $350 per day. For a private tour, approach Kedma Israel Travel, GUY Tours, or Genesis Boutique Travel.

Genesis Boutique Travel. This intimate operation provides guide-driven vehicles and customized ground services throughout the Jerusalem area and the rest of the country. ⊠ *Jerusalem* ☎ *02/676–5868, 052/286–2650* ⊕ *www.genesis-boutique-travel.com.*

GUY Tours. In business for more than 50 years, GUY Tours is the country's largest private tour company. It offers guided tours both in and around Jerusalem, as well as the rest of the country. ⊠ *Jerusalem* ☎ *02/638–3318* ⊕ *guy-tours.com.*

Kedma Israel Travel. This boutique agency prides itself on its personal touch in handling everything for your tailor-made trip. Guide-driven tours are its strong suit. ☎ *08/970–4139, 054/345–1808* ⊕ *www.kedmatravel.com.*

WALKING TOURS

Sandeman's New Europe. This European company offers free two-hour tours of the most famous sights, led by licensed guides, as well as longer, in-depth routes in and around the Old City (the latter for payment). ⊠ *Jerusalem* ☎ ⊕ *www.newjerusalemtours.com* 🎟 *NIS 100–NIS 120.*

VISITOR INFORMATION

Christian Information Centre. Run by the Franciscans (Roman Catholic), the CIC is a source of information about Christian holy sites, and the times, places, and language of Catholic masses and Protestant services. It is closed Sunday. ⊠ *Omar ibn el-Khatab Sq., Jaffa Gate* ✚ *Just inside Jaffa Gate* ☎ *02/627–2692* ⊕ *www.cicts.org.*

Jerusalem Tourist Information Center. Open daily and run by the Israel Ministry of Tourism, the center is a useful stopping point for orientation information and more. ⊠ *Omar Ibn Hatab Sq., Jaffa Gate* ✚ *Just inside Jaffa Gate* ☎ *02/627–1422* ⊕ *www.goisrael.com.*

EXPLORING JERUSALEM

Immerse yourself in Jerusalem. Of course, you can see the primary sights in a couple of days—some visitors claim to have done it in less—but don't short-change yourself if you can help it. Take time to wander where the spirit takes you, to linger longer over a snack and people-watch, to follow the late Hebrew poet, Yehuda Amichai, "in the evening into the Old City / and...emerge from it pockets stuffed with images / and metaphors and well-constructed parables..." The poet struggled for breath in an atmosphere "saturated with prayers and dreams"; but the city's baggage of history and religion doesn't have to weigh you down. Decompress in the markets and eateries of the Old City, and the jewelry and art stores, coffee shops, and pubs of the New.

The city is built on a series of hills, part of the country's north–south watershed. To the east, the Judean Desert tumbles down to the Dead Sea, the lowest point on Earth, less than an hour's drive away. The main highway to the west winds down through the pine-covered Judean

Hills toward the international airport and Tel Aviv. North and south of the city—Samaria and Judea, respectively—is what is known today as the West Bank. Since 1967, this contested area has been administered largely by Israel, though the major concentrations of Arab population are currently under autonomous Palestinian control.

OLD CITY

The city's primary religious sites in the Christian and Muslim quarters, and at the Western Wall, are the very essence of historical Jerusalem: explore and touch the different cultures that share it. The Old City's 35,000 inhabitants jostle in the cobblestone lanes with an air of ownership, at best merely tolerating the "intruders" from other quarters. Devout Jews in black and white scurry from their neighborhoods north and west of the Old City, through Damascus Gate and the Muslim Quarter, toward the Western Wall. Arab women in long, embroidered dresses flow across the Western Wall plaza to Dung Gate and the village of Silwan beyond it. It's not unusual to stand at the Western Wall, surrounded by the sounds of devotions, and hear the piercing call to prayer of the Muslim *muezzin* above you, with the more distant bells of the Christian Quarter providing a counterpoint.

Sites such as the Western Wall, Calvary, and the Haram esh-Sharif bring a thrill of recognition to ancient history. The devout can't fail to be moved by the holy city, and its special, if sometimes dissonant, moods and modes of devotion tend to fascinate the nonbeliever as well.

GETTING HERE AND AROUND

To explore the key sites in one day, keep in mind opening times and geography, and plan accordingly. Beat the security line for the Temple Mount (Muslim shrines) with a really early start; the only entrance is above the Western Wall and visiting times are limited. Exit the northern end of the mount to the Via Dolorosa and Holy Sepulcher. Entering the Old City via Jaffa Gate will take you right to the Holy Sepulcher and on to the Western Wall. Lions' Gate is best for beginning with St. Anne's Church and the Via Dolorosa. Damascus Gate plunges you into the bazaar, and thence to whatever sequence of sights you prefer. Of course, you can spread your visit over more than one day.

TIMING AND PRECAUTIONS

Avoid the Muslim Quarter, and thus the first six stations of the Via Dolorosa, between noon and 2 pm Friday, the time of important weekly Muslim prayers. All the holy places demand modest dress: no shorts or short capris, no sleeveless tops, no low necklines.

JEWISH QUARTER

This is at once the Old City's oldest quarter and its newest neighborhood. Abandoned for a generation after the War of Independence, the quarter was restored and resettled after the Six-Day War of 1967. The subsequent archaeological excavations exposed artifacts and structures that date back 27 centuries and more. If you have a photographer's eye, get off the main streets and stroll at random. The limestone houses and alleys—often counterpointed with a shock of bougainvillea or palm fronds and ficus trees—offer pleasing compositions.

If you like to people-watch, find a shaded café table and sip a good latte while the world jitterbugs by. The population of the Jewish Quarter is almost entirely religious, roughly split between "modern" Orthodox (devout, but integrated into contemporary Israeli society at every level) and the more traditional ultra-Orthodox (men in black frock coats and black hats, in many ways a community apart). The locals, especially the women, tend to dress very conservatively. Several religious-study institutions attract a transient population of young students, many of them from abroad. Religious Jewish families tend to have lots of kids, and little ones here are given independence at an astonishingly early age. It's quite common to see three- and four-year-olds toddling home from preschool alone or shepherded by a one-year-more-mature brother or sister. And if you see a big group of Israeli soldiers, don't assume the worst. The army maintains a center for its educational tours here, and the recruits are more likely than not boisterously kidding around with each other as they follow their guide. Shopping is good here—especially jewelry and Judaica—and there are decent fast-food options when hunger strikes.

A renewed landmark of the quarter is the high, white-domed Hurva Synagogue. It was built and soon destroyed in the 18th century, rebuilt in the 19th, and blown up when the Jordanian Arab Legion captured the area in the 1948 war. The current building, rededicated in spring 2010, is a faithful reconstruction of its predecessor.

GETTING HERE AND AROUND
It's best to approach the Jewish Quarter on foot. From Jaffa Gate, you can plunge directly ahead into the Arab bazaar and follow David Street until it becomes a T-junction: the right turn becomes Jewish Quarter Street. Alternatively, after you enter Jaffa Gate, follow the vehicle road to the right and through a small tunnel, then turn left (on foot) onto St. James Street and down to the quarter. A third idea is to begin your tour on Mount Zion, and then continue to the Jewish Quarter through Zion Gate.

TIMING AND PRECAUTIONS
Allow at least two hours to explore the Jewish Quarter, not counting shopping and eating. If you're pressed for time, absorb the scene over the rim of a glass or mug, and take time to visit the Herodian Quarter. Avoid visiting on Saturday, when everything is closed, and some religious locals may resent you taking pictures on their Sabbath. Sites with entrance fees close by midday Friday.

TOP ATTRACTIONS
Burnt House. "We could almost smell the burning and feel the heat of the flames," wrote archaeologist Nahman Avigad, whose team uncovered evidence of the Roman devastation of Jerusalem in AD 70. The affluent residence was part of a larger complex under today's Jewish Quarter. Charred cooking pots, sooty debris, and—most arresting—the skeletal hand and arm of a woman clutching a scorched staircase recaptured the poignancy of the moment. Stone weights inscribed with the name Bar Katros—a Jewish priestly family known from ancient sources—suggested that this might have been a basement industrial workshop,

The Old City

MOUNT OF OLIVES

Jericho Rd.

Ophel Rd.

Golden Gate

al-Aqsa Mosque

Lions' (St. Stephen's) Gate

Church of St. Anne

Bab al-Asbat

El-Omari Rd.

Rockefeller Archaeological Museum

Sultan Suleiman Rd.

Bab Hutta Rd.

Pools of Bethesda **5**

Dome of the Rock **4**

Bab el-Silsila

2 Western (Wailing) Wall Plaza

3

Bab el-Qattanin

Aqabat Shaddad

Bab al-Ghawanmeh

Bab al-Nadhir

Aqabat el-Bustami

Monastery of the Flagellation

Al-Mujahideen Rd.

El-Wad Rd.

Herod's Gate

Saladin St.

Aqabat el-Mawlawiyeh

Aqabat el-Rahbat

Ibn Al-Jarrah Rd.

MUSLIM QUARTER

Aqabat esh-Sheikh Rihan

6 Via Dolorosa **7**

Aqabat el-Khalidieh

Aqabat el-Saraya

El-Hakkari Rd.

Bab el-Silsila (St. of the Chain)

El-Wad Rd.

Via Dolorosa

Aqabat el-Takiyeh (Khaski Sultan)

Suq el-Attarin

Suq el-Lahhamin

MURISTAN

Suq Khan ez-Zeit

Damascus Gate

8

9

Der el-Habes

St. Francis Rd.

Christian Quarter Rd.

Nablus Rd.

Hatzanchanim

Greek Orthodox Patriarchate Rd.

Greek Catholic Patriarchate Rd.

CHRISTIAN QUARTER

Casa Nova Rd.

Casa Nova Hospice

Rd. 1

Notre Dame de France

New Gate

KEY

🛈 Tourist information
--- Path
— Light rail

OPHEL

KIDRON VALLEY

Gihon Spring
Hezekiah's Tunnel

Robinson's Arch **1**

Warren's Shaft **14**

CITY OF DAVID

Dung Gate

Ophel Rd.

Pool ◆
Pool ◆

Wall Plaza

Steps to Western Wall

Western Wall

Misgav Ladach St.

12

13

JEWISH QUARTER

Hurva Square

Steps to Western Wall

Bab al-...

11

Hurva Synagogue

Jewish Quarter St.

10

Habad St.

Melchizedek Rd.

Ma'alot Hashalom

Beit El St.

Via Dolorosa **7**
Western Wall **2**
Western Wall Tunnel **3**

David St.

Christ Church

Ara St.

St. James's St.

Cathedral of St. James

Armenian Orthodox Monastery

ARMENIAN QUARTER

Armenian Orthodox Patriarchate Rd.

16

Citadel

Zion Gate

19

20 **21** **22**

MT. ZION

Hativat Etzioni

Hativat Yerushalayim

Pools of Bethesda and
Church of St. Anne **5**
Ramparts Walk **15**
Room of the Last Supper . **20**
Tomb of David **21**
Tower of David Museum .. **16**

Herodian Quarter/
Wohl Archaeological
Museum **13**
Hinnom Valley **18**
Jerusalem Archaeological
Park and Davidson Center .. **1**
Park Teddy **17**

MOUNT HERZL

Hospice

Jaffa Gate

15

🛈 **7**

17

Hutzot Hayotzer
(Arts and Crafts La.)

18

Jaffa Rd.

Yitzhak Kariv (Mamilla)

Mishkenot Sha'anannim

0 ___ 1/8 mile
0 ___ 1/8 kilometer

City of David **14**
Dome of the Rock
and Haram esh-Sharif
(Temple Mount) **4**
Dormition Abbey **19**
Ecce Homo Convent of
the Sisters of Zion **6**
Ethiopian Monastery **8**

Broad Wall **11**
Burnt House **12**
Cardo **10**
Chamber of
the Holocaust **22**
Church of the
Holy Sepulcher **9**

possibly for the manufacture of sacramental incense used in the Temple. A video presentation re-creates the bitter civil rivalries of the period and the city's tragic end; book online for the English showing. ✉ *2 Tiferet Israel St., Jewish Quarter* ✛ *At end of line of eateries before descent to Western Wall* ☎ *02/626–5922* ⊕ *www.rova-yehudi.org.il* ✏ *NIS 29* ⊘ *Closed Sat. and Jewish religious holidays.*

Fodor'sChoice   **Herodian Quarter/Wohl Archaeological Museum.** Excavations in the 1970s
★   exposed the Jewish Quarter's most visually interesting site: the remains of sumptuous mansions from the late Second Temple period. Preserved in the basement of a modern Jewish seminary—but entered separately—the geometrically patterned mosaic floors, still-vibrant frescoes, and costly glassware and ceramics provide a peek into the life of the wealthy in the days of Herod and Jesus. Several small plastered cisterns, with broad steps descending into them, have been identified as private *mikvahs* (Jewish ritual baths); holograms depict their use. Large stone water jars are just like those described in the New Testament story of the wedding at Cana (John 2). Rare stone tables resemble the dining-room furniture depicted in Roman stone reliefs found in Europe.

On the last of the site's three distinct levels is a mansion with an estimated original floor area of some 6,000 square feet. None of the upper stories has survived, but the fine, fashionable stucco work and the quality of the artifacts found here indicate an exceptional standard of living, leading some scholars to suggest this may have been the long-sought palace of the high priest. The charred ceiling beams and scorched mosaic floor and fresco at the southern end of the reception hall bear witness to the Roman torching of the neighborhood in the late summer of AD 70, exactly one month after the Temple itself had been destroyed. Allow about 45 minutes to explore the site. ✉ *1 Hakara'im Rd., Jewish Quarter* ✛ *Entrance a few steps east of Hurva Sq.* ☎ *02/626–5922* ⊕ *www.rova-yehudi.org.il* ✏ *NIS 20* ⊘ *Closed Sat. and Jewish religious holidays.*

Jerusalem Archaeological Park and Davidson Center. Though strictly speaking outside the Jewish Quarter, this site is related to it historically, and is often visited at the same time. A gold mine for Israeli archaeologists, its most dramatic and monumental finds were from the Herodian period, the late 1st century BC. The low-rise, air-conditioned **Davidson Center** (on your right as you enter the site) offers visual aids, some artifacts, two interesting videos (which alternate between English and Hebrew), and modern restrooms. Allow 30 minutes for the center and another 40 minutes for the site.

The best place to start a tour is the high corner, off to the left as you enter the site. King Herod the Great rebuilt the Second Temple on the exact site of its predecessor, more or less where the Dome of the Rock now stands. He expanded the sacred enclosure by constructing a massive, shoebox-shaped retaining wall on the slopes of the hill, the biblical Mount Moriah. The inside was filled with thousands of tons of rubble to level off the hill and create the huge platform, the size of 27 football fields, known today as the Temple Mount. The stones near the corner, with their signature precision-cut borders, are not held together with

With its cobblestone streets and limestone houses, the Jewish Quarter of the Old City is a favorite of tourists.

mortar; their sheer weight gives the structure its stability. The original wall is thought to have been a third higher than it is today.

To the left of the corner is the white pavement of an impressive main street and commercial area from the Second Temple period. The protrusion high above your head is known as **Robinson's Arch,** named for a 19th-century American explorer. It is a remnant of a monumental bridge to the Temple Mount that was reached by a staircase from the street where you now stand: look for the ancient steps. The square-cut building stones heaped on the street came from the top of the original wall, dramatic evidence of the Roman destruction of AD 70. A piece of Hebrew scriptural graffiti (Isaiah 66:14) was etched into a stone, possibly by a Jewish pilgrim, some 15 centuries ago.

Climb the wooden steps and turn left through the shaded square. A modern spiral staircase descends below present ground level to a partially reconstructed labyrinth of Byzantine dwellings and mosaics; from here you reemerge outside the present city walls. Alternatively, stay at ground level and continue east through a small arched gate. The broad, impressive **Southern Steps** on your left, a good part of them original, once brought hordes of Jewish pilgrims through the now-blocked southern gates of the Temple Mount. The rock-hewn ritual baths near the bottom of the steps were used for the purification rites once demanded of Jews before they entered the sacred temple precincts. This section of the site, directly below the al-Aqsa Mosque, closes at 11 am on Friday, before the Muslim prayer time. ⊠ *Inside Dung Gate, Jewish Quarter* ✛ *South of Western Wall* ☎ *02/627–7550* ⊕ *www.archpark.org.il* ⌦ *NIS 30* ☺ *Closed Sat. and Jewish religious holidays.*

CLOSE UP

Jews in the Old City

The history of Jewish life in the Old City has been marked by the trials of conflict and the joys of creating and rebuilding community. Here are some highlights from the medieval period on.

1099. Crusaders conquer Jerusalem and massacre much of its population. Jews lived at the time in today's Muslim Quarter.

1267. Spanish rabbi Nachmanides ("Ramban") reestablishes Jewish community. (His synagogue is on Jewish Quarter Street.)

1517. Ottoman Turks conquer Palestine and allow Sephardic Jews (expelled from Spain a generation earlier) to resettle the country. A cluster of four interlinked synagogues gradually emerges in the quarter.

1700. A large group of Ashkenazi Jews from Eastern Europe settles in Jerusalem.

1860. The first neighborhood is established outside the walls (Mishkenot Sha'ananim). Initially, very few Old City Jews had the courage to move out.

1948. Israel's War of Independence. The Jewish Quarter surrenders to Jordanian forces and is abandoned. By then, the residents of the quarter represent only a tiny percentage of Jerusalem's Jewish population.

1967. Six-Day War. The Jewish Quarter, much of it ruined, is recaptured. Archaeological excavations and restoration work begin side by side.

1980s to present. The Jewish Quarter becomes revitalized, with the conservation and construction of housing, educational institutions, synagogues, and stores, and the opening of new archaeological sites.

Fodor'sChoice
★
Western Wall. Judaism is more a religion of time than of place. Historically, Jews have tended to emphasize the significance of an important event rather than the place where it may have occurred. But among the exceptions to that rule, the 2,000-year-old Western Wall is in a class of its own. Its status as the most important existing Jewish shrine derives from its connection with the ancient Temple, the House of God. It was not itself part of the Temple edifice, but of the massive retaining wall King Herod built to create the vast platform now known as the Temple Mount.

After the destruction of Jerusalem by the Romans in AD 70, and especially after the dedication of a pagan town in its place 65 years later, the city was off-limits to Jews for generations. The memory of the precise location of the Temple—in the vicinity of today's Dome of the Rock—was lost. Even when access was eventually regained, Jews avoided entering the Temple Mount for fear of unwittingly trespassing on the most sacred, and thus forbidden, areas of the long-gone ancient sanctuary. With time, the closest remnant of the period took on the aura of the Temple itself, making the Western Wall a kind of holy place by proxy.

Jewish visitors often just refer to the site as "the Wall" (*Kotel* in Hebrew); the "Wailing Wall" is a Gentile appellation, describing the sight—more common once—of devout Jews grieving for God's House.

It is a telling point that, for many Jews, the ancient Temple was as much a national site as a religious one, and its destruction as much a national trauma as a religious cataclysm.

The Western Wall is in the southeast corner of the Old City, accessible from the Dung Gate, the Jewish Quarter, and the Muslim Quarter's el-Wad Road and the Street of the Chain. It functions under the aegis of the Orthodox rabbinic authorities, with all the trappings of an Orthodox synagogue. ■ TIP→ **Modest dress is required: for women, this means no shorts or bare shoulders. Men must cover their heads in the prayer area.** There is segregation of men and women in prayer, and smoking and photography on the Sabbath and religious holidays are prohibited. The cracks between the massive stones are stuffed with slips of paper bearing prayers and petitions. (These are collected several times a year and buried in a Jewish cemetery.) The swaying and praying of the devout reveal the powerful hold this place still has on the hearts and minds of many Jews.

The Wall is often crowded, but many people find that it's only when the crowds have gone (the Wall is floodlit at night and always open), and you share the warm, prayer-drenched stones with just a handful of bearded stalwarts or kerchiefed women, that the true spirituality of the Western Wall is palpable. (Expect a routine security check at all four entrances to the modern plaza, including a magnetic gate—visitors with pacemakers can avoid this—and examination of bags.) *For more information about this sight, see the "Jerusalem: Keeping the Faith" feature in this chapter.* ⊠ *Near Dung Gate, Jewish Quarter* ⊕ *english. thekotel.org* ⊠ *Free.*

Western Wall Tunnel. The long tunnel beyond the men's side of the Western Wall is not a rediscovered ancient thoroughfare, but was deliberately dug in recent years with the purpose of exposing a strip of the 2,000-year-old Western Wall along its entire length. The massive construction, part of the retaining wall of King Herod's Temple Mount, includes two building stones estimated to weigh an incredible 400 tons and 570 tons, respectively. Local guided tours in English are available and are recommended—you can visit the site only as part of an organized tour—but the times change from week to week (some include evening hours). The tour takes about 75 minutes and includes computer-generated graphics of how the area might have looked in its heyday. During daylight hours, tours end at the beginning of the Via Dolorosa, in the Muslim Quarter. After dark, that exit is closed, and the tour retraces its steps through the tunnel. The ticket office is under the arches at the northern end of the Western Wall plaza, but advance booking online is essential. ⊠ *North of Western Wall, Jewish Quarter* ☎ *02/627–1333* ⊕ *english.thekotel.org* ⊠ *NIS 30* ⊙ *Closed Sat. and Jewish religious holidays.*

WORTH NOTING

Broad Wall. The discovery in the 1970s of the massive 23-foot-thick foundations of an Old Testament city wall was hailed as one of the most important archaeological finds in the Jewish Quarter. Hezekiah, King of Judah and a contemporary of the prophet Isaiah, built the wall in 701 BC to protect the city against an impending Assyrian invasion. The unearthing of the Broad Wall—a biblical name—resolved a long-running scholarly debate about the size of Old Testament Jerusalem: a large on-site map shows that the ancient city was far more extensive than was once thought. ✉ *Plugat Hakotel St., off Jewish Quarter St., Jewish Quarter* ⊕ *www.rova-yehudi.org.il* ✉ *Free.*

Cardo. Today it's known for shopping, but the Cardo has a long history. In AD 135, the Roman emperor Hadrian built his town of Aelia Capitolina on the ruins of Jerusalem, an urban plan essentially preserved in the Old City of today. The *cardo maximus,* the generic name for the city's main north–south street, began at the present-day Damascus Gate, where sections of the Roman pavement have been unearthed. With the Christianization of the Roman Empire in the 4th century, access to Mount Zion and its important Christian sites became a priority, and the main street was eventually extended south into today's Jewish Quarter. The original width—today you see only half—was 73 feet, about the width of a six-lane highway. A strip of good stores (jewelry, art, and Judaica) occupies the Cardo's medieval reincarnation. ✉ *Jewish Quarter St., Jewish Quarter* ⊕ *www.rova-yehudi.org.il* ✉ *Free.*

CHRISTIAN AND MUSLIM QUARTERS

Fragmented into a dozen denominational domains, the Christian Quarter is capped by the great gray dome of the Church of the Holy Sepulcher. (The struggle for visibility in the holy city seems to be as much about dominating the skyline as about controlling real estate.) The numerous churches and religious institutions in this quarter, which is west of the Muslim Quarter, make for low population density.

The Muslim Quarter, located between Damascus Gate and the Western Wall, and west of Lions' Gate, is by far the largest in both area and population. The famous Via Dolorosa (Way of the Cross) that begins in and winds through this quarter on its way to the Holy Sepulcher, is lined with stores displaying Christian souvenirs and artifacts. It's a facade: the side streets, with their little grocery stores, neighborhood mosques, and stenciled pictures of Mecca, bespeak the real character of this residential area. Short dead-end alleys give tantalizing glimpses of the enormous gold Dome of the Rock on the Haram esh-Sharif (aka the Temple Mount).

TOP ATTRACTIONS

Fodor's Choice ★ **Church of the Holy Sepulcher.** This church, which was built by the Crusaders in the 12th century (the fourth to be built on this site), is believed to be the place where Jesus was crucified by the Romans, was buried, and rose from the dead. The site was officially consecrated, and the first church built here, following the visit in AD 326 by Helena, mother of the Byzantine emperor Constantine the Great. It and the adjacent Via Dolorosa encompass the stations of the cross.

Steep steps take you up from the church to **Golgotha**, or Calvary, as the site of the crucifixion is described in the New Testament. At the foot of the hill, opposite the main entrance, is the rectangular pink **Stone of Unction**, where, it is said, the body of Jesus was cleansed and prepared for burial. The **tomb of Jesus**, encased in a pink marble edifice (and under a restoration that is expected to be completed during 2017) is in the rotunda to the left of the main entrance of the church.

The church is shared, albeit unequally and uncomfortably, by six Christian denominations: Roman Catholic, Greek Orthodox, Armenian Orthodox, Syrian Orthodox, Egyptian Coptic, and Ethiopian, under an agreement imposed by the Ottoman Turkish authorities in 1852. Each section guarded by its own denomination.

If you visit in the late afternoon (the time changes with the seasons), you can watch the groups in turn—Greek Orthodox, Latins (as Roman Catholics are known in the Holy Land), Armenian Orthodox, and Egyptian Copts—in procession from Calvary to the tomb. A modern agreement among the Greeks, the Latins, and the Armenians on the interior restoration of the great dome was hailed as an almost miraculous breakthrough in ecumenical relations. *For information about the church, see the feature "Jerusalem: Keeping the Faith" in this chapter.* ✉ *Between Suq Khan e-Zeit and Christian Quarter Rd., Christian Quarter* ☎ *02/626–7000* ⊕ *www.holysepulchre.custodia.org/* ✉ *Free.*

Fodor's Choice
★ **Dome of the Rock and Haram esh-Sharif (Temple Mount).** The magnificent golden **Dome of the Rock** dominates the vast 35-acre Temple Mount, the area known to Muslims as *Haram esh-Sharif* (the Noble Sanctuary). At its southern end, immediately in front of you as you enter the area from the Western Wall plaza (the only gate for non-Muslims), is the large, black-domed **al-Aqsa Mosque,** the third in holiness for Muslims everywhere.

Herod the Great built the Temple Mount in the late 1st century BC, and included the center of the plaza was the Second Temple, the one Jesus knew.

Jewish tradition identifies the great **rock** at the summit of the hill—now under the gold dome—as the foundation stone of the world, and the place where Abraham bound and almost sacrificed his son Isaac (Genesis 22). With greater probability, this was where the biblical King David made a repentance offering to the Lord (II Samuel 22), and where his son Solomon built "God's House," the so-called First Temple. The Second Temple stood on the identical spot, but the memory of its precise location was lost after the Roman destruction and the banning of Jews from Jerusalem.

The Haram today is a Muslim preserve, and tradition has it that Muhammad rose to heaven from this spot in Jerusalem to meet God face-to-face, received the teachings of Islam, and returned to Mecca the same night, and the great rock was the very spot from which the Prophet ascended.

The Muslim shrines are closed to non-Muslims to leave the faithful alone to enjoy the wondrous interiors of stained-glass windows, granite columns, green-and-gold mosaics, arabesques, and superb medieval masonry. Even if you can't get inside, the vast plaza is both visually and historically arresting and worth a visit. Take a look at the bright exterior tiles of the Dome of the Rock and the remarkable jigsaws of fitted red, white, and black stone in the 14th- and 15th-century Mamluk buildings that line the western edge of the plaza.

Security check lines to enter the area are often long; it's best to come early. Note that the gate near the Western Wall is for entrance only. You can exit through any of the other eight gates on the site. The Muslim

The Via Dolorosa often teems with pilgrims but can sometimes offer a quiet path.

attendants are very strict about modest dress, and prohibit Bibles in the area. *For information about these sites, see the feature "Jerusalem: Keeping the Faith" in this chapter.* ⊠ *Access between Western Wall and Dung Gate, Muslim Quarter* ☎ *02/595–5820* ⊕ *www.noblesanctuary. com/* ⊠ *Free* ☉ *Closed Fri. and Sat.*

NEED A BREAK

✕ **Jafar Sweets.** Jafar specializes in *kunafe*, the Nablus sweet made of goat cheese topped with syrupy semolina crumbles. You may be tempted to split your first plate, but the treat soon grows addictive. Jafar also makes sheets of golden baklava topped with nuts. It's a landmark, so anyone in the Old City can help you find it. ⊠ *Khan A-Zeit St., Muslim Quarter* ☎ *02/628–3582.*

Via Dolorosa. Commonly called "the Way of the Cross" in English, the Latin *Via Dolorosa* literally translates as "the Way of Sorrow." It's venerated as the route Jesus walked, carrying his cross, from the place of his trial and condemnation by the Roman governor Pontius Pilate to the site of his crucifixion and burial. (Stations I and II are where the Antonia fortress once stood, widely regarded as the site of the "praetorium" referred to in the Gospels.) The present tradition jelled no earlier than the 18th century, but it draws on much older beliefs. Some of the incidents represented by the 14 Stations of the Cross are scriptural; others (III, IV, VI, VII, and IX) are not. Tiny chapels mark a few of the stations; the last five are inside the Church of the Holy Sepulcher. Catholic pilgrim groups, or the Franciscan-led Friday afternoon procession, take about 45 minutes to wind their way through the busy market streets of the Muslim and Christian quarters, with prayers and chants at each station of the almost-mile-long route.

Here are the 14 stations on the Via Dolorosa that mark the route that Jesus took, from trial and condemnation to crucifixion and burial.

Station I. Jesus is tried and condemned by Pontius Pilate.

Station II. Jesus is scourged and given the cross.

Station III. Jesus falls for the first time. (Soldiers of the Free Polish Forces built the chapel here after World War II.)

Station IV. Mary embraces Jesus.

Station V. Simon of Cyrene picks up the cross.

Station VI. A woman wipes the face of Jesus, whose image remains on the cloth. (She is remembered as Veronica, apparently derived from the Latin word *vera* and the Greek word *icon,* meaning "true image.")

Station VII. Jesus falls for the second time. (The chapel contains one of the columns of the Byzantine Cardo, the main street of 6th-century Jerusalem.)

Station VIII. Jesus addresses the women in the crowd.

Station IX. Jesus falls for the third time.

Station X. Jesus is stripped of his garments.

Station XI. Jesus is nailed to the cross.

Station XII. Jesus dies on the cross.

Station XIII. Jesus is taken down from the cross.

Station XIV. Jesus is buried. ⊠ *Christian Quarter* ✛ *Winds east to west, ending in Church of the Holy Sepulcher* ⌦ *Free.*

NEED A BREAK

Holy Rock Café. Between Stations VI and VII of the Via Dolorosa is the very good Holy Rock Café. The name may be a little hokey, but there's nothing wrong with its freshly squeezed orange and pomegranate juice, Arab coffee, mint tea, and superb *bourma,* a tubular Arab confection filled with whole pista-chio nuts. You get Julio Iglesias in the background for free. ⊠ *Via Dolorosa, Between Stations VI and VII, Muslim Quarter* ☽ *Closed Sun. No dinner.*

WORTH NOTING

Ecce Homo Convent of the Sisters of Zion. The arch that crosses the Via Dolorosa, just beyond Station II, and continues into the chapel of the adjacent convent, was once thought to have been the gate of Herod's Antonia fortress, perhaps the spot where the Roman governor Pontius Pilate presented Jesus to the crowd with the words *"Ecce homo!"* ("Behold, the man!"). Recent scholarship has determined otherwise: it was a triumphal arch built by the Roman emperor Hadrian in the 2nd century AD after his suppression of the second Jewish revolt and the dedication of a new Roman town, Aelia Capitolina, in place of Jerusalem.

The basement of the convent has several points of interest: an impressive reservoir with a barrel-vault roof, apparently built by Hadrian in the moat of Herod's older Antonia fortress; a tiny but attractive collection of ancient artifacts found on-site; and the famous *lithostratos,* or stone pavement, etched with games played by Roman legionnaires. The origin of one such diversion—the notorious Game of the King—called for the execution of a mock king, a sequence tantalizingly reminiscent of the New Testament

A Walk on the Via Dolorosa

The Old City's main Jewish and Muslim sites can be visited individually, but the primary Christian shrines—the **Via Dolorosa** (or Way of the Cross) and the Holy Sepulcher—are best experienced in sequence. This walk will keep you oriented in the confusing marketplace through which the Via Dolorosa winds its way. (Beware of slick pickpockets.) The route takes a leisurely 40 minutes; plan additional time if you want to linger at specific sites. About 200 yards up the road from St. Anne's Church (near Lions' Gate), look for a ramp on your left leading to the dark metal door of a school. This is the site of the ancient Antonia fortress. On Friday afternoons at 4 (April to September; at 3 from October to March), the brown-robed Franciscans begin their procession of the Via Dolorosa outside the metal door. This is Station I; Station II is across the street. Just beyond it, on the right, is the entrance to the **Ecce Homo Convent of the Sisters of Zion**, with a Roman arch in the chapel. The continuation of the arch crosses the street outside; just beyond it, a small vestibule on the right has a view of the chapel's interior.

The Via Dolorosa runs down into El-Wad Road, one of the Old City's most important thoroughfares. To the right, the street climbs toward the Damascus Gate, and beyond it to East Jerusalem. To the left, it passes through the heart of the Muslim Quarter and reaches the Western Wall. Black-hatted Hasidic Jews hurry on divine missions, nimble local Arab kids in T-shirts and jeans play in the street, and Christian pilgrims pace out ancient footsteps.

As you turn left onto El-Wad Road, Station III is on your left. Right next to it is Station IV and, on the next corner, 50 yards farther, Station V. There the Via Dolorosa turns right and begins its ascent toward Calvary. Halfway up the street, a brown wooden door on your left marks Station VI.

Facing you at the top of the stepped street, on the busy Suq Khan e-Zeit, is Station VII. The little chapel preserves one of the columns of the Byzantine Cardo (main street). Step to the left, and walk 30 yards up the street facing you to Station VIII, marked by nothing more than an inscribed stone in the wall opposite a souvenir store. Return to the main street and turn right. (If you skip Station VIII, turn left as you reach Station VII from the stepped street.) About 100 yards along Suq Khan e-Zeit from Station VII, turn onto the ramp on your right that ascends parallel to the street and becomes a lane. (Stay alert: the clutter of market merchandise makes it easy to miss.) At the end of the lane is a column that represents Station IX.

Step through the open door to the left of the column into the courtyard of the **Ethiopian Monastery** known as Deir es-Sultan. From the monastery's upper chapel, descend through a lower one and out a small wooden door to the court of the **Church of the Holy Sepulcher**. Most Christians venerate this site as that of the death, burial, and resurrection of Jesus—you'll find Stations X, XI, XII, XIII, and XIV within the church. A good time to be here is in the late afternoon, after 4 pm, when the different denominations in turn chant their way between Calvary and the tomb.

description of the treatment of Jesus by the Roman soldiers. Contrary to tradition, however, the pavement of large, foot-worn brown flagstones is apparently not from Jesus's day, but was laid down a century or two later. Allow 30 minutes for the visit. ⊠ *41 Via Dolorosa, Muslim Quarter* ☎ *02/627–7292* ⊕ *www.eccehomopilgrimhouse.com/* ✉ *NIS 9.*

Ethiopian Monastery. Stand in the monastery's courtyard beneath the medieval bulge of the Church of the Holy Sepulcher, and you have a cross-section of Christendom. The adjacent Egyptian Coptic monastery peeks through the entrance gate, and a Russian Orthodox gable, a Lutheran bell tower, and the crosses of Greek Orthodox, Armenian Orthodox, and Roman Catholic churches break the skyline.

The robed Ethiopian monks live in tiny cells in the rooftop monastery. One of the modern paintings in their small, dark chapel depicts the visit of the Queen of Sheba to King Solomon, as described in the Bible (I Kings 10). Ethiopian tradition holds that more passed between the two than the Bible is telling—she came to "prove" his wisdom "with hard questions"—and that their supposed union produced an heir to both royal houses. In Solomon's court, the prince was met with hostility by the king's legitimate offspring, says the legend, and the young man was sent home—with the precious Ark of the Covenant as a gift. To this day (say the Ethiopians), it remains in a sealed crypt in their homeland. The script in the paintings is Ge'ez, the ecclesiastical language of the Ethiopian church. Taking in the rooftop view and the chapel will occupy about 15 minutes. The exit, via a short stairway to another, lower-level chapel, deposits you in the courtyard of the Church of the Holy Sepulcher. ⊠ *Off Suq Khan e-Zeit, near the Church of the Holy Sepulcher, Christian Quarter* ✉ *Free.*

Pools of Bethesda and Church of St. Anne. The transition is sudden and complete, from the raucous cobbled streets and persistent vendors to the pepper trees, flower beds, and birdsong of this serene Catholic monastery of the amiable White Fathers. The Romanesque **Church of St. Anne** was built by the Crusaders in 1140, and restored in the 19th century. Its austere and unadorned stone interior and extraordinarily reverberant acoustics make it one of the finest examples of medieval architecture in the country. According to local tradition, the Virgin Mary was born in the grotto over which the church is built, and the church is supposedly named after her mother (although "Anne" is never mentioned in the Gospels). In the same compound are the excavated **Pools of Bethesda,** a large public reservoir in use during the 1st century BC and 1st century AD. The New Testament speaks of Jesus miraculously curing a lame man by "a pool, which is called in the Hebrew tongue Bethesda" (John 5). The actual bathing pools were probably the small ones, east of the reservoir, but it was over the big pools that both the Byzantines and the Crusaders built churches, now ruined, to commemorate the miracle. A visit to both sites takes no more than 30 minutes. The good bathrooms here are a welcome addition. ■ **TIP➔ Wait for one or two pilgrim groups who often test the acoustics in the church with some hymn-singing.** ⊠ *Al-Mujahideen Rd., Muslim Quarter* ⊹ *Just inside Lions' Gate* ☎ *02/628–3285* ⊕ *www.africamission-mafr.org/jerusalem_presentationgb.htm* ✉ *NIS 10.*

Continued on page 86

JERUSALEM: KEEPING THE FAITH

✡ ✝ ☪

Unforgotten and unforgettable, the city of Jerusalem is holy ground for the three great monotheistic religions, whose numbers embrace half the world's population. Its Old City is home to some of the most sacred sites of Judaism, Christianity, and Islam: the Western Wall, the Temple Mount/Haram esh-Sharif, the Church of the Holy Sepulcher, and the Dome of the Rock and al-Aqsa Mosque. Some travelers visit them to find their soul, others to seek a sense of communion with ancient epochs. Whether pilgrim or tourist, you'll discover that history, faith, and culture commingle here as perhaps nowhere else on earth.

By Mike Rogoff

(right) The Western Wall, (opposite left) Dome of the Church of the Holy Sepulcher, (opposite right) The Dome of the Rock

ONE CITY UNDER GOD

Jerusalem is a composite of three faith-civilizations: Jewish, Christian, and Muslim. They cohabit the Old City uneasily, burdened by centuries of struggle with each other for rights and real estate. But at the level of day-to-day routine, each draws its adherents to, respectively, the Western Wall, the Church of the Holy Sepulcher, and the al-Aqsa Mosque. To the visitor, the collage of spiritual traditions is often bewildering, sometimes alien, always fascinating. The intricate choreographies of devotion have been known to move nonbelievers as well as the devout.

HISTORY AND HOLY STONES

Wander the cobblestone lanes of historical Jerusalem and you can hear in your mind's ear the echoes of King David's harp, trace the revered footsteps of Jesus of Nazareth, and sense the presence of

(left) Woman praying, (top right) Miracle of Holy Fire, Church of the Holy Sepulcher, (bottom right) Men praying near the Dome of the Rock

the Prophet Muhammad. In the space of just a few hours, you can visit Golgotha and the tomb of Jesus, gaze at the shrine that caps "the farthermost place" from which Islam's founder rose to heaven, and stand before the only extant remnant of the Second Temple compound. Not without reason do some visitors imagine their fold-out atlases to be road maps leading to heaven itself.

Great dramas played out on these stones—occasionally, it is claimed, on the very same stone. The rock capped by the gold dome is the summit of Mount Moriah, identified in Jewish tradition with the biblical site where Abraham erected an altar and prepared to sacrifice his son Isaac. It was here on the Temple Mount that the "First" and "Second" Jewish Temples stood for a total of one thousand years. In the same rock, devout Muslims point to the imprint of a foot, regarded as that of Muhammad himself, as evidence that it was here that the Prophet ascended to heaven for his meeting with God. The Dome of the Rock and the nearby al-Aqsa Mosque enshrine that tradition.

On the one hand, Jerusalem is a layer-cake of time, each period leaving distinct strata. The biblical kings David and Solomon transformed a small and already-ancient Jebusite town into an important metropolis. The march of history proceeded through destruction and the Babylonian captivity, Helleni-zation, Roman rule and another de-struction, Byzantine Christianity, the Muslim invasions, the 12th-century Crusades, the Muslim reconquest, Eu-ropean rediscovery of the Holy Land and British control, and down to Je-rusalem's contemporary status as the capital (though some dispute it) of the State of Israel.

At another level—change the meta-phor—Jerusalem is a complex tangle, a Gordian knot of related but competing faith traditions, historical narratives, and national dreams. The knot seems fated to be around for a while yet, with no hero in sight to slice it through with one bold stroke.

FINDING YOUR FEET

Each of the three religious sites is infused with its own unique tradition. Making a connection between these stone struc-tures of the past and the wellsprings of religious faith or cultural identity can be uplifting. Many pilgrims focus on their own shrines; some take the time to explore the others so close at hand. The Western Wall is just steps from the Jerusalem Archaeological Park, where excavations turned up remnants of King Herod the Great's grand structures that Jesus almost certainly knew. The bridge between the Western Wall and the park leads up to the vast plaza—the Temple Mount or Haram esh-Sharif—now dominated by the Muslim shrines. Any of the gates at its far northern end will deposit you on the Via Dolorosa. A twenty-minute stroll through the bus-tling bazaar brings you to the Church of the Holy Sepulcher, revered as the site of Jesus's death and burial.

Whichever site you start with (this fea-ture lists them in historical order: Wall, Church, Dome), a tour of all three unfailingly provokes a powerful ap-preciation of Jerusalem as an epicenter of faith.

Israelites enslaved during the Babylonian Captivity after the fall of Jerusalem in 586 BC

THE WESTERN WALL

No Jewish shrine is holier than the Western Wall, the remains of the ancient Second Temple compound, whose stones are saturated with centuries of prayers and tears.

The status of the Western Wall as the most important existing Jewish shrine derives from its connection with the ancient Temple, the House of God. The 2,000-year-old Wall was not itself part of the Temple edifice, but of the massive retaining wall King Herod built to create the vast plaza now known as the Temple Mount.

After the destruction of Jerusalem by the Romans in AD 70, and especially after the dedication of a pagan town in its place 65 years later, the city became off-limits to Jews for generations. The precise location of the Temple—

in the vicinity of today's Dome of the Rock—was lost. Even when access was regained, Jews avoided entering the Temple Mount out of fear of trespassing on the most sacred, and thus forbidden, areas of the ancient sanctuary. With time, the closest remnant of the period took on the aura of the Temple itself, making the Western Wall a kind of holy place by proxy.

Jewish visitors often just refer to the site as "the Wall" (*Kotel* in Hebrew); "Wailing Wall" is a Gentile term, describing the sight—once more common—of devout Jews grieving for God's House. For many Jews, the ancient Temple was as much a national site as a religious one, and its destruction as much a national trauma as a religious cataclysm.

(top) Jewish man praying at the Western Wall,
(right) Western Wall

VISITING THE WALL

The swaying and praying of the devout reveal the powerful hold this place has on the hearts and minds of many Jews.

On Monday and Thursday mornings, the Wall bubbles with colorful bar-mitzvah ceremonies, when Jewish families celebrate the coming of age of their 13-year-old sons. The excitement is still greater on Friday evenings just after sunset, when the young men of a nearby yeshiva, a Jewish seminary, often come dancing and singing down to the Wall to welcome in the "Sabbath bride." The fervor reaches its highest point three times a year during the three Jewish pilgrimage festivals—Passover, Shavuot (Feast of Weeks), and Sukkot (Feast of Tabernacies), when many Jews come to pray. But many people find that it's only when the crowds have gone (the Wall is floodlit at night and always open), and you share the warm, prayer-drenched stones with just a handful of bearded stalwarts or kerchiefed women, that the true spirituality of the Western Wall is palpable.

The Wall precinct functions under the aegis of the rabbinic authorities, with all the trappings of an Orthodox synagogue. Modest dress is required (men must cover their heads in the prayer area), there is segregation of men and women in prayer, and smoking and photography on the Sabbath and religious holidays are prohibited. Expect a routine check of your bags.

NOTES IN THE WALL

The cracks between the massive stones of the Western Wall are stuffed with slips of paper bearing prayers and petitions. "They reach their destination more quickly than the Israeli postal service," it has been said, with a mixture of serious faith and light cynicism. The cracks are cleared several times a year, but the slips are never simply dumped. Since they often contain God's name, and are written from the heart, the slips are collected in a sack and buried with reverence in a Jewish cemetery.

THE TEMPLE MOUNT, OR HARAM ESH-SHARIF

The size of 27 football fields, the Temple Mount is the vast plaza constructed around the Second Temple in the late 1st century BC by King Herod the Great.

In order to rebuild the Temple on a grand scale, and significantly expand the courts around it, Herod leveled off the top of Mt. Moriah with thousands of tons of rubble. The massive retaining walls include some of the largest building stones known. Structurally, the famous Western Wall is simply the western side of the huge shoebox-like project.

Some scholars regard the Temple Mount as perhaps the greatest religious enclosure of the ancient world, and the splendid Temple, the one Jesus knew, as an architectural wonder of its day. The Romans reduced the building to smoldering ruins in the summer of AD 70, in the last stages of the Great Revolt of the Jews (AD 66–73). Many of its treasures, including the gold menorah, were carried off to Rome as booty.

Jewish tradition identifies the great rock at the summit of the hill—now under the golden Dome of the Rock—as the foundation stone of the world, and the place where Abraham bound and almost sacrificed his son Isaac (Genesis 22). With greater probability, this was where the biblical King David made a repentance offering to

(top) Aerial view of the Jewish Quarter and the Temple Mount, (top left) al-Aqsa Mosque, (top right) Drawing of a reconstruction of the First Temple the Lord (II Samuel 22), and where his son Solomon built "God's House," the so-called First Temple. The Second Temple stood on the identical spot, but the precise location of its innermost holy of holies is a question that engages religious Jews and archaeologists to this day.

Christian tradition adds the New Testament dimension. Here Jesus disputed points of law with other Jewish teachers, angrily overturned the tables of money changers, and, looking down at the Temple precinct from the Mount of Olives, predicted its destruction. The Byzantines seem to have neglected the place (perhaps believing it cursed); the medieval Templars took their name from the area in which they set up their headquarters.

Muslims identify it as "the farthermost place," from which Muhammad rose to heaven, and call this area Haram esh-Sharif, the Noble Sanctuary.

JERUSALEM ARCHAEOLOGICAL PARK

Immediately south of the Western Wall, in the shadow of the Temple Mount, is an important archaeological site, still popularly known as the Western and Southern Wall excavations. The dominant monumental structures were the work of King Herod the Great, some 2,000 years ago, though there are Byzantine and early Arab buildings of interest. Robinson's Arch, named for a 19th-century American explorer, once supported a monumental stairway leading up to the Temple Mount. Also discovered were numerous "mikva'ot" (singular "mikveh," a Jewish ritual bath) and a Herodian street, once lined with shops. In the southern part of the site is the low-rise Davidson Center; its exhibits range from ancient artifacts to computer-animated recreations of the Second Temple. *For complete information, see the separate entry for Jerusalem Archaeological Park in this chapter.*

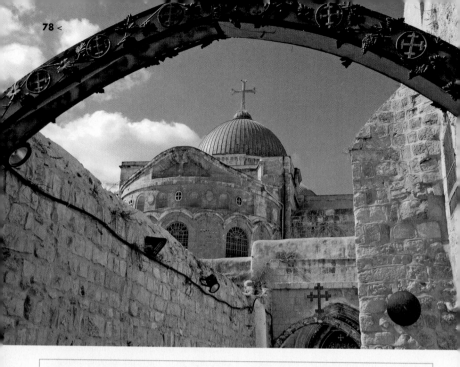

THE CHURCH OF THE HOLY SEPULCHER

Follow the footsteps of Jesus along the Via Dolorosa to the hallowed church that enshrines Golgotha—the hillside of Jesus's crucifixion, burial, and resurrection.

Vast numbers of Christians, especially adherents of the older "mainline" churches, believe that this church marks the place where Jesus was crucified by the Romans and buried by his followers, and where he rose from the dead three days later. Some claim that the antiquity of the Holy Sepulcher tradition argues in favor of its authenticity, since the fervent early Christian community would have striven to preserve the memory of such an important site. The church is outside the city walls of Jesus's day—a vital point, for no executions or burials took place within Jerusalem's sacred precincts.

The site was officially consecrated, and the first church built here, following the visit in AD 326 by Helena, mother of the Byzantine emperor Constantine the Great. The present imposing structure, the fourth church on the site, was built by the Crusaders in the 12th century. Interior additions over the years have distorted the Gothic plan, but look for the Norman-style vault at the far end of the Greek Orthodox basilica (facing the tomb), and the ceiling of the dim corridor leading to the adjacent Catholic chapel. After a fire in 1808, much of the church was rebuilt in 19th-century style.

(top) Church of the Holy Sepulcher, (top right) Greek Orthodox chapel, Calvary, (bottom right) Monk kissing the Stone of Unction

HOLIEST LANDMARKS

On the floor just inside the entrance of the church is the rectangular pink **Stone of Unction**, where, it is said, the body of Jesus was cleansed and prepared for burial. Pilgrims often rub fabric or religious trinkets on the stone to absorb its sanctity, and take them home as mementos. Nearby steep steps take you up to **Golgotha**, or Calvary, meaning "the place of the skull," as the site is described in the New Testament. Up the steps, the chapel on the right is Roman Catholic: a window looks out at Station X of the Via Dolorosa, a wall mosaic at the front of the chapel depicts Jesus being nailed to the cross (Station XI), and a bust of Mary in a cabinet to the left of it represents Station XIII where Jesus was taken off the cross. The central chapel—all candlelight, oil lamps, and icons—is Greek Orthodox. Under the altar, and capping the rocky hillock on which you stand, is a silver disc with a hole, purportedly the place—Station XII—where the cross actually stood.

The **tomb** itself (Station XIV), encased in a pink marble edifice, is in the rotunda to the left of the main entrance of the church, under the great dome that dominates the Christian Quarter. The only hint of what the tomb must have been like 2,000 years ago is the ledge in the inner chamber (now covered with marble) on which Jesus's body would have been laid. You can see a more pristine example of an upscale Jewish tomb of the period in the gloomy Chapel of St. Nicodemus, opposite the Coptic chapel in the back of the sepulcher.

SHARING THE CHURCH

An astonishing peculiarity of the Holy Sepulcher is that it is shared, albeit unequally and uncomfortably, by six Christian denominations. Centuries of sometimes-violent competition for control of key Christian sites culminated in the Status Quo Agreement of 1852.

Via Dolorosa and Church of the Holy Sepulcher

Ecce Homo Arch

Monastery of the Flagellation

Convent of the Sisters of Zion

Via Dolorosa

Station II

Station III

Station IV

Station I

School

Station VII

Via Dolorosa

St. Francis Rd.

Station VIII

Station VI

Station V

Greek Orthodox Patriarchate Rd.

Station IX

Aqabat el-Takiyeh (Khaski Sultan)

TO LIONS' GATE

Deir el-Hades

Suq Khan ez-Zeit Rd.

El-Wad Rd.

Church of the Holy Sepulcher

Stations X–XIV

Aqabat el-Saraya

Christian Quarter Rd.

0   1/4 mile

0   1/4 km

Tomb of Joseph of Arimathea

Western apse, 4th-century church

Southern apse, 4th-century church

Coptic Chapel

Station XIV (Tomb of Jesus)

Franciscan Convent

Northern apse, 4th-century church

Chapel of the Angel

Altar of Mary Magdalene

Chapel of the Apparition

Chapel of St. James

Chapel of St. John

Chapel of 40 Martyrs

Twelfth-century facade and entrance to church

Calvary/ Golgotha steps

Stone of Unction

"Center of the World"

Arches of the Virgin

Entrance Courtyard

Main Entrance

See Inset

Tomb of Phillip d'Aubigny

Chapel of Adam

Chapel of the Franks

Crusader church

Chapel of St. Michael and exit from Ethiopian Monastery

Rock of Golgotha

Chapel of the Mocking

Prison of Christ

Chapel of St. Longinus

Calvary/Golgotha—Upper level detail

Chapel of the Division of the Rainments

Calvary/ Golgotha steps

Station X

Station XI

Chapel of St. Helena

Station XIII

Station XII

Chapel of the Holy Cross

Byzantine wall etching of ship

Mosaic of Jesus near the Stone of Unction

Under the pressure of Orthodox Russia, the Ottoman Turks recognized the precedence of the Greek Orthodox as on-the-ground representatives of the Eastern Rite churches.

Each denomination guards its assigned privileges, and minor infringements by one of its neighbors can flare up into open hostility. At the same time, the phenomenon gives the place much of its color. Try visiting in the late afternoon (the exact time changes with the seasons), and watch the groups in turn—Greek Orthodox, Latins (as Roman Catholics are known in the Holy Land), Armenian Orthodox, and Egyptian Copts—in procession from Calvary to the tomb. The candlelight and swinging censers are passingly similar; the robes and lusty hymn-singing are different.

A modern agreement among the Greeks, the Latins, and the Armenians on the interior restoration of the great dome was hailed as a breakthrough in ecumenical relations, and it was rededicated in January 1997 in an unprecedented interdenominational service.

SUGGESTIONS FOR YOUR VISIT

While the first nine Stations of the Cross are to be found along the Way of the Cross—the Via Dolorosa—the final and most holy ones are within the Church of the Holy Sepulcher itself. The best time to visit may be around 4pm when many denominations are found worshipping. *For more information, see the separate entry for the Via Dolorosa elsewhere in this chapter.*

As in many religious sites, modest dress and discreet behavior are required here, but it's difficult for the clergy of any particular community to assert authority. Come early or late to avoid the worst crowds; be patient, too. A small flashlight or some candles will help you explore the small tomb of St. Nicodemus, an authentic Jewish tomb of the period.

Entrance of the Church of the Holy Sepulcher

THE DOME OF THE ROCK AND AL-AQSA MOSQUE

The focal point of these sanctuaries, whose interiors are currently open only to Muslims, is the Rock—the place from which Muhammad is believed to have ascended to heaven to be given the divine precepts of Islam.

The magnificent golden **Dome of the Rock** dominates the vast 35-acre Temple Mount, the area known to Muslims as Haram esh-Sharif (the Noble Sanctuary). This is the original octagonal building, completed in AD 691. It enshrines the great rock—the summit of Mount Moriah—from which the prophet Muhammad is said to have risen to heaven. Jerusalem is not mentioned in the Qur an, but Muhammad's

"Night Ride" is. Awakened by the archangel Gabriel, he was taken on the fabulous winged horse el-Burak to the *masjid al-aqsa*, the "farthermost place." From there he rose to heaven, met God face to face, received the teachings of Islam, and returned to Mecca the same night. Tradition has it that the *masjid al-aqsa* was none other than Jerusalem, and the great rock the very spot from which the prophet ascended.

To be sure, Muhammad's triumphant successors venerated Jerusalem's biblical sanctity; but some modern scholars suggest they did not like the feeling of being Johnnies-come-lately in the holy city of rival faiths. The impressive Dome of the Rock, built by the Ummayad caliph Abd el-Malik, was almost certainly intended to proclaim the ascendancy of the "true faith."

A SPLENDID SHRINE

Considering the original builders and craftsmen adopted the artistic traditions of their Byzantine predecessors, it's hardly surprising that the plan of the shrine resembles those of its Christian contemporaries, like the Byzantine Church of San Vitale in Ravenna, Italy. Take a close look at the bright exterior tiles in variegated shades of blue. The marvelous gold dome was restored in the 1990s, with 176 pounds of 24-carat gold electroplated on copper.

At the time of this writing, non-Muslims were denied entry to the interior of the building, with its beautiful granite columns supporting arches, some of which bear the original green-and-gold mosaics set in arabesque motifs. In obedience to Islamic religious tradition, no human or animal forms appear in the artwork. The mosaics were restored in 1027, but preserved much of the original work.

All this splendor was designed to emphasize the importance of the rock itself, directly under the great dome. The faithful reach out and touch an inden-

tation which, they believe, was nothing less than the Prophet's footprint, left there as he ascended to heaven.

THE THIRD-HOLIEST OF ALL

At the southern end of the Haram, immediately in front of you as you enter the area from the Western Wall plaza (the only gate for non-Muslims), is the large, black-domed **Al-Aqsa Mosque**. The Dome of the Rock is a shrine, the place where a hallowed event is believed to

THE DOME'S MOSAICS

Some of the Arabic inscriptions in the mosaics are quotations from the Qur an, others are dedications. One of the latter originally lauded Abd el-Malik, caliph of the Damascus-based Ummayad dynasty, who built the shrine. Some 140 years later, the caliph of a rival dynasty removed el-Malik's name and replaced it with his own, but he neglected to change the date.

have taken place. Individuals go there to pray, but al-Aqsa is a true mosque, attracting thousands of worshippers on Fridays and Muslim holidays. It is third in holiness for Muslims everywhere, after the great mosques of Mecca and Medina, both in Saudi Arabia.

Built by the Ummayad dynasty in the early 8th century AD, it has been destroyed and restored several times. In the 12th century, the al-Aqsa Mosque became the headquarters of the Templars, a Crusader monastic order that took its name from the ancient temple that once stood nearby. The spot has been the setting for more recent dramas, most importantly the assassination of King Abdullah I of Jordan (the present king's great-grandfather) in 1951.

EXPLORING THE HARAM

The Haram today is a Muslim preserve, a legacy that dates back to AD 638, when the Arab caliph Omar Ibn-Khatib

seized Jerusalem from the Byzantines. At the time of this writing, the Muslim shrines were closed to non-Muslims indefinitely, leaving the faithful alone to enjoy their wondrous interiors.

Even if you can't get inside, the vast plaza is visually and historically arresting, and worth a visit. Fifteenth-century Mamluk buildings line the western edge. Overlooking the plaza at its northwestern corner is a long building, today an elementary school, built on the artificial scarp that protected Herod's Antonia fortress. Christian tradition, very possibly accurate, identifies the site as the praetorium where Jesus was tried.

Security check lines to enter the Haram esh-Sharif are often long; it's best to come early. Note that the Muslim attendants prohibit Bibles in the area.

(top) Parts of columns on the Haram, (right) Mosaics and arches grace the Dome's interior

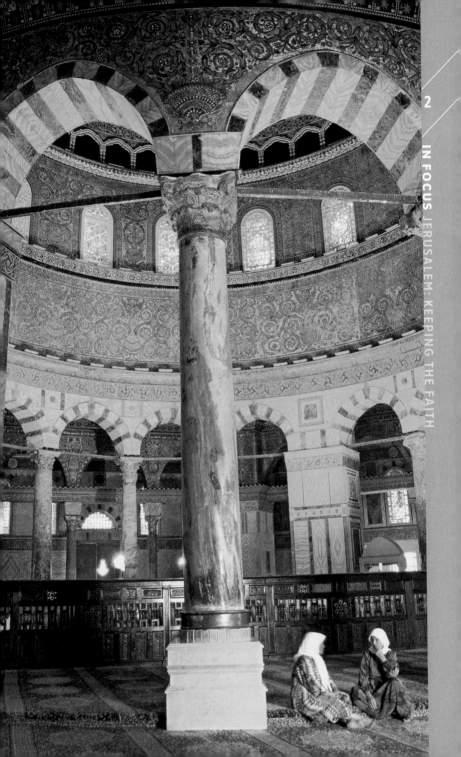

JAFFA GATE

Jaffa Gate got its name from its westerly orientation, toward the Mediterranean harbor of Jaffa, now part of Tel Aviv. Its Arabic name of Bab el-Khalil, "Gate of the Beloved," points you south, toward the city of Hebron (in the West Bank of today) where the biblical Abraham, the "Beloved of God" in Muslim tradition, is buried. The old pedestrian gate, like most of the Old City wall itself, was built by the Ottoman Turkish sultan, Suleiman the Magnificent, in the 16th century. The vehicle road is a newer, grand entrance created in 1898 for the royal visit of the German emperor, Kaiser Wilhelm II. The British general, Sir Edmund Allenby, took a different approach when he seized the city from the Turks in December 1917: eschewing pomp and ceremony, he and his staff officers dismounted from their horses to enter the holy city on foot with the humility befitting pilgrims. Outside the walls is the deep Hinnom Valley, the natural western defense of the ancient city.

Behind the railings just inside the imposing gate are, traditionally, the graves of the two Muslim architects who built Suleiman's city walls. According to legend, they were executed by order of the Sultan, either (says one version) because they angered Suleiman by not including Mount Zion and the venerated Tomb of David within the walls, or (relates another) because the satisfied Sultan wanted to make sure they would never build anything grander for anyone else.

Directly ahead is the souk (bazaar), engaging in itself, but also a convenient route to the Christian and Jewish quarters.

The huge stone tower on the right as you enter Jaffa Gate is the last survivor of the strategic fortress built by King Herod 2,000 years ago to secure the city's weak point: the saddle between the deep Hinnom Valley to the west and the shallow valley to the north (today's bazaar). The massive Citadel, as it's still often known, houses the Tower of David Museum—well worth your time as a springboard for exploring this part of the historical city. Opposite the museum entrance (once a drawbridge) is the Gothic-style Christ Church (Anglican), built in 1849 as the first Protestant church in the Middle East.

The vehicle road continues through the Armenian Quarter, the Old City's smallest neighborhood. Its closed enclave perpetuates the life and faith of a far-off land, the first to embrace Christianity. A short walk beyond it brings you to Zion Gate (and through it, Mount Zion) and to the Jewish Quarter.

GETTING HERE AND AROUND

Jaffa Gate, a logical entry point for visits to the Old City, is an easy walk from the Downtown or King David Street areas. Many Downtown bus stops are within striking distance as well.

TIMING AND PRECAUTIONS

Jaffa Gate is always open, though within the Old City itself some sites have limited hours or are closed Friday, Saturday, or Sunday.

TOP ATTRACTIONS

Fodor'sChoice ★

Ramparts Walk. The narrow stone catwalks of the Old City walls provide great panoramic views and interesting perspectives of this intriguing city. But they also offer an innocent bit of voyeurism as you look down

2

into gardens and courtyards and become, for a moment, a more intimate partner in the secret domestic life of the different quarters you pass. Across the rooftops, the domes and spires of the three religions that call Jerusalem holy compete for the skyline, just as their adherents jealously guard their territory down below. Peer through the shooting niches, just as watchmen and snipers did in the not-so-distant past. The hotels and high-rises of the new city dominate the skyline to the west; Mount Zion is immediately to the south; the bustle of East Jerusalem is almost tangible to the north; and the churches and cemeteries quietly cling to the Mount of Olives to the east. ■TIP→ There are many high steps on this route; the railings are secure, but small children should not walk alone; good footwear, a hat, and water are recommended.

The two sections of the walk are separated by Jaffa Gate, though the same ticket covers both (available from the commercial tourist services office just inside Jaffa Gate and at the entrance to the southern route). The shorter southern section is accessible only from the end of the seemingly dead-end terrace outside Jaffa Gate at the exit of the Tower of David Museum. Descent is at Zion Gate or just before Dung Gate. The longer and more varied walk begins at Jaffa Gate (up the stairs immediately on the left as you enter the Old City), with descent at New, Damascus, Herod's, or Lions' Gates. Allow 30 to 40 minutes for the shorter section to Zion Gate, adding 10 to 15 minutes to get to Dung Gate. For the longer section, it takes 20 minutes to walk north-northeast to the New Gate, another 20 minutes east to Damascus Gate, 15 minutes from there to Herod's Gate, and about 20 minutes more to Lions' Gate. ■TIP→ Since much of the long northern route passes through or above Palestinian areas, it's advisable to end your walk at the New Gate during times of tension. ⊠ *Entry near Jaffa Gate, Jaffa Gate* ☎ *02/627–7550* ⊕ *www.pami.co.il/eng* ✉ *NIS 16* ☉ *Northern route closed Fri.*

Fodor'sChoice **Tower of David Museum.** Many visitors find this museum invaluable in
★ mapping Jerusalem's often-confusing historical byways. Housed in a series of medieval halls, known locally as the Citadel (*Hametzuda* in Hebrew), the museum tells the city's four-millennium story through models, maps, holograms, and videos. The galleries are organized by historical period around the Citadel's central courtyard, where the old stone walls and arches add an appropriately antique atmosphere. Walking on the Citadel ramparts provides unexpected panoramas: don't miss the wonderful view from the top of the big tower. The basement has a model of 19th-century Jerusalem, constructed for the Ottoman pavilion at the Vienna World Fair in 1873. Guided tours in English are offered weekdays at 11. You'll need 90 minutes to do justice to this museum.

The outdoor "Night Spectacular" is a stunning 45-minute sound-and-light pageant of historical images played onto the ancient stone walls and towers. The event runs throughout the year, but days and times change with the seasons. Reserve in advance. ⊠ *Armenian Orthodox Patriarchate Rd., Jaffa Gate* ⊕ *On the vehicle road, just inside Jaffa Gate* ☎ *02/626–5333* ⊕ *www.towerofdavid.org.il* ✉ *NIS 40 for museum, NIS 55 for Night Spectacular, NIS 70 for combined ticket.*

The City of David, just south of the Temple Mount, is one of the oldest parts of Jerusalem.

WORTH NOTING

FAMILY **Park Teddy.** The most recent attraction in the Hinnom Valley, just west of Jaffa Gate, is Park Teddy, named for Teddy Kollek, the popular mayor of Jerusalem from 1965 to 1993. On the park's upper terrace, a small mirrorlike globe is designed as a jigsaw of the continents. Entering the globe through the "oceans," you encounter a floor engraving of a famous Renaissance map that shows Jerusalem as the center of the world. The middle terrace boasts an intriguingly innovative sundial that not only tells time, but also tracks the solstices, equinoxes, and a few memorable dates. In the summer, a large square platform on the lower terrace becomes a cool children's playground when multiple water jets spurt unpredictably into the air for 20 minutes, four times daily (at 10, noon, 2, and 4). ■ TIP➔ **Bring a towel and a change of clothes for your kids.** At night, the fountain plays to an orchestration of light and music (April–October at 8, 9, and 10 pm; November–March at 7, 8, and 9 pm). ⊠ *Outside Old City walls, below Jaffa Gate, Jaffa Gate* 🔊 *Free* 🕑 *Visitor center closed Fri.*

MOUNT ZION

Thousands of years ago, Mount Zion lay within the compass of the city walls, protected in the west and south by the virtually unassailable slopes of the Hinnom Valley. No more. The 16th-century Turkish wall slashes across Mount Zion, leaving it outside the Old City, connected to it by the narrow Zion Gate. The faiths that call Jerusalem holy cross paths on this hilltop. For Judaism—and, by extension, Islam—this is where King David was buried 30 centuries ago: his supposed tomb is venerated to this day. Christianity identifies the area with key scriptural events, and churches, monasteries, institutions, and graveyards are visible landmarks. There are few must-see sites here; but if you enjoy less compulsive sightseeing, Mount Zion is worth an hour or two of your time.

GETTING HERE AND AROUND

Get to Mount Zion on foot from Jaffa Gate. Most interesting is taking the southern Ramparts Walk (coming down at Zion Gate), or strolling the path that skirts the outside of the Old City wall: both offer fine views across the Hinnom Valley. Or share the road through the Armenian Quarter with the cabs and minivans.

TIMING AND PRECAUTIONS

Modest dress is de rigueur for David's Tomb and the churches. Pay attention to opening times on Friday and Saturday (for the tomb) and Sunday (for the churches).

TOP ATTRACTIONS

Room of the Last Supper. Tradition has enshrined this spare, 14th-century second-story room as the location of the New Testament "upper room," where Jesus and his disciples celebrated the ceremonial Passover meal that would become known in popular parlance as the Last Supper (Mark 14). At that time, archaeologists tell us, the site was inside the city walls. Formally known as the Cenacle or the Coenaculum (dining room), the room is also associated with a second New Testament tradition (Acts 2) as the place where the disciples gathered on Pentecost, seven weeks after Jesus's death, and were "filled with the Holy Spirit."

A little incongruously, the chamber has the trappings of a mosque as well: restored stained-glass Arabic inscriptions in the Gothic windows, an ornate *mihrab* (an alcove indicating the Muslim direction of prayer, toward Mecca), and two Arabic plaques in the wall. The Muslims were not concerned with the site's Christian traditions but with the supposed Tomb of King David—the "Prophet" David in their belief—on the level below. Allow 10 minutes to imbibe the atmosphere. ⊠ *Off Ma'ale HaShalom, Mount Zion* ✥ *Above David's Tomb, by means of outside staircase* ⬛ *Free.*

Tomb of David. According to the Hebrew Bible, King David, the great Israelite king of the 10th century BC, was buried in "the City of David"—the Bible's dynastic name for his capital, Jerusalem. Archaeologists have identified and excavated that site, on a low ridge to the east; but medieval Jewish pilgrims erroneously placed the ancient city on this hill, where they sought—and supposedly found—the royal tomb. Its authenticity may be questionable, but a millennium of tears and prayers has sanctified the place.

The tomb is capped by a cenotaph, a massive stone marker draped with a velvet cloth embroidered with symbols and Hebrew texts traditionally associated with David. Ultra-Orthodox religious authorities have divided the shrine, already cramped, into two tiny prayer areas to separate men and women. Modest dress is required, especially for women; men must cover their heads. There's no photography on the Sabbath and Jewish religious holidays, and the unusual opening hours may be subject to change. ⊠ *Off Ma'ale HaShalom, Mount Zion* ✥ *Just beyond Dormition Abbey when coming from Zion Gate, beneath the Room of the Last Supper* ☎ *02/581–1911* ⬛ *Free* ☉ *Closed Fri. afternoon.*

WORTH NOTING

Chamber of the Holocaust (*Martef Hasho'ah*). This small museum is dedicated to the memory of the 6 million European Jews annihilated by the Nazis in the Second World War. Among the artifacts salvaged from the Holocaust are items that the Nazis forced Jews to make out of sacred Torah scrolls. One Jewish tailor fashioned a vest for his Nazi "customer" out of the inscribed parchment, but with grim humor he chose sections that contained the worst of the biblical curses. Plaques commemorate many of the 5,000 European Jewish communities destroyed from 1939 to 1945. ⊠ *Ma'ale Shazakh, Mount Zion* ✧ *On east side of Tomb of David* ☏ *052/770–2906* ⊕ *www.martefhashoah.org* ▧ *Free (donation expected)* ⊙ *Closed Sat. and Jewish religious holidays.*

Dormition Abbey. The large, round Roman Catholic church, with its distinctive cone-shaped roof, ornamented turrets, and landmark clock tower, is a Jerusalem landmark. It was built on land bought by the German emperor Kaiser Wilhelm II when he visited Jerusalem in 1898. The German Benedictines dedicated the echoing main church, with its Byzantine-style apse and mosaic floors, in 1910. The lower-level crypt houses a cenotaph with a carved-stone figure of Mary in repose (*dormitio*), reflecting the tradition that she fell into eternal sleep. Among the adjacent little chapels is one donated by the Ivory Coast, with wooden figures and motifs inlaid with ivory. The premises include a bookstore and a coffee shop. A visit takes about 25 minutes. ⊠ *Off Har Tsiyon St., near the Room of the Last Supper, Mount Zion* ☏ *02/565–5330* ⊕ *www.dormitio.net/english/en/places/en.abbey/index.html* ▧ *Free.*

Hinnom Valley. A few minutes from the Jaffa Gate is the deep Hinnom Valley, which offers some fine views of Mount Zion and the Old City walls. The area achieved notoriety in the 7th century BC during the long reign of the Israelite king Menasseh (697–640 BC). He was not merely an idolater, the Bible relates, but supported a cult of child sacrifice by fire in the Valley of the Son of Hinnom. Over time, the biblical Hebrew name of the valley—*Gei Ben Hinnom*, contracted to *Gehennom* or *Gehenna*—became a synonym for a hellish place of burning, in both Hebrew and New Testament Greek.

In the late 1970s, Israeli archaeologist Gabriel Barkai discovered a series of Old Testament–period rock tombs at the bend in the valley, below the fortress-like St. Andrew's Scots Church. The most spectacular finds were two tiny rolled strips of silver, designed to be worn as amulets around the neck. The painstaking opening of the little cylinders revealed the biblical "priestly benediction" (Nos. 6), inscribed in the ancient Hebrew script. This 7th-century-BC sample, beginning "The Lord bless you and keep you," is the oldest biblical passage ever found. The tombs are an open site, accessed through the Menachem Begin Heritage Center during its visiting hours. ⊠ *6 Nachon St., Mount Zion* ✧ *Below St. Andrew's Scots Church* ☏ *02/565–2020* ⊕ *www.begincenter.org.il/en/* ▧ *Free* ⊙ *Tomb site closed Sat.*

CITY OF DAVID

If you thrill to the thought of standing where the ancients once stood, you'll be in your element in this city of memories, from Old Testament walls and water systems to Second Temple streets and stones.

GETTING HERE AND AROUND

Parking is nonexistent: come by cab, or walk down from the Old City by way of Dung Gate.

TIMING AND PRECAUTIONS

Allow 2 to 2½ hours for a full unhurried tour of the City of David (though you can cover a lot of ground in less time). The site is in the heart of the predominantly Arab Silwan neighborhood, with occasional tension between Palestinians and Jewish settlers, but the layout of the enclosure and the security arrangements should dispel concerns.

TOP ATTRACTIONS

Fodor'sChoice
★

City of David. Lying just south of today's Old City walls, the City of David was the very core of Old Testament Jerusalem, built more than four millennia ago on a 15-acre spur over the vital Gihon Spring. It was given its royal Israelite sobriquet 1,000 years later, when the legendary King David conquered the city and made it his capital (II Samuel 5). Begin with the great rooftop observation point above the visitor center. Consider the 15-minute 3-D movie, despite its ideological bias; it's a good historical introduction to the site, especially for kids (call ahead for English-language show times). Below the floorboards of the center are the excavated remains of a large building of the 10th century BC, identified by some archaeologists as King David's fortified palace; others demur. A few flights of steps down from the center is Area G, dominated by a sloping structure of the same period, possibly a support ramp for the "palace" above. The most intriguing artifacts found here were 51 *bullae*, clay seal impressions no bigger than a fingernail, used for sealing documents or official correspondence. Some were inscribed, in ancient Hebrew, with the names of personages mentioned in the biblical book of Jeremiah. There is strong circumstantial evidence to suggest that the bullae were baked into permanent pottery by the Babylonian burning of Jerusalem in 586 BC.

Take the steps about a third of the way down the hillside: a small sign on the right directs you to Warren's Shaft and the descent to the spring. Charles Warren, a British army engineer, discovered the spacious, sloping access tunnel—note the ancient chisel marks and rough-cut steps—in 1867. The deep vertical shaft that drops into the Spring of Gihon may not have been the actual biblical "gutter" or "water-shaft" through which David's warriors penetrated the city 3,000 years ago—it was apparently hewn in a later era—but an alternative access to the spring has kept the biblical story alive. Three centuries later, King Hezekiah of Judah had a horizontal tunnel dug through solid rock to bring the spring water safely into a new inner-city reservoir.

The tunnel—variously called Siloam, Shilo'ach, or Hezekiah's Tunnel—can be waded today. You will need water shoes or sandals, a flashlight (cheap LED ones are on sale at the visitor center), and appropriate clothing: the water is thigh-deep for the first few minutes, and then below the knees for almost the entire length of the tunnel (a 30-minute walk). The visitor center has lockers for your gear. In this very conservative neighborhood, it's advisable for women to wear covering over their swimsuits when walking outside. The wade is not recommended for very small children or for claustrophobes of any age.

If you don't fancy getting wet, you can still view the spring, and then continue through the dry Canaanite tunnel to emerge above ground.

The tunnel ends in the Pool of Siloam, mentioned in the New Testament as the place where a blind man had his sight restored (John 9); the current pool is its Byzantine successor. From the exit, modern wooden steps take you down and over the large flagstones of a 1st-century-BC commercial street to the edge of an ancient pool unearthed in 2004 by city workers repairing a sewage pipe. Archaeologists exposed finely cut steps and two corners of the pool, apparently a large public mikvah, or Jewish ritual bath, for pilgrims who flocked here 2,000 years ago—and arguably the very pool of the Gospel miracle. Hezekiah's original pool remains hidden.

An underground Roman-period drainage ditch is the adventurous route back up the hill. For an additional fee you can continue still further north through the ditch (bypassing the visitor center), to the Jerusalem Archaeological Park inside the city walls. ■TIP→ There is a shuttle van (NIS 5) from the pool up the steep hill back to the visitor center, but currently not from the dry exit. ⊠ *Off Ophel Rd., Silwan* ✛ *South of Old City walls, 200 yards down from Dung Gate* ☎ *02/626–8700* ⊕ *www. cityofdavid.org.il* ⊠ *City of David NIS 29; guided tour including admission NIS 60* ☉ *Closed Sat. and Jewish religious holidays.*

EAST JERUSALEM

Loosely speaking, East Jerusalem refers to the Arab neighborhoods controlled by Jordan in the years when the city was divided (1948–67). That includes the Mount of Olives, and the areas north and southeast of the Old City.

The sights in this area are for the most part distinctly Christian. A few are a little off the beaten path, and the best way to explore them—if you're energetic enough—is on foot. If you're driving, however, you can sometimes find free parking at the Seven Arches Hotel on the Mount of Olives and paid parking at the cluster of large hotels near the American Colony; or take a cab.

GETTING HERE AND AROUND

If you enjoy a bit of a walk and the weather is fine, it's no more than a 25-minute walk from Hebrew University's Mount Scopus campus (served by West Jerusalem bus routes 19, 34, and 68) across to the Mount of Olives. The panoramic view of the Judean Desert to the east is a bonus. A cab ride is an alternative, but if you skip the top of the mountain, the rest of the sights are accessible by foot from the Old City.

The Church of All Nations stands at the base of the Mount of Olives, next to the Garden of Gethsemane.

TIMING AND PRECAUTIONS

Morning views are best from the Mount of Olives. Some of the sites are closed on Sunday. Watch out for pickpockets on the Mount of Olives, on the road down to Gethsemane, and on Nablus Road outside the Garden Tomb.

TOP ATTRACTIONS

Garden of Gethsemane. After the Last Supper, the New Testament relates, Jesus and his disciples walked to the Mount of Olives, to a "place" called Gethsemane, where he was betrayed and arrested. Gethsemane derives from the Aramaic or Hebrew word for "oil press," referring to the precious olive that has always flourished here. The enormous, gnarled, and still-productive olive trees on the site may be older than Christianity itself, according to some botanists. They make a fine picture, but a fence prevents pilgrims from taking home sprigs as a more tangible souvenir.

The **Church of All Nations,** with its brilliantly colorful, landmark mosaic facade, was completed in 1924 on the scanty remains of its Byzantine predecessor. The prolific architect, Antonio Barluzzi, filled the church's interior domes with mosaic symbols of the Catholic communities that contributed to its construction. The windows are glazed with translucent alabaster in somber browns and purples, creating a mystical feeling in the dim interior. At the altar is the so-called Rock of the Agony, where Jesus is said to have endured his Passion; this is the source of the older name of the church, the **Basilica of the Agony.**

A popular approach to Gethsemane is walking down the steep road from the top of the Mount of Olives—identified by pilgrims as the Palm

Sunday Road—perhaps stopping in on the way at the Dominus Flevit church where, tradition has it, Jesus wept as he foretold the destruction of the city (Luke 19). The entrance to the well-tended garden at the foot of the hill is marked by a small platoon of vendors outside. ⊠ *Jericho Rd., corner of El-Mansuriya Rd., Kidron Valley* ✛ *Foot of Mount of Olives and its Palm Sunday Rd.* ☎ *02/626–6444* ⊕ *www.gethsemane-en.custodia.org* 🎫 *Free.*

Garden Tomb. A beautifully tended English-style country garden makes this an island of tranquillity in the hurly-burly of East Jerusalem. What Christian pilgrims come for, however, is an empty ancient tomb, and a moving opportunity to ponder the Gospel account of the death and resurrection of Jesus. It is a favorite site for the many Protestant visitors who respond less or not at all to the ornamentation and ritual of the Holy Sepulcher.

In 1883, British general Charles Gordon spent several months in Jerusalem. From his window looking out over the Old City walls, he was struck by the skull-like features of a cliff face north of the Damascus Gate. He was convinced that this, rather than the Church of the Holy Sepulcher, was "the place of the skull" (Mark 15) where Jesus was crucified. An ancient rock-cut tomb had already been uncovered there, and subsequent excavations exposed cisterns and a wine press, features typical of an ancient garden.

According to the New Testament, Jesus was buried in the fresh tomb of the wealthy Joseph of Arimathea, in a garden close to the execution site, and some archaeologists identified the tomb as an upper-class Jewish burial place of the Second Temple period. Recent research, however, indicates that this tomb is apparently from the Old Testament period, making it too old to have been that of Jesus. In general, the gentle guardians of the Garden Tomb do not insist on the identification of the site as that of Calvary and the tomb of Christ, but are keen to provide a contemplative setting for the pilgrim, in a place that just might have been historically significant. ⊠ *Conrad Schick St., off Nablus Rd., East Jerusalem* ☎ *02/539–8100* ⊕ *www.gardentomb.com* 🎫 *Free* ☾ *Closed Sun.*

NEED A BREAK

✕ **American Colony Hotel.** This upscale hotel is an elegant 19th-century limestone building with cane furniture, Armenian ceramic tiles, and a delightful courtyard. The food is generally very good, and a light lunch or afternoon tea in the cool lobby lounge, at the poolside restaurant, or on the patio under the trees can make for a well-earned break. ⊠ *1 Louis Vincent St., American Colony, at Nablus Rd., East Jerusalem* ☎ *02/627–9777* ⊕ *www.americancolony.com.*

Fodor'sChoice
★

Mount of Olives Observation Point. The Old City, with its landmark domes and towers, is squarely within your lens in this classic, picture-postcard panoramic view. It's best in the early morning, with the sun at your back, or at sunset on days with some clouds, when the golden glow and sunbeams more than compensate for the glare.

East Jerusalem

KEY

⊢—⊣ *Light rail*

Church of
Mary Magdalene **5**

Dominus Flevit **4**

Garden of
Gethsemane **6**

Garden Tomb **9**

Kidron Valley **1**

Mount of Olives
Observation Point **2**

Pater Noster Convent **3**

Rockefeller
Archaeological
Museum **8**

Tomb of the Virgin **7**

The magnificent, gold Dome of the Rock and the black-domed al-Aqsa Mosque to the left of it dominate the skyline; but look behind them for the large gray dome of the Holy Sepulcher and (farther left) the white one of the Jewish Quarter's Hurva Synagogue for a hint of the long-running visibility contest among faiths and nations. To the left of the Old City, the cone-roof Dormition Abbey and its adjacent clock tower crown Mount Zion, today outside the walls but within the city of the Second Temple period.

The Mount of Olives has been bathed in sanctity for millennia. On the slope beneath you, and off to your left, is the vast Jewish cemetery, reputedly the oldest still in use anywhere in the world. For more than 2,000 years, Jews have been buried here to await the coming of the Messiah and the resurrection to follow. The raised structures over the graves are merely tomb markers, not crypts; burial is belowground.

Camel and donkey drivers (usually one of each) are always pushing to give you a short ride (not cheap!), and the vendors can be persistent, but a polite "no thank you" is sometimes enough for them to go bother someone else. ■TIP➜ **Beware of pickpockets here and on the road down to Gethsemane.** Fairly good bathrooms are a welcome feature. ✉ *E-Sheikh St., in front of Seven Arches Hotel, Mount of Olives.*

Rockefeller Archaeological Museum. Built in the 1930s, and now a branch of the Israel Museum, the museum has echoing stone halls and somewhat old-fashioned displays that recall the period of the British Mandate. Among the most important exhibits are stucco and other decorations from the 8th-century AD Hisham's Palace (Umayyad dynasty) just north of Jericho, the doors of the original al-Aqsa Mosque (also 8th century), and gold Canaanite jewelry. Stone bas-reliefs by Eric Gill, representing different ancient cultures, overlook the pool in the inner courtyard. The museum's octagonal white stone tower is an East Jerusalem landmark. Parking is only available on Saturday. ■TIP➜ **For winter visitors, note that the buildings have no heating.** ✉ *27 Sultan Suleiman St., East Jerusalem* ✛ *Opposite Herod's Gate (northeastern corner of Old City)* ☎ *02/670–8074* ⊕ *www.english.imjnet.org.il/page_1684* ✉ *Free* ☽ *Closed Tues., Fri., and Jewish holiday eves.*

WORTH NOTING

Church of Mary Magdalene. With its sculpted white turrets and gold onion domes, this Russian Orthodox church looks like something out of a fairy tale. It was dedicated in 1888, when the competition among European powers for influence in this part of the world was at its height. Princess Alice, the mother of Prince Philip, Duke of Edinburgh, is buried here, near her aunt, Elizabeth, the Russian grand duchess–turned-nun, who was murdered by the Bolsheviks in 1918. The church has limited hours, but its icon-studded interior and tranquil garden are well worth a visit if your plans bring you to the area at the right time. ✉ *Palm Sunday Rd., off El-Mansuriya Rd., Mount of Olives* ✛ *Above the Garden of Gethsemane* ☎ *02/628–4371* ⊕ *www.jerusalem-mission. org/convent_magdalene.html* ✉ *Free* ☽ *Closed Fri.–Mon. and Wed., and Tues. and Thurs. afternoon.*

Dominus Flevit. Designed by Antonio Barluzzi in the 1950s, the tear-shaped church—its name means "The Lord Wept"—preserves the New Testament story of Jesus's sorrowful prediction of the destruction of Jerusalem (Luke 19). The remarkable feature of its simple interior is a picture window facing west, the iron cross on the altar silhouetted against a superb view of the Old City. Many archaeological items were unearthed here, including a group of ancient stone ossuaries, or bone boxes, preserved in a grotto on the right as you enter the site. The courtyard is a good place to enjoy the view in peace between waves of pilgrim groups. (Equally worthy of mention are the restrooms, rare in this area.) The church is about one-third of the way down the steep road that descends to Gethsemane from the Mount of Olives observation point. ⚠ **Beware of pickpockets on the street outside.** ✉ *Palm Sunday Rd., Mount of Olives* ✛ *Below Mount of Olives Observation Point* ☎ *02/626–6450* ✆ *Free.*

Kidron Valley. This deep valley separates the Old City and the City of David from the high ridge of the Mount of Olives and the Arab neighborhood of Silwan. In the cliff face below the neighborhood are the symmetrical openings of tombs from both the First Temple (Old Testament) and Second Temple (Hellenistic-Roman) periods. You can view the impressive group of 2,200-year-old funerary monuments from the lookout terrace at the southeast corner of the Old City wall, down and to your left, or wander down into the valley itself and see them close up. The huge, square, stone structure with the conical roof is known as **Absalom's Pillar.** The one crowned by a pyramidal roof, a solid block of stone cut out of the mountain, is called **Zachariah's Tomb.** The association with those Old Testament personalities was a medieval mistake, and the structures more probably mark the tombs of wealthy Jerusalemites of the Second Temple period who wished to await the coming of the Messiah and the resurrection to follow in the style to which they were accustomed. ✉ *Jericho Rd., between Mount of Olives and the Old City, Kidron Valley* ✆ *Free.*

Pater Noster Convent. The church built here in the 4th century AD by Constantine the Great became known as the Eleona (olive), and was associated back then with the ascension of Jesus to heaven. By the Middle Ages, tradition had firmly settled on a small grotto—the focal point of the site—as the place where Jesus taught his disciples the Lord's Prayer: "Our Father [Pater Noster]..." (Matthew 6). The land was purchased by the Princesse de la Tour d'Auvergne of France in 1868, and the Carmelite convent stands on the site of the earlier Byzantine and Crusader structures. An ambitious basilica, begun in the 1920s, was designed to follow the lines of the 4th-century church, but was never completed: its aisles, open to the sky, are now lined with pine trees. The real attractions of the site, however, are the many large ceramic plaques adorning the cloister walls and the small church, with the Lord's Prayer in more than 100 different languages. (Look for the high wall, metal door, and French flag on a bend 200 yards before the Mount of Olives Observation Point.) ✉ *E-Sheikh St. at Rub'a el-Adawiya, Mount of Olives* ☎ *02/626–4904* ⊕ *www.cicts.org* ✆ *NIS 10* ☾ *Closed Sun.*

Tomb of the Virgin. The Gothic facade of the underground Church of the Assumption, which contains this shrine, clearly dates it to the Crusader era (12th century). Tradition has it that this is where the Virgin Mary was interred and then "assumed" into heaven, hence the more common name, the Tomb of the Virgin. In an otherwise gloomy church—hung with age-darkened icons and brass lamps—the marble sarcophagus, apparently medieval, remains illuminated. The 1852 Status Quo Agreement in force in the Church of the Holy Sepulcher and Bethlehem's Church of the Nativity pertains here, too: the Greek Orthodox, Armenian Orthodox, and even the Muslims control different parts of the property. The Roman Catholic Franciscans were expelled in 1757, a loss of privilege that rankles to this day. ⊠ *Jericho Rd., Kidron Valley* ✢ *A few steps away from Garden of Gethsemane* ☎ *02/628–4613* ✆ *Free.*

WEST JERUSALEM

Visitors tend to focus, naturally enough, on the historical and religious sights in the Old City, on the eastern side of town; but West Jerusalem houses the nation's institutions, is the repository for its collective memory, and—together with Downtown—gives more insight into contemporary life in Israel's largest city. The world-class Israel Museum and the Yad Vashem Holocaust museum are located here, as well as poignant Mount Herzl and the picturesque neighborhood of Ein Kerem. These attractions, which are spread out over a number of West Jerusalem neighborhoods, are most easily accessed by car or by a combination of buses, light-rail, and short cab rides.

GETTING HERE AND AROUND
There are good city bus services and the single-line light-rail in this part of town (ask at each site how to get to the next), but a few cab rides will be a much better use of limited time.

TIMING AND PRECAUTIONS
Pay attention to the closing times of sites: several aren't open on Saturday and close early on Friday. Some museums have evening hours on particular days—a time-efficient option. Avoid burnout by staggering visits to the museums and combining them on any given day with other kinds of experiences.

TOP ATTRACTIONS
Bible Lands Museum. Most archaeological museums group artifacts according to their place of origin, but the curators here favor a chronological display, seeking cross-cultural influences within any given era. The exhibits cover a more than 6,000 years—from the prehistoric Neolithic period (Late Stone Age) to that of the Byzantine Empire—and sweep geographically from Afghanistan to Sudan. Rare clay vessels, fertility idols, cylinder seals, ivories, and sarcophagi fill the soaring, naturally lighted galleries. Look for the ancient Egyptian wooden coffin, in a stunning state of preservation.

The concept of the museum is intriguing, but some have criticized its methodology. A concept was imposed on a largely preexisting collection, rather than a collection being created item by selected item to illustrate a concept. Plan on an hour to see the permanent exhibition—a guided tour will enhance the experience—and check out the temporary exhibitions downstairs. ⊠ *25 Granot St., Givat Ram* ✛ *Adjacent to Israel Museum* ☎ *02/561–1066* ⊕ *www.blmj.org* ✉ *NIS 44.*

Chagall Windows and Hadassah Hospital. Marc Chagall's vibrant stained-glass windows are the jewels in the crown of Hadassah Hospital's huge Ein Kerem campus. When the U.S.-based Hadassah organization began planning this hospital on the western edge of town back in the 1950s, it asked the Russian-born Jewish artist to adorn the small synagogue. Chagall was reportedly so delighted that he created the windows for free: Hadassah only paid for materials and labor. Taking his inspiration from the Bible—Jacob's deathbed blessings on his sons and, to a lesser extent, Moses's valediction to the tribes of Israel—he created 12 windows in luminous primary colors, with an ark-full of characteristically Chagallian beasts and a bag of Jewish and esoteric symbols. The innovative techniques of the Reims glassmakers give the wafer-thin windows an illusion of depth. Recorded explanations in the synagogue are available in several languages. Buses 12, 19, 27, and 42 head to the Ein Kerem campus. ⊠ *Hadassah Hospital, Henrietta Szold Rd., Ein Kerem* ☎ *02/677–6271* ⊕ *www.hadassah-med.com* ✉ *NIS 10* ☉ *Closed Fri. and Sat.*

> ## BRIDGE OF STRINGS
>
> The "Bridge of Strings" (or "Cords") was designed by Spanish architect Santiago Calatrava to suspend the new light-rail over the busy intersection at Jerusalem's western entrance (Tel Aviv Highway, Route 1). The commission was intended to provide the city with a contemporary icon. "What do we need it for?" complained some residents. Judge for yourself from the best angle: not as you enter the city but from the sidewalk outside the International Convention Center (*Binyanei Ha'ooma, Zalman Shazar Blvd.*).

Ein Kerem. The neighborhood of Ein Kerem still retains much of its old village character. Tree-framed stone houses spill across its hillsides with a pleasing Mediterranean nonchalance. Artists and professionals who have joined the older working-class population over the last 40 or 50 years have marvelously renovated many homes and made an effort to keep developers at bay. Back alleys provide an off-the-beaten-path feel, and occasionally a serendipitous art or craft studio.

Tradition identifies Ein Kerem as the birthplace of John the Baptist, and its most prominent landmarks are the orange-roofed Church of St. John the Baptist in the heart of the village, the Church of the Visitation up the hillside above the Spring of the Virgin—both Roman Catholic—and the gold-domed Russian church above that along the road to Hadassah Hospital. The neighborhood is served by city Bus 28 from Mount Herzl. There is free underground parking in the neighborhood center. Ein Kerem is less than five minutes from Mount Herzl by bus or taxi, and about 15 minutes by taxi from Downtown. ⊠ *Ein Kerem.*

West Jerusalem

KEY

┼─┼─┼ Light rail

Mitzpeh Nof ▲

1–4

Bible Lands Museum	**11**
Bloomfield Science Museum	**9**
Chagall Windows and Hadassah Hospital	**2**
Church of St. John the Baptist........	**3**

Church of the Visitation	**4**
Ein Kerem	**1**
Israel Museum	**12**
Knesset	**10**
L.A. Mayer Museum for Islamic Art	**13**

Mount Herzl Military Cemetery	**7**
Mount Herzl National Memorial Park	**6**
Tisch Family Zoological Gardens	**8**
Yad Vashem.................	**5**

0 ─────── 1/4 mile
0 ─────── 400 meters

FAMILY **Israel Museum.** This world-class museum shines after a massive makeover
Fodor's Choice that brought with it modern exhibits and state-of-the-art technology.
★ The **Dead Sea Scrolls** are certainly the museum's most famous—and
most important—collection. A Bedouin boy discovered the first of the
2,000-year-old parchments in 1947 in a Judean Desert cave, overlooking the Dead Sea. Of the nine main scrolls and bags full of small fragments that surfaced over the years, many of the most important and
most complete are preserved here; the Antiquities Authority holds the
rest of the parchments, and a unique copper scroll is in Jordan. The
white dome of the Shrine of the Book, the separate pavilion in which
the scrolls are housed, was inspired by the lids of the clay jars in which
the first ones were found.

The scrolls were written in the Second Temple period by a fiercely
zealous, separatist, and monastic Jewish sect, widely identified as the
Essenes, a group described by contemporary historians. Archaeological,
laboratory, and textual evidence dates the earliest of the scrolls to the
2nd century BC; none could have been written later than AD 68, the
year in which their home community, known today as Qumran, was
destroyed by the Romans. The parchments, still in an extraordinary
state of preservation because of the dryness of the Dead Sea region, contain the oldest Hebrew manuscripts of the Old Testament ever found,
authenticating the almost identical Hebrew texts still in use today. The
sectarian literature provides an insight into this esoteric community.
The early-medieval Aleppo Codex, on display in the small lower gallery
under the white dome, is considered the most authoritative text of the
Hebrew Bible in existence.

The quarter-acre outdoor **1:50 scale model,** adjacent to the Shrine of
the Book, represents Jerusalem as it was on the eve of the Great Revolt
against Rome (AD 66). Designed in the mid-1960s by the late Professor Michael Avi-Yonah, it stood on the grounds of the Holyland Hotel
in West Jerusalem until 2006, when new (and controversial) urban
development brought it here. Avi-Yonah relied on considerable data
gleaned from Roman-period historians, important Jewish texts, and
even the New Testament, and based some of his generic reconstruc-
tions (villas, a theater, markets, etc.) on Roman structures that have
survived across the ancient empire. Later archaeological excavations
have sometimes confirmed and sometimes challenged Avi-Yonah's sharp
intuition, and the model has been updated occasionally to incorporate
new knowledge. The available audio guide is a worthwhile aid in deci-
phering the site.

Taken together, the Dead Sea Scrolls, the huge model, and Roman-
period exhibits in the Archaeology Wing evoke the turbulent and historically momentous Second Temple period. That was the era from
which Christianity emerged; and when the Romans razed the Temple
in Jerusalem, it compelled a slow revolution in Jewish life and religious
practice that has defined Judaism to this day.

The **Archaeology Wing** has been reorganized to highlight particular treasures in galleries that follow a historical sequence. If you know a bit of
Bible, many artifacts in the Canaanite, Israelite, and Hellenistic-Roman

sections offer evocative illustrations of familiar texts. Don't miss the small side rooms devoted to glass, coins, and the Hebrew script.

Jewish Art and Life is the name for the wing made up mostly of finely wrought Jewish ceremonial objects (Judaica) from widely disparate communities. The "synagogue route" includes reconstructed old synagogues from India, Germany, Italy, and Suriname.

The **Art Wing** is a slightly confusing maze spread over different levels, but if you have patience and time, the payoff is great. Older European art rubs shoulders with modern works, contemporary Israeli art, design, and photography. The flyer available at the museum entrance lists new and temporary exhibitions. Landscape architect Isamu Noguchi designed the open-air **Art Garden.** Crunch over the gravel amid works by Daumier, Rodin, Moore, Picasso, and less-legendary local luminaries.

The **Youth Wing** mounts one major new exhibition a year, interactive and often adult-friendly, designed to encourage children to appreciate the arts and the world around them, or to be creative in a crafts workshop. Parents with younger kids will also be grateful for the outdoor play areas.

The vegetarian/dairy café, Mansfeld, is a great place for a light meal or coffee. The more expensive Modern has tempting meat and fish combinations and remains open beyond museum hours. The lockers and ATM in the museum's entrance hall are useful. Large bags or packs have to be checked. Photography (without flash) is allowed everywhere except in the Shrine of the Book. Check the website for summer days with longer hours and free entrance for kids. ✉ *11 Ruppin Rd., Givat Ram* ✛ *Near Knesset* ☏ *02/670–8811* ⊕ *www.imj.org.il* 🎟 *NIS 54.*

Knesset. Both the name of Israel's one-chamber parliament and its number of seats (120) were taken from *Haknesset Hagedolah,* the Great Assembly of the Second Temple period, some 2,000 years ago. The free hour-long public tour, offered Sunday and Thursday, includes the session hall and three enormous, brilliantly colored tapestries designed by Marc Chagall on the subjects of the Creation, the Exodus, and Jerusalem. Arrive at least 30 minutes before the tour (especially in summer, when the lines are longer), and be sure to bring your passport. Bags and cameras have to be deposited with security. On other days, when in session, Knesset proceedings (conducted in Hebrew) are open to the public—call ahead to verify.

Across the road from the Knesset main gate is a 14-foot-high, 4-ton bronze menorah, based on the one that once stood within the sanctuary of the ancient temple in Jerusalem. The seven-branch candelabrum was adopted soon after independence as the official symbol of the modern State of Israel. This one, designed by sculptor Benno Elkan, and given as a gift by British parliamentarians to the Knesset in 1956, is decorated with bas-relief depictions of events and personages in Jewish history, from biblical times to the modern day. Behind the menorah is the Wohl Rose Garden, which has hundreds of varieties of roses, many lawns for children to romp on, and adult-friendly nooks in its upper section (entry from outside the Knesset complex). ✉ *Kiryat Ben-Gurion, Givat Ram* ✛ *Near Israel Museum* ☏ *02/675–3337* ⊕ *www.knesset.gov.il* 🎟 *Free.*

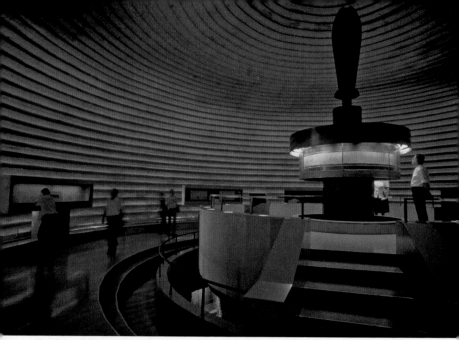
The Shrine of the Book at the Israel Museum dramatically displays fragile sections of the Dead Sea Scrolls.

L.A. Mayer Museum for Islamic Art. The considerable and diverse artistic achievements of Islamic culture are what this small museum is all about. Its rich collections—ceramics, glass, carpets, fabrics, jewelry, metalwork, and painting—reflect a creativity that spanned half a hemisphere, from Spain to India, and from the 7th century to the 19th. Unconnected to the main theme is a unique and stunning collection of rare (some priceless) antique European clocks and watches, the pride of the founder's family: this alone is worth the visit. ⊠ *2 Hapalmach St., Hapalmach* 🕾 *02/566–1291* ⊕ *www.islamicart.co.il* ✆ *NIS 40* ☉ *Closed Sun.*

Mount Herzl National Memorial Park. Cedars of Lebanon and native pine and cypress trees surround the entrance to Mount Herzl National Memorial Park, the last resting place of Zionist visionary Theodor Herzl and many Israeli leaders.

In 1894, the Budapest-born Herzl was the Paris correspondent for a Vienna newspaper, covering the controversial treason trial of Alfred Dreyfus, a Jewish officer in the French army. Dreyfus was later exonerated, but Herzl was shocked by the anti-Semitic outbursts that accompanied the trial. He devoted himself to the need for a Jewish state, convening the first World Zionist Congress, in Basel, Switzerland, in 1897. Herzl wrote in his diary that year: "If not in five years, then in 50 [a Jewish state] will become reality." True to his prediction, the United Nations approved the idea exactly 50 years later, in November 1947. Herzl died in 1904, and his remains were brought to Israel in 1949. His simple tombstone, inscribed in Hebrew with just his last name, caps the hill.

To the left (west) of his tomb, a gravel path leads down to a section containing the graves of Israeli national leaders—among them prime ministers Golda Meir and Yitzhak Rabin, and presidents Zalman Shazar, Chaim Herzog, and Shimon Peres—and the country's main military cemetery.

The Herzl Center (on the left as you enter the park) presents an engaging, multimedia introduction to the life, times, and legacy of Israel's spiritual forebear, Theodor Herzl. The program takes 50 minutes and costs NIS 25. Call ahead for English time slots. ✉ *Herzl Blvd., Mount Herzl* ☎ *02/632–1515* ⊕ *www.wzo.org.il/mount-herzl* ✆ *Free* ⊘ *Closed Sat.*

OFF THE BEATEN PATH

Tisch Family Zoological Gardens. Spread over a scenic 62-acre ridge among Jerusalem's hilly southern neighborhoods, this zoo has many of the usual species that delight zoo visitors everywhere: monkeys and elephants, snakes and birds, and all the rest. But it goes much further, focusing on two groups of wildlife. The first is creatures mentioned in the Bible that have become locally extinct, some as late as the 20th century. Among these are Asian lions, bears, cheetahs, the Nile crocodile, and the Persian fallow deer. The second focus is on endangered species worldwide, among them the Asian elephant and rare macaws. At the time of this writing, the new aquarium was planned to be completed in mid-2017.

This is a wonderful place to let kids expend some energy—there are lawns and playground equipment—and allow adults some downtime from touring. Early morning or late afternoon are the best hours in summer; budget 2½ hours to see (almost) everything. A wagon train does the rounds of the zoo, at a nominal fee of NIS 2 (not on Saturdays and Jewish holidays). The Noah's Ark Visitors Center has a movie and computer programs. The zoo is served by city routes 26A (from Central Bus Station) and 33 (from Mount Herzl). The ride is about 30 minutes; a cab would take 15 minutes from Downtown hotels. ✉ *1 Derech Aharon Shulov, near Jerusalem Mall, Malcha* ☎ *02/675–0111* ⊕ *www.jerusalemzoo.org.il* ✆ *NIS 55.*

Fodor's Choice
★

Yad Vashem. The experience of the Holocaust—the annihilation of 6 million Jews by the Nazis during World War II—is so deeply seared into the Jewish national psyche that understanding it goes a long way toward understanding Israelis themselves. Yad Vashem was created in 1953 by an act of the Knesset, and charged with preserving a record of those times. The multifaceted campus includes a museum, an archive and research facility, an energetic education department, art galleries, and numerous monuments. (The name Yad Vashem—"a memorial and a name"—comes from the biblical book of Isaiah [56:5].) The Israeli government has made a tradition of bringing almost all high-ranking official foreign guests to visit the place.

The riveting **Holocaust History Museum**—a well-lit, 200-yard-long triangular concrete "prism"—is the centerpiece of the site. Powerful visual and audiovisual techniques in a series of galleries document Jewish life in Europe before the catastrophe and follow the escalation of persecution and internment to the hideous climax of the Nazi's "Final Solution." Video interviews and personal artifacts individualize the experience. ■ TIP→ Note that children under 10 are not admitted, photography is not allowed in the exhibition areas, and large bags have to be checked.

In Yad Vashem's Holocaust History Museum, the Hall of Names includes 600 photos of Jews who perished.

The small **Children's Memorial** is dedicated to the 1.5 million Jewish children murdered by the Nazis. Architect Moshe Safdie wanted to convey the enormity of the crime without numbing the visitor's emotions or losing sight of the victims' individuality. The result is a single dark room, lit by just a few candles infinitely reflected in hundreds of mirrors. Recorded narrators intone the names, ages, and countries of origin of known victims. The effect is electrifying. Also focusing on children is a poignant exhibition called "No Child's Play," about children's activities during the Holocaust. It's in an art museum beyond the exit of the Holocaust History Museum.

The **Avenue of the Righteous** encircles Yad Vashem with thousands of trees marked with the names of Gentiles in Europe who risked and sometimes lost their lives trying to save Jews from the Nazis. Raoul Wallenberg, King Christian X of Denmark, Corrie ten Boom, Oskar Schindler, and American journalist Varian Fry are among the more famous honorees. The **Hall of Remembrance** is a heavy basalt-and-concrete building that houses an eternal flame, with the names of the death camps and main concentration camps in relief on the floor.

A detour takes you to the **Valley of the Communities** at the bottom of the hill, where large, rough-hewn limestone boulders divide the site into a series of small, man-made canyons. Each clearing represents a region of Nazi Europe, laid out geographically. The names of some 5,000 destroyed Jewish communities are inscribed in the stone walls, with larger letters highlighting those that were particularly important in prewar Europe.

There is an information booth (be sure to buy the inexpensive map of the site), a bookstore, and a cafeteria at the entrance to Yad Vashem.

Allow about two hours to see the Holocaust History Museum, more if you rent an audio guide. If your time is short, be sure to see the Children's Memorial and the Avenue of the Righteous. To avoid the biggest crowds, come first thing in the morning or around noon. The site is an easy 10-minute walk or a quick free shuttle from the Mount Herzl intersection, which in turn is served by many city bus lines and the light-rail. ⊠ *Hazikaron St., Mount Herzl* ✛ *Near Herzl Blvd.* ☎ *02/644–3565* ⊕ *www.yadvashem.org* 🎫 *Free* ☉ *Closed Sat.*

WORTH NOTING

FAMILY **Bloomfield Science Museum.** For kids, this may be the city's best rainy-day option, but don't wait for a rainy day to enjoy the museum. Along with a range of intriguing, please-touch interactive equipment that demonstrates scientific principles in an engagingly fun environment, there is lots of innovation and creativity—not least of all in the changing exhibits. Explanations are in English, and Hebrew University science students, as many as 20 at a time on busy weekends, are on hand to explain stuff. ⊠ *Museum Blvd., Givat Ram* ☎ *02/654–4888* ⊕ *www.mada.org.il/en* 🎫 *NIS 60* ☉ *Closed Sun.*

Church of St. John the Baptist. The village of Ein Kerem is not mentioned by name in the New Testament, but its identification as the birthplace of John the Baptist is a tradition that apparently goes back to the Byzantine period (5th century AD). The grotto associated with that event is enshrined in the large, late-17th-century Franciscan church that bears his name, its orange tile roof a prominent landmark in the heart of Ein Kerem. The walls of the sanctuary are covered in age-darkened paintings and glazed tiles. ⊠ *Mevo Hasha'ar, off Ein Kerem St., Ein Kerem* ☎ *02/632–3000* 🎫 *Free.*

Church of the Visitation. Built over what is thought to have been the home of John the Baptist's parents, Zechariah and Elizabeth, this church sits high up the hillside in Ein Kerem, with a wonderful view of the valley and the surrounding wooded hills. It is a short but stiff walk up from the spring at the center of the village. When Mary, pregnant with Jesus, came to visit her cousin, the aging Elizabeth, who was also with child, "the babe leaped in [Elizabeth's] womb" with joy at recognizing the unborn Jesus. Mary thereupon pronounced the paean to God known as the Magnificat ("My soul doth magnify the Lord" [Luke 1]). One wall of the church courtyard is covered with ceramic tiles quoting the Magnificat in 41 languages. The upper church is adorned with large wall paintings depicting the mantles with which Mary has been endowed—Mother of God, Refuge of Sinners, Dispenser of All Grace, Help of Christians—as well as the Immaculate Conception. Other frescoes depict Hebrew women of the Bible also known for their "hymns and canticles," as the Franciscan guide puts it. Ring the bell for entry on Saturday. ⊠ *Madreigot Habikur, Ein Kerem* ✛ *At end of Hama'ayan St., beyond spring* ☎ *02/641–7291* 🎫 *Free.*

Mount Herzl Military Cemetery. The tranquillity and well-tended greenery of Israel's national military cemetery almost belie its somber purpose. Different sections are reserved for the casualties of each war the nation has fought. The large number of headstones, all identical, are a sobering reminder of the price Israel has paid for its national independence and security. Note that officers and privates are buried alongside one another—lost lives are mourned equally, regardless of rank. ⊠ *Herzl Blvd., Mount Herzl.*

CENTER CITY

West Jerusalem's Downtown and near-Downtown areas, just west of the Old City, are a mix of old neighborhoods, new limestone edifices, monuments, and markets. There are plenty of hotels and restaurants here, too. Few of the attractions appear on a Jerusalem don't-miss checklist, but you'll rub shoulders with the locals in the vibrant Machaneh Yehuda produce market, breathe the atmosphere of day-to-day life on Ben-Yehuda and Jaffa Streets, get a feel for the city's more recent history in Nahalat Shiva and Yemin Moshe—in short, for a few brief hours you can be a bit less of a tourist.

GETTING HERE AND AROUND
There's paid parking in the Center City, but you're better off walking, grabbing a cab, or riding the light-rail. The area is served by many bus lines from the Central Bus Station; 34 and 77 from the German Colony and Talbieh; and 7 and 9 from the Knesset and the Israel Museum.

TIMING AND PRECAUTIONS
Jaffa Street, Ben-Yehuda Street, and Machaneh Yehuda are ghostly quiet from Friday afternoon until after dark Saturday because of the Jewish Sabbath. Friday morning through early afternoon is the most bustling, as Jerusalemites meet friends for coffee or lunch, and do their weekend shopping.

TOP ATTRACTIONS
Ben-Yehuda Street. Most of the street is an open-air pedestrian mall, in the heart of Downtown, forming a triangle with King George Street and Jaffa Street. It is known locally as the **Midrachov**, a term concocted from two Hebrew words: *midracha* (sidewalk) and *rechov* (street). The street is named after the brilliant linguist Eliezer Ben-Yehuda, who in the late 19th century almost single-handedly revived Hebrew as a modern spoken language; he would have liked the clever new word. Cafés have tables out on the cobblestones, and buskers are usually around in good weather, playing tunes old and new. It's a great place to sip coffee or munch falafel and watch the passing crowd. On Saturday and Jewish holidays, only a few restaurants and convenience stores are open, but after nightfall (especially in warm weather) the area comes back to life. ⊠ *Ben-Yehuda St., Center City* ⊹ *Between King George St. and Zion Sq.*

Fodor'sChoice ★ **Machaneh Yehuda.** For a unique local experience, head to this two-block-long covered lane and its adjacent alleys, filled with the brilliant colors of the city's best-quality produce, cheeses, and baked goods. It's fun to elbow your way through this decidedly unslick market anytime,

CLOSE UP

A Good Walk in Center City

Jerusalem is a good city to stroll. The limestone buildings, shaded courtyards, and colorful peoplescapes of the Center City make for an absorbing experience. The first part of the walk—up to the YMCA—is good anytime; avoid the rest of it late Friday and on Saturday, when the Downtown area shuts down for the Jewish Sabbath. The route will take 1½ hours to walk, not counting stops.

MONTEFIORE'S WINDMILL TO THE YMCA

Begin at the landmark **Montefiore's Windmill,** across the valley from Mount Zion. Immediately below the adjacent patio is the long, crenellated roof of Mishkenot Sha'ananim, the first neighborhood outside the walls of Jerusalem, built by Sir Moses (Moshe) Montefiore in 1860.

Separating you from Mount Zion and the Old City is the deep **Hinnom Valley,** the biblical border between the Israelite tribes of Judah (to the south) and Benjamin (to the north). A few hundred yards off to your right is the fortresslike St. Andrew's Scots Church, right above the bend in the valley known as Ketef Hinnom (the Hinnom Shoulder). An excavation in the late 1970s on the rock scarp below the church uncovered hewn-out Old Testament–period tombs and a treasure trove of archaeological finds.

Stroll through the attractive cobblestone streets of the **Yemin Moshe** neighborhood, abutting the windmill, and up through the small park that separates it from King David Street. The landmark King David Hotel is a handsome, rectangular limestone building with a back terrace overlooking the Old City walls. Drinks and desserts aren't cheap, but the location and Hollywood echoes (Paul Newman and Eva Marie Saint in *Exodus*) count for something. Across the street is the **Jerusalem YMCA:** its tower has stunning panoramas.

INDEPENDENCE PARK TO MACHANEH YEHUDA

Turn onto Abraham Lincoln Street, alongside the YMCA and opposite the gas station. From the intersection 70 yards beyond it, a pedestrian lane (George Eliot Street) continues in the same direction, emerging at Agron Street, next to the U.S. Consulate General. Cross Agron and walk over the lawns of **Independence Park.** The park's crossroad, 50 yards to your right, emerges at Hillel Street, where there are excellent coffee shops.

Across Hillel is Yoel Salomon Street, and to the right and parallel to it is Yosef Rivlin Street, named after two of the seven founders of **Nahalat Shiva,** the second neighborhood built outside the city walls, in 1869. Hidden courtyards, funky stores, and eateries make this a fun time-out option. At the other end of Salomon Street is Zion Square, where Jaffa Street, Jerusalem's main thoroughfare, meets **Ben-Yehuda Street,** a pedestrian-only commercial street.

At the top of Ben-Yehuda Street, cross King George Street, turn right, and take your first left onto Agrippas Street. (The corner falafel stand is your landmark.) A short walk up the street, on your right, is the entrance to the colorful **Machaneh Yehuda** produce market. It extends for two city blocks, to Jaffa Street. *For more information on the sights in bold type, see the listings in Center City.*

Center City

but it's riotously busy on Friday, when Jewish Jerusalem does its last-minute shopping for the Sabbath. Its traditional Mediterranean-Middle Eastern character, going back generations, still dominates; but a liberal sprinkling of stall-size Western eateries, wine shops, and bars, and a few arts-and-crafts or souvenir shops, have given Machaneh Yehuda a more cosmopolitan feel. The market links Jaffa Street and Agrippas Street, parallel to and just a five-minute walk up from King George Street. Many of the Downtown bus lines stop on King George, and several on Agrippas itself, while the light-rail runs the length of Jaffa Street (which is otherwise closed to traffic). There is some paid parking close to the market, but it is most easily approached on foot. ⊠ *Etz Hayim St., at Agrippas St., Center City* ☉ *Closed Sat.*

Montefiore's Windmill. This limestone, wind-driven flour mill was built by Sir Moses Montefiore in 1857 to provide a source of income for his planned neighborhood of Mishkenot Sha'ananim, the first outside the city walls. Its usefulness was cut short when steam mills made their appearance; but in 2012, with Dutch and English expertise, the landmark windmill was restored to working order.

Montefiore was a prominent figure in the financial circles of mid-19th-century London—a rare phenomenon for a Jew at the time. He married into the legendary Rothschild family, becoming the stockbroker of its

London branch, and retired early. The larger-than-life philanthropist—he stood a remarkable 6 feet 3 inches tall—devoted much of his long life, and his wealth, to aiding fellow Jews in distress, wherever they might be. To this end he visited Palestine, as this district of the Ottoman Empire was then known, seven times. A replica of the carriage that conveyed him around the country is behind thick glass: vandals torched its predecessor. ⊠ *Yemin Moshe St., Center City* ☜ *Free.*

Nahalat Shiva. This small neighborhood has a funky feel, with worn flagstones, wrought-iron banisters, and defunct water cisterns. Its name translates roughly as "the Estate of the Seven," so called by the seven Jewish families that founded the quarter in 1869. The alleys and courtyards have been refashioned as a pedestrian district, offering equal opportunities for photographers, shoppers, and gastronomes. An eclectic variety of eateries, from Israeli to Italian, Asian to Arabic, tempt you to take a break from the jewelry and ceramics. ⊠ *Bordered by Salomon, Rivlin, Jaffa, and Hillel Sts., Center City* ✛ *Near Zion Sq.*

NEED A BREAK

✕ **Halitatea.** This teahouse in an alley, barely visible from the street, imports dozens of organic, fair-trade specialty leaves, especially from India, Sri Lanka, Japan, China, and South Africa. It's all served in glass teapots on wooden trays carved by the shop owner. There's a tempting vegetarian and vegan menu of light fare, and an espresso machine for diehard coffee drinkers: all this and free Wi-Fi, too. ⊠ *5 Hillel St., Center City* ☎ *077/411–0224* ⊕ *halitatea.com/* ⊗ *Closed Sat. and Jewish religious holidays.*

Umberto Nahon Museum of Italian Jewish Art. A little-known gem, the museum shares its classic old stone building with a cultural center (ask to see the frescoes in the ground-floor hall). The second-floor galleries include the interior of an ornate Italian synagogue from 1701; illustrated manuscripts; and ritual artifacts in metal, wood, and embroidered fabric from the Italian Renaissance to modern times. The attention to detail characteristic of the best Italian art was adopted and adapted by skilled Jewish craftspeople. The result is a feast for the eyes, even if the spiritual significance of some exhibits may be less familiar to some visitors. ⊠ *27 Hillel St., Center City* ☎ *02/624–1610* ⊕ *www.ijamuseum.org* ☜ *NIS 25* ⊗ *Closed Mon. and Sat.*

WORTH NOTING

Independence Park. This is a great area for lounging around, throwing Frisbees, or eating a picnic lunch in warm weather. Some of the Muslim graves at the bottom of the park date from the 13th century. The large defunct reservoir nearby, known as the Mamilla Pool, is probably late medieval, though it may have much earlier Roman origins. ⊠ *Between Agron and Hillel Sts., Center City* ☜ *Free.*

Jerusalem YMCA. The YMCA exudes old-world charm: its high-domed landmark bell tower thrusts out of a palatial white-limestone facade, full of carved arcane symbols and ancient scripts. The complex boasts the usual YMCA fitness facilities, a hotel, a concert hall, a restaurant, and a bilingual preschool. For NIS 20 you can ride the small elevator (they insist on two people minimum) to tiny balconies, with

The Machaneh Yehuda covered market offers a unique traditional shopping experience.

breathtaking views of the city in all directions. A bit of trivia: the building, dedicated in 1933, was designed by Arthur Loomis Harmon, one of the architects of New York City's Empire State Building. ⊠ *26 King David St., Center City* ⊕ *Opposite King David Hotel* ☎ *02/569–2692* ⊕ *ymca.org.il* 🎟 *Tower NIS 20.*

Ticho House (*Beit Ticho*). This handsome, two-story, 19th-century building was the home of Dr. A. A. Ticho, a renowned Jewish ophthalmologist, and his wife, Anna. He moved from Vienna to Jerusalem in 1912, and his cousin, Anna, followed soon after, to assist him in his pioneering struggle against the endemic scourge of trachoma. They were soon married, and in 1924 they bought and renovated this stone house. Anna's artistic talent gradually earned her a reputation as a brilliant chronicler—in charcoal, pen, and brush—of the landscape around Jerusalem. Ticho House, which operates as a branch of the Israel Museum, has recently been restored, giving more exhibition space for the Ticho story, a selection of Anna Ticho's works, and changing, intimate exhibitions of contemporary Israeli art. The upper level houses an Italian café called Anna. ⊠ *10 Harav Agan St., Center City* ☎ *02/624–5068* ⊕ *www.english.imjnet.org.il/page_1712* 🎟 *Free* ⊙ *Closed Sat.*

Yemin Moshe. Attractive old stone buildings, bursts of greenery and bougainvillea, and well-kept cobblestone streets distinguish a now-affluent neighborhood that grew up a century ago alongside the older Mishkenot Sha'ananim, and was named for that project's founder, Sir Moses (*Moshe* in Hebrew) Montefiore. In the 1950s and '60s, the area overlooked the armistice line that gashed through the city, and was dangerously exposed to Jordanian sniper positions on the nearby Old

City walls. Most families sought safer lodgings elsewhere, leaving only those who couldn't afford to move, and the neighborhood ran to seed. The reunification of Jerusalem under Israeli rule after the Six-Day War in 1967 changed all that. Developers bought up the area, renovated old buildings, and built new and spacious homes in a compatible style. Yemin Moshe is now a place to wander at random, offering joy to photographers and quiet nooks for meditation. ⊠ *Between King David St. and Emile Botta St., Center City.*

GERMAN COLONY AND BAKA

The German Colony got its name from a group of breakaway Lutherans known as the Templers (not the medieval ones: these are spelled with an "*e*"). They established half a dozen communities around the country in the 1860s and '70s in the belief that their presence in the Holy Land would hasten the Second Coming. Feelings of German patriotism ran high among the Templers in World War I, and many were interned as enemy aliens by the victorious British forces in 1918. Pro-Nazi sentiments and symbols surfaced in the 1930s, and the British deported most of the group en masse when World War II broke out. Look for the row of private stone houses towards the northern end of Emek Refa'im, many with German inscriptions and dates over the doorways.

Israelis have discovered the old-world charms of "the Moshava" (the German Colony) and its environs, and so should you. This isn't the place for headline sights, but take in the good eateries and cafés, some memorable restaurants and pubs in the First Station and Colony compounds, and a sprinkling of little stores, particularly along Emek Refa'im Street. Relax with the residents, especially daytime Friday or on warm summer evenings (except Friday), when the area is at its liveliest.

The Baka neighborhood, just across the old train tracks east of the German Colony, has its busy thoroughfares, stores, and coffee shops, to be sure, but its true character lies in a maze of eucalyptus-shaded backstreets and century-old homes built in the Jerusalem style with honey-color limestone. Many have been preserved or restored, while others have given way to (mercifully) low-rise modernization.

TOP ATTRACTIONS

FAMILY **First Station.** This was once the terminus of the old Jaffa–Jerusalem railroad, inaugurated in 1892. It survived two world wars and two regime changes until the suspension of rail service in 1998. Despite being boarded up, the handsome building's limestone facade, gabled roof, and arched doorways stood as a reminder of its glory days. A creative renovation has won accolades, especially from Jerusalemites. In a city not known for its contemporary attractions, First Station made a splash with its cafés and restaurants, shaded crafts stalls, and play equipment for the kids (and sometimes balloon artists or puppeteers). Evening performances and other cultural events have become popular, especially in the warmer months. The compound is open on Saturday, but only really comes alive in the evening. ⊠ *4 David Remez St., German Colony* ✛ *Entrance also from Derech Beit Lehem (Bethlehem Rd.)* ☎ *02/653–5239* ⊕ *firststation.co.il/en* ✉ *Free.*

Me'a She'arim

The name of this neighborhood just north of Downtown is the biblical "hundredfold," describing the bountiful blessing God gave Isaac (Genesis 26). The appearance of that verse in the cyclical Torah reading the very week the neighborhood was founded, in 1874, was regarded as a good omen. This is a stronghold of 24/7 ultra-Orthodox Judaism, mostly of the charismatic Hasidic variety. The community is insular and uncompromising and clings to an old-world lifestyle: residents have no TVs; many reject the legitimacy of modern secular Israel; and Yiddish rather than the "sacred" Hebrew tongue is the conversational language of choice.

Modesty in dress and behavior is imperative for anyone entering the neighborhood. Visitors (best in tiny groups) must avoid male-female contact; women should wear long skirts, long sleeves, and nothing exposed below the neck. Sternly worded street banners (in English) emphasize the public norms, and some discourage casual tourists altogether. It's a voyeuristic experience, to be sure; but if you do choose to go, avoid the Sabbath and photograph very discreetly at other times.

Me'a She'arim is traversed by Me'a She'arim Street, and most of the historic neighborhood is on the slope above it (in the direction of Hanevi'im Street and the Downtown area). To the west it's bounded by Strauss Street; to the east it almost touches Road No. 1.

Haas Promenade. Get your bearings in Jerusalem by taking in the panorama from the Haas Promenade, an attractive 1-km (½-mile) promenade along one of the city's highest ridges. Hidden behind a grove of trees to the east (your right as you pan the view) is a turreted limestone building, the residence of the British High Commissioner for Palestine in the 1930s and 1940s. In Hebrew, the whole ridge is known as Armon Hanatziv, the Commissioner's Palace. In 1949, the building became the headquarters of the U.N. Truce Supervision Organization (UNTSO), charged with monitoring the armistice line that divided the city. It remained a neutral enclave between Israeli West Jerusalem and Jordanian-controlled East Jerusalem until the reunification of the city in the Six-Day War of 1967. You can reach the promenade by car from Hebron Road—consult a map, and look for signs to East Talpiot and the Haas Promenade—by Bus 78 from the Central Bus Station, Downtown, and the First Station; Bus 12 from Hadassah Ein Kerem and Malkha Mall; or by cab. If the traffic flows well, it's a 10-minute drive from Downtown, five minutes from the German Colony. There are restrooms just off the sidewalk at the "city" end of the ridge, before the promenade dips down into the valley. ⊠ *Daniel Yanovsky St., East Talpiot* 🖾 *Free.*

WORTH NOTING

Train Track Park. This park separates the picturesque neighborhoods of Baka and the German Colony, to your left and right respectively as you leave the First Station. It was a swath of stones and weeds after the trains stopped running, but residents could see its potential, and

2

(for once) successfully fought the city and the developers. The old train tracks now bracket a boardwalk and are flanked by pedestrian and bike paths, lovely greenery, and conveniently placed benches. A charming series of signs along the route relates the story of the railway, illustrated by photos and anecdotes. The path is about 7 km (4½ miles) long, but the most popular section for visitors is the first kilometer (roughly a half mile) as you walk south from the First Station. ⊠ *David Remez St., Baka* ✛ *Behind First Station, then south toward Katamon* 🖾 *Free.*

WHERE TO EAT

Jerusalem's dining scene is smaller and more modest than Tel Aviv's, but is steeped in 4,000 years of culinary traditions. Among Jewish residents, more than a century of immigration has infused the local fare with the best of Kurdish, Moroccan, French, Polish, Yemenite, and Italian flavors. On the Palestinian side, most restaurants rely on a rich heritage of family cooking. On both sides, an elite class of chefs has begun combining the best of local ingredients with advanced cooking techniques and imaginative serving styles.

All this is to say that when you're in Jerusalem you can enjoy the best of both worlds: hole-in-the-wall eateries brimming with aromatic stews and garlicky hummus or high-end dining rooms serving inspired and elegant riffs on the city's flavors and produce.

Some cuisine designations are self-explanatory, but other terms may be confusing. A restaurant billing itself as "dairy" will serve meals without meat; many such places do serve fish, in addition to pasta, soup, and salads. "Oriental" usually means Middle Eastern (in contrast to Western), often meaning hummus, kebabs, and stews.

The term *kosher* doesn't imply a particular style of cooking, only that the cooks followed Jewish dietary law in selecting and preparing the food. In Jerusalem, where there are many kosher standards from which to choose, the selection can be dizzying. But unless specific kosher standards govern your eating habits, don't worry. Jerusalem is home to dozens of kosher restaurants preparing excellent food. Remember that most kosher restaurants are closed for Friday dinner and Saturday lunch in observation of the Jewish Sabbath. A generous handful of nonkosher cafés, bars, and restaurants remain open all weekend.

Dress codes are pretty much nonexistent in Jerusalem's restaurants (as in the rest of Israel). People tend to dress casually—jeans are perfectly appropriate almost everywhere anytime. A modicum of neatness and modesty (trousers instead of jeans, a button-down shirt instead of a T-shirt) might be expected in the more exclusive establishments. In conservative neighborhoods, women will feel more comfortable covered up. If you brought the kids, you're in luck: nearly every Israeli restaurant is kid-friendly, and many have special menus and high chairs.

Use the coordinates at the end of each listing (✛ A1) to locate a site on the corresponding map.

WHAT IT COSTS				
	$	$$	$$$	$$$$
Restaurants	Under NIS 50	NIS 50–NIS 75	NIS 76–NIS 100	over NIS 100

Restaurant prices are the average cost of a main course at dinner in NIS (Israeli shekels) or, if dinner isn't served, at lunch.

OLD CITY

The walled Old City pretty much shuts down at night, so most watering holes cater to the lunch customer. There are several outstanding hummus and shawarma places in the Christian Quarter and a broader range of options in and around the Jewish Quarter's Hurva Square and on the route to the Western Wall.

JEWISH QUARTER

$$ ✕ **Holy Cafe.** With wooden tables in the tile-floored dining room and
ISRAELI under the trees in the nearby square, this is one of the few full-service
FAMILY restaurants in the Jewish Quarter of the Old City. The modest menu ranges from fresh salads to salmon burgers, and there is beer and wine. Try one of several fish dishes, or just enjoy a coffee while you rest from your tour of the Old City. $ *Average main: NIS 50* ⊠ *2 Tiferet Israel St., Jewish Quarter* ☎ *02/628–7515* ⊗ *Closed Sat. No dinner Fri.* ✣ *G5.*

CHRISTIAN AND MUSLIM QUARTERS

$ ✕ **Abu Shukri.** In the heart of the Old City, this place has some of the best
MIDDLE EASTERN hummus in town, served fast to locals crammed around rickety tables under fluorescent lights. Enjoy the excellent falafel, eggplant salad, and *labaneh* (a slightly sour cheese served with olive oil and spices). Eat family style and don't order too much, as you can get additional portions on the spot. $ *Average main: NIS 25* ⊠ *63 El-Wad Rd., Muslim Quarter* ☎ *02/627–1538* ▭ *No credit cards* ⊗ *No dinner* ✣ *G4.*

$ ✕ **Austrian Hospice Café.** This Viennese-style second-floor garden café
AUSTRIAN in a guesthouse for pilgrims is a refined retreat from the chaos of the Old City markets down below. Lunch and dinner are available, but the café is most renowned for its apple strudel and Sachertorte, which must be complemented with a frothy coffee. Deep burgundy walls, wooden tables, and classical music make this a lovely wintertime spot for light fare or dessert. Ask at reception about visiting the rooftop for a small fee: the views of the Old City are gorgeous. $ *Average main: NIS 40* ⊠ *37 Via Dolorosa, Muslim Quarter* ☎ *02/626–5800* ⊕ *www.austrianhospice.com* ✣ *G4.*

$ ✕ **Costa.** Steps from the Church of the Holy Sepulcher, Palestinians
MIDDLE EASTERN crowd into this tiny spot to tuck into *hammam mehshi,* or stuffed pigeon. It's a delicately flavored specialty served with salads and rice. You can also opt for stuffed chicken, grilled lamb chops, or fried liver, all made fresh by the friendly proprietor. Get here early, as the place closes at 6. $ *Average main: NIS 45* ⊠ *28 Hakoptim St., Christian Quarter* ☎ *02/627–4480* ▭ *No credit cards* ✣ *G4.*

JERUSALEM'S CAFÉS

Sitting down for coffee and cake in one of Jerusalem's fine cafés is something of a tradition. Yeast cakes and strudels recall the past, but today's palate craves flaky brioches and savory tarts. Italian coffee machines have driven a rise in quality and a demand for the perfect *hafuch*, the strong Israeli version of a cappuccino.

Two Jerusalem coffee chains have expanded across the country. Aroma has excellent coffee and fresh sandwiches and salads. Hillel is a favorite with locals for breakfast, with its good food and good prices.

In Jerusalem, the open-air mall of Ben-Yehuda Street has several venerable hangouts, but the newer

cafés along the bars and restaurants of Shlomzion Hamalka Street offer more sophisticated menus—and better coffee. The upscale Mamilla Mall, outside Jaffa Gate, is known for its coffee places, but don't overlook Emek Refa'im Street in the German Colony or Bethlehem Road in Baka.

Most popular coffee spots serve decent light, affordable meals for lunch and dinner as well, and courtyard seating gets full in fine weather and on summer evenings. Coffee and a pastry are about NIS 30 to NIS 40; sandwiches, salads, quiche, and pasta will cost NIS 30 to NIS 60. If you're not a coffee drinker, consider trying a *gazoz*, a fizzy drink made of soda water and syrup.

$ ✕ **Hummus Lina.** With an upstairs dining area, Lina offers a respite from
MIDDLE EASTERN   the hubbub of the Old City. Hand-ground hummus is the main event here, and you can order it topped with chickpeas, fava beans, or pine nuts. You can also sample the yogurt-cheese called labaneh and wash it down with freshly pressed fruit juice. ⑤ *Average main: NIS 20* ⊠ *42 Al Khanka St., Christian Quarter* ☎ *02/627–7230* ◷ *No dinner* ✛ *G4.*

$$ ✕ **Nafoura.** Just inside the Jaffa Gate, Nafoura offers a tranquil court-
MIDDLE EASTERN   yard for alfresco lunchtime dining. Your table might even lean against
FAMILY   the Old City wall. The pleasant if unremarkable interior is a comfortable refuge in inclement weather. Start with the traditional array of salads, enough for two people to share. Focus on the excellent local dishes (hummus, eggplant salad, tahini, and so on). Ask for the *kibbeh*, delicacies of cracked wheat and ground beef, or the Armenian sausage. From the typical selection of entrées, try the lamb cutlets or the grilled sea bream. ⑤ *Average main: NIS 75* ⊠ *26 Latin Patriarchate Rd., Christian Quarter* ☎ *02/626–0034* ⊕ *nafoura-rest.com* ◷ *Closed Sun.* ✛ *F5.*

EAST JERUSALEM

The heart of East Jerusalem runs through Salah A-Din Street, lined with hummus joints, colorful vegetable shops, fresh juice stands, and a few modest coffee spots. Palestinian students and foreign journalists and aid workers gravitate toward the more upscale eateries.

$$ ✕ **Askadinya.** At this East Jerusalem bistro, the stone walls are hung
ECLECTIC   with local art and antique musical instruments. In summer, you can enjoy your meal on a lovely patio. The menu emphasizes salads—the

tabbouleh is a refreshing mix of parsley and cracked wheat—simple pastas, and heavy-hitting meat dishes. The service is efficient and unpretentious, and the well-stocked bar includes local Palestinian Taybeh beer and wine from Bethlehem, along with European imports. Most Thursdays feature live music. $ *Average main: NIS 75* ⊠ *11 Shimon Hatzadik, East Jerusalem* ☎ *02/532–4590* ✛ *F1.*

$$ ✕ **Azzahra.** On a quiet alley off the main East Jerusalem thoroughfare,
MIDDLE EASTERN this white-tablecloth restaurant in a hotel has long been popular with
FAMILY journalists, NGO workers, and local families, who flock here for piz-
Fodor'sChoice zas from the olive-wood-burning brick oven and Palestinian favorites.
★ High wooden ceilings, stone walls, and a simple outdoor garden create a lovely setting perfect for groups of any size. Enjoy a glass of wine or local beer along with the tasty *mansaf,* a regional lamb dish cooked in yogurt; or the *mulukhiya,* an earthy vegetarian stew served over rice. Save a little room for the complimentary Arabic sweets and hot tea served at the end of the meal by friendly waiters. $ *Average main: NIS 65* ⊠ *13 Azzahra St., East Jerusalem* ☎ *02/628–2447* ⊕ *www.azzahra-hotel.com* ✛ *G3.*

$$$ ✕ **Cardo.** The terraced restaurant atop the Legacy Hotel has a beauti-
MIDDLE EASTERN ful view, but the real art is on the plate. Award-winning chef Johnny Goric is a judge on the TV show *Master Chef,* and you can watch him preparing traditional Palestinian dishes and more in his open kitchen. Focaccias and pizzas come hot and crusty from the clay oven, and pastas are fresh and flavorful. The hummus with meat is a quiet stunner; grilled lamb is a regal repast, and desserts include both chocolate delights and classic Lebanese sweets. $ *Average main: NIS 90* ⊠ *Legacy Hotel, 29 Nablus Rd., East Jerusalem* ☎ *02/627–0800* ⊕ *www.cardo.rest-e.co.il* ✛ *F3.*

$ ✕ **Educational Bookshop.** Part coffee shop, part bookstore, this spot has
MIDDLE EASTERN an endless trove of literature exploring the Arab-Israeli conflict from a Palestinian perspective. Take a volume upstairs and peruse it over a lunch of a savory *manaqeesh* bread topped with thyme and olive oil, freshly made labaneh cheese, or salmon sandwiches. Turkish coffee is brewed fresh on an orange camping stove. Ask about upcoming lectures and movie screenings. $ *Average main: NIS 20* ⊠ *19 Salah A-Din St., East Jerusalem* ☎ *02/627–5858* ⊕ *educationalbookshop.com* ✛ *G3.*

$$$ ✕ **Philadelphia.** Steps from the Old City, this East Jerusalem landmark
MIDDLE EASTERN has been in business for decades—a thank-you note from President
FAMILY Jimmy Carter proves it. Starters like the hummus or the eggplant spread are reliably executed. Traditional fare like stuffed carrots and onions, or *musakhan* chicken cooked in sumac and onions, show Palestinian home cooking at its finest. If owner Zouheir Izhiman is around, ask him to share his years of local lore. $ *Average main: NIS 100* ⊠ *9 Azzahra St., East Jerusalem* ☎ *02/532–2626* ⊕ *thephiladelphiarestaurant.com* ✛ *G3.*

$ ✕ **Sarwa Street Kitchen.** Brothers Mo and Mick Tahhan opened this
ECLECTIC cheery café in the space that was once their father's travel agency with
Fodor'sChoice the vision of creating a gathering spot as comfy and as fun as your living
★ room at home. Staff often joins patrons for a chat on the bright blue couches and encourages them to add or take from the in-house library stocked with a selection of English-language books. Changing daily

specials include *maqloubeh*, a Palestinian rice and chicken dish, or the bright orange *knaffeh*, the traditional cheese pastry soaked in syrup, for dessert. Excellent coffee, pastries, Wi-Fi, and in-house printers create a kind of coworking vibe during the day, but the wine list and excellent pastas also attract more serious diners later on. ⑤ *Average main: NIS 40* ⊠ *42 Salah A-Din St., East Jerusalem* ☎ *02/627–4626* ✛ *G3.*

CENTER CITY

The area extends from the Machaneh Yehuda market and Nachla'ot neighborhood, through the central Downtown triangle, to King David Street. The range is vast, from funky budget or takeaway joints to upscale fine-dining specialists, from Middle Eastern food to European cuisine, and several surprises in between. Nonkosher restaurants do a roaring trade on Friday night, after the Sabbath begins, when their kosher counterparts are closed and the city streets quiet.

$$$$
MODERN ISRAELI

✕ **Angelica.** This popular eatery with a geometric mirrored ceiling is steps from the King David Street hotel district. Sashimi with wasabi reduction comes elegantly arranged in shades of bright pink and fuchsia, and the brandied duck breast with asparagus and sweet potato is a delight. The desserts are among the city's finest, including the dark-chocolate mousse and the fresh fruit over tapioca pudding. The staff is helpful and friendly, and the knowledgeable sommelier will guide you to unusual Israeli vintages. ⑤ *Average main: NIS 120* ⊠ *4 George Washington St., Center City* ☎ *02/623–0056* ⊕ *angelicarest.com* ⊗ *Closed Fri. and Sat.* ✛ *E5.*

$$
ITALIAN

✕ **Anna.** This imposing 200-year-old stone building called Beit Ticho (Ticho House) was once the home of artist Anna Ticho, whose evocative drawings of Jerusalem adorn its walls. Anna has a number of hit dishes for moderate prices, but the pizzas and fish dishes like the whole sea bream baked with lemony herb potatoes are especially popular. The portions are perfect for a light lunch or dinner, and the lemon pie is sinful. Like the food, the dining room is rustic chic, with sturdy wooden tables bathed in the natural sunlight from the large arched windows. If the weather's good, angle for a table on the patio overlooking a beautiful olive tree. ⑤ *Average main: NIS 64* ⊠ *Ticho House, 10 Harav Agan St., Center City* ☎ *02/543–4144* ⊕ *annarest.co.il* ⊗ *No dinner Fri. Closed Sat.* ✛ *B1.*

$
MIDDLE EASTERN
Fodor's Choice
★

✕ **Azura.** Jerusalem is famous for its Kurdish *kubbeh* soup, made with softball-size meat-and-semolina dumplings, and Azura is the perfect place to try this classic dish. Tucked away in a plaza off the Machaneh Yehuda market, the cavelike kitchen is packed with massive pots simmering on kerosene burners. Try the velvety beet kubbeh soup, or the tangy *hamusta* soup made with lemon and chard. Delicious hummus is made daily, and on some days the oxtail stew has the pungent flavors of the market. If weather permits, grab an outdoor table to watch groups of old Iraqi men drink coffee and play backgammon on the benches nearby. The restaurant closes when the food runs out, so don't come too late. ⑤ *Average main: NIS 45* ⊠ *4 Haeshkol St., Center City* ☎ *02/623–5204* ⊗ *Closed Sat. No dinner* ✛ *D3.*

$$$
MIDDLE EASTERN

✕ **Barood.** Jerusalemite Daniella Lerer combines her family's Sephardic culinary traditions with modern Israeli cooking techniques and personal favorites from two decades in the business. Starters include picked herring, *boyikos* (cheesy biscuits) and *pastelikos*—meat dumplings that Lerer stuffs with seasoned ground meat. Main dishes include *sufrito* (braised dumplings with Jerusalem artichokes) and shrimp in wine and lemon. For dessert, look for the traditional *sutlach,* a cold rice pudding topped with cinnamon, nuts, and halva. Barood's other face is its well-stocked bar serving more familiar fare like spareribs and sausages, along with homemade citrus schnapps and 20 other flavors of schnapps. Reservations are a must for dinner Friday night and on Saturday, when there are often live performances outside. ⓢ *Average main: NIS 88* ⊠ *Feingold Courtyard, 31 Jaffa St., Center City* ☎ *02/625–9081* ⊕ *www.rol.co.il/images/sites/barood/eng.html* ⊘ *Closed Sun.* ✛ *C1.*

$$
AMERICAN

✕ **Black.** This national chain lends bling to burgers: try the Popeye, made with beef and spinach, or the lamb patty. All burgers are served with a range of toppings including sunny-side-up eggs and goose breast. The menu also includes plenty of chicken options, like Thai chicken skewers and panfried chicken breast. The bar, with its good range of drinks, exudes youthful cool with its black-and-red decor, illuminated liquor bottles, and large-screen TVs. ⓢ *Average main: NIS 70* ⊠ *18 Shlomzion Hamalka St., Center City* ☎ *02/624–6767* ⊘ *No dinner Fri. No lunch Sat.* ✛ *C2.*

$
FAST FOOD
FAMILY

✕ **Burgers Bar.** At this popular kosher place, the hamburgers are more like cakes than patties. They come with your choice of tasty sauces, and all are made to order. Lamb and chicken wraps and robust salads reflect Israeli tastes. Vegetarians will delight in the portobello burger. ⓢ *Average main: NIS 43* ⊠ *12 Shammai St., Center City* ☎ *02/622–1555* ⊕ *www.burgersbar.co.il/en* ⊘ *No dinner Fri. No lunch Sat.* ✛ *B1.*

$$
AMERICAN
FAMILY
Fodor'sChoice
★

✕ **Café Yehoshua.** One of the restaurants that locals flock to for breakfast, lunch, or dinner, Café Yehoshua offers an Israeli take on American diner food. The menu includes everything from tahini pancakes to spaghetti tossed with shrimp. A laid-back yet vibrant atmosphere and a location just a few minutes' walk from the prime minister's residence make it a great spot for some quality people-watching in one of Jerusalem's quaintest neighborhoods. In good weather, the rooftop dining area lets you enjoy the fresh air. Evening is a great time to stop by for a drink and a bite-sized burger ⓢ *Average main: NIS 55* ⊠ *17 Azza St., Center City* ☎ *02/563–2898* ⊕ *www.cafeyehoshua.com* ⊘ *No dinner Fri. No lunch Sat.* ✛ *D6.*

$$$$
MODERN ISRAELI
Fodor'sChoice
★

✕ **Chakra.** Despite being one of the city's best-known restaurants, Chakra still feigns anonymity: its name is nowhere in sight. It draws a lively thirtysomething crowd of hip Jerusalemites who appreciate the tasty fare from the open kitchen. The tables are arranged around the striking semicircular bar, and the patio enjoys a park view. Daily specials enhance the expansive menu, which changes every three months. Some good starters include focaccia, beef carpaccio with arugula, or black tiger shrimp with chili. Try the sea bream, grilled to perfection on a mound of mashed cauliflower and wild mushrooms. The well-stocked bar includes Israeli boutique beers and bitters, along with a list of expertly balanced cocktails. $ *Average main: NIS 120* ⊠ *41 King George St., Center City* ☎ *02/625–2733* ⊕ *www.chakra-rest.com* ⊘ *No lunch Sun.–Fri.* ⊕ *E4.*

$$$$
ITALIAN
Fodor'sChoice
★

✕ **Cielo.** Personable chef Adi Cohen has been serving the same classic dishes from his family's native northern Italy for a couple of decades—and they are still fantastic. The decor is understated and cheery, with bright green tablecloths, warm brick floors, and flowers in the windows. A starter menu includes great traditional dishes like ravioli (the stuffings change: look for seafood or truffles), and a superb lasagna and cannelloni combination. Especially interesting among the entrées are the tender *piccatina con funghi* (thinly sliced veal with lemon and mushrooms), *tournedo dello chef* (beef with white wine, truffles, and porcini mushrooms) and *tournedo Modena* (beef with a balsamic vinegar and leek sauce). The house red wine is excellent, as is the homemade limoncello served at the end of the meal. $ *Average main: NIS 105* ⊠ *18 Ben Sira St., Center City* ☎ *02/625–1132* ⊕ *www.cielo.rest-e. co.il* ⊘ *No lunch Fri.* ⊕ *E4.*

$$$$
MOROCCAN

✕ **Darna.** A vaulted tunnel sets you down in a corner of Morocco, complete with imported tiles, inlaid chairs, and a delightful outdoor garden. The salads include beet greens with lemon and spicy green olives with red peppers. Don't miss the *harira* soup of veal, chickpeas, and lentils flavored with cumin or any of the stews cooked in clay pots and flavored with olives or sweet dried fruit. The house specialty is the roast lamb shoulder with almonds and couscous—listed as a two-person dish but could easily serve three to four. The wine cellar holds 1,000 bottles. $ *Average main: NIS 115* ⊠ *3 Horkanos St., Center City* ☎ *02/624–5406* ⊕ *www.darna.co.il* ⊘ *Closed Fri. and Sat.* ⊕ *C1.*

$
POLISH

✕ **Deitsch.** *Cholent* is a dish that evolved from necessity: Jewish law forbids cooking on the Sabbath, and so observant Jews often start a stew on Friday that will be ready the following afternoon. Every Jewish community has its own recipe, but in Jerusalem the best place to try cholent is in the ultra-Orthodox quarter of Mea Shearim, where on Thursday nights locals crowd into Deitsch for a plate straight out of Poland. You'll be served a rich brown stew with a few vegetables and a dumpling. Dress modestly, and expect to be the only patrons not wearing black and white. $ *Average main: NIS 40* ⊠ *32 Mea Shearim St., Center City* ☎ *02/582–9529* ▭ *No credit cards* ⊘ *Closed Sat. No dinner Fri.* ⊕ *D3.*

$$$
SEAFOOD
FAMILY

✕ **Dolphin Yam.** Hebrew for "Sea Dolphin," this lively eatery serves some of the city's best seafood. The decor is pleasant enough—pale yellow stucco walls, recessed wine racks, arched windows, and an outdoor patio—but it's not a place for intimacy. Food is what draws the mixed clientele, including plenty of families. Start with appetizers like the excellent wild roasted eggplant with tahini and pine nuts, then move on to the shrimp in a mushroom-cream sauce or the drum fish in a tasty broth. You can also experiment with the generous seafood platter for two that includes crab, scallops, and calamari. $ *Average main: NIS 95* ⊠ *9 Ben Shetach St., Center City* ☎ *073/759–8522* ⊕ *www.rol.co.il/ images/sites/dolphin-yam/menu/english.html* ⊕ *C2.*

Where to Eat and Stay in Jerusalem

KEY

☐ Hotels
■ Restaurants
■ Restaurants in Hotels

⬦ following reviews indicates map-grid coordinates

$$$$
MODERN ISRAELI
Fodor'sChoice
★

✕ **1868.** In an old stone house with a delightful back garden, 1868 is Jerusalem's most innovative, exacting kosher restaurant, on par with the city's best. Jerusalemite chef Yankele Turjeman combines the flavors of the city with high-quality ingredients and exquisite cooking techniques to create an unforgettable dining experience. Most of the fruits and vegetables are organic, and the menu changes monthly to incorporate the best of the season. If it's on the menu, don't miss the charcoal-grilled veal sweetbreads, served with steamed slices of baguette and pickled onion. The duck is spectacular, served with fruits of the season. The whiskey selection is endless, as is the list of local Israeli wines. Cocktails are beautifully balanced. ⑤ *Average main: NIS 110* ⊠ *10 King David St., Center City* ☎ *02/622–2312* ⊕ *1868.co.il* ⊙ *Closed Fri. No lunch Sat.* ✛ *E5.*

$$$$
MIDDLE EASTERN
Fodor'sChoice
★

✕ **Eucalyptus.** Chef Moshe Basson, repeated winner of international couscous contests, has mined the kitchens of older Jewish and Arab women to revive nearly forgotten recipes and ingredients. Grab a seat on the outside porch, adjacent to the Old City walls on one side and overlooking the picturesque Hutzot Hayotzer artists colony on the other. The appetizers are all tasty, but try the crepelike pastilla filled with duck confit and pumpkin jam, or the extraordinary stuffed mallow leaves (instead of the more conventional grape leaves). Two exquisite mains include traditional *makloubeh* with chicken and rice, and the clay-baked lamb with okra. Vegetarians will also find plenty of options, and there are a few tasting menus if you want to try it all. Finish with unusual desserts and herbal tea. If you're in the mood, ask Basson to share some of his culinary lore. Reservations are imperative. ⑤ *Average main: NIS 110* ⊠ *14 Hativat Jerusalem St., Center City* ☎ *02/624–4331* ⊕ *www.the-eucalyptus.com* ⊙ *Closed Fri. No lunch Sat.* ✛ *F5.*

$
BRITISH
FAMILY

✕ **Fishenchips.** Shlomi Ohana's tiny fish-and-chips emporium in the heart of the vegetable market offers fresh selections direct from his father Haim's seafood stall down the alley. Everything is garnished with a range of tasty dressings and accompanied by great fries. Try classic British-style battered cod, or a range of interesting dishes including tuna, salmon, or whatever "today's fresh catch" happens to be. There are also good beers on tap. Ohana tripled the seating area because of the huge demand, so there's plenty of space. ⑤ *Average main: NIS 37* ⊠ *10 HaEgoz St., Center City* ☎ *02/624–9503* ⊕ *fnc.menu.pics* ⊙ *No dinner Fri. No lunch Sat.* ✛ *D3.*

$$
ITALIAN

✕ **Focaccia Bar.** This popular haunt has been baking fluffy focaccias for 20 years. There are many toppings (don't miss the black-olive spread), and some tasty starters (try the mushrooms stuffed with goat cheese or the fried calamari). The chicken livers stir-fried with shallots and fried onions are delicious. There are generous sandwich options, including the sirloin strips. This is also one of the city's few restaurants to flout Passover restrictions on eating leavened dough. Reserve a table on weekends. ⑤ *Average main: NIS 63* ⊠ *4 Rabbi Akiva St., Center City* ☎ *02/625–6428* ⊕ *bar.focaccia.co* ✛ *B2.*

$$$$
ECLECTIC

✕ **Gabriel.** Canadian immigrant Harvey Sandler bought this kosher landmark and added innovative cooking techniques and elegant service to transform it into something to write home about. The menu is

2

seasonal and fusion-inspired, with lots of Asian and French influences. The ceviche is accented with zippy lemon zest and a citrus soy sauce, and the grass-fed rib-eye steak is beautifully grilled and served with carrot sauce and crisp zucchini. Stop by for happy hour from 4 to 6, where you can try unlimited wine or beer and two appetizers while enjoying the delightful alfresco dining space. $⑤ Average main: NIS 129 ⊠ 7 Ben Shatakh St., Center City ☎ 02/624–6444 ⊕ gabriel-jerusalem. co.il ⊙ Closed Fri. No lunch Sat. ⊹ C2.

$ ⑤ **✕Hamarakia.** Share a long wooden table with university students
ISRAELI at this restaurant named for a soup pot and enjoy an ever-changing menu of hearty soups and stews served with white bread, butter, and pesto. *Shakshuka* (a tangy dish of eggs, tomatoes, garlic, and onions), interesting salads, and other vegetarian and vegan options complete the menu. There's a piano in the corner, a box of old records, and a chandelier made of spoons. In winter, ask about evening live jazz, usually Wednesday. $⑤ Average main: NIS 30 ⊠ 4 Koresh St., Center City ☎ 02/625–7797 ▬ No credit cards ⊙ Closed Fri. No lunch Sat. ⊹ C2.

$ ⑤ **✕Hasabichiya.** The sign is only in Hebrew at this hole-in-the-wall stand,
ISRAELI which features what many say is the best *sabich* in the city. Thin slices of fried eggplant are combined with hard-boiled egg and your choice of greens and wrapped in a *laffa* (flatbread) or stuffed into a pita. The hours? Until the eggplant runs out. $⑤ Average main: NIS 20 ⊠ 9 Shamai St., Center City ⊙ Closed Fri. and Sat. ⊹ B1.

$ ⑤ **✕Hummus Ben Sira.** Everyone from students to sanitation workers
MIDDLE EASTERN shares elbow space at this casual eatery's long bar inlaid with Armenian painted tiles. The hummus here is especially tasty and is served from morning until well after midnight. $⑤ Average main: NIS 30 ⊠ 3 Ben Sira St., Center City ☎ 02/625–3893 ▬ No credit cards ⊙ No dinner Fri. No lunch Sat. ⊹ C2.

$$ ⑤⑤ **✕Ima.** With a name that means "Mom," Ima honors the owner's
MIDDLE EASTERN Kurdish-Jewish mother, who inspired many of the excellent traditional Middle Eastern offerings served in this century-old stone house just a few minutes from the Machaneh Yehuda market. This is a great place to try Kurdish kubbeh soups, made with beets or pumpkin and blessed with softball-sized meat-and-semolina dumplings. The modest array of salads includes hummus and baba ghanoush, as well as stuffed grape leaves, stuffed vegetables, and wonderful kibbeh (seasoned ground meat deep-fried in a jacket of bulgur wheat). The restaurant is open until late at night. $⑤ Average main: NIS 70 ⊠ 55 Shmuel Baruch St., Center City ☎ 02/624–6860 ⊕ www.ima-rest.co.il/en ⊙ No dinner Fri. Closed Sat. ⊹ C3.

$$ ⑤⑤ **✕Iwo's.** Consistently ranked among the country's best burger places,
FAST FOOD Iwo's was founded by a butcher and serves expertly grilled patties on pillowy rolls. Black-and-white-tiled walls evoke American diner traditions, but this is a sleeves-up, self-service destination. You can top your burger with sunny-side-up eggs, crispy bacon, grilled onions, and a rainbow of sauces. The veggie portobello option is just as good, and there are several salads as well. Beer makes this a great place to start or end an evening. $⑤ Average main: NIS 55 ⊠ 28 Hillel St., Center City ☎ 02/622–2513 ⊕ www.iwos.co.il ⊹ B2.

$$ ✕**Kohinoor.** Jerusalem's beloved
INDIAN (and only) Indian restaurant offers
a tantalizing menu of expertly pre-
pared curries, tikkas, and biryanis.
Owner Beni Binyamin immigrated
here from Mumbai, and the menu
maintains a taste of home. Espe-
cially delicious are the vegetables
with rice, the fluffy naan bread, and
the mango-flavored lassi. The *kulfi*
ice cream flavored with pistachio
is to die for. ⑤ *Average main: NIS
55* ✉ *13 Shamai St., Center City*
☎ *02/940–0444* ✛ *B1.*

$$$ ✕**Lavan.** At the in-house eatery of
ITALIAN the popular Cinematheque, diners
delight at the Italian-inspired menu.
Many people opt for the fresh fish
of the day, but there's also more
substantial fare like polenta with
truffles and a poached egg, lamb
sausages with beans, and veal gnoc-
chi. Locals and visitors alike enjoy the superb Old City views from the
glassed-in patio. It's open Friday night and Saturday, which is another
plus. ⑤ *Average main: NIS 80* ✉ *Cinematheque, 11 Hebron Rd., Center
City* ☎ *02/673–7393* ⊕ *lavan.rest.co.il* ✛ *F6.*

$$$$ ✕**Machneyuda.** On the edge of its namesake market, this restaurant is
ISRAELI considered one of the best in Jerusalem, possibly the country. Celebrity-
Fodor'sChoice chef Asaf Granit grew up in Jerusalem and pays homage to the city's
★ colors and cacophony in his elegant dishes. You can wait for your
reservation across the street at Yudaleh, a lively cocktail bar by the
same owners. Once in, grab a seat at the bar to watch the exuberant
chefs slice, dice, and sauté while banging on the pots and pans to the
beat of zippy music. The menu changes twice daily, but nearly always
includes *chamshuka,* a fusion of chopped meat and hummus; a creamy
polenta topped with crisp asparagus, mushroom ragout, and shaved
Parmesan; and a raucous dessert ceremony of ice cream flung on tables
covered in aluminum foil. To enjoy the full range of flavors, order the
tasting menu. Reserve at least two weeks in advance. ⑤ *Average main:
NIS 140* ✉ *10 Beit Yaakov St., Center City* ☎ *02/533–3442* ⊕ *www.
machneyuda.co.il/en* ⊘ *No dinner Fri. No lunch Sat.* ✛ *C3.*

$$$ ✕**Menza.** Sink into one of Menza's retro-style banquettes or take a seat
MODERN ISRAELI around a robust wooden table for a deliciously prepared meal in this
Fodor'sChoice lovely café between downtown and Machaneh Yehuda market. Israeli
★ breakfast or brunch dishes like croque monsieur are served as late as 1
pm, but be sure to stop by again in the evening to try the creative ver-
sions of bistro classics such as seared tuna nicoise salad. The burger here
is in the running for being the best in the city, and the menu also lists
vegan options. ⑤ *Average main: NIS 84* ✉ *10 Bezalel St., City Center*
☎ *02/625–5222* ⊕ *www.menza.today* ✛ *A1.*

FAST FOODS TO TRY

Falafel and hummus are ubiqui-
tous in Jerusalem, as is the
sabich, a pita stuffed with deep-
fried eggplant and a hard-boiled
egg. Tasty **shawarma** is grilled
lamb or turkey, also served in
pita bread. Try the stands in the
Ben-Yehuda Street open-air mall.

If you crave meat, the **me'orav
Yerushalmi** (Jerusalem-style
mixed grill) is a specialty of the
eateries on Agrippas Street, near
the Machaneh Yehuda market.
It's a deliciously seasoned meal
of pitas stuffed with grilled
chicken hearts, livers, and other
offal meats.

$$$$ ✗ **Mona.** Nestled into a stonewalled garden, Mona has a working fire-
MODERN ISRAELI   place and a tree growing through the indoor section, creating a rustic
Fodor'sChoice   setting for eminently modern Israeli cooking overseen by two chef-
★   owners. Start your night with the light red tuna sashimi with chili or
the award-winning crab bisque. Continue to a hearty polenta with
mushroom ragout and asparagus. Do not miss the beautifully prepared
beef fillet with sweetbreads and purple cabbage. Vegetarians will seek
refuge in a few salads. For dessert, try the sour cream and Szechuan
sorbet over nectarine compote. Wait until later in the evening if you
just want to order cocktails based on homemade liquor at the excellent
bar. Reservations are essential on weekends. ⑤ *Average main: NIS 108*
✉ *12 Shmuel Hanagid, Center City* ☎ *02/622–2283* ⊕ *monarest.co.il/
mona/en/* ⊘ *No lunch Sun.–Thurs.* ✛ *A2.*

$$ ✗ **Nadi.** Nadi has great food all day but shines in the morning, when
ISRAELI   the breakfast plates come crowded with mouthwatering spreads of sun-
dried tomato, olive tapenade, local cheeses, tuna, and tahini, all meant
to be slathered on fabulous sourdough bread. Other offerings are deli-
cious, colorful salads; earthy asparagus and spinach pasta; shakshuka
made out of tomatoes, spinach, or beets; croissant sandwiches; quiches;
or fresh coffee. ⑤ *Average main: NIS 50* ✉ *10 Shatz St., Center City*
☎ *02/625–1737* ⊘ *Closed Sat. No dinner Fri.* ✛ *A1.*

$ ✗ **Nocturno.** Part of a workshop space for local artists, this landmark
CAFÉ   café has a fun and funky atmosphere. The menu is rich with sandwiches
filled with delectable ingredients like avocado, feta cheese, or grilled
vegetables, and they all come with side salads drizzled with a delightful
basil dressing. If a sandwich isn't your style, try a quiche or a pasta dish.
There's a slew of vegan-friendly dishes as well. At night, Jerusalem's
hipsters come to drink beer or arak while discussing politics. There's
live music throughout the week. ⑤ *Average main: NIS 41* ✉ *7 Bezalel
St., Center City* ☎ *077/700–8510* ⊕ *www.nocturno.co.il* ⊘ *No dinner
Fri. No lunch Sat.* ✛ *A1.*

$$$ ✗ **Olive & Fish.** Its location near many of the major hotels is part of
MODERN ISRAELI   the appeal, but Olive & Fish also pleases locals with its dependable
contemporary Israeli dishes. For starters, try the tasty grilled eggplant
with tahini, or the excellent hot salmon salad. Great fish options include
whole grilled trout or St. Peter's fish on a bed of pasta with zucchini,
sun-dried tomatoes, garlic, mint, and lemon. Other temptations include
a half duck cooked in pears, apple cider, and white wine, or delectable
chicken and beef kebabs. Save room for homemade apple pie or one of
the chocolate creations. ⑤ *Average main: NIS 95* ✉ *2 Jabotinsky St.,
Center City* ☎ *02/566–5020* ⊘ *Closed Fri. No lunch Sat.* ✛ *E6.*

$ ✗ **Oren and Yani.** Locals swear by this deli's inexpensive sandwiches,
DELI   which come piled high with smoked meats, exotic cheeses, or pickled
herring. Meat and dairy are prepared in separate kitchens, so you have
an unusually wide range of choices for a kosher eatery. It's also a great
place to pick up a fresh pastry, a bottle of wine, or a block of cheese,
which you can enjoy at one of the deli's few street-side tables. ⑤ *Average main: NIS 25* ✉ *8 Schatz St., Center City* ☎ *02/579–7378* ⊘ *Closed
Sat. No dinner Fri.* ✛ *A2.*

$$
ITALIAN

✕ **Piccolino.** Inside an atmospheric old building, this kosher Italian restaurant has stone walls, graceful arches, and a sunny courtyard. The house salad, made with seasonal fruit and drizzled with a mustard-orange dressing, is delicious. For a main course, try the pappardelle cooked with flavorful wild mushrooms, or the earthy beet gnocchi served in a cashew cream sauce. Ask about the whole-wheat or gluten-free pasta. After dinner, take a sip of the hot chocolate, dark chocolate, and whiskey topped with whipped cream and served in a shot glass. The wine list includes foreign and local choices. ⑤ *Average main: NIS 70* ✉ *12 Yoel Solomon St., Center City* ☎ *02/624–4186* ⊕ *piccolino. co.il* ⊗ *No dinner Fri. No lunch Sat.* ✛ *B1.*

$
MIDDLE EASTERN

✕ **Pinati.** When aficionados of local standards like garlicky hummus, skewered shish kebabs, fried chicken schnitzel, and bean soup argue hotly about the merits of *their* favorite eateries, Pinati—which means "corner" in Hebrew—comes up as a leading contender. It's now a chain, but this simple downtown spot remains a convenient place to rub shoulders with locals while eating expertly prepared food. Not for long, though: your table will soon be in demand, and you will have to share at peak times. ⑤ *Average main: NIS 40* ✉ *13 King George St., Center City* ☎ *02/625–4540* ⊗ *Closed Sat. No dinner Fri.* ✛ *A1.*

$$
ITALIAN

✕ **P2 Pizza.** Grab a seat at the bar and sip a Peroni while you watch the young, friendly staff roll out extra-thin pizza dough in this narrow temple to Italian fast food. Toppings are tasty combinations of cheese, vegetables, and meats. If you'd rather enjoy pasta, the cooks will crank out fresh fettuccine on the countertop. There's an abundant supply of red and white wine. ⑤ *Average main: NIS 55* ✉ *36 Keren Hayesod St., Center City* ☎ *02/563–5555* ⊗ *Closed Fri.* ✛ *E6.*

$$
ISRAELI

✕ **Rahmo.** You'll probably smell this eatery long before you see it: rich stews of eggplant, potatoes, and meat cook all day on kerosene burners, and the aromas waft into the narrow alleys of Nahalat Shiva. This is an outpost of Rahmo's original location in the vegetable market, and it's a down-to-earth spot in which to take a break from shopping. Try the stuffed grape leaves, scoop up hummus with freshly baked pitas, or order beef heaped over rice for a meal that will stick to your ribs. ⑤ *Average main: NIS 55* ✉ *25 Yoel Salomon St., Center City* ☎ *02/624–0468* ⊕ *www.rol.co.il/sites/ rachmo-nahalat-shiva* ⊗ *Closed Sat. No dinner Fri.* ✛ *B2.*

$$$$
MODERN ISRAELI

✕ **Rooftop.** On the top of the Mamilla Hotel, this open-air restaurant lays claim to one of the best views of Jerusalem, and you can enjoy it from a cushioned chair as you sip spiked iced tea and dine on seared sea bass or grilled lamb chops with Swiss chard. The extensive wine list features more than 20 local boutique labels. If you're on a budget, opt for the tasty grilled focaccia. During the Sabbath, the Rooftop serves a cold menu of salads and fish. The atmosphere is lovely and the view is unbeatable, so advance reservations are a must in summer. ⑤ *Average main: NIS 125* ✉ *Mamilla Hotel, 11 King Solomon St., Center City* ☎ *02/548–2230* ⊕ *www.mamillahotel.com/rooftop* ⊗ *No lunch Sun.–Thurs.* ✛ *F4.*

$$$
MIDDLE EASTERN

✕ **Steakiyat Hatzot.** Down the block from the Machaneh Yehuda produce market, Agrippas Street has some of Jerusalem's best-known greasy spoons. Loyalists claim that Steakiyat Hatzot, which means "Midnight Grill," actually pioneered the local favorite known as me'orav

Yerushalmi. Jerusalem mixed grill is a substantial and delicious meal-in-a-pita of cumin-flavored bits of chicken hearts, livers, and other organ meats. A bulging pita sandwich, eaten standing up, will set you back 42 shekels; you can also sit down at a table in the well-decorated dining area and pay about twice that amount for skewers of grilled meat, duck breast, or fish. There are plenty of vegan and children's options. $ *Average main: NIS 97* ⊠ *121 Agrippas St., Center City* ☎ *073/758–4204* ⊕ *www.hatzot.co.il* ⊗ *No dinner Fri. No lunch Sat.* ✛ *C3.*

$
HUNGARIAN
✕ **Sweet Moment.** Embroidered doilies cover every table and wall at this adorable eatery, transforming it into a bistro straight out of Budapest. Owner Yigal Fisher stuffs cabbage leaves, crepes, and strudels with delicious vegetarian fillings—don't miss the chestnut cream. The coffee is out of this world, and make sure to ask for mulled wine in winter. Fisher's father ran the storied Goulash Inn restaurant in Jerusalem for 30 years; ask to see the packed guest books full of yellowing photos and notes from Israeli prime ministers. $ *Average main: NIS 37* ⊠ *16 Yoel Salomon St., Center City* ☎ *077/400–2098* ⊗ *Closed Sat. No dinner Fri.* ✛ *B2.*

$$$$
FRENCH
Fodor'sChoice
★
✕ **Talbiye.** Just beside the Jerusalem Theatre, Talbiye is a cozy neighborhood restaurant and wine bar specializing in French-Israeli cuisine. The soundtrack of classical music during the day and jazz at night, as well as the rustic-chic decor, provide a sophisticated atmosphere for a solid clientele of politicians, judges, and Jerusalemite intelligentsia. Don't miss the *moules frites* (mussels served with french fries) or the sea bream cooked in white wine, and finish off the rich meal with a baba au rhum, a small bundt cake doused in sweet rum. $ *Average main: NIS 102* ⊠ *5 Chopin St., Center City* ✛ *On side of Jerusalem Theater* ☎ *02/581–1972* ⊕ *www.talbiye.com* ✛ *F6.*

$$
VEGETARIAN
✕ **Te'enim.** In the classic limestone Confederation House—with stone arches, flagstone floors, and tantalizing views of the Old City walls—Te'enim finds a delicate balance between traditional and innovative in its vegetarian fare. Great choices include the spinach salad with baked ricotta or the endive salad with Roquefort and arugula. Standard main dishes include polenta with black beans and corn, mushroom and seaweed pie, and the *maharajah majadra,* with bulgur, lentils, onions, ginger chutney, and yogurt. The homemade sorbets and ice creams are excellent. $ *Average main: NIS 54* ⊠ *12 Emile Botta St., Center City* ☎ *02/625–1967* ⊕ *www.teenim.rest-e.co.il* ⊗ *Closed Sat. No dinner Fri.* ✛ *F5.*

$$
ISRAELI
✕ **Tmol Shilshom.** The name—a Hebrew literary phrase that translates roughly as "yesteryear"—is a clue to the character of the place. A tiny passageway leads to a rear courtyard and an iron stairway, which takes you up to this funky restaurant and bookstore in two separate rooms on the top floor of a 19th-century house. Hosting Hebrew (and occasionally English) poetry readings, lectures, and modest book parties, T'mol Shilshom has long been a popular spot for folks who enjoy lingering over a novel. No meat is served, but choose from a tempting selection of salads, pastas, and fish dishes like salmon in an orange sauce. Desserts are luscious, and the array of hot drinks served in chunky ceramic mugs is always welcome on a rainy day. $ *Average main: NIS 54* ⊠ *5 Yoel Salomon St., Center City* ☎ *02/623–2758* ⊗ *No dinner Fri. No lunch Sat.* ✛ *B2.*

$$ ✕ **Trattoria Haba.** The son of a prominent family of Iraqi bakers founded
MODERN ISRAELI this airy, spacious bistro featuring fresh breads, pastries, and pastas.
It's considered a top spot for brunch as well as Italian-style aperitivo in
the evening, and the large wooden communal table is the perfect way
to share a light meal with strangers. Try the salad dressed in Campari
vinaigrette, the focaccia dotted with goat cheese and dates, or the ricotta
gnocchi. If you're just passing through, consider taking home some of
the expertly selected prepared foods and local offerings, like Israeli
wines, olive oils, and liquors. $ *Average main: NIS 69* ⊠ *119 Jaffa St.,
Center City* ☎ *02/623–3379* ☼ *No dinner Fri. No lunch Sat.* ✛ *D3.*

$$$$ ✕ **Touro.** On a hillside opposite Jerusalem's Old City, this is one of the
MODERN ISRAELI best spots to dine when the stone walls reflect the golden sunset. The
menu is heavy on meat and draws from Mediterranean influences. For
starters, try the leek patties or the earthy bean soup with truffle oil.
Ceviche is served with grated tomatoes, a nod to Yemenite kitchens.
The standout dish is *shpondra,* or thin rib, cooked for seven hours. Veg-
etarians will find grilled artichokes or black risotto with mushrooms.
Desserts are tasty, and the extensive wine list features local and foreign
bottles. Look around while you dine; Touro is underneath the Jerusalem
Press Club and is frequented by prominent local and foreign journalists.
$ *Average main: NIS 120* ⊠ *2 Nachon St., Center City* ☎ *02/570–2189*
☼ *Closed Fri. No lunch Sat.* ✛ *F5.*

$ ✕ **Village Green.** Near Zion Square, this airy vegetarian restaurant prides
VEGETARIAN itself on the quality of its soups, salads, and quiches. Many ingredients
are organic, and the options for vegans are abundant. The hot buffet
and cold salad bar are self-service (charged by plate), and every meal
comes with a choice of sourdough, whole wheat, or spelt rolls. For a
coffee-time option, take a fine organic latte and a slice of home-baked
cake or pie (gluten-free and sugar-free options available) out to a table
on the shaded sidewalk. There's another vegan branch at nearby 5 Yoel
Salomon Street. $ *Average main: NIS 42* ⊠ *33 Jaffa St., Center City*
☎ *02/625–3065* ☼ *Closed Sat. No dinner Fri.* ✛ *C1.*

$$$ ✕ **Zuni.** In this elegantly clubby version of the 24-hour diner, you can
AMERICAN enjoy a wide variety of breakfast options, from the traditional English
FAMILY breakfast of bacon, sausage, baked beans, and a sunny-side-up egg to
the classic Israeli breakfast of eggs, cheeses, and fresh vegetables. Later
on you can sample the house-made pumpkin tortellini or the famous
French toast. There's a discount when you dine from noon to 5 on
weekdays. There's a good kids' menu that's served fast to keep little
ones happy. $ *Average main: NIS 93* ⊠ *15 Yoel Salomon St., Center
City* ☎ *02/625–7778* ⊕ *www.zuni.rest-e.co.il* ✛ *B1.*

GERMAN COLONY AND BAKA

South of Downtown, the German Colony is a hot spot for eateries,
cafés, and little shops. It's a fun, if crowded, spot to pass a morning,
afternoon, or evening. The First Station compound is home to nearly
a dozen restaurants. Nearby Baka has its own set of quirky cafés and
delis. It's worth the 10-minute walk.

2

$$$ ✕**Adom.** The name means "red" in Hebrew, referring to the 150 kinds
MODERN ISRAELI of wine that decorate every wall in this large yet cozy restaurant. The
menu has roots in Mediterranean kitchens, and includes loads of meat
and seafood options. Try the fantastic Jerusalem mixed grill—it's a
gussied-up version of the city's famed street food. Desserts include
tahini ice cream and a dark chocolate, gluten-free "Nemesis cake." If
you're seated at the bar, look up: when Adom moved to the First Sta-
tion complex, the old restaurant's plates were converted into intricate
light fixtures. After 10 pm, smoking is allowed at the bar. Don't arrive
Friday evenings without reservations. Ⓢ *Average main: NIS 90* ✉ *First
Station, 4 David Remez St., German Colony* ☎ *053/427–5330* ⊕ *adom.
rest.co.il* ✛ *F6.*

$$ ✕**Caffit.** This German Colony institution, part of a chain, is well-known
CAFÉ for its sweet potato soup and juicy salmon skewers. Morning meals
FAMILY are generous and varied, including classic Israeli breakfast of eggs and
salads. The personable staff and the warm, welcoming space make this
a favorite spot for locals. There is a branch downtown on Shlomzion
Hamalka Street as well as at the Botanical Garden. Ⓢ *Average main:
NIS 66* ✉ *36 Emek Refa'im St., German Colony* ☎ *02/563–5284*
⊕ *www.caffit-jr.co.il* ☽ *No dinner Fri. No lunch Sat.* ✛ *E6.*

$$$ ✕**Focaccia Moshava.** This kosher cousin of the popular Downtown res-
ITALIAN taurant welcomes you with a large display of fresh vegetables and an
FAMILY open *taboon* oven where the focaccias are baked. The inventive menu
offers eight different focaccias, including an excellent roast beef variety.
For starters, try the Peruvian-style chicken strips blanched with mint
and seasoned with lime and cilantro, or the beef carpaccio with aru-
gula. Other good choices include the veal bruschetta served with rib-eye
skewers, sweetbreads, and grilled portobello mushrooms; or the fish
fillet baked with a crust of panko bread crumbs. The menu has several
vegetarian options as well. Ⓢ *Average main: NIS 76* ✉ *35 Emek Refaim
St., German Colony* ☎ *02/538–7182* ⊕ *m.focaccia.co* ☽ *No dinner Fri.
No lunch Sat.* ✛ *F6.*

$$$$ ✕**HaChazer.** In a former train station, this spacious eatery's dark-wood
MODERN ISRAELI tables and white cloth napkins might be unremarkable, but the inter-
esting menu, with its welcome departure from the standard Jerusalem
dishes, more than makes up for it. The chef takes meat eating seri-
ously, adding Mediterranean, South American, and Asian touches to
the menu. There's a fine selection of house stews—including some made
with beef cheeks—and a selection of juicy steaks. Specialties include
beef carpaccio in truffle aioli, broiled sweetbreads served on eggplant
cream, and grilled fish. The desserts change according to season and
are definitely worthwhile. Ⓢ *Average main: NIS 105* ✉ *7 Bethlehem
Rd., Baka* ☎ *02/671–9922* ⊕ *www.thecourtyard.rest-e.co.il* ☽ *Closed
Sat. No dinner Fri.* ✛ *F6.*

$$ ✕**Hamiznon Kitchen Station.** In the former cafeteria of Jerusalem's train
MODERN ISRAELI station, this casual eatery prints its menus on newspaper broadsheet
and has maintained more than a century of peeling paint on the walls.
Come in as late as 2 pm on weekdays for generous European-inspired
breakfasts like the "Barcelona," a frittata served with a salad. Later
in the day, sample the grilled sea bass, a colorful salad, or one of the

sandwiches served in shoeboxes. ⑤ *Average main: NIS 64* ⊠ *6 David Remez St., German Colony* ☎ *02/561–1497* ⊕ *www.hamiznon.co.il* ☉ *No dinner Fri. No lunch Sat.* ✛ *G6.*

$$
MIDDLE EASTERN

✕ **Hasandwich Shel Rachel.** This Tunisian hole-in-the-wall offers pillowy hand-rolled couscous, slow-cooked stews, and zingy tuna and egg sandwiches, served outside on tiny tables or packed up to go. There is no menu, just whatever owner Motti Hadad is cooking in the shoebox-sized kitchen. ⑤ *Average main: NIS 52* ⊠ *17 Beit Lechem St., Baka* ☎ *02/671–3918* ▭ *No credit cards* ☉ *Closed Sat. No dinner Fri.* ✛ *G6.*

$$
ITALIAN
FAMILY

✕ **Roza.** The varied menu, generous portions, and reasonable prices have made this kosher restaurant a hit with locals in the German Colony. Start with one of nine types of focaccia—the sliced roast beef with arugula or the smoked goose breast are big hits—before moving on to entrées like fettuccine with chicken and cilantro, chicken liver with date honey, or steak sandwiches. The tasty tortilla wraps are a lighter option. Decorated with cobalt blue tiles, the dining room is friendly and informal. ⑤ *Average main: NIS 50* ⊠ *2 Rachel Imenu St., German Colony* ☎ *02/563–8000* ⊕ *www.rozajerusalem.rest-e.co.il* ☉ *No dinner Fri. No lunch Sat.* ✛ *F6.*

WHERE TO STAY

Some travelers insist on a hotel in a central location; others prefer to retreat to a haven at the end of the day, with atmosphere more important than accessibility. Jerusalem has more of the first kind than the second, and many hotels once considered remote are really no more than 10 minutes by cab or train from the city center. Most hotels are contemporary and modern, but a few have retained an old-world allure. There are also guesthouses, B&Bs, and other lodgings that offer more of the local charm coupled with often-cheaper prices.

Defining high season is not an exact science. Some hotels may talk about peak periods in addition to or instead of high season, typically the weeklong Jewish holiday of Passover (March or April), and a similar period around Sukkot (September or October). Because of variations in hotel policy, and because the dates of Jewish holidays shift annually in accordance with the Hebrew calendar, the difference in room rates can be significant.

Almost all West Jerusalem hotels are kosher.

Hotel reviews have been shortened. For more information, visit Fodors. com. Use the coordinates at the end of each listing (✛ A1) to locate a site on the corresponding map.

WHAT IT COSTS				
	$	**$$**	**$$$**	**$$$$**
Hotels	Under $200	$200–$300	$301–$400	over $400

Hotel prices, given in U.S. dollars, are the lowest cost of a standard double room in high season. Non-Israeli citizens paying in foreign currency are exempt from the 17% V.A.T. on hotel rooms.

OLD CITY

The Old City, the historic walled heart of Jerusalem, includes the Armenian Quarter, the Christian Quarter, the Jewish Quarter, and the Muslim Quarter. Lodging options here are limited, and you'll trade luxurious amenities for the ability to step out of your room and into the ancient cobbled streets.

JAFFA GATE

$
B&B/INN
Christ Church Guest House. Inside the Jaffa Gate, this guesthouse is part of the oldest Protestant church in the Middle East. **Pros:** tranquil haven; free parking; excellent for sightseeing. **Cons:** not always comfortable for non-Christian guests. $ *Rooms from: $170 ⊠ 55 Armenian Orthodox Patriarchate Rd., Armenian Quarter ☎ 02/627–7727 ⊕ cmjisrae.w16. wh-2.com ⬦ 32 rooms* ꙳⨀꙳ *Breakfast ⊕ G5.*

$
B&B/INN
Lutheran Guesthouse. Tucked into an alleyway behind the souk in the Armenian Quarter, this guesthouse is a maze of stone buildings and tranquil gardens. **Pros:** free Internet access; leaf-framed panoramas; free hot drinks. **Cons:** Old City location difficult to reach. $ *Rooms from: $115 ⊠ 7 St. Mark Rd., Armenian Quarter ☎ 02/626–6888 ⊕ www.luthguesthouse-jerusalem.com ⬦ 36 rooms* ꙳⨀꙳ *Breakfast ⊕ G5.*

$
HOTEL
New Imperial Hotel. Tiny iron balconies overlooking Jaffa Gate make this century-old hotel a solid choice for a historic—if humble—night near the Old City walls. **Pros:** great location; authentic feel; budget-friendly rates. **Cons:** can be noisy; room updates not especially attractive; spotty Wi-Fi access. $ *Rooms from: $120 ⊠ Omar Ibn El-Khattib St., Jaffa Gate ☎ 02/628–2261 ⊕ www.newimperial.com ⬦ 40 rooms* ꙳⨀꙳ *Breakfast ⊕ F5.*

EAST JERUSALEM

The cluster of hotels here, some Israeli run, some Palestinian, are within yards of each other. They are on the old "seam" (as it's sometimes called) that once divided Jerusalem into East and West. At some levels, the old divisions remain, but the seam area itself has become a comfortable middle ground.

$
HOTEL
Addar Hotel. This intimate boutique hotel sits between East and West Jerusalem, just a 10-minute walk from the Old City. **Pros:** English-speaking manager; reasonably priced meals; near the Old City. **Cons:** neighborhood dark at night; no pool. $ *Rooms from: $190 ⊠ 53 Nablus Rd., East Jerusalem ☎ 02/626–3111 ⊕ www.addar-hotel.com ⬦ 30 rooms* ꙳⨀꙳ *Breakfast ⊕ F2.*

$
HOTEL
Ambassador Hotel. One of East Jerusalem's longtime favorites, the Ambassador has been tastefully renovated with loads of Jerusalem stone. **Pros:** outdoor dining; lovely views; comfortable rooms. **Cons:** far from attractions; area dead at night. $ *Rooms from: $180 ⊠ 5 Nablus Rd., East Jerusalem ☎ 02/541–2222 ⊕ www.jerusalemambassador.com ⬦ 115 rooms* ꙳⨀꙳ *Breakfast ⊕ G1.*

$$$
HOTEL
Fodor'sChoice
★
American Colony Hotel. Once a pasha's palace, this cool limestone oasis with its flower-filled inner courtyard and gorgeous garden is in a class of its own—no wonder it's a favored haunt of statesmen, stars, and spies. **Pros:** atmospheric cellar bar in winter, lovely garden bar in summer;

good English bookstore and gift shop; beautiful pool. **Cons:** quiet neighborhood at night; a cab or light-rail ride from most attractions. $ *Rooms from: $310* ✉ *1 Louis Vincent St., East Jerusalem* ☎ *02/627–9777* ⊕ *www.americancolony.com* ✎ *100 rooms* ⎮⊙⎮ *Breakfast* ✛ *G2.*

$ 🖼 **Dan Jerusalem Hotel.** Cascading down Mount Scopus, the sprawling
HOTEL Dan Jerusalem has spectacular views, an oasislike pool, and a bold design. **Pros:** impressive architecture; memorable lobby; impressive spa and Turkish bath. **Cons:** remote location; a bit overpriced. $ *Rooms from: $175* ✉ *32 Lehi St., East Jerusalem* ☎ *02/533–1234* ⊕ *www.dan-hotels.com* ✎ *505 rooms* ⎮⊙⎮ *Breakfast* ✛ *H1.*

$ 🖼 **Grand Court Hotel.** This huge hotel is a celebration of light and space:
HOTEL from the large, airy lobby, with its limestone walls and marble arches,
FAMILY to the well-lighted, comfortable guest rooms, with their soft decor and bright bathrooms. **Pros:** 10-minute walk from Damascus Gate; close to light-rail; gym and pool on-site. **Cons:** neighborhood dead at night. $ *Rooms from: $171* ✉ *15 St. George St., East Jerusalem* ☎ *02/591–7777* ⊕ *www.grandhotels-israel.com* ✎ *450 rooms* ⎮⊙⎮ *Breakfast* ✛ *F2.*

$ 🖼 **Leonardo Hotel Jerusalem.** A huge circular skylight in the middle of
HOTEL the lobby gives this hotel a sense of light and space. **Pros:** comfortable rooms; lots of space; 10-minute walk from Damascus Gate. **Cons:** neighborhood dead at night; no distinctive character. $ *Rooms from: $160* ✉ *9 St. George St., East Jerusalem* ☎ *02/532–0000* ⊕ *www.leonardo-hotels.com* ✎ *400 rooms* ⎮⊙⎮ *Breakfast* ✛ *F2.*

$ 🖼 **National Hotel.** Five minutes from the Old City, this hotel is once
HOTEL again attracting the journalists, diplomats, and government officials who patronized it during its glory days. **Pros:** free parking; reasonable rates; great service. **Cons:** a bit out of the way; no pool. $ *Rooms from: $120* ✉ *4 Al Zahra St., East Jerusalem* ☎ *02/627–8880* ⊕ *www.nationalhotel-jerusalem.com* ✎ *120 rooms* ⎮⊙⎮ *Breakfast* ✛ *G3.*

$$ 🖼 **Olive Tree Hotel.** The stone arches, lacey latticework, and bronze orna-
HOTEL ments in the reception area help create a distinctly regional atmosphere, as do the old flagstones in the skylit atrium and polished floorboards in the comfortable lounge. **Pros:** 10-minute walk from Damascus Gate; superior sports facilities; elegant atmosphere. **Cons:** smallish rooms; neighborhood is dead at night. $ *Rooms from: $239* ✉ *23 St. George St., East Jerusalem* ☎ *02/541–0410* ⊕ *www.olivetreehotel.com* ✎ *304 rooms* ⎮⊙⎮ *Breakfast* ✛ *F2.*

CENTER CITY

This vast area is more about central locations than leafy retreats. Parking is at a premium: this is discouraging territory for those with rental cars. However, you'll enjoy feeling the pulse of West Jerusalem, watching locals as they hang laundry, walk dogs, and sip coffee.

$$ 🖼 **Arthur Hotel.** In this stylish boutique lodging, named after Arthur
HOTEL Balfour of the famed Balfour Declaration that promised the Jews a
Fodor's Choice state, an abundant breakfast is served in the charming lobby with
★ wooden furniture or outside in a small garden. **Pros:** excellent service; central location; friendly staff. **Cons:** none of the amenities of

larger hotels. $ *Rooms from: $250* ✉ *13 Dorot Rishonim St., Center City* ☎ *02/623–9999* ⊕ *www.atlas.co.il/arthur-jerusalem* ⤴ *54 rooms* ⦿⦿ *Breakfast* ✛ *B1.*

$$$ 🏨 **Dan Panorama Jerusalem.** The guest rooms at this 11-story landmark
HOTEL   in the middle of the hotel district are a bit compact, but thoughtful light-
ing, well-placed furnishings, and interesting artwork make a difference.
Pros: excellent location; pleasant staff; thoughtful renovations. **Cons:** a
bit overpriced; pool is small. $ *Rooms from: $340* ✉ *39 Keren Hayesod St., Center City* ☎ *02/569–5695* ⊕ *www.danhotels.com* ⤴ *289 rooms* ⦿⦿ *Breakfast* ✛ *E5.*

$$$$ 🏨 **David Citadel.** Talk about a great first impression—this hotel's lobby,
HOTEL   by noted Italian architect Piero Lissoni, is modern and welcoming, illu-
FAMILY minated by the natural sunlight streaming in from the arched glass roof.
Pros: five minutes from Jaffa Gate; year-round outdoor pool; fantastic
breakfast. **Cons:** rooms have little character; expensive rates. $ *Rooms from: $470* ✉ *7 King David St., Center City* ☎ *02/621–1111* ⊕ *theda-vidcitadel.com* ⤴ *380 rooms* ⦿⦿ *Breakfast* ✛ *F5.*

$$ 🏨 **Eldan Hotel.** The address in the heart of a prestigious hotel district—
HOTEL   just a five-minute walk from Downtown or from Jaffa Gate—is a major
draw here. **Pros:** prime location; cheerful rooms; some nice views. **Cons:**
few frills; no pool; limited parking. $ *Rooms from: $220* ✉ *24 King David St., Center City* ☎ *02/567–9777* ⊕ *www.eldanhotel.com* ⤴ *75 rooms* ⦿⦿ *Breakfast* ✛ *E5.*

$ 🏨 **Eyal Hotel.** An unbeatable location and lovely rooftop terrace make
HOTEL   this a welcome addition to the neighborhood's growing list of boutique
hotels. **Pros:** great location; pleasant balconies; USB outlets in every
room. **Cons:** small standard rooms face an external wall; can get noisy
at night; entrance is a bit cheap looking. $ *Rooms from: $170* ✉ *21 Shamai St., Center City* ☎ *02/623–1000* ⊕ *eyalhotel.co.il* ⤴ *68 rooms* ⦿⦿ *Breakfast* ✛ *B1.*

$$ 🏨 **Harmony Hotel.** A combination of stellar service and delightful rooms
HOTEL   heralded this first of many boutique hotels in the historic Nahalat Shiva
Fodor's Choice neighborhood, in the heart of downtown Jerusalem. **Pros:** free Wi-Fi
★   access; perfect location; free leaflets for self-guided tours. **Cons:** down-
town noise when you open windows; small rooms. $ *Rooms from: $200* ✉ *14 Shammai St., Center City* ☎ *02/621–9999* ⊕ *www.atlas. co.il/harmony-hotel-jerusalem* ⤴ *60 rooms* ⦿⦿ *Breakfast* ✛ *B2.*

$$ 🏨 **Herbert Samuel Hotel Jerusalem.** Named after the British-Jewish poli-
HOTEL   tician who governed Israel during the Mandate, Herbert Samuel is a
Fodor's Choice widely celebrated addition to the downtown area. **Pros:** gorgeous heated
★   pool; beautiful design; great location. **Cons:** service can be slow; street
noise is loud when the windows are open. $ *Rooms from: $285* ✉ *25 Shamai St., Center City* ☎ *02/560–0600* ⊕ *www.herbertsamuel.com* ⤴ *137 rooms* ⦿⦿ *Breakfast* ✛ *B1.*

$$$$ 🏨 **Inbal Jerusalem Hotel.** Jerusalem stone lends a warm glow to this
HOTEL   low-slung hotel, which is wrapped around a central courtyard and
FAMILY atrium. **Pros:** excellent location; free parking; relaxing lobby. **Cons:**
Fodor's Choice restaurant is mediocre. $ *Rooms from: $450* ✉ *3 Jabotinsky St.,*
★   *Center City* ☎ *02/675–6666* ⊕ *www.inbalhotel.com* ⤴ *283 rooms* ⦿⦿ *Breakfast* ✛ *E6.*

$ · HOTEL — 🏨 **Jerusalem Tower Hotel.** Steps from the Old City, this hotel's prime location makes it a great option if you want to be close to the action. **Pros:** good value; in the heart of things; free Wi-Fi access. **Cons:** not many amenities; no room to spread out; parking for a fee. $ *Rooms from: $105* ✉ *23 Hillel St., Center City* ☎ *02/620–9209* ⊕ *www.jerusalemtowerhotel.com* ↪ *120 rooms* ❄ *Breakfast* ✛ *B2.*

$$$$ · HOTEL · Fodor's Choice ★ — 🏨 **King David.** This grande dame of Israeli luxury hotels opened in 1931 and it has successfully defended its title ever since, adding modern amenities like a well-appointed gym and luxuries like a French-style restaurant called La Régence. **Pros:** outstanding pool and garden; terrific location and views; historic building. **Cons:** limited parking; older rooms are quite small and shabby. $ *Rooms from: $560* ✉ *23 King David St., Center City* ☎ *02/620–8888* ⊕ *www.danhotels.com* ↪ *233 rooms* ❄ *Breakfast* ✛ *E5.*

$$$$ · HOTEL — 🏨 **Leonardo Plaza Hotel Jerusalem.** Overlooking Independence Park, the 22-story Leonardo Plaza is a Jerusalem landmark with terrific views, especially from upper floors. **Pros:** 10-minute walk from the Old City; good restaurants; up-to-date gym. **Cons:** business hotel feel; pay parking; pricey rates. $ *Rooms from: $415* ✉ *47 King George St., Center City* ☎ *02/629–8666* ⊕ *www.leonardo-hotels.com* ↪ *300 rooms* ❄ *Breakfast* ✛ *D5.*

$ · B&B/INN — 🏨 **Little House in Rechavia.** The small hotel makes no pretensions about being a full-service facility, but it is comfortably furnished, a good value, and within walking distance of the Old City. **Pros:** neighborhood feel; reasonable rates; rooftop terrace. **Cons:** no restaurant; no pool; no parking. $ *Rooms from: $168* ✉ *20 Ibn Ezra St., Center City* ☎ *02/563–3344* ⊕ *www.jerusalem-hotel.co.il* ↪ *28 rooms* ❄ *Breakfast* ✛ *D5.*

$$$$ · HOTEL · Fodor's Choice ★ — 🏨 **Mamilla Hotel.** With clever and soaring architectural flourishes by starchitect Moshe Safdie and a restrained yet luxurious modern interior design by Piero Lissoni, the Mamilla is a sleek and comfortable haven with bars and restaurants that appeal to locals and travelers alike. **Pros:** contemporary design; central location; good service; great spa. **Cons:** Happy Fish restaurant is uncharacteristically mediocre. $ *Rooms from: $600* ✉ *11 King Solomon St., Center City* ☎ *02/548–2222* ⊕ *www.mamillahotel.com* ↪ *194 rooms* ❄ *Breakfast* ✛ *F4.*

$$ · HOTEL — 🏨 **Montefiore Hotel.** The side-street location in the center of town—on a pedestrian-only block with shops and restaurants just outside the front door—adds to the serenity of this reasonably priced hotel. **Pros:** 10-minute walk from Old City; interesting shops and cafés nearby; free Wi-Fi access. **Cons:** a bit old-fashioned; paid parking; elevator is loud and stops on every floor on the Sabbath. $ *Rooms from: $230* ✉ *7 Shatz St., Center City* ☎ *02/622–1111* ⊕ *www.montefiorehotel.com* ↪ *48 rooms* ❄ *Breakfast* ✛ *A2.*

$$ · B&B/INN — 🏨 **Notre Dame Guest House.** Pilgrim tour groups have long been drawn to the modest rooms and stellar location (a 10-minute walk from the Church of the Holy Sepulcher in the Old City) of this gorgeous stone castlelike building owned by the Vatican and dating back to the 1880s. **Pros:** free parking; a short walk to the Old City; affordable for Jerusalem. **Cons:** few room amenities; only twin mattresses in standard rooms; no TVs in rooms. $ *Rooms from: $270* ✉ *3 HaTsanhanim*

Rd., *Center City* ☎ *02/627–9111* ⊕ *notredamecenter.org* ⤴ *150 rooms* �‖ *Breakfast* ✛ *F4.*

$ ⬚ **Palatin Hotel.** Proprietor Tody Warshavsky's grandfather built the Pal-
HOTEL atin Hotel in 1936, and members of the Knesset, which used to be just
up the road, stayed here when parliament was in session. **Pros:** central
location; multilingual staff; free coffee all day. **Cons:** no elevator; can get
noisy; no parking. ⑤ *Rooms from: $139* ✉ *4 Agrippas St., Center City*
☎ *02/623–1141* ⊕ *palatinhotel.com* ⤴ *25 rooms* �‖ *Breakfast* ✛ *B1.*

$ ⬚ **Prima Kings Hotel.** "The Kings"—the name by which it's still
HOTEL known—sits on a busy intersection, less than a 10-minute walk from
FAMILY Downtown and the Old City. **Pros:** near the Great Synagogue; adjacent
late-night supermarket. **Cons:** a bit overpriced; traffic noise when win-
dows are open. ⑤ *Rooms from: $153* ✉ *60 King George St., Center*
City ☎ *02/620–1201* ⊕ *www.prima-hotels-israel.com* ⤴ *210 rooms*
�‖ *Breakfast* ✛ *D5.*

$ ⬚ **Prima Royale Hotel.** The centerpiece of this centrally located boutique
HOTEL hotel is a spectacular rooftop deck where you can sip cocktails, listen to
classical or jazz music on summer evenings, or gaze through telescopes
at the 360-degree panorama. **Pros:** live music; tasteful decor; quiet location. **Cons:** no pool; limited parking. ⑤ *Rooms from: $170* ✉ *3 Mendele*
St., Center City ☎ *02/560–7111* ⊕ *www.prima-hotels-israel.com* ⤴ *133*
rooms �‖ *Breakfast* ✛ *E6.*

$$$$ ⬚ **Waldorf Astoria Jerusalem.** In a former treasury building, this luxuri-
HOTEL ous lodging wraps around a four-story-high courtyard flooded with
natural light and sparkling with greenery. **Pros:** unmitigated luxury;
beautiful courtyard; breakfast includes Champagne and the work of an
in-house French bakery. **Cons:** limited outdoor space; few rooms have
view of Old City; expensive rates. ⑤ *Rooms from: $775* ✉ *26 Agron*
St., Center City ☎ *02/542–3333* ⊕ *waldorfastoria.com* ⤴ *226 rooms*
�‖ *Breakfast* ✛ *E5.*

$ ⬚ **YMCA Three Arches Hotel.** Built in 1933, this limestone building with
HOTEL its famous domed bell tower has long been a Jerusalem landmark, and
FAMILY its basic guest rooms have fabulous Old City views. **Pros:** great location; complimentary sports facilities; affordable rates. **Cons:** dated
decor; smallish rooms. ⑤ *Rooms from: $169* ✉ *26 King David St.,*
King David St., Center City ☎ *02/569–2692* ⊕ *ymca3arches.com* ⤴ *56*
rooms �‖ *Breakfast* ✛ *E5.*

WEST JERUSALEM

This cluster of hotels in Givat Ram and Romema is near the point where
the Tel Aviv Highway (Route 1) enters Jerusalem. Some properties are
near the Central Bus Station, others closer to the Israel Museum and
the Knesset. Many hotels lie along the light-rail line that connects the
western and eastern parts of the city. Ein Kerem, a leafy enclave, is
included here, too, along with Mount Herzl and Givat Massuah, close
to the Malcha Mall. Downtown is some distance away, the Old City
even farther—a long walk, but 10 to 15 minutes by cab or bus, and bus
lines are plentiful. If you're after hotel deals or if other places in town
are booked, this area makes a great option.

$$$
B&B/INN
🏨 **Alegra Boutique Hotel.** In the picturesque village of Ein Kerem, this boutique hotel occupies a century-old house famous for the true-life-Romeo-and-Juliet story of a Jewish-Arab couple. **Pros:** modern design; gorgeous rooms; free parking. **Cons:** far from attractions; not for families; brusque staff. ⑤ *Rooms from: $333* ✉ *13 Derech HaAchayot, Ein Kerem* ☎ *02/650–0506* ⊕ *www.hotelalegra.com* ↝ *13 suites* ⏹ *Breakfast* ✛ *A3.*

$
HOTEL
🏨 **Crowne Plaza Jerusalem.** Although this gleaming white tower with sweeping city views is a classic business hotel, it's also a comfortable option when you're on vacation. **Pros:** away from city noise; nice spa, tennis, and pool facilities; close to light-rail. **Cons:** few attractions within walking distance; limited parking. ⑤ *Rooms from: $108* ✉ *1 HaAliyah St., Givat Ram* ☎ *02/658–8888* ⊕ *www.ihg.com/crowneplaza* ↝ *397 rooms* ⏹ *Breakfast* ✛ *B3.*

$
HOTEL
FAMILY
🏨 **Hotel Yehuda.** This popular hotel makes a practical—if a bit remote—base for families, since rooms are reasonably priced and there's plenty of space for kids to run around. **Pros:** large swimming pool; great views of Jerusalem; close to train station to Tel Aviv; lovely spa. **Cons:** remote location; dining hall feels institutional; two-night minimum stays over weekends. ⑤ *Rooms from: $117* ✉ *11 Haim Kulitz St., Malcha* ☎ *02/632–2777* ⊕ *www.byh.co.il* ↝ *129 rooms* ⏹ *Breakfast* ✛ *A6.*

$
HOTEL
🏨 **Prima Park Hotel.** This West Jerusalem hotel right on the light-rail line has a good reputation thanks to its pretty stone courtyard, reasonable prices, and tastefully decorated rooms. **Pros:** friendly staff; intimate atmosphere; close to light-rail. **Cons:** far from Downtown; area dead at night; limited parking. ⑤ *Rooms from: $128* ✉ *2 Vilnai St., Givat Ram* ☎ *02/658–2222* ⊕ *www.prima-hotels-israel.com* ↝ *217 rooms* ⏹ *Breakfast* ✛ *A3.*

$$$
HOTEL
FAMILY
🏨 **Ramada Jerusalem.** This massive hotel's marble lobby, with its reflective ceiling, clubby leather chairs, and frilly potted palms, has a feeling of grandeur. **Pros:** close to the light-rail; well-equipped gym; wonderful for families. **Cons:** neighborhood is dead at night; expensive rates; staff are not always informative. ⑤ *Rooms from: $400* ✉ *Ruppin Bridge at Herzl Blvd., Givat Ram* ☎ *02/659–9999* ⊕ *jerusalemramadahotel.com/en* ↝ *615 rooms* ⏹ *Breakfast* ✛ *A3.*

GERMAN COLONY AND BAKA

This area lies in Jerusalem's southwest quadrant, due south of Jaffa Gate. Baka is some distance away, but all other listed properties are a fairly easy walk from the Old City. The German Colony is an excellent place for people-watching, or for a relaxed afternoon of boutique shopping. The opening of Isrotel's luxurious Orient Hotel in 2017 will be an elegant addition to the German Colony.

$$
HOTEL
🏨 **Dan Boutique Jerusalem.** A lovely sundeck, deluxe rooms with delightful views, and a funky lobby lounge give this hotel a contemporary appeal. **Pros:** great design; inviting public area; close to First Station dining and shopping complex. **Cons:** limited free parking; no pool. ⑤ *Rooms from: $220* ✉ *31 Hebron Rd., German Colony* ☎ *02/568–9999* ⊕ *www.danhotels.com* ↝ *160 rooms* ⏹ *Breakfast* ✛ *F6.*

$ ⊞ **Little House in Bakah.** This handsome Ottoman-style mansion with
B&B/INN dramatic arched windows sits on the edge of a residential neighborhood dotted with many shops and restaurants. **Pros:** intimate vibe; good value; near public transportation. **Cons:** a bit dowdy; no elevator; traffic noise. ⑤ *Rooms from: $100* ⊠ *1 Yehuda St., corner of Hebron Rd., Baka* ☎ *02/673–7944* ⊕ *www.jerusalem-hotel.co.il* ↘ *33 rooms* ⦿| *Breakfast* ✛ *G6.*

$ ⊞ **Little House in the Colony.** On a quiet street, this small inn was built by
B&B/INN the original settlers of the German Colony, and the creaking wooden floors attest to its European roots. **Pros:** quiet and intimate feel; shops and eateries nearby; a bargain in Jerusalem. **Cons:** basic amenities; no elevator; some bathrooms are minuscule. ⑤ *Rooms from: $149* ⊠ *4a Lloyd George St., German Colony* ☎ *02/566–2424* ⊕ *www.jerusalem-hotel.co.il* ↘ *23 rooms* ⦿| *Breakfast* ✛ *E6.*

$$$$ ⊞ **Mount Zion Hotel.** Arched doorways and windows in golden-hue Jerusalem stone frame this hotel's ethereal views of the Hinnom Valley.
HOTEL
Fodor'sChoice **Pros:** wonderful mix of old and new; inviting pool area; easy walk
★ to Old City, First Station, and German Colony. **Cons:** staff could be cheerier; some dated decor. ⑤ *Rooms from: $420* ⊠ *17 Hebron Rd., German Colony* ☎ *02/568–9555* ⊕ *www.mountzion.co.il* ↘ *139 rooms* ⦿| *Breakfast* ✛ *F6.*

$ ⊞ **Rafael Residence.** In the heart of leafy Baka, this apartment hotel offers
HOTEL mostly two-room suites with well-equipped kitchenettes and extra space for the kids. **Pros:** great value for families; modern vibe; underground parking. **Cons:** far from Downtown; breakfast costs extra. ⑤ *Rooms from: $180* ⊠ *70 Bethlehem Rd., Baka* ☎ *077/777–2222* ⊕ *www.rafael-residence.com* ↘ *34 suites* ⦿| *No meals* ✛ *G6.*

$ ⊞ **St. Andrew's Scottish Guesthouse.** Built in the early 1930s as part of
B&B/INN St. Andrew's Church, this inexpensive guesthouse is a well-tended and
Fodor'sChoice homey place to hang your hat. **Pros:** serene atmosphere; close to the
★ German Colony; delightful library, garden, and terrace. **Cons:** no elevator; no restaurant; scant breakfast options. ⑤ *Rooms from: $170* ⊠ *1 David Remez St., German Colony* ☎ *02/673–2401* ⊕ *www.scotsguesthouse.com* ↘ *20 rooms* ⦿| *Breakfast* ✛ *F6.*

NIGHTLIFE AND PERFORMING ARTS

Jerusalem is not known for its nightlife, but there are a handful of excellent pubs and clubs, and finding them can feel like spotting a diamond in the rough. You can combine a great meal or tasty snack with a concert, pub, or dance bar for a lively evening out on the town. Thursday and Friday nights are the hot times for bars and clubs and late-night shows; classical music and dance performances tend to avoid Friday nights, and take place over the rest of the week. Check out listings in English-language publications you find in hotels, or search for upcoming events at ⊕ *www.gojerusalem.com* or ⊕ *www.itraveljerusalem.com.*

NIGHTLIFE

Although Jerusalem can't compete with Tel Aviv in terms of the number of nightlife attractions, what the city lacks in quantity it more than makes up for in quality. Pubs, bars, and nightclubs in Jerusalem tend to be more relaxed than those in Tel Aviv—they're friendlier, more informal, and often less expensive. As in Tel Aviv, the nightlife scene in Jerusalem starts very late: some places only begin to fill up after midnight, and most pubs are open until the early hours of the morning. Given the university presence in the city, there's often a younger crowd at many places.

EAST JERUSALEM

BARS AND PUBS

Borderline. A haunt for reporters from around the world, Borderline has a delightful summer garden and a huge screen for watching soccer games. In winter, seats are plentiful inside the century-old building. This Palestinian place is a great place to try anise-flavored arak from Ramallah. Borderline is connected to Pasha's, a reliable source for great Middle Eastern cooking. ⊠ *13 Shimon Hatzadik, East Jerusalem* ☎ *02/532–8342* ⊕ *www.pashasofjerusalem.com.*

Fodor'sChoice ★ **Cellar Bar.** This place has the feel of an intimate wine cellar, with small tables, quiet corners, and a mix of languages that makes you feel far away from all the political problems of the day. It's open only during the winter months, but from June to October you can enjoy the same well-made cocktails at the outdoor Summer Bar. ⊠ *American Colony Hotel, 1 Louis Vincent St., at Nablus Rd., East Jerusalem* ☎ *02/627–9777* ⊕ *www.americancolony.com.*

WEST JERUSALEM

MUSIC CENTER

Yellow Submarine. A not-for-profit music center, Yellow Submarine offers free jazz concerts once a week, as well as popular sing-along evenings and performances by major Israeli and international rock and pop artists. A decent bar also serves salads and other light fare. ⊠ *13 HaRechavim St., East Talpiot* ☎ *02/679–4040* ⊕ *www.yellowsubmarine.org.il.*

CENTER CITY

BARS AND PUBS

Fodor'sChoice ★ **Casino de Paris.** Owned by Israeli rock star Shaanan Streett, this bar in the heart of the vegetable market occupies what was once a British Army brothel. It serves a fine selection of original cocktails and beers from local microbreweries, along with stellar cured fish platters. ⊠ *Georgian Market, 3 Machaneh Yehuda St., Center City* ☎ *02/650–4235.*

Gatsby. An unmarked door opens to a library with bookshelves that slide apart to reveal a bar inspired by the Roaring '20s. Eager young bartenders mix classic cocktails and drinks of their own creation, accented by crushed star anise, arak liquor, absinthe, or honey syrup. ⊠ *18 Hillel St., Center City* ☎ *054/814–7143.*

Hashchena. Hebrew for "Neighbor," Hashchena is a youthful bar steps from the Mahaneh Yehuda market that greets you with hanging laundry and a wall of beer cans from around the world. There are plenty of local and imported brews along with a satisfying food menu. ⊠ *11 Beit Yaacov St., Center City* ☎ *02/537–5916* ⊙ *Closed Fri. night and Sat. until 8 pm.*

HaTaklit. The name means "The Record," a nostalgic tribute by the three young, musically inclined owners. This is a great place for beer, especially during happy hour. There's live music, occasional dance parties, and a back room where international soccer games are screened. ⊠ *7 Helene Hamalka St., Center City* ☎ *02/624–4073.*

Link. Popular with a professional crowd, this all-day restaurant has a deck that's a great spot on warm evenings. The grilled chicken wings are terrific. Unlike a lot of nearby places, it's open Friday night. ⊠ *3 Hama'alot St., Center City* ☎ *02/625–3446* ⊕ *www.2eat.co.il/eng/link.*

Mirror Bar. This chic bar in Jerusalem's elegant Mamilla Hotel appeals to a cross section of locals, travelers, and expats. The intimate space (and yes, there are plenty of mirrors) is perfect for a nightcap or a table of excellent tapas. ⊠ *Mamilla Hotel, 11 King Solomon St., Center City* ☎ *02/548–2230* ⊕ *www.mamillahotel.com/mirrorbar.*

Fodor'sChoice ★ **Notre Dame Cheese and Wine Restaurant.** Across from the New Gate of the Old City, this rooftop eatery offers an unrivaled vista of Old Jerusalem and the hills beyond. Take it all in while nibbling on some of the 45 local and imported cheeses and sipping one of the 85 wines. There's also a rather pricey menu, but the best reasons to come here are the drinks and the view. ⊠ *Notre Dame Guest House, 3 HaTsanhanim Rd., Center City* ☎ *02/627–9177* ⊕ *notredamecenter.org.*

Yudaleh. Across the street from the well-regarded Machneyuda, this bar serves smaller versions of the classics served at the restaurant. It's good for a drink before dinner or before hitting the town. ⊠ *11 Beit Yaacov St., Center City* ☎ *02/533–3442.*

DANCE CLUBS

Fodor'sChoice ★ **The Distillery** (*Hamazkeka*). This austere open space in the center of town once served as a cistern and a storage area, but today the Distillery is the center of Jerusalem's art and alternative music scene. During the day it's an artists' workspace, and at night this spot is a performance space where you can get Palestinian beer on tap and dance alongside throngs of art students. Try to make it when local DJ mini-celebrities Tali Ben Itzhak or Markey Funk are on the lineup. ⊠ *3 Shoshan St., Center City* ☎ *02/582–2090* ⊕ *www.mazkeka.com.*

Sira. A great watering hole with a gritty edge, Sira features a variety of music spun by DJs. Open until the wee hours, it's one of the most fun places in the city to dance. Here you'll find a hodgepodge of students and young professionals who gather on weekend afternoons. ⊠ *4 Ben-Sira St., Center City* ☎ *02/623–4366.*

GERMAN COLONY AND BAKA

BARS AND PUBS

Fodor'sChoice ★ **Hasadna Culinary Workshop.** Housed in an old factory, this is a temple to the craft of cocktails near Jerusalem's First Station shopping and dining complex. The drinks—mixed with outstanding homemade syrups and juices—change frequently, but if it's on the menu try a celery daiquiri.

Tapas-style dishes emphasize expertly prepared seafood and include a sea-bass bruschetta, seafood curry, and smoked octopus. ⊠ *28 Hebron Rd., German Colony* ☎ *053/934–4990* ⊕ *www.hasadna.rest-e.co.il.*

PERFORMING ARTS

Classical music is the capital's strong suit. Artists in other musical genres pass through from time to time, but Jerusalem is seldom their main focus. For English-language schedules of performances and other cultural events, consult the Friday weekend section of the *Jerusalem Post* and its insert "In Jerusalem," Friday's "The Guide" of *Haaretz's* English edition, *Time Out Jerusalem*, and the free weekly and monthly booklets available at hotels and information bureaus. Ticket prices typically range from NIS 75 to NIS 350, depending on venue size and artist.

TICKETS

Bimot. This is the main ticket agency for performances in Jerusalem. ⊠ *8 Shammai St., Center City* ☎ *02/623–7000* ⊕ *www.bimot.co.il.*

ARTS CENTERS

Beit Avi Chai. This 270-seat auditorium hosts lectures, concerts, and theater in Hebrew and English throughout the year, often on topics related to Jewish culture and history. ⊠ *44 King George St., Center City* ☎ *02/621–5300* ⊕ *www.bac.org.il.*

Beit Shmuel. Musical and theatrical performances fill the season at this theater. Most of the plays are in Hebrew, but some are in English. Beit Shmuel also offers themed walking tours around Jerusalem. ⊠ *6 Eliyahu Shama'a St., Center City* ☎ *02/620–3555* ⊕ *www.beitshmuel. com/en-us.*

Jerusalem Theatre. Also known as the Jerusalem Centre for the Performing Arts, this venue hosts some of the city's best plays, music, dance, and film screenings. The 760-seat Henry Crown Auditorium is the home of the Jerusalem Symphony Orchestra. The Israeli Camerata Orchestra plays occasional concerts here at 11 am on Friday. Some of the Hebrew plays have English subtitles. ⊠ *20 Marcus St., Center City* ☎ *02/560–5755* ⊕ *www.jerusalem-theatre.co.il.*

DANCE

Gerard Behar Center. Look out for performances by two excellent Jerusalem-based contemporary dance companies, Vertigo and Kolben, both of which are based at the Gerard Behar Center. ⊠ *11 Bezalel St., Center City* ☎ *02/545–6868* ⊕ *gerard-behar.jerusalem.muni.il.*

FESTIVALS

Fodor's Choice ★ **Hutzot Hayotzer Arts and Crafts Festival.** The fine crafts and lively concerts presented at this festival are a highlight of August. Located in the Sultan's Pool, an ancient reservoir in the Hinnom Valley beneath the walls of the Old City, the 10-day event showcases crafts by Israeli and international artisans and features open-air concerts by top Israeli rock and pop performers. Arrive early for the best seats. ⊠ *Hativat Yerushalayim, Center City* ☎ *02/623–7000* ⊕ *www.itraveljerusalem. com/evt/hutzot-hayotzer-intl-arts-and-crafts-fair.*

FAMILY **International Festival of Puppet Theater.** Each August, puppeteers from around the globe bring their productions to venues around the city in a festival organized by Jerusalem's Train Theater. The shows are generally geared toward youngsters, although some are entertaining for the whole family. Many shows are in English or without words. ⊠ *Gan Hapa'amon, Center City* ☎ *02/561–8514* ⊕ *traintheater.co.il/en.*

Fodor'sChoice ★ **Israel Festival.** Top national and international orchestras, theater companies, choirs, dance troupes, and street entertainers participate in this festival, usually held for three weeks in late May or early June. Styles range from classical to avant-garde. The Jerusalem Theatre is the main venue, but a dozen secondary locations around the city get some of the smaller acts. ⊠ *Jerusalem* ☎ *02/623–7000* ⊕ *israel-festival.org/en/.*

Fodor'sChoice ★ **Jerusalem Film Festival.** Held in July each year, this festival attracts large crowds for screenings of Israeli and international films. Some screenings and the awards ceremony are held at the Cinematheque, while other screenings are at a number of venues throughout the city. Reserve tickets in advance. ⊠ *11 Hebron Rd., Center City* ☎ *02/565–4333* ⊕ *www.jff. org.il* ✆ *NIS 46 for screenings.*

Jerusalem International Chamber Music Festival. The 600-seat YMCA Concert Hall is the main venue for the much-acclaimed Jerusalem International Chamber Music Festival, held over 10 days each year in late August or early September. ⊠ *YMCA Three Arches Hotel, 26 King David St., Center City* ☎ *02/569–2692* ⊕ *jcmf.org.il.*

Jerusalem Season of Culture. Held for three weeks in September, this diverse selection of events highlights local and international artists, musicians, dancers, and other types of performers. Many of the offerings are delightfully offbeat. ⊠ *Hutzot Hayotzer, Center City* ☎ *02/653–5880* ⊕ *en.mekudeshet.com.*

Jerusalem Wine Festival. Held in September, this event presents the latest vintages from 200 national and international wineries. ⊠ *Israel Museum, Ruppin Blvd., Givat Ram* ☎ *02/625–9703* ⊕ *www.imj.org. il* ✆ *NIS 95.*

Oud Festival. This festival paying homage to the Arabic lute presents a range of ethnic music from Turkey, Iraq, India, and a host of other cultures, often including Israeli rock. Performances are held at various concert halls around town in November. ⊠ *Confederation House, 12 Emile Botta St., Center City* ☎ *02/624–5206* ⊕ *www.confederation-house.org.*

Palestine Festival of Literature. The five-day festival brings together local and international artists to read prose and poetry related to Arab culture. Free events take place in East Jerusalem and the Old City in May, and the festival travels to other cities in Israel, the West Bank, and Gaza. ⊠ *Shimon Hatsadik St., East Jerusalem* ⊕ *www.palfest.org.*

FILM

Israeli films have been garnering international praise in recent years; they and other non-English-speaking movies are almost always subtitled in English.

Jerusalem Cinematheque. Specializing in old, rare, and art films, this complex has four theaters, a restaurant, and splendid views of the Old City and the Hinnom Valley from the terrace. Its monthly programs focus on specific directors, actors, or subjects. The annual Jerusalem Film Festival, held in July, attracts large crowds, as does December's Jewish Film Festival. ⊠ *11 Hebron Rd., Center City* ☎ *02/565–4333* ⊕ *www.jer-cin.org.il.*

FAMILY **Lev Smadar.** In the German Colony, this venue is a bit of a throwback to yesteryear's movie atmosphere. It's a single-screen cinema with a snack bar in an older building on a narrow lane. Its local following watches independent films, as well as the occasional blockbuster. ⊠ *4 Lloyd George St., German Colony* ☎ *02/566–0954* ⊕ *www.lev.co.il* ◩ *NIS 39.*

MUSIC

Classical music abounds in Jerusalem, with Israeli orchestras and chamber ensembles performing year-round and a trickle of international artists passing through.

Israel Philharmonic Orchestra. This world-renowned orchestra, which is based in Tel Aviv, performs locally at the International Convention Center, opposite the Central Bus Station. The venue also hosts traveling art exhibits and musicians from around the world. ⊠ *1 Zalman Shazar Blvd., Givat Ram* ☎ *02/655–8558* ⊕ *iccjer.co.il.*

Zappa at the Lab. This popular music venue hosts the country's top jazz, rock, and pop performers. Small and intimate, it's a great place to see Israel's best musicians close up. Dinner and drinks are usually available. Posters around town announce upcoming concerts. ⊠ *28 Hebron Rd., German Colony* ☎ *03/762–6666* ⊕ *www.zappa-club.co.il.*

THEATER

The Israel Festival, held in May or June in the Jerusalem Theatre, is your best bet for quality English-language productions.

Khan Theater. Set in a former stable, this intimate venue offers some special events in English. There's a beautiful courtyard and a charming coffee shop and bar. ⊠ *2 David Remez Sq., German Colony* ☎ *02/630–3600* ⊕ *www.khan.co.il.*

SHOPPING

Jerusalem offers distinctive gifts from modern jewelry to traditional crafts to religious icons. The top shopping spots are the Downtown area, the Old City, and the Mamilla outdoor mall. The Hutzot Hayotzer artists' collective just outside the Old City walls is another popular and particularly beautiful spot, where during the August Arts and Crafts Festival you can visit the studios of resident artists and enjoy open-air music performances at night.

Prices are generally fixed in the Center City and the Jewish Quarter of the Old City, although you can sometimes negotiate for significant discounts on expensive art and jewelry. However, bargaining is common practice in the Old City's colorful Arab bazaar, or souk (pronounced "shook" in Hebrew—rhymes with "book"); it's fascinating but can be a trap for the unwary.

Young fashion designers, often graduates of Jerusalem's Bezalel Academy of Arts and Design, have opened a stream of shops and boutiques. They're scattered throughout the city. Several galleries representing Israeli artists are close to the hotels on King David Street.

Stores generally open by 8:30 am or 9 am, and some close between 1 pm and 4 pm. A few still close on Tuesday afternoon, a traditional but less and less observed half day. Jewish-owned stores (that is, all of West Jerusalem and the Old City's Jewish Quarter) close on Friday afternoon by 2 pm or 3 pm, depending on the season and the kind of store (food and souvenir shops tend to stay open later), and reopen on Sunday morning. Some stores geared to the tourist trade, particularly Downtown, reopen on Saturday night after the Jewish Sabbath ends, especially in summer. Arab-owned stores in the Old City and East Jerusalem are busiest on Saturday and quietest on Sunday, when many (but not all) Christian storekeepers close for the day.

OLD CITY

JEWISH QUARTER
ART
Blue and White Art Gallery. Udi Merioz, the artist and owner of this gallery, does "soft painting," a special appliqué technique that uses synthetic fibers on canvas. The gallery also represents Israeli artist Yaacov Agam. ⊠ *1 Cardo St., Jewish Quarter* ☎ *02/628–8464* ⊕ *www.blueandwhiteart.com.*

MALLS AND SHOPPING CENTERS
Cardo. In the Old City's Jewish Quarter, the Cardo began life as the main thoroughfare of Byzantine Jerusalem. It was a commercial street during the Crusader era, and has now been converted into an attractive shopping area. Beyond souvenirs and Judaica, you'll find good-quality jewelry and artwork, although at quite high prices. ⊠ *Jewish Quarter St., Jewish Quarter.*

CHRISTIAN AND MUSLIM QUARTERS
ART
Elia Photo Service. Kevork Kahvedjian's collection of 3,500 photographic prints of Jerusalem and the Holy Land dating back to 1860 provides a window into a vanished world. Many of them have been published in history books and adorn the walls of local hotels and restaurants. All are available as high-quality prints in various sizes, mounted and ready for framing. ⊠ *14 Al-Khanka St., Christian Quarter* ☎ *02/628–2074* ⊕ *www.eliaphoto.com.*

CLOTHING
Fodor's Choice ★ **Bilal Abu Khalaf.** The family of Bilal Abu Khalaf has been trading in fine fabrics for Jerusalem's elite for three generations. The shop is an Aladdin's cave of Damascene silks woven with golden thread, Moroccan brocade set with semiprecious stones, and the finest fabrics from Kashmir. Phone ahead to arrange a riveting 20-minute presentation of the shop's most beautiful treasures, and an explanation of the Crusader church visible through the glass floor. ⊠ *164 Suq Aftimus, Muristan, Christian Quarter* ☎ *02/626–1718.*

Stores along the narrow streets of the souk in the Old City tempt passersby with food, fabrics, and ceramics.

CRAFTS

Jerusalem Pottery. Through a tiny passageway opposite the sixth Station of the Cross is the store of two fine local artisans, Stefan Karakashian and his son Hagop. Their particularly high-quality work includes plates, bowls, tiles, and plaques painted with peacocks and flowers. ⊠ *15 Via Dolorosa, Muslim Quarter* ☎ *02/626–1587* ⊕ *www.jerusalempottery.biz.*

Fodor's Choice
★

Sandrouni. This shop just inside the New Gate stocks intricately hand-painted ceramic tiles in any shape or size, from small decorative tiles to elaborate tiled mirrors, tables, and trays. From the Jaffa Gate, take the first left onto Latin Patriarch Road. ⊠ *New Gate Rd., Christian Quarter* ☎ *02/626–3744* ⊕ *www.sandrouni.com.*

MARKETS

Fodor's Choice
★

Souk. Jerusalem's main market is the souk in the Old City, spread over a warren of intersecting streets. This is where much of Arab Jerusalem shops. It's awash with color and redolent with the clashing scents of exotic spices. Baskets of produce vie for attention with hanging shanks of lamb, fresh fish on ice, and fresh-baked delicacies. Food stalls are interspersed with purveyors of fabrics and shoes. The baubles and trinkets of the tourist trade often seem secondary, except along the well-trodden paths of the Via Dolorosa, David Street, and Christian Quarter Road.

Haggling with merchants in the Arab market—a time-honored tradition—is not for everyone. If you know what you want and what you are willing to pay, it can be fun to try to knock the price down; if not, enjoy the local color and seek out shops with set prices, either in the Old City or outside its walls. ■ **TIP→** Women should dress modestly, and everyone should keep an eye on their purses and wallets. ⊠ *Muslim Quarter.*

ARMENIAN QUARTER

CRAFTS

Hagop Antreassian's. The standouts in Armenian Hagop Antreassian's studio are his wonderful large bowls. They won't fit in your carry-ons, but the owner is happy to ship your orders. You can often find him painting or firing his clay creations in his studio just inside Zion Gate. ⊠ *Armenian Patriarchate St., opposite Zion Gate, Armenian Quarter* ☎ *054/300–8577.*

WEST JERUSALEM

CRAFTS

Klein. Israeli prime ministers have been shopping for gifts here since 1951. This is the factory showroom, and it stocks everything from high-quality olive-wood cutting boards to attractive trays decorated with Armenian pottery tiles. ⊠ *3 Ziv St., at Bar Ilan St., Tel Arza* ☎ *02/538–9992* ⊕ *www.aklein.co.il.*

Ruth Havilio. Artist Ruth Havilio makes hand-painted tiles that can make your table shine, give your floors a shot of Middle Eastern color, or brighten up a child's room. You can have your tiles personalized, but keep in mind that this can't be done on the spot. To get there, take the alley to the left of St. John's Church. Part of the charm of the gallery is its evocative courtyard setting. ⊠ *18 Ein Kerem St., Ein Kerem* ☎ *02/641–7912.*

MALLS AND SHOPPING CENTERS

Malcha Mall. Known locally as Kenyon Malcha, this huge shopping mall is—at 500,000 square feet—one of the largest in the Middle East. It includes a department store, a supermarket, and almost 200 shops and eateries, all near the train station to Tel Aviv. ⊠ *1 Agudat Sport Maccabi St., Malcha* ☎ *02/679–1333* ⊕ *www.azrielimalls.co.il.*

CENTER CITY

ART

Motke Blum Studio. On Arts and Crafts Lane, Motke Blum does everything from soft-color oil paintings of abstract shapes to vivid cityscapes of Jerusalem. Visits are by appointment only. ⊠ *20 Hutzot Hayotzer, Center City* ☎ *02/623–4002* ⊕ *www.motkeblum.com.*

BEAUTY

Ahava Center. The store stocks all the company's products using minerals from the Dead Sea, but at less attractive prices than elsewhere. ⊠ *5 Ben-Yehuda St., Center City* ☎ *02/625–2592.*

Laline. This shop is known for its trademark white-and-black setting for luxe creams and soaps, all made in Israel. Additional branches are in the Malcha Mall and on Ben Yehuda Street. ⊠ *Alrov Mamilla Ave., Center City* ☎ *054/334–5032* ⊕ *www.laline.co.il.*

CLOTHING

Adi Kilav. This shop sells striking handmade leather shoes that you definitely won't find back home. Adi Kilav's classic lines reflect his training in architecture. ✉ *6 Shatz St., Center City* ☎ *02/563–3701* ⊕ *www. adikilav.com.*

Daniella Lehavi. Local designer Daniella Lehavi makes distinctive, well-crafted leather bags, shoes, and accessories. ✉ *Mamilla Ave., Center City* ☎ *02/624–3791* ⊕ *daniellalehavi.com.*

Him with the Shirts. Here's where to find a great array of T-shirts with clever slogans and designs, primarily in Hebrew. ✉ *3 Ben Sira St., Center City* ☎ *077/783–3499* ⊕ *www.h-i-h.co.il.*

Mikanmor. The Jerusalem outpost of a Tel Aviv design shop features beautifully executed leather bags, wallets, belts, and jewelry, including distinctive collar necklaces. You will probably spot some of the designers working on new pieces in the back. ✉ *18 Shlomzion HaMalka St., Center City* ☎ *02/650–9077* ⊕ *www.mikanmor.com.*

Naama Bezalel. Naama Bezalel specializes in decidedly feminine lines for a range of ages, as well as a selection of distinctly beautiful bridal dresses. ✉ *27 King George St., Center City* ☎ *02/625–5611* ⊕ *naama-bezalel.com.*

Poenta. This store offers a distinctive selection of Israeli designer clothing, bags, and jewelry. ✉ *5 Shlomzion Hamalka St., Center City* ☎ *02/628–7258.*

Ronen Chen. Simple, classic styles in very comfortable fabrics are this well-known Israeli clothing designer's hallmark. ✉ *6 Yitzhak Kariv St., Center City* ☎ *02/930–9463* ⊕ *www.ronenchen.com.*

Shoofra. Hip shoes from Europe, Israel, and the United States are the specialty at this shop, including mod boots and loafers from brands like the French Bensimon, the Dutch Bullboxer, and the Swedish Sneaky Steve. There's a second branch in the Malcha Mall. ✉ *18 Shlomzion Hamalka St., Center City* ☎ *02/623–3414* ⊕ *www.shoofra.co.il.*

Sofia. Owner Miri Ashur Zuta offers a well-honed selection of Israeli designer clothing and accessories. ✉ *2 Bezalel St., Center City* ☎ *02/625–2765.*

Sweet-T. Head here for a good selection of T-shirts ready for custom decoration. ✉ *5 Ben-Yehuda St., Center City* ☎ *02/624–9269* ⊕ *www. jerusalemtshirts.com.*

Tashtari. This exclusive boutique features owner Amos Sadan's outstanding "wearable art"—much of which is influenced by Japanese aesthetics—predominantly as elaborately beaded or woven headbands, scarves, and belts. ✉ *25 King George St., Center City* ☎ *02/625–3282* ⊕ *www. tashtari.com.*

CRAFTS

Cadim. A decidedly contemporary selection of ceramics is on view at this shop showcasing the works of 15 artists. ✉ *4 Yoel Salomon St., Center City* ☎ *02/623–4869.*

Fodor's Choice **Charlotte.** This 80-year-old shop carries colorful ceramics, weavings,
★ painted silks, and jewelry. ⊠ 4 Koresh St., Center City ☎ 02/625–1632.

Danny Azoulay. These delicate items in fine porcelain are all hand-painted
in rich shades of blue, red, and gold. Traditional Jewish ritual objects
include fine papercuts and a range of ornamental *ketubot* (wedding con-
tracts). Less expensive items include napkin rings and bottle stoppers.
⊠ 5 Yoel Salomon St., Center City ☎ 02/623–3918 ⊕ www.ketuba-
hazoulayart.com.

Darian Armenian Ceramics. Arman Darian's exacting painting can be seen
in prestigious buildings around Israel and the world. Besides ceramic
pieces with Jewish themes, the shop carries hand-painted tables and
mirrors and has a plentiful selection of bargain-priced seconds. You
can often catch Darian and his staff working on new designs. ⊠ 12
Shlomzion Hamalka St., Center City ☎ 02/623–4802.

Guild of Ceramicists. This shop beckons with its delightfully colorful tiled
steps. The functional and ornamental pottery is made by a dozen Israeli
artists, and many pieces are bright and cheerful. ⊠ 27 Yoel Salomon St.,
Center City ☎ 02/624–4065.

Judaicut. This shop sells traditional and affordable papercuts, a well-
established Jewish art form. These pieces make unusual gifts—to say
nothing of being both light and easy to pack. They can be customized
with your name. ⊠ 21 Yoel Salomon St., Center City ☎ 02/623–3634
⊕ www.judaicut.co.il.

Salomon. This is the Jerusalem outpost for David Gerstein, who creates brightly painted metal cutouts of bikers, flowers, butterflies, and
streetscapes. There's also a wide selection of handmade jewelry. ⊠ 6
Yoel Salomon St., Center City ☎ 02/623–6031.

Sari Srulovitch. The shop's award-winning hand-crafted silver tableware
and Jewish ceremonial objects combine traditional and modern themes
in distinctive designs with a clean, contemporary feel. ⊠ 7 Hutzot Hayotzer, opposite Jaffa Gate, Center City ☎ 02/628–6699 ⊕ www.sarisru-
lovitch.com.

Shemonah Beyachad. Roughly translated as "Eight All Together," this
cooperative shop shows and sells original ceramics, often in surprisingly
light, airy forms. ⊠ 11 Yoel Salomon St., Center City ☎ 02/624–7250.

HOME FURNISHINGS

A.B.C. A.B.C. is a homegrown label selling well-made gifts and accessories for the home. Their wooden boxes and apothecary bottles
wrapped in bamboo make unique gifts. ⊠ 25 King George St., Center
City ☎ 02/624–2549 ⊕ mygiftshop.co.il.

JEWELRY

Dan Alsberg. Jeweler Dan Alsberg has crafted outstanding modern gold
and silver pieces for more than 40 years. ⊠ 15 Hutzot Hayotzer, outside
Jaffa Gate, Center City ☎ 02/627–1430 ⊕ www.studioalsberg.com.

H. Stern. The Jerusalem flagship store of this international company offers high-quality pieces. ⊠ Alrov Mamilla Ave., Center City
☎ 02/624–2855 ⊕ www.hstern.co.il.

Hedya. This boutique carries the collections of owners Ze'ev and Sharon Tammuz, as well as other local artists. Necklaces and earrings are made from antique gold, silver, amber, and other materials that retain a feel of the past. ✉ *23 Hillel St., Center City* ☎ *02/622–1151.*

Idit. Offering an intriguing range of in-house designs, this family jewelry business is run by the children of the founder, craftsman Chaim Paz. ✉ *23 King George St., Center City* ☎ *02/622–1911* ⊕ *www.iditjewelry.com.*

Michal Negrin. Whimsical, vintage-inspired jewelry and fashion accessories have made Michal Negrin a girly favorite in Israel and around the world. There is another branch in the Malcha Mall. ✉ *Alrov Mamilla Ave., Center City* ☎ *02/624–2112* ⊕ *www.michalnegrin.com.*

Turquoise. Itzik Sasson has been creating chunky jewelry from pounded gold since 1989. He also has an intriguing collection of baubles made with aqua-color Roman glass from Caesarea. ✉ *8 Yoel Salomon St., Center City* ☎ *02/624–1192.*

LOCAL SPECIALTIES

Jerusalem Experience. This is the place for items of religious interest and handmade Judaica. The friendly staff is happy to show you Israeli perfumes, Dead Sea skin-care products, olive wood, boutique wines, and books about Jerusalem and other aspects of Israel. ✉ *17 Jaffa St., opposite Safra Sq., Center City* ☎ *02/622–3030.*

MALLS AND SHOPPING CENTERS

Arts and Crafts Lane. Outside Jaffa Gate, Hutzot Hayotzer is home to goldsmiths and silversmiths specializing in jewelry, fine art, and Judaica, generally done in a modern, minimalist style. The work is of extremely high quality and priced accordingly. ✉ *Hutzot Hayotzer, Center City.*

Fodor's Choice
★
Designers in the City. More than 20 Israeli jewelry designers, leather workers, clothing makers, and ceramics artists have studios here, where you can watch them work and buy original items. ✉ *7 Bezalel St, Center City.*

King David Street. Prestigious stores and galleries, most with an emphasis on art, antiquities, jewelry, and Jewish ritual objects, line this avenue. ✉ *King David St., Center City.*

Mamilla Mall. Bordered by Old City's Jaffa Gate on one end and the Mamilla Hotel on the other, this open-air shopping center features such familiar clothing chains as Topshop and Zara. There's also a growing number of independent Israeli fashion and jewelry designers. The restaurants and cafés all have spectacular views. ✉ *Alrov Mamilla Ave., Center City* ⊕ *www.alrovmamilla.com.*

Midrachov. This pedestrian-only strip of Ben-Yehuda Street makes for a fun shopping experience. Street musicians serenade passersby and those seated at the many outdoor cafés. Summer evenings are lively, as the mall fills with peddlers of cheap jewelry and crafts. Some of the city's best restaurants are tucked into the nearby alleys. ✉ *Ben-Yehuda St., Center City.*

Yoel Moshe Salomon Street. In the old neighborhood of Nahalat Shiva, just off Zion Square, is the pedestrian-only Yoel Moshe Salomon Street. Between the restaurants on the main drag and in the adjacent alleys and courtyards, you'll find several crafts galleries, unique ceramics stores, and artsy jewelry and clothing shops. ✉ *Yoel Moshe Salomon St., Center City.*

MARKETS

Bezalel Arts Fair. Every Friday, local artists and craftspeople hawk handmade jewelry and bags, whimsical puppets, hefty wooden cutting boards, and other pieces at this art market in central Jerusalem. The pace is relaxed and friendly. Stalls run from the pedestrian section of Bezalel Street and continue onto Shatz Street to the small Schieber Park. ⊠ *Bezalel St., Center City.*

TOYS

Gaya. Well-crafted wooden toys and games fill the shelves of this vaulted underground shop. Kids are welcome to try out many of them. Gaya also has a branch at the First Station. ⊠ *7 Yoel Salomon St., Center City* ☎ *02/625–1515* ⊕ *gaya-game.co.il.*

GERMAN COLONY AND BAKA

BEAUTY

Fodor's Choice ★ **Sabon Shel Paam.** Sabon—Hebrew for soap—sells its aromatic herb-infused soaps, creams, and lotions all around the world. The ritual hand washing in the shop is a delight. There's another branch in the Malcha Mall. ⊠ *35 Emek Refa'im St., German Colony* ☎ *02/650–6644* ⊕ *www.sabon.co.il/en.*

CLOTHING

Osfa. Carrying well-chosen pieces by local designers, this small but well-stocked boutique has a friendly staff that knows its wares. ⊠ *53 Bethlehem Rd., Baka* ☎ *02/672–8815* ⊕ *www.osfacollect.com.*

Pashmina. Here you'll find a wonderful selection of Israeli-designed clothing, jewelry, shoes, belts, and bags. Let the owner, Michal, or her skilled assistants advise you; they know their inventory and are helpful without being pushy. ⊠ *4 HaMelitz St., German Colony* ☎ *02/561–0567.*

CRAFTS

Barbara Shaw. Australian immigrant Barbara Shaw has put her colorful, contemporary stamp on a selection of household gifts, from crisp dish towels and whimsical aprons to soft pillows and roomy tote bags. ⊠ *26 Emek Refa'im St., German Colony* ☎ *02/579–9621* ⊕ *www.barbarashawgifts.com.*

Hoshen. Jewelry and attractive items in wood, ceramics, and fabric are available at Hoshen. ⊠ *32 Emek Refa'im St., German Colony* ☎ *02/563–0966.*

Jerusalem House of Quality. Here you'll discover the work of 20 excellent Israeli craftspeople working in ceramics, glass, jewelry, sculpture, and wood. You can join them for a crafts workshop in their studios on the second floor. The store offers guided tours in English on the history of art in Jerusalem as well as on the building itself, which served as a hospital during the British Mandate. ⊠ *12 Hebron Rd., German Colony* ☎ *02/671–7430* ⊕ *www.art-jerusalem.com.*

Nisha. This shop displays an ample selection of reasonably priced Israeli crafts, from FIMO clay jewelry to whimsical pottery. There's a second branch at 43 Emek Refa'im Street. ⊠ *31 Bethlehem Rd., Baka* ☎ *02/674–6060.*

Set. Solve your gift problems here with an array of different objects, from jewelry to art pieces, dishes to handbags, in both traditional and modern styles. A second branch is in the Mamilla Mall. ✉ *26 Emek Refa'im St., German Colony* ☎ *02/566-3366* ⊕ *set-gifts.com.*

JEWELRY

Keo. Handmade jewelry in delicate, modern designs is the specialty of this shop. ✉ *25 Emek Refa'im St., German Colony* ☎ *02/563-7026.*

Sheshet. The shop carries a solid selection of contemporary Israeli gold and silver jewelry, as well as locally designed leather bags, belts, and wallets. ✉ *34 Emek Refa'im St., German Colony* ☎ *02/566-2261.*

Stav. Exquisite, and exquisitely priced, pieces in gold or silver show a graceful mix of modern and traditional influences. ✉ *40 Emek Refa'im St., German Colony* ☎ *02/563-7059* ⊕ *www.stavjewelry.com.*

MALLS AND SHOPPING CENTERS

Emek Refa'im Street. This area is a great destination for shopping and people-watching from early morning to late at night. Jewelry is easy to find in a rainbow of styles and tastes. Food choices can be limited, so check out the options at First Station. ✉ *Emek Refa'im St., German Colony.*

AROUND JERUSALEM AND THE DEAD SEA

With Masada and Bethlehem

WELCOME TO AROUND JERUSALEM AND THE DEAD SEA

TOP REASONS TO GO

★ **Ein Gedi:** This oasis rich in flora, fauna, and archaeology—praised in the Bible for its beauty and today one of Israel's most impressive national parks—offers spectacular hiking near waterfalls and canyons.

★ **Masada:** The awe-inspiring remains of this mountaintop palace overlooking the Dead Sea recall its history as a retreat for Herod the Great and as the last stand of the Jewish rebels against Rome in AD 73.

★ **Dead Sea:** At the lowest point on Earth, float effortlessly on one of the world's saltiest bodies of water, renowned for its therapeutic qualities. In Ein Bokek, cover yourself with the mud and check in to a resort.

★ **Bethlehem:** Follow in the footsteps of Jesus from the Church of the Nativity to the grotto where Mary nursed him.

★ **Judean Hills wineries:** Close to Jerusalem, this area is home to more than two dozen wineries that produce some excellent and highly prized wines.

1 Masada and the Dead Sea. Herod the Great's desert retreat would be an extraordinary archaeological site even if it had never made it into the history books. But Masada is also famous for being where hundreds of Jews committed suicide rather than surrender to Rome. Hike (or take the cable car) to the top of the plateau for sunrise over the Dead Sea. Afterward, take a relaxing dip in this saltiest of all lakes. Combine a visit with a trip to Ein Gedi or Ein Bokek, both near the Dead Sea, for unforgettable desert adventures.

2 West of Jerusalem. The picturesque Judean Hills are dotted with natural springs and forested nature reserves, as well as outstanding wineries, boutique breweries, rustic restaurants, and farms making great goat cheese. Pack a picnic and take the winding road to visit Soreq Cave and Beit Guvrin National Park.

3 Bethlehem. A few miles south of Jerusalem in the West Bank, visit the birthplace of Jesus, today marked by the Church of the Nativity on Manger Square, and try some tasty Palestinian cuisine.

GETTING ORIENTED

3

The wealth of beautiful land-scapes, historical treasures, and biblical sites within an easy drive of Jerusalem makes a number of good day trips. To the west lie the Judean Hills, covered with vineyards and farms. To the south is Bethlehem, an age-old pilgrimage site for Christians. To the east is the Judean Desert, graced with fertile oases like Jericho and Ein Gedi. Descending from Jerusalem's peaks, you quickly arrive at the Dead Sea—the lowest point on the face of Earth. Ein Bokek, near the Dead Sea's southern end, is a good place to float in its warm, salty water.

Updated by
Shira Rubin

The Judean Hills that encircle Jerusalem, together with the wilderness that slopes precipitously eastward to the Dead Sea, host an astonishing range of scenery: springs and oases, forests and fields, caves, hiking trails, and impressive archaeological sites such as Masada. West of the city, farmers are coaxing grapes from the valley where David once battled Goliath. The area is becoming more popular with a wide range of travelers, thanks to its wineries, breweries, and boutique cheese and olive oil producers.

The Judean Desert–Dead Sea area—little changed from when Abraham wandered here with his flocks—contrasts sharply with the lush greenery of the oases of Ein Gedi, Ain Fashkha, and the verdant fields of Jericho. Nomadic Bedouin still herd sheep and goats, though you notice some concessions to modernity: pickup trucks are parked beside camels.

The route along the Dead Sea shore is hemmed in by towering brown cliffs fractured by *wadis,* or dry riverbeds. Ein Gedi has two of the most spectacular of these wadis, Nahal David and Nahal Arugot. In Ein Bokek, near the southern end of the Dead Sea, you can settle into one of the numerous health and beauty spas that make use of the Dead Sea's saline waters and medicinal mud.

North of Ein Bokek is Masada, Herod the Great's mountaintop palace-fortress built more than 2,000 years ago, which is a UNESCO World Heritage Site. Overlooking the Dead Sea, the king's extravagant architectural feat still displays ingenious water systems, elaborate frescoes, mosaic floors, and bathhouses. Add the human drama of the last Jewish stand against Rome during the Great Revolt, and it's easy to understand why this is one of the most visited sights in Israel.

Just south of Jerusalem, Bethlehem is a major site of Christian pilgrimage. The Church of the Nativity, the oldest church in the country, erected in the 4th century, is built over the grotto where Christian tradition holds Jesus was born. The West Bank Palestinian city of roughly 30,000 sits on the ancient highway through the rocky Judean Hills. Farmers tend century-old terraces of olives, figs, and grapes all around the ancient city.

AROUND JERUSALEM AND THE DEAD SEA PLANNER

WHEN TO GO

The Dead Sea region is pleasant between October and April but suffers from searing dry heat during the summer. Beginning the day with a tour of Masada can help beat the heat and the crowds. Ein Bokek, with its unique hotels and spas by the Dead Sea, attracts visitors even in broiling hot summer. Bethlehem is best early or late in the day if you want to avoid the crowds. Before you set out, check the hours for the Church of the Nativity. The area to the west of Jerusalem is agreeable any time of the year.

Some advance planning pays off if you want to visit this region during a religious holiday, since transportation can be difficult during Jewish holidays like Yom Kippur and the Muslim observance of Ramadan. On Passover, Israelis tend to mob the Dead Sea. Similarly, Christmas is celebrated three times in Jerusalem and Bethlehem, according to the Western, Orthodox, and Armenian rites. Visit Bethlehem's Manger Square on Christmas Eve for an unforgettable holiday, but book hotels far in advance.

PLANNING YOUR TIME

The Dead Sea can be a great day trip from Jerusalem, but you have a richer experience if you spend a few nights in Ein Bokek or other hotels in the area. An ideal itinerary might be: On the first morning, climb Masada and marvel at the views, then head to your Ein Bokek hotel for an afternoon at the Dead Sea; watch the hills of Jordan redden as the sun sets. On the second day, drive to Ein Gedi (a half hour north of Ein Bokek) for the waterfalls and a dip in the pools. On the third day, stop in Jericho on the way back to Jerusalem.

When traveling to Bethlehem, Jericho, and other areas under Palestinian control, you need to present your passport at the checkpoint. This usually just takes a minute if you're traveling by car. There can be traffic crossing back from Bethlehem to Jerusalem, so allow extra time. Be aware that some of the Dead Sea beaches and the Ahava factory store mentioned in this section are actually in the West Bank, though under Israeli control.

GETTING HERE AND AROUND

BUS TRAVEL

Egged buses are modern, air-conditioned, and reasonably priced. Service is dependable on main routes but infrequent to outlying rural districts. Egged buses don't run from sunset Friday to sunset Saturday.

From the Beersheva Central Bus Station, buses depart four times a day for Arad, Ein Bokek, and other southern points. For Ein Bokek, there's also a daily 8:40 am bus from Tel Aviv's Arlozorov Bus Station (a three-hour ride) and several buses, departing on the hour, from Jerusalem (a two-hour journey). There is a bus line that drops passengers at the front door of the Ein Gedi Hotel. Buses can be crowded, especially on Friday and Sunday. You can't buy tickets or reserve seats by phone for the above routes; go to the bus station early and be aware that buses often are off schedule.

Buses to Bethlehem and Beit Jala run from the Palestinian bus station at Damascus Gate in Jerusalem's Old City. Expect to be stopped and checked by Israeli troops on the way back to Jerusalem.

CAR TRAVEL

Driving is preferable to relying on public transportation here, as some sights are on secondary roads where bus service is scarce. Highway conditions are good, and most destinations are signposted in both Hebrew and English. The steep road between Arad and Ein Bokek has one hairpin turn after another. Unless otherwise posted, stick to the intercity speed of 90 kph (56 mph). Budget extra time for leaving Jerusalem during rush hours. Gas stations are plentiful; some are open 24 hours, but play it safe and keep the tank at least half full.

If you plan to drive to areas controlled by the Palestinian Authority, several East Jerusalem car-rental companies have insurance for the West Bank. Always check whether there's political unrest that could make roads unsafe. Throw a *keffiyeh,* the traditional checkered headscarf, onto your dashboard for extra security.

SHERUT TRAVEL

Sheruts, or shared taxis seating up to 10 passengers, run set routes (usually along major bus routes) and charge a nominally more expensive fare. These run on Saturday between Tel Aviv and Jerusalem. Known in Arabic as *serveeses,* they run to Bethlehem and Jericho from East Jerusalem's Damascus Gate, though an Arab taxi may be delayed at military checkpoints.

TRAIN TRAVEL

Israel Railways has regular—but slow—train service between Jerusalem and Tel Aviv, hourly from 6 am to 8 pm, from the southern neighborhood of Malcha; there are occasional departures from the Jerusalem Biblical Zoo. The beautiful 40-minute ride through forested hills to the Judean lowlands is spectacular for the scenery alone and includes a stop at Beit Shemesh.

RESTAURANTS

Some Judean Hills wineries serve fancy meals along with their tastings, but these should be reserved in advance. Abu Gosh, on the way to Latrun, is known for its hummus and kebab restaurants. There are also some passable cafeterias west of Jerusalem and a handful of excellent restaurants set in the hills. An alternative is to take a packed lunch or have a picnic west of Jerusalem with wine and cheese. At the Dead Sea, it's always a good idea to make reservations in Ein Bokek restaurants, especially on Friday and Saturday night.

HOTELS

Visitors, national and international, who come to "take the waters" and enjoy the serene desert scenery, heavily use the lodgings in the Dead Sea region. On the northern shore, facilities range from youth hostels to kibbutz inns. Although they might conjure up visions of spartan plain-ness, the kibbutz inns are surprisingly comfortable. They also give you a chance to see life on the communal settlements firsthand.

Along the southern shore, hotels in sunny Ein Bokek run from family-style simplicity to huge resorts, many of which were once hailed as the country's finest but have in recent years been subject to some neglect. Shuttle buses link hotels with each other and the center of town. A beauti-ful and luxurious spa with a wide range of facilities is an important fea-ture of each large hotel and many smaller hotels as well. The high seasons are mid-March to mid-June, and mid-September to the end of November.

Since visitors typically explore the area west of Jerusalem on a day trip, lodgings are few and far between. The exceptions are some fine bed-and-breakfast–style guesthouses known as *zimmers*.

Hotel reviews have been shortened. For more information, visit Fodors.com.

WHAT IT COSTS			
$	$$	$$$	$$$$
Restaurants	Under NIS 50	NIS 50–NIS 75	NIS 76–NIS 100	over NIS 100
Hotels	Under $200	$200–$300	$301–$400	over $400

Restaurant prices are the average cost of a main course at dinner in NIS (Israeli shekels) or, if dinner isn't served, at lunch. Hotel prices, given in U.S. dollars, are the lowest cost of a standard double room in high season. Non-Israeli citizens pay-ing in foreign currency are exempt from the 17% V.A.T. on hotel rooms.

TOURS

Bus tours pick you up and return you to your hotel in Jerusalem: very convenient. Egged and United have full-day tours of Masada, the Dead Sea, and Ein Gedi daily for about $100 per person from Jerusalem. *For more information see Tours in Travel Smart.*

Abraham Tours. This well-regarded company offers a variety of packages to Masada and the Dead Sea, as well as the West Bank. ☎ *02/566–0045* ⊕ *www.abrahamtours.com.*

Eshcolot Tours. This Jerusalem-based company runs tours of the region, including around the Dead Sea. ☎ *02/566–5555, 052/321–1377.*

MASADA AND THE DEAD SEA

The 4,000-foot descent from Jerusalem to the Dead Sea is only 24 km (15 miles) but takes you on a journey from one climate to another. Annual precipitation plummets from 22 inches in Jerusalem to 2 inches at the Dead Sea. Still, the desert's proximity has always made it part of that city's consciousness. Refugees fled here, hermits sought its solitude; and when the Temple stood, on the Day of Atonement a scapegoat bearing the sins of the Jewish people was symbolically driven off its stark precipices.

GOOD SAMARITAN MUSEUM

20 km (13 miles) east of Jerusalem on Rte. 1 and 500 yards east of the junction with Rte. 458.

A popular spot for many tours, this site just east of Jerusalem is steeped in New Testament lore.

GETTING HERE AND AROUND

Follow Route 1 east from Jerusalem for 20 km (13 miles). The site is clearly signposted on the south side of the road. You need your own car, as buses do not stop here.

EXPLORING

FAMILY **Genesis Land.** On the scrubby mountains where Abraham likely walked, ride camels with actors dressed up as the patriarch and his manservant Eliezer. Young children find the reenactment of biblical stories enchanting, especially when they can enjoy making pita bread or eating lunch in a Bedouin-style tent overlooking the desert. Older children roll their eyes at the actors wearing simple robes over jeans and sneakers. ✉ *Off Rte. 458* ☎ *02/997–4477* ⊕ *www.genesisland.co.il* 🎟 *NIS 89* ☽ *Closed Sat.*

Good Samaritan Museum. About 2,000 years ago, thieves ambushed a man traveling the Jerusalem–Jericho road, and only one passing Samaritan bothered to help him, dragging him to a nearby inn (Luke 10). Today, on what may be the same spot, is this museum, housed in a restored Ottoman inn. It's an extensive collection of intricate mosaics scraped off the floors of churches, synagogues, and Samaritan houses of worship in Gaza and the West Bank. When you visit, ask to see the silent film about the parable dating from the 1920s, filmed on the very same arid hills that stretch for miles from the museum. The staff here has plenty of information and maps about nearby sites and trails as well. The museum is 8 km (5 miles) east of Maaleh Adumim. ✉ *Rte. 1, Maaleh Adumim* ☎ *02/633–8230* ⊕ *www.parks.org.il* 🎟 *NIS 22.*

JERICHO

35 km (22 miles) east of Jerusalem.

The sleepy oasis of Jericho—full of date palms, orange groves, banana plantations, bougainvillea bushes, and papaya trees—is aptly called *Ariha,* or "fragrant," in Arabic. This oldest continuously inhabited city in the world is immortalized as the place where "the walls came tumblin' down" at the sound of Joshua's trumpets. Those ramparts haven't been found, but the ruins of Hisham's Palace give you an idea of the devastating power of an earthquake at a time when cities were built of mud, wood, and stone.

The Palestinian population of about 25,000 is mostly Muslim, but the tiny Christian minority is well represented by a number of landmark churches and monasteries. These biblical and archaeological sites are what draws most tourists today.

Continued on page 164

THE DEAD SEA
A NATURAL WONDER

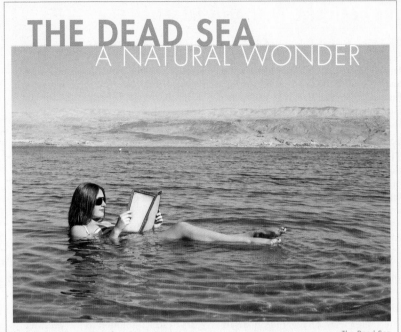

The Dead Sea

Taking a dip in the Dead Sea is a must-do experience in Israel. This unique body of water—the shores of which are the lowest point of dry land on Earth—was a resort for King Herod in the 1st century BC and the site of Queen Cleopatra's cosmetics empire.

Today, though, the Dead Sea is slowly dying. A combination of less rainfall in the region and Israeli and Jordanian diversion of the Jordan river for irrigation has caused its waters to recede at a rapid rate, threatening the area's ecology.

Israel started developing the Dead Sea as a tourist destination in the 1950s. Today, more than a dozen hotels in the area take advantage of the Dead Sea's mineral-rich mud and waters, known for nourishing, cleansing, and stimulating the skin, as well as for therapeutic benefits for treating medical conditions. Spas offer an array of services: body wraps, mud massages, facial peels, and the like, in addition to general amenities such as Jacuzzis and saunas.

It's an easy day-trip from Jerusalem, but spending the night allows you to watch the sun rise over Jordan. After a day on the beach, you can head back to your hotel for lunch and a spa treatment, followed by a Turkish bath or a dip in a warm sulfur pool.

THE DEAD SEA: PAST AND PRESENT

The stark, beautiful shores of the Dead Sea are literally the lowest point of dry land on Earth, at 1,373 feet below sea level. It's called the Dead Sea because virtually nothing can live in it; with a salt concentration of about 32%, the water is almost 9 times saltier than the ocean.

WHY IS THE DEAD SEA SALTY?

The Dead Sea is salty because water flows in from the Jordan River and other sources, but has no way of flowing out. Evaporation leaves a massive amount of salt behind. Beaches here aren't sandy—they're caked with hardened crystals of salt. The consistently dry air surrounding the Dead Sea has a high oxygen content, low pollution and allergen levels, and weakened ultraviolet radiation.

HOW DID THE DEAD SEA FORM?

The high mesas of the Judean desert nearby, also below sea level, bear testimony to the millions of years of geological changes that created this unique place. The Dead Sea was formed by fault lines shifting in the Earth's crust, a process that began about 15 million years ago and created the basin where the Dead Sea is now located.

WHY IS THE DEAD SEA IN DANGER?

Since it receives a maximum of 2 to 4 inches of rain per year, the Dead Sea's main source of water is the Jordan River, and by extension, the Sea of Galilee to the north.

The Dead Sea's water levels have fluctuated greatly over the last 10,000 years. However, its shores have significantly receded in the past few decades—about one meter per year—due to the lack of rainfall in Israel's north and human activity. Israel, Jordan, and Syria all divert water away from the Jordan River for drinking and irrigation. Less than 7% of the river's original flow reaches the Dead Sea.

WHAT'S BEING DONE TO STOP IT?

Israel and Jordan have been in talks for years to seek a solution to this pressing environmental problem. Currently the countries hope to build a canal to pump water into the Dead Sea from the Red Sea. Environmentalists are concerned about the possible negative impacts of such a canal both on the Dead Sea and on the Arava region. No firm plans to move forward have been announced. To find out more, visit www.foeme.org.

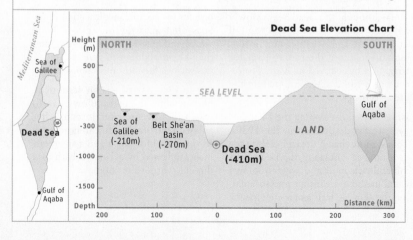

EXPERIENCING THE SPAS AND BEACHES

Before booking at a hotel or spa, carefully check what services it offers and whether any particular areas are closed for the season or for repairs. Quality of treatments at the spas can vary widely.

ENJOYING THE WATER

When entering the Dead Sea, wear flip flops or waterproof sandals, as the sea's floor has a rough, rock salt surface. Before getting in the water, check for the nearest source of fresh water, in case you get painful salt water in your eyes. Lean back slowly and rise gently, and be careful not to splash water toward yourself or others.

Small wounds such as scratches will burn for a few moments, but avoid getting salt water in any deep or open wounds. Don't stay in the Dead Sea (or in the spas' warmed mineral pools) for more than 15 minutes at a time, and drink plenty of water afterward.

GETTING MUDDY

It can be surprisingly difficult to find free Dead Sea mud. Some hotels pump the mud to their grounds, or provide vats of it at their beach. You can also purchase more refined mud in packets and apply it at the beach for your photos.

(top) People sunbathing on the shores of the Dead Sea. (bottom) Covered in Dead Sea mud

Bring a friend to the mudbaths so that you can help each other slather the dark goo on every inch of exposed skin. Cake it on evenly but thinly, so that it will dry within 15–20 minutes in the sun. You might need a third person to take pictures, unless you want mud on your camera!

Dead Sea products, including salts and mud, make great gifts and are available at all the spas, but note that similar items may be available at your local health food store at home.

GETTING HERE AND AROUND

Follow Route 1 east from Jerusalem for 35 km (21 miles), then turn north on Old Route 90. Jericho is clearly signposted. Egged bus drivers drop you off at the side of Route 1, but it's still 5 km (3 miles) to Jericho. Arab serveeses from Damascus Gate go to Azariya (Abu Dis); another shared taxi goes from there to Jericho. Serveeses also travel from Bethlehem to Jericho.

TIMING

Jericho is very pleasant during the winter months but swelteringly hot in the summer.

SAFETY AND PRECAUTIONS

As always, it's wise to check on the political situation before venturing into the Palestinian Authority. There are seldom problems in Jericho, however. Although there are no restrictions on tourists in private cars visiting the town, you need to present your foreign passport to reenter Israeli-controlled territory. Only Palestinian car-rental companies have insurance for driving in the West Bank. Another option is to hire a driver or visit with a tour group.

EXPLORING

TOP ATTRACTIONS

Hisham's Palace. Known as Khirbet al-Mafjar in Arabic, this restored palace has exquisite stonework and a spectacular mosaic floor. Hisham was a scion of the Umayyad dynasty, which built the Dome of the Rock and al-Aqsa Mosque in Jerusalem. Although the palace was severely damaged by the great earthquake of AD 749 while still under construction, the surviving mosaics and stone and plaster reliefs are evidence of its splendor. A small gatehouse leads into a wide courtyard dominated by a star-shape stone window that once graced an upper floor. Several sections of the fine geometric mosaics have been left exposed; others are covered by sand. The most impressive part of the complex is the reception room, off the plaza. Its intricate mosaic floor, depicting a lion hunting gazelles, is one of the most beautiful in the country. (At the time of this writing, a carpet covered the floor during renovation work.) The balustrade of an ornamental pool reflects the artistic influences of both East and West. Fragments of ornate stucco reliefs are still visible on some of the walls.

To get here go north from the traffic circle that constitutes downtown Jericho, follow Hisham's Palace Road for 4 km (2½ miles), turn right at the sign to Hisham's Palace after the Police Intelligence Building, and then take an immediate left down a 1-km (½-mile) access road. ⊠ *Hisham's Palace Rd.* ☎ *02/232–2522* ⊠ *NIS 10.*

Fodor'sChoice
★

Jericho Cable Car. To the west of Tel Jericho is the Mount of Temptation, identified by tradition as the "exceedingly high mountain" from which Satan tempted Jesus with dominion over "all the kingdoms of the world" (Matthew 4). Departing from a ticket booth facing Tel Jericho, a cable car (locals know it by the French: "Téléphérique") brings riders up and down the mountain. You can see all of Jericho and parts of Jordan from the restaurant at the cable car's upper station. Halfway down the mountain sits the remarkable Greek Orthodox monastery of

Qarantal, the name being a corruption of *quarantena*—a period of 40 days (the source of the English word *quarantine*)—the period of Jesus's temptation. Built into the cliff face in 1895 on Byzantine and Crusader remains, it is flanked by caves that once housed hermits. ⌧ *Ain as-Sultan St.* ☎ *02/232–1590* ⊕ *www.jericho-cablecar.com* ⌧ *NIS 60 round-trip.*

Qasr Al Yahud. This is the site where Jesus is said to have been baptized (Matthew 3:13–17), and where the Israelites crossed the Jordan River to enter the Promised Land (Joshua 3). Back then, the Jordan was a mighty, roaring river; today, it is little more than a silty creek which environmentalists say is polluted, but the Parks Authority says is certifiably clean. Facilities include a wooden deck, changing rooms, and an inexpensive gift shop. You can almost shake hands with the Jordanian soldier guarding the opposite bank. The route to the water is lined on either side by mines and barbed wire, but old monasteries lend a holy air to the place. Bring modest clothing if you plan to go under. ⌧ *Off Rte. 90* ☎ *02/650–4844* ⊕ *www.parks.org.il* ⌧ *Free.*

Russian Museum. Russian funding has given a glorious status to the gnarled sycamore that tradition identifies as the Tree of Zacchaeus, which the chief tax collector climbed to get a better look at Jesus (Luke 19:1–4). The Russian Museum was built as a Greek-style palace just behind the tree and houses an extensive collection of Palestinian artifacts and archaeological finds. Behind the museum is a sprawling garden complex with lush green lawns and towering palm trees. ⌧ *Medvedev St.* ✛ *As you reach Jericho via Rte. 1, take left fork at traffic island. When road swings to left, look for museum on right* ☎ *02/231–3007* ⌧ *NIS 20.*

Tel Jericho. Also called Tel es-Sultan (Sultan's Hill), the archaeological site of Tel Jericho covers the legendary ancient city. Nearly 200 years of excavations have still not uncovered the walls that fell when Joshua stormed the city in the mid-13th century BC. The most impressive ruins unearthed are a massive tower and wall, remains of the world's oldest walled city. Little is known about these early urbanites, who lived here in the Neolithic period between 7800 and 6500 BC, or why they needed such fortifications thousands of years before they became common in the region. Across the road is Ain as-Sultan, or the Sultan's Spring. The name comes from the prophet Elijah's miracle of sweetening the water with a bowl of salt (II Kings 2:19–22). The waters are still eminently drinkable if you wish to refill your bottles. To the east in Jordan are the mountains of the biblical kingdoms of Ammon and Moab, among them the peak of Mount Nebo, from which Moses viewed the Promised Land before dying at the ripe old age of 120.

To get to Tel Jericho by car, drive along Old Route 90, the main road through Jericho, and turn left at the traffic circle onto Ain as-Sultan Street. The parking lot is about 2 km (1 mile) down the road. ⌧ *Ain as-Sultan St.* ☎ *02/232–4815* ⌧ *NIS 10.*

WORTH NOTING

FAMILY **Auja Eco Center.** This tiny Palestinian village north of Jericho has turned an acute water shortage into an ecotourism opportunity at this center. Established by Friends of the Earth Middle East, it brings together Palestinian, Israeli, and Jordanian environmentalists. The knowledgeable staff leads hikes in the surrounding areas, including a moonlit trek in the stark desert and visits to nearby Bedouin communities that are also suffering from diminished water supplies. A rooftop restaurant offers traditional food with lovely views of the area. Curious teens enjoy the displays on recycling, while younger children can enjoy the playground. There's an 11-room B&B should you wish to sleep over. ✉ *Rte. 90 ✛ 13 km (9 miles) north of Jericho* ☎ *02/231–0424, 059/884–4006* ⊕ *www. aujaecocenter.org* ✍ *NIS 1,000 for group hike (6–18 people), including lunch; NIS 400 for group tour and visit to Bedouin village.*

WHERE TO EAT

$$ ✕ **Abu Omar Shaabi Restaurant.** Sheets of golden baklava line the walls
MIDDLE EASTERN of this bakery, steps from Jericho's main square. The *bourma*, a sugary rope of angel-hair-like dough wrapped around whole pistachios, is the ideal complement to strong, black Arabic coffee. Locals flock to the attached restaurant for grilled chicken or lamb served with fresh salads and hummus. ⑤ *Average main: NIS 50* ✉ *Arrasheed St. ✛ Off main square* ☎ *02/232–3429* ▭ No credit cards.

$$ ✕ **Limonah.** Sun-dappled tables under green palm leaves and passion-
MIDDLE EASTERN fruit plants provide a delightful setting for Palestinian basics done right
FAMILY on Jericho's main restaurant street. The minty lemonade is a revela-
Fodor'sChoice tion after a hot day. Middle Eastern mezze salads are delicious, as is
★ the whole grilled fish drenched in a garlicky lemon sauce. For dessert, there's an attached ice-cream shop, or you can ask for sweets like baklava. Kids can escape to an on-site playground while parents enjoy beer or a water pipe. Look for the giant lemon outside the entrance. ⑤ *Average main: NIS 70* ✉ *1 Muntazahat St.* ☎ *02/231–2977.*

$$ ✕ **Sultan.** Reached by the Jericho Cable Car, this restaurant is the only
MIDDLE EASTERN cup of coffee (and the only place selling lunch) near the Qarantal mon-
FAMILY astery. Tables are scattered on terraces built into the mountainside. Try sipping a cup of coffee or a fresh fruit juice while taking in the views of the oasis below. The menu includes grilled meats, hummus, salads, and some Western foods like pasta. Sultan closes at 7 pm daily, except for Thursday and Friday, when it is open later. ⑤ *Average main: NIS 50* ✉ *Qarantal St.* ☎ *02/232–1590* ⊕ *jericho-cablecar.com.*

$$ ✕ **Temptation.** The closest restaurant to Tel Jericho (they share a park-
MIDDLE EASTERN ing lot), this touristy spot serves standard versions of grilled meat and chicken, Palestinian standards like hummus and salads, and a wide range of mezzes (Middle Eastern salads). Buffet lunches are a good value, though some customers note inattentive service and unclean facilities. ⑤ *Average main: NIS 50* ✉ *Ain as-Sultan St.* ☎ *02/232–2614* ⊕ *www.temptationcenter.com/restaurants.html.*

WHERE TO STAY

$$ ☖ **Oasis Hotel.** A Moorish-inspired lobby decorated with soaring stone
RESORT arches lets you know that you've arrived at a sumptuous desert resort, as do the pools that sparkle in the arid valley. **Pros:** lovely pools; plenty of amenities; great value. **Cons:** smoking allowed in some public areas; not within walking distance of downtown. ⑤ *Rooms from: $210* ✉ *Jerusalem– Jericho Rd.* ☎ *02/231–1200* ⊕ *oasis-jericho.ps* ⤷ *181 rooms* ◎*Breakfast.*

The dryness of Qumran helped preserve the Dead Sea Scrolls stored in caves in the sculpted rock.

QUMRAN NATIONAL PARK

13 km (8 miles) south of the Almog Junction on Rte. 90, 20 km (13 miles) south of Jericho, 50 km (31 miles) east of Jerusalem.

If you're interested in archaeology, Qumran definitely should be on your itinerary. This is where the famous Dead Sea Scrolls were unearthed, and the museum here recounts the amazing story of how they were discovered and how they contributed to our understanding of the world.

GETTING HERE AND AROUND

Follow Route 1 east from Jerusalem for 50 km (31 miles), turning south on Route 90. Qumran is on the right. Not far from Qumran are some Dead Sea beaches worth a stop if you have a car. Qumran is in the West Bank, but cars are routinely waved through the checkpoints.

SAFETY AND PRECAUTIONS

Check the weather forecast before hiking in the winter. On rare occasions, flash floods cause closures on Route 90.

EXPLORING

Fodor's Choice ★ **Qumran National Park.** The sandy caves in the cliffs north of the Dead Sea yielded the most significant archaeological find ever made in Israel: the Dead Sea Scrolls. These biblical, apocryphal, and sectarian religious texts were found under extraordinary circumstances in 1947 when a young Bedouin goatherd stumbled on a cave containing scrolls in earthen jars. Because the scrolls were made from animal hide, he first went to a shoemaker to turn them into sandals. The shoemaker alerted a local antiquities dealer, who brought them to the attention of Professor Eliezer Sukenik of the Hebrew University of Jerusalem. Six other major scrolls and hundreds of fragments have since been discovered in 11 of the caves, and some are on display in Jerusalem's Israel Museum.

Most scholars believe that the Essenes, a Jewish separatist sect that set up a monastic community here in the late 2nd century BC, wrote the scrolls. During the Jewish revolt against Rome (AD 66–73), they apparently hid their precious scrolls in the caves before the site was destroyed in AD 68. Others contend the texts were brought from libraries in Jerusalem, possibly even the library of the Jewish Temple.

Almost all books of the Hebrew Bible were discovered here, many of them virtually identical to the texts still used in Jewish communities today. Sectarian texts were also found, including the constitution or "Community Rule," a description of an end-of-days battle ("The War of the Sons of Light Against the Sons of Darkness"), and the "Thanksgiving Scroll," containing hymns reminiscent of biblical psalms.

A short film at the visitor center introduces the mysterious sect that once lived here. Climb the tower for a good view, and note the elaborate system of channels and cisterns that gathered precious floodwater from the cliffs. Just below the tower is a long room some scholars have identified as the scriptorium. A plaster writing table and bronze and ceramic inkwells found here suggest that this may have been where the scrolls were written. You shouldn't need more than an hour to tour this site. ✉ *Rte. 90 ✛ 13 km (8 miles) south of Almog Junction* ☎ *02/994–2235* ⊕ *www.parks.org.il* ◉ *NIS 29.*

BEACHES AND POOLS

Qumran is conveniently located near some beaches on the Dead Sea. You can't actually swim in the briny water; you take a leisurely float in its incredible salinity, about 10 times that of the ocean. Anyone can enjoy the benefits of the mineral concentration in the Dead Sea water and mud, and the oxygen-rich atmosphere at the lowest point on Earth. Beach shoes or rubber sandals are a must, as the salt in the hypersaturated water builds up into sharp ridges that are hard to walk on. Any open cuts on your body sting when they encounter the briny water, so avoid shaving the day you go to the sea.

Biankini Beach. This beautiful beach has a spa with mineral treatments and massages and a Moroccan restaurant serving couscous on imported crockery. There is also a modest collection of cabins and a campsite for overnighters, plus a half-Olympic-sized freshwater pool for adults; kids can enjoy a wading pool and petting zoo. **Amenities:** food and drink; parking (free); showers; toilets. **Best for:** walking; swimming; sunset. ✉ *Off Rte. 90 ✛ 3 km (2 miles) north of Qumran* ☎ *02/940–0266* ⊕ *www.biankini1.com* ◉ *Fri., Sat. NIS 80; Sun.–Thurs. NIS 60.*

FAMILY **Einot Tzukim Nature Reserve.** Known for its freshwater springs, Einot Tzukim (also called Ein Fashkha) is a nature reserve with many species of trees and reeds not often found in the arid Judean Desert. You can swim in two shallow spring-fed pools, peek at the receding Dead Sea water, and visit an archaeological site from the Second Temple period and a manor from the Herodian period. Call ahead for free English tours on Sunday. Last entry is an hour before closure. **Amenities:**

food and drink; lifeguards; parking (free); showers; toilets. **Best for:** walking; swimming. ⊠ *Rte. 90* ⊕ *3 km (2 miles) south of Qumran* ☎ *02/994–2355* ⊕ *www.parks.org.il* ✉ *NIS 29.*

Kalia Beach. On the Dead Sea, Kalia Beach (the name derives from *kalium*, the Latin name for potassium, found in abundance here) is the place to go for a free mud bath. Slather your whole body with the mineral-rich black mud and let it dry before showering. The beach also has chair and towel rentals, a gift shop, and snack bar. The adjacent kibbutz has a swimming pool and guest rooms. **Amenities:** food and drink; lifeguards; parking (free); showers; toilets. **Best for:** swimming; walking. ⊠ *Off Rte. 90, 3 km (2 miles) north of Qumran* ☎ *02/994–2391* ⊕ *www.hof-kalia.co.il* ✉ *NIS 53.*

Neve Midbar Beach. South of Biankini Beach, Neve Midbar Beach stays open all night for camping and sometimes weddings, although swimming is allowed during daylight hours only. **Amenities:** food and drink; lifeguards; parking (free); showers; toilets. **Best for:** partiers; sunset; swimming. ⊠ *Rte. 90, 3 km (2 miles) north of Qumran* ☎ *050/202–8233* ⊕ *www.nevemidbar-beach.com* ✉ *NIS 85.*

EN ROUTE
Ahava Factory Visitors Center. Kibbutz Mitzpe Shalem manufactures the excellent Ahava skin- and hair-care products based on (but not smelling like) Dead Sea minerals, and the factory outlet here is 20 km (12½ miles) south of Qumran. There are plans to move the factory to the area of Ein Gedi. ⊠ *Rte. 90* ☎ *02/994–5123* ⊕ *www.ahavaus.com.*

EIN GEDI NATURE RESERVE

33 km (21 miles) south of Qumran, 20 km (12½ miles) north of Masada, 83 km (52 miles) southeast of Jerusalem.

After miles of burned brown and beige desert rock, the green lushness of the Ein Gedi oasis leaps out in vivid and unexpected contrast. This nature reserve is one of the most beautiful places in Israel—with everything from hiking trails to ancient ruins. Settled for thousands of years, it inspired the writer of the *Song of Songs* to describe his beloved "as a cluster of henna in the vineyards of Ein Gedi." Loads of waterfalls and gurgling springs make this an option for summer hiking, too.

GETTING HERE AND AROUND
Follow Route 1 east from Jerusalem for 50 km (31 miles), turning south on Route 90. Ein Gedi is on the right. Egged bus drivers drop you off at the side of Route 90. From there, it's a short walk to the gate of the nature reserve.

SAFETY AND PRECAUTIONS
Check the weather forecast before hiking in the winter. Flash floods are an occasional danger.

EXPLORING

FAMILY
Fodor'sChoice
★
Ein Gedi Nature Reserve. This beautiful nature reserve has a number of well-marked trails to explore, all of which are off the main entrance. It is home to Nahal David (David's Stream), and the cave at Nahal David is believed to be the place where David hid while Saul hunted him down 3,000 years ago (I Samuel 24:1–22). Walkers can also visit the canyon

Waterfalls, pools, and desert landscapes are among the pleasures awaiting hikers in Ein Gedi's nature reserve.

of Nahal Arugot and the remains of an ancient synagogue. Get a map from the admission booth and you can spend anywhere from an hour to a day here, depending on your interest in nature and hiking. Reaching Ein Gedi from the north, the first turnoff to the right is the parking lot at the entrance to the reserve.

The clearly marked trail to Nahal David rises past several pools and small waterfalls to the upper waterfall. There are many steps, but it's not too daunting. Allow at least 1¼ hours to include a dip under one of the lower waterfalls. Look out for ibex (wild goats), especially in the afternoon, and for the small, furry hyrax, often seen on tree branches. Leopards here face extinction because of breeding problems and are seldom seen nowadays.

If you're a serious hiker, don't miss the trail that breaks off to the right 50 yards down the return path from the top waterfall. It passes the remains of Byzantine irrigation systems and has breathtaking views of the Dead Sea. The trail doubles back on itself toward the source of Nahal David. Near the top, a short side path climbs to the remains of a 4th-millennium-BC Chalcolithic temple, the treasures of which can be seen in Jerusalem's Israel Museum. The main path leads on to the streambed, again turns east, and reaches Dudim Cave, formed by boulders and filled with crystal clear spring water. Swimming in "Lover's Cave" is one of the most refreshing and romantic experiences in Israel. Since this trail involves a considerable climb (and hikers invariably take time to bathe in the "cave"), access to the trail is permitted only up to 3½ hours before closing time.

Although not as lush as Nahal David, the deep canyon of Nahal Arugot is perhaps more spectacular. Enormous boulders and slabs of stone on the opposite cliff face seem poised in midcataclysm. The hour-long hike to the Hidden Waterfall (not too difficult) passes by spots where the stream bubbles over rock shelves and shallow pools give relief from the heat. If you're adventurous and have water shoes, you can return through the greenery of the streambed. Experienced hikers can ascend the Tsafit Trail to Mapal Hachalon (translated as "window waterfall"), where there are stunning views over the Dead Sea.

A Jewish community lived in Ein Gedi for more than 1,200 years, beginning in the 7th century BC. In the 3rd century AD, they built a synagogue between Nahal David and Nahal Arugot with a beautiful mosaic floor. The mosaic includes an inscription in Hebrew and Aramaic invoking the wrath of heaven on troublemakers including "whoever reveals the secret of the town." The secret is believed to refer to a method of cultivating a now-extinct balsam tree, which was used to make the prized perfume for which Ein Gedi was once famous. ⊠ *Rte. 90, Ein Gedi* ☎ *08/658–4285* ⊕ *www.parks.org.il* ⊠ *NIS 28, NIS 14 synagogue only.*

SPAS

Fodor'sChoice ★ **Synergy Spa.** At the Ein Gedi Hotel's impressive spa, you can float in an indoor pool rich in sulfur, magnesium, and potassium as you enjoy the stunning view of mountains on one side and the Dead Sea on the other. Treatment rooms, like the rest of the spa, are elegantly simple, decorated in soft hues that showcase the surrounding oasis. Try the Turkish hammam, and get a smoothie from the bar and lounge beside the freshwater pool. Body peels use materials like myrrh and frankincense; the cost is NIS 295 for 40 minutes. The spa's tranquillity and superior services make it a better option than the hectic Ein Gedi Spa nearby. Hotel guests have free access to pools and saunas, and receive a discount on treatments. Nonguests should call at least a day in advance to make reservations. ⊠ *Ein Gedi Hotel, Rte. 90, Ein Gedi, Ein Gedi* ☎ *08/659–4058* ⊕ *www.ein-gedi.co.il* ⊠ *NIS 225 for 50-min massage, NIS 305 for day package with 30-min massage and breakfast.*

WHERE TO EAT

$$
ISRAELI

✕ **Baobar.** The café at the Ein Gedi Hotel is a great option in the area for fresh salads, pastas, and coffee after a hike at the nearby Ein Gedi Nature Reserve. Sit on the outdoor deck amid the baobob trees and landscaped gardens and enjoy the gorgeous views and the aromatic botanical gardens. The café is open for evening drinks as well as lunch and dinner, and there is live music on Friday evening and during holidays. ⑤ *Average main: NIS 53* ⊠ *Ein Gedi Hotel, Rte. 90, Ein Gedi* ☎ *08/659–4220* ⊕ *www.en.ein-gedi.co.il.*

WHERE TO STAY

$$
HOTEL
FAMILY
Fodor'sChoice
★

Ein Gedi Hotel. Desert ibexes, kibbutz members, and tourists share the footpaths of this hotel, surrounded by majestic baobab trees, aromatic herbs, and hundreds of species of tropical flora. **Pros:** serene oasis atmosphere; fantastic spa; grounds and activities great for families. **Cons:** some dingy rooms; limited hours at the beach; dining hall and pool get crowded and loud when hotel is full. ⑤ *Rooms from: $209* ⊠ *Rte. 90, Ein Gedi* ☎ *08/659–4220* ⊕ *www.ein-gedi.co.il/en* ⇆ *166 rooms* ⊠ *Breakfast.*

MASADA

19 km (12 miles) south of Ein Gedi on Rte. 90, 103 km (64 miles) east and south of Jerusalem, 20 km (12½ miles) north of Ein Bokek.

The isolated flattop rock of Masada commands the surrounding desert, its ancient remains bearing witness to long-ago power and conflict. One of Israel's most stunning archaeological sites, Masada earned fame and a place in history first as one of King Herod's palace-fortresses and later as the site of the last stand of Jewish rebels against the legions of Rome, almost 2,000 years ago.

EXPLORING

Fodor's Choice ★ **Masada.** A symbol of the ancient kingdom of Israel, Masada (Hebrew for "fortress") towers majestically over the western shore of the Dead Sea. Its unusual natural form—a plateau set off on all sides by towering cliffs—attracted Herod the Great, who built an opulent desert palace here in the 1st century AD. Masada became the last refuge of the Jews in AD 73 to 74, during their final fight against Rome. The historian Flavius Josephus wrote that the rebels (almost 1,000 people) chose to commit suicide rather than surrender, although no one can be sure what happened at the end. In recognition of its historical significance, this was the first site in Israel to be added to the UNESCO World Heritage List in 2001.

To reach the top, most visitors make use of the speedy cable car (NIS 74 round-trip). More intrepid visitors climb the eastern Snake Path (at least 45 minutes of steep walking), some even starting before dawn to watch the sunrise. Others take the less arduous western Roman Ramp path, accessible only from the road that descends from Arad. ■TIP→ **Water fountains (but no other refreshments) are available on Masada itself, so save bottles for refilling.** Allow no less than 1½ hours to explore the site. The most popular route heads counterclockwise. If time allows, be sure to visit the southern area as well (especially the huge cistern and echo wall). Maps, a detailed brochure, and a very useful audio guide are available at the top entrance.

The entire mountaintop—less than 20 acres—is surrounded by a 4,250-foot-long casemate, a double wall that included living quarters and guardrooms. Most of the important buildings are concentrated in the high northern area.

The Northern Palace, Masada's most impressive structure, is an extraordinary three-tiered structure that seems to hang off the highest and most northerly point of the mountain. The panoramic effect is awesome: baked brown precipices and bleached valleys shimmer in the midday glare.

Clearly visible from the upper terrace are the Roman camps—the remains of the most complete Roman siege system in the world—and "runner's path" (used for communication between the camps).

The synagogue, one of only four that have been uncovered from the Second Temple period, can be seen in the western casemate. The building's orientation toward Jerusalem suggested its function, but the stone benches (*synagogue* means "place of assembly") and the man-made pit for damaged scrolls (a *genizah*) confirmed it.

Continued on page 179

DID YOU KNOW?

King Herod built a dam in the valley so that reservoir water could be carried to cisterns atop Masada. His engineers also created channels, visible today, that guided water from streams into cisterns hewn into the mountainside.

MASADA: DESERT FORTRESS

The isolated flattop rock of Masada commands the surrounding desert, its ancient remains bearing witness to long-ago power and conflict. One of Israel's most stunning archaeological sites, Masada earned fame and a place in history first as one of King Herod's opulent palace-fortresses and later as the site of the last stand of Jewish rebels against the legions of Rome, almost 2,000 years ago.

A KING'S PALACE

Surrounded by steep cliffs and with spectacular views of the Dead Sea and the desert, the Masada plateau offers nearly impregnable natural protection.

Herod the Great, the brilliant builder and paranoid leader who reigned over Israel as king of the Jews by the grace of the Roman Empire in the 1st century BC, developed the 18-acre site. Both for his relaxation and as a possible refuge from his enemies (including Cleopatra) and hostile subjects, Herod built atop Masada a fantastic, state-of-the-art complex of palaces, storehouses, and water systems.

THE REVOLT OF THE JEWS

Herod died around 4 BC, and the Jews rebelled against Rome in AD 66. By AD 70, the Roman Empire had destroyed Jerusalem and crushed the Jewish revolt there. Around AD 72, the last Jewish rebels took refuge at Masada. For at least a year, 960 Israelite men, women, and children lived here, protected from thousands of Roman soldiers by cliffs more than 1,400 feet high.

The Roman general and governor Flavius Silva, determined to end the rebellion, built eight legionnaire camps around the mountain. Silva's forces gradually erected an assault ramp on Masada's western side.

THE REBELS' "TERRIBLE RESOLVE"

According to a few survivors who related the story to the 1st-century historian Flavius Josephus, the night before the Romans reached Masada's walls, the rebel leader Elazar Ben-Yair gave a rallying speech. He reminded his community that they had resolved "neither to serve the Romans nor any other save God." After discussion, the Jews agreed to commit suicide rather than be taken captive.

The men drew lots to choose the ten who would kill the others. Those ten, having carried out "their terrible resolve," Josephus wrote, drew additional lots to select the one who would kill the other nine and then himself. When the Romans breached the walls the next morning, they found hundreds of corpses. The zealots' final action made the Roman victory at Masada a hollow one.

Although Josephus' physical description of Masada is accurate, some historians doubt his narrative. Several artifacts, including pottery shards bearing names (the lots, perhaps?), support the accuracy of Josephus' text, but no one can be sure what happened at the end. Masada continues to inspire debate.

TOURING MASADA'S TOP SIGHTS

Ride the cable car up Masada, hike the Snake Path, or walk the easier Ramp Path. Take in these highlights of Herod's buildings and the Jewish rebels' presence—and awesome desert views.

Museum

① Museum. The fine museum, near the cable car, interprets the history of Masada and has archaeological artifacts.

② Roman Camps. The eight military camps around Masada are the most complete Roman siege works in the world. Museum visitors may also enter a restored Roman camp. From Masada's top, note the square camps and the remnants of the siege wall connecting them.

③ Cable Car. The fastest way to ascend is also near the Masada Museum and a Roman siege camp on the east side.

④ Snake Path. You can still climb the steep path on the eastern side of Masada used by Herod's workers and the Jewish rebels.

TO
← DEAD SEA, EIN GEDI,
AND EIN BOKEK

⑫ Casemate Wall

⑬ Mikveh

⑪ Church

Snake Path **④**

Cable Car

③

⑤ Commandant's Residence
and Storerooms

Synagogue
⑧

⑦

Bathhouse

Northern Palace

⑥

Path

KEY	
🛈	Tourist information
🚶	Trail
🚡	Cable car
💧	Drinking water
🚻	Restroom
♿	Wheelchair access
🔭	Observation Point

Frescoed walls

⑤ Commandant's Residence and Storerooms. With its frescoed walls, this area may have housed Herod's commanders. Simple ovens here indicate that the Jews, too, used the complex as living quarters. The undecorated rooms stored grain, dry fruit, and wine.

Inauguration of the synagogue: blowing the shofar (2005)

7 Bathhouse. This spa on a desert cliff demonstrates Herod's grandiosity, his dedication to Roman culture, and the success of Masada's water systems. The building has cold and lukewarm baths, a sauna, frescoes, and tile work. Jewish rebels incorporated a ritual bath.

Bathhouse

8 Synagogue. Built into the wall, the synagogue is oddly shaped, but its benches and geniza (burial for damaged scrolls) indicate its function. Here, perhaps, the rebels agreed to die at their own hands. Today the synagogue is used for bar and bat mitzvahs.

Roman Ramp on the western slopes of Masada

9 Roman Ramp. You can stand on the western edge where Romans breached Masada's defenses. The original ramp is below, as well as a modern path for walkers.

10 Western Palace. Believed to have been an administrative base and a guest house, this palace retains frescoed walls and mosaics in Greek style; unusual for Herodian mosaics, one has a fruit motif.

11 Church. During the 5th to 7th centuries, monks lived at Masada, choosing it for its isolation. This 5th-century chapel is Byzantine in design, with mosaic floors.

12 Casemate Wall. Despite Masada's strategic advantages, Herod built a casemate (double-layered) wall around the oblong flattop rock, including offices

and storerooms. The Jewish rebels used these rooms as dwellings.

13 Mikveh. In Jewish culture, the mikveh, or ritual bath, is a symbol of life and purity. Two found on Masada were built in accordance with Jewish laws still followed today. The presence of mikvehs indicates the rebels' religious piety.

14 Water Cistern. Like other cisterns at Masada, the southern cistern—into which you may descend—was built underground to prevent evaporation. Also make your way to see the spectacular canyon view to the south, and test the echoes.

Mikveh

**Map labels:**

14 Water Cistern

Casemate Wall

12

Western Palace

10

Western gate

Ramp path

9 Roman Ramp

12

Casemate Wall

TO ARAD →

Northern Palace

6 Northern Palace. Herod's personal living quarters is an extraordinary three-tiered structure that seems to hang from the cliffs. The amazing, terraced buildings feature colorful frescoes, Greek-inspired architecture, and Herod's personal bathhouse.

MAKING THE MOST OF YOUR VISIT

WHEN TO VISIT

The weather at Masada is fairly consistent year-round; it's hot during the day. Visit in the early morning or late afternoon, when the sun is weakest. ■TIP→ It's popular to hike up before dawn via the Snake or Ramp Path, and watch the sun rise from behind Jordan and the Dead Sea. After 9 or 10 am, extreme heat may dictate that you use the cable car.

WHAT TO WEAR AND BRING

Layered clothing is recommended, as cool early-morning temperatures rise to uncomfortable heat. Good walking shoes and hats or bandanas are musts. Free drinking water is available at Masada, but bring plenty to start with. Food is not sold atop the site. The museum cafeteria sells lunch after 11 am, Sunscreen and a camera are essential.

TIMING AND HIGHLIGHTS

Visiting Masada, a UNESCO World Heritage Site, can take three to seven hours, depending on your interest. The museum takes about an hour. Going up can take from three minutes (cable car) to sixty minutes (Snake Path). Your tour at the top might take ninety minutes or up to three hours.

The **Masada Museum**, near the cable car, offers an excellent combination of life-size scenes depicting the history of Masada; archaeological artifacts; and audio guide (available in English). Watch the short English-language film near the cable-car entrance. Atop Masada, many highlights such as Herod's **Northern Palace** and the **bathhouse** are toward the site's

Cable car heading down from Masada

northern end. On the sparser southern side, the views and echo point near the southern **water cistern** are notable.

OTHER THINGS TO DO

If you're traveling or staying overnight on the Dead Sea side, combine your excursion with a hike in **Ein Gedi** or a visit to a spa in **Ein Bokek.** You'll find plenty of hotels in Ein Bokek and its beaches are good for a float in the Dead Sea. Masada's western side has a seasonal sound-and-light show. For information, see www.parks.org.il.

Cooking pots at Masada

THREE WAYS TO GET UP AND DOWN MASADA

On Masada's east side, the cable car takes only three minutes. The quickest way up, the **cable car** is convenient to the Masada Museum and a restored Roman siege camp. The long, steep **Snake Path** up the east side is an arduous but rewarding one-hour hike, recommended for visitors who are fit or determined to ascend Masada the same way the Jewish rebels did. Accessible from Arad on the west side, the **Ramp Path** is less grueling and takes fifteen to thirty minutes to ascend; it's equivalent to climbing about twenty flights of stairs.

At an opening in the walls on the western edge, you can stand where the Roman legionnaires breached Masada's defenses. The original wedge-shape ramp is below, though its upper part has since collapsed. The Western Gate leads to a modern trail down this side of the mountain (access via Arad only).

Adjoining the lower cable-car station is the Masada Museum, with hundreds of artifacts from the site. Especially moving is a set of 12 pottery shards, each bearing a single name. Archaeologists believe these might have been lots drawn to decide the order in which the last remaining rebels would die. All the artifacts are placed within scenes of daily life.

A fine summer-night diversion is the sound-and-light show at Masada's western base. The show runs every Tuesday and Thursday from March to October and costs NIS 45. ⊠ *Off Rte. 3199, Ein Gedi* ☎ *08/658–4207/8* ⊕ *www.parks.org.il* ⊠ *NIS 28, entrance and round-trip cable car NIS 74, museum NIS 20.*

WHERE TO STAY

$

B&B/INN

🛏 **Masada Hostel.** This moderately priced hostel at the foot of Masada is the most convenient lodging for those intent on watching the spectacular sunrise over the Dead Sea; it has single, double, and family rooms, each with private bath. **Pros:** convenient to Masada; swimming pool; air-conditioned rooms. **Cons:** rowdy teenage groups; no evening entertainment; minimalist twin beds; plain decor. ⑤ *Rooms from: $113* ⊠ *Off Rte. 90, Ein Gedi* ✛ *At entrance to Masada* ☎ *08/995–3222* ⊕ *www.iyha.org.il/eng* ⟲ *88 rooms* ⦿ *Breakfast.*

ARAD

64 km (40 miles) south of Ein Gedi, 20 km (12½ miles) west of Masada, 25 km (15½ miles) west of Ein Bokek and the Dead Sea, 45 km (28 miles) east of Beersheva.

Breathe deeply: Arad sits 2,000 feet above sea level and is famous for its dry, pollution-free air and mild climate, ideal for asthma sufferers. The modern town was established by ex-kibbutzniks as a planned community in 1962 and today hosts a growing alternative music and art scene. Its population of nearly 25,000 now includes immigrants from Russia and Ethiopia, and until recently, Arad was home to acclaimed Israeli writer Amos Oz.

Arad is often used as a base for excursions to sites in the Dead Sea area. It has an archaeological site and is near Yatir, one of the country's finest desert wineries. You can also take a stroll through the galleries and workshops of Eshet Lot, the artists' quarter.

GETTING HERE AND AROUND

Arad is accessible by Route 31; the city is 45 km (28 miles) east of Beersheva. From Ein Gedi, the trip is around an hour, starting from Route 90 south and continuing onto Route 31. Driving from Jerusalem by Route 40 takes about 2½ hours; avoid Route 60 and Hebron in the West Bank. Egged bus lines run to Arad from Beersheva, Tel Aviv and

Jerusalem. A small supply of maps, brochures, and hiking information is available; a simple 24/7 café called Yellow sits next to the gas pumps.

VISITOR INFORMATION

Contacts Arad Tourist Information Center. ✉ *34 Chen St., inside Arad municipality* ☎ *08/995–1871* ⊕ *www.travelarad.com.*

EXPLORING

Glass Art Museum. Israeli glass artist Gideon Friedman uses recycled glass to capture three-dimensional movement in his mesmerizing sculptures of human bodies and faces. Works by other artists are also on display. A guided tour, included in the price, helps reveal the magic in the works. The museum is in Arad's artist quarter and near several other galleries and the Midbar winery. ✉ *11 Sadan St.* ☎ *08/995–3388* ⊕ *www.warmglassil.com/english* ⬚ *NIS 50* ⊘ *Closed Fri.*

Tel Arad National Park. The 250-acre site of the biblical city of Arad (to the northwest of the modern city) contains the remains of a major metropolis from the Bronze Age and the Israelite period. The lower city, with its meticulously planned streets and plazas, was inhabited in the Early Bronze Age (3150–2200 BC), when it was one of the largest cities in this region. Here you can walk around a walled urban community and enter the carefully reconstructed dwellings, whose style became known as the "Arad house."

After the Early Bronze Age, Arad was abandoned. The book of Numbers (21:1–3) relates that the Canaanite king of Arad battled the Israelites during the exodus from Egypt but that his cities were "utterly destroyed." The upper city was first settled in the Israelite period (1200 BC). It's worth the trek up the somewhat steep path to see the Israelite temple, a miniature version of Solomon's Temple in Jerusalem.

At the entrance, pick up a free pamphlet explaining the ongoing excavations and purchase a map of the Canaanite city of Arad, with its recommended walking route and diagrams of a typical Arad house. Tel Arad is 8 km (5 miles) west of Arad. At the Tel Arad Junction on Route 31, turn north on Route 80 for 3 km (2 miles). ✉ *Rte. 80* ☎ *08/699–2444* ⊕ *www.parks.org.il* ⬚ *NIS 14.*

Yatir Winery. At the foot of the ancient Tel Arad, this boutique vineyard, now a subsidiary of Carmel Wines, was established in 2000. Yatir Forest (a Cabernet Sauvignon blend) is the premier label. The adjacent Yatir Forest, after which the winery is named, is the largest planted forest in Israel. Call ahead and speak to Etti to arrange an appointment for a visit and tasting. ✉ *Rte. 80* ☎ *052/830–8196, 054/645–8725 Etti Edry* ⊕ *yatirwinery.com/en* ⬚ *NIS 40* ⊘ *Closed Sat.*

WHERE TO EAT

$ ✗ **Kaparuchka.** A neighborhood spot attached to a yoga studio, this
ITALIAN unpretentious pizzeria makes everything from scratch. The simple Italian
FAMILY fare is lovingly prepared by the owner-chefs, a young couple who made the trek back home from Tel Aviv. Grab a table in the outside patio and enjoy a ricotta-and-dill "Moldovan calzone" along with an Israeli beer. ⑤ *Average main: NIS 49* ✉ *Akhva 19* ☎ *08/860–6615* ⊘ *Closed Sat.*

$$
MIDDLE EASTERN

✕**Muza.** Every inch of wall, ceiling, and bar real estate is plastered with the scarves of worldwide soccer teams at this beloved, more than 30-year-old roadside eatery on Route 31 at the entrance to Arad. Burgers are best here, served with spicy potato wedges and washed down with a large selection of Israeli and imported beers. Vegetarian dishes exist but are not as well executed. The atmosphere is cozy and warm, with cheery waitstaff and a big-screen TV always tuned to a soccer match. ⑤*Average main: NIS 55* ✉*Rte. 31* ✛*Near Alon gas station* ☎*08/997–5555* ⊕*www.muza-arad.co.il.*

WHERE TO STAY

$$
B&B/INN
Fodor'sChoice
★

🏠**Yehelim Boutique Hotel.** The main terrace and every room of this luxurious, award-winning small hotel face the desert. **Pros:** lovely views; friendly staff; delicious breakfast. **Cons:** books up fast; no pool. ⑤*Rooms from: $230* ✉*72 Moav St.* ☎*052/652–2718,* ⊕*www.yehelim.com* ⥲*12 rooms* ⦿*Breakfast.*

$
B&B/INN

🏠**Zimmer Mantur.** Several entrepreneurs in Arad have opened small B&Bs, or zimmers, and Mantur stands out for owner Anat Rubinstein's heartfelt hospitality. **Pros:** reasonable price; close to Masada and the Dead Sea; warm hospitality; outstanding showers. **Cons:** uninspired design; no desert view. ⑤*Rooms from: $135* ✉*Mivtza Lot 30* ☎*054/766–9308* ✍*mantur11@walla.com* ⥲*3 suites* ⦿*No meals.*

EIN BOKEK

40 km (25 miles) east of Arad, 8 km (5 miles) north of Zohar–Arad Junction on Rte. 90.

Fodor'sChoice
★

The sudden and startling sight, in this bare landscape, of gleaming, ultramodern hotels surrounded by waving palm trees signals your arrival at the spa-resort area of Ein Bokek, near the southern tip of the Dead Sea. According to the Bible, it was along these shores that the Lord rained fire and brimstone on the people of Sodom and Gomorrah (Genesis 19:24) and turned Lot's wife into a pillar of salt (Genesis 26). Here, at the lowest point on Earth, the hot, sulfur-pungent air hangs heavy, and a haze often shimmers over the water. You can float, but you can't sink, in the warm, salty water.

Once upon a time, Ein Bokek comprised a handful of hotels, each with a small "spa," and a pebbly beach out front. Today, it's a collection of large resorts with curvy pools, rooftop solariums, and landscaped outdoor areas. While the downsides of many hotels are the outdated decor and buffet-style dining options, the pools and state-of-the-art spas are a welcome relief from the often sweltering heat on the rocky Dead Sea beaches. There are no full-service restaurants outside the hotels, although a few casual eating places are along the beach and in two tiny shopping centers. The central cluster of hotels is linked by a promenade to two hotels at the southern end of the area. At this writing, construction of the promenade is slated for completion in spring 2017; until it opens, half of the beach is closed, and all hotels are sharing the public beaches.

GETTING HERE AND AROUND

To drive to Ein Bokek from Jerusalem, take Route 1 eastbound, marked Jericho–Dead Sea. At the Dead Sea, take Route 90 south, passing Qumran, Ein Gedi, and Masada, until you reach Ein Bokek. From Arad, head southeast on Route 31 and continue onto Route 90 north. Egged buses run between Jerusalem and Ein Bokek several times a day. The trip is 1½ hours.

EXPLORING

Arava Road. Traversing the Arava Valley from Ein Bokek to Eilat, the 177-km (111-mile) Route 90 parallels the Israel-Jordan border, almost touching it at some points. To the east rise the spiky, red-brown mountains of Moab, in Jordan. The road follows an ancient route mentioned in biblical descriptions of the journeys of the Children of Israel.

The *Arava* (meaning "wilderness") is part of the Great Rift Valley, the deep fissure in the earth stretching from Turkey to East Africa, the result of an ancient shift of landmasses. Just south of Ein Bokek, you pass signs for the communities Neot HaKikar and Ein Tamar (home to many metalwork and jewelry artists), whose date palms draw water from underground springs rather than irrigation.

With the Edom Mountains rising in the east, the road continues along the southern Dead Sea valley, where you cross one of the largest dry riverbeds in the Negev, Nahal Zin, and pass several sprawling date orchards that belong to neighboring kibbutzim. ⊠ *Ein Bokek.*

WHERE TO STAY

$$$
RESORT
🏨 **Daniel Dead Sea Hotel.** At this upscale lodging, an undulating front wall swirls around a huge flower-shape pool. **Pros:** lovely pool; all-inclusive option; video games for kids. **Cons:** drab, outdated decor; staff can be brusque. $ *Rooms from: $304* ⊠ *Off Rte. 90* ☎ *08/668–9999* ⊕ *www. tamareshotels.com/daniel_dead_sea* ⇗ *300 rooms* ⭥ *Breakfast.*

$$$
RESORT
🏨 **David Dead Sea Resort and Spa.** Reached via a trail of baby palm trees, Ein Bokek's largest hotel stands out for its cavernous lobby, wonderful views, delightful spa, and endless swimming pool. **Pros:** lovely rooms; pretty grounds; option to include all meals in the price. **Cons:** up a steep hill; can seem immense and impersonal; inconsistent service. $ *Rooms from: $360* ⊠ *Off Rte. 90* ☎ *08/659–1234* ⊕ *www.david-deadsea.com* ⇗ *600 rooms* ⭥ *Breakfast.*

$$$$
RESORT
Fodor'sChoice
★
🏨 **Herods Dead Sea.** On the Dead Sea beach is this palatial hotel, decorated in relaxing blues, teals, and grays to echo the natural landscape. **Pros:** on the beach; gleaming furnishings; good food; pillow menu. **Cons:** pricey. $ *Rooms from: $425* ⊠ *Off Rte. 90* ☎ *08/659–1591* ⊕ *www.fattal-hotels.com* ⇗ *223 rooms* ⭥ *Breakfast.*

$$
RESORT
Fodor'sChoice
★
🏨 **Isrotel Dead Sea Resort and Spa.** Walk into the nine-story Isrotel and look to your left at the gorgeous wooden wall carved with date palms and fruit; this hotel puts an emphasis on being a part of the natural world. **Pros:** sparkling pool; beer on tap for dinner; good business lounge. **Cons:** across the sometimes blisteringly hot street from the Dead Sea; in summer, can be overrun with kids; service can be brusque. $ *Rooms from: $290* ⊠ *Off Rte. 90* ☎ *08/668–9666* ⊕ *www.isrotel. com/isrotel_dead_sea* ⇗ *296 rooms* ⭥ *Breakfast.*

$$ **Isrotel Ganim.** Compared to some of the palatial resorts of Ein Bokek,
RESORT Isrotel Ganim is a smaller and less expensive property distinguished by a
lobby of vintage furniture and loads of large windows overlooking the
Dead Sea. Rooms are average in size, and some of the third-floor ones
have balconies. **Pros:** spa; every room faces the Dead Sea; two Dead
Sea–water pools at different temperatures; meal plans include one for
all meals. **Cons:** small gym; private Dead Sea beach across the street
requires golf cart on hot days; room decor is uninspired. $ *Rooms from:
$223 ⊠ Off Rte. 90* ☎ *08/668–9090* ⊕ *www.isrotel.com/isrotel-ganim*
↪ *200 rooms* ⦿ *Breakfast.*

$$ **Leonardo Club Dead Sea.** Bring the whole family to this all-inclusive
RESORT property, where adults can enjoy a midnight supper or the spa and
FAMILY kids can cool off with ice pops around the clock. **Pros:** the area's only
all-inclusive hotel; excellent kids' programs; nice views; on the beach.
Cons: small rooms; drab entry; noisy lobby; many children. $ *Rooms
from: $250 ⊠ Off Rte. 90* ☎ *08/668–9444* ⊕ *www.fattal-hotels.com*
↪ *388 rooms* ⦿ *All-inclusive.*

SPORTS AND THE OUTDOORS

The beaches of Ein Bokek are free to the public and are usually fairly
crowded. A lifeguard is on duty year-round, and there's ample parking
alongside the promenade. Most don't have facilities.

Dead Sea Divers. In the sea where everyone floats, diving requires lots
of weights just to keep you below the surface. Under the sea is another
world of rocky, white salt crystals. A day's training and diving costs NIS
2,400. Avi Bresler picks you up from your hotel in Ein Bokek. ⊠ *Ein
Bokek* ☎ *077/710–9100* ⊕ *deadseadivers.com.*

SHOPPING

Several companies manufacture excellent Dead Sea skin and beauty
products made from mud, salts, and minerals; the actual mud is sold
in squishy, leak-proof packages. Ahava and Jericho are popular brands
sold at the shopping centers of Ein Bokek and shops in most hotels.

Dead Sea Diamond Center. Unique, handcrafted jewelry by Israeli designers
is sold at this establishment just outside the David Dead Sea Resort and
Spa. Call for a free shuttle to pick you up. ⊠ *Rte. 90* ☎ *08/995–8777.*

WEST OF JERUSALEM

The rugged Judean Hills tumble down from Jerusalem to the west, eventually easing into the gentler terrain of the coastal lowlands (known in
Hebrew as the *Shfela*). This is a region of forests, springs, monasteries,
battlefields, national parks, and archaeological treasures. It's the fastest-
growing wine-producing area in the country, encompassing more than
two-dozen vineyards. A number of locals also produce goat and sheep
cheese, as well as craft beers. For Jerusalemites, the Judean Hills are
a place to hike and picnic. For many visitors, this sparsely populated
region with its ancient terraced hills evokes the landscape of the Bible
with none of the distractions of a big city.

ABU GOSH

11 km (7 miles) west of Jerusalem on Rte. 1.

The Arab village of Abu Gosh is said to be the biblical site of Kiryat Yearim, where the Ark of the Covenant rested for 20 years, out of the reach of the Israelites (1 Samuel 7:2). In modern times, Abu Gosh is better known as the national capital of hummus, that lemony chickpea spread ubiquitous around the Middle East. Jerusalem's secular Jews flock to Abu Gosh on weekends to escape the religious Sabbath with hummus and water pipes. But it's not all escapism: Abu Gosh retains a spiritual quality, with Crusader-era churches and a recently built mega-mosque bankrolled by the Islamic Republic of Chechnya. These religious buildings provide an evocative background for the village's annual summer music festival.

GETTING HERE AND AROUND

Coming from Jerusalem, Abu Gosh is easily accessible via Route 1. There are no good public transportation options.

EXPLORING

Our Lady of the Ark of the Covenant Church. Built in 1924, this church is said to be on the site where the Ark of the Covenant remained for 20 years in the ancient town of Kiryat Yearim. A statue of Mary holding Jesus in her arms towers above the church and can be seen across the village. The Byzantines built a church on the same site in the 5th century, and pieces of floor mosaic and other telltale leftovers give this church a patina far richer than its age. ⊠ *1 Notre Dame St.* ☎ *02/534–2818* ⊘ *Closed Sun.*

St. Mary of the Resurrection Abbey. The Crusaders believed that Abu Gosh was the site where Jesus revealed himself after his resurrection, and in the 12th century they built this Benedictine monastery to commemorate the event. Parts of it still stand today, with magnificent frescoes covering the walls and a small stream bubbling out of the underground crypt. Here you can see some of the best-preserved Crusader architecture in the country. There is still a religious community here: try to visit during prayers, which are recited to Gregorian music. ⊠ *3 Mahmoud Rashid St.* ☎ *02/534–2798* ⊕ *abbaye-abugosh.info/* ⊘ *Closed Sun. except for services.*

WHERE TO EAT

$$
MIDDLE EASTERN

✕ **Abu Ghosh Restaurant.** Jawdat Ibrahim won the Illinois state lottery in 1991 and plowed his earnings back into his village, creating a local restaurant as well as a scholarship fund for Arab and Jewish students. In 2010, Jawdat was the driving force behind Israel's Guinness World Record for the largest plate of hummus, served on a satellite dish. Taste the hummus yourself at his restaurant, along with freshly cut salads, tasty bean soup, stuffed vine leaves, and juicy meat skewers. Ⓢ *Average main: NIS 60* ⊠ *Hashalom 65* ☎ *02/533–2019.*

WHERE TO STAY

There are some very good kibbutz guesthouses in the wooded enclaves of the Judean Hills, a 15- to 20-minute drive west of Jerusalem. All have commanding hilltop views, quiet surroundings, very comfortable if not luxurious accommodations, and good swimming pools.

$$$
HOTEL
FAMILY
C Hotel Neve Ilan. A cut above its neighbors, this hotel has spacious, nicely furnished rooms, a sparkling heated pool, and a well-equipped exercise room. **Pros:** panoramic views; children's activities; choice of meal plans. **Cons:** gym and pool are at nearby sports facility; inattentive staff. $ Rooms from: $355 ⊠ North of Rte. 1, Neve Ilan ✛ 15 km (10 miles) west of Jerusalem ☎ 03/919–0669 ⊕ www.c-hotels.co.il ⟿ 160 rooms ⦿ Breakfast.

$$$
HOTEL
Fodor's Choice
★
Cramim Spa & Wine Hotel. The name of this hotel, part of the Isrotel chain, translates to "vineyards," and grapes are the inspiration for every facet of this spa hotel set in the beautiful Jerusalem hills. **Pros:** serene, gorgeous setting; fantastic spa treatments; great food. **Cons:** books up months in advance; cramped parking; staff can be brusque. $ Rooms from: $324 ⊠ Off Rte. 425, Kiryat Anavim ☎ 02/548–9800 ⊕ www.isrotel.com/kiryat_anavim ⟿ 156 rooms ⦿ Breakfast.

$
HOTEL
FAMILY
Hotel Tzuba. Great views, delicious brunches, and a nearby Galita chocolate factory offering children's workshops make this hotel a great choice for families. **Pros:** great place for young children; interesting tours; panoramic views. **Cons:** no evening entertainment; meals eaten in the kibbutz dining hall; minimum stays on weekends. $ Rooms from: $141 ⊠ Rte. 39, Tzuba ✛ 12 km (7½ miles) west of Jerusalem ☎ 02/534–7000 ⊕ www.tzubahotel.co.il/en ⟿ 65 rooms ⦿ Breakfast.

$$
HOTEL
Ye'arim Hotel. This large guesthouse, spread over beautifully landscaped gardens, is ideal for nature lovers and families. **Pros:** panoramic views; sunlit pool; parklike setting; free calls to the United States from lobby. **Cons:** can get crowded with tour groups or families; older wings are in dire need of renovation; some small rooms. $ Rooms from: $205 ⊠ Rte. 1, Maaleh Hahamisha ✛ 14 km (9 miles) west of Jerusalem ☎ 02/533–1331 ⊕ eng.yearimhotel.com ⟿ 230 rooms ⦿ Breakfast.

LATRUN

14 km (8 miles) west of Abu Gosh, 25 km (16 miles) west of Jerusalem on Rte. 1.

Latrun is the ridge that projects into and dominates the western side of the Ayalon Valley. A natural passage between the coastal plain and the Judean Hills, the strategic valley has served as a battleground throughout history, from the conquests of the biblical Israelite leader Joshua in the 13th century BC, through the Hasmonean campaigns of the 2nd century BC, to the bloody defeat of the newly established Israel Defense Force by Jordan's Arab Legion in 1948. Today, the Trappist monastery is known for its olive oil and wine, and Mini Israel is a favorite for children of all ages.

GETTING HERE AND AROUND

Coming from Jerusalem on Route 1, exit onto Route 3 (the Modi'in and Ashkelon–Beersheva road), about 5 km (3 miles) west of the Sha'ar Hagai gas station. At the T-junction, turn left for the Trappist Abbey of Latrun, the Latrun Armored Corps Museum, and Mini Israel. There are no good public transportation options.

EXPLORING

TOP ATTRACTIONS

Domaine du Castel. This vineyard consistently produces some of the country's best wines. The small winery, with its exquisite cellar, runs tours and tastings of wine and cheese. ⊠ *Rte. 4115, Yad Hashmona* ☎ *02/534–2249* ⊕ *www.castel.co.il* ✆ *Tour and tasting NIS 130* ⊘ *Closed Fri. afternoon and Sat. By appointment only.*

FAMILY **Latrun Armored Corps Museum.** The name Latrun is thought to derive from "La Toron de Chevaliers" (the Tower of the Knights), the French name of the Crusader castle that occupied the crest of the hill in the 12th century. Eight centuries later, in 1940, the British erected the concrete fortress that today holds the museum. In the 1948 War of Independence, Israeli forces attempted five times to capture the fortress from Jordanian soldiers. The names of 142 Israeli soldiers who fell in these unsuccessful attempts are engraved on the walls. There are more than 100 assorted antique tanks on which children love to climb. ⊠ *Rte. 3* ✛ *1 km (½ mile) south of Rte. 1* ☎ *08/630-7400* ⊕ *www.yadlashiryon.com* ✆ *NIS 30.*

FAMILY
Fodor'sChoice
★
Mini Israel. One of the most popular attractions in Israel, this theme park spreads over 13 acres and contains nearly 400 models of the most important historical, national, religious, and natural sites in the country, all scaled down to 1:25. Worth at least an hour's visit, it is especially fun for children. About 25,000 miniature "residents" have been meticulously created to present not just the physical, but also the cultural, religious, and social aspects of contemporary Israel. A walk through the park—along with a 3-D film about Israel—lets you see and hear the people of different faiths and cultures that make up the country's human landscape. ⊠ *Rte. 424* ☎ *700/559–559* ⊕ *www.minisrael.co.il/en* ✆ *NIS 69.*

Pepo Beer. Moti Bohadana named his brewery for his father and the eight beers for all the women in his life. Elisheva, named after his grandmother, is a bitter, hoppy IPA. Tamara is a red, flowery ale and Tirza is an Irish stout. There's also hard apple and cherry cider. Call ahead about visits and occasional music events held Thursday nights, or to reserve a table at unlimited Friday brunch for NIS 60 per person. To get here from Latrun, take Route 3 toward Ashkelon and turn left on Route 44. Follow signs for the Navot Winery. ⊠ *49 Hate'ena St., Tzlafon* ☎ *054/530–4576, 02/999–2291* ⊕ *tour-yehuda.org.il/1216/* ⊘ *Closed Sat.*

FAMILY
Fodor'sChoice
★
Sataf. Just outside Jerusalem, Sataf was one of many Arab villages that were abandoned in the 1948 War of Independence. You can hike here on well-marked trails amid ancient terraces shaded with pine, fig, and almond trees. Hikes last two or four hours and pass springs where you

West of
Jerusalem

can get your feet wet. There's a small coffee shop on site serving Israeli breakfasts, salads, and sandwiches along with ice cream and drinks. On weekends, follow the pictures of goats to get to Shai Seltzer, who raises goats in the forest and ages unique and delicious cheese in an old Byzantine cave. You can walk to Sataf from Ein Kerem in about an hour. ⊠ *Sataf Junction, intersection of Rtes. 395 and 3965, Sataf* ☎ *054/440–3762 Seltzer farm, 02/579–8830 Cafe Sataf* ⊕ *www.goat-cheese.co.il* ▨ *Free.*

WORTH NOTING

Neot Kedumim. At Israel's only Biblical Landscape Reserve, paved paths wind around ancient olive terraces, bushes of sage and hyssop, and millennia-old winepresses. The name of the site means "Oases of Antiquity." Show yourself around well-planned trails with the help of the available English map, or take a guided tour to fully appreciate the threshing floors, the Dale of the Song of Songs, and the Valley of Milk and Honey. Tours focus on Jewish, Christian, or interfaith themes. Ask about Biblical meals as well. Allow two hours minimum for the visit. ⊠ *Rte. 443 ⊕ 20 km (12 miles) north of Latrun* ☎ *08/977–0777* ⊕ *www.neot-kedumim.org.il* ▨ *NIS 25* ☾ *Closed Sat.*

**OFF THE
BEATEN
PATH**

WINERIES IN THE JUDEAN HILLS

For years, good Israeli wine was an oxymoron, but the days of producing only sweet sacramental wines are long gone. In the past few decades, a viniculture revolution has yielded an abundance of wines that easily compete against those from older vineyards. The Judean Hills area is now home to more than two dozen vineyards, the majority of them close to Route 38, north and south of Beit Shemesh. Since most vineyards are "boutique"—producing fewer than 100,000 bottles per year—few have visitor centers that encourage drop-in visits or have regularly scheduled tours, so call ahead. The wineries are convenient to Tel Aviv (40 minutes away) as well as Jerusalem (about 20 minutes). Every October, the area's more than 20 wineries sponsor a wine festival; the venue changes.

Trappist Abbey of Latrun. Trappist monks have been producing wine here since the 1890s. The interior of the 19th-century abbey is an odd mix of round neo-Byzantine arches and apses and the soaring ceiling that seems Gothic in inspiration. Survivors of the Cistercian Order suppressed in the French Revolution, the Trappists keep a vow of silence. But the staff of the wine shop chats with you in English, French, Hebrew, or Arabic. The setting in the foothills is lovely. ⊠ *Rte. 3 ✛ 2 km (1 mile) off Rte. 1* ☎ *08/922–0065* ⊕ *www.holy-wine.com* ◱ *Free.*

WHERE TO EAT

$$
DINER
FAMILY
✕ **Elvis Inn.** At the edge of the gas station by Neve Ilan, this American-style diner has the largest collection of Elvis memorabilia this side of Graceland, including 1,700 photos, two statues that tower outside, and three inside. Grab some classic American food like burgers and fries, or stay local and order hummus. Serious fans should come on the anniversary of his birth (January 8) or death (August 16), when Israel's aging Elvis impersonators come to get all shook up. ⑤ *Average main: NIS 55* ⊠ *Rte. 4115, Neve Ilan* ☎ *02/534–1275* ☉ *No dinner Fri. and Sat.*

$$$
EUROPEAN
✕ **Yad Hashmona Restaurant.** Finnish Christians built this moshav, a kind of cooperative farm, outside Jerusalem with pine beams imported from home, lending a Scandinavian setting to the famously abundant Friday brunch of salads, cheeses, quiche, and fish (NIS 95 per person). The moshav is called Yad Hashmona, or "memorial to the eight," to atone for the Finnish government's turning over of eight Jewish fellow countrymen to the Nazis. Call ahead to reserve a space. At other times, this place is open for meals only by request. From Jerusalem, take Route 1 toward Tel Aviv, exit at Neve Ilan, and follow signs to Yad Hashmona. ⑤ *Average main: NIS 95* ⊠ *Off Rte. 1, Yad Hashmona* ☎ *02/594–2004* ⊕ *www.yadha8.co.il* ☉ *Closed Sat.–Thurs. No dinner Fri.*

BEIT SHEMESH

16 km (10 miles) south of Latrun, 35 km (22 miles) west of Jerusalem.

The modern town of Beit Shemesh, Hebrew for "House of the Sun," takes its name from an ancient city now entombed by the tell on a rise on Route 38, 2 km (1 mile) south of the main entrance. Nearby are a number of wineries and breweries worth exploring.

This is Samson country. Samson, one of the judges of Old Testament Israel, is better known for his physical prowess and lust for Philistine women than for his shining spiritual qualities, but it was here, "between Tzorah and Eshta'ol," that "the Spirit of the Lord began to stir him" (Judges 13). Today, Eshta'ol is a moshav (a cooperative settlement composed of individual farms) a few minutes' drive north, and Tzora is the wine-producing kibbutz immediately to the west.

GETTING HERE AND AROUND

Follow Route 1 west from Jerusalem, then head south on Route 38 to Beit Shemesh. Israel Railways provides regular train service between Jerusalem and Tel Aviv via Beit Shemesh on an hourly basis from 6 am to 8 pm.

EXPLORING

TOP ATTRACTIONS

Fodor's Choice ★

Clos de Gat. Winemaker Eyal Rotem puts a premium on quality at this boutique estate winery that produces 90,000 bottles a year. While it's not kosher, the winery prides itself on its participation in ancient and Jewish history: it houses a 3,000-year-old-winepress and during the 1948 war served as the base for Itzhak Rabin and his Har'el Brigades. Many Clos de Gat wines age beautifully, including the Sycra series, which has garnered international accolades. The tour and tasting fee is deductible with the purchase of six bottles. ☒ *Har'el Vineyards, Rte. 44* ☏ *02/999–3505* ⊕ *closdegat.com* ☛ *Tours and tastings NIS 100* ⊗ *Closed Sat. Other days, by appointment only.*

Flam Winery. Family owned, this well-regarded winery sources grapes from the Judean Hills and the Upper Galilee. Many of its bottles, including the Bordeaux blend called The Noble, have garnered international praise for their complexity. Wine-and-cheese tastings are held at an elegantly rustic communal table. ☒ *Yaar Hakodshim, Eshtaol, Rte. 38* ☏ *02/992–9923, 054/211–3324 Mireia (for appointments)* ⊕ *flamwinery.com* ☛ *Tasting NIS 130, by appointment only* ⊗ *Closed Sat.*

Soreq Cave. At the heart of the Avshalom Nature Reserve, on the western slopes of the Judean Hills, the Soreq Cave contains a wondrous variety of stalactites and stalagmites. Some formations are at least 300,000 years old and allow scientists to track climate changes over the millennia. The cave was discovered in 1968 when a routine blast in the nearby Har-Tuv quarry tore away the rock face, revealing a subterranean wonderland.

Colored lights are used to highlight the natural whites and honey browns of the stones. Local guides have given the stalactite forms nicknames like "macaroni," "curtains," and "sombreros." In a series of "interfaith" images, some find rocky evocations of Moses, the Madonna and Child, Buddha, and the Ayatollah Khomeini.

Photography is allowed only at certain times, when there are no guided tours. Despite the high humidity, the temperature in the cave is comfortable year-round.

The 150 steps down to the cave mean it's not ideal for visitors with mobility concerns. Local guides take groups as they arrive into the cave every 25 minutes for a 45-minute tour (English tours on request). An English-language video explains how the cave was formed. ⊠ *Rte. 3866, Avshalom Nature Reserve* ☎ *02/991–1117* ⊕ *www.parks.org. il* ☜ *NIS 28.*

WORTH NOTING

Buster's Beverage Co. South African Denny Neilson brews alcoholic apple cider and hard lemonade in Beit Shemesh. The brewery is named for the family dog; the cider—dry or sweet—is crisp and delicious. Factory tours, tastings, and occasional barbecues take place Friday; call ahead to reserve. Ask about Danny's beer, known as Isra-Ale. ⊠ *Nacham Industrial Park* ✦ *Off Rte. 38* ☎ *054/638–1103* ⊕ *www.busters.co.il* ☾ *Closed Sat.–Thurs.*

Kadma Wines. Born in the Republic of Georgia, former software engineer Lina Slutzkin remembers how wine was once made there in egg-shaped clay casks. At Kadma Wines, she uses these unusual vessels to produce a range of red wines. Tours run every hour from 11 to 2 on Friday and Saturday and include a sampling of fresh goat cheese and tasty bread to accompany the wine. ⊠ *Rte. 44, 14½ km (9 miles) northwest of Beit Shemesh, Kfar Uriya* ☎ *02/992–7894, 054/919–5156* ⊕ *www.kadma-wine.co.il* ☜ *Tours NIS 35, by appointment only.*

Shapiro Beer. "Jerusalem's Beer" is actually brewed in Beit Shemesh, but brothers Dani, Itzik, and Avi learned how in their Jerusalem basement. The three main beers are an oatmeal stout, wheat beer, and pale ale, all labeled with a Jerusalem lion downing a bottle. Call in advance to tour the brewery and sip a few samples in the tiny kitchen overlooking the floor. ⊠ *Off Rte. 38* ☎ *02/561–2622* ⊕ *shapirobeer.co.il* ☜ *NIS 400 for tour and tasting for groups up to 15 people* ☾ *Closed Fri. and Sat.*

Tel Beit Shemesh. This low-profile archaeological site has fine views of the fields of Nahal Soreq, where Samson dallied with Delilah (Judges 16). When the Philistines captured the Israelite Ark of the Covenant in battle (11th century BC), they found that their prize brought divine retribution with it, destroying their idol Dagon and afflicting their bodies with tumors and cities with rats (I Samuel 5). The Philistines rid themselves of the jinxed ark by sending it back to the Israelites at Beit Shemesh. The stone ruins of the tell—including the oldest iron workshop in the world—are hard to interpret without an archaeologist on hand. ⊠ *Rte. 38, 2 km (1 mile) from Tzora turnoff* ☜ *Free.*

Tzora Vineyard. Overlooking the Soreq Valley, this kibbutz winery sells and serves reds and whites, including their Shoresh signature red blend of single-vineyard Cabernet Sauvignon, Syrah, and Merlot. Wine-tasting workshops cost NIS 60, though you get NIS 30 back if you purchase a bottle. ⊠ *Rte. 3835* ☎ *02/990–8261* ⊕ *www.tzorawines.com* ☜ *Tasting NIS 60* ☾ *Closed Sat.*

Tzuba Vineyard. Part of the eponymous kibbutz, this winery produces excellent Cabernet Sauvignon, Syrah, and Chardonnay. Call winemaker

Paul Dubb to coordinate a visit. ⊠ *Rte. 395, Tzuba ✛ 12 km (7½ miles) west of Jerusalem* ☎ *02/534–7000, 054/563–7788 Paul Dubb* ⊕ *www. tzubawinery.co.il* ⊠ *NIS 35* ⊗ *Closed Sat.*

WHERE TO EAT

$$
MIDDLE EASTERN

✕ **Derech Hagefen.** Just outside Jerusalem, a leafy garden and a wood-burning stove make a rustic setting for delicious takes on new Israeli cooking. Try the Beit Zayit salad with mushrooms, cherry tomatoes, and asparagus. Mullet kebabs are juicy skewers of grilled fish. More traditional eaters can find pizza and pasta. The wine list has a generous range of local and foreign bottles. The restaurant is kosher. ⑤ *Average main: NIS 70* ⊠ *Derech Hagefen 1, Beit Zayit* ☎ *02/650–2044* ⊕ *www.d-hagefen.co.il* ⊗ *Closed Sat. and Jewish holidays. No dinner Fri.*

$$$
MIDDLE EASTERN

✕ **Majda.** An earnest Jewish-Arab couple makes fresh food straight from their garden in this picturesque spot a few miles west of Jerusalem. Yakub Barhum built the outdoor deck and pergola overhead. Michal Baranc, the chef, dreamed up the menu. Dishes change regularly; sardine *siniyeh* features fresh cherry tomatoes with sardines served rustically on a tin plate. The fig salad is a celebration of the summer's juicy abundance, while fish cooked in grape leaves stays toothsome and aromatic. The *knafeh* dessert—usually goat cheese served hot and covered with semolina dough—gets a makeover here with poppy seed and a hint of lavender. It beautifully draws on both Jewish and Arab influences to become a uniquely new yet familiar concept. From Jerusalem, take Route 1 toward Tel Aviv and get off at Route 3975 toward Ein Rafah. ⑤ *Average main: NIS 97* ⊠ *Off Rte. 3975, Ein Rafah* ☎ *02/579–7108* ⊕ *majda.co.il* ⊗ *Closed Sun.–Wed.*

SHOPPING

Ya'aran Farm. This small but popular farm, run by Yavshi and Bar Ya'aran, produces more than 10 types of hard and soft organic goat cheese from their herd of 130 goats that enjoy a life of grazing. It's best to come on a Saturday, when the couple bakes their own bread. If Bar isn't too busy, she'll explain her vision of living off the land, using only rainwater and solar power and windmills for energy. The farm is 8 km (5 miles) east of Beit Shemesh. It's open daily, but you must call ahead to visit any day except Friday and Saturday. ⊠ *Rte. 3866* ☎ *050/750–0253, 054/683–0183* ⊗ *Closed Mon.–Thurs. and Sun. except by appointment.*

ELLA VALLEY

10 km (6 miles) south of Beit Shemesh, 42 km (26 miles) west of Jerusalem.

The Ella Valley is one of those delightful places—not uncommon in Israel—where you can relate the scenery to a specific biblical text and confirm the maxim that once you've visited this country, you'll never read the Bible in quite the same way again. Beyond the junction of Route 38 with Route 383, and up to the right above the pinewood slopes of Park Britannia, is a distinctively bald flattop hill, **Tel Azekah,** the site of an ancient Israelite town. The hills are especially delightful in March and April when the wildflowers are out; hiking paths are plentiful.

Beit Guvrin-Maresha National Park preserves ancient caves used for storage, industry, and tombs.

In the Ella Valley, the southernmost of the great valleys that cut from the Judean highlands toward the coast, Route 38 crosses a usually dry streambed; 200 yards beyond is a place to pull off and park. If you have a Bible, open it to I Samuel 17 and read about the dramatic duel between the Israelite shepherd David and the Philistine champion Goliath. The battle probably took place close to where you're standing:

And Saul and the men of Israel were gathered, and encamped in the valley of Ella, and drew up in line of battle against the Philistines. And the Philistines stood on the mountain on the one side, and Israel stood on the mountain on the other side, with a valley between them.

Look east up the valley to the mountains of Judah in the distance and the road from Bethlehem—the same road by which David reached the battlefield. The white northern ridge, a spur of the mountains of Judah, may have been the camp of the Israelite army. The southern ridge (where the gas station is today) is where the Philistines gathered. The creek, the only one in the valley, is where David "chose five smooth stones." The rest, as they say, is history: Goliath was slain, the Philistines were routed, and David went on to become the darling of the nation and eventually its king.

GETTING HERE AND AROUND
Follow Route 1 west from Jerusalem, then head south on Route 38, passing Beit Shemesh on your left.

EXPLORING
TOP ATTRACTIONS

Abeer Haela. Aram Dekel was the first to brew beer in the rolling green hills of the Ella Valley, brimming with biblical history. Some of his bottles evoke ancient recipes with date syrup and honey. The allspice beer stays on your tongue with its crisp and potent flavor. Make sure to ask about the mead and ginger liqueur. You must call ahead to reserve a tasting and a workshop on the secrets of home brewing. ⊠ *Farm 25, Rte. 3554, Tzafririm* ☎ *054/700–0512* ✉ *NIS 1100 for 1-hr group workshop.*

FAMILY
Fodor'sChoice
★

Beit Guvrin–Maresha National Park. This national park encompasses some 1,250 acres of rolling hills in the Judean lowlands, where for thousands of years people dug quarries, burial caves, storerooms, hideouts, and dovecotes in a subterranean labyrinth of unparalleled complexity. In the Second Temple period, millions of pilgrims ascended to Jerusalem to offer animal sacrifices. At Beit Guvrin, doves were raised on a vast scale to supply the pilgrims' need. Unlike many ruins, this national park allows you to readily envision life 2,000 years ago, both above- and underground.

The antiquities sprawl around the kibbutz of Beit Guvrin, just beyond the junction of Routes 38 and 35. These are bits and pieces of the 2nd- to 3rd-century AD Beit Guvrin, renamed (around the year 200) *Eleuthropolis*, "the city of free men." The amphitheater—an arena for Roman blood sports and mock sea battles—is one of only a few discovered in Israel.

After entering the park, drive south toward the flattop mound of ancient Maresha, known today as Tel Maresha. King Rehoboam of Judah fortified it, but it was during the Hellenistic period (4th to 2nd centuries BC) that the city reached its height and the endless complexes of chalk caves were dug. Maresha was finally destroyed by the Parthians in 40 BC and replaced by the nearby Roman city of Beit Guvrin. The view from the tell is worth the short climb.

Ancient Mareshans excavated thousands of underground chambers to extract soft chalk bricks, with which they built their homes aboveground. Residents then turned their "basement" quarries into industrial complexes, with water cisterns, olive-oil presses, and columbaria (derived from the Latin word *columba*, meaning dove or pigeon). The birds were used in ritual sacrifice and as food, producers of fertilizer, and message carriers.

The most interesting and extensive cave system is just off the road on the opposite side of the tell (the trail begins at a parking lot). It includes water cisterns, storerooms, and a restored ancient olive press. The excitement of exploration makes this site a must for kids (with close parental supervision, though the safety features are good), but the many steps are physically demanding.

The great "bell caves" of Beit Guvrin date from the late Roman, Byzantine, and early Arab periods (2nd to 7th century AD), when the locals created a quarry to extract lime for cement. At the top of each bell-shape space is a hole through the 4-foot-thick stone crust of the ground. When the ancient diggers reached the soft chalk below, they began reaming out their quarry in the structurally secure bell shape, each bell eventually cutting into the one adjacent to it. Although not built to be inhabited, the caves may have been used as refugees by early Christians. In the North Cave, a cross high on the wall, at the same level as an Arabic inscription, suggests a degree of coexistence even after the Arab conquest of the area in AD 636. More recently, Beit Guvrin was an Arab village, depopulated in 1948.

After leaving this system, continue walking down the hill to visit the Sidonian Burial Caves. These magnificent 3rd- to 2nd-century BC tombs—adorned with colorful, restored frescoes and inscriptions—have important archaeological evidence as to the nature of the town's ancient Phoenician colonists.

> ### MICROBREWERIES IN ISRAEL
>
> In the last decade, microbreweries have taken off in Israel. Importers are bringing in more exotic varieties of barley and hops, and well-traveled Israelis are re-creating favorites they sipped in Belgium, Germany, England, and the United States. The area around the Ella Valley, Beit Shemesh, and Latrun is especially easy to tour because most breweries are a short distance from each other. It's worth calling in advance, as the hours change frequently.

The undeveloped complexes of caves near the tell are off-limits to visitors. Keep to the marked sites only. The brochure at the entrance has a good map of the site. ⊠ *Off Rte. 35, Beit Shemesh* ✢ *21 km (13 miles) south of Beit Shemesh* ☎ *08/681–1020* ⊕ *www.parks.org.il* ☑ *NIS 28.*

Dig for a Day. Archaeological Seminars, in Jerusalem, runs this program at Beit Guvrin-Maresha National Park. The three-hour activity includes supervised digging in a real excavation site inside a cave, into which local inhabitants dumped earth and artifacts 21 centuries ago. Participants then sift the buckets of dirt they have hauled out of the cave, looking for finds. Some museum-quality artifacts of the 3rd to 2nd centuries BC (Hellenistic period) have been uncovered here. (No, you can't take home what you find!) You are then led on a fun 30-minute exploration through caves not yet open to the public. This involves some crawling, because some spaces are too tight or too low for walking upright. The tour ends with a short talk in the pottery shed about how clay vessels are reconstructed. You must reserve ahead. ⊠ *Beit Shemesh* ☎ *02/586–2011* ⊕ *www.archesem.com* ☑ *$30 plus park entrance fee.*

WORTH NOTING

Srigim Brewery. Ohad Eilon and Ofer Ronen fell in love with European and American beers while traveling for work in the Israeli high-tech industry, and they quit their jobs to found this award-winning brewery. The two take great care when crafting their fantastic Bavarian-style wheat beer, dark ale, and India pale ale, which you can sip while overlooking the Ella Valley. Call ahead for guided tours Sunday to Thursday, or stop by for free tastings and pub fare on Friday and Saturday. ⊠ *Rte. 353, Srigim* ☎ *052/622–7679, 052/593–8287* ⊕ *www. srigim-beer.co.il* ☑ *Tour NIS 27.*

WHERE TO EAT

$$
MODERN ISRAELI
FAMILY
Fodor'sChoice
★

✕ **Hans Sternbach Vineyards.** It's worth the drive here to sample the rustic and delicious creations by vintner Gadi Sternbach, who makes nearly everything on the menu, from the bread to the ricotta and the outstanding cured beef, tuna, and salmon. The succulent beef stew and unforgettable glazed onions are cooked in a sauce that uses the winery's own red wines. Seating is in the dining room or on a terrace shaded by leafy trees and flowers. Sternbach is a former tour guide and can explain the biblical history of the surrounding hills and show you around the vineyards. Tours and tastings are offered hourly on Friday and Saturday, and can be arranged on weekdays if you call in advance. ⑤ *Average main: NIS 75* ✉ *Farm 83, Rte. 3544, Givat Yeshayahu* ☎ *02/999–0162* ⊕ *www.hsw.co.il.*

**EN
ROUTE**
Instead of the Tel Aviv–Jerusalem expressway, an attractive alternative route back to Jerusalem is Route 375 through the Ella Valley, past Israel's main satellite communications receiver, and up through wooded hill country to Tzur Hadassah (look out for the rock-hewn Roman road on the right). Route 386 heads off to the left and runs north to Jerusalem through rugged mountain scenery, emerging in the Ein Kerem neighborhood on the city's western edge.

BETHLEHEM

8 km (5 miles) south of Jerusalem.

Fodor'sChoice
★

Even from a distance, it's easy to identify the minarets and steeples that symbolically vie for control of the skyline of Bethlehem, home to one of the oldest Christian communities in the world. Although a few decades ago most residents were Christians, today the great majority of greater Bethlehem's 30,000 residents are Muslim, as elsewhere in the West Bank.

For Christians the world over, the city is synonymous with the birth of Jesus and the many shrines that celebrate that event. Bethlehem is also the site of the Tomb of Rachel, Jacob's wife, who died in childbirth here. Rachel's Tomb today lies in Israeli-controlled territory, immediately to the north of the wall that divides the area.

GETTING HERE AND AROUND

The birthplace of Jesus is 15 minutes south of Jerusalem, although the ride seldom goes so quickly. This is because Bethlehem is part of the Palestinian Authority and set off from Jerusalem by the controversial security barrier that snakes roughly along the border with the West Bank. The wall is especially intimidating around the Bethlehem border crossing, as it stands taller than most of the surrounding buildings and is constructed of solid concrete. Graffiti artists have covered the Bethlehem side with demands for rights for Palestinians. British artist Banksy also left his mark, inspiring a falafel stand and souvenir stand named after him. As daunting as it seems, tourists with a foreign passport have no difficulty visiting Bethlehem. Simply show the cover of your passport and be whisked through, usually without a single question.

Christmas in Bethlehem includes a colorful Greek Orthodox procession in Manger Square.

TIMING
Allow at least two hours for a visit to the Church of the Nativity and Manger Square.

SAFETY AND PRECAUTIONS
Tourists are unlikely to be bothered in Bethlehem, but check travel advisories before your trip. You can also ask your hotel concierge if there have been any recent issues.

TOURS
In recent years Bethlehem has made a concerted effort to woo tourists. Several companies like the Alternative Tourism Group organize people-to-people meetings and unusual hiking trips through farming villages.

Alternative Tourism Group. This West Bank–based organization offers everything from day trips to overnight visits to Bethlehem and other spots in the West Bank. Tours of Bethlehem and Hebron run every Monday and Thursday and cost NIS 335. ☎ 02/277–2151 ⊕ *www.atg.ps*.

VISITOR INFORMATION
Contacts Bethlehem Tourist Information Office. ⊠ *Peace Center, Manger Sq.* ☎ *02/275–1315* ⊕ *www.travelpalestine.ps.* **Visitor Information Center.** ⊠ *Manger Sq.* ☎ *02/275–4235* ⊕ *vicbethlehem.wordpress.com.*

EXPLORING

TOP ATTRACTIONS

Church of St. Catherine. Built by Franciscans in 1882, Bethlehem's Roman Catholic parish church incorporates remnants of its 12th-century Crusader predecessor. Note the bronze doors with reliefs of St. Jerome, St. Paula, and St. Eustochium. From this church, the midnight Catholic Christmas mass is broadcast around the world. Steps descend from within the church to a series of dim grottoes, clearly once used as living quarters. Chapels here are dedicated to Joseph, the Innocents killed by Herod the Great, and to the 4th-century St. Jerome, who wrote the Vulgate—the Latin translation of the Bible—supposedly right here. St. Catherine is adjacent to the Church of the Nativity, and accessible by a passage from its Armenian chapel. Next to the church is a lovely cloister, restored in 1949. A small wooden door (kept locked) connects the complex with the Grotto of the Nativity. Call ahead to check hours, as they change frequently. ⊠ *Manger Sq.* ☎ *02/274–2425* ⊕ *www.bethlehem. custodia.org/default.asp?id=476.*

Fodor's Choice ★ **Church of the Nativity.** At this church marking the traditional site of the birth of Jesus, the stone exterior is crowned by the crosses of the three denominations sharing it: the Greek Orthodox, Latins (Roman Catholic, represented by the Franciscan order), and Armenian Orthodox. The blocked, square entranceway dates from the time of the Byzantine emperor Justinian (6th century); the arched entrance (also blocked) within the Byzantine one is 12th-century Crusader; and the current low entrance was designed in the 16th century to protect the worshippers from attack by hostile Muslim neighbors.

The church interior is vast and gloomy. In the central nave, a large wooden trapdoor reveals a remnant of a striking mosaic floor from the original basilica, built in the 4th century by Helena, mother of Constantine the Great, the Roman emperor who first embraced Christianity. Emperor Justinian's rebuilding two centuries later enlarged the church, creating its present-day plan and structure, including the 44 red-stone columns with Corinthian capitals that run the length of the nave in two paired lines.

This is the oldest standing church in the country. When the Persians invaded in 614, they destroyed every Christian church and monastery in the land except this one. Legend holds that the church was adorned with a wall painting depicting the Nativity, including the visit to the infant Jesus by the Three Wise Men of the East. For the local artist, "east" meant Persia, and he dressed his wise men in Persian garb. The Persian conquerors did not understand the picture's significance, but "recognized" themselves in the painting and so spared the church. In the 8th century, the church was pillaged by the Muslims and was later renovated by the Crusaders. Patches of 12th-century mosaics high on the walls, the medieval oak ceiling beams, and figures of saints on the Corinthian pillars hint at its medieval splendor.

The elaborately ornamented front of the church serves as the parish church of Bethlehem's Greek Orthodox community. The right transept is theirs, too, but the left transept belongs to the Armenian Orthodox.

Bethlehem

❶ ↑
TO JERUSALEM

KEY

i *Tourist information*

Hebron Rd.

HARAT
AL-HURAYZAT

Jacir Palace
Bethlehem ♦

TO
BEIT JALA ←
HWY 60

Beit Jala St.

Al-Karkafa St.

♦ Hosh Jasmin
♦ Ka'abar

Manger St.

Paul VI St.

John Paul II St.

♦
Bethlehem
University

HARAT
AL-TARAGMA

Singer Café ♦
Tent ♦ →

HARAT
AL-BATIN

Al-Fawaghreh St.

Star St.

Hosh al-Syrian
♦ guesthouse

Hebron Rd.

Jamal Abdel Hasser St.

Bethlehem
Lutheran
Guest House ♦

THE
OLD CITY

Beit Sahour St.

❻ →

Peace Center Restaurant ♦

i ❷ ❸

Afteem

❹

Attan St.

Al-Saff St.

Anatre St.

Wad

Milk Grotto St.

Dar Sitti Aziza ♦

❺

The altar in the left transept is known as the altar of the kings, because tradition holds this to be the place where the three magi dismounted. For centuries, all three "shareholders" in the church have vied for control of the holiest Christian sites in the Holy Land. The 19th-century Status Quo Agreement that froze their respective rights and privileges in Jerusalem's Church of the Holy Sepulcher and the Tomb of the Virgin pertains here, too: ownership, the timing of ceremonies, number of oil lamps, and so on are all clearly defined.

From the right transept at the front of the church, descend to the Grotto of the Nativity, encased in white marble. Long lines can form at the entrance to the grotto, making the suggestion of spending just an hour to see the church an impossibility. Once a cave—precisely the kind of place that might have been used as a barn—the grotto has been reamed, plastered, and decorated beyond recognition. Immediately on the right is a small altar, and on the floor below it is the focal point of the entire site: a 14-point silver star with the Latin inscription *"hic de virgine maria jesus christus natus est"* (Here of the Virgin Mary, Jesus Christ was born). The Latins placed the original star here in 1717 but lost control of the altar 40 years later to the more influential Greek Orthodox. In 1847 the star mysteriously disappeared, and pressure from the Turkish sultan compelled the Greeks

CLOSE UP

The West Bank

The West Bank is a kidney-shape area, a bit larger than the U.S. state of Delaware. The large majority of the approximately 2 million Palestinians are Muslim, with the Christian minority living mostly in the greater Bethlehem area and Ramallah, and a tiny community of Samaritans living on Mount Gerizim near Nablus.

The West Bank gets its name from the Jordan River. Under the British, it was part of the state of Palestine. The newly formed Kingdom of Transjordan occupied the West Bank in its war with the nascent State of Israel in 1948. Israel conquered the West Bank from Jordan in the Six Days' War of 1967. At first, Israeli leaders assumed they would return the territory in exchange for peace, but soon changed tack and saw it as a resource of land, water, and heritage.

In Israel itself, the region is often referred to as "the territories," "over the Green Line" (a term denoting the 1949 armistice line between the West Bank and Israel), or by its biblical names of Judea (the area south of Jerusalem) and Samaria (the much larger area north of Jerusalem).

Following the Oslo Accords in 1993, much of the West Bank was, on paper, turned over to the Palestinian Authority. However, a comprehensive agreement has proven elusive due to seemingly irreconcilable differences on the thorny issues of land, settlements, refugees, and Jerusalem.

In addition to the 2 million Arabs in the West Bank, half a million Israelis also live there in hundreds of small settlements and a number of cities. The larger urban settlements are really satellite communities of

Jerusalem and Tel Aviv; however, nationalist Israelis have also set up smaller, ideological caravan sites and settlements deep into the West Bank in a drive to maintain Jewish control in the Biblical homeland.

With its prime location within 14 km (9 miles) of the Mediterranean Sea, and its mountain heights—dominating Israel's main population centers—the West Bank has a strategic value that has convinced even many Israelis that it would be folly to relinquish it to potentially hostile Arab control. Other Israelis favor some kind of two-state solution. Meanwhile, Palestinians say Israeli rule has isolated their cities, stunted their economy, drawn down their water supply, and forced them to depend on low-wage work in Israel and international aid.

In late 2000, the simmering crisis exploded with lethal ferocity as young Palestinians took to the streets in riots known as the Second Intifada. In 2002, Israel began building a separation barrier roughly along the 1967 border. In 2005, Israel unilaterally withdrew from the Gaza Strip and four remote settlements in northern Samaria. Although violence has subsided significantly, some visitors still avoid the West Bank. Others, while exercising caution, visit such worthwhile West Bank sites as Bethlehem and Jericho.

Tourists can travel to Bethlehem and Jericho as security conditions permit; they need to take passports with them. At this writing, Israeli citizens are prohibited from entering areas under full Palestinian control. Please check your government's travel advisory before visiting these areas.

to allow the present Latin replacement to be installed in 1853. The Franciscan guardians do have possession, however, of the little alcove a few steps down on the left at the entrance to the grotto, said to be the manger where the infant Jesus was laid. ✉ *Manger Sq.* ☎ *02/274–2440* ⊕ *www. bethlehem.custodia.org* ✉ *Free* ⊙ *Grotto closed Sun. morning.*

Manger Square. Bethlehem's central plaza and the site of the Church of the Nativity, Manger Square is built over the grotto thought to be the birthplace of Jesus. The end of the square opposite the church is the Mosque of Omar, the city's largest Muslim house of worship. The square occupies the center of Bethlehem's Old City and has a tourist information office, several good souvenir shops, and restaurants where you can drink a coffee

CHRISTMAS IN BETHLEHEM

In Bethlehem, Christmas is celebrated three times: December 25 by the Roman Catholics and Protestants; January 6 by the Greek, Coptic, and Russian Orthodox; and January 19 by the Armenian Orthodox. For nearly a month, Manger Square is brilliantly illuminated and bursting with life. On December 24, choirs from around the world perform carols and sacred music in the square between 8:30 pm and 11:30 pm, and at midnight at the Franciscan Church of St. Catherine. That service is relayed on closed-circuit television onto a large screen in Manger Square and, via satellite, to all parts of the globe.

while people-watching. On Christmas, it is filled with lights, music tents, Palestinian children's marching bands, and merrymakers in Santa hats.

Fodor'sChoice **Shepherds' Fields.** Just east of Bethlehem is the town of Beit Sahour, ★ famous in Christian tradition for the Shepherds' Fields, where herdsmen received the "tidings of great joy" that Jesus was born in Bethlehem (Luke 2). The same fields are also said to be where the biblical Ruth the Moabite, daughter-in-law of Naomi, "gleaned in the field" (Ruth 2:2). Local Christians disagree about where the real Shepherds' Fields are, and two chapels and gardens give rival interpretations, complete with rival Byzantine relics. Entrance is free to both.

The Greek Orthodox Der El Rawat Chapel is a small white building with a charming red dome; inside, bright paintings of the Stations of the Cross cover the walls and soaring ceilings. A mosaic dating to a 5th-century Byzantine church lies just outside. A Catholic church— Shepherds' Field of the Franciscan Custody of the Holy Land—is a short walk away. This tiny, minimalist chapel built over a cave is tucked away in a lush garden, with walking paths surrounded by soaring pines and bright aloe plants. Outside are a number of souvenir stores and coffee shops. ✉ *Beit Sahour* ⊕ *www.bethlehem.custodia.org* ✉ *Free* ⊙ *Greek Orthodox chapel closed Sun.*

WORTH NOTING

Fodor'sChoice **Milk Grotto.** Legend has it that when Mary stopped here to nurse the ★ baby Jesus, a drop of milk fell on the floor in this cavelike grotto and the walls turned white. The grotto and the church above are beautiful, especially just before sunset when the light catches the stained-glass windows. ⊠ *Milk Grotto St.* ☏ *02/627–2692* ⊕ *www.bethlehem.custodia.org* 🎫 *Free* ☯ *Closed Sun. Apr.–Sept.*

Rachel's Tomb. The Bible relates that the matriarch Rachel, second and favorite wife of Jacob, died in childbirth on the outskirts of Bethlehem, "and Jacob set up a pillar upon her grave" (Genesis 35:19–20). There is no trace of that pillar, but observant Jews for centuries have hallowed the velvet-draped cenotaph inside the building as the site of Rachel's tomb. People come to pray here for good health, fertility, and a safe birth. Some pilgrims wind a red thread seven times around the tomb, and give away snippets of it as talismans to cure all ills. Today, Rachel's Tomb is an Israeli enclave in the Palestinian area of Bethlehem.

Islam as well venerates Rachel. Next to the tomb is a Muslim cemetery, reflecting the Middle Eastern tradition that it is a special privilege to be buried near a great personage. Note that men and women are separated here and have different entrances. Egged Bus 163 runs from Jerusalem to the tomb. The site is surrounded by a concrete barrier, so for access from Bethlehem you must return to Jerusalem. ⊠ *Rte. 60* ☏ *02/580–0863* ⊕ *www.keverrachel.com* 🎫 *Free* ☯ *Closed Sat. and holidays.*

WHERE TO EAT

$ | MIDDLE EASTERN | Fodor's Choice | ★

✕ **Afteem.** Just off Manger Square, Afteem draws locals and tourists alike for its falafel, hummus, and chicken platters. Enjoy them sitting inside a stone cave or standing on the steps outside. Taybeh beer, local wine, and fresh fruit juices are available to wash it all down. The best part is that the prices are unbeatable. ⑤ *Average main: NIS 20* ⊠ *Manger Sq.* ☏ *02/274–7940* ▬ *No credit cards.*

$$ | MIDDLE EASTERN | FAMILY | Fodor's Choice | ★

✕ **Hosh Jasmin.** Filmmaker Mazen Saadeh learned organic farming techniques in Oregon and returned to his native West Bank to cook what he grows on the rocky terraces outside Bethlehem. Sit at a table, order rabbit cooked in a *zarb*, or underground oven, wash it down with freshly distilled arak liquor or red wine made on-site, and gaze at olive trees that have been growing here for centuries. To get here, go to the DCO checkpoint in Beit Jala and call Mazen for precise directions. The site is in Area C, meaning it is open to Israeli cars and taxis. ⑤ *Average main: NIS 55* ⊠ *Al Makhrour, Beit Jala* ☏ *059/986–8914.*

$ | MIDDLE EASTERN | Fodor's Choice | ★

✕ **Ka'bar.** Just west of Bethlehem in Beit Jala, this fluorescent-lit hole-in-the-wall has perfected the art of grilled chicken—a good thing, since it's the only item on the menu. The birds are butterflied and charred on a six-foot-long grill outside. Half or whole chickens are served with colorful salads, creamy hummus, and an unforgettable light garlic sauce whipped with olive oil. Taxi drivers can take you here from Manger Square, and it's worth the trip. ⑤ *Average main: NIS 40* ⊠ *Near Beit Jala Municipality Bldg., Beit Jala* ☏ *02/274–1419* ▬ *No credit cards* ☯ *Closed Sun.*

$ | MIDDLE EASTERN

✕ **Peace Center Restaurant.** Palestinian classics are the main draw at this eatery steps from the Church of the Nativity. Try the *maqloubeh,* a spiced and baked chicken leg served with a colorful pilaf of yellow

rice and eggplant, cauliflower, and carrots. Another great option is *musakhan*, chicken and onion baked in sumac spice over flatbread. There are also a wide range of pasta dishes. Palestinian Taybeh beer is on tap, and you can end with local baklava pastry or tiramisu. $ *Average main: NIS 35* ⊠ *20 Manger Sq.* ☎ *02/276–6677.*

$ ✕ **Singer Café.** Reflecting the backgrounds of the Dutch-Palestinian
CAFÉ couple that founded this coffee shop for the literati of Bethlehem, old Singer sewing machines are the tables and portraits of Palestinian poet laureate Mahmoud Darwish dot the walls. Besides good coffee, you can enjoy fresh juice or lighter fare like sandwiches and salads. Keep an eye on the bulletin boards for upcoming book readings and local tours. The café is a 15-minute walk from the Church of the Nativity. $ *Average main: NIS 25* ⊠ *Near Beit Sahour municipality, Beit Sahour* ☎ *059/992–9989* ⊕ *www.singercafe.com.*

$ ✕ **Stars and Bucks.** Come to this Palestinian-owned chain for the freshly
CAFÉ pressed orange and pomegranate juices or a potent cup of thick Arabic coffee. Take home a souvenir mug printed with a green circle that looks strikingly like one from a certain U.S. coffee behemoth. $ *Average main: NIS 12* ⊠ *Manger St.* ☎ *02/275–8787.*

$$ ✕ **Tent Restaurant.** Slip into a bright red chair, order a water pipe, and
MIDDLE EASTERN wait for waiters in white shirts and black vests to bring out well-spiced grilled meats, hummus, and salads. This massive restaurant with wide windows is a great way to end a day of sightseeing; it's in Beit Sahour. $ *Average main: NIS 70* ⊠ *Shepherd's Field St., Beit Sahour* ☎ *02/277–3875* ⊕ *tent.ps.*

WHERE TO STAY

$ ▦ **Bethlehem Lutheran Guest House** (*Abu Jubran*). Rooms are named for
B&B/INN nearby villages in this stone-walled, clean, and modest guesthouse that overlooks a busy market street a few steps from Manger Square. **Pros:** inexpensive; central location; charming. **Cons:** can get noisy; bathrooms are quite basic. $ *Rooms from: $102* ⊠ *Dar Annadwa, Paul IV St. 109* ☎ *02/277–0047* ⊕ *www.diyar.ps* ⬐ *13 rooms* ⦿❘ *Breakfast.*

$ ▦ **Dar Sitti Aziza.** Scientist Nabil Rishmawi renovated his grandmoth-
B&B/INN er's house and created Bethlehem's first heritage hotel, with each room named for its original function: the wine room, olive room, and horse room, and so on. **Pros:** unique restoration property; personal service; great location near all the major sites. **Cons:** basic rooms and bathroom; a bit overpriced. $ *Rooms from: $160* ⊠ *Anatra St.* ☎ *02/274–4848* ⊕ *www.darsittiaziza.ps/en* ⬐ *9 rooms* ⦿❘ *Breakfast.*

$ ▦ **Hosh al-Syrian Guesthouse.** This charming guesthouse, in the quar-
B&B/INN ter formerly home to city's once-vibrant Assyrian community (some
Fodor'sChoice of whom still remain), has great rooftop views and thoughtfully
★ designed stone-walled rooms with Palestinian soaps from Nablus and vintage portraits of local Bethlehem families. **Pros:** walking distance to all the sites; sophisticated ambience; reasonable rates. **Cons:** none of the amenities of larger hotels. $ *Rooms from: $100* ⊠ *Assyrian Quarter, Children St.* ☎ *02/274–7529* ⊕ *www.hoshalsyrian.com* ⬐ *11 rooms* ⦿❘ *Breakfast.*

$ 🔲 **Jacir Palace Bethlehem.** Bethlehem's most luxurious accommodation
HOTEL   is in a century-old mansion, and the stunning stone building and five-
Fodor's Choice   star service make you feel like a sultan. **Pros:** amazing atmosphere;
★   excellent service; swimming pool. **Cons:** navigating the hallways can
be tough; long walk to main Bethlehem sites. $ *Rooms from: $150*
⊠ *Jerusalem–Hebron Rd.* 🕾 *02/276–6777* ⊕ *www.jacirpalace.ps* ↴ *250
rooms* ⦿| *Breakfast.*

SHOPPING

In the city's 300 workshops, Bethlehem craftspeople make carved
olive-wood and mother-of-pearl objects, mostly of a religious nature,
but many stores along the tourist route in town sell jewelry and trinkets. For quality and reliability, most of the large establishments on
Manger Street are worth investigating, but some of the merchants
near the Church of the Nativity, on Manger Square, have good-quality
items as well.

FAMILY   **Christmas House.** At this olive-wood factory, the gracious owner is happy
to show you how the well-known souvenirs are made—by a small
army of Palestinian craftsmen whittling away the local wood. Ask to
go up to the roof, which has a great view of Manger Square. The
shop ships worldwide. Don't forget to bargain. ⊠ *74 Milk Grotto St.*
🕾 *02/275–7233* ⊕ *mychristmashouse.com.*

TEL AVIV

WELCOME TO TEL AVIV

TOP REASONS TO GO

★ **Lively neighborhoods:** Check out Neve Tzedek's pastel-color homes and boutiques, Jaffa's jumble of a flea market, Tel Aviv Port's undulating board-walk, and Florentine's urban hipster feel.

★ **Mediterranean beaches:** Hit the sand, walk along the promenade, or watch the sun dip into the Mediterranean with the locals in the evening.

★ **Bauhaus architecture:** Tel Aviv is also known as "The White City" because it is home to the largest concentration of Bauhaus architecture in the world. Explore it on a walking tour.

★ **Nahalat Binyamin Pedestrian Mall:** Stalls of this twice-weekly street fair offer a range of handmade crafts from pottery to jew-elry at reasonable prices.

★ **Israel's best modern cuisine:** Inventive chefs have put the city on the gastronomic map—all good news for the hun-gry traveling foodie.

1 **Center City.** Most of Tel Aviv's major sites can be found in this warren of small side streets and hidden parks. Look for Rothschild Boulevard brimming with Bauhaus buildings, Carmel Market, and the Nahalat Binyamin Pedestrian Mall.

2 **Neve Tzedek.** Restoration has meant a renaissance for this neighborhood of narrow roads lined with boutiques, galleries, and cafés. The Suzanne Dellal Centre for Dance and Theatre, with its orange tree-studded square, is magical.

3 **Florentine.** Those seeking reasonable rents have brought a youthful, hipster vibe to this rough-around-the-edges part of town south of Neve Tzedek. Bars and restaurants make it lively at night.

4 **Jaffa.** This port—where a certain whale is said to have swallowed Jonah—is one of the oldest in the world. Here you'll find a flea market crammed with antique furniture and a growing number of trendy boutiques and restaurants.

GETTING ORIENTED

Tel Aviv's compact size and flat landscape make it easy to get around on foot. The city's main north–south thoroughfares of Hayarkon, Ben Yehuda (which becomes Allenby), Dizengoff, and Ibn Gvirol Streets run more or less parallel to the Mediterranean shoreline. Closest to the water is Hayarkon and the beachfront Tayelet. At the northern end of Hayarkon is the Tel Aviv Port. Most hotels are on the beachfront along Hayarkon.

5 **North Tel Aviv.** The abandoned warehouses of the Tel Aviv Port have been transformed into upscale restaurants, cafés, and clubs. Cyclists and strolling families pack the undulating boardwalk.

STREET FOOD IN ISRAEL

Fast, faster, fastest! If you're hungry right now, the streets of the Holy Land await your eating pleasure. Israel has a refined culture of noshing on the run, because everyone is always in a hurry and apparently hungry most of the time. Put food and drink in hand and join the locals.

To find the goods from falafel to papayas, look for the food stalls and kiosks that line Israel's main streets and shopping areas. Fruit and vegetable markets, notably Carmel Market in Tel Aviv and Machaneh Yehuda in Jerusalem, offer snack opportunities. In Tel Aviv, Rothschild Boulevard and Ben-Gurion Boulevard have popular food kiosks offering made-to-order sandwiches and fresh-squeezed juices. In Jerusalem, try the Old City's hummus spots or home-style restaurants. Most fast-food stalls serve lunch only. The outdoor markets in Tel Aviv and Jerusalem close in late afternoon and on Shabbat. In Jerusalem, no food stalls open on Shabbat, but in the Old City (except the Jewish Quarter) hummus and falafel joints do business.

GRAB IT AND GO

Some street fare is substantial, whether it's falafel or the sandwiches on five-nut artisanal breads that are edging out traditional favorites in Tel Aviv. Other choices are lighter. Sold in markets, in bakeries, and on street stands are sweet pastries called *rugelach*: these two-bite-size twists are rolled up with cinnamon or oozing with chocolate. Just-roasted nuts or sunflower seeds are a quick pick-me-up; or sip fresh-squeezed juices such as pomegranate or carrot. Frosty frozen yogurt is perfect on hot days. In winter, try a cup of hot custardlike *sahlab*, perhaps sprinkled with cinnamon.

FALAFEL

The region's ultimate fast-food snack consists of deep-fried chickpea balls—the best are crispy outside with soft centers. "Falafel" also refers to the whole production of the balls served in pita pockets with an array of chopped vegetable salads plus hummus, tahini, and pickles that you add yourself and then eat (watch for drips!) with a waxed paper napkin for further refinement. Vendors compete with extra touches such as free salads. It's filling, nutritious, and cheap.

HUMMUS

Ubiquitous in the Middle East, hummus is a creamy paste made from mashed chickpeas, olive oil, garlic, and tahini, a sesame sauce. You eat it in a pita or scoop it up from a plate with the same. In Hebrew, there's a verb for this action specifically related to hummus: *lenagev*, which means "to wipe." Heartfelt arguments prevail among Israelis over where to find the best hummus, but you should try it at a Middle Eastern specialty place; some of the best are on market alleys and side streets—even at gas stations.

SHAWARMA

For this fast-food favorite, marinated lamb or turkey slices are stacked and grilled on a vertical spit, then sliced off and stuffed into a pita. Accompaniments are usually the same as for falafel, though

onion rings and french fries are other extras. Jerusalem mixed grill (*me'orav Yerushalmi*) is unique to the holy city; look for it on Agrippas Street, alongside the outdoor fruit and vegetable market. It's a well-seasoned meal of grilled chicken hearts and other organ meats eaten in a pita with grilled onions.

TAHINI

Silky in texture, this sauce with a nutty, slightly sweet taste is made from ground sesame seeds, fresh lemon juice, and sometimes garlic. The tasty green variety has parsley chopped in. Tahini is used as a sauce and is the main ingredient in halvah, the famous Middle Eastern sweet. A popular dessert—among those not watching their calories—is a dish of vanilla ice cream topped with tahini and crumbled halvah and flooded with date syrup.

BOUREKAS

From the Balkans comes Israel's favorite snack: flaky, crispy, golden-brown *bourekas*. Best eaten warm, these pastry triangles, squares, or crescents are deliciously filled with tangy cheese or mashed potato or creamy spinach and sometimes mushrooms. Small (two bites) or large (four bites), they can be made of several kinds of dough: puff pastry, phyllo, and short pastry.

—By Judy Stacey Goldman

BAUHAUS STYLE IN TEL AVIV

Viewing Bauhaus, the defining architectural style of Tel Aviv, is a great way to explore the city. The geometric forms and pastel colors of this modern design ethos, transplanted in the 1930s by Jewish architects fleeing Europe, fit both the landscape and Zionist notions of a socialist Utopia.

The rounded corner balconies, rooftop garden, and staircase with windows are classic Bauhaus elements in this restored building at 17 Emile Zola Street.

The so-called White City, the central part of Tel Aviv that is home to the largest concentration of Bauhaus buildings, was named a World Cultural Heritage Site by UNESCO in 2003. Bauhaus-inspired architecture, more accurately referred to as the Modern or International Style, was based on the idea that art should serve society and that form should also have function. For example, balconies were not designed to be merely decorative but to serve as a source of shade, fresh air, and a place from which to interact with neighbors. Today conservation efforts are making headway, but many classic buildings need repair, their beauty lost under peeling paint and cracked concrete. It's a work in progress as the city offers incentives to owners to restore their properties.

STYLE ELEMENTS

Signature **vertical staircases** offset horizontal lines and are recognizable by the steel-frame windows that provide light. **Roof gardens,** identifiable by pergolas of beams and columns, were designed with the expectation that neighbors would socialize on their rooftops. **Balconies** can be curved or square or rectangular in shape, and are often overhung with ledges that provide shade.

A BAUHAUS WALK

The city's Bauhaus bounty is best discovered by foot. A good place to stroll is along Rothschild Boulevard and its side streets, which also have pleasant cafés and restaurants. A walking tour can begin at **90 Rothschild Boulevard,** at the corner of Balfour Street. Here a three-story, mustard-color building, with the clean lines that are a trademark of the style, stands in contrast to the highly decorated building next door. Note the front door with horizontal strips of wood inlaid in the glass. Its wooden shutters aren't necessarily an element that would be seen in European Bauhaus examples, but here became a necessity because of the sun. Walk to **89 and 91 Rothschild Boulevard,** twin buildings in need of renovation, and see the small vertical windows indicating the placement of a central staircase and the two main styles of balcony, rounded and rectangular.

Walk back across the boulevard and look for Engel Street, a pedestrian-friendly lane lined with Bauhaus buildings. **7 Engel Street** features horizontal bands of balconies and windows. The front door has an asymmetrical overhang and canopy. For an example of the city's restoration efforts, look up to its top floor, which continues the horizontal theme.

Returning to Rothschild Boulevard, walk to **113 and 115 Rothschild Boulevard.** Here again you can see the "thermometer" staircase and its small, elegant windows. On the right-hand side the balconies wrap around the building, mimicking the corner of the street; on the left-hand side the balconies are aligned with the side of the building.

SEEING MORE

Check the city tourist office for free Bauhaus walking tours. The **Bauhaus Center** at 99 Dizengoff Street sells books and more, and offers excellent walking tours. Another resource is the **Bauhaus Foundation Museum** at 21 Bialik Street, open Wednesday and Friday. Bialik Street has many attractive older buildings.

Exploring on your own? Here are a few key buildings around the city.

9 Gordon Street. Take in this 1935 building's elegant cube-within-a-cube design, wooden shutters, and rooftop pergola.

Haaretz Print Works, 56 Mazeh Street. The 1934 building where *Haaretz* newspaper was once printed has steel-framed glass windows and balconies with rounded railings and cantilevered roofs.

25 Idelson Street. Designed in 1931, this family villa has interesting balconies, an asymmetric form, and a mix of small horizontal and vertical windows.

Updated by
Inbal Baum

Tel Aviv, Israel's ever-growing metropolis, would be unrecognizable to its founders, a small group of Jewish immigrant families in what was then Ottoman-ruled Palestine. A skyline of shimmering skyscrapers has replaced the towering sand dunes of just over a century ago. The city is now known for its boxy Bauhaus apartment buildings, theaters, and concert halls, as well as its legions of sidewalk cafés that host overflowing crowds every night of the week.

The city manages to pull off the seemingly impossible task of being both hip and homey: witness the happy mix of wine bars, clothing boutiques, hardware shops, and greengrocers—often on the same block. High-end restaurants mingle with old-school eateries where elderly men hold noisy court about the issues of the day over black coffee and apple turnovers.

Sometimes described as an urban village, Tel Aviv is made for walking (or biking, now that it has an extensive network of more than 100 km [62 miles] of bike paths and a bike-share system). From most parts of the city, the sea is never more than a 20-minute walk. In this combination beach town, business center, and arts mecca, people spend Friday afternoon bumping into friends, wandering from café to café, and pausing to hear live jazz trios, all the while strolling with their dogs down boulevards lined with 1940s-era newspaper kiosks that have been transformed into gourmet sandwich stands.

Tel Aviv isn't the most beautiful of cities, although its charms have a way of making you forgive its aesthetic shortcomings. It was declared a UNESCO World Cultural Heritage Site in 2003 because its collection of International Style architecture, known more commonly as Bauhaus, is the largest in the world. Although restoration efforts are moving along, many of these buildings are in need of a face-lift. It might take an hour or two of wandering on the tree-lined side streets for you to appreciate their graceful lines and subtle architectural flourishes.

There's a spirit of freedom in Tel Aviv, where it's possible to escape from the difficult political realities that are closer to the surface in places like Jerusalem. After all, the city's nickname among Israelis is "the Bubble." Residents tend to be politically and socially liberal. The gay scene is thriving, as are the arts and music communities. It's an exciting city, one that newcomers, returning visitors, and longtime residents all find captivating.

TEL AVIV PLANNER

WHEN TO GO

Tel Aviv's mild Mediterranean climate means that any time is a good time to visit. Nevertheless, midday summer temperatures in the 90s may mean choosing museums and other air-conditioned sites until the sun dips and the sea breeze stirs. Weekends (in Israel this means Thursday night, Friday, and Saturday) are the busiest times, but also the most fun in terms of people-watching and special events.

PLANNING YOUR TIME

With two to four days, you can explore most of Tel Aviv and still have time for the beach. Although it's not a huge area to cover, see the city in geographical order. Start with Old Jaffa in the south, and amble through the art galleries, flea market, and fishing port. Jaffa can also be a good choice in the evening for strolling, low-key restaurants, and wine bars. From here, it's a short walk north to Neve Tzedek. Shop, dine, check out the well-restored buildings, and catch an evening dance performance at the Suzanne Dellal Centre. In the center of town, don't miss the Bauhaus buildings of the White City or the Nahalat Binyamin market (on Tuesday or Friday). If you have more time, head to the Museum of the Jewish People, the Palmach Museum, and the Eretz Israel Museum, as well as Hayarkon Park for boating or cycling. Tel Aviv Port is a good place for trendy dining and nightlife.

GETTING HERE AND AROUND

AIR TRAVEL

Ben Gurion International Airport, a few miles southeast of Tel Aviv, is the country's main airport and has both international and domestic flights.

For full information about air travel and transfers, see Getting Here and Around in Travel Smart Israel.

BIKE TRAVEL

Tel Aviv has more than 100 km (62 miles) of designated bike lanes and a user-friendly bike rental system called Tel-O-Fun. Look for the bright green bike stands throughout the city. The basic access fee is NIS 17 Sunday through Friday and NIS 23 on Saturday and on holidays. There's even a weekly basic access fee of NIS 70. Beyond the access fee, you pay an extra fee based on how long you keep the bike: NIS 10 for up to 90 minutes or NIS 70 for 3½ hours, for example.

BUS TRAVEL

Bus fare is a fixed NIS 6.90 within the city center, and you buy your tickets onboard. There's a small discount for a 10-ride card. Combined train-and-bus tickets are also available. Privately run minibuses, called "service taxis," run along two of the major lines: Bus 4 (Ben Yehuda and Allenby Streets) and Bus 5 (Dizengoff Street and Rothschild Boulevard). You can flag these down and ask to get off at any point along their routes; the fare is the same as on regular buses. Minibuses also run on Saturday, when regular buses don't.

From Tel Aviv's Central Bus Station, Jerusalem-bound buses depart every 15 minutes.

CAR TRAVEL

Driving in Tel Aviv isn't for the fainthearted; Israeli drivers are aggressive, and motorbikes weave in and out of traffic. Major highways lead in and out of Tel Aviv: Route 1 from Jerusalem, Route 4 from the northern coast, and Route 5 from the east. Take advantage of Tel Aviv's belt road, the Ayalon Freeway, to access various parts of the city. The city has started work on a light-rail system, causing some street closures that change frequently.

TAXI TRAVEL

The fastest and easiest way into the city from Ben Gurion International Airport is by taxi, and costs NIS 170. During rush hour, allow 45 minutes for a trip that would otherwise be 20 minutes.

Taxis can be any car model or color and have lighted signs on top. They're plentiful, even in bad weather; drivers honk to catch your attention, even if you're not trying to catch theirs. If traveling within the metropolitan area, make sure the driver turns the meter on when you get in. Rates are NIS 13.10 for the first 18 seconds and 30 *agorot* in increments thereafter. *Sherut* taxis consist mainly of a fleet of vans at the Central Bus Station that run the same routes as the buses, at comparable one-way prices. They run on Saturday at a higher charge.

TRAIN TRAVEL

From Ben Gurion International Airport, the train is a money and time saver for NIS 15 and takes about 20 minutes. There are taxis waiting outside each train station to get you to your final destination.

The train is an excellent way to travel between Tel Aviv and cities and towns to the north, such as Netanya, Hadera, Haifa, and Nahariya. To Jerusalem, buses are a better option until the high-speed line is completed. Northbound trains depart from the Central Railway Station (Savidor/Mercaz) and the Azrieli Station. Trains run roughly every hour on weekdays from between 5 am and 6 am to between 10 pm and 11 pm depending on the destination; there are fewer trains on Friday and Jewish holiday eves and no service on Saturday or on holidays. There's also a line to Beersheva. The information office is open Sunday to Thursday 6 am to 11 pm and Friday 6 to 3.

Train Contacts Central Railway Station. ✉ *Arlozoroff St.* ☎ *08/683–1222* ⊕ *www.rail.co.il/en.*

TOURS

The Tel Aviv–Jaffa Municipality has laid out three self-guided tours. The White Route relates Tel Aviv's history, the Blue Route its coastline, and the Green Route its natural wonders. Free walking tours sponsored by the Tel Aviv–Jaffa Municipality are available as follows: Old Jaffa, beginning at the clock tower on Wednesday at 10 am; neighborhood evening historical tour beginning at the corner of Rothschild Boulevard and Herzl Street, Tuesday at 8 pm; and the Bauhaus White City, Saturday at 11 am, beginning at 46 Rothschild Boulevard. No prior registration is required. Personal guides can also be arranged through most hotels.

FAMILY **Bauhaus Center Tour.** Expert guides lead the center's popular introductory walking tours of Tel Aviv's Bauhaus district. After a 20-minute presentation on historical background, the tour visits a variety of prominent Bauhaus buildings. A two-hour tour in English departs every Friday at 10 am from the Bauhaus Center; groups may be as large as 50 people. Reservations are required; other options are an audio-guide tour or a private tour. ⊠ *77 Dizengoff St., Center City* ☏ *03/522–0249* ⊕ *www. bauhaus-center.com* ⊠ *NIS 60 for 2-hr tour.*

Fodor's Choice **Delicious Israel.** An ideal way to learn the history of Tel Aviv is through ★ the lens of food. This culinary tour company offers six guided tasting tours that visit the backstreets of the city's markets, as well as "Shuk + Cook" workshops that include a visit to the market followed by preparing an Israeli meal with a chef. ⊠ *Tel Aviv* ☏ *052/569–9499* ⊕ *www. deliciousisrael.com* ⊠ *$100 for 4-hr walking tour, including food; $175 for 5-hr cooking class.*

VISITOR INFORMATION

The Israeli Government Tourist Office operates a 24-hour information desk in the arrivals hall at Ben Gurion International Airport that will make same-day reservations. The city tourist office, on the oceanfront promenade, stocks maps of walking tours around the city and is open Sunday to Thursday 9:30 to 5:30, Friday 9:30 to 1.

Contacts Israel Government Tourist Office. ☏ *050/900–0400* ⊕ *www.goisrael.com.* **Tel Aviv Tourist Information Office.** ⊠ *46 Herbert Samuel St., Center City* ☏ *03/516–6188* ⊕ *www.visit-tlv.co.il.*

EXPLORING TEL AVIV

From the city center, it's easy to head south to Jaffa and its ancient port and lively flea market—to get there the scenic way, saunter along the seaside promenade overlooking the beach—and the other southern neighborhoods like the gentrified Neve Tzedek and the more rough-edged Florentine.

Farther north, at the edge of Tel Aviv proper, lies the sprawling green lung of Tel Aviv, Hayarkon Park. You'll also discover the city's renovated port area, an ideal setting for a seaside breakfast or a toast at sunset with which to usher in Tel Aviv's famous inexhaustible nightlife.

CENTER CITY

Think of downtown Tel Aviv as a cat's cradle of boulevards and side streets leading to all of the city's great sights. These few square miles are the heart and soul of the city; they also hold the thousands of Bauhaus buildings, known as the White City, that have been named a UNESCO World Cultural Heritage Site. As you explore, you might see surfers heading up from the beach, film crews shooting commercials, and couples walking their dogs along leafy boulevards.

GETTING HERE AND AROUND

Most of the main bus lines travel through the center of the city, but two in particular are of interest to travelers: Bus 4 on Ben Yehuda Street and Bus 5 on Dizengoff Street. Both run at frequent intervals. Both of these thoroughfares also have minibuses that can be hailed like taxis and are often an even faster option for getting around. The flat landscape makes strolling along streets like Dizengoff, King George, Rothschild, and Ibn Gvirol very easy.

TIMING

Give yourself the better part of a day to savor some highlights of this part of the city, as there is a lot to see. It's well lighted at night and safe for evening strolls.

TOP ATTRACTIONS

Bauhaus Foundation Museum. A good stop for those who love architecture, this one-room museum on historic Bialik Street occupies the ground floor of an original Bauhaus building, built in 1934. You'll discover that the pristine lines and basic geometric forms typical of the Bauhaus school extend to everyday objects as well, from furniture to light fixtures to glazed stoneware. There's even a door handle designed by Walter Gropius (1883–1969), founder and first director of the Bauhaus in Germany. ⊠ *21 Bialik St., Center City* ☎ *03/620–4664* ☐ *Free* ⊗ *Closed Sat.–Tues., Thurs.*

Fodor's Choice ★ **Beit Ha'ir.** Catch up on Tel Aviv's remarkable history at this historical museum in the original 1924 municipal building, an architectural masterpiece that has been lovingly restored. Among the exhibits highlighting the progress of the last century is a brief film tracing the city's development from huts in the sand to gleaming apartment towers. There's also a pretty patchwork floor made up of colorful tiles typical of vintage buildings and the restored office of the city's first mayor, Meir Dizengoff, with the original map of Tel Aviv hanging on a wall. ⊠ *27 Bialik St., Center City* ☎ *03/724–0311* ⊕ *www.beithair.org* ☐ *NIS 20* ⊗ *Closed Sun.*

Fodor's Choice ★ **Carmel Market.** The northern half of the Carmel Market (commonly referred to as the *shuk*) consists of cheap clothing and housewares, but continue farther down to the fruit and vegetable section, where the real show begins. Vendors loudly hawk their fresh produce, and the crowded aisles reveal Israel's incredible ethnic mix. Don't pass by the small side streets filled with unusual treats. The market is busiest on Tuesday and Friday, when it can be combined with a visit to the Nahalat Binyamin Pedestrian Mall's crafts fair. If you don't like crowds, though, avoid Fridays, when shoppers preparing for Shabbat pack the market. ⊠ *Along HaCarmel St., Center City* ✛ *Enter from intersection of Allenby, Nahalat Binyamin, Sheinkin, and King George Sts.* ⊗ *Closed Sat.*

FAMILY **Habima Square.** Here you'll find a number of cultural institutions, including the Habima Theatre, the Charles Bronfman Auditorium, and the Helena Rubinstein Pavilion for Contemporary Art. A great place for

Dizengoff Street is a favorite nighttime destination for its many bars, restaurants, and cafés.

kids to run around, the square also has a relaxation garden with music wafting from the ecologically designed seating. ⊠ *Rothschild Blvd. at Marmorek St., Center City* ☒ *Free.*

Independence Hall Museum. This impressive building was originally the home of the city's first mayor, Meir Dizengoff. The country's leaders assembled here on May 14, 1948, to announce to the world the establishment of the State of Israel. Today the museum's **Hall of Declaration** stands as it did on that dramatic day, with the original microphones on the long table where the dignitaries sat. Behind the table is a portrait of the Zionist leader Theodor Herzl. Call ahead to reserve a tour. ⊠ *16 Rothschild Blvd., Center City* ☎ *03/517–3942* ⊕ *eng.ihi.org.il* ☒ *NIS 20* ☉ *Closed Sat.*

Fodor's **Choice**
★
Nahalat Binyamin Pedestrian Mall. Everything from plastic trinkets to handmade silver jewelry can be found at this bustling artisans street market, open on Tuesday and Friday along this pedestrian mall. A profusion of buskers compete to entertain you. For a finishing touch of local color, cafés serving cakes and light meals line the street. At the end of the market is a large Bedouin tent, where you can treat yourself to a *laffa* with *labaneh* and *za'atar* (large pita bread with tangy sour cream, sprinkled with hyssop, an oregano-like herb). ⊠ *Nahalat Binyamin St., off Allenby St., Center City* ⊕ *www.nachlat-binyamin.com* ☒ *Free* ☉ *Closed Sat.–Mon., Wed., and Thurs.*

Fodor's **Choice**
★
Rothschild Boulevard. Half a century ago, this magnificent tree-lined boulevard was one of the most exclusive streets in the city. Today it's once again what visionaries at the beginning of the 20th century meant it to be—a place for people to meet, stroll, and relax. Along the street are

Center City,
Neve Tzedek,
and Florentine

The former city hall on Bialik Square is now the Beit Ha'ir a museum about Tel Aviv's history.

some of the city's best restaurants and bars, and many Bauhaus gems are on or just off the street. ⊠ *Center City* ✛ *Runs for 1½ km (1 mile) from Herzl St. to Marmorek St./Habima Sq.*

Rubin Museum. Recognized as one of Israel's major painters, Reuven Rubin (1893–1974) bequeathed his house to Tel Aviv along with 45 of his works, which make up the permanent collection here. The house, built in 1930, is now an art gallery, with changing exhibits by Israeli artists. Upstairs is a small but well-stocked library where you can pore over press clippings and browse through books. A moving audiovisual presentation tells the story of Rubin's life, and his original studio can still be seen on the third floor. ⊠ *14 Bialik St., Center City* ☎ *03/525–5961* ⊕ *www.rubinmuseum.org.il* ⊠ *NIS 20* ⊗ *Closed Sun.*

Sarona. Shaded by leafy trees, this area was formerly an agricultural colony established by German Templers in 1871. The picturesque houses have been transformed into a bustling complex with a visitor center, restaurants, bars, boutiques, and cultural institutions. The Sarona Market's 90 food stalls and shops showcase some of Israel's top chefs and bakeries, as well as locally produced wine and craft beer. Pick up some essentials at the Friday morning Farmers' Market for a picnic in one of Sarona's grassy open areas. ⊠ *Kaplan St., near Begin Rd., Center City* ☎ *03/609–9028* ⊕ *www.saronatlv.co.il* ⊠ *Free.*

Fodor'sChoice ★ **Tel Aviv Museum of Art.** This museum houses a fine collection of Israeli and international art, including changing exhibits as well as a permanent section with works by prominent Jewish artists like Marc Chagall and Roy Lichtenstein. There's also an impressive French impressionist collection and many sculptures by Aleksandr Archipenko. The Herta

Shop for local foods in the Sarona Market.

and Paul Amir Building, designed by Preston Scott Cohen, is a dramatic, light-filled modern addition to the 1971 main building. The gift shop sells unique pieces of jewelry and other items that make memorable souvenirs. Visiting on Saturday is a great option, as many other places are closed for the Sabbath. ⊠ *27 Shaul Hamelech Blvd., Center City* 🕾 *03/607–7020* ⊕ *www.tamuseum.org.il* 🖀 *NIS 50* ☉ *Closed Sun.*

FAMILY **Yemenite Quarter.** Bordering the Carmel Market, this small area hides several cheap and satisfying third-generation eateries owned by Yemenite families whose traditional foods have been passed down since their arrival to the neighborhood in the 1920s and '30s. Wash your meal down with a beer as you gaze out onto the warren of cobblestone lanes. Some streets that are nice to stroll include Nahliel and Haim Havshush, lined with restaurants serving tasty hummus and flatbread. This is a soothing place for a stroll on a Friday afternoon, as the neighborhood hushes to a close for the Sabbath. Though the Yemenite Quarter was once a haven to families who could not afford living in central Tel Aviv, the historic buildings are slowly being renovated by foreign investors as vacation rental properties. ⊠ *Around Kehilat Eden St. and Yishkon St., Center City.*

WORTH NOTING

Azrieli Towers. A spectacular 360-degree view of Tel Aviv and beyond awaits on the 49th-floor observation deck of the circular building in this office complex, which consists of one triangular, one circular, and one square tower. Call ahead, as the observation deck sometimes closes early for special events. ⊠ *Azrieli Towers, 132 Menachem Begin Rd.,*

Center City ☎ *03/608–1990* ⊕ *www.mitzpe49.co.il/home* ✉ *NIS 22 for observatory* ⊘ *Closed Sat.*

Beit Bialik (*Bialik House*). Bold colors and many original furnishings enhance the charming two-story home of Chaim Nachman Bialik (1873–1934), considered the father of Hebrew poetry. An exhibit explores the significance of his writings and cultural activity. Bialik was already a respected poet and publisher by the time he moved to Tel Aviv from Russia in 1924; in the remaining 10 years of his life, his house, built in 1927, became the intellectual center of Tel Aviv. It's said that when Bialik lived here, the street was closed to traffic in the afternoon in order to let him write in peace and quiet. English-language tours can be arranged in advance. ⊠ *22 Bialik St., Center City* ☎ *03/525–4530* ⊕ *eng.shimur.org/Bialik* ⊘ *Closed Sun.*

Bialik Street. This area has been more successful than many other Tel Aviv neighborhoods in maintaining its older buildings. Bialik has long been a popular address with many of the city's artists and literati, so it's not surprising that some of the houses have been converted into small museums, including Beit Ha'ir, Beit Bialik, the Rubin Museum, and the Bauhaus Foundation Museum. ⊠ *Bialik St., Center City.*

Founders' Monument and Fountain. Dedicated in 1949, the Founders' Monument honors those who founded Tel Aviv. This large slab of stone also encapsulates the city's past in three copper bas-relief panels representing the earliest pioneer days of planting and building as well as modern architecture. ⊠ *Rothschild Blvd., at Nahalat Binyamin St., Center City* ✉ *Free.*

FAMILY **Gan Meir** (*Meir Park*). In the midst of crowded, noisy King George Street, you can wander through Meir Park and relax on benches shaded by beautiful old trees. The first trees were planted in 1936 when the city offered to name the park after its first mayor, Meir Dizengoff, in honor of his 70th birthday. The feisty Dizengoff objected, so the park only got its official name in 1944, years after he passed away. There's a large playground that's extremely popular with local kids. ⊠ *King George and Hashmonim Sts., Center City* ⊕ *Near Dizengoff Center* ✉ *Free.*

Helena Rubinstein Pavilion. This annex of the Tel Aviv Museum of Art houses changing contemporary art exhibits in an intimate space that's perfect for one-person shows. It's also a great escape from the midday sun. ⊠ *6 Tarsat St., Center City* ☎ *03/528–7196* ⊕ *www.tamuseum.org.il* ✉ *NIS10* ⊘ *Closed Sun.*

Kikar Magen David. This meeting point of six streets is named for the six-point Magen David, or Star of David. Faded historic buildings flank it on one side, shops and eateries on the other. It's the gateway to the Carmel Market, the open-air fruit and vegetable market. Musicians and street performers find their way to the open area in the middle of the hustle and bustle. ⊠ *King George and Allenby Sts., Center City.*

King Albert Square. Named after the Belgian monarch who was a personal friend of Mayor Meir Dizengoff, this prominent square is surrounded by some interesting monuments. The Bauhaus-style Pagoda House, now luxuriously restored as a private home, was built in 1924. The rooftop ornament gives the building its name. Inside the elegant

THE ORIGINS OF TEL AVIV

Having risen from desolate sand dunes starting in the late 19th century, Tel Aviv lacks the ancient aura of Jerusalem (which some say is part of its attraction). Still, the city's southern border, the port of Jaffa, is as old as they come: Jonah set sail from here for what turned out to be his journey to the belly of a whale. The cedars of Lebanon used to build Solomon's Temple arrived in Jaffa before being transported to Jerusalem.

Jaffa was founded in the Middle Canaanite period, around 1600 BC. For the next 1,000 years, one ancient people after another—Egyptians, Philistines, Israelites, Phoenicians, and Greeks—dominated it. After being taken by Crusaders twice, in the 11th and 12th centuries, it was recaptured by the Muslims and remained largely under Arab control until the 20th century.

In the second half of the 19th century, Jewish pioneers began immigrating here in numbers that strained the small port's capacity. By the late 1880s, a group of Jewish families moved from the overcrowded city to the empty sands north of Jaffa to found Neve Tzedek, now a beautifully restored shopping, cultural, and residential area. The next move was to Ahuzat Bayit (literally, "housing estate"), an area to the north of Neve Tzedek that became the precursor of Tel Aviv. The city was named Tel Aviv in 1909; Arab riots in Jaffa in the 1920s then drove more Jews to Ahuzat Bayit, spurring further growth.

Immigrants from Europe joined these Jews. These new, urban arrivals—unlike the pioneers from earlier immigrant waves—brought with them an appreciation for the arts and a penchant for sidewalk cafés, and left a strong social and cultural mark on Tel Aviv. The wave of immigration included some of the world's leading architects of the time, who saw their new home as virtually a blank slate on which they could realize their innovative and exciting ideas about urban planning. Scottish urban planner Patrick Geddes developed the 1929 plan for a functionalist, humanistic Garden City, and architects from Germany's Bauhaus School designed and built modern buildings for the growing city. Today Tel Aviv's many Bauhaus-style buildings, now protected as a UNESCO World Cultural Heritage Site, are a major attraction for architecture lovers.

stairwell of Shifrin House, at 2 Melchett Street, are crumbling remnants of frescoes of the Western Wall and Rachel's Tomb. ⊠ *Nahmani and Montefiore Sts., Center City.*

Rabin Square. The square was renamed for Prime Minister Yitzhak Rabin after he was assassinated here on November 4, 1995. Passersby often pause at the small monument of black stones, rippled and uneven as if after an earthquake. This quiet memorial is the work of Israeli artist Danny Karavan. The southeast corner of the square is a great place to grab a coffee, reflect, and people-watch. ⊠ *Ibn Gvirol St. and Frishman St., Center City.*

Sheinkin Street. This popular thoroughfare off Allenby Street has plenty of cafés and restaurants where you can watch passersby. This is where

If you're looking for a "bird's-eye" view of the city, it doesn't get better than from the top of Azrieli Towers.

young people shop for the latest fashions: the sizes are tiny, the favored color is black, and some of the boutiques are so minuscule you'll think you walked straight into the dressing room. ⊠ *Sheinkin St., Center City.*

Simtat Plonit. Wander down this alley to see old Tel Aviv decorative architecture at its best. Two plaster obelisks at the entrance mark the city's first "gated" community. Note the stucco lion in front of **Number 7**, which used to have glowing eyes fitted with lightbulbs. The original apartment house is painted pale yellow with garish orange trim. An outspoken builder named Meir Getzel Shapira bought Simtat Plonit in the 1920s and insisted that this pint-size street be named after him. Tel Aviv's first mayor, Meir Dizengoff, argued that another street already had that name. The mayor emerged victorious and named it Simtat Plonit, meaning "John Doe Street." ⊠ *Simtat Plonit, Center City* ✛ *Off King George St., near HaAvoda St.*

NEVE TZEDEK

Made up of about a dozen tiny streets crammed with one- and two-story dwellings in various stages of renovation, Neve Tzedek is rich with history. This is where the saga of Tel Aviv began, when a small group of Jewish families from Jaffa laid the cornerstone for their new neighborhood, naming it Neve Tzedek (Oasis of Justice). When Tel Aviv was busy expanding to the north and the east in the early days of the state, Neve Tzedek was allowed to deteriorate. But in recent years the beautiful old buildings were rediscovered, and the lovingly restored homes here are now among the most prestigious addresses in the city.

Full of restaurants and cafés, Neve Tzedek is where you'll find the fantastic dance and theater complex, the Suzanne Dellal Centre for Dance and Theatre, as well as a growing number of trendy galleries and boutiques. Though bordered on three sides by major thoroughfares (Eilat Road to the south, Herzl Street to the east, and Kaufman Street along the sea), this quarter is very tranquil.

GETTING HERE AND AROUND

The spine of Neve Tzedek is Shabazi Street, which runs the length of the neighborhood. Most shops and restaurants are either on or near Shabazi Street. The roads here are notoriously narrow, and pedestrians have the right-of-way.

TIMING

Neve Tzedek is the perfect place to spend a few leisurely hours exploring the interesting shops and tasty eateries. The neighborhood can get pretty crowded on weekends, and most of the action is in the bars and restaurants along and around Shabazi Street.

TOP ATTRACTIONS

Fodor'sChoice ★ **Suzanne Dellal Centre for Dance and Theatre.** A pair of whitewashed buildings—one built in 1892, the other in 1908—make up this attractive complex. The square, designed by noted landscape architect Shlomo Aronson, has hints of a medieval Middle Eastern courtyard in its scattering of orange trees connected by water channels. One side of the square is decorated with a tile triptych that illustrates the neighborhood's history and famous people who lived here in the early years, including S. Y. Agnon, who went on to win the Nobel Prize in Literature. There's a café-bar on the premises and a number of great restaurants nearby for pre- or postperformance meals. It's worth a stroll here even if you aren't seeing a performance. ⊠ *5 Yehieli St., near Shabazi St., Neve Tzedek* ☎ *03/510–5656* ⊕ *www.suzannedellal.org.il.*

WORTH NOTING

Gutman Museum. In the 1920s, a number of Tel Aviv's most famous writers lived in this building, whose renovations have somewhat obscured its original look. One of the first houses in Neve Tzedek, the building now displays the art of Nahum Gutman, colorful chronicler of early Tel Aviv. Tours in English are available by appointment. ⊠ *21 Rokach St., Neve Tzedek* ☎ *03/510–8554* ⊕ *www.gutmanmuseum.co.il* ☑ *NIS 24* ☉ *Closed Sun.*

HaTachana. On the edge of Neve Tzedek, this Turkish-era train station is where travelers once embarked to Jerusalem on the first piece of railroad in the Middle East. Even Theodor Herzl, founder of modern Zionism, passed through here. Dubbed HaTachana, Hebrew for "The Station," the 49-acre complex includes 22 different buildings, among them the former station that now houses art exhibits. A pair of restored train cars tells the story of the station's days as a major travel hub in the region. You'll also find restaurants, cafés, and boutiques peddling handcrafted jewelry and homegrown designer clothes. At the entrance is a tourist information stand. ⊠ *Koifman and Ha'Mered Sts., Neve Tzedek* ⊕ *www.hatachana.co.il* ☑ *Free.*

Rokach House. Built in 1887, the home of Neve Tzedek founder Shimon Rokach had fallen into disrepair and was slated for demolition before being reclaimed and restored in the 1980s by his granddaughter, artist Leah Majaro-Mintz. It now houses an exhibit of items from the quarter's early days, as well as pieces of her own art. Guided tours in English are available by calling ahead. A cabaret-style performance (in Hebrew) showcasing Neve Tzedek's history, preceded by samples of the period's cuisine, is offered on Thursday and Friday evening at 8:30 pm. ⊠ *36 Rokach St., Neve Tzedek* ☎ *03/516–8042* ⊕ *www.rokach-house. co.il* 🖵 *NIS 10.*

FLORENTINE

A gritty section of town that once served as a base to Greek and Turkish Jewish immigrants in the '20s and '30s is experiencing a slow and steady hipster renaissance. Moving away from the high rental costs of central Tel Aviv, musicians, artists, and students adopted the neighborhood and are bringing a youthful vibe that's felt in the street art, vegan eateries, and plant-filled green balconies. Spend an afternoon exploring the Levinsky Market and the evening in the colorful bohemian bars. The neighborhood is bounded by Eilat Street to the north, Salame Street to the south, Elifelet Street to the west, and HaAliya Street to the east.

GETTING HERE AND AROUND
The neighborhood is an easy 10- or 15-minute walk from Rothschild Boulevard or a 10- or 15-minute cab from most hotels. Shared taxis drop you off near the Central Bus Station area; walk south and west toward Florentine Street.

TIMING AND PRECAUTIONS
Since there are no real sights, our best advice is to just wander around. If you're heading here for bars and clubs, stick to the area around the intersection of Florentine and Vital Streets, as a block or two in most directions will leave you in a less interesting residential part of the neighborhood.

TOP ATTRACTIONS
Levinsky Market. The Levinsky Market is known as a spice-and-herb market but it also has wonderful Mediterranean delicacies. Nearby you'll find good Persian eateries. Once considered off the beaten path, the Levinsky Market is now a central destination for foodies. ⊠ *43 Levinsky St., Florentine* ⊘ *Closed Sat.*

JAFFA

Part of the sprawling municipality of Tel Aviv, the ancient port city of Jaffa is a mix of Jews, Christians, and Muslims. It's an ideal place for strolling down cobblestone streets and for dining at one of the no-frills fish restaurants that line the quay. Don't miss the Old City, where art galleries and shops occupy the centuries-old buildings along the narrow roads. At the Jaffa Flea Market, you can be part of the trading and bargaining for treasures—real and perceived—that are a hallmark of the Middle East.

The streets around Clock Tower Square bustle on weekday afternoons, when school children stop by the open-air eateries for flaky pastries, and weekend evenings, when the bars empty out and their patrons go in search of a late-night bite. An oceanfront promenade connects Tel Aviv with Jaffa. The sprawling park that runs parallel to the promenade was once a landfill, but is now one of the city's greenest areas. Kids love the playgrounds and vast stretches of grass.

South of Jaffa are two worthwhile excursions. Design Museum Holon, in the suburb of that name, is an exciting contemporary art museum. Even farther south, in Rehovot, is the Weizmann Institute of Science.

Some historians claim that Jaffa was named after its founder, Japhet, son of Noah; others think its name is from the Hebrew *yafeh* (beautiful). What's certain is its status as one of the world's oldest ports—perhaps the oldest. The Bible says the cedars used in the construction of the Holy Temple passed through Jaffa on their way to Jerusalem; the prophet Jonah set off from Jaffa before being swallowed by the whale; and St. Peter raised Tabitha from the dead here. Napoléon was but one of a succession of invaders who brought the city walls down; these walls were rebuilt for the last time in the early 19th century by the Turks and torn down yet again as recently as 1879.

GETTING HERE AND AROUND

From central Tel Aviv, Dan Buses 18 and 10 take you to Jaffa. You can also walk or bike along the seafront promenade to get here. A cab ride costing about 50 shekels will also get you to Jaffa.

TIMING

A few hours is enough time to soak up the atmosphere in Jaffa. Some less-traveled streets in Jaffa can feel deserted at night. Although the flea market and the port area are safe, at night you should stay away from dark streets and avoid walking alone.

TOP ATTRACTIONS

Jaffa Flea Market. One of many small bazaars surrounding the clock tower in the mid-19th century, the Jaffa Flea Market is the only survivor of that era. Along the cobblestone streets you can find everything from European antiques to Israeli memorabilia. As some antiques sellers close their doors with no family to continue the business, chic design boutiques are arriving and shifting the Flea Market neighborhood to an upscale vibe. The market's main street is Olei Zion, but there are a number of smaller streets and arcades to explore. Watch the locals bargain, and do what they do: *never* agree to the first price a seller demands. Combine the Flea Market's shopping and cafés with the Old City of Jaffa for a relaxed half-day stroll. ⊠ *Olei Zion St., Jaffa* ☉ *Closed Sat.*

NEED A BREAK

✕ **Capitolina Ice Cream.** An artisanal ice-cream shop in every sense of the word, this corner store makes everything using fresh ingredients from the nearby spice and food markets. A cool haven in the hubbub of the bustling Jaffa Flea Market, it's the place to treat yourself to a taste of dark chocolate toffee, pistachio, or a refreshing lemon-mint sorbet. Soy milk and sugar-free options are available. ✉ *Jaffa Flea Market, 9 Olei Tzion St., Jaffa* ☎ *03/603–6275.*

Fodor's Choice **Jaffa Port.** This small, intimate-feeling marina (one of the most ancient
    ★   ports in the world) is home to bobbing wooden fishing boats and a
waterfront of restaurants, cafés, and a small number of art galleries.
Some of its warehouses have been converted into public spaces for
rotating art exhibits. From here, enjoy a fish lunch or a snack from one
of the food stalls, and then hop on a boat for a cruise along the city's
coastline. ✉ *Retsef Aliyah Ha'Shniyah, Jaffa.*

Kedumim Square. The focus of Kedumim Square is an archaeological site
that exposes 3rd-century BC catacombs; the site has been converted into
a free underground visitor center with large, vivid, illustrated descriptions of Jaffa's history. A labyrinthine network of tiny alleys snakes in
all directions from Kedumim Square down to the fishing port; a good
selection of galleries and jewelry stores can be found south of the square
around Mazal Dagim Street. ✉ *Kedumim Square St., Jaffa* 🎟 *Free.*

St. Peter's Monastery. Jaffa is famous as a meeting point of East and
West, and as soon as you step into this century-old Franciscan church
you'll find yourself steeped in a European atmosphere. St. Peter's was
built over the ruins of a citadel dating from the Seventh Crusade, led

If you visit Jaffa, sit at the old port and watch the sun dip down into the Mediterranean.

by King Louis IX of France in the mid-13th century. A monument to Louis stands at the entrance to the friary. Napoléon is rumored to have stayed here during his Jaffa campaign of 1799. To enter, ring the bell on the right side of the door; you will probably be greeted by one of the custodians, most of whom speak Spanish and some English. ⊠ *Kedumim Sq., Jaffa* ☎ *03/682–2871* ☞ *Free.*

Summit Park. Seven archaeological layers have been unearthed in a part of this park called Ramses II Garden. The oldest sections of wall (20 feet thick) have been identified as part of a Hyksos city dating from the 17th century BC. Other remains include part of a 13th-century BC city gate inscribed with the name of Ramses II; a Canaanite city; a Jewish city from the time of Ezra and Nehemiah; Hasmonean ruins from the 2nd century BC; and traces of Roman occupation. At the summit is a stone sculpture called *Faith*, in the shape of a gateway, which depicts biblical stories. ⊠ *Kedumim Square St., Jaffa* ☞ *Free.*

WORTH NOTING

Andromeda's Rock. From Kedumim Square, a number of large boulders can be seen out at sea not far from shore. Greek mythology says one of these (pick your own, everyone does) is where the people of Jaffa tied the virgin Andromeda in sacrifice to a sea monster to appease Poseidon, god of the sea. But the hero Perseus, riding the winged horse Pegasus, soared down from the sky to behead the monster, rescue Andromeda, and promptly marry her. ⊠ *Jaffa.*

Clock Tower Square. Completed in 1906, in time to mark the 30th anniversary of the reign of Sultan Abdul Hamid II, this eye-catching limestone spire imarks the entrance of Jaffa and is a city landmark. The stained-glass windows from 1965 depict events in Jaffa's history. The centuries-old buildings around the square have been carefully restored, preserving their ornate facades. Since Jaffa was a major port in Turkish times, it's not surprising to find the Turkish Cultural Center here. ⊠ *Clock Tower Square, Yefet St., Jaffa.*

OFF THE BEATEN PATH

Design Museum Holon. Israeli-born architect Ron Arad designed this striking, much-acclaimed structure made of rounded ribbons of orange-and-red steel that rises off a drab street like a modernist mirage. Inside is a two-story space with changing exhibits on contemporary design, including fashion, jewelry, and textiles. English-language recorded tours are available for free. A good café known for tasty pastries and cakes is located at the entrance. The museum is in Holon, a suburb south of Tel Aviv that is easily reachable by taxi. ⊠ *8 Pinhas Eilon St., Holon* ☎ *073/215–1515* ⊕ *www.dmh.org.il* ⊠ *NIS 35* ⊙ *Closed Sun.*

El-Mahmoudiye Mosque. Tucked behind the shops along Jaffa's Clock Tower Square is the El-Mahmoudiye Mosque, whose hexagonal minaret and pink-granite-and-marble fountain can be seen from the square. When Turkish governor Muhammed Abu Najat Aja built the fountain in the early 19th century, it had six pillars and an arched roof. The fountain's foundation is still visible in the parking lot west of the minaret. The mosque is closed to the public, though you may be able to sneak a peek through the ornate carved doors on the western side into the spacious restored courtyard. The archway on the south side formed the entrance to the hammam, or old Turkish bath. ⊠ *Yefet St., at Mifratz Shlomo St., Jaffa* ⊙ *Closed to the public.*

NEED A BREAK

✕ **Abulafia Bakery.** There's always a crowd forming outside Abulafia Bakery, south of Jaffa's clock tower. For a simple snack with an exquisite flavor, order a pita topped with za'atar (a mixture of herbs, spices, and seeds), or stuffed with salty cheese, calzone style. In winter, Abulafia is a good place to try *sahlab*, a warm drink sprinkled with coconut and cinnamon. ⊠ *7 Yefet St., Jaffa.*

Ilana Goor Museum. Veteran Israeli artist Ilana Goor works and resides in this restored 18th-century house with romantic stone arches and high ceilings. She's turned part of it into a museum of her sculptures in wood, stone, and metal, some reminiscent of the "found-art" genre. A gift shop occupies part of the complex. ⊠ *4 Mazal Dagim St., Jaffa* ☎ *03/683–7676* ⊕ *www.ilanagoor.com* ⊠ *NIS 32.*

San Antonio Roman Catholic Church. Although its white bricks look new, this church actually dates from 1932, when it was built to accommodate the growing needs of Jaffa's Roman Catholic community. The church is named for St. Anthony of Padua, friend and disciple of St. Francis of Assisi. ⊠ *51 Yefet St., Jaffa* ☎ *03/513–3800* ⊠ *Free.*

OFF THE BEATEN PATH

Weizmann Institute of Science. On the grounds of one of Israel's finest science research centers, the Weizmann Institute's indoor Levinson Visitors Center and the open-air Clore Garden of Science are educational and fun for kids of all ages. Experience how it feels to walk on the moon and climb on or through dozens of other interactive exhibits that explain various scientific phenomena. Also worth a visit is the glass-and-steel Eco-Sphere, which houses educational exhibits on the environment. Call ahead for reservations and guided tours. By car, the institute is about 40 minutes from Tel Aviv. Bus routes 174, 201, 301, and 274 take about an hour from central Tel Aviv. The train takes about 35 minutes; it's a 15-minute walk from the train station. ⊠ *234 Herzl St., Rehovot* ☎ *08/934–4500* ⊕ *www.weizmann.ac.il* ☜ *NIS 30 for guided group tours* ⊘ *Closed Fri. and Sat.*

Yefet Street. Think of Yefet as a sort of thread between eras: beneath it is the old market area, while all around you stand schools and churches of the 19th and 20th centuries. Several deserve mention. At No. 21 is the Tabitha School, established by the Presbyterian Church of Scotland in 1863. Behind the school is a small cemetery where some fairly prominent figures are buried, including Dr. Thomas Hodgkin, the first to define Hodgkin's disease. No. 23 was once a French Catholic school, and it still carries the sign "Collège des Frères." At No. 25, the fortress-like Urim School was set up as a girls' school in 1882. ⊠ *Jaffa.*

NORTH TEL AVIV

While still considered Center City, from the east–west cross street of Arlozorov, North Tel Aviv flows into blocks of tranquil residential streets of small apartment houses, up to the banks of the Yarkon River and its beautiful park. At Hayarkon Park, a welcome swath of green on the Yarkon River, families picnic not far from joggers and bikers on well-paved paths. The Tel Aviv Port is a delightful area for eating, shopping, and strolling. Just north of the river are three important museums. The Eretz Israel Museum is close to Tel Aviv University, the Palmach Museum is next door to it, and the Museum of the Jewish People is farther north on the university campus.

GETTING HERE AND AROUND
Dan Bus Company's Route 4 is an easy way to reach the port. The museums are about 8 km (5 miles) from the downtown hotels; Dan Buses 7, 25, and 45 will take you to the area. Allow at least two hours to visit each museum.

TIMING
The port area can feel a bit overrun on the weekends, especially with families and young children. North Tel Aviv tends to be bustling by day, sleepy at night.

TOP ATTRACTIONS
Eretz Israel Museum. This large museum's eight pavilions span 3,000 years of culture and history in Israel, covering everything from ethnography and folklore to ceramics and other handicrafts. In the center is the ancient site of Tel Kassile, where archaeologists have uncovered 12 layers of settlements. There is also a daily sound-and-light show in the adjacent planetarium. ⊠ *2 Levanon St., North Tel Aviv* ☎ *03/641–5244* ⊕ *www.eretzmuseum.org.il* ☜ *Museum NIS 52, planetarium NIS 84.*

FAMILY **Ganei Yehoshua** (*Hayarkon Park*). Tel Avivians go to this sprawling park to stretch out on the grass for a picnic or a nap in the shade. For those seeking more activity, a bike ride on one of its paths can be combined with a visit to the tropical garden and the rock garden. Or you can rent a pedal boat, rowboat, or motorboat to ride on the Yarkon Stream. There's even a pleasure boat, which takes up to 80 people for 20-minute rides. ⊠ *Rokach Blvd., North Tel Aviv* ☎ *03/642–2828* ⊕ *www.park. co.il* 🎟 *Free.*

Museum of the Jewish People (*Beit Hatfutsot*). Presented here is the story of 2,500 years of the diaspora (Jews who settled outside Israel). It begins with the destruction of the First Temple in Jerusalem in 586 BC and chronicles such major events as the exile to Babylon and the expulsion from Spain in 1492. Photographs and text labels provide the narrative, and films and music enhance the experience. One highlight is a replica collection of miniature synagogues throughout the world, both those destroyed and those still functioning. Another is the computerized genealogy section, where it's possible to look up Jewish family names to determine their origins. There's a music center with Jewish music from around the world and a children's gallery with interactive exhibits. The museum is on the Tel Aviv University Campus in the Ramat Aviv neighborhood. ⊠ *Tel Aviv University, Klausner St., Ramat Aviv, North Tel Aviv* ☎ *03/745–7800* ⊕ *www.bh.org.il* 🎟 *NIS 45* ⊗ *Closed Sat.*

See art that reflects aspects of Jewish life, past and present, at the Museum of the Jewish People on the Tel Aviv University campus.

Tel Aviv Port. Once a cluster of decrepit warehouses, the old port is buzzing with cafés, restaurants, and, late at night, clubs. It ends where the pavement gives way to a wooden platform designed with moderate dips and curves, pleasing to the eye and fun for roller skaters. On weekends, restaurants are all packed by 1 pm. There's a very appealing Friday farmers' market and a small swap meet good for finding handmade jewelry, old books, and Israeli memorabilia. ⊠ *Nemal Tel Aviv St., Tel Aviv Port* ✉ *Free.*

WORTH NOTING

Palmach Museum. This museum makes you feel as if you were back in the days of the Palmach, the pre-State underground, with a group of young defenders. Visitors are led through rooms, each of which encompasses one part of the Palmach experience. There's the "forest," which has real-looking trees; a room with a falling bridge and faux explosions; and a chilling mock-up of an illegal-immigrants' ship. Call ahead for reservations. ⊠ *10 Levanon St., North Tel Aviv* ☎ *03/643–6393* ⊕ *www. palmach.org.il* ✉ *NIS 30* ⊙ *Closed Sat.*

Tel Aviv Port Farmers' Market. After wandering through the stalls selling organic produce, sample the fresh offerings at eateries like the in-house pasta bar or the specialty-sandwich stand. Don't miss the stand selling just-squeezed seasonal juice. Friday afternoons are particularly active with farmers and food vendors selling artisanal goodies. It's closed Sunday. ⊠ *Hangar 12, Tel Aviv Port* ⊕ *www.shukhanamal.co.il.*

WHERE TO EAT

The city's cosmopolitan character is happily represented in its food, although stands selling the Middle Eastern fast food for which this part of the world is famous—such as falafel and shawarma—still occupy countless street corners. You'll find restaurants serving everything from American-style burgers to sushi and chili con carne. In contrast to Jerusalem, diners who keep kosher have to search for a kosher restaurant, aside from those in the hotels. A spate of new kosher establishments caters to a significant slice of the discerning dining market, but with the fairly rapid turnover of some Tel Aviv eateries, the concierge is still the best person to ask about the latest in kosher restaurants.

Most Tel Aviv restaurants, except those that keep kosher, are open seven days a week. Many serve business lunches at reasonable prices, making them less-expensive options than the price categories suggest. As elsewhere in the Mediterranean, Israelis dine late; chances are there will be no trouble getting a table at 7 pm, whereas past 10, diners may face a long line. Casual attire is always acceptable in Tel Aviv.

Tel Aviv's restaurants are concentrated in a few areas: Sheinkin and Rothschild Streets, Basel, Ibn Gvirol Street, and the Tel Aviv Port.

Use the coordinates at the end of each listing (✛ A1) to locate a site on the corresponding map.

WHAT IT COSTS				
	$	$$	$$$	$$$$
Restaurants	Under NIS 50	NIS 50–NIS 75	NIS 76–NIS 100	over NIS 100

Restaurant prices are the average cost of a main course at dinner in NIS (Israeli shekels) or, if dinner isn't served, at lunch.

CENTER CITY

Home of the historic White City, the center of town is chock-full of cafés and restaurants that run the gamut from simple storefront eateries to chic dining rooms run by celebrity chefs. When you just want a quick bite, the boulevards are lined with food kiosks.

$$$$
ISRAELI
✕ **Abraxas North.** For one of the best meals in the city, take your place at one of the tables spilling out onto the sidewalk or alongside the small, chic bar. The menu changes daily, depending on what Eyal Shani, its celebrity chef, finds to be the freshest produce or catch of the day. A couple of delectable dishes are often featured, including lamb shawarma marinated overnight in wine grapes from the Judean Hills, and cold shrimp with green onions and tomatoes served in piping-hot homemade pita. If you arrive without reservations, you may be able to find room at the bar. ⑤ *Average main: NIS 129* ⊠ *40 Lilienblum St., Center City* ☎ *03/516–6660* ✛ *B5.*

$$
ITALIAN
✕ **Allora.** The well-stocked wooden bar is the centerpiece of this tiny eatery, where the roaring brick oven and pizza-dough kneaders are in

full view. The focaccia makes a great starter, served with a variety of dips including Clemente-olive spread, garlic confit, and, for Middle Eastern good measure, labaneh (yogurt cheese). Balkan pizza, topped with grilled eggplant, peppers, and feta cheese, is especially tasty. The narrow porch is your perch to watch the people strolling and cycling along the tree-lined center of Rothschild Boulevard. $ *Average main: NIS 70* ✉ *60 Rothschild Blvd., Center City* ☎ *03/566–5655* ⊕ *allora.co.il* ✛ *B5.*

$$
CAFÉ
FAMILY
✕ **Benedict.** Celebrating the love that Israelis have for breakfast, this restaurant with simple and sunny decor features many variations on the morning meal, served around the clock. Choose the classic Israeli breakfast with all the trimmings, the Mexican egg scramble, or several different styles of eggs Benedict. French toast and pancakes satisfy anyone's sweet tooth. Despite the dish's unusual name, it is worth tasting the signature "egg balls," cooked omelet style, formed into a dumpling shape, and served with a choice of sauces such as spinach and cream. $ *Average main: NIS 67* ✉ *29 Rothschild Blvd., Center City* ☎ *03/686–8657* ⊕ *www.benedict.co.il* ✛ *B5.*

$$$$
ITALIAN
✕ **Bindella.** Tel Aviv might be an unexpected city for the Bindella family's first foray outside their native Switzerland, but this Italian food outlet has enjoyed impressive success. Engaging a sophisticated local design team and utilizing chef Roy Sofer's vast experience—and capitalizing on Swiss-style service—the restaurant is a welcome addition to the city's ever-growing food scene. For starters, tempt your taste buds with the tangy yellowtail or finely sliced octopus carpaccio, the crunchy cauliflower and hazelnut Sicilian salad, or the ravioli with plenty of king crab meat. The broad variety of local fish and made-on-the-premises pastas are all fresh and light and will leave you room for desserts like cannoli with fresh figs, mascarpone, and pistachio ice cream. $ *Average main: NIS 109* ✉ *27 Montefiore St., Center City* ☎ *03/650–0071* ⊕ *www.bindella.co.il* ✛ *B5.*

$$
FRENCH
✕ **Brasserie.** The dark upholstery, mustard-color walls, and menu in French (as well as Hebrew and English) are all meant to recall Paris, and the wide selection of excellently prepared food is a credit to French cuisine. It's open around the clock, and always seems to have a crowd. Brunch is popular, with dishes like eggs Creole and eggs Norwegian style (poached with salmon and spinach), as well as pancakes and club sandwiches. For lunch or dinner, try the ravioli with crab, steak tartare, or the salade Nicoise. $ *Average main: NIS 65* ✉ *70 Ibn Gvirol St., Center City* ☎ *03/696–7111* ⊕ *www.brasserie.co.il* ✛ *C3.*

$$
BAKERY
FAMILY
✕ **Bread & Co.** The aromas emanating from this street-corner bakery and café make it well worth the visit. Choose from the savory or sweet section of French-style baked goods, made throughout the day by chefs trained in Paris. A plentiful Israeli breakfast is upgraded with housemade jams, French butter, and a diverse bread basket filled with sourdoughs, brioches, and sweet croissants. This place is obviously not for the gluten averse. $ *Average main: NIS 55* ✉ *128 Ben Yehuda St., Center City* ☎ *03/624–7100* ✛ *B3.*

$$
ASIAN FUSION
✕ **The Bun.** The Asian-influenced fare at this tiny casual eatery at the entrance to the Carmel Market is some of the freshest you will find in Israel. Each dish is made on the spot in an open kitchen by friendly

Where to Eat in Tel Aviv

KEY

■ Restaurants

↔ following dining reviews indicates map-grid coordinates

brothers Shai and Ayal. The creative steamed buns veer from tradition, and the result is innovative without reaching too far—try the ones with braised short ribs, pickles, and miso barbecue sauce. The great Vietnamese salad with green papayas, green beans, cherry tomatoes, and chili is a healthy addition alongside a steaming bowl of ramen or udon noodle soups. Finish off with the crème caramel miso, a smooth dessert with the consistency of flan, combining both salty and sweet flavors. ⑤ *Average main: NIS 56* ✉ *18 Hillel Hazaken St., Center City* ☎ *03/604–4725* ✛ *B4.*

$$ ✕ **Café Batia.** A longtime favorite, this café has a full menu of old-
EASTERN fashioned Eastern European favorites. Try a bowl of matzoh-ball soup,
EUROPEAN leg of goose, or stuffed cabbage for a taste of what Grandma used to prepare. If you're adventurous, sample some of the less well-known dishes, such as *pupiks*, which is Yiddish for gizzards. Vegetarians can enjoy a spread of specialty deli salads. ⑤ *Average main: NIS 62* ✉ *95 HaHashmonaim St., Center City* ☎ *03/522–1335* ✛ *C4.*

$ ✕ **Café Bialik.** This veteran of Tel Aviv café culture is the perfect comple-
CAFÉ ment to a stroll down historic Bialik Street. Plenty of restaurants serve more or less the same menu as Café Bialik—an "Israeli breakfast," which is a wide selection of chopped salads with eggs done in a variety of ways, toast, coffee, and juice, and sometimes smoked salmon and small sandwiches. But it's the neighborhood-hangout feel and the old-fashioned chrome bar stools and wooden tables that make this place stand out. Evenings ring with live music. ⑤ *Average main: NIS 46* ✉ *2 Bialik St., Center City* ☎ *03/620–0832* ⊕ *www.cafebialik.co.il* ✛ *B4.*

$ ✕ **Café Mersand.** For a taste of the best of the local hipster scene, score
CAFÉ a table on this eatery's sunny sidewalk. The older customers, some of whom have been coming since the place opened its doors in 1955, mingle unusually well with the younger crowd. Everyone enjoys the specials from the original menu, including the poppy-seed cake and the brownie cheesecake. In the morning, try the Turkish breakfast, which includes couscous, cheese, a hard-boiled egg, and halvah. ⑤ *Average main: NIS 40* ✉ *18 Frishman St., Center City* ☎ *03/523–4318* ✛ *B3.*

$$ ✕ **Café Metzada.** A varied but simple menu—including steak, salads,
CAFÉ sandwiches, and pasta—makes this a good place to recharge after a day at the beach or a nice spot to relax with a glass of wine at sunset. The highlight of this café is not the food but the indoor or outdoor seating with fabulous Mediterranean views. ⑤ *Average main: NIS 60* ✉ *83 Hayarkon St., Center City* ☎ *03/510–3353* ✛ *A3.*

$ ✕ **Café Xoho.** Doubling as an art-and-music haven for locals, this inviting
CAFÉ neighborhood café will make you feel as if you're in someone's fun and
FAMILY relaxing living room. The service is personal, the patrons are friendly (you will most likely end up in a conversation with many of them), and the extensive menu has options for everyone. The in-house baked goods including homemade bagels, and the ever-changing array of muffins makes for a light breakfast or afternoon snack. The salads and sandwiches are made fresh, so you can choose any toppings you like. ⑤ *Average main: NIS 35* ✉ *17 Gordon St., Center City* ☎ *072/249–5497* ⊕ *www.cafexoho.com* ☾ *Closed Mon. No dinner* ✛ *B3.*

$ ✕ **Falafel Benin Johnny.** Passed down from father to son, this local land-
MIDDLE EASTERN   mark has been serving some of the best falafel for more than 50 years.
For a few shekels, you'll get a pita filled with plentiful, perfectly prepared falafel balls, fried potatoes (called "chips" here) and just the
right amount of salad. Sit on the outdoor bench or stand and enjoy
this classic Israeli street food done right. ⑤ *Average main: NIS 16* ⊠ *2
Tchernikovsky St., Center City* ▭ *No credit cards* ⊹ *B4.*

$ ✕ **Giraffe Noodle Bar.** Generous portions of noodles in a variety of Japa-
ASIAN   nese, Thai, and other Asian styles attract a loyal clientele. There's a
selection of soups and sushi for starters. Save room for the meringue-
based, berry-topped pavlova for dessert. Lunch is a particularly good
bargain. ⑤ *Average main: NIS 49* ⊠ *49 Ibn Gvirol St., Center City*
☎ *03/691–6294* ⊕ *www.giraffe.co.il* ⊹ *C3.*

$$$$ ✕ **HaBasta.** This tiny restaurant and wine bar, just a clutch of round tables
MEDITERRANEAN   on an alley just off Carmel Market, draws its inspiration from the market's
Fodor'sChoice   fresh offerings. (The name is Hebrew for "market stall.") The choices
★   change daily, and the kitchen is well-known for dishing out organ meats
you might not see much back home. For the less adventurous, the seafood
and pork options are sure to be fresh and aesthetically appealing. Try also
the white pizza with black truffles when in season. The paella with bacon,
sausage, shrimp, and mussels is about as nonkosher as it gets for a place
whose chef refers to the nearby market as the "Holy of Holies," a Biblical
reference to where the Ark of the Covenant was kept. ⑤ *Average main: NIS
169* ⊠ *4 HaShomer St., Center City* ☎ *03/516–9234* ⊹ *B4.*

$$$$ ✕ **Hotel Montefiore Restaurant.** The restaurant at this boutique hotel serves
FRENCH   modern brasserie fare, throwing in a few Vietnamese touches for good
Fodor'sChoice   measure. For starters, sample the raw tuna with yuzu or the mussels
★   with lemongrass. Main dishes include baked drum fish with tomatoes
and olive oil, grilled lamb chops, and sirloin steak with wild mushrooms. The dining room is in a lovingly restored home on Montefiore
Street in the heart of historic Tel Aviv. White walls, potted plants, slatted
wooden blinds, and the silver-plated sugar servers selected by co-owner
Ruthie Brouda evoke old-world colonial days. The impeccable service,
well-prepared food, and interesting wine list compare very favorably
with the city's more expensive restaurants. ⑤ *Average main: NIS 110*
⊠ *Hotel Montefiore, 36 Montefiore St., Center City* ☎ *03/564–6100*
⊕ *www.hotelmontefiore.co.il/restaurant* ⊹ *B4.*

$ ✕ **Lilush.** At this cozy neighborhood bistro, the portions are generous, the
MEDITERRANEAN   prices extremely reasonable, and the atmosphere a friendly hubbub of clat-
FAMILY   tering dishes and animated conversations. Tables are packed close together,
both in the small dining room and on the sidewalk. The thick menu is
filled with hearty salads and pastas, as well as the signature paninis. In the
warmer months, there are creative daily specials like tasty risotto. During
the winter, there's a daily selection of a dozen different soups. The all-day
happy hour will keep your mouth and wallet smiling. ⑤ *Average main: NIS
42* ⊠ *73 Frishman St., Center City* ☎ *03/529–1852* ⊹ *B3.*

$ ✕ **Max Brenner.** Chocolate lovers should run, not walk, to this eatery
ECLECTIC   for a mouthwatering, *Charlie and the Chocolate Factory* experience.
FAMILY   Beneath pipes of imaginary chocolate crisscrossing the ceiling, children
of all ages can order the likes of chocolate pizza—topped with chocolate

4

chips, of course—or chocolate fondue for dipping toasted marshmallows and fruit like melon, dates, and bananas. There's even chocolate soup! For a souvenir, take home some hand-stenciled pralines in artfully designed tins. And yes, there are nonchocolate options, including pastas and salads. ⑤ *Average main: NIS 49* ⊠ *45 Rothschild Blvd., Center City* ☎ *03/560–4570* ⊕ *www.max-brenner.co.il* ✛ *B4.*

$$$$ ✕ **Messa.** Chef Aviv Moshe serves traditional dishes like the shredded-
MODERN ISRAELI wheat type of pastry called *kadaif,* but his method of preparation is in a class of its own. This Mediterranean–Middle Eastern haute cuisine is enlivened with French and Italian touches. White is the dominant color in the lavish dining room, with marble floors and tented ceiling lamps on which video art is projected. A long, white central table with stylish high-back chairs is the room's centerpiece, perfect for mingling with fellow diners while the attentive staff serves such dishes as seared red tuna over an eggplant-and-goat-cheese roll with pomegranate dressing or sea bass with shallot ravioli. Adjacent to the restaurant is the bar, a much more chaotic affair done up in stark black. ⑤ *Average main: NIS 148* ⊠ *19 Ha'arbaa St., Center City* ☎ *03/685–6859* ⊕ *www.messa.co.il* ✛ *C4.*

$$ ✕ **Moses.** This bar and grill is part retro lounge, part bistro. Best known
AMERICAN for its burgers, the place has an extensive menu that includes everything
FAMILY from shish kebabs to calamari and quesadillas. It's good for the whole family, with children's dishes and, for the adults, an interesting selection of cocktails. The ribs in molasses are a real treat, as is the chicken Caesar salad. Drop by after midnight, when late-night specials add to the mix. ⑤ *Average main: NIS 60* ⊠ *35 Rothschild Blvd., Center City* ☎ *03/566–4949* ⊕ *www.mosesrest.co.il* ✛ *B5.*

$$$ ✕ **Night Kitchen** (*Mitbach Layla*). As the name suggests, this popular eat-
MEDITERRANEAN ery is geared toward the city's night owls. Using local ingredients and highlighting modern takes on traditional Israeli cuisine, the menu items are meant to be shared like tapas. Tomato carpaccio with za'atar leaves, calamari with fennel and spinach, and gnocchi with oyster mushrooms and roasted cherry tomatoes are a few of the colorful options. For dessert there's a lollipop-shape crème brûlée wrapped around tonka-bean puree and drizzled with fruit syrup. ⑤ *Average main: NIS 88* ⊠ *43 Lilienblum St., Center City* ☎ *03/566–0481* ⊕ *www.nightkitchen.co.il* ✛ *B5.*

$$$$ ✕ **Oasis.** Chef Rima Olivera's 30 years of experience in the world's best
CONTEMPORARY kitchens and her principles of cooking set this eatery apart from the rest in the Tel Aviv food scene. The menu changes constantly based on the choicest seasonal ingredients, including those that are locally grown and those that are hand-picked from abroad. An open kitchen at this tastefully designed location lets you watch Olivera in action. The natural flavors emanating from each dish have just a hint of butter or cream, if any at all. Taste the gently seasoned zucchini salad with truffle oil for starters. Also recommended is the Vietnamese-style sea bream with shallots, lemongrass, and caramel. Be sure to end the meal with a perfectly balanced dessert and green-tea milk with jasmine cream. ⑤ *Average main: NIS 145* ⊠ *17 Montefiore St., Center City* ☎ *03/620–6022* ⊕ *www.oasistlv.co.il* ☽ *No lunch* ✛ *B4.*

$$$
JAPANESE
✕ **Onami.** This distinguished Japanese restaurant is consistently ranked among the best in a city with no shortage of sushi. The expansive bar is the restaurant's centerpiece, and the surrounding tables are filled with all sorts of locals, from extended families enjoying an early meal to young people who arrive in clusters later in the evening. Onami presents a large variety of tastefully presented Japanese dishes, including agedashi tofu (fried and served with a sweet soy sauce), that can be combined with sushi or sashimi. ⑤ *Average main: NIS 78* ✉ *18 Ha'arba'a St., Center City* ☎ *03/562–1172* ⊕ *www.onami.co.il* ✛ *C4.*

$$
MODERN ISRAELI
✕ **Orna and Ella.** As the loyal clientele will attest, Orna and Ella is worth the trip because of its comfort-food-with-a-twist menu. Entrées might be anything from moussaka to a tomato-and-cucumber salad piled high with feta cheese and topped with a yogurt-mint dressing. The house specialty, a mound of sweet-potato pancakes, is not to be missed. Desserts include a scrumptious pear-and-almond-cream tart. Innovative vegan offerings, such as macadamia nut dip, are worth a taste. There's often a long wait, especially Friday afternoons and weekday evenings. ⑤ *Average main: NIS 56* ✉ *33 Sheinkin St., Center City* ☎ *03/620–4753* ⊕ *www.ornaandella.com* ✛ *B4.*

$$$$
ITALIAN
✕ **Pronto.** This elegant dining room's owner was made a Knight of the Italian Republic for his contribution to Italian culture around the globe. At this small oasis of Roman cuisine, the kitchen serves dishes that are imaginative yet uncomplicated. The menu, which changes seasonally, includes favorites like a cold antipasti platter appetizer and lamb osso buco. The homemade pastas are delicate and seasoned to highlight the high-quality ingredients. Finish off the meal with one of the interesting house-made ice-cream flavors such as salted caramel. ⑤ *Average main: NIS 128* ✉ *4 Herzl St., Center City* ☎ *03/566–0915* ⊕ *www.pronto. co.il* ✛ *B5.*

$$$$
ITALIAN
✕ **Quattro.** Acclaimed Israeli chef Aviv Moshe turns his plating charm on high at the Italian-Mediterranean Quattro. A playfully colorful chandelier centerpiece contrasts with the stark black-and-white walls also found in Moshe's sister restaurant, Messa. Photo-friendly plated starters include pickled rump steak carpaccio with mustard sorbet and egg-yolk cream, as well as the more classic Italian bruschetta with balsamic vinegar pearls served with creamy burrata. Business-lunch deals and a bright patio encourage daytime visits, and the sophisticated after-work scene means the dinner crowd is a winner as well. ⑤ *Average main: NIS 120* ✉ *Platinum Bldg., 21 HaArba'a St., Center City* ☎ *03/919–1555* ✛ *C4.*

$$$$
MEDITERRANEAN
✕ **Raphael.** This place bills itself as a bistro (to be exact, a "resto-bistro"), but that term doesn't begin to conjure up the elegant setting with touches of the Far East. The Mediterranean (framed by picture windows) is the perfect backdrop for the sophisticated cuisine. Try a first course like market vegetables stuffed with lamb, goat cheese, and basmati rice, then move on to main dishes like swordfish accented with white Madagascar pepper and tomato confit. The service is particularly attentive and pleasant. ⑤ *Average main: NIS 125* ✉ *87 Hayarkon St., Center City* ☎ *03/522–6464* ⊕ *raphaeltlv.co.il* ✛ *A3.*

4

$ ✕ **Sabich Tchernikovsky.** This food stand is one of the best spots to sample
ISRAELI   the Iraqi-Israeli street food called *sabich*. The Zen-like concentration
of the owner results in a hearty and thoughtful dish consisting of fried
eggplant, hard-boiled eggs, potatoes, and tahini—a perfect combination of flavors. Here you have the rare options of a whole-wheat or
gluten-free pita. $ *Average main: NIS 17* ✉ *2 Tchernichovsky, Center
City* ▭ *No credit cards* ✛ *B4.*

$ ✕ **Sonya Getzel Shapira.** This quirky café, decorated with antique glass
CAFÉ   lamps and other flea-market finds, has a refreshingly relaxed feel. A
FAMILY   black-and-white-checked floor adds to the retro vibe. Regulars ask for
the *shakshuka*, a North African dish of panfried tomatoes and spices
topped with an egg, as well as the market salad with sweet potatoes and
feta cheese with a roasted-pepper dressing. If the weather is pleasant,
you can sit in the garden and let the kids roam. $ *Average main: NIS
45* ✉ *1 Simtat Almonit St., Center City* ☎ *077/526–1234* ✛ *B4.*

$$$$ ✕ **Taizu.** Part of the city's influx of Asian restaurants, the "Asia-ter-
ASIAN FUSION   ranean" kitchen of Taizu is a nod to the street food of India, China,
FodorsChoice   Thailand, Vietnam, and Cambodia. The interior design is based on the
★   five elements of Chinese philosophy: water, wood, fire, earth, and metal,
each of which is also represented in the style of food. Visit in a group
and share plates like the aromatic tandoori calamari served with a sour
cream sauce, the rump steak with lemongrass and herbs, or the creative
sesame-covered fish tartare, served in a cone to resemble ice cream. The
buttery chicken and scallop dumplings will leave you licking the sauce
on the plate. Temptingly sweet cocktails are a great way to start or end
the meal; try the Green Tai made with Stoli vodka, sake, lychee cream,
and green tea. $ *Average main: NIS 108* ✉ *23 Menachem Begin St.,
Center City* ☎ *03/522–5005* ⊕ *www.taizu.co.il* ✛ *C4.*

NEVE TZEDEK

Elegant wine bars and contemporary dining rooms are what you will
find in historic Neve Tzedek. As the home of the Suzanne Dellal Centre
for Dance and Theatre, this neighborhood is the ideal place for a pre- or
postperformance meal.

$$$ ✕ **Bellini.** With indoor and outdoor seating, this Tuscan-style establish-
ITALIAN   ment facing the open square across from the Suzanne Dellal Centre is
useful primarily if you are need of a postperformance nosh. Try the
gnocchi with truffle oil accompanied by the namesake beverage. $ *Aver-
age main: NIS 80* ✉ *Suzanne Dellal Centre, 6 Yehieli St., Neve Tzedek*
☎ *072/334–0485* ⊕ *www.bellini.co.il* ✛ *B5.*

$$$$ ✕ **Dallal.** Inside a beautifully restored historic building, this bistro has
MEDITERRANEAN   a rarefied atmosphere and an on-the-premises bakery that turns out a
luscious array of French-style pastries. The breakfast menu highlights
some of the baked delights, including smoked-salmon croissants and
the indulgent strawberry–French toast sandwich. An enclosed patio,
with its wrought-iron tables and chairs, is a lovely place to enjoy a
late-afternoon coffee among a mixed crowd of business executives,
surfers, and families. The business lunch is a good value while the
dinner menu offers more extensive (and higher-priced) fish and meat

options. $ *Average main: NIS 110* ⊠ *10 Shabazi St., Neve Tzedek* ☎ *03/510–9292* ⊕ *www.dallal.co.il* ✛ *A5.*

$$$
STEAKHOUSE
✕**Hatraklin.** At this bistro in the heart of Neve Tzedek, the warm environment, hearty food, fine wine, and excellent service will leave you feeling satisfied. The wine menu boasts over 160 Israeli boutique wines, and the friendly owner-sommelier, Yossi Ben Odis, will let you know exactly which wine pairs well with your meal. The house special is the "seared sirloin" that you cook yourself at the table on a specially heated rock. The menu is mostly meat and chicken dishes complemented with a few options for vegetarians. $ *Average main: NIS 98* ⊠ *4 Heichal Hatalmud St., Neve Tzedek* ☎ *03/566–0013* ⊕ *www.hatraklin.co.il* ⊗ *No lunch* ✛ *B5.*

$$$$
CONTEMPORARY
✕**NG.** Tucked away in a quiet corner of the city, this small, elegant bistro specializes in fine cuts of expertly prepared meat. It's purported to be the only place in Israel where you can enjoy a real porterhouse steak. And for dessert? That depends on the time of year. Tangy strawberry-vanilla pie is a winter specialty, and fig-vanilla pie is a summer favorite. The building is historic, yet the interior is contemporary, with Mediterranean tile floors in geometric patterns. $ *Average main: NIS 150* ⊠ *6 Ahad Ha'am St., Neve Tzedek* ☎ *03/516–7888* ⊕ *www.ngrestaurant.co.il* ⊗ *No lunch Sun., Mon., Wed., and Thurs.* ✛ *B5.*

$$
MEDITERRANEAN
✕**Suzanna.** In a century-old building near the Suzanne Dellal Centre for Dance and Theatre, this popular eatery bustles day and night. Sample the Kurdish *kubbeh* (meat-filled semolina dumplings) and pumpkin soup, or the Moroccan *harira*, a thick soup with chickpeas, veal, and coriander. To start things off, the savory antipasti platter is a welcome sight for the hungry traveler. Opt for a table on the terrace beneath the massive branches of an old ficus tree. $ *Average main: NIS 69* ⊠ *9 Shabazi St., Neve Tzedek* ☎ *03/517–7580* ✛ *A5.*

FLORENTINE

Bordering Neve Tzedek, the up-and-coming Florentine neighborhood has a reputation as a foodie favorite. The crowd here is young and hip, and so are the eateries. Restaurants here tend to come and go quickly, so take a stroll and see which places are drawing the crowds.

$$
MEXICAN
✕**Mezcal.** This lively neighborhood restaurant and bar hits the spot with refreshing margaritas and straightforward, tasty Mexican fare. Share a few plates from the "street food" menu of tostadas, tacos, chimichangas, and enchiladas. A multicourse tasting menu on Sunday night is an opportune time to sample the chef's favorites. Happy hour starts every day at 6 pm, a good time to try the Bloody Maria, chili martini, or classic margarita. Try the churros—sweet tubes of fried dough—if you have room for dessert. $ *Average main: NIS 62* ⊠ *2 Vital St., Florentine* ☎ *03/518–7925* ✛ *B5.*

JAFFA

This ancient fishing port is great for sampling local fish and other authentic local delights. The Flea Market has new and trendy eateries opening each week, so wander around and find a place that's filled with locals, a sure sign that it's a hot spot.

$$
SEAFOOD

✕**Abdu Hadayag.** Neighborhood lore says that this eatery's namesake was a fisherman in his early years. His simple establishment has long been a fixture of Jaffa's main street. The fishing nets, lanterns, and other marine accoutrements are refreshingly down-to-earth in a city where the interior design of restaurants has sometimes become as important as the menu. The favorites here include grouper, red snapper, gray mullet, and mackerel, as well as melita, an Israeli fish in the barracuda family. ⑤ *Average main: NIS 75* ⊠ *37 Yefet St., Jaffa* ☎ *03/518–2595* ✛ *A6.*

$
MIDDLE EASTERN

✕**Abu Hassan.** This shop serves what is often called the country's best hummus, which is not an easy task with so many places serving this addictive chickpea dish. For something quite different, order the *masabacha* with chunks of chickpeas served in warm hummus, or the hummus *ful*, made from Egyptian fava beans. Get here early and expect to wait in line, because once the pot is empty the restaurant closes (usually around 2:30 pm). ⑤ *Average main: NIS 25* ⊠ *1 Dolphin St., Jaffa* ☎ *03/682–0387* ▭ *No credit cards* ✛ *A6.*

$$$
ITALIAN
FAMILY

✕**Cafe Yaffo.** The Italian-style ice creams and sorbets prepared daily by chef Ronnie Rivlin are the highlight of this light, airy corner café in the middle of the Jaffa Flea Market. Apple pie and berry frozen yogurt are among the most popular choices. The kosher menu also includes an extensive list of pastas and pizzas, making it a good choice for families with kids longing for something familiar. The Friday brunch buffet is a good value and will fill you up for the day. ⑤ *Average main: NIS 84* ⊠ *11 Olei Tzion St., Jaffa* ☎ *03/518–1988* ⊕ *www.caffeyaffo.com* ☾ *No breakfast or lunch Sat.* ✛ *A6.*

$$
SEAFOOD

✕**The Container.** The surprises at Jaffa Port include this waterfront eatery, whose name and decor are inspired by the shipping containers once unloaded along this dock. In fact, its sleek bar is fashioned from the metal shell of one discarded container. Steps away from bobbing fishing boats, diners feast on a mostly fish and seafood menu on high tables made from wooden crates. The menu varies, but red snapper with horseradish and Jerusalem artichokes with truffles are among its delights. Local art graces the walls, and live music reverberates throughout the week. ⑤ *Average main: NIS 75* ⊠ *Jaffa Port, Warehouse 2, Jaffa* ☎ *03/683–6321* ⊕ *www.container.org.il* ✛ *A6.*

$$
MEDITERRANEAN

✕**Kalamata.** With an unbeatable view of the Mediterranean Sea on one side and the Old City on the other, this Greek-influenced eatery will add a romantic touch to your visit to Jaffa. Sip ouzo or arak (a locally produced anise-flavored liqueur) alongside fresh-baked kalamata olive bread and colorful small dishes like grilled artichokes over lentils or fish kabobs with cilantro-mint salad. The small dining space is set in an old stone building on the water, so be sure to request one of the few tables by the window to watch the special sunset view. ⑤ *Average main: NIS 66* ⊠ *10 Kedumim Sq., Jaffa* ☎ *03/681–9998* ⊕ *www.kalamata. co.il* ✛ *A6.*

$$$
SEAFOOD

✕ **Manta Ray.** A Tel Aviv institution, this boisterous restaurant boasts indoor and outdoor dining options and a great beach view. It appeals to everyone from families to couples looking for romance, and attracts a loyal clientele. The imaginative appetizers vary from day to day, but some standards include the shrimp with spinach, mango, and cracked wheat, or goat cheese with beets. The baked sea bream with rosemary and olive oil is simple Mediterranean fare at its best, especially with a spicy chili and pepper sauce on the side. ⑤ *Average main: NIS 90* ⊠ *Alma Beach, near the Dolphinarium, Jaffa* ☎ *03/517–4773* ⊕ *www. mantaray.co.il* ✛ *A5.*

$$$
SEAFOOD

✕ **Margaret Tayar.** Just off the main entrance to Jaffa, this slightly ramshackle spot treats you to a view of the city's coastline. Mediterranean-style grilled fish is the specialty, but the menu also includes favorites like fried sardines stuffed with caviar. Owner Margaret Tayar is a gregarious presence, serving up steaming plates from her tiny kitchen off a small wooden bar topped with jars of pickled red peppers and kumquats. The snug interior is fine for cold winter days, but when the weather is good, opt for a spot on the garden patio overlooking the sea. ⑤ *Average main: NIS 90* ⊠ *8 Razif Ha'Aliyah Ha'Shnia St., at Clock Tower Sq., Jaffa* ☎ *03/682–4741* ▭ *No credit cards* ✛ *A6.*

$$$$
MODERN ISRAELI
Fodor'sChoice
★

✕ **OCD.** The name (an acronym for obsessive-compulsive disorder) refers to the meticulous care chef Raz Rahav and his team pour into each elaborate dish in this nine-course adventure tasting menu. A first of its kind for Tel Aviv, OCD offers two nightly seatings with no menu to choose from, and the dishes change monthly based on seasonal offerings. Exquisitely concocted selections like steamed drum fish over barley in a shrimp stock with vanilla and shiso leaves, though seemingly overwhelming, taste great and make conversation pieces for what feels like an intimate dinner party. Guests are invited to join the chefs and photograph the creative action. Advance reservations are required, and guests can inform the restaurant of any dietary restrictions at the time of booking. ⑤ *Average main: NIS 270* ⊠ *17 Tirtsa St., Jaffa* ☎ *03/556–6774* ⊕ *www.ocdtlv.com* ✛ *A6.*

$
CAFÉ

✕ **Puaa.** In the heart of the Jaffa Flea Market, Puaa's lumpy sofas and slightly battered tables and chairs make for a kick-your-shoes-off atmosphere—and some patrons oblige. It's a popular gathering place for thirtysomething Tel Avivians, as well as young families. All the cakes, cookies, and croissants are baked fresh on the premises. There's a good selection of vegetarian dishes, including the Middle Eastern favorite *majadarah* (rice with lentils), served with salad and yogurt. One of the prize meat dishes is sautéed chicken with mushrooms, onions, shatta peppers, and pieces of apple. ⑤ *Average main: NIS 46* ⊠ *8 Rabbi Yohanan St., Jaffa* ☎ *03/682–3821* ⊕ *www.puaa.co.il* ✛ *A6.*

$$
AMERICAN

✕ **Pundak Deluxe.** Been traveling for a while and need a familiar taste of home? This American-style barbecue joint in the heart of the Jaffa Flea Market slow cooks its meats in an imported meat smoker and serves them alongside coleslaw and mac 'n' cheese. Wooden tables with colorful plastic chairs keep things casual as you enjoy baby back ribs, open-faced sandwiches, and sausages made from locally sourced lamb, pork, and beef. The homemade toppings are a highlight: horseradish

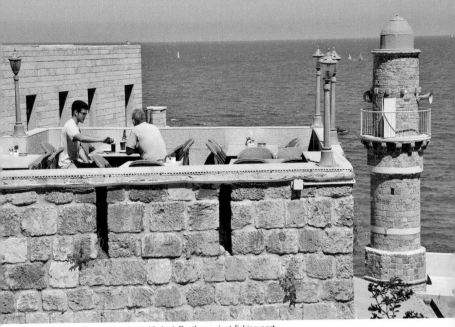

There are plenty of spots to eat outside in Jaffa, the ancient fishing port.

mayonnaise, sweet ketchup, and beet barbecue sauce add just the right touch. $ *Average main: NIS 70* ✉ *7 Olei Tzion St., Jaffa* ☎ *03/523–3186* ⊕ *www.de-luxe.co.il* ✛ *A6.*

NORTH TEL AVIV

Primarily a residential area, North Tel Aviv has many long-established family favorites. Most eateries are at Tel Aviv Port, where you can enjoy views of the ocean and refreshing sea breezes.

$$ ✕ **Ashtor.** This small corner café, a neighborhood favorite, is where
CAFÉ you can catch a glimpse of the beauty of European café culture. Coffee is the main event, over which you can linger for hours along with your newspaper, computer, or friends from the neighborhood. Because it's in the heart of the upscale Basel area, patrons include celebrities that live nearby. The menu includes sandwiches and salads, pastas, and schnitzel. $ *Average main: NIS 56* ✉ *37 Basel St., North Tel Aviv* ☎ *03/546–5318* ✛ *B2.*

$$$ ✕ **Kitchen Market.** On the top floor of the farmers' market at the Tel Aviv
MODERN ISRAELI Port, this eatery's stellar views of the sea make it an ideal rendezvous spot for a romantic lunch or dinner. Because of the location, you can bet that the ingredients are as fresh as possible. With a menu full of modern Israeli dishes to choose from, the restaurant makes it hard for you to pick, but you almost can't lose. For a few lighter dishes, try the mushroom ragout with boiled egg and truffle oil or the colorful tomato, mozzarella, and labaneh (yogurt cheese) salad. $ *Average main: NIS 98* ✉ *Hangar 12, Tel Aviv Port* ☎ *03/544–6669* ⊕ *www.kitchen-market.co.il* ✛ *B1.*

$ | × **Sabich.** The specialty at this hole-in-the-wall eatery is sabich, a
MIDDLE EASTERN | meal-in-a-pita popular in the region. It's considered a breakfast food (the word comes from the Arabic for "morning") because it includes a hard-boiled egg, in addition to hummus, tomatoes, peppers, and spices. It's a filling snack at any time of day, however. Another popular menu item is the platter of meatballs served in a light tomato sauce. The indoor dining area consists of three or four stools at a counter, and there are a few tables outside as well. $ *Average main: NIS 16* ✉ *99 Ibn Gvirol St., North Tel Aviv* ☎ *03/523–1810* ⊟ *No credit cards* ☉ *No dinner* ⊹ *C2.*

$$$ | × **Shtsupak.** Diners crowd the tables inside and out at this simple seafood
SEAFOOD | place. They've been doing so for years, despite the fact that the trendy Tel Aviv Port, with several fish places of its own, is a few steps away. Locals agree that the fish here is reasonably priced, well prepared, and always fresh. For the main course, there's a catch of the day, which may include whole trout, fried calamari, or oysters in cream sauce. All the entrées come with an assortment of salads. $ *Average main: NIS 98* ✉ *256 Ben Yehuda St., North Tel Aviv* ☎ *03/544–1973* ⊕ *www.shtsupak.co.il* ⊹ *B2.*

HERZLIYA PITUACH

A seaside suburb north of Tel Aviv, Herzliya Pituach has a cluster of chain restaurants in the Arena Mall at the marina, with a picturesque view of the yachts at anchor. The excellent Herbert Samuel is also here.

$$$$ | × **Herbert Samuel.** Walking through the door of this understated but
MEDITERRANEAN | elegant dining room, you hear the energetic hum of good conversation.
Fodor's Choice | The upscale but accessible kosher menu has a strong Mediterranean
★ | influence and changes every season. Staples include the nine-variety tomato salad, barbecue lamb sliders, and the daily catch from the adjacent marina. Leave room for the luscious house-made, dairy-free desserts. An open kitchen is on full view and is a must-see for anyone who loves to cook. The extensive wine list and refreshing cocktails are professionally created. $ *Average main: NIS 120* ✉ *The Ritz-Carlton Herzliya , 4 HaShunit St., Herzliya Pituach* ☎ *073/203–7596* ⊕ *www.herbertsamuel.co.il* ☉ *Closed Sat.* ⊹ *B1.*

WHERE TO STAY

Nothing stands between Tel Aviv's luxury hotels and the Mediterranean Sea except the golden beach and a promenade outfitted with chairs and gazebos. Tel Aviv's hotel row is on Hayarkon Street, which becomes Herbert Samuel Esplanade as you proceed south between the Tel Aviv Port area and Jaffa. Across the street from the luxury hotels are a number of more economical ones. Boutique hotels are becoming more popular and are also centrally located, so you're never far from the trendy shops and outdoor cafés of Ben Yehuda and Dizengoff Streets or the buzzy restaurants and bars of Rothschild Boulevard.

Hotel reservations are essential during all Jewish holidays and are advised throughout the year. Some hotels have parking lots, but a few rely on public lots that can be at least a short walk away.

Hotel reviews have been shortened. For more information, visit Fodors. com. Use the coordinates (✛A1) at the end of each listing to locate a site on the corresponding map.

WHAT IT COSTS				
	$	**$$**	**$$$**	**$$$$**
Hotels	Under $200	$200–$300	$301–$400	over $400

Hotel prices, given in U.S. dollars, are the lowest cost of a standard double room in high season. Non-Israeli citizens paying in foreign currency are exempt from the 17% V.A.T. on hotel rooms.

CENTER CITY

For convenience, the center of the city is the ideal place to rest after long days of sightseeing. These hotels put you within walking or biking distance of just about anywhere you'll want to visit in Tel Aviv.

$$$$ 🏨 **Alma Hotel.** Housed in a 1920s building that once served as a private
HOTEL residence, this meticulously designed hotel is filled with warm colors, fine fabrics, and original artwork. **Pros:** free Wi-Fi connections; handy espresso machines; breakfast in gourmet lounge downstairs. **Cons:** very pricey; intensely musky perfumed lobby; windows are not double glazed. ⑤ *Rooms from: $480* ⊠ *23 Yavne St., Center City* ☎ *03/630–8777* ⊕ *www.almahotel.co.il* ⟿ *15 rooms* ⍔ *No meals* ✛ *A4.*

$$ 🏨 **ArtPlus Hotel Tel Aviv.** Designed as a showcase of modern Israeli art,
HOTEL this boutique hotel manages to pull off the look of a gallery and the feel of a homey oasis. **Pros:** a fun happy hour for guests; friendly atmosphere; chic but accessible style. **Cons:** small rooms; on a slightly run-down section of Ben Yehuda Street. ⑤ *Rooms from: $250* ⊠ *35 Ben Yehuda St., Center City* ☎ *03/797–1700* ⊕ *www.atlas.co.il* ⟿ *62 rooms* ⍔ *Breakfast* ✛ *B3.*

$$ 🏨 **Brown TLV.** As hip as the city around it, this fun boutique hotel offers
HOTEL luxurious pampering at a remarkably reasonable price, making it a great find. **Pros:** warm and attentive service; included breakfast is at local eateries; walk to the beach. **Cons:** small rooms; no breakfast on-site. ⑤ *Rooms from: $280* ⊠ *25 Kalisher St., Center City* ☎ *03/717–0200* ⊕ *www.browntlv.com* ⟿ *30 rooms* ⍔ *Breakfast* ✛ *B4.*

$$$ 🏨 **Carlton.** The lobby of this massive hotel has intimate sitting areas,
HOTEL each of which features the work of a different artist. **Pros:** homey feel; great service; close to public beach. **Cons:** location near Atarim Square, which is rather shabby. ⑤ *Rooms from: $350* ⊠ *10 Eliezer Peri St., Center City* ☎ *03/520–1818* ⊕ *www.carlton.co.il* ⟿ *280 rooms* ⍔ *Breakfast* ✛ *A2.*

$$ 🏨 **Center Chic Hotel Tel Aviv.** This member of the Atlas chain of bou-
HOTEL tique hotels has a cozy lobby filled with books about Tel Aviv and a lounge area that screens vintage black-and-white films about Israel.

Pros: free bicycles for guests; trendy Bauhaus design; rooftop view. **Cons:** small rooms. ⑤ *Rooms from: $250* ✉ *2 Zamenhoff St., Center City* ☎ *03/542–5555* ⊕ *www.atlas.co.il* ↗ *56 rooms* ⓘⓄⓘ *Breakfast* ✢ *B3.*

$$ ⛺ **Cinema Hotel Tel Aviv.** In the 1930s this was the Esther Cinema, one
HOTEL of the first movie theaters in Tel Aviv. **Pros:** a sense of history and style; careful renovation; complimentary afternoon coffee. **Cons:** no pool. ⑤ *Rooms from: $245* ✉ *1 Zamenhoff St., Center City* ☎ *03/520–7100* ⊕ *www.atlas.co.il* ↗ *82 rooms* ⓘⓄⓘ *Breakfast* ✢ *B3.*

$$$$ ⛺ **Dan Tel Aviv.** Return visitors say they love the sense of history at the
HOTEL Dan, built in 1953 and billed as Tel Aviv's very first hotel. **Pros:** historic premises; close to the beach; suites have stereo systems. **Cons:** guest lounge bans children. ⑤ *Rooms from: $475* ✉ *99 Hayarkon St., Center City* ☎ *03/520–2525* ⊕ *www.danhotels.com* ↗ *329 rooms* ⓘⓄⓘ *Breakfast* ✢ *A3.*

$$$$ ⛺ **Hilton Tel Aviv.** Perched on a cliff, this sprawling hotel is buffered on
HOTEL three sides by Independence Park. **Pros:** the lap of luxury; quiet loca-
FAMILY tion; separate shower stalls in many rooms. **Cons:** at the end of the hotel strip, somewhat detached from the city. ⑤ *Rooms from: $560* ✉ *Hayarkon St., at Independence Park, Center City* ☎ *03/520–2222* ⊕ *www3.hilton.com* ↗ *584 rooms* ⓘⓄⓘ *Breakfast* ✢ *B2.*

$$$$ ⛺ **Hotel Montefiore.** This stunning boutique hotel shows off what restora-
HOTEL tion can bring to the historic buildings of Tel Aviv. **Pros:** crisp service;
Fodor's Choice historic building; excellent breakfast. **Cons:** front entrance is not wheel-
★ chair accessible; rather pricey. ⑤ *Rooms from: $475* ✉ *36 Montefiore St., Center City* ☎ *03/564–6100* ⊕ *www.hotelmontefiore.co.il* ↗ *12 rooms* ⓘⓄⓘ *Breakfast* ✢ *B4.*

$ ⛺ **Maxim Hotel Tel Aviv.** Located across from the beach, Maxim has sim-
HOTEL ply decorated rooms, many with sea views. **Pros:** complimentary coffee and cake in lobby; free parking; nice location near the ocean. **Cons:** small rooms; drab character. ⑤ *Rooms from: $120* ✉ *86 Hayarkon St., Center City* ☎ *03/517–3721* ⊕ *www.telavivmaxim.com* ↗ *71 rooms* ⓘⓄⓘ *Breakfast* ✢ *B3.*

$$ ⛺ **Mendeli Street Hotel.** A location on a side street between Hayarkon
HOTEL Street and Ben Yehuda means this amiable five-story hotel is a short walk from the beach and a growing crop of cafés and restaurants. **Pros:** excellent breakfast; modern renovations. **Cons:** no sea views; limited parking. ⑤ *Rooms from: $220* ✉ *5 Mendeli St., Center City* ☎ *03/520–2700* ⊕ *www.mendelistreethotel.com* ↗ *66 rooms* ⓘⓄⓘ *Breakfast* ✢ *B3.*

$$$$ ⛺ **The Norman Hotel.** Two immaculately restored historic buildings
HOTEL in central Tel Aviv make up this contemporary urban hot spot that
Fodor's Choice evokes Bauhaus-era elegance and old-world charm. **Pros:** outstanding
★ service; excellent on-site bar and restaurant; rooftop pool. **Cons:** pricey. ⑤ *Rooms from: $500* ✉ *23–25 Nachmani St., Center City* ☎ *03/543–5555* ⊕ *www.thenorman.com* ↗ *50 rooms* ⓘⓄⓘ *Breakfast* ✢ *B4.*

$$ ⛺ **Poli House.** Star designer Karim Rashid chose the iconic Polishuk
HOTEL House, a Bauhaus building, for his first venture into Tel Aviv's bou-tique hotel scene. **Pros:** rooftop infinity pool; helpful staff; trendy bar. **Cons:** design overlooks practicality at times. ⑤ *Rooms from: $250* ✉ *1 Nahalat Binyamin St., Center City* ✢ *Entrance accessible from pedes-trian street* ☎ *03/710–5000* ⊕ *www.thepolihouse.com* ↗ *40 rooms* ⓘⓄⓘ *Breakfast* ✢ *B4.*

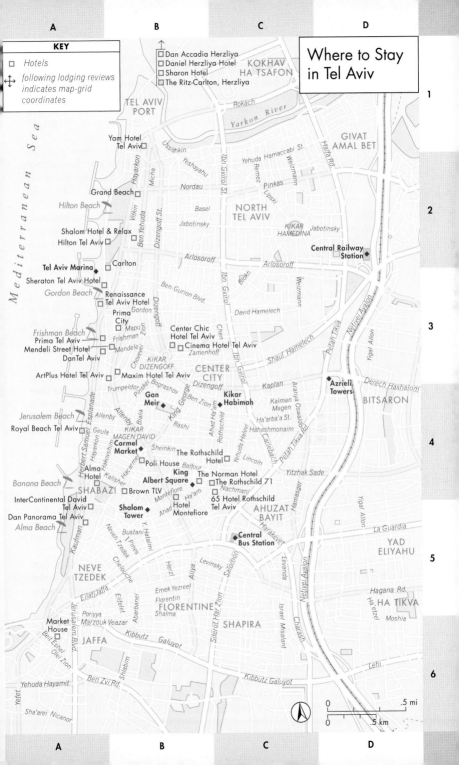

$$ ⬜ **Prima City.** A block from the beach, this six-story hotel on a street
HOTEL lined with small apartment houses has a light, airy lobby with a small
sitting area on one side and a simple restaurant on the other. **Pros:**
friendly staff; adjoining rooms for families; kosher restaurant offers
special meals. **Cons:** outdated. ⑤ *Rooms from: $200* ✉ *9 Mapu St.,
Center City* ☎ *03/552–2220* ⊕ *www.prima.co.il* ⤶ *96 rooms* ⦿ *Break-
fast* ✛ *B3.*

$$ ⬜ **Prima Tel Aviv.** Excellent views of the sea are available from many of
HOTEL the subtly decorated rooms at the Prima Tel Aviv. **Pros:** near the sea; cozy
rooms; lots of interesting art. **Cons:** charge for Wi-Fi. ⑤ *Rooms from:
$205* ✉ *105 Hayarkon St., at Frishman St., Center City* ☎ *03/520–6666*
⊕ *www.prima.co.il* ⤶ *55 rooms* ⦿ *Breakfast* ✛ *B3.*

$$$ ⬜ **Renaissance Tel Aviv Hotel.** All the rooms and suites have spectacular
HOTEL sea-facing balconies at this comfortable luxury hotel with a geometric
facade. **Pros:** pretty sundecks; beautiful indoor pool; direct access to
beach. **Cons:** business lounge closes at midnight. ⑤ *Rooms from: $321*
✉ *121 Hayarkon St., Center City* ☎ *03/521–5555* ⊕ *www.marriott.com*
⤶ *346 rooms* ⦿ *Breakfast* ✛ *A3.*

$$$ ⬜ **The Rothschild Hotel.** On Rothschild Boulevard, this boutique hotel
HOTEL has a color scheme and design aesthetic intended to evoke the Tel Aviv
of days gone by. **Pros:** free Wi-Fi; top-notch restaurant with excellent breakfast; espresso machine in each room. **Cons:** on a busy street.
⑤ *Rooms from: $301* ✉ *96 Rothschild Blvd., Center City* ☎ *03/957–
8888* ⊕ *www.the-rothschild-hotel.com* ⤶ *29 rooms* ⦿ *Breakfast* ✛ *C4.*

$$ ⬜ **The Rothschild 71.** When you enter this nicely renovated International
HOTEL Style building you'll feel right at home, thanks to a living-room-style
lobby where you can enjoy coffee and tea. **Pros:** personal service;
espresso machine in each room; good value for the area. **Cons:** included
breakfast is at inferior restaurant. ⑤ *Rooms from: $220* ✉ *71 Roths-
child Blvd., Center City* ☎ *03/629–0555* ⊕ *www.the-rothschild.com*
⤶ *30 rooms* ⦿ *Breakfast* ✛ *B4.*

$$$ ⬜ **Royal Beach Tel Aviv.** A relative newcomer along the coastline, this
HOTEL is the most modern and updated of the large hotel chains to set up
overlooking the sea along the Tel Aviv promenade. **Pros:** infinity pool
overlooking the sea; fantastic kosher restaurant in hotel. **Cons:** additional cost for gym and spa area. ⑤ *Rooms from: $375* ✉ *19 Hayar-
kon St., Center City* ☎ *03/740–5000* ⊕ *www.isrotel.com* ⤶ *230 rooms*
⦿ *Breakfast* ✛ *A4.*

$$ ⬜ **Shalom Hotel & Relax.** At this boutique hotel, the attentive staff, always
HOTEL friendly and accommodating, greets you with a cold beverage and a
chocolate treat, and the daily happy hour includes a complimentary
15-minute massage—a great way to revive yourself after a day of sight-
seeing. **Pros:** rooftop lounge with sea view; complimentary Wi-Fi access;
free use of bikes. **Cons:** no pool. ⑤ *Rooms from: $295* ✉ *216 Hayar-
kon St., Center City* ☎ *03/762–5400* ⊕ *www.atlas.co.il* ⤶ *51 rooms*
⦿ *Breakfast* ✛ *B2.*

$$$ ⬜ **Sheraton Tel Aviv Hotel.** Combining a personal touch with the efficiency
HOTEL of an international chain, this hotel is an attractive option on the beach
of Tel Aviv. **Pros:** fine restaurant; dog beds for visiting canines; wine
tasting of local wines three times a week. **Cons:** hard to find parking.

The colorful Design Museum Holon hosts changing exhibits that explore the importance of design in daily life.

$ *Rooms from: $305* ✉ *115 Hayarkon St., Center City* ☎ *03/521–1111* ⊕ *www.sheratontelaviv.com* ↘ *349 rooms* ⧆ *Breakfast* ✛ *B3.*

$$
HOTEL
Fodor's Choice
★

🛏 **65 Hotel Rothschild Tel Aviv.** The Atlas hotel chain's most sophisticated design to date harmonizes with the central business location in the heart of Rothschild Boulevard. **Pros:** daily happy hour with drinks and snacks; great value for the money; ideal location for business travelers. **Cons:** no pool or gym. $ *Rooms from: $275* ✉ *65 Rothschild Blvd., Center City* ☎ *03/767–7677* ⊕ *www.atlas.co.il/65-hotel-tel-aviv/* ↘ *74 rooms* ⧆ *Breakfast* ✛ *C4.*

NEVE TZEDEK

Historic Neve Tzedek has a few modern lodgings with a convenient location a short distance from the sea.

$$
HOTEL

🛏 **Dan Panorama Tel Aviv.** At the southern end of the beach, this high-rise is a short walk from Jaffa and Neve Tzedek. **Pros:** across the street from the beach; handy location; efficient service. **Cons:** staid atmosphere; feels more business hotel than luxury vacation spot. $ *Rooms from: $235* ✉ *10 Koifman St., Neve Tzedek* ☎ *03/519–0190* ⊕ *www.danhotels.com* ↘ *500 rooms* ⧆ *Breakfast* ✛ *A5.*

$$$
HOTEL

🛏 **InterContinental David Tel Aviv.** At the southern end of the beach, this luxurious hotel has suites that are often reserved by visiting celebrities—and with the gorgeous views of the sea, it's easy to understand why. **Pros:** ocean views; tasty breakfast; near Neve Tzedek. **Cons:** no balconies. $ *Rooms from: $310* ✉ *12 Kaufman St., Neve Tzedek* ☎ *03/795–1111* ⊕ *www.ihg.com* ↘ *555 rooms* ⧆ *Breakfast* ✛ *A5.*

JAFFA

The city's boutique-hotel boom is about to spread south from central Tel Aviv toward Jaffa. With the openings of the W Hotel and the Setai set for 2017, travelers can expect other boutiques to appear on the scene.

$$$
HOTEL
Fodor'sChoice
★

🏨 **Market House.** In an area with few hotel options, this gem is the first in a coming wave of high-end boutique hotels in Jaffa. **Pros:** unique location; friendly and helpful front-desk staff; excellent breakfast. **Cons:** small rooms; a short distance from Center City attractions. $ *Rooms from: $305* ⊠ *5 Beit Eshel St., Jaffa* ☎ *03/797–4000* ⊕ *www.atlas.co.il* ↪ *44 rooms* ❤️*Breakfast* ✛ *A6.*

NORTH TEL AVIV

With proximity to the sea, the Hayarkon Park and the Tel Aviv Port, the northern area of Tel Aviv is great for sports enthusiasts, sun seekers, and those seeking respite from the hustle of the Center City.

$
HOTEL

🏨 **Grand Beach.** There's a small but inviting rooftop pool and sundeck at this basic hotel, located less than five minutes from the beach. **Pros:** close to restaurants; comfortable lobby bar; reasonable rates. **Cons:** many tour groups. $ *Rooms from: $190* ⊠ *250 Hayarkon St., North Tel Aviv* ☎ *03/543–3333* ⊕ *www.grandbeach.co.il* ↪ *212 rooms* ❤️*Breakfast* ✛ *B2.*

$
HOTEL

🏨 **Yam Hotel Tel Aviv.** While not directly on the sea, the Yam, meaning "beach" in Hebrew, goes to lengths to remind visitors of their location close to the water. **Pros:** abundant complimentary happy-hour spread; playful design; free bicycles. **Cons:** very small rooms. $ *Rooms from: $190* ⊠ *16 Kaf Gimel Yordei ha-Sira St., Tel Aviv Port* ☎ *03/542–5555* ⊕ *www.atlas.co.il* ↪ *42 rooms* ❤️*Breakfast* ✛ *B1.*

HERZLIYA PITUACH

Don't want to stay in a city? Herzliya Pituach is a resort area 12 km (7½ miles) up the coast from Tel Aviv. It has a number of beachfront hotels, a public square with outdoor cafés that's a short walk from the beach, and a marina and adjacent Arena Mall with a selection of high-end shops, restaurants, and pubs. The area has a cosmopolitan air, as affluent suburbanites live here, along with diplomats and foreign journalists. A car is useful, but it's possible to get around with taxis; parking in Tel Aviv is a challenge.

$$$
HOTEL

🏨 **Dan Accadia Herzliya.** The three buildings of this seaside hotel are surrounded by flower-filled gardens that lead to a swimming pool overlooking the sea. **Pros:** lovely views; gorgeous grounds; dinner buffets on summer nights. **Cons:** little local atmosphere; away from the city's attractions. $ *Rooms from: $340* ⊠ *22 Ramat Yam St., Herzliya Pituach* ☎ *09/959–7070* ⊕ *www.danhotels.com* ↪ *209 rooms* ❤️*Breakfast* ✛ *B1.*

$$$
HOTEL

🏨 **Daniel Herzliya Hotel.** The high-ceiling lobby at this hotel has a glass wall that lets you gaze out at the Mediterranean—and the rooms have even better views. **Pros:** in-house spa. **Cons:** some rooms are small and

Herzilya Pituach is a popular beach resort area north of Tel Aviv.

plain; public parking is first-come, first-served. $ *Rooms from: $310* ✉ *60 Ramot Yam St., Herzliya Pituach* ☎ *09/952–8282* ⊕ *www.tamareshotels.com* ⌁ *200 rooms* ⦿| *Breakfast* ✛ *B1.*

$$$$
HOTEL
🎞 **The Ritz-Carlton, Herzliya.** The exclusive Herzliya Pituach Marina is the setting for Ritz-Carlton's first hotel and residences in Israel, a striking, modern building that makes up for being 12 km (7 miles) north of central Tel Aviv with grandly plush public areas and guest rooms with large windows and balconies for viewing seaside sunsets. **Pros:** well-equipped gym; abundant breakfast; large rooms and suites. **Cons:** need car or taxi to get to Tel Aviv; wind noise on the marina side can be loud. $ *Rooms from: $405* ✉ *4 HaShunut St., Herzliya Pituach* ✛ *Entrance through Arena Mall* ☎ *09/373–5555* ⊕ *www.ritzcarlton.com* ⌁ *160 rooms* ⦿| *Breakfast* ✛ *B1.*

$$
HOTEL
🎞 **Sharon Hotel.** The northernmost hotel on the strip overlooking the water is a little far from the neighborhood's shopping and dining options. **Pros:** homey atmosphere; nice location; sense of local color. **Cons:** rooms on lower floors have uninspiring views; noisy lobby. $ *Rooms from: $234* ✉ *5 Ramat Yam St., Herzliya Pituach* ☎ *09/952–5777* ⊕ *www.sharon.co.il* ⌁ *173 rooms* ⦿| *Breakfast* ✛ *B1.*

NIGHTLIFE AND PERFORMING ARTS

"When do they sleep?" That's what visitors tend to ask about Tel Avivians because they always seem to be out and about, coming or going from a bar, restaurant, or a performance. Tel Aviv's reputation for having some of the world's best nightlife is well deserved, and the city is also Israel's cultural center.

NIGHTLIFE

On Lilienblum and Allenby Streets, and in Florentine, where many of the pubs and bars are clustered, things don't really get started until at least 10 pm, especially on Friday night. Most places stay open "until the last customer," which means it's at least 3 am when things finally begin to wind down, although some places are still crowded at 5 am.

For those who want to start and finish the evening early, some night-spots—particularly wine bars—open before the night owls descend. Happy hours are becoming more and more popular.

CENTER CITY

BARS AND CLUBS

Aria Lounge Bar. This Manhattan-style lounge bar offers the rare combination of classy food, cocktails, and dancing in the same space. Seats in the lounge circle the DJ booth, where top local and international DJs, and occasional live-music performers, hold forth. A full dinner menu is available from the upstairs restaurant, along with craft cocktails like the Lady in Red: gin, house-made lavender and hibiscus syrup, and fresh lemon, finished with roses and lilies. ⊠ *66 Nahalat Binyamin St., Center City* ☎ *03/529–6054* ⊕ *www. ariatlv.co.il.*

Bar Barbunia. Aptly named for a small fish that's a staple of the city's old-time restaurants, Bar Barbunia draws a mixed crowd that ranges from fishermen to financial planners. It manages to be both smoky and cheerful, and the music tends toward classics from the '70s. ⊠ *192 Ben Yehuda St., Center City* ☎ *03/524–0961.*

Fodor's Choice ★ **Bellboy.** Many of the cocktails here are lit up with a fiery uproar, and some come with garnishes straight out of a toy shop. It's definitely worth watching the skilled bartenders do their stuff in a room that takes you straight back to the 1920s. Small dishes are served with a bit less drama and include beef tartare, crispy calamari, and house-made fried kale chips (hard to find in Israel). It's on a side street near the northern end of Rothschild Boulevard. ⊠ *14 Berdichevsky St., Center City* ☎ *03/728–9213* ⊕ *www.bellboybar.com.*

Café Europa. At this place to see and be seen, especially in summer evenings, the sparkling cocktails and creative small plates draw attractive customers to a packed outdoor patio. Be adventurous and taste one of the cocktails made with a local product, such as the anise-flavored arak. ⊠ *9B Rothschild Blvd., Center City* ☎ *03/525–9987.*

Cafe Noga. This sticky-floored Tel Aviv institution doubles as a pool hall, with 19 tables drawing a fun-loving crowd. If darts is your sport, stop in on Wednesday nights for the weekly contest. The music runs from oldies to hip-hop, depending on which staff is working. ⊠ *4 Pinsker St., near Allenby St., Center City* ☎ *03/629–6457.*

Evita. One of Tel Aviv's best gay bars, Evita is a small, classy place with some of the city's top DJs. The long line outside in the later hours attests to its popularity. ⊠ *31 Yavne St., Center City* ☎ *03/566–9559* ⊕ *www.evita.co.il.*

HaMaoz. The quirky interior of this bar geared toward the twenty- and thirtysomething crowd resembles someone's apartment, down to the black-and-white family photos on the walls. There's even a refrigerator in the kitchen and a working shower in the bathroom. It's always crowded in the living room, where there's a flat-screen TV. ⊠ *32 King George St., Center City* ☎ *03/620–9458.*

HaMinzar. One of the oldest bars in Tel Aviv, the Monastery is a gritty, down-to-earth pub that's popular with a slightly older after-work crowd, as well as with students later in the evening and on weekends. The kitchen serves up some fine food, too. ⊠ *60 Allenby St., Center City* ☎ *03/517–3015.*

Hashoftim. At this neighborhood tavern rich with history, the regulars tend to be older and mellower. Groups of friends congregate outside in the beer garden or inside at the small bar while enjoying jazz or blues. ⊠ *39 Ibn Gvirol St., at Hashoftim St., Center City* ☎ *03/695–1153.*

Fodor's Choice ★ **Imperial Craft Cocktail Bar.** Head to the hidden back entrance of a somewhat lackluster hotel lobby and discover this colonial-British-themed playground run by five of Tel Aviv's top mixologists. Nightly specials enhance the standard menu of 150 precisely concocted cocktails. Happy-hour specials (50% off) are particularly appealing, or reserve for late night, when you may be sitting next to the city's top chefs. ⊠ *Imperial Hotel, 66 Hayarkon St., Center City* ☎ *073/264–9464.*

Jimmy Who? In an old bank building, this place creatively uses the space for three connected bars that each have a different feel. Push your way through the turnstile in the middle, and you'll find yourself dancing in and through this dimly lighted maze. ⊠ *24 Rothschild Blvd., Center City* ☎ *050/666–7337.*

Kuli Alma. A two-level subterranean courtyard adorned by local graffiti artists draws bohemian music addicts and casual partiers for alternative music, not to mention fresh baked pizza and mojito slushies. Any night of the week you can find a relaxed crowd enjoying either a live band or an international DJ playing hip-hop, soul, or electronic music. ⊠ *10 Mikveh Israel St., Center City* ☎ *03/656–5155* ⊕ *www. kulialma.com.*

Levontin 7. This is a vibrant spot to experience the local music scene. Two shows every night feature the widest possible mix of musical offerings, from solo singers to bands blasting indie rock in Arabic. There's a cozy bar upstairs. ⊠ *7 Levontin St., Center City* ☎ *03/560– 5084* ⊕ *www.levontin7.com.*

Library Bar. In the lobby of the elegant Norman Hotel, the stately 1940s colonial-style Library Bar is ideal for refreshment at any time of day. Open from 9 am to 1 am, this posh refuge serves a traditional English high tea by day and pours wines from one of Tel Aviv's most luxurious wine lists throughout the evening. Look out for the bar's art and fashion evenings, which bring together the city's tastemakers for cultural conversation. ⊠ *The Norman Hotel, 23–25 Nachmani St., Center City* ☎ *03/543–5400* ⊕ *www.thenorman.com.*

M.A.S.H. A sports bar catering to soccer and rugby fans (that is, mostly Brits and Aussies), M.A.S.H. is the place to go when you want to see a live event on satellite TV. ⊠ *98 Hayarkon St., Center City* ☎ *03/605–1007* ⊕ *www.mash.co.il.*

Mike's Place. This well-stocked bar with multiple locations throughout the city has live music that appeals to the over-30 crowd. Its primary location, on the promenade facing the beach, makes it popular with tourists. ⊠ *86 Herbert Samuel St., Center City* ☎ *03/510–6392* ⊕ *www. mikesplacebars.com.*

Molly Bloom. The country's most authentic Irish pub is—no surprise—run by an Irishman, Robert Segal. Live music reverberates on Monday and Friday afternoon. There's a full menu, including such Emerald Isle favorites as shepherd's pie and beef stew. ⊠ *100 Hayarkon St., corner of Mendeli St., Center City* ☎ *03/522–1558* ⊕ *www.molly-blooms.com.*

Nanuchka. This ornate bistro and bar occupies a courtyard and a large interior space adorned with tapestries and paintings. The dancing gets going around 10 pm every night. Drinks include specialties of the house—a selection of sweet but light wines from the country of Georgia. The vegan menu is delicious and is surprising considering Georgian food is generally rich with meat. ⊠ *30 Lilienblum St., Center City* ☎ *03/516–2254* ⊕ *www.nanuchka.co.il.*

Rothschild 12. Entered through a back gate, this hipster hangout hosts live music most nights. Things can get very loud under the exposed concrete ceiling, so you may want to escape to the cozy courtyard. The front section of the bar is a café that's open all day. ⊠ *12 Rothschild St., Center City* ☎ *03/510–6430.*

Fodor's Choice ★ **Tasting Room.** Showcasing Israeli vintages is the name of the game at this wine bar in the Sarona complex. Winemaker Roni Saslove brought high-tech tasting machines from Napa Valley so patrons could sample more than 30 different Israeli wines. Tastings are available by the sip, half glass, or full glass. If you particularly enjoy a certain wine, you can purchase a bottle to drink at the sleek bar or to take with you. ⊠ *Sarona, 36 Kaplan St., Center City* ☎ *03/533–3213* ⊕ *www. tastingroom.co.il.*

223. This stylish neighborhood bar has the feel of Prohibition-era New York City. The suspender-wearing bartenders specialize in excellent mixed drinks. Order a spicy apple martini to go alongside the expertly crafted bar food. ⊠ *223 Dizengoff St., Center City* ☎ *03/544–6537* ⊕ *www.223.co.il.*

Zizi. This hot club's focus is on dancing, but some secluded corners can be found for quiet conversation. Bartenders wave their hands in the air to the beat of the music, adding to the feel of escapist abandon. Check the schedule for gay party nights. ⊠ *7 Carlebach St., Center City* ☎ *03/561–1597.*

Tel Aviv is a music lover's paradise, and it's not hard to find live performances in bars, restaurants, or even on the street.

NEVE TZEDEK

After many years of neglect, Neve Tzedek has been rediscovered, becoming one of Tel Aviv's most popular neighborhoods by day and night. It brims with laid-back wine bars and other places perfect for an afternoon drink or a night on the town.

BARS AND CLUBS

Fodor's Choice
★

Jajo. The elegant Jajo Vino and Jajo Bar face each other in the heart of Neve Tzedek, and both are designed with an elegant character. Each location seats only about 20 people, but these dimly lit jewels are as chic as could be. The chandeliers hanging from the high ceilings, the flickering candles on the tables, the gracefully arched windows, and the oh-so-hip clientele make them ideal for intimate conversations. ⊠ *44 Shabazi St., Neve Tzedek* ☎ *03/510–0620* ⊕ *www.jajotlv.com.*

Vicky Cristina. In a renovated train station, this tapas bar evokes a Latin atmosphere with its sultry mood music. Sangria and other Spanish-style beverages are the theme of the large outdoor bar, where you may be lucky enough to catch some live music. ⊠ *HaTachana, 1 Koifman St., Neve Tzedek* ☎ *03/736–7272.*

FLORENTINE

Ranked internationally as a top hipster living spot, Florentine has bohemian nightlife that is filled with youthful, creative energy.

BARS AND CLUBS

Hoodna. This place attracts students and young professionals who lean toward the left on the political spectrum. The bar is split in two, with an alley down the middle that's ideal for kicking back and enjoying a pint.

Gobble up a burger and fries, or try some of the excellent homemade hummus. ⊠ *13 Abarbanel St., Florentine* ☏ *03/518–4558.*

Norma Jean. With an attractive brick facade, this bistro and bar on the edge of Florentine serves more than 200 kinds of whiskey, said to be the biggest collection in the country. The kitchen serves full meals, with a focus on pleasing the carnivorous. ⊠ *23 Elifelet St., Florentine* ☏ *03/683–7383* ⊕ *www.normajean.co.il.*

JAFFA

The winding stone alleyways of Jaffa make it a fun place to explore, and its perch on a hill in the southern end of Tel Aviv means there are alluring nighttime views of the twinkling coastline.

BARS AND CLUBS

Saloona. In the Noga neighborhood of Jaffa, this swank bar retains a hip, artistic feel that draws people to the area. Enjoy a drink under the gigantic chandeliers while you listen to live music. ⊠ *17 Tirza St., Jaffa* ☏ *03/518–1719.*

NORTH TEL AVIV

Tel Aviv's hottest, loudest nightlife destination is the Tel Aviv Port, located in the city's northern reaches. With its cutting-edge music, DJ-spun grooves, and raucous crowds, the port has contributed in no small measure to Tel Aviv's newly acquired status as a major player in the club world.

BARS AND CLUBS

Shablul Jazz Club. This intimate jazz club presents everything from hip-hop to ethno jazz Monday through Saturday nights. Performers range from veteran jazz artists to up-and-coming young talents. ⊠ *Hangar 13, Tel Aviv Port* ☏ *03/546–1891* ⊕ *www.shabluljazz.com.*

TLV. This megaclub doesn't start jumping until around 2 am. The state-of-the-art speaker system keeps the young crowd moving until sunrise. ⊠ *3 Hataarucha St., Tel Aviv Port* ☏ *03/544–4194.*

Zappa Club. One of Tel Aviv's best venues for live music, the Zappa Club is in the Ramat HaHayal neighborhood, just a short cab ride away from downtown. ⊠ *24 Raoul Wallenberg St., North Tel Aviv* ☏ *03/762–6666* ⊕ *www.zappa-club.co.il.*

PERFORMING ARTS

Tel Aviv is Israel's cultural capital, and it fulfills this role with relish. The Tel Aviv Museum of Art, the city's major artistic venue (for concerts and lectures as well as the fine arts), is complemented by a host of galleries, especially along Gordon Street. Tel Aviv is also home to a dynamic performing arts scene, including the iconic Batsheva Dance Company and the Israel Philharmonic Orchestra led by Zubin Mehta.

The Friday editions of the English-language *Jerusalem Post* and *Haaretz* contain extensive entertainment listings for the entire country. There are a handful of mostly online ticket agencies for performances in Tel Aviv.

The relaxation garden in Habima Square is surrounded by major cultural institutions like the Habima Theatre and the Charles Bronfman Auditorium.

TICKETS

Castel. ☎ 03/604–5000 ⊕ www.eventim.co.il.

Hadran. ☎ 03/521–5200 ⊕ www.hadran.co.il.

Leaan. ☎ 03/524–7373 ⊕ www.leaan.co.il.

DANCE

Most of Israel's dance groups, including the contemporary Batsheva Dance Company and Inbal Pinto, perform in the Suzanne Dellal Centre for Dance and Theatre (⊕ www.suzannedellal.org.il) in Neve Tzedek. The complex itself is an example of new Israeli architectural styles used to restore some of the oldest buildings in Tel Aviv.

MUSIC

Fodor'sChoice
★

Charles Bronfman Auditorium. Israel's largest concert hall is the home of the Israel Philharmonic Orchestra, led by maestro Zubin Mehta. The low-slung gray building, among the most architecturally sophisticated cultural buildings in the country when it was completed in 1957, was magnificently restored in 2013. It has excellent acoustics and a seating capacity of 3,000 people. The hall also hosts pop and rock concerts. ⊠ 1 Huberman St., Center City ☎ 03/543–0777 ⊕ www.hatarbut.co.il.

Enav Cultural Center. Run by the city, the Enav Cultural Center is a 300-seat venue offering eclectic music and theater. ⊠ 71 Ibn Gvirol St., Center City ☎ 03/521–7760, 03/521–7763 ⊕ www.telavivfoundation.org.

Mayumana. This exciting troupe of drummers and dancers bangs in perfect synchronicity on anything from garbage pails to the floor. It also plays actual drums from cultures all over the world. ⊠ 15 Louis Pasteur St., Jaffa ☎ 03/681–1787 ⊕ www.mayumana.com.

Tel Aviv Performing Arts Center. The Tel Aviv Performing Arts Center is home to the Israeli Opera, as well as the Israel Ballet and the Cameri Theatre. It's possible to book a behind-the-scenes tour 75 minutes prior to the performance. ⊠ *19 Shaul Hamelech St., Center City* ☎ *03/692–7777* ⊕ *www.israel-opera.co.il.*

THEATER

While there are a few exceptions, theater performances are almost always in Hebrew, so inquire before booking.

Beit Lessin Theatre. One of Israel's largest repertory theaters, the Beit Lessin Theatre hosts works by Israeli playwrights in Hebrew. ⊠ *101 Dizengoff St., at Frishman St., Center City* ☎ *03/725-5333* ⊕ *www. lessin.co.il.*

Fodor'sChoice   **Cameri Theatre of Tel Aviv.** Started in 1944, this long-standing Hebrew
★   performance theater, located in the Tel Aviv Performing Arts Center, offers a useful "See it in Hebrew, Read it in English" program in which the most popular productions are simultaneously translated into English. Shows range from popular international dramas and comedies to local pieces. ⊠ *19 Shaul Hamelech St., Center City* ☎ *03/606–1900* ⊕ *www.cameri.co.il.*

Habima National Theater. This troupe is rooted in the Russian Revolution, when a group of young Jewish artists established a theater company that performed in Hebrew—this at a time when Hebrew was barely a living language. Subsequent tours through Europe and the United States in the 1920s won wide acclaim. Many of the group's members moved to Israel and helped establish a theater company that now inhabits multiple spaces, including a nicely renovated complex at Habima Square. ⊠ *Habima Sq., end of Rothschild Blvd., Center City* ☎ *03/629–5555, 03/526–6666* ⊕ *www.habima.co.il.*

HaSimta Theatre. In Old Jaffa, HaSimta Theatre features avant-garde and fringe performances in Hebrew (or sometimes without words at all). ⊠ *8 Mazal Dagim St., Jaffa* ☎ *03/681–2126* ⊕ *www.hasimta.com.*

Nalaga'at Center. This cultural and entertainment center features deaf and blind performers. Shows can be combined with a preperformance snack at the BlackOut Restaurant (eating in the dark) or Café Kapish (ordering in sign language). ⊠ *Retsif Haaliya Hashniya St., Jaffa* ☎ *03/633–0808* ⊕ *www.nalagaat.org.il.*

SHOPPING

The Tel Aviv shopping scene is the most varied in the country. It's Israel's fashion capital, and you'll find styles quite different from what you might see back home in terms of design and color. The real pleasure of shopping in Tel Aviv is access to the exciting creations of its cadre of young designers who have made waves around the world. Dizengoff Street, north of Arlozoroff Street, is where you'll find the shops of many of Israel's best-known designers.

If it's crafts and jewelry you're shopping for, Neve Tzedek is the place to go, especially along the main drag of Shabazi Street. Local crafts and jewelry also star in the Tuesday and Friday Nahalat Binyamin Pedestrian Mall, where prices can be lower than at regular stores and you can almost always meet the artist who made them. As for Judaica, there are a number of stores on Ben Yehuda and Dizengoff Streets.

CENTER CITY

CLOTHING

Couple Of. This shop is known for making beautiful and comfortable shoes for hard-to-fit feet. ⊠ *207 Dizengoff St., Center City* ☎ *054/421–0936.*

Fodor'sChoice ★ **Gideon Oberson.** Sexy and stylish beach apparel is the focus of Gideon Oberson's boutique. The vibrant and colorful swimsuits are meant to complement the skin and figure of each person. ⊠ *36 Gordon St., Center City* ☎ *03/524–3822* ⊕ *gideon-oberson.com.*

Kisim. This designer is influenced by Japanese origami, which you'll notice in the handbags, clutches, and wallets. The designer's informal style has an elegant twist. One of the bags was famously used by Sarah Jessica Parker in *Sex and the City.* ⊠ *8 HaHashmal St., Center City* ☎ *03/560–4890* ⊕ *www.kisim.com.*

Maya Bash. These designer clothing collections made from wearable cottons and other light materials are great for the Tel Aviv climate. The unique cuts and comfortable materials are making Maya Bash a hit in Germany and Japan as well. ⊠ *13 Barzilay St., Center City* ☎ *03/560–0305* ⊕ *www.mayabash.com.*

CRAFTS

Raphael. One of the most pleasant shopping experiences in Tel Aviv, this shop carries a large selection of Judaica, jewelry, and handcrafts by some of the best Israeli artists. ⊠ *94 Ben Yehuda St., Center City* ☎ *03/527–3619* ⊕ *www.raphaels.co.il.*

JEWELRY

Hagar Satat. Weaving together leather with gold and silver, Hagar Satat's jewelry is great for special occasions or everyday wear. Pick up bargain-priced pieces from the outlet store in the trendy Gan HaHashmal fashion neighborhood. ⊠ *13 Levontin St., Center City* ☎ *03/560–6095.*

JUDAICA

Miller. Specializing in Judaica, Miller has a particularly wide selection of silver items, including a jewelry collection. ⊠ *157 Dizengoff St., Center City* ☎ *03/524–9383* ⊕ *www.miller.co.il.*

LOCAL SPECIALTIES

Bauhaus Center. The attractive displays of books, maps, posters, furnishings, dishes, and even Judaica, all inspired by Bauhaus design, are a reminder that this school of design embraced more than buildings. There's a gallery of changing exhibits related to Bauhaus style and history, and the center organizes both group and private Bauhaus (and other) walking tours. ⊠ *99 Dizengoff St., Center City* ☎ *03/522–0249* ⊕ *www.bauhaus-center.com.*

Fodor's Choice **Zalmania** (*The PhotoHouse*). Established in 1940, the Zalmania Pho-
★ toHouse is the oldest photography shop in Israel and has been family
owned and operated for generations. With more than a million nega-
tives documenting Israel's history, this nostalgic shop sells historical
photographs, books, postcards, posters, and gifts, many of which are
only found in this shop. ⊠ *5 Tchernichovsky St., Center City* ☎ *03/517–
7916* ⊕ *www.pri-or.com.*

NEVE TZEDEK

CRAFTS

Chomer Tov Ceramics Gallery. A cooperative of 14 local artists, this ceramics gallery is on Neve Tzedek's main drag. ⊠ *27 Shabazi St., Neve Tzedek* ☎ *03/516–6229* ⊕ *www.chomertov.co.il.*

Shlush Shloshim Ceramics Gallery. This gallery is a cooperative of 11
ceramic artists who display a pleasingly eclectic mix of both decorative and practical items in a variety of colors, shapes, and textures. ⊠ *31
Shabazi St., Neve Tzedek* ☎ *03/510–6067* ⊕ *www.shlushshloshim.com.*

JEWELRY

Ayala Bar. Israeli designer Ayala Bar's sparkling, multicolor bracelets,
earrings, and necklaces, now famous around the world, can be seen
from time to time in shops throughout the country, but the best selection
is at this flagship store. ⊠ *36 Shabazi St., Neve Tzedek* ☎ *03/510–0082*
⊕ *www.ayalabar.com.*

Fodor's Choice **Dave + Esty.** This talented husband-and-wife team work together to
★ create playful and memorable jewelry. Their whimsical takes on pomegranates and Jewish stars result in Israel-inspired pieces that make
meaningful gifts. The store is filled with charm, so take your time while
searching, as there is something for everyone. ⊠ *67 Shabazi St., Neve
Tzedek* ☎ *054/442–2204.*

LOCAL SPECIALTIES

Fodor's Choice **Made in TLV.** This fun-spirited souvenir shop sells all kinds of locally
★ designed items like postcards, stationery, T-shirts, and large photos
depicting both old and modern Tel Aviv. ⊠ *HaTachana, Koifman and
Ha'Mered Sts., Hangar 5, Neve Tzedek* ☎ *03/510–4333.*

SOHO Design Center. Carrying pieces by Israeli and international designers,
this store is filled to the brim with interesting items, from kitchen accessories to handbags to children's toys. ⊠ *HaTachana, Koifman and Ha'Mered
Sts., Hangar 12, Neve Tzedek* ☎ *03/716–7010* ⊕ *www.sohocenter.co.il.*

JAFFA

JEWELRY

Adina Plastelina. This gallery and jewelry studio in the heart of Old Jaffa
sells handcrafted jewelry in sterling silver and gold that's combined with
polymer clay in the ancient technique called *millefiori,* which means "a
thousand flowers" in Italian. The combination of metals and modern
materials creates an innovative and classy look. ⊠ *23 Netiv Hamazalot
St., Jaffa* ☎ *03/518–7894* ⊕ *www.adinaplastelina.com.*

JUDAICA

Dar-Fez. An extensive and colorful selection of Judaica adorned with silver and copper and inlaid with mother-of-pearl is the focus of this shop. ✉ *23 Raziel St., Clock Tower Sq., Jaffa* ☎ *03/518–1417.*

Fodor'sChoice ★ **Frank Meisler.** A specialist in Jewish fine art and a pioneer in pewter pieces, Frank Meisler has a magical studio and gallery located in the heart of the artist's quarter in Old Jaffa. Here you'll find his regal Judaica as well as a display of caricature sculptures. ✉ *25 Simtat Mazal Arie, Jaffa* ☎ *03/512–3000* ⊕ *www.frank-meisler.com.*

NORTH TEL AVIV

CLOTHING

Rina Zin. The European cuts of this designer's chic styles appeal to older women. ✉ *280 Dizengoff St., North Tel Aviv* ☎ *03/523–5746* ⊕ *rinazin.com.*

LOCAL SPECIALTIES

Fodor'sChoice ★ **Kelim Shloovim.** Run by the nonprofit organization Shikum Acher (A Different Rehabilitation), this stylish store sells high-quality housewares made by various community groups. Handmade candles, soaps, jewelry, and toys are just some of the creative and chic products on the shelves. ✉ *229 Dizengoff St., North Tel Aviv* ☎ *03/535–3810* ⊕ *www. kelimshloovim.org.il.*

SPORTS AND THE OUTDOORS

Almost all outdoorsy activity in Tel Aviv centers on its gorgeous beaches, from boating to surfing, or relaxing by spreading out a towel in the sand to get some sun.

BEACHES

Tel Aviv's western border, an idyllic stretch of Mediterranean sand, has miles of beaches and a beachfront promenade. Just after dawn, it's the territory of joggers, cyclists, and yoga enthusiasts. As the sun rises, so does the number of beachgoers, from bikini-clad young women to middle-aged men playing the ever-popular (and noisy) ball-and-paddle game called *matkot*. Sunsets here are spectacular.

The city beaches have many of the same amenities: restrooms, changing areas, towel and umbrella rentals, and restaurants or cafés. Beaches are generally named after something nearby—a street or a hotel, for example. They're hugely popular, especially on weekends. If you'd rather not battle the crowds, you'll find fewer people during the week. The lapping of gentle waves offers respite and relaxation for most of the year. There's a strong undertow on these beaches, so exercise caution.

Dolphinarium Beach. At the southern end of Hayarkon Street, Dolphinarium Beach (sometimes known as Aviv Beach) has a festive atmosphere, especially on Friday around sunset. Young Israelis, many of whom have returned from post-army trips to Asia or South America, gather for drumming circles and other group activities. **Amenities:** food and drink; lifeguards; showers; toilets; water sports. **Best for:** partiers; sunset. ⊠ *Shlomo Lahat Promenade, Center City* ⊕ *Facing InterContinental David Tel Aviv* ⊠ *Free.*

Frishman Beach. Facing a strip of restaurants and cafés on the seaside promenade, Frishman Beach is across from many of the larger hotels and gets its fair share of tourists. Saturday morning it attracts Israeli dancing circles. Lounge chairs are available for a fee, but there's not much quiet because of the lifeguards constantly screeching over the loudspeaker. **Amenities:** food and drink; lifeguards; showers; toilets. **Best for:** sunset. ⊠ *Frishman St. and Hayarkon St., Center City* ⊠ *Free.*

FAMILY   **Gordon Beach.** At the end of Gordon Street, this wide beach is popular with local families because of its calm water and tidal pool. Weekends you'll find both sunbathing travelers and youngsters lining the beach with sand castles. Gordon Pool, just north of the beach, is a saltwater pool that's good for swimming laps. **Amenities:** food and drink; lifeguards; toilets. **Good for:** swimming; walking. ⊠ *Gordon St., at Hayarkon St., Center City* ⊠ *Free.*

Herzliya Pituach Beach. About 10 km (7 miles) north of Tel Aviv is this white-sand beach lined by well-manicured lawns. Nearby are restaurants, cafés, and a handful of luxury high-rise hotels. From central Tel Aviv, Dan's Bus 90 heads to this beach. **Amenities:** food and drink; lifeguards; toilets; water sports. **Best for:** snorkeling; swimming; walking. ⊠ *Ramat Yam St., at Medinat Hayehudim St., Herzliya Pituach* ⊠ *Free.*

Fodor'sChoice   **Hilton Beach.** In front of the hotel of the same name, Hilton Beach is very ★   popular, especially with enthusiastic matkot players. The northern end of the beach is a gay-friendly area known as Gay Beach, which can get packed on sunny summer afternoons. Here you'll also find Dog Beach, which got its name because pampered pooches are let off their leashes to play. There is no car access, so walk or bike down the promenade to reach this stretch of sand. **Amenities:** food and drink; lifeguards; showers; toilets; water sports. **Best for:** surfing; swimming; walking; windsurfing. ⊠ *Shlomo Lahat Promenade, north of Tel Aviv Marina, Center City* ⊠ *Free.*

Jerusalem Beach. At the bottom of Allenby Road, Jerusalem Beach is known for its beachside café featuring Brazilian bands that get the crowd dancing. **Amenities:** food and drink; showers; toilets; water sports. **Best for:** partiers. ⊠ *Allenby Rd., at Herbert Samuel St., Center City* ⊠ *Free.*

FAMILY   **Metzizim Beach.** This stretch of sand near the Yarkon River attracts a younger crowd. It's an especially good choice for families because it has a long sandbar that keeps the waves gentle. Many people nurse a beer at the nearby pub and watch the sunset. Just south of Metzizim Beach is a private area for Orthodox Jews who prefer gender-separated swimming. Women come on Sunday, Tuesday, and Thursday, while men are here on Monday, Wednesday, and Friday. Everyone is welcome on Saturday, and it's one of the area's mellowest beaches.

Amenities: food and drink; lifeguards; parking (fee); showers, toilets. **Best for:** partiers; swimming. ⊠ *Havakuk Ha'navi St., near Tel Aviv Port, North Tel Aviv* 🕸 *Free.*

FAMILY **Tel Baruch Beach.** In the northern reaches of Tel Aviv, Tel Baruch Beach is popular among families with young children because it has a breakwater that softens the waves. Because it's the farthest beach from downtown, it can often be less crowded. The section to the north has an unsavory reputation after dark. **Amenities:** food and drink; lifeguards; parking (fee); showers; toilets; water sports. **Best for:** swimming; walking. ⊠ *Propes St., North Tel Aviv* 🕸 *Free.*

BIKING

4

Tel-O-Fun. Tel Aviv runs this convenient bike-sharing system—pick up a bike at one station and return it there or at any other station around the city. The fees (NIS 23 daily, plus an additional hourly fee when more than ½ hour) must be paid by credit card at the pick-up bike station. The bikes are quite heavy and are useful for getting from point to point throughout the city or for riding along the seafront promenade. ⊠ *Center City* ☎ **6070* ⊕ *www.tel-o-fun.co.il/en.*

BOATING

FAMILY **Ganei Yehoshua Boating** (*Hayarkon Park*). In the northern part of the city, Ganei Yehoshua (Hayarkon Park) rents pedal boats and rowboats and motorboats. ⊠ *Rokach Blvd., Center City* ☎ *03/642–0541* 🕸 *From NIS 95 per hour.*

Sea Kayak Club. This club offers two-hour kayaking tours of the coastline throughout the year. Beginners are welcome when conditions are calm. ⊠ *Jaffa Port, Jaffa* ☎ *03/681–4732* ⊕ *www.kayak4all.com* 🕸 *NIS 150.*

SAILING

Ofek Yachts. Charter a weeklong yacht journey with a skipper or a day party boat for up to 22 people at Ofek Yachts at the Tel Aviv Marina. ⊠ *Tel Aviv Marina, 14 Eliezer Peri St., Center City* ☎ *03/529–9988* ⊕ *www.ofek-yachts.co.il.*

Sea Tel Aviv. You can charter a variety of boats here for daytime excursions or romantic sunset sails leaving from Tel Aviv Marina. It's also possible to arrange scuba diving, snorkeling, and other activities. ⊠ *Tel Aviv Marina, 10 Eliezer Peri St., Center City* ☎ *052/869–8080* ⊕ *www.seatelaviv.co.il.*

Via Maris. At Herzliya Marina, Via Maris is the place to charter a sailboat or other vessel for a catered, private, romantic sunset cruise; a family outing; or an overnight sea stay. Options include with or without skipper. ⊠ *1 Yordei Yam St., Herzliya* ☎ *09/957–8811* ⊕ *www.yamonline.co.il.*

SURFING

Topsea. Teaching surfing at every level, Topsea offers both private and group lessons, as well as surfboard rental (by the hour or by the day) for those with previous experience. ⊠ *Kikar Atarim, 165 Hayarkon St., North Tel Aviv* ☎ *050/432–9001* ⊕ *www.topsea.co.il* 🖃 *NIS 180 for 1-hr private lesson; rental from NIS 50.*

SWIMMING

FAMILY **Gordon Pool.** This outdoor complex includes an Olympic-size swimming pool with a separate section for kids. There are also dressing rooms and lounge chairs. ⊠ *14 Eliezer Peri St., Center City* ☎ *03/762–3300* ⊕ *www.gordon-pool.co.il* 🖃 *NIS 67.*

FAMILY **Meymadiyon Water Park.** Open from June to September, Meymadiyon is a 25-acre water park featuring a swimming pool, a wave pool, a kiddie pool, waterslides, and lawns dotted with plastic chairs. ⊠ *Ganei Yehoshua, North Tel Aviv* ☎ *03/642–2777* ⊕ *www.meymadion.co.il* 🖃 *NIS 115.*

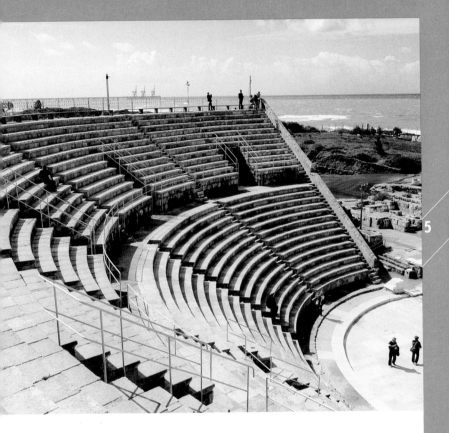

HAIFA AND THE NORTHERN COAST

With Caesarea, Akko, and Rosh Hanikra

WELCOME TO HAIFA AND THE NORTHERN COAST

TOP REASONS TO GO

★ **Caesarea:** Originally built by Herod the Great, these 2,000-year-old Roman ruins occupy a strategic spot on the sea. They include Byzantine bathhouses and Crusader moats.

★ **Baha'i Gardens:** In Haifa, this unforgettable series of gardens tumbles down from Mount Carmel into 19 terraces that enclose a gold-domed shrine.

★ **Underground Akko:** At this fascinating archaeological site, you can descend into Crusader knights' halls, navigate a secret tunnel toward the sea, and rest in a Turkish bathhouse.

★ **Glorious beaches:** The coast means beaches, and this is Israel's finest stretch of golden sand. Haifa's beaches are particularly beautiful. Scuba diving and paragliding are options.

★ **Great wine:** Taste and toast internationally known wines at the many wineries on the hillsides of the northern coast. Tishbi and Carmel are especially worth visiting.

1 **Haifa.** This steep-sloped port city, the largest in northern Israel, rewards you at every turn with hillside breezes and breathtaking vistas of the Mediterranean. At the base of the hill are the beaches, some of the area's best.

2 **The Northern Coast.** Besides an especially lovely string of beaches, the Mediterranean coast south of Haifa is home to wonderfully preserved archaeological sites at Caesarea and Nahsholim-Dor.

3 **The Wine Country and Mount Carmel.** The quality of Israeli wines has risen to heady heights on the international scene. One of the country's very first wineries is here, along with several others of equal stature. They're in or near charming towns such as Zichron Ya'akov, making access as easy as saying "l'chaim."

4 **Akko and the Far Northern Coast.** Exploring Akko's atmospheric Old City, with its souk and Crusader remains, is a highlight here. This section of the northern coast is also known for its fine-sand beaches and nature reserves. The sea-battered caves at Rosh Hanikra are worth the trip north.

GETTING ORIENTED

Two seaside cities anchor this stretch of coastline. Haifa, a hilltop city on a peninsula jutting into the Mediterranean, offers the magnificent Baha'i Shrine and Gardens, the bustling German Colony, fine restaurants, the Carmelite Monastery, maritime museums, and more. The ancient port of Akko, north of Haifa, features underground ruins dating from the era of the Crusaders. Many people come to this area for the beaches, but the coastal Route 2 and the slightly more inland Route 4 can whisk you to such sites as King Herod's port city of Caesarea, the 19th-century town of Zichron Ya'akov, and the artists' colony of Ein Hod. Farther to the north, near the border with Lebanon, are the cliffs and grottoes of Rosh Hanikra.

5

Updated by
Shari Helmer

Stretched taut on a narrow coastal strip between Tel Aviv and the Lebanese border, this gorgeous region has a rare blend of Mediterranean beaches, fertile fields and citrus groves of the Sharon Plain, and seaside historical sights. Whether you succumb to the delights of the ancient port of Caesarea, with its spectacularly restored Roman ruins, the alleyways and beautifully vaulted Crusader halls of the Old City of Akko, or the vistas and gardens of modern Haifa, this lovely part of Israel doesn't disappoint.

It was in the softly contoured foothills of Mount Carmel that philanthropist Baron Edmond de Rothschild helped found the country's wine industry in the 19th century, now one of the region's most successful enterprises. The Carmel range rises dramatically to its pine-covered heights over the coast of Haifa, an amiable and thoroughly modern port city. Across the sweeping arc of Haifa Bay lies Akko, a jewel of a Crusader city that combines Romanesque ruins, Muslim minarets, and swaying palms. To the north, the resort town of Nahariya draws droves of vacationing Israelis. Just south of the Lebanese border, don't miss the amazing seaside coves of Rosh Hanikra, which have been scooped from the cliffs by the pounding surf.

As the scenery changes, so does the ethnic mix of the residents: Druze, Carmelite monks, Baha'is, Christian and Muslim Arabs, and Jews. In the caves of Nahal Me'arot on Mount Carmel, paleontologists continue to study the artifacts of the most ancient, prehistoric native people. The Baha'is, dedicated to the idea that all great religions teach the same fundamental truths about an unknowable God, dominate Haifa's mountainside. Their terraced gardens spill down the slope toward a gleaming golden-domed shrine. White Friars of the Carmelite order preside over their serene monasteries in Haifa and on Mount Carmel. The monastery in Mukhraka sits in the outskirts of Daliyat el Carmel, one of the two large Druze villages on Mount Carmel. The

Druze of the Galilee and Carmel, now numbering more than 125,000, have lived here for 1,000 years. Although they consider themselves an integral part of Israeli society, they maintain a unique cultural and religious enclave on Mount Carmel, with the esoteric rites and rituals of their faith and the distinctive handlebar moustaches and white head scarves favored by the older men. Akko's vast subterranean Crusader vaults and halls, Ottoman skyline of domes and minarets, and outdoor *shuk* (market) are enchanting.

As you drive north, enjoy long stretches of unimpeded views of the sparkling blue Mediterranean. Beautiful beaches lie beside (and in between) Netanya, Haifa, and Achziv, with soft sand, no-frills hummus joints, and seaside restaurants. You can learn to scuba dive, explore underwater shipwrecks, hike the pine-scented slopes of Mount Carmel, tread the winding lanes of Ein Hod artists' village, and taste local wines and tangy cheeses at some excellent wineries.

HAIFA AND THE NORTHERN COAST PLANNER

WHEN TO GO
There's really no bad time to visit this region. Spring (April and May) and fall (October and November) are balmy and crisp, making them the most pleasant seasons for travelers. Summer (June to September) is hot, but humidity remains low, and soft sea and mountain breezes cool things down. Winter (December to March) brings cold weather (sun interspersed with rain) and chilly sea winds.

As in the rest of Israel, hotels are often booked solid on weekends. On Saturday and national holidays, Israelis hit the road, so north–south traffic out of Tel Aviv can be heavy. If you're taking a few days to explore the region, traveling Sunday to Thursday guarantees you plenty of peace and quiet. If you can only go on Friday and Saturday, make reservations well in advance, and be prepared for crowds at the beaches and tourist sights.

PLANNING YOUR TIME
Haifa, the country's third-largest city, can be a useful base for exploring sights both to the south (Caesarea and the wine country) and north (the Crusader city in historic Akko and the coast up to Rosh Hanikra). Ein Hod, an artists' colony, and the Carmel Caves are also nearby. Haifa itself is notable for the Baha'i Gardens and Germany Colony. However, the coast's southern sights can also be seen easily if you're staying in Tel Aviv. Several companies run day tours to Caesarea and Akko from Jerusalem, Tel Aviv, and Netanya; this may be a useful option.

Not counting time in Haifa, you could see the area's highlights in a couple of days, starting with King Herod's port city, Caesarea, and the wine country in the Carmel Hills. Check tour information for the wineries in Benyamina and Zichron Ya'akov. The picturesque Druze villages of Daliyat el Carmel and Isfiya are well worth a visit, too. You can also spend a full day exploring Akko, to the north; the grottoes at Rosh Hanikra are lovely, but far north. Plan time for swimming or hiking; the Mediterranean coast has great beaches and scenic trails.

GETTING HERE AND AROUND

AIR TRAVEL

Ben Gurion International Airport, the country's main gateway, is near Tel Aviv and is 105 km (65 miles) south of Haifa, about a 90-minute drive. A convenient *sherut* (shared taxi minibus) service to Haifa costs NIS 106, and runs 24 hours a day, seven days a week. For sherut service, call ☎ 04/866-2324. Private taxi service costs NIS 545 for two passengers with two suitcases, plus a charge for extra suitcases of approximately NIS 4 per bag.

BUS TRAVEL

Egged serves the coastal area from Jerusalem Central Bus Station to Tel Aviv Central Station. There's service to Netanya, Hadera, Zichron Ya'akov, and Haifa from both cities. From Jerusalem, a direct bus to Haifa takes one hour and 40 minutes. Getting to Caesarea requires a change at Hadera. To get to Akko, change at Haifa. Crowds are heavy at bus stations on Thursday night and Sunday morning. Buses don't operate from Friday evening to Saturday evening; in Haifa, select buses run on Saturday.

CAR TRAVEL

Driving is the most comfortable and convenient way to tour this region. You can take Route 2 (the coastal road) or Route 4 (parallel to Route 2, but slightly inland) north along the coast from Tel Aviv to Haifa, continuing on Route 4 up to the Lebanese border. From Jerusalem follow Route 1 to Tel Aviv; connect via the Ayalon Highway to Herzliya and Route 2. Toll road Route 6 also connects to Route 1 and saves time.

TAXI TRAVEL

In towns, taxis can be hailed on the street day or night. Ask the driver to turn on the meter, or *moneh*.

TRAIN TRAVEL

The northern coast is one part of Israel where train travel is both practical and scenic. As always, remember that service is interrupted Friday evening to Saturday evening. Israel Railways trains from Jerusalem and Tel Aviv travel several times a day to Netanya, Benyamina, Caesarea, Haifa, Atlit, Akko, and Nahariya. You'll have to change trains in Tel Aviv when coming from Jerusalem.

The train line from Ben Gurion International Airport travels to Tel Aviv, Benyamina, Atlit, Haifa, Akko, and Nahariya. The trip from Tel Aviv to Haifa takes about one hour. Sunday to Thursday, trains depart every 20 minutes from 6 am until 10:30 pm; on Friday they run from 6 am until an hour before sundown. On Saturday there are four departures after 8:30 pm. Train travel from Jerusalem to Haifa is feasible only if you have plenty of time, as you have to change in Tel Aviv.

RESTAURANTS

You don't have to look hard for a restaurant, whether simple or fancy, with a striking view of the Mediterranean. Fish, served with a variety of sauces, is usually grilled or baked. The most common types are *locus* (grouper), *mulit* (red mullet), *churi* (red snapper), and *farida* (sea bream). Also fresh, but from commercial ponds and the Sea of Galilee, are the ubiquitous tilapia, *buri* (gray mullet), and *iltit* (a hybrid of salmon and trout). Fresh seafood, such as shrimp and calamari, is available in abundance. Many casual restaurants serve schnitzel (breaded and fried chicken cutlets) with french fries, which kids often love.

Until recently, coastal restaurants weren't as refined as those in Tel Aviv, but no longer. Haifa now has several first-class restaurants with creative chefs. The artists' village of Ein Hod offers sumptuous Argentinean dining, and there's locally famous falafel in the Druze village of Daliyat el Carmel. Netanya boasts the area's highest concentration of kosher establishments. Dress is always informal.

HOTELS

Options range from small inns to luxury hotels, though the selection and quality of accommodations doesn't equal that of, say, Tel Aviv. Gracious bed-and-breakfasts (known in Israel as *zimmers*) are tucked into coastal rural settlements, mostly north of Nahariya. The splendid spa hotel in the Carmel Forest near Haifa deserves its reputation. In some places, such as Zichron Ya'akov, pickings are slim; but because this region is so compact, you can cover many coastal sights from one base, such as Haifa. *Hotel reviews have been shortened. For more information, visit Fodors.com.*

WHAT IT COSTS				
	$	$$	$$$	$$$$
Restaurants	Under NIS 50	NIS 50–NIS 75	NIS 76–NIS 100	over NIS 100
Hotels	Under $200	$200–$300	$301–$400	over $400

Restaurant prices are the average cost of a main course at dinner in NIS (Israeli shekels) or, if dinner isn't served, at lunch. Hotel prices, given in U.S. dollars, are the lowest cost of a standard double room in high season. Non-Israeli citizens paying in foreign currency are exempt from the 17% V.A.T. on hotel rooms.

HAIFA

Spilling down from the pine-covered heights of Mount Carmel to Haifa Bay, Haifa is a city with a vertiginous setting that has led to comparisons with San Francisco. The most striking landmark on the mountainside is the gleaming golden dome of the Baha'i Shrine, set amid utterly beautiful garden terraces. The city is the world center for the Baha'i faith, and its members provide informative walking tours of the flower-edged 100-acre spot, a UNESCO World Heritage Site. At the top of the hill are some small but interesting museums, the larger hotels, and two major universities. At the bottom is the lovingly restored German Colony, a perfect area for strolling.

Israel's largest port and third-largest city, Haifa was ruled for four centuries by the Ottomans and gradually spread its tendrils up the mountainside, becoming a cosmopolitan city whose port served the entire Middle East. The climate is gentle, the beaches beautiful, and the locals friendly.

You don't see the religious garb of Jerusalem or the tattoos and piercings of Tel Aviv in this diverse but fairly conservative city. In fact, you can't always tell at a glance who is part of an Arab or Jewish Israeli family, or if someone is a more recent immigrant from the former Soviet Union.

GETTING HERE AND AROUND

A direct bus operated by Egged leaves Tel Aviv for Haifa every 20 minutes between 5:20 am and 11 pm; travel time is one hour. Trains from Tel Aviv to Haifa also take one hour and cost NIS 28. Trains depart every half hour from 6 am until 10:30 pm; on Friday from 6 am until an hour before sundown. During the day on Saturday trains don't run, but there are four departures after 8:30 pm.

There are plenty of nice walks in the city, but to see the sights, a car or a taxi is required; another option is the local buses. The Carmel Tunnels, which bypass the most congested parts of Haifa by boring below Mount Carmel, cut a 30- to 45-minute drive down to less than 10. The toll is NIS 18 and can be paid with cash at the tollbooths. The tunnels aren't much use to visitors, but if you're just passing through, they could save you time. Coming north from Tel Aviv, the entrance is at the end of Route 2. From the north, it's off Route 4 near the Checkpoint Interchange.

You can hail a taxi in the city, or use an app like Gett to summons one. You can also call to arrange a taxi pickup.

Haifa has the six-station Carmelit subway—actually a funicular railway—that runs from Gan Ha'em Park on Hanassi Boulevard (adjacent to the Dan Panorama) in Central Carmel down to Kikar Paris in the port area in six minutes. The fare is NIS 6.60 for a single ticket (NIS 15 for a day pass), and the train operates Sunday to Thursday 6 am to midnight, Friday 6 to 3, and Saturday sundown to midnight.

The Haifa Cable Car travels from the lower station at Bat Galim to the upper station at Stella Maris, and has panoramic views of the bay. It's accessible by bus routes 41 and 42 from Bat Galim and 25, 26, 27, 30, and 31 from Stella Maris. Free parking is available at both ends.

Bus Contacts Egged. ☎ 03/694–8888 ⊕ www.egged.co.il.

Taxi Contacts Carmel. ☎ 04/838–2626, 04/838–2626. **Horev.** ✉ Horev 15 ☎ 04/888–8888.

Train Contacts Israel Railways. ☎ *5770 ⊕ www.rail.co.il/EN.

VISITOR INFORMATION

Contacts Haifa Tourist Board. ✉ 48 Ben Gurion Blvd., German Colony ☎ 04/853–5606 ⊕ www.visit-haifa.org//eng/.

EXPLORING HAIFA

Israel's "city on the hill" is divided into three main levels, each crisscrossed by parks and gardens: the port down below; Hadar, a commercial area in the middle; and Merkaz Carmel (known as "the Merkaz"), with the posher hotels and many restaurants, on the crest of Mount Carmel.

Thanks to the beneficence of the Baha'is, you can enjoy a walking tour that takes you through the stunning terraces that lie like multicolor jewels from the crest of the city at Mount Carmel to the German Colony below.

TOP ATTRACTIONS

Fodor's Choice
★
Baha'i Shrine and Gardens. The most striking feature of the stunning gardens that form the centerpiece of Haifa is the Shrine of the Bab, whose brilliantly gilded dome dominates the city's skyline. The renovated shrine gleams magnificently with 11,790 gold-glazed porcelain tiles.

Haifa is the world center for the Baha'i faith, founded in Iran in the 19th century. It holds as its central belief the unity of mankind. Religious truth for Baha'is consists of progressive revelations of a universal faith. Thus the Baha'is teach that great prophets have appeared throughout history to reveal divine truths, among them Moses, Zoroaster, Buddha, Jesus, Muhammad, and most recently, the founder of the Baha'i faith, Mirza Husayn Ali, known as Baha'u'llah—"the Glory of God." The Shah and then the Ottomans exiled Baha'u'llah (1817–92) from his native Persia to Akko, where he lived as a prisoner for almost 25 years. The Baha'is' holiest shrine is on the grounds of Baha'u'llah's home, where he lived after his release from prison and is now buried, just north of Akko.

Here in Haifa, at the center of the shrine's pristinely manicured set of 19 garden terraces, is the mausoleum built for the Bab (literally, the "Gate"), the forerunner of this religion, who heralded the coming of a new faith to be revealed by Baha'u'llah. The Persian authorities martyred Bab in 1850. Baha'u'llah's son and successor built the gardens and shrine and had the Bab's remains reburied here in 1909. The building, made of Italian stone and rising 128 feet, gracefully combines the canons of classical European architecture with elements of Eastern design and also houses the remains of Baha'u'llah's son. The dome glistens with some 12,000 gilded tiles imported from the Netherlands. Inside, the floor is covered with rich Oriental carpets, and a filigree veils the serene inner shrine.

The magnificent gardens, with their gravel paths, groomed hedges, and 12,000 plant species, are a sight to behold: stunningly landscaped circular terraces extend from Yefe Nof Street for 1 km (½ mile) down the hillside to Ben Gurion Boulevard, at the German Colony. The terraces are a harmony of color and form—pale pink-and-gray-stone flights of stairs and carved urns overflowing with red geraniums set off the perfect cutouts of emerald green grass and floral borders, dark green trees, and wildflowers, with not a leaf out of place anywhere. The gardens, tended by 120 dedicated gardeners, are one of Israel's 11 UNESCO World Heritage Sites.

Three areas are open to the public year-round, except on Baha'i holidays: the shrine and surrounding gardens (*80 Hatzionut Avenue, near Shifra Street*); the upper terrace and observation point (*Yefe Nof Street*); and the entry at the lower terrace (*Hagefen Square, at the end of Ben Gurion Boulevard*). Free walk-in tours in English are given at noon every day except Wednesday. These depart from 45 Yefe Nof Street, near the top of the hill. Note: the Shrine of the Bab is a pilgrimage site for the worldwide Baha'i community; visitors to the shrine are asked to dress modestly (no shorts). ✉ *80 Hatzionut Ave., Merkaz Carmel* ☎ *04/831–3131* ⊕ *www.ganbahai.org.il/en/haifa/* ⌗ *Free* ⊘ *Shrine closed daily after noon.*

Fodor's Choice ★ **German Colony.** Although it runs along a single boulevard, "The Colony" packs in history (with explanatory placards), interesting architecture, great restaurants, and wonderful spots for people-watching. Ben Gurion Boulevard was the heart of a late-19th-century colony established by the German Templer religious reform movement. Along either side are robust two-story chiseled limestone houses with red-tile roofs. Many bear German names, dates from the 1800s, biblical inscriptions on the lintels, and old wooden shutters framing narrow windows.

Neglected for years, the German Colony is now one of the city's loveliest (and flattest) strolls. It's best to start your exploration around Yaffo (Jaffa) Street so that you're walking toward the stunning Baha'i Gardens. Along the way you can have a meal or cup of coffee, explore the shops in the City Centre Mall, and learn about the history of the Templers. Any time of day is pleasant, but evening, when the cafés and restaurants are brimming with people, is best.

The Templers' colony in Haifa was one of seven in the Holy Land. The early settlers formed a self-sufficient community; by 1883 they had built nearly 100 houses and filled them with as many families. Industrious workers, they introduced the horse-drawn wagon—unknown before their arrival—to Haifa. They also built with their own funds a pilgrimage road from Haifa to Nazareth. The Germans' labors gave rise to modern workshops and warehouses, and it was under their influence that Haifa began to resemble a modern city, with well-laid-out streets, gardens, and attractive homes.

Haifa's importance to Germany was highlighted in 1898, when Kaiser Wilhelm II sailed into the bay, on the first official visit to the Holy Land by a German emperor in more than 600 years. In the 1930s, many Templers began identifying with German nationalism and the Nazi party, and during World War II the British deported them as nationals of an enemy country. ✉ *Ben Gurion Blvd.*

Tikotin Museum of Japanese Art. Established in 1957 by renowned collector Felix Tikotin, this graceful venue on the crest of Mount Carmel adheres to the Japanese tradition of displaying beautiful objects in harmony with the season, so exhibits change every three months. The Japanese atmosphere, created in part by sliding doors and partitions of wood and paper, enhances a display of scrolls, screens, pottery and porcelain, lacquer and metalwork, paintings from several schools, and fresh-flower arrangements. The library houses some 3,000 volumes related to Japanese art. ✉ *89 Hanassi Blvd., Merkaz Carmel* ☎ *04/838–3554* ⊕ *www. tmja.org.il* ⌗ *NIS 35.*

Yefe Nof Street. Also known as Panorama Road, this gently curving street high above the city skirts behind Haifa's biggest hotels, providing remarkable views. Enjoy the beauty of the lushly planted Louis Promenade, with shaded benches along the way, beginning behind the Dan

5

Mediterranean Sea

Harbor

Sderot Hameginim

Hagalim St.

Ben Gurion Blvd.

Rutberg

**GERMAN
COLONY**

DOWNTOWN

Yaffo

Sderot Ha'atzma'ut

③

Khouri St.

④

Y. L. Peretz St.

Shivat Zion St.

Nathanson

Carmelit Funicular

Shabbetai Levy St.

Hassan Shukri

Gid'on St.

Baerwald St.

Bialik

PORT

Herzl St.

Nordau St.

Kibbutz Galuyot St.

Balfour St.

Pevsner St.

⑭

Arlosoroff St.

HADAR

Bilu

⑮

Somora

Hakishon

Hapoel St.

Sderot Wingate

Geula St.

Sderot Krish

TEL AMAL

0   1/4 mile

0   1/4 kilometer

Haifa's History

The city's tumultuous past includes reminders of many of the events that shaped Israel and the region over the centuries. First mentioned in the Talmud, the area around Haifa had two settlements in ancient times. To the east, in what is today a congested industrial zone in the port, lay Zalmona, and 5 km (3 miles) west around the cape was Shiqmona. The city was under Byzantine rule until the Arab conquest in the 7th century, when it became a center of glass production and dye making from marine snails.

CRUSADERS AND OTTOMANS
In 1099, the Crusaders conquered the city and maintained it as a fortress along the coastal road to Akko for 200 years. In the 12th century, a group of hermits established the Order of Our Lady of Mount Carmel (the Carmelite order) over Elijah's Cave. After Akko and Haifa succumbed to the Mamluk Sultan Baybars in 1265, Haifa was destroyed and left derelict. It was a sleepy fishing village for centuries.

The city reawakened under the rule of the Bedouin sheikh Dahr el-Omar, who in 1750 ordered the city to be demolished and moved about 3 km (2 miles) to the south. The new town was fortified by walls and protected by a castle, and its port began to compete with that of Akko across the bay.

From 1775 until World War I, Haifa remained under Turkish control with a brief interruption: Napoléon came to Haifa en route to ignominious defeat at Akko during his Eastern Campaign. General Bonaparte left his wounded at the Carmelite Monastery when he beat a retreat in 1799, but the French soldiers there were killed and the monks driven out by Ahmed al-Jazzar, the victorious pasha of Akko. A small memorial stands before the monastery to this day.

THE 19TH CENTURY
The religious reform movement known as the Templers founded Haifa's German Colony in 1868, and in 1879 European Jews settled in the city.

Under the auspices of Sultan Abdul Hamid II, Haifa was connected to the legendary Hejaz Railway through the Jezreel Valley to Damascus. Although the line is long dormant, a Turkish-built monument to the sultan stands in Haifa to this day.

MODERN TIMES
After World War I, Haifa was taken from the Turks by the British, and during the British Mandate period (1921–48), the city was the scene of many dramatic confrontations between the British who sought to keep Jews from entering Palestine and the clandestine efforts of the Haganah to smuggle in immigrants and survivors of the Holocaust. One of the ships used to run the British blockade, an old American craft called the *Af Al Pi Chen*, can be seen in the Clandestine Immigration and Maritime Museum.

The city became the center of the Baha'i faith in the early 20th century. With the creation of a deep-water port in 1929, Haifa's development as a modern city began. By the time the State of Israel was declared in 1948, Haifa had a population of more than 100,000. Today it's the country's third-largest city, home to 270,000 Jews and Arabs.

Carmel Hotel. On a clear day, from any of several lookouts you can see the port below, Akko across the bay, and the cliffs of Rosh Hanikra, with Lebanon in the distance. Panorama Road is spectacular during both day and night. ⊠ *Merkaz Carmel.*

WORTH NOTING

Carmelite Monastery and Stella Maris Church. The imposing Stella Maris (Latin for "Star of the Sea") is graced by wall and ceiling paintings that bring to life to the dramatic story of the prophet Elijah, the patron of the Carmelite order, as well as depicting King David, the Holy Family, and the four evangelists. During the Crusader period, hermits emulating Elijah's ascetic life lived in caves on this steep mountain slope. In the early 13th century, they united under the leadership of St. Berthold, who petitioned the patriarch of Jerusalem for a charter. Thus was born the Carmelite order, which spread across Europe. The Carmelite monks were forced to leave their settlements on Mount Carmel at the end of the 13th century and could not return for nearly four centuries. When they found Elijah's cave inhabited by Muslim dervishes, they set up a monastery nearby.

The church of the present monastery dates from 1836 and was built with the munificence of the French monarchy, hence the name of the surrounding neighborhood: French Carmel. A small pyramid memorial topped with an iron cross commemorates those French who were slaughtered here by the Turks in 1799 after the retreating Napoléon left his ailing troops behind at the monastery. Inside, paintings in the dome depict Elijah in the chariot of fire in which he ascended to heaven, and other biblical prophets. The small grotto a few steps down at the end of the nave is traditionally associated with Elijah and his pupil, Elisha. ⊠ *Stella Maris Rd., French Carmel* ☎ *04/833–7758* 🖾 *Free.*

Clandestine Immigration and Naval Museum. The rather dull name of this museum belies the dramatic story it tells of the heroic efforts to bring Jewish immigrants to Palestine from war-torn Europe in defiance of British policy. In 1939, on the eve of World War II, the British issued the so-called White Paper, which effectively strangled Jewish immigration to Palestine. Out of 63 clandestine ships that tried to run the blockade after the war's end, all but five were intercepted, and their passengers were deported to Cyprus. The museum—full of moving stories of courage and tenacity—is centered on the *Af Al Pi Chen* (Hebrew for "Nevertheless"), a landing craft, which attempted to bring 434 Jewish refugees ashore. A photomural and model of the celebrated ship the *Exodus* recalls the story of the 4,530 refugees aboard who were forcibly transferred back to Germany in 1947, but not before the British forces opened fire on the ship. The history of Israel's navy, told here in impressive detail, begins with the transformation of these clandestine immigration craft into warships. ⊠ *204 Allenby Rd., Kiryat Eliezer* ☎ *04/853–6249* ⊕ *www.navy.idf.il/1285-he/Navy.aspx* 🖾 *NIS 15* 🕓 *Closed Fri. and Sat.*

Elijah's Cave. Jews, Christians, and Muslims consider this site sacred; an early Byzantine tradition identified it as the cave in which Elijah found refuge from the wrath of Ahab, king of Israel from 871 to 853

The blue Mediterranean, Haifa's hills, and the terraced Baha'i Gardens make for irresistible photos.

BC. Graffiti from pilgrims of various faiths and centuries are scrawled on the right wall, and written prayers are often stuffed into crevices. Modest dress is required. The cave is a pretty 20-minute walk down the fairly steep path that begins across from the entrance to the Carmelite Monastery and Stella Maris Church and descends past the lighthouse and World War II fortification. It is more easily accessible by a short flight of stairs that rises from Allenby Road not far from the Bat Galim cable-car station. ✉ *230 Allenby Rd., Ein Hayam* ☎ *04/852–7430* 🎟 *Free* 🕙 *Closed Sat.*

FAMILY **Haifa Museum of Art.** This museum, on the southern edge of the Wadi Nisnas neighborhood, displays artwork from all over the world, dating from the mid-18th century to the present. It also serves as a special repository of contemporary Israeli art. Included are 20th-century graphics and contemporary paintings, sculptures, and photographs. The print collection is of special note, as are frequent solo exhibitions by young Israeli artists. The museum also houses an interactive children's wing. ✉ *26 Shabbetai Levy St., Hadar* ☎ *04/911–5991* ⊕ *www.hma. org.il* 🎟 *NIS 45.*

FAMILY **Haifa Zoo.** Amid masses of trees and lush foliage in the Gan Ha'Em park is a seemingly happy collection of roaring lions and tigers, big brown bears, chattering monkeys, stripe-tailed lemurs, a placid camel, lots of snakes and reptiles, one croc, a kangaroo, and fierce-eyed eagles and owls—plus a bat cave and a waterbird pond. It's a hilly place, but there's a tram to take visitors up the steepest terrain. A small natural history museum and petting zoo complement the regular educational exhibits.

✉ *124 Hatishbi St., Merkaz Carmel* ☎ *04/837–2390* ⊕ *www.haifazoo. co.il* 🖾 *NIS 38* ☉ *Closed Fri. and Sat.*

Hecht Museum. It's worth the trip to Haifa University to see this museum's archaeological treasures. At the summit of Mount Carmel, in the main campus tower (called Eshkol Tower), the museum has a collection that spans the millennia from the Chalcolithic era to the Roman and Byzantine periods, concentrating on "The People of Israel in Eretz Israel." The artifacts include religious altars and lamps, Bronze Age figurines, inscribed seals from the biblical period, and a 2,400-year-old ship. Featured prominently are finds from the excavations of Jerusalem's Temple Mount. A separate art wing displays a small collection of paintings, mostly impressionist works by Monet, Soutine, and Modigliani, among others. The roof observation deck, on the 27th floor, has spectacular views. ✉ *199 Abu Hushi St., Hadar* ☎ *04/825–7773, 04/824–0308* ⊕ *mushecht.haifa.ac.il* 🖾 *Free.*

Mané Katz Museum. This whitewashed building on Panorama Road is the house and studio where the expressionist painter Emmanuel Katz (1894–1962) lived and worked for the last four years of his life. Katz spent the 1920s in Paris, where he exhibited with a group of avant-garde Jewish artists from the École de Paris. As in the canvases of fellow members Marc Chagall and Chaim Soutine, a recurring theme in his work is the village life of Eastern European Jews. Besides Katz's paintings, drawings, and sculptures are the Ukrainian-born artist's collection of rugs, 17th-century antiques from Spain and Germany, and Judaica. ✉ *89 Yefe Nof St., Merkaz Carmel* ☎ *04/911–9372* ⊕ *mkm. org.il* 🖾 *NIS 35.*

National Maritime Museum. About 5,000 years of maritime history in the Mediterranean and Red Sea are told with model ships, ancient anchors, coins minted with nautical symbols, navigational instruments, and other artifacts. There are also intriguing underwater finds from nearby excavations and shipwrecks. The ancient-art collection is one of the finest in the country, comprising mostly Greek and Roman stone and marble sculpture, Egyptian textiles, Greek pottery, and encaustic grave portraits from Fayyum, in Lower Egypt. Particularly rare are the figures of fishermen from the Hellenistic period, as well as a 1st-century wooden boat rescued in the 1980s from the muddy bottom of the Sea of Galilee. ✉ *198 Allenby Rd., Kiryat Eliezer* ☎ *04/853–6622* ⊕ *www. nmm.org.il* 🖾 *NIS 35.*

FAMILY **National Museum of Science, Technology, and Space (MadaTech).** Housed in a landmark building (designed by Alexander Baerwald, a German Jewish architect, in the early 20th century) that was the original home of the Technion, Israel's MIT, this museum features excellent interactive exhibits sure to captivate children and adults alike. Explore the mysteries of DNA, the disorientations of mirrors and visual illusions, or the promises of green energy. ✉ *12 Balfour St., Hadar* ☎ *04/861–4444* ⊕ *www.madatech.org.il* 🖾 *NIS 89.*

Technion. Israel's top university for science and technology, the 300-acre Israeli Institute of Technology is highly fertile ground for cutting-edge research in such fields as engineering, medicine, architecture, and computer science. Founded in 1912, it is the country's oldest university and a key to Israel's reputation and success as a "start-up nation" of innovators. The Coler-California Visitors Center has a virtual tour of the institute and multimedia touch-screen videos. ⊠ *Kiryat Ha-Technion, Neve Sha'anan* ☎ *04/829–3775* ⊕ *pard.technion.ac.il/coler-visitors-center/* ⌕ *Free* ⊘ *Closed Fri. and Sat.* ☞ *Reservations must be made 24 hrs in advance.*

Vista of Peace Sculpture Garden. You can contemplate one of the 29 buoyant life-size bronzes of children and animals from a bench on the winding path through this little jewel of a garden, which commands a sweeping view of Haifa Bay and beyond. Sculptor Ursula Malbin, who came to Israel as a refugee from Nazi Germany, created this oasis west of the Baha'i Shrine. It opens at sunrise and closes at 6. ⊠ *112 Hazionut Ave., Bahai* ⊕ *www.malbin-sculpture.com* ⌕ *Free.*

WHERE TO EAT

There are plenty of restaurants near the large hotels at the top of the city in Merkaz Carmel. Another popular place to eat is along Ben Gurion Boulevard in the German Colony, where the evening hours are whiled away at sidewalk terraces. The port area is being gentrified, so there are always new restaurants opening up. Dress is casual, Israeli style.

In a city known for its falafel, the universally beloved Israeli food, check out the falafel joints called Michel and Hazkenim on Wadi Street, the circular street in the Wadi Nisnas market, and George's on Yohanan Hakadosh. You get plenty of fresh, steaming chickpea balls stuffed into warm pita bread with crunchy cucumber and tomatoes.

Use the coordinates (✛ A1) at the end of each listing to locate a site on the corresponding map.

$$
VEGETARIAN
✕ **Café Louise.** At this nutritious vegetarian eatery, breakfast, lunch, and dinner are served in the cheerful dining room (good feng shui) or on the glass-enclosed patio. Grains are the mains here: choose from among such creative dishes as red-quinoa salad with sweet-carrot vinaigrette, whole-wheat-and-spelt quiche, and vegetable curry stew with cashews. If you prefer fish, try the fillet of salmon in lemongrass sauce with whole-wheat couscous. For dessert, there's tapioca in coconut milk with seasonal fruit. Consider indulging in an Israeli-style Bellini—arak and fresh-squeezed red-grapefruit juice. Many Israeli wines are also available, as is organic coffee, which you can purchase along with health products in the café-run shop next door. ⑤ *Average main: NIS 60* ⊠ *58 Moriah Blvd., Merkaz Carmel* ☎ *04/834–9950* ⊕ *www.cafelouise.co.il* ✛ *A6.*

$$$
MEDITERRANEAN
✕ **Douzan.** Inside this old German Templer building with a pleasant outdoor terrace, a huge metal lamp studded with colored glass casts lacy designs on the walls, lending to the Middle Eastern design. The food, much of it prepared by the owner's mother, is an eclectic combination of French and local Arabic cuisines. Her specialty is *kubbeh,* deep-fried torpedoes of cracked wheat kneaded with minced beef, pine nuts, onions, and exotic spices. A variation on the dish is *sfeeha,* puff pastry topped with delicately minced beef, onions, and pine nuts. For dessert, try the *mouhalabieh,* a delicious Middle Eastern custard topped

Where to
Eat and Stay
in Haifa

KEY
□ Hotels
■ Restaurants
-•- Funicular
✛ following reviews
indicates a map-grid
coordinate

Mediterranean Sea

A   B   C   D

1

2

3

4

5

6

BAT GALIM

Hasharon
Ha'aliya Hashnia
Yonatan

Bat Galim
□ Boutique hotel

Hof Carmel ◆
Train and Bus Station

KIRYAT
ELIEZER

Zahal St.
Sderot Hahagana
Hey Hayam St.
A. Zisu

Goldfish

Yaffo St.

Allenby Road
Stella Maris Rd.

■ Shawatina

Tel Aviv St.

KIRYAT
ELIAHU

Deror

Sderot James
de Rothschild
Yrzhac Sade St.

Sderot Hameginim

Ben Gurion Blvd.
Rutberg

Harbor

✛
Zebra

Allenby Rd.

Colony Hotel □

Fattoush ■ ■ Douzan

Hagefen Blvd.
Hagefen St.

GERMAN
COLONY

Hatsyonut

Yaffo St.

DOWNTOWN

Port Inn Hostel □

Sderot Ha'atzma'ut

PORT

Yere Nof
Hanass Blvd.

Baha'i
Shrine and
Gardens ◆

Sderot Hatsyonut

Shabetai Levy St.
Wadi
Khouri St.

Maayan Habira ■

Jacko's ■

Shivat Zion St.

Hassan Shukri

KIKAR
PARIS

Hanamal 24 ■

Nathanson

PORT

✛

Giraffe ■

MERKAZ
CARMEL
(THE TOP
OF THE
MOUNTAIN)

Dan Panorama
Haifa ●

□ Hotel Beth Shalom

Carmelit Funicular

Y. L. Peretz St.

Gid'on St.

Baerwald St.
Bialik

Herzl St.
Nordau St.

Kibbutz Galuyot St.

Carmel Forest
Spa Resort
✛

Nof □

Dan Carmel □

Crowne
Plaza
□ Haifa

Hacarmel St.
Havam

Moriah St.

Eliahu Golumb St.
Hahashmona'im St.

Spinoza

Baffour St.
Arlosoroff St.

Peissner St.

HADAR

Bilu
Hakishon

Villa Carmel □

■ Café Louise

■ Minna Tomei
■ Raffaello

0   1/4 mile
0   1/4 kilometer

by dried fruits. $ *Average main: NIS 90* ⊠ *35 Ben Gurion Blvd., German Colony* ☎ *04/852–5444* ⊕ *douzan.rest.co.il* ✛ *C4.*

$$$
MIDDLE EASTERN

✕ **Fattoush.** At this attractive restaurant-bar at the foot of the Baha'i Gardens, olive trees hung with blue and green lights set the tone for the elaborate interior, which contains several intimate rooms. One is a "cave" with Arabic script on the walls, low banquettes, wooden stools, and filigree lamps; another is modern with leather seats, embroidered cushions, and a changing art exhibit set against burnt orange walls. The eponymous Fattoush Salad is a favorite, consisting of a generous helping of chopped tomato, cucumber, onion, and mint and sprinkled with crisp toasted pita pieces. You might follow it with *emsakhan,* roast chicken topped with sumac and served on oven-baked pita. $ *Average main: NIS 80* ⊠ *38 Ben Gurion Blvd., German Colony* ☎ *04/852–4930* ✛ *B4.*

$$
ASIAN

✕ **Giraffe.** Here's a welcome combination of jolly atmosphere and casual pan-Asian cuisine. It's sort of a New York lounge–style hangout: stainless-steel open kitchen; black tables, chairs, bar, and stools; silver photography-studio ceiling lights; and a staff in bright white T-shirts, jeans, and long black aprons. Noodles are the specialty, and most dishes are prepared in a wok. You might start with a crispy Thai salad in peanut sauce; then feast on spicy egg noodles with chicken, coconut milk, and red Thai curry; or try your luck with black egg noodles (dyed with squid ink) with calamari and green onions. $ *Average main: NIS 55* ⊠ *131 Hanassi Blvd., Merkaz Carmel* ☎ *04/810–4012* ⊕ *www.giraffe. co.il* ✛ *A5.*

$$
SEAFOOD

✕ **Goldfish.** Over the shabby doorway, a crooked sign announces that the fish is "fresh every day." That's all you need to know about this barebones, old-time favorite seafood restaurant. Take a seat at one of the 16 tables, each covered with rough white paper, and be treated to lots of what Israelis call *salatim,* or little dishes of roasted eggplant, fish roe, and homemade hummus. There's no menu in English, and no need for one, as only three dishes are offered: shrimp, calamari, and deep-fried fish. There's no dessert, just jangling-strong espresso. $ *Average main: NIS 55* ⊠ *26 A.L. Zissu St., Downtown* ☎ *04/855–2663* ▭ *No credit cards* ⊗ *Closed Sun.* ✛ *B2.*

$$$$
MODERN ISRAELI
Fodor's Choice
★

✕ **Hanamal 24.** Hands down, this is the finest gastronomic experience in Haifa. Tasteful renovations have transformed this old wheat-and-corn warehouse in Haifa's rather run-down port into an elegant Tuscan country inn. Climbing the stairs, you arrive at four rooms of various sizes and levels of privacy (one's the bar, with leather sofas) with original stone floors, brick walls, and lofty ceilings. Starters such as cream of onion soup with truffle cream and bok choy leaves and delectable entrées such as fillet of sea bass in a Tomme-cheese crust are highlights. Wash it down with a splash of the house wine, a blend made for Hanamal 24 by the Vitkin boutique winery. $ *Average main: NIS 130* ⊠ *24 Hanamal St., off Sha'ar Palmer St., Haifa Port* ☎ *04/862–8899* ⊕ *hanamal24.rest.co.il/en/* ⊗ *Closed Sun.* ✛ *D4.*

$$
SEAFOOD

✕ **Jacko's.** If ever there was a beloved eating place in Haifa, Jacko's is it. Give the name to your taxi driver; he'll nod approvingly, gun the motor, and drop you at a nondescript building with a Hebrew sign. Since 1976, this family-run restaurant founded by a Turkish fisherman has been serving delicious seafood in a rowdy, informal setting with shared tables. The specialties at this lunch spot are fish and seafood sautéed in butter, white wine, and garlic. There are piles of soft-shell crab, mussels, and calamari served with a variety of sauces, large shrimp grilled in their shells, and Mediterranean lobster (in summer). Ask for the catch of the day. For dessert try the Turkish cookies. ⑤ *Average main: NIS 70* ⊠ *12 Kehilat Saloniki St., Downtown* ☎ *04/866–8813* ⊗ *No dinner Sat.–Thurs.* ✛ *D4.*

$$
EASTERN
EUROPEAN
✕**Maayan Habira.** The decor of this meat-lovers' haven is informal: beer kegs piled in a corner; the walls covered with photos of glowing restaurant reviews; and a mural of the customers painted by an art student in 1989. The Romanian family-run business has been around since 1962; today Reuven and his son Shlomi do the excellent cooking. To start, savor chopped liver, jellied calf's foot, gefilte fish, and oxtail soup. Then go to work on delectable pork spareribs, goose, or beef pastrami, which they smoke themselves. As befits a place whose name means "beer spring," an impressive selection of imported beers is on tap. In summer, diners sit outside and enjoy live music. It's usually a lunch place, but Tuesday and Thursday nights it's open for dinner. ⑤ *Average main: NIS 70* ⊠ *4 Natanson St., Downtown* ☎ *04/862–3193* ⊗ *Closed Sat. No dinner Sun., Mon., Wed., and Fri.* ✛ *D4.*

$$
ASIAN
✕**Minna Tomei.** This pan-Asian gem on the top floor of the Castra mall is a bit hard to find, but worth the effort. Five kitchens (Japan, India, Korea, Vietnam, and Thailand) offer flavorful dining options in unusual juxtaposition. Relax with inspired cocktails or a Thai beer before dinner. Standout options are the Bombay butter chicken and red Thai curry. End the evening on a sweet note with a coffee-infused Saigon crème brûlée. The kitchen operates on a you-get-it-when-it's-ready concept, so your food will arrive at different times. Give your order one course at a time to keep the table paced together. ⑤ *Average main: NIS 65* ⊠ *Castra Shopping Center, 8 Filman St., South Haifa* ☎ *170/050–4506* ⊕ *www. minna-tomei.co.il* ✛ *B6.*

$$$
ITALIAN
✕**Raffaello.** Pasta made on the premises with imported ingredients from Italy speaks to the close attention and high quality of this premier Italian restaurant with an open kitchen and a pleasant atmosphere. Beautiful wood furnishings and a light, bright interior provide a backdrop to innovative dishes like pizza with pear, truffle, and blue cheese, or salmon pappardelle with spinach and beets. Desserts are really the standout: Homemade ice cream and a pistachio crème brûlée have the locals lining up for a table. Reservations are required. ⑤ *Average main: NIS 100* ⊠ *Castra Shopping Center, 8 Filman St., South Haifa* ☎ *170/050–7107* ⊕ *raffaellocc.co.il* ▭ *No credit cards* ✛ *B6.*

$$$
MIDDLE EASTERN
Fodor'sChoice
★
✕**Shawatina.** No visit to Stella Maris Monastery is complete without a meal at this local favorite, where you can marvel at the eye-popping harbor view from the floor-to-ceiling windows in the exposed brick dining room while you enjoy traditional Middle Eastern fare. Start the meal with an array of salads and appetizers served family style; inventive grilled halumi cheese with crunchy peanuts and a sweet mango salad are more unusual additions to the traditional plates of eggplant, hummus, pickles, and cabbage salads. Grilled meats and fresh fish are

the house specialties. Reservations are essential at this popular spot. The restaurant has a second branch on the beach. $ *Average main: NIS 90* ⊠ *100 Stella Maris St., French Carmel* ☎ *04/833–3037* ✛ *A3.*

$ ✕ **Zebra.** One of Haifa's best-kept secrets, this intimate bar serves terrific

AMERICAN   hamburgers and salads, but the artistic vibe is what keeps 'em coming back. Owner Vicki paints, and her artwork, along with works by other locals, is featured. Her husband, Gil, runs the restaurant, books the music, and in his off-hours, manages a theater company. There's music most nights, and Tuesday-night jams are a treat, or try a Thursday evening when the Daniel Dworsky Trio is in town. $ *Average main: NIS 45* ⊠ *39 Tchernikovsky St.* ☎ *077/321–2290* ⊗ *Closed Sun.* ✛ *A4.*

WHERE TO STAY

Haifa's best-known hotels are at the top of the hill in the Merkaz Carmel area. The Colony hotel is in the downtown area, as is the Port Inn hostel-guesthouse; both have more affordable stays. Within easy reach of the city, the Carmel Forest Resort Spa is quiet and pampering, though it's pricey.

Use the coordinates (✛ A1) at the end of each listing to locate a site on the corresponding map.

$ 🏨 **Bat Galim Boutique Hotel.** Opened in 2015, this romantic boutique

HOTEL   hotel has great views of the sea. **Pros:** short walk to restaurants; close to the beach; convenient to train and bus station. **Cons:** no elevator; no restaurant; small rooms. $ *Rooms from: $120* ⊠ *10 Yonatan St., Kiryat Eliezer* ☎ *04/603–7800* ⊕ *www.batgalim-boutique-hotel.co.il* ⛨ *12 rooms* ⊺◎⊦ *Breakfast* ✛ *A2.*

$$$$ 🏨 **Carmel Forest Spa Resort.** Set by itself in the Carmel Forest, this spa-

RESORT   resort 25 km (15 miles) south of Haifa is the ultimate escape: a top-of-

Fodor's Choice   the-line spa with tasteful lodgings designed to pamper guests in a calm

★   and healthy setting (no cell phones or children under 16). **Pros:** serene setting; lovely forest walks. **Cons:** no public transportation; rather pricey. $ *Rooms from: $800* ⊠ *Rte. 721, Beit Oren* ✛ *About 1 mile on Rte. 721 from Hwy. 4* ☎ *04/830–7888* ⊕ *www.isrotel.com* ⛨ *126 rooms* ⊺◎⊦ *Breakfast* ✛ *D5.*

$ 🏨 **Colony Hotel.** Step into this palm-shaded courtyard and you're in the

HOTEL   world of the German Templers: the three-story lodging is in the center of the German Colony, amid the neighborhood's carefully restored red-roofed homes. **Pros:** uniquely charming setting; discounts at local restaurants. **Cons:** no pool; no restaurant. $ *Rooms from: $180* ⊠ *28 Ben Gurion Blvd., German Colony* ☎ *04/851–3344* ⊕ *www.colony-haifa.com* ⛨ *40 rooms* ⊺◎⊦ *Breakfast* ✛ *C3.*

$ 🏨 **Crowne Plaza Haifa.** Catering to a business crowd, this modern, well-

HOTEL   designed chain hotel is built into a pine-shaded slope. **Pros:** indoor pool and Jacuzzi open until 9 pm; spa; free Wi-Fi in rooms and lobby. **Cons:** mediocre breakfast by Israeli standards. $ *Rooms from: $180* ⊠ *111 Yefe Nof St., Merkaz Carmel* ☎ *04/835–0801* ⊕ *www.ichotelsgroup. com/crowneplaza/hotels/us/en/haifa/hfail/hoteldetail* ⛨ *100 rooms* ⊺◎⊦ *Breakfast* ✛ *B6.*

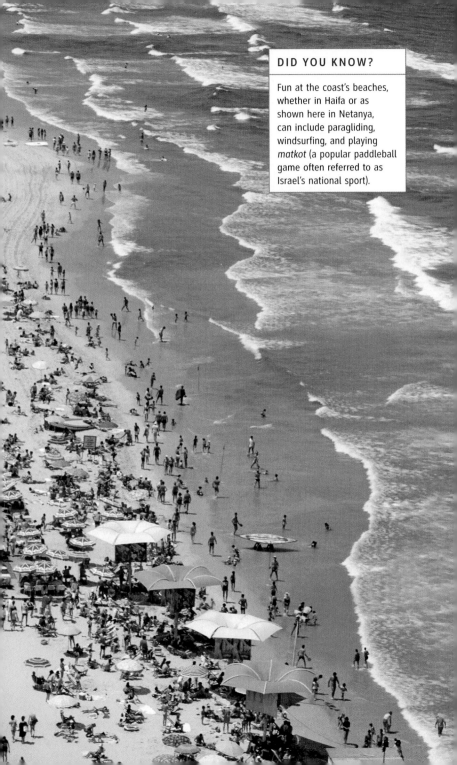

DID YOU KNOW?

Fun at the coast's beaches, whether in Haifa or as shown here in Netanya, can include paragliding, windsurfing, and playing *matkot* (a popular paddleball game often referred to as Israel's national sport).

$$$
HOTEL 🛏 **Dan Carmel.** The Dan Carmel, beautifully situated on the heights of Merkaz Carmel, is a longtime favorite with stately charm and a devoted staff. **Pros:** superb views; attentive staff. **Cons:** pool closed in winter. ⑤ *Rooms from: $330* ✉ *87 Hanassi Blvd., Merkaz Carmel* ☎ *04/830–3030* ⊕ *www.danhotels.com* ⟿ *227 rooms* ❘◯❘ *Breakfast* ⊹ *B6.*

$$
HOTEL 🛏 **Dan Panorama Haifa.** The glitzier younger sister of the Dan Carmel up the road, this 21-story hotel is popular with business executives (especially the comfortable second-floor lobby with its circular bar). **Pros:** welcoming staff; splendid views; large fitness center. **Cons:** no balconies; dated decor. ⑤ *Rooms from: $220* ✉ *107 Hanassi Blvd., Merkaz Carmel* ☎ *04/835–2222* ⊕ *www.danhotels.com* ⟿ *266 rooms* ❘◯❘ *Breakfast* ⊹ *A5.*

$
B&B/INN 🛏 **Hotel Beth Shalom.** Plain but pleasant, this Christian-run lodging has three floors of small rooms; each room has wicker furniture, beds with fluffy duvets, and good reading lights. **Pros:** central location close to Carmel Center and promenade; modest prices. **Cons:** no restaurant; basic decor. ⑤ *Rooms from: $110* ✉ *110 Hanassi Blvd., Merkaz Carmel* ☎ *04/837–7481* ⊕ *www.beth-shalom.co.il* ⟿ *30 rooms* ❘◯❘ *Breakfast* ⊹ *B5.*

$
B&B/INN 🛏 **Port Inn Hostel.** A haven for budget travelers, this inn with a pleasant guest lounge is in a neighborhood filled with interesting shops. **Pros:** cheerful garden; small rooms good for solo travelers. **Cons:** far from tourist sites; not a lot of privacy. ⑤ *Rooms from: $90* ✉ *34 Yaffo St., Downtown* ☎ *04/852–4401* ⊕ *www.portinn.net* ⟿ *18 rooms, 10 with bath* ❘◯❘ *Breakfast* ⊹ *C4.*

$
HOTEL 🛏 **Villa Carmel.** The facade may look ordinary, but this chic boutique hotel's interior is unlike anything else in Haifa. **Pros:** stylish atmosphere; attention to detail; on a quiet street. **Cons:** no pool. ⑤ *Rooms from: $180* ✉ *1 Heinrich Heine Sq., off 30 Moriah Blvd., Merkaz Carmel* ☎ *04/837–5777* ⊕ *www.villacarmel.co.il* ⟿ *15 rooms* ❘◯❘ *Breakfast* ⊹ *A6.*

NIGHTLIFE AND PERFORMING ARTS

Haifa at night may not pulse like Tel Aviv, but there are more than a few things to do after dark. For information on performances and other special events in and around Haifa, check Friday's *Jerusalem Post* or the *Haaretz* newspaper; both publish separate weekend entertainment guides. In balmy weather, a stroll along the Louis Promenade and then along Panorama Road, with lovely views of nighttime Haifa, is a relaxing way to end the day.

NIGHTLIFE

For a festive evening, try the restaurants and cafés-cum-pubs in the German Colony. Night spots in Haifa come and go, and some open only on certain evenings, so call ahead if possible.

Colony Bar. Opened in 2016, the Colony Bar at the hotel of the same name opens nightly to both guests and visitors. Grab a drink in the heart of the German Colony, right on the boulevard; the location can't be beat. This classy, intimate bar caters to a more mature crowd. ✉ *Colony Hotel, 38 Ben Gurion Blvd., German Colony* ☎ *04/851–3344* ⊕ *colonyhaifa.com.*

Duke. The lovely Duke is a civilized old-world Irish pub with good draft beers, other libations from whiskey to wine, and a menu with such standbys as fish-and-chips. Bottles on display and plenty of dark wood add to the convivial atmosphere. ⊠ *107 Moriah Blvd., Merkaz Carmel* ☎ *04/834–7282* ⊕ *www.duke-pub.co.il/en/.*

Pundak HaDov. One of Haifa's oldest and most reliable pubs and sports bars, the cozy Pundak HaDov (The Bear Inn) tends to fill with enthusiastic sports fans cheering on their favorite teams in front of four big screens. The menu has ample choices for snacks and full meals. ⊠ *135 Hanassi Blvd., Merkaz Carmel* ☎ *04/838–1703* ⊕ *www.pundakhadov. rest-e.co.il.*

PERFORMING ARTS

Haifa Symphony Orchestra. The orchestra performs at the Haifa Auditorium (Krieger Center) four to five times a month from October through July. For ticket and performance information, contact the box office. ⊠ *6 Eliyahu Hakim St., French Carmel* ☎ *04/833–8888 box office* ⊕ *www.haifasymphony.co.il.*

Israel Philharmonic Orchestra. The world-class Israel Philharmonic Orchestra gives 20 concerts at the Haifa Auditorium (Rappaport Hall) from October through July. ⊠ *138 Hanassi Blvd., Merkaz Carmel* ☎ *04/810–1558* ⊕ *www.ipo.co.il.*

SHOPPING

Haifa is studded with modern shopping malls with boutiques, eateries, and movie theaters, not to mention drugstores, photography stores, and money-exchange desks.

Castra Shopping Center. Near the Hof Carmel railway station, this popular mall has three floors of jewelry stores, clothing boutiques, and art workshops. It is easily spotted by Eric Brauer's large ceramic-tile mural outside depicting Old Testament themes. ⊠ *8 Fliman St., South Haifa* ☎ *04/859–0000.*

Panorama Center. Located in the heart of the Carmel Center next to the Dan Panorama Haifa hotel, the Panorama Center has everything from a pharmacy and newspaper stand to a wine outlet and clothing shops. ⊠ *109 Hanassi Blvd., Merkaz Carmel* ☎ *04/837–5011* ☉ *Closed Sat.*

Sara's Gift Shop. This boutique in the Dan Carmel Haifa hotel is crammed with jewelry made exclusively for it, including silver inlaid with Roman glass, gold Baha'i pendants, and art-deco earrings. ⊠ *Dan Carmel Haifa, 87 Hanassi Blvd., Merkaz Carmel* ☎ *04/830–3098.*

SPORTS AND THE OUTDOORS

BEACHES

Haifa's coastline is one fine, sandy public beach after another. They span 5 km (3 miles) of coast and have lifeguard stations, changing rooms, showers, toilets, refreshment stands, sports areas, restaurants, and a winding stone promenade. In the north are the Bat Galim and Surfers Beaches. Moving south, you come across the Carmel Beach, Nirvana,

Zamir, Dado, Dado South, and the Students Beach. To be on the safe side, never swim when a lifeguard isn't on duty. There's parking at every beach, and all are free. All city beaches are reachable by local buses.

Carmel Beach. With its attractive boardwalk and beachside kiosks, Carmel Beach sits in front of the Leonardo Hotel at the southern entrance to Haifa. **Amenities:** food and drink; parking (fee); lifeguards; showers; toilets. **Best for:** swimming. ⊠ *Access via Andrei Sakharov St., South Haifa* ⌲ *Free.*

Dado Beach. On Saturday at Dado Beach, Haifa's longest stretch of sandy beach, Israelis of all ages come and find folk dance to the delight of onlookers. You can also find exercise equipment, picnic areas, and a small bathing pool for young children The northern part of the beach is wheelchair accessible, as are the restrooms and showers. **Amenities:** food and drink; lifeguards; parking (fee); showers; toilets; water sports. **Best for:** swimming. ⊠ *David Elazar St., South Haifa* ⌲ *Free.*

Hof HaShaket. North of the Leonardo Hotel, and next to the Rambam Medical Center, the quiet Hof HaShaket has separate gender days: Sunday, Tuesday, and Thursday for women; Monday, Wednesday, and Friday for men; Saturday for everyone. **Amenities:** food and drink; lifeguards; parking (fee); showers. **Best for:** solitude; swimming. ⊠ *Entrance from Cheyl HaYam St., South Haifa* ⌲ *Free.*

Zamir Beach. Just next to Dado Beach, Zamir Beach is regarded as one of the best Haifa beaches, with fine golden sand and many amenities, including coffeehouses, restaurants, access for the disabled, and even Wi-Fi. **Amenities:** food and drink; lifeguards; parking (fee); showers; toilets. **Best for:** swimming; walking. ⊠ *David Elazar St., South Haifa* ⌲ *Free.*

> **BEACH BASICS**
>
> Between Tel Aviv and the Lebanese border are miles of beautiful sandy beaches, most of them public and attended by lifeguards from early May to mid-October. Many Israeli beaches are left untended off-season, but they're generally cleaned up and well maintained once warm weather returns. Beachside restaurants can make for rough-and-tumble eating because of loud music, but it's fun to eat fresh food by the beach. *Never* swim in the absence of a lifeguard, as undertows can be dangerous.

THE NORTHERN COAST

Beaches abound, the sea sparkles, and skies are sunny most of the year in the coastal area south of Haifa. Archaeological sites, such as the outstanding Roman, Byzantine, and Crusader ruins at Caesarea, house beautiful restored treasures, and historical museums are fun and not fusty. Netanya and Nahsholim-Dor have plenty for seekers of sun and fun, including paragliding and other adventures. Fresh fish, seafood, and good local wine please every palate.

NAHSHOLIM-DOR

29 km (19 miles) south of Haifa.

The beautiful beach at Dor is fit for a king—not surprising since it has a royal history. Founded 3,500 years ago, biblical Dor was once the maritime capital of the Carmel coast. The best harbor between Jaffa (near present-day Tel Aviv) and Akko, it was a target for many with imperial ambitions, from the ancient Egyptians and the "Sea Peoples" through to King Solomon and on down. It was renowned in antiquity for its precious purple dye; reserved for royalty, this hue was extracted from a mollusk that was abundant along the coast. Today, as you watch fishing boats bob in the sheltered bays, you can complement your suntanning with a swim to a small offshore island, a visit to a diving site, or a break at a pub.

GETTING HERE AND AROUND

Take Route 2, getting off at the Zichron Ya'akov exit. At the Fureidis Junction, drive north about 1 km (½ mile) until you reach the small sign for Nahsholim-Dor. There's no public transportation here.

EXPLORING

FAMILY **Mizgaga Museum.** This very worthwhile museum next to Kibbutz Nahsholim and the Nahsholim Seaside Resort holds a rich trove of finds from local nautical digs and excavations at nearby Tel Dor. It's in the partly restored former glass factory opened by Baron Edmond de Rothschild in 1891 to serve the wineries of nearby Zichron Ya'akov. The sequence of peoples who settled, conquered, or passed through Dor—from the Canaanites to Phoenicians to Napoléon—can be traced through these artifacts. Of particular interest is the bronze cannon that Napoléon's vanquished troops dumped into the sea during their retreat from Akko to Egypt in May 1799. An informative film in English illuminates the history of the ancient port city of Dor. ⊠ *Kibbutz Nahsholim, Rd. 7011* ☎ *04/639–0950* ⊕ *www.mizgaga.com* ⊠ *NIS 20* ⊙ *Closed Sat.*

WHERE TO STAY

$$ ⌂ **Nahsholim Seaside Resort.** You'd have to travel quite a distance to find
HOTEL a prettier beach cove, though this one is just 30 km (18½ miles) south of
FAMILY Haifa, for a hotel setting; the low-slung white buildings, steps from the beach and separated by lawns with hammocks, contain airy, modern, pastel-hue rooms (many with sea views) and apartments that accommodate up to five people. **Pros:** fabulous beach; family-friendly vibe. **Cons:** expensive for what you get; limited access to Haifa attractions. $ *Rooms from: $200* ⊠ *Kibbutz Nahsholim, Rd. 7011* ☎ *04/639–9533* ⊕ *www.nahsholim.co.il* ⊅ *150 rooms* ⍝ *Breakfast.*

SPORTS AND THE OUTDOORS

Fodor's Choice **Dor Beach.** Part of a coastal nature reserve, Dor Beach, also known as
★ Tantura Beach, is a dreamy stretch of beige sand. Rocky islets form breakwaters and jetties provide calm seas for happy bathers. Amenities are ample: chair and umbrella rentals, a first-aid station, a restaurant, and changing rooms. The beach, beside Kibbutz Nahsholim, gets crowded on summer weekends and holidays. **Amenities:** food and drink; lifeguards; parking; showers; toilets. **Best for:** partiers; swimming; walking. ⊠ *Off Rte. 4* ⌚ *Nature reserve NIS 35, beach entrance free.*

Paradive. The company organizes thrilling tandem skydives 14,000 feet over the Mediterranean. No experience is required. It's about 3 km (2 miles) north of Kibbutz Nahsholim. ⊠ *Habonim Beach* ✛ *Off Rte. 4* ☎ *04/639–1068* ⊕ *www.paradive.co.il.*

Underwater Archaeological Center. Kurt Raveh, a marine archaeologist and resident of Kibbutz Nahsholim, runs the Underwater Archaeological Center. Raveh conducts underwater expeditions and "dives into history" where divers (even those without experience) get to tour ancient shipwrecks (many of which he discovered) and explore reefs under his experienced eye. You can also arrange kayaking trips along the coast. ⊠ *Kibbutz Nahsholim* ☎ *052/516–2795* ⊕ *www.northern-wind.co.il.*

EN ROUTE **Atlit Detention Camp.** Atlit, a peninsula with the jagged remains of an important Crusader castle, also holds a more recent historical site: to the west (about 1,500 feet from the highway) is the Atlit detention camp used by the British to house refugees smuggled in during and after World War II. The reconstructed barracks, fences, and watchtowers stand as reminders of how Jewish immigration was outlawed under the British Mandate after the publication of the infamous White Paper in 1939. More than a third of the 120,000 illegal immigrants to Palestine passed through the camp from 1934 to 1948. In 1945, Yitzhak Rabin, then a young officer in the Palmach, planned a raid that freed 200 detainees. The authenticity of the exhibit is striking: it was re-created from accounts of actual detainees and their contemporaries; you see the living quarters, complete with laundry hanging from the rafters. The camp is 15 km (9 miles) south of Haifa. ⊠ *Rd. 7110* ✛ *Off Rte. 2* ☎ *04/984–1980* 🖃 *NIS 32* ☉ *Closed Sat.* ☞ *Reservations required.*

CAESAREA

49 km (29½ miles) south of Haifa.

The Phoenicians discovered it, and the Romans fell in love with it: Caesarea is most famous for its intriguing Roman, Byzantine, and Crusader ruins, but also offers a stroll through artists' galleries, an underwater archaeological park, and culinary delights. This popular tourist center juxtaposes a vibrant past and bustling present. Near the archaeological site is the well-to-do community of Caesarea, a group of homes on the sea. Here you'll find the Ralli Museum and the famed Roman aqueduct.

GETTING HERE AND AROUND

A car is your best option for reaching Caesarea. It's off Route 2, about one hour by car from Tel Aviv or Haifa. You can also opt for a guided bus tour of this and other sites, departing from a number of cities, with Egged Tours or United Tours, two well-regarded companies.

EXPLORING

FAMILY **Caesarea Maritima National Park.** By turns an ancient Roman port city, Fodor's Choice Byzantine capital, and Crusader stronghold, Caesarea is one of the ★ country's major archaeological sites and a delightful place to spend a day of leisurely sightseeing among the fascinating ruins. You can browse in souvenir shops and art galleries, take a dip at the beach, snorkel or dive around a submerged port, and enjoy a seaside meal. Caesarea is

Caesarea

an easy day trip from Tel Aviv and Haifa or even Jerusalem. A good strategy is to start at the Roman Theater, at the southern entrance. After exploring, you can then leave through the northern entrance. If you're short on time, enter through the northern entrance and take a quicker tour of the site. At either of the two entrances to this intriguing site, pick up the free brochure and map.

Entry to the Roman Theater is through one of the vomitoria (arched tunnels that served as entrances for the public). Herod's theaters—here as elsewhere in Israel—were the first of their kind in the ancient Near East. The theater today seats 3,600 and is a spectacular venue for summer concerts and performances. What you see today is largely a reconstruction. Only a few of the seats of the *cavea* (where the audience sat) near the orchestra are original, in addition to some of the stairs and the decorative wall at the front of the stage.

The huge Herodian Amphitheater is a horseshoe-shape stadium with sloping sides filled with rows of stone seats. It's most likely the one mentioned by 1st-century AD historian Josephus Flavius in *The Jewish War*. A crowd of 10,000 watched horse and chariot races and various sporting events here some 2,000 years ago. Up the wooden steps, you see the street's beautiful and imaginative mosaic floors in the bathhouse complex of the Roman-Byzantine administrative area.

King Louis IX of France built the walls that surround the Crusader City. The bulk of what you see today—the moat, escarpment, citadel, and walls, which once contained 16 towers—dates from 1251, when the French monarch spent a year pitching in with his own two hands to help restore the existing fortifications. As you enter the southern wall gate of the Crusader city, you see the remains of an unfinished cathedral with three graceful apses.

At the observation point, you can gaze out over the remains of Herod's Port, once a magnificent sight that writers of the day compared to Athens' Port of Piraeus. An earthquake devastated the harbor in AD 130, which is why Crusaders utilized only a small section of it when they conquered the city in 1101.

In the harbor area, don't miss the Time Trek. Inside, you meet 12 of Caesarea's fascinating historic personages—among them Herod the Great, Rabbi Akiva, and St. Paul. These realistic-looking, larger-than-life figures answer questions about their lives in Caesarea. If you climb the stairs of the nearby squarish stone tower of the re-created fortress on the pier, you can view three-dimensional animations on giant screens that explain the amazing construction of the port.

East of the northern entrance to the site, a fenced-in area encloses Caesarea's Byzantine Street. During the Byzantine period and late Roman times, Caesarea thrived as a center of Christian scholarship. In the 7th century, Caesarea boasted a famous library of some 30,000 volumes that originated with the collection of the Christian philosopher Origen (185–254), who lived here for two decades. Towering over the street are two headless marble statues, probably carted here from nearby Roman temples. The provenance of the milky-white statue is unknown; Emperor Hadrian might have commissioned the reddish figure facing it when he visited Caesarea.

A wonderful finale to your trip to Caesarea, especially at sunset, is the beachfront Roman Aqueduct. The chain of arches tumbling northward until they disappear beneath the sand is a captivating sight. During Roman times, the demand for a steady water supply was considerable, but the source was a spring about 13 km (8 miles) away in the foothills of Mount Carmel. Workers cut a channel approximately 6½ km (4 miles) long through solid rock before the water was piped into the aqueduct. In the 2nd century, Hadrian doubled its capacity by adding a new channel. Today you can walk along the aqueduct and see marble plaques dedicated to the troops of various legions who toiled here. ⊠ *Off Rte. 2, near Kibbutz Sdot Yam* ☎ *04/626–7080* ⊕ *www. parks.org.il* ⊠ *NIS 40.*

Caesarea Maritima Museum. In Kibbutz Sdot Yam just outside Caesarea, this excellent museum houses many of the remarkable artifacts found by kibbutz members as they plowed their fields in the 1940s; archaeological excavations have discovered more. The small museum has arguably the best collection of late-Roman sculpture and figurines in Israel, with impressive holdings of rare Roman and Byzantine gemstones; a large variety of coins minted in Caesarea over the ages; and oil lamps, jewelry, and urns excavated from the sea floor. ⊠ *Kibbutz Sdot Yam* ✛ *Near*

Ancient Caesarea, which has ruins from a variety of historical periods, is one of Israel's most popular destinations.

southern entrance to Caesarea ☎ *04/636–4367* ⊕ *www.caesareamuseum.com* ⊠ *NIS 18* ⊗ *Closed Fri. and Sat.*

Ralli Museum. In Caesarea's villa area, you can't miss the two Spanish colonial–style buildings of the Ralli Museum, with their red-tile roofs and terraces: one of these dazzling white buildings houses an exhibit on the ancient city's history, and the second building, in a Moorish style, examines the golden age of Spanish Jewry in the Middle Ages. It's a pleasure to wander along the walls of the courtyard and gaze at the sculptures of various dignitaries such as Maimonides and Spinoza. Inside are paintings with biblical themes by European artists of the 16th to 18th centuries. Rotating exhibitions display contemporary Latin American art. ⊠ *Rothschild Blvd., next to water tower* ☎ *04/626–1013* ⊕ *www.rallimuseums.com* ⊠ *Free* ⊗ *Mar.–Dec., closed Wed., Sun.; Jan. and Feb., closed Sun.–Thurs.*

WHERE TO EAT

$$　✕ **Agenda.** If you're one of those people who could eat breakfast three
ISRAELI　times a day, Agenda is for you. Try the *shakshuka*, an Israeli dish in
FAMILY　which eggs are poached in a sharp tomato sauce. For lunch and dinner there are also pizzas, sushi, and other light fare, plus cocktails and wine. The staff is friendly, the atmosphere casual. Like many of the tastiest good-value restaurants in Israel, this one is in a gas station (next to Minato, a sushi place). It has a bright interior with indoor, outdoor, and bar seating. ⑤ *Average main: NIS 60* ⊠ *Caesarea Junction, Off Rte. 2* ✛ *At Paz gas station* ☎ *04/626–2092* ⊕ *agenda.rest.co.il* ⊗ *No dinner Fri. No breakfast or lunch Sat.*

Herod's Amazing Port at Caesarea

The port's construction at Caesarea was an unprecedented challenge—there was no artificial harbor of this size anywhere in the world. But Herod wasn't one to avoid a challenge and spent 12 years, from 22 to 10 BC, building a port for the luxury-goods trade (including spices, textiles, and precious stones) that would make Caesarea the economic capital of the country and the most modern harbor in the whole Roman Empire.

During underwater research in the 1970s, archaeologists were stunned to discover concrete blocks near the breakwater offshore, indicating the sophisticated use of hydraulic concrete (which hardens underwater).

Historians knew that the Romans had developed such techniques, but before the discoveries at Caesarea, they never knew hydraulic concrete to have been used on such a massive scale. The main ingredient in the concrete,

volcanic ash, was probably imported from Italy's Mount Vesuvius, as were the wooden forms. Teams of professional divers actually did much of the trickiest work, laying the foundations hundreds of yards offshore.

Once finished, two massive breakwaters—one stretching west and then north from the Citadel restaurant some 1,800 feet and the other 600 feet long, both now submerged—sheltered an area of about 3½ acres from the waves and tides.

Two towers, each mounted by three colossal statues, marked the entrance to the port; and although neither the towers nor the statues have been found, a tiny medal bearing their image was discovered in the first underwater excavations here in 1960. The finished harbor also contained the dominating temple to Emperor Augustus and cavernous storage facilities along the shore.

$$$
SEAFOOD
FAMILY

✕ **Crusaders' Restaurant** (*HaTzalbanim*). Sitting by the old port of Caesarea in Caesarea National Park, and with ample seating overlooking the bay, this cavernous seaside restaurant is famous for its fish. The menu features fresh seafood, caught right from the water below, as well as juicy steaks and kebabs. An excellent starter is the salad of grilled eggplant, hummus, and fried cauliflower. Crunchy pita rounds toasted with olive oil and local spices are served alongside. House specialties include baked red snapper topped with chopped vegetables and black mussels sautéed in garlic, butter, and wine. Still hungry? Creamy cheesecake or warm apple pie with ice cream will do the trick. This place is a favorite with tour groups. ⑤ *Average main: NIS 100* ⊠ *Caesarea* ⌖ *Northern end of port* ☎ *04/636–1679* ⊕ *pundakazalbanim.rest.co.il.*

$$$
MEDITERRANEAN
Fodor's Choice
★

✕ **Helena.** Two of Israel's best-known culinary personalities, Amos Sion and Uri Yarmias, opened this restaurant to create a first-rate yet affordable dining experience. It occupies a beautifully restored stone building in the ancient harbor. Large windows everywhere maximize the sea view under a wooden pergola. The chef puts an Israeli spin on Mediterranean-style cooking, turning out such tantalizing appetizers as calamari with lemon and hyssop leaves on sheep-milk yogurt, and sliced sirloin in aged balsamic vinegar with Cambozola cheese and pistachios. Main dishes include an aromatic fish stew made of red mullet,

Caesarea: Roman City

Herod the Great gave Caesarea its name, dedicating the magnificent Roman city he built to his patron, Augustus Caesar. It was the Roman emperor who had crowned Herod—born to an Idumean family that had converted to Judaism—King of the Jews around 30 BC.

Construction began in 22 BC; Herod spared nothing in his elaborate designs for the port and the city itself, which included palaces, temples, a theater, a marketplace, a hippodrome, and water and sewage systems. When Caesarea was completed 12 years later, only Jerusalem outshined it. Its population under Herod grew to around 100,000, and the city covered some 164 acres.

In AD 6, a decade after Herod died, Caesarea became the seat of the Roman procurators, one of whom was Pontius Pilate, governor of Judea when Jesus was crucified. With Jerusalem predominantly Jewish,

the Romans preferred the Hellenistic Caesarea, with its Jewish minority, as the seat of their administration.

But religious harmony did not prevail. The mixed population of Jews and Gentiles (mainly Greeks and Syrians) repeatedly clashed, with hostilities exploding during the Jewish revolt of AD 66. Vespasian, proclaimed emperor by his legions in AD 69, squelched the first Jewish rebellion. A year later, his son Titus razed Jerusalem and celebrated his suppression of the Jewish revolt.

Henceforth, Caesarea was a Roman colony and the local Roman capital of Palestine for nearly 600 years. It was here that Peter converted the Roman centurion Cornelius to Christianity—a milestone in the spread of the new faith—and Paul preached and was imprisoned for two years. In the 2nd century, Rabbi Akiva, the spiritual mentor of the Bar Kochba revolt, was tortured to death here.

spinach, and Swiss chard, and grilled *barbuni* (sardine-sized fish). The wine room holds the chef's private collection. A children's menu is available. $ *Average main: NIS 100* ⊠ *Caesarea* ✛ *Southern end of port* ☎ *04/610–1018* ⊕ *www.hellena.co.il.*

$$ ✕ **Minato.** In a gas station (and next door to the restaurant Agenda), this
JAPANESE place is perfect for beachgoers craving sushi. The name means "port" in Japanese, and Minato does a brisk take-out business, serving sashimi and nigiri as well as a variety of tempura dishes. You can also eat in at the long sushi bar and watch the chefs' knives flash in front of you. Try the *temaki*, a cone of seaweed filled with rice, vegetables, and the fish of your choice. $ *Average main: NIS 60* ⊠ *Caesarea Junction, Rte. 2* ✛ *At Paz gas station* ☎ *04/636–0812* ⊕ *www.minato.co.il* ⊗ *No dinner Fri. No lunch Sat.*

WHERE TO STAY

$$ 🏨 **Dan Caesarea.** Equidistant from Tel Aviv and Haifa, this chain hotel
HOTEL suits business executives and vacationers alike, and the 15 acres of land-
FAMILY scaped lawns, sparkling swimming pool, and 18-hole minigolf course make it great for families. **Pros:** beautiful grounds; family-friendly vibe; helpful staff. **Cons:** no public transportation; far from restaurants;

pool closed during the winter. $ *Rooms from: $300* ✉ *1 Rothschild St.* ☎ *04/626–9111* ⊕ *www.danhotels.com* ⌁ *113 rooms* ⚬ *No meals.*

SPORTS AND THE OUTDOORS

BEACHES

Caesarea Beach Club. In a calm cove in Caesarea's ancient harbor, the Caesarea Beach Club has chairs and umbrellas. A lifeguard is on duty in season, and the restaurant sells sandwiches and other light fare. **Amenities:** food and drink; lifeguards; showers. **Best for:** sunset; swimming. ✉ *Northern entrance to archaeological site* ⌁ *Free.*

FAMILY **Hof Shonit.** The largest and most popular beach in the area is the exceptionally well-kept Hof Shonit (translated as "Reef Beach"), with a refreshment stand and a restaurant, as well as restrooms and cold showers. In addition to the beach there is a water park with extreme slides for the kids (open only on Saturdays in-season) and adult and toddler swimming pools. Parking is NIS 15. **Amenities:** food and drink; lifeguards; parking (fee); showers; toilets; water sports. **Best for:** swimming. ✉ *South of archaeological site* ⊹ *Off Rte. 2.*

Roman Aqueduct. Caesarea's Roman aqueduct frames a spacious beach with the dramatic backdrop of arches disappearing into the sand. There is no entrance fee but few amenities—no restaurants or promenade. The beach and swimming areas have been cleared of rocks and debris, but swimming outside the designated area is prohibited. Never swim unless the seasonal lifeguard is on duty. **Amenities:** lifeguards; parking (fee) **Best for:** sunset; walking. ✉ *North of archaeological site.*

GOLF

Caesarea Golf Club. The country's only 18-hole golf course is the Caesarea Golf Club, adjacent to the Dan Caesarea. Although it was first established by the Rothschilds in the 1960s, noted golf course architect Pete Dye remodeled the course to high standards in 2009. There's a pro shop and the Albatross restaurant. ✉ *Caesarea* ⊹ *Off Rte. 2* ☎ *04/610–9618* ⊕ *www.caesarea.com* ⌁ *NIS 480–NIS 540; NIS 150 for golf club rental* ⚲ *18 holes, 7200 yards, par 72* ⌁ *Closed Mon.*

Ga'ash Golf Club. At the 9-hole Ga'ash Golf Club, you can play a second time from alternative tees to make for an 18-hole experience. There's a shop and a restaurant here, too. ✉ *Off Rte. 2* ☎ *09/951–5111* ⊕ *www.golfgaash.co.il* ⌁ *NIS 350–430 for 9 holes, NIS 460–530 for 18 holes; NIS 100 for golf bag; NIS 115–175 for golf cart* ⚲ *9 holes, 2955 yards, par 35.*

SCUBA DIVING

Old Caesarea Diving Center. Located inside the national park, this diving center runs a full range of courses for novices, experts, and everyone in between. Snorkelers are welcome, and divers can use a plastic map and four underwater trails marked by ropes to follow a route of numbered artifacts in the submerged port built by King Herod 2,000 years ago. Half-hour introductory dives to a depth of 6 meters range from NIS 240 to NIS 350; another option is to explore the nocturnal marine life on a night dive. You must make diving reservations in advance. ✉ *Caesarea Harbor* ⊹ *Behind Time Trek* ☎ *04/626–5898* ⊕ *www.caesarea-diving.com.*

NETANYA

65 km (43 miles) south of Haifa, 30 km (18 miles) north of Tel Aviv.

The lively resort city of Netanya (literally, "gift of God") has a pretty seaside promenade along the cliffs, endless sandy beaches, a pleasant town square, and plenty of cafés and restaurants. Once a sleepy place surrounded by orange groves, the town—named after Jewish philanthropist Nathan Straus, co-owner of Macy's—has steadily grown from a few settlers in 1929 to some 210,000 residents today. Since the 1930s, it has been a center for the diamond-cutting industry. More recently Netanya has become known for its large immigrant population, most notably from France and the former Soviet Union.

Just south of the city are several nature reserves: the Iris Reserve, where purple irises flower in February and March; the Nahal Poleg Reserve, with fauna unique to the area; and the Udim Reserve, which includes a pool with turtles, fish, and birds.

Though citrus farming is still evident on Netanya's outskirts, there are few traces of small-town charm. Tracts of residential development since 2010 can be seen all along the southern approach to the city following the shoreline, with high-rise towers dotting the landscape. Vacationers from abroad have purchased many of the apartment units.

GETTING HERE AND AROUND

To get here by car from Tel Aviv or Haifa, take coastal Route 2. Trains from Haifa depart on the hour and take about 25 minutes. Egged buses from Haifa leave at least every 30 minutes and take one hour 40 minutes.

VISITOR INFORMATION

Contacts Netanya Tourist Information Office. ⊠ *12 Ha'atzmaut Sq.* ☎ *09/882-7286* ⊕ *www.gonetanya.com.*

EXPLORING

Ha'atzmaut Square. Benches sit among palm trees and surround a large fountain at this lively central square with open-air cafés and restaurants that are crowded from morning until late into the evening. Netanya attracts droves of French visitors, and in summer their lilting tones float above the café au lait and croissants. Saturday nights are often enlivened by folk dancing, and the amphitheater hosts free concerts in summer and an arts-and-crafts fair on Friday morning. ⊠ *Netanya.*

NEED A BREAK

Tony Ice Café. Cool off at this authentic gelateria, which scoops a huge array of flavors, all made by hand by a family of immigrants from Italy. Coffee, milk shakes, and pastries are also for sale. ⊠ *Ha'atzmaut Sq., 5 Herzl St.* ☎ *09/834-0406* ☉ *Closed Fri. evening and Sat. until sundown.*

FAMILY **Seaside Promenade.** Also known as "the boulevard," the seaside promenade extends north and south of the city for about 6 km (4 miles) with beautifully landscaped walkways that wind around the contours of the sandstone cliffs overlooking the sea; every angle affords a gorgeous view. It's dotted with pergola-shaded benches, wooden bridges, colorful playground areas, and waving palm trees. An elevator at the center of the promenade eases the climb up and down the seaside cliff. ⊠ *Netanya.*

WHERE TO EAT

$$$$
STEAKHOUSE

✕**El Gaucho.** Inside the Carmel Hotel, this is one of Israel's best kosher steak houses, part of a small chain. Decorated in a rustic style, the restaurant is dominated by a dramatic view of the sea. South American–style meat specialties, among them thick slabs of entrecôte steaks and veal *asado,* are cooked over embers on a giant grill. The kitchen also serves grilled sea bream and skewered chicken, and the wine list is extensive. Ⓢ *Average main: NIS 130* ✉ *Carmel Hotel, 2 Oved Ben Ami St.* ☎ *09/884–1264* ⊕ *www.elgaucho.co.il* ◔ *No dinner Fri. No lunch Sat.*

$$
MEDITERRANEAN

✕**Miriam's Grill.** A stone's throw from the main approach to the beach, the well-known Shipudei Miriam has a nice location facing a bubbling fountain. Moroccan-style grilled fish and lamb dishes are served both indoors and outdoors. Reward an appetite sharpened by sea breezes and splashes in the surf with appetizers like creamy hummus, tasty couscous, or shakshuka. Main dishes come with crispy fries or green salads, and wine and beer are available. Ⓢ *Average main: NIS 60* ✉ *11 Gad Maknes* ☎ *09/834–1376* ⊕ *http://62810590.rest.co.il* ◔ *No dinner Fri. No lunch Sat.*

$$$
FRENCH

✕**Mul Hayam.** Perched on a cliff overlooking the sea, this eatery has a wonderful view from every table. Seating is available in an outdoor plaza, with a pleasant sea breeze, or in the dining room with comfortable upholstered banquettes. Its menu has a French accent: trout amandine in butter and herbs, for example, and mushroom or spinach quiche. There's also an extensive wine menu. Ⓢ *Average main: NIS 80* ✉ *1 David HaMelech, Gan Hamelech* ☎ *09/884–5885* ⊕ *mulyam.rest. co.il* ◔ *No dinner Fri. No lunch Sat.*

$$$
SEAFOOD

✕**Rosemarine.** At this tiny seaside haven for fish lovers you can enjoy fresh and tasty fare indoors or on the terrace overlooking Netanya's famous promenade. The kitchen serves a wide range of excellent fish dishes, such as tilapia, cod, and gray mullet, grilled, baked, or sautéed. Entrées come with salad or roasted potatoes. Ⓢ *Average main: NIS 90* ✉ *8 Nitza Blvd.* ☎ *09/832–3322* ◔ *Closed Sat. No dinner Fri.*

WHERE TO STAY

$
HOTEL

▦ **Mizpe Yam.** Don't expect luxury at this family-owned five-story hotel; what you can count on is good value and a warm welcome. **Pros:** near the promenade and beach; nice rooftop sundeck. **Cons:** no sea views; no-frills decor. Ⓢ *Rooms from: $115* ✉ *1 Jabotinsky St.* ☎ *09/862–3730* ⊕ *www.mizpe-yam.co.il* ⇌ *35 rooms* ◍|*Breakfast.*

$$$
HOTEL

▦ **Seasons Netanya.** Consistently good service is the hallmark of this hotel with spacious guest rooms that have private terraces and sea views; the bathrooms are luxurious. **Pros:** free Wi-Fi; sea views. **Cons:** not for those seeking peace and quiet. Ⓢ *Rooms from: $350* ✉ *1 Nitza Blvd.* ☎ *09/860–1555* ⊕ *www.seasons.co.il* ⇌ *170 rooms* ◍|*Breakfast.*

During the Jewish holiday of Purim, revelers in Netanya and around the country dress up in costume.

SPORTS AND THE OUTDOORS
BEACHES

Showers, restrooms and changing rooms, lifeguards, and first-aid stations are available free at all of Netanya's beaches, which cover 14 km (8½ miles) of soft, sandy coastline. Most beaches rent beach chairs and umbrellas.

Beit Yanai. About 5 km (3 miles) north of Netanya is lovely Beit Yanai, named after ancient Judean king Alexander Yanai. Amenities include barbecue grills, picnic tables, restrooms with showers, and chair and umbrella rentals. There's a seafood restaurant right on the beach, and you can stroll along the Alexander Stream, shaded by eucalyptus trees. Parking is NIS 24 on weekdays and NIS 33 on Saturday. **Amenities:** food and drink; lifeguards; parking (fee); showers; toilets; water sports. **Best for:** walking; windsurfing. ⊠ *Rte. 2* ☎ *09/866–6230* ⎘ *Free.*

FAMILY **Herzl.** Netanya's most popular beach, Herzl, has a broad staircase that leads down to the waterfront. For fitness nuts there's a shaded exercise area with all sorts of equipment, volleyball nets, and a paved basketball court. You can rent kayaks and windsurfing gear in the summer. The beach is wheelchair accessible. There is also a café and two lifeguard stations. **Amenities:** food and drink; lifeguards; showers; toilets; water sports; parking (fee). **Best for:** swimming; windsurfing. ⊠ *Ha'atzmaut Square* ⎘ *Free.*

Mikhmoret. The beach at Mikhmoret, a tiny moshav 7½ km (4½ miles) north of Netanya, is popular with swimmers as well as those who laze away the day under umbrellas. The huge dirt parking lot, which charges per car, is 1 km (½ mile) after the turnoff from Route 2. There are three lifeguard stations, a restaurant, café, and chair and umbrella rentals. This is a backpacker favorite, and the Resort Hostel is on the beach. **Amenities:** food and drink; lifeguards; parking (fee); toilets; water sports. **Best for:** sunset; swimming. ⊠ *Netanya* 🔊 *Free.*

Sironit. This main beach is the largest stretch of sand on the Netanya coast. An elevator takes you down the sandstone cliff to this beach. There are two cafés and two drink kiosks with seating inside and out. Fridays are filled with salsa and folk dancing. The parking lot is on the beach, just south of Ha'atzmaut Square. Handicapped accessible, the beach has a paved road that allows wheelchairs and walkers access almost to the shoreline. The lifeguard stand has ultralight wheelchairs for use that can drive right into the water. **Amenities:** food and drink; lifeguards; parking (fee); showers; toilets; water sports. **Best for:** partiers; swimming. ⊠ *Gad Machness St.* 🔊 *Free.*

HORSEBACK RIDING

The Ranch (*Hachava*). In northern Netanya, The Ranch has horseback riding for NIS 120 per hour. It's necessary to reserve ahead for weekend trips or for sunset rides along the beach. ⊠ *Havatzelet Hasharon St., Neurim Beach* 🕾 *09/866–3525* ⊕ *www.the-ranch.co.il.*

PARAGLIDING

Netanya's cliffs make for exciting paragliding. Under the guidance of experienced instructors, you take off from a specially designed field along the promenade about half a mile south of the city center.

Dvir Paragliding. This established paragliding company leads thrilling adventures throughout the year, but the ideal time is from May to October. Make reservations at least two days in advance. The company offers different activities at two locations, both Netanya-based, depending on the time of year and the activity. ⊠ *Netanya* 🕾 *054/655–4466* ⊕ *dvirparagliding.co.il* 🔊 *NIS 190 for 10 mins; NIS 350 for 20 mins.*

Sky Paragliding School. Founded in 1998, the company arranges a one-time guided experience as well as two-day introductory courses. The onetime experience offers a 10–20 minute paragliding adventure in Netanya during the summer, and in northern Israel during the winter, for NIS 250–NIS 450. Call ahead to make reservations. ⊠ *Netanya* 🕾 *054/671–4440* ⊕ *www.paragliding.co.il.*

THE WINE COUNTRY AND MOUNT CARMEL

Wine has been produced in this fertile region for thousands of years. In the biblical book of Deuteronomy, the fruit of the vine was listed as one of the seven blessed species of fruit found in the land of Israel. The Sharon Plain near the Mediterranean coast south of Haifa, including the towns of Zichron Ya'akov and Benyamina, is the largest grape-growing area in Israel. Though the Rothschilds updated viniculture around Zichron Ya'akov in the 1880s, truly world-class wines began to appear only in the 1990s. After a tour of a winery, it's delightful to sit under the grapevines and sample the vintages along with fresh salad, warm bread, and good local cheese.

The Druze villages high in the Carmel serve traditional confections like *knafeh* and baklava as well as excellent olive oil and homemade *labaneh* (yogurt cheese). A meal in one of the towns isn't only a tasty experience, but also a warmly welcoming one.

Route 4, which runs north to south parallel to Route 2, is a more scenic drive, with Mount Carmel looming to the east beyond cultivated fields and banana plantations (though you may not see the bananas, as they're usually bagged in blue or gray plastic to protect them from bugs). The road leads through undulating countryside dotted with cypresses, palms, and vineyards.

In 2010, a forest fire—the most severe in Israel's history—raged for several days on Mount Carmel. The area damaged was estimated at about one-third of the entire forested area of the Carmel mountain range. As a result, you may notice bare swathes along the mountainside when traveling along Route 2 or Route 4. In the aftermath of the fire replanting was initiated, and many areas show bright-green new growth, along with the gradual natural regeneration of oak, pistachio, and pine trees.

EIN HOD

15 km (10 miles) south of Haifa, 5 km (3 miles) west of Isfiya.

Fodor's Choice ★ A charming village nestled in ancient olive groves on the western slope of Mount Carmel, Ein Hod is home to some 500 residents, most of them sculptors, painters, ceramicists, architects, jewelers, and other artists. The setting is an idyllic one, with rough-hewn stone houses built on the hillside and sweeping views down to the Mediterranean. The Dadaist painter Marcel Janco (1895–1984) wrote upon his first visit in 1950, "The beauty of the place was staggering."

Parking is across the road, opposite the entrance to the village. Climbing up the hill, you soon come to a winding street on the left that starts a lovely walk through the small village. Signs along the way indicate studios and workshops where artists paint, sculpt, and make jewelry, pottery, silkscreen prints, and clothing. You can continue straight to the town square, bordered by a restaurant and a large gallery where works by Ein Hod artists are exhibited.

GETTING HERE AND AROUND

Your best option is to get here by car via Route 4, because buses are few and far between. The village itself is small and quite walkable.

EXPLORING

Janco-Dada Museum. On the village square is this museum dedicated to the art and life of one of the founders of the Dada movement. The Romanian-born Marcel Janco had already established a considerable professional reputation by the time he moved here in 1941. The museum houses a permanent collection of the artist's work in various media, reflecting Janco's 70-year output both in Europe and Israel. A 20-minute slide show chronicles the life of the artist and the Dada movement, and the DadaLab offers hands-on activities for children.

Don't miss the view from the roof. ✉ *Ein Hod* ✛ *Near village square* ☎ *04/984–2350* ⊕ *www.jancodada.co.il* 🎫 *NIS 24.*

FAMILY

Fodor's Choice

★

Nahal Me'arot Nature Reserve. The prehistoric Carmel Caves, recognized in 2012 as a UNESCO World Heritage Site, are a highlight of this nature reserve, 3 km (2 miles) south of Ein Hod. They form a key site for the study of human evolution in general and the prehistory of the Levant in particular.

The three excavated caves are up a steep flight of stairs, on a fossil reef covered by the sea 100 million years ago. The first discoveries of prehistoric remains were made when this area was being scoured for stones to build the Haifa port. In the late 1920s, Dorothy Garrod of England headed the first archaeological expedition, receiving assistance from a British feminist group on the condition that only women carry out the dig.

In the Tannur cave, the first on the tour, the strata Garrod's team excavated are clearly marked, spanning about 150,000 years in the life of early humans. The most exciting discoveries were Homo sapiens and Neanderthal skeletons; evidence that raised fascinating questions about the relationship between the two and whether they lived side by side. A display on the daily life of early man as hunter and food gatherer occupies the Gamal cave. The last and largest cave, called the Nahal, cuts deep into the mountain and was the first discovered. A burial place with 84 skeletons was found outside the mouth of the cave along with stone tools, which suggest that people who settled here, about 12,000 years ago, were the forebears of early farmers, with a social structure more developed than that of hunters and gatherers. There is also evidence that the Crusaders once used the cave to guard the coastal road. There's a snack bar at this site. ✉ *Off Rte. 4* ☎ *04/984–1750* ⊕ *www. parks.org.il* 🎫 *NIS 22.*

FAMILY **Nisco Museum of Mechanical Music.** Nisan Cohen, a colorful and charming character who knows everything there is to know about old mechanical musical instruments, has amassed 150 music boxes, hand-operated automatic pianos, manivelles, antique gramophones on which to play his collection of old Yiddish records, and more antique musical marvels. Cohen is pleased to give you a guided tour and then treat you to a personal concert. His sense of humor and gift of the gab make for a touching and intriguing experience. Before the entrance to Ein Hod, watch for a brown wooden sign with yellow letters. ✉ *Off Rte. 7111* ☎ *052/475–5313* ⊕ *ein-hod.info/nisco* 🎫 *NIS 30.*

WHERE TO EAT

$

ISRAELI

✕ **Abu Yakov.** You reach Abu Yakov's by climbing the stone seats of Ein Hod's amphitheater. There are a few seats inside, but most people prefer outside in the blue plastic chairs beneath a ragged plastic tarp. It feels a bit makeshift, but the fresh food counts for everything. Dine on what locals often call "Oriental" (meaning Middle Eastern) food: hummus, fluffy pita bread, chopped vegetable salad, and grilled meat on skewers. Call ahead for oven-roasted lamb. Ⓢ *Average main: NIS 49* ✉ *Ein Hod* ✛ *Near village square* ☎ *04/984–3377* ▭ *No credit cards* ☾ *Closed Sun. No dinner.*

$ ✕ **Café Ein Hod.** Climb up the stairs beside the Doña Rosa restaurant
CAFÉ and keep an eye out for this local favorite: a two-level collection of mismatched chairs and odd tables, complete with cat sunning itself on a stool. Inside the old stone building, handmade clothes and handbags are for sale. You can sit outside to sip coffee and fruit smoothies alongside homemade *bourekas* (filled pastry triangles), shakshuka (eggs in tomato sauce), carrot cake, grilled cheese sandwiches, and apple pie. Beer and wine are available, too. Indian cuisine is served every Thursday night. From Thursday night through Sunday you can get vegetarian meals; the rest of the week, pastries and coffee are offered. ⑤ *Average main: NIS 35* ⊠ *Near village square* ☎ *054/667–6089* ☉ *Closed Mon.*

$$$ ✕ **Doña Rosa.** If you can't read the restaurant's sign in Hebrew, just
ARGENTINE follow the tantalizing aroma up the steps of this wooden building on the town square: Rosa's grandsons, Uri and Doron, import meat and special charcoal from Argentina and roast the food in the true Argentinean style. The bar is decorated with a drawing of a hefty cow that illustrates each cut of meat. Highlights include grilled pork spareribs; seafood simmered with fragrant yellow rice; and asado: delicious, chunky ribs (available only on Saturday). There's beer and Chilean and Argentinean wine, too. ⑤ *Average main: NIS 90* ⊠ *Near village square* ☎ *04/954–3777, 057/934–5520* ⊕ *doniarosa. rest.co.il* ☉ *Closed Sun.*

$ ✕ **Yanooki's Tavern.** The perfect place for a light meal and coffee, this
CAFÉ casual outdoor café with mismatched chairs and tables is next to the post office in the town center, making it also a good spot to people-watch. Enjoy homemade quiche or a Greek salad, or relax with a glass of wine or cup of coffee. Occasionally there's live music. ⑤ *Average main: NIS 45* ⊠ *Ein Hod* ✛ *Past post office in town center* ☉ *No dinner* ▭ *No credit cards.*

WHERE TO STAY

$ ⛺ **B&B Batia & Claude.** Batia's and Claude's bed-and-breakfast is quiet
B&B/INN and private, hidden behind masses of hot pink bougainvillea. **Pros:** pretty, private building; fun shop. **Cons:** often gets booked well in advance; breakfast not included. ⑤ *Rooms from: $120* ⊠ *Ein Hod* ✛ *Second (east) entrance to Ein Hod* ☎ *04/984–1648* ⊕ *www.eisen-wasser-jancourt.co.il* ⤵ *2 rooms* ◯║ *No meals.*

$ ⛺ **Yakir Ein Hod.** If you'd enjoy a dip in a pool ringed by olive trees while
B&B/INN you gaze at the blue Mediterranean, consider this delightful lodging. **Pros:** quiet location; private pool; lovely sea views. **Cons:** minimum stay required on weekends. ⑤ *Rooms from: $190* ⊠ *Ein Hod* ✛ *Second (east) entrance to Ein Hod* ☎ *050/554–3982* ⊕ *www.yakireinhod.co.il* ⤵ *3 suites* ◯║ *No meals.*

SHOPPING

Many of the artists living in the winding lanes of Ein Hod throw open their workshops to visitors, who are welcome to browse and buy. Between the olive trees and behind painted gates, look for signs on homes that indicate the sale of art and crafts from jewelry to artistic photography. Either start at the entrance to the village where signs point to the left or head for the village square straight ahead.

Art & Wear Gallery. Owners Dan and Lea Ben-Arye have lived and worked in Ein Hod for more than three decades, creating and selling their art. Their gallery features paintings, sculptures, jewelry, Judaica, and wearable art. They act as village ambassadors, running an information center from their shop. Private workshops can be arranged ahead of time with Lea. ⊠ *Ein Hod* ✛ *Across from Janco-Dada Museum* ☎ *054/481–1968.*

Central Gallery. The Ein Hod Central Gallery, an integral part of the artistic community here since 1953, carries a wide selection of handicrafts and art by resident artists at its space on the main square. Displayed in the front room are ceramics, enamel, and silver and gold jewelry, while through the arch into another room are paintings, sculptures, and graphic works. ⊠ *Ein Hod* ☎ *04/984–2548* ⊕ *www.ein-hod.org/ en/maingallery.asp* ☉ *Closed Mon.*

Silver Print. This lovely little studio holds Vivienne Silver-Brody's collection of vintage works by Israel's best photographers. The emphasis is on the building of the State of Israel. There's also a wide range of 19th-century photos of the Holy Land. A digital print costs NIS 150. Call or email for hours and the address. ⊠ *Ein Hod* ☎ *04/954–1673* ✉ *vivroy@netvision.net.il* ⊕ *www.viviennesilver-brody.com.*

DALIYAT EL CARMEL AND ISFIYA

5 km (3 miles) east of Daliyat el Carmel and Isfiya, 16 km (11 miles) south of Haifa.

Daliyat el Carmel (Vine of the Carmel) is Israel's largest Druze village, and its weekend market, oil press, and *hilweh* (house of worship) are worth exploring. Though most of the younger generation wears jeans and T-shirts, older people tend to wear traditional garb. Head coverings indicate the degree of religious belief, from the high white turban resembling a fez to the white kerchief covering the head and shoulders. Many men sport a bushy moustache, a hallmark of the Druze, and some older ones wear dark robes and black pantaloons.

Very similar to neighboring Daliyat el Carmel, Isfiya is a village of flat-roof homes built closely together into the hillside, many of them raised on pillars and cut with arched windows. It stands on the remains of a Jewish village dating back to Roman times. Hospitality is second nature to the Druze here; you may be able to visit a village home and eat pita bread with yogurt cheese and spices while hearing about Druze life. The village is about 1 km (½ mile) from Daliyat el Carmel.

GETTING HERE AND AROUND
Coming from Haifa, drive south on Route 672.

TOURS
House of Druze Hospitality. To really get to know Isfiya and the Druze, arrange a tour through this company. Your guide will take you to visit their place of prayer, an olive oil press, and then to a private home where the matriarch bakes pita bread in a *tabun* (oven). You'll hear about the distinctive Druze way of life. Tours are available every

CLOSE UP

The Druze

The Druze are an Arabic-speaking minority whose remarkable cohesion and esoteric faith have enabled them to maintain their close-knit identity through almost a thousand years of turbulent history. In Israel, they number about 130,000 and live in 17 villages in the Carmel, the Galilee, and Golan Heights. Larger kindred communities exist in Syria and Lebanon.

So exclusive is this sect that only a fraction of the community is initiated into its religious doctrine, one tenet of which is a belief in continuous reincarnation. The Druze broke away from Islam about 1,000 years ago, incorporating other traditions and also believing in the divinity of their founder, al-Hākim bi-Amr Allāh, the Caliph of the Egyptian Fatimid dynasty from AD 996 to 1021. They don't permit gambling or the use of alcohol.

The Druze who live in the two existing villages on Mount Carmel (Daliyat el Carmel and Isfiya) serve in the Israeli army, a mark of their loyalty to Israel.

day except Saturday, but make reservations at least a week ahead of time. The price is NIS 120 per person. ⊠ *Isfiya* ☎ *04/839–0125* 🖾 *NIS 120.*

EXPLORING

Daliyat el Carmel Marketplace. About 1 km (½ mile) inside town, take a right turn into the marketplace, a colorful jumble of shops lining the street. You can be assured of finding excellent falafel and fresh produce at any of the roadside stands or restaurants. ⊠ *Daliyat el Carmel* ⊙ *Closed Sun.*

WHERE TO EAT

$$ ✕ **Halabi Brothers.** At this storefront eatery, brothers Fouad and Ahmad
MIDDLE EASTERN Halabi greet you with a handshake and a "Hello, my cousin!" The delicious falafel and shawarma are wrapped in thin, lightly browned Druze-style pitas, a nice change from the fluffy ones served at most other places in the country. A refreshing splash of lemon tops the platter of salads. Watch everything being prepared in the glass-front kitchen that opens onto a series of tile-floor dining rooms. The adjoining gift shop, also run by the siblings, displays locally woven tablecloths and pillowcases. ⑤ *Average main: NIS 50* ⊠ *14 Commercial Center St., Daliyat el Carmel* ☎ *04/839–3576.*

$$ ✕ **House of Druze Heritage.** Dine à la Druze on skewers of grilled lamb or
MIDDLE EASTERN steak and big, flat pita bread. Plenty of salads will be on your table, and you'll get a warm welcome from Fadal, the congenial owner. Baklava and Turkish coffee provide the finishing touches. The Druze are justly famous for their hospitality. This house formerly belonged to the British traveler and diplomat Laurence Oliphant. Order a tour in advance for NIS 20, and Fadal will explain the Druze way of life and demonstrate Druze farm implements, household objects, and handicrafts. ⑤ *Average main: NIS 75* ⊠ *4 Ahat St., Daliyat el Carmel* ☎ *04/839–3242.*

$$ ✕ **Nof HaCarmel.** People come from all over the Carmel for the fine
MIDDLE EASTERN Middle Eastern fare at this excellent Druze restaurant, especially the homemade hummus with pine nuts, olive oil, garlic, and lemon juice,

and the well-seasoned kebabs on skewers. Those with a sweet tooth should sample the *sahlab* (a warm, custardlike pudding of crushed orchid bulb with thickened milk and sugar). To find this place, drive to the northern edge of the village. The eatery is on your left; look for a few tables outside under the trees. $ *Average main: NIS 70* ⊠ *Rte. 672, Isfiya* ☏ *04/839–1718.*

SHOPPING

Along a brief stretch of the main road that winds through Daliyat el Carmel are shops selling lightweight throw rugs, handwoven baskets, brightly colored pottery, brass dishes, characteristic woven wall hangings, and embroidered skullcaps worn by men. Bargaining is expected. Some shops close on Friday; the strip is crowded on Saturday.

MUKHRAKA

18 km (12 miles) south of Haifa, 2 km (1 mile) west of Daliyat el Carmel.

You can't miss Mukhraka, a site on the southeastern peak of Mount Carmel that is marked by a tall white statue of Elijah the Prophet with his sword raised on high. Just beyond is the graceful Carmelite monastery with a sweeping rooftop view of the Jezreel Valley. The site has well-marked hiking trails.

GETTING HERE AND AROUND

Mukhraka is an interesting stop if you're on the way to Isfiya and Daliyat el Carmel on Route 70. It's not accessible for those without a car.

EXPLORING

Carmelite Monastery. Past open, uncultivated fields and a goatherd's rickety shack, Mukhraka's Carmelite monastery stands on the spur of the Carmel range, at an altitude of 1,580 feet, on the site where the struggle between the prophet Elijah and the priests of Ba'al is believed to have taken place. Climb to the roof for an unforgettable panorama: to the east stretches the Jezreel Valley and the hills of Nazareth, Moreh, and Gilboa. On a clear day, you can even see Jordan's Gilead Mountains beyond the Jordan River and Mount Hermon. The stark stone monastery was built in 1883 over Byzantine ruins. There's a small gift shop in the monastery, but no place to buy drinks or snacks.

Mukhraka is the Arabic word for a place of burning, referring to the fire that consumed the offering on Elijah's altar. The conflict developed because the people of Israel had been seduced by the pagan cults introduced by King Ahab's wife, Jezebel. Elijah demanded a contest with the priests of Ba'al in which each would erect an altar with a butchered ox as an offering and see which divinity sent down fire. Elijah drenched his altar with water, yet it burst into flames. On his orders, the pagan priests were taken down to the Kishon ravine and slain, an event depicted by the impressive statue of Elijah inscribed in Hebrew, Arabic, and Latin. ⊠ *Off Rte. 672* ⊕ *www.muhraqa.org* ☏ *Free.*

Continued on page 318

In a land where grapes have been grown and enjoyed since biblical times, a modern winemaking revolution has taken hold. Whether the vintage is from big producers or boutique up-and-comers, the improved quality of Israeli wine has catapulted all things oenological into the spotlight. This tiny country is now home to over 250 wineries large and small. It was Baron Edmond de Rothschild—the proprietor of France's prestigious Château Lafite winery and an early Zionist—who jumpstarted the modern Israeli wine industry by providing money to found wineries in the 1880s. After a few false starts, Carmel Mizrachi, which his funds helped support, flourished; to this day it is Israel's most prolific wine producer.

by Adeena Sussman

(top) Ancient floor mosaic depicting wine vase at Eretz Israel Museum, Tel Aviv. (right) Golan Heights Winery

The
Wines
of
Israel

WINEMAKING IN ISRAEL

(top left) Winemaking barrel shop in Zichron Ya'akov, 1890s. (bottom left) Golan Heights Winery. (right) Wine fair in Tel Aviv.

Israel manufactured mostly mediocre wines until the late 1970s, when the first *moshavim* and *kibbutzim* (living cooperatives) planted vines in the Golan Heights on the advice of scientists from California, who saw a grape-growing diamond in the rough amid the mountain ranges of this northern region. Soon thereafter Golan Heights Winery was born, and awards and accolades were uncorked almost immediately.

GROWTH AND CHALLENGE

Besides two dozen or so larger operations, more than 250 smaller wineries now operate, many less than 15 years old and some producing just a few thousand bottles per year. Five large wineries account for 75 percent of production. Winemaking is a relatively young industry, sparked by a new crop of winemakers with experience at outstanding wineries. Though top wine writers have given some Israeli wines high marks, confirming internationally that these are vintages worth seeking out, there is still room for improvement in the ongoing, so-called "quality revolution."

Per capita wine consumption in Israel has nearly doubled since the late 1990s but remains low. A culture of wine appreciation is gradually fomenting, although the lion's share of bottles are exported to the United States and Europe. Despite challenges, winemakers continue to experiment: up-and-coming regions include the Judean Hills outside Jerusalem and even the Negev desert.

KOSHER & MEVUSHAL: MESSAGE ON A BOTTLE

For a wine to be certified kosher, as many Israeli wines are, a religious supervisor must oversee the process to ensure that no non-kosher tools or ingredients are used. Only rigorously observant Jews can handle equipment. Critics agree that these regulations don't affect the quality of wine. *Mevushal* wines, with more stringent kosher requirements, are flash-pasteurized, and then rapidly chilled; this can affect quality. However, many top-tier Israeli wines today are non-Mevushal, or are unsupervised altogether.

WINE REGIONS AND GRAPES

Sea Horse winery

GRAPE EXPECTATIONS

After commercial vines were first planted in the 19th century, Israeli winemakers focused on a small group of grape varietals that seemed to take well to Israeli terrain. The country has no indigenous grapes. With the help of technology, experience, and trial and error, a wide range of grapes are now raised with success.

Some of Israel's red wines are world-class, notably those that blend Cabernet Sauvignon grapes with Merlot, Cabernet Franc, and Petit Verdot. Chardonnays also do well here—the warm days and cool nights of the northern region seem particularly advantageous for this varietal.

Winemakers consistently push the envelope, introducing exciting new wines into the market. Two recent examples? Viognier, which has been one of the darlings of the current Israeli wine market, and Syrah, a grape that flourishes amid the country's hot days and cool, breezy nights.

Israel's wine-growing areas are typically divided into five regions, although no official, European-style government-regulated classification system exists. Since the country is so small—about the size of New Jersey—grapes are often shared among the regions. This is especially true of the northern plains, which provide grapes to many of the country's best wineries. Still, each area is geographically unique.

GALILEE Actually two regions, this area covers a lot of geographical ground in the north. The Galilee is a rocky area, and the Golan Heights, which borders Syria, sees winter snowfall at its highest altitudes. With cool climes and rich soil, the Galilee and Golan claim bragging rights as home to many of the country's premier grapes.

SHOMRON/CARMEL The advantageous growing conditions of the lush Carmel Mountains make this coastal plain south of Haifa the most prolific grape-growing region in Israel, if not the most prestigious. The climate and soil variety make it the most traditionally Mediterranean of the regions.

SAMSON/CENTRAL COAST Situated west of Jerusalem and stretching north toward Tel Aviv and south toward Ashkelon, this region has hot, humid summers and mellow winters that make for good growing conditions. If you're in Tel Aviv, this is an easy region for accessing great wineries.

JUDEAN HILLS In 2000, barely a winery or tasting room existed here, though ancient winemaking equipment has been unearthed. Thin limey or rocky soil, sunny days, and breezy nights have helped this region's wines shine. With its winding roads, and lush, shallow mountainsides, the region west and south of Jerusalem is day-trip perfect from Jerusalem and Tel Aviv.

THE NEGEV Thanks to drip-irrigation technology and an influx of talented winemakers, grapes are thriving in the desert. Since there are relatively few wineries in the southern part of the Negev, they're best included in a trip to Eilat or Mitzpe Ramon; call to schedule a visit.

Clos de Gat Winery in the Judean Hills

5

IN FOCUS THE WINES OF ISRAEL

WINE TOURING AND TASTING

Visiting wineries in Israel can require a different approach from touring vineyards in California, and your touring strategy may depend on the size of the winery.

Most of the **bigger players,** including Golan Heights, Carmel, and Barkan/Segal, offer tasting rooms. You can simply stop by and visit to sample and purchase wines, though generally it's good to call in advance if you want to include a winery tour. Many **medium- and smaller-sized wineries** are often happy to accommodate visitors, but always call ahead to ensure that English-speaking staff will be on hand and to confirm hours.

Many **boutique** wineries welcome tourists, but some of the best aren't equipped for a regular onslaught of visitors. While you can call yourself, this is where private tour guides come in handy. Often, these individuals have the connections to get you inside wineries you'd otherwise never see—not to mention the knowledge of the back roads in some of the harder-to-find locales.

PICK OF THE VINEYARDS
These wineries either have open tasting rooms, or visits can be arranged with an advance phone call. Note: most kosher wineries are open only a half-day on Friday, and are closed on Saturdays and Jewish holidays. Small tastes are usually free, but expect to pay $10 or more per person for a guided tasting of three to five wines at most wineries.

Carmel Winery

GALILEE
❶ Golan Heights Winery Still the standard bearer for Israeli wines, this large producer has a welcoming visitor center and tours. Wines are made under the Yarden, Gamla, and Golan labels. Kosher. *Try: Single-vineyard Odem Organic Chardonnay; Yarden Syrah.* ✉ Derech Ha'Yayin St., Katzrin ☎ 04/696–8435 ⊕ www.golanwines.co.il

❷ Lotem Winery One of Israel's two organic wineries offers tours and tapas near the Sea of Galilee. Call in advance. Not kosher. Try Rosé, Cabernet Franc-Merlot blend, Nebbiolo. ⊠Kibbuts Lotem, off Rte. 804, Lotem ☎054/791–5868 www.lotemwinery.co.il.

❸ Galil Mountain Winery A sleek, modern low-lying stone-and-wood build-

WINES IN RESTAURANTS AND SHOPS

Look for vintages from these superior regional producers in restaurants or shops in Israel.
Galilee: Golan Heights, Pelter and Chateau Golan in the Golan; Dal-
Clos de Gat

ton and Galil Mountain in the Galilee
Shomron/Carmel: Recanati, Margalit, Amphorae
Samson/Central Coast: Carmel, Barkan, Soreq

Judean Hills: Sea Horse, Domaine du Castel, Clos de Gat
The Negev: Yatir, La Terra Promessa, Rota, Kadesh Barnea

Galil Mountain

ing offers views of the vineyards and the winemaking facilities. These are great-value wines for the money. Kosher. *Try: Fruity, mineral-tinged Sauvignon Blanc.* ✉ Kibbutz Yiron, off Rte 899, Merom, ☎ 04/686–8748 ⊕ www.galilmountain. co.il.

4 Tabor Winery Set amid almond groves near Mount Tabor in the Galilee, this intimate visitor center offers tastings and tours, in a lovely setting. Kosher. *Robust single-vineyard limited edition Cabernet Sauvignon.* ✉ Kfar Tavor, ☎ 04/676–0444 ⊕ www.twc.co.il/en

SHOMRON/ CARMEL

5 Tishbi Winery The vistor center at this fourth-generation winery offers a special chocolate and wine tasting. Kosher. *Try: Woodsy, berry-rich Pinot Noir.* ✉ Rte. 652, Benyamina, Zichron Ya'akov ☎ 04/638–0434 ⊕ www.tishbi. com/en

6 Amphorae Winery This boutique winery nar Zichon Ya akov is set in a series of rustic, Tuscan-style stone build-

ings. Call in advance to arrange a visit. Not kosher. *Try: Balanced, full-bodied Cabernet Sauvignon.* ✉ Makura Farm, Kerem Maharal ☎ 04/984–0702 ⊕ www.amphoraewines. com.

7 Carmel Winery The Center for Wine Culture at the country's largest winery offers a restaurant, a tour encompassing Israel's viticultural history, several tasting options, and a visit to a historic wine cellar built by founder Baron Edmond de Rothschild.

JUDEAN HILLS

8 Ella Valley Vineyards Domaine du Costel This family-run winery produces some of Israel's finest wines. Call for a tour and wime and cheese tasting. ERte. 4115, Yad Hasmona P02/534–2449 wwww. castel.co.il

9 Flam Winery Two dynamic brothers, the sons of a former chief winemaker for Carmel Mizrachi, run this well-regarded producer. Call to arrange a cheese and wine tasting. *Try: Woodsy, berry-rich Flam Reserve Merlot.* ✉ Eshtal Junction, Ya'ar Ha'kodshim ☎ 02/992–9923 ⊕ www.flamwinery. com.

Mediterranean Sea

Haifa

3 GOLAN HEIGHTS
1
2
GALILEE
4

6 5 7

SHOMRON/ CARMEL

Tel Aviv

Jerusalem
SAMSON/ CENTRAL **8**
COAST **9**
JUDEAN
GAZA HILLS

10
Beersheva

THE NEGEV

THE NEGEV

10 Yatir Winery Generating great excitement, Yatir is a desert gem with promise. Call in advance. Kosher. *Try: Yatir Forest, whose grape blend varies from year to year; fruity, light Viognier.* ✉ Off Rte. 80, Tel Arad ☎ 052/830–8196

Yatir Winery

⊕ www.yatircoinery. com/en

ZICHRON YA'AKOV

25 km (15 miles) southwest of Mukhraka, 35 km (22 miles) south of Haifa, 61 km (40 miles) north of Tel Aviv.

Fodor's Choice
★

Zichron Ya'akov, the country's first moshava, or cooperative farming community, was founded in 1882 with the help of Baron Edmond de Rothschild. From the beginning, it centered on its vineyards and large winery. A visit to the charming town should start on its main street, Hameyasdim, a cobblestone pedestrian mall lined with small, restored, red-roofed, 19th-century homes. Pick up a town map in the tourist office at the entrance to the town.

GETTING HERE AND AROUND

If driving from Haifa or Tel Aviv, take Route 2 to the Zichron Ya'akov exit. Buses run from Haifa and Tel Aviv.

VISITOR INFORMATION

Contacts **Zichron Ya'akov Tourist Office.** ✉ *HaMeyasdim St.* ✛ *Southern entrance to town, opposite cemetery* ☎ *04/639–8811.*

EXPLORING

TOP ATTRACTIONS

Amphorae Wines. The setting of one of Israel's leading boutique wineries, in a pastoral landscape overlooking the forests of the Carmel Mountains, couldn't be prettier. Call ahead to tour the winery, see the demonstration vineyard, and learn about these attention-getting wines. For your tasting, select a flight of three to five wines: the reds, including blends, are notable. Order a generous tasting platter of bread and fine cheeses (extra charge) to accompany them. ✉ *Makura Farm, Off Rte. 7021, Kerem Maharal* ✛ *14 km (9 miles) north of Zichron Ya'akov via Rte. 4* ☎ *04/984–0702* ⊕ *www.amphoraewines.com* ✉ *Tour and tasting of 5 wines NIS 100.*

Fodor's Choice
★

Carmel Winery. Rare among Israel's many wineries are Carmel Winery's underground vaulted-ceiling wine cellars. Dating from 1892, the huge, old, and chilly rooms are a contrast to the state-of-the art facility aboveground, where top wines are produced. Founder Baron Edmond de Rothschild, owner of France's famous Château Lafite, would be pleased at the success of his viniculture venture, now the country's largest winery. At the Center for Wine Culture, a guided 45-minute tour outlines the stages of local wine production. Included in the tour are a tasting of some four varieties and a seven-minute audiovisual presentation screened in the original wine cellar. Tours depart between 9 and 4 and must be reserved in advance. Other wine tastings and workshops are also available by reservation. ✉ *2 Yekev Way* ☎ *04/639–1788* ⊕ *www.carmelwines.co.il* ✉ *NIS 30 tour* ⊘ *Closed Sat.*

FAMILY

Ramat Hanadiv. In the hills near Zichron Ya'akov, this sprawling garden is a fitting tribute to Baron Edmond de Rothschild. (*Hanadiv* means "the benefactor.") At its center is the dignified tomb where Rothschild and his wife Ada lie buried. A 20-minute film in the welcoming Visitors Pavilion tells of his legacy in Israel: the last screening on weekdays is at 3:30. Outside, curving paths framed rolling green lawns, abundant patches of flowers, carob trees, waving palms, and 42 rare plant species. Clearly marked trails lead to a 2,000-year old Roman farmhouse and a hidden spring. After all that legwork, the terraces of the on-site café beckon. A children's playground is set off to one side. ⊠ *Rte. 652 ✛ Southern end of Mount Carmel, south of Zichron Ya'akov* ☎ *04/629–8111* ⊕ *www.ramat-hanadiv.org.il* ⊡ *Free.*

WORTH NOTING

Beit Aaronson (*Aaronson House*). About halfway down Hameyasdim Street is Beit Aaronson, whose late-19th-century architecture successfully combines art nouveau and Middle Eastern traditions. This museum was once the home of the agronomist Aaron Aaronson (1876–1919), who gained international fame for his discovery of an ancestor of modern wheat. The house remains as it looked after World War I, with family photographs and French and Turkish furniture, as well as Aaronson's library, diaries, and letters. Aaronson and his two sisters became local heroes as leaders of an underground group called NILI, dedicated to ousting the Turks from Palestine. A tour in English is provided; the last one takes place at 1:30. You must reserve ahead by phone or online. Credit cards aren't accepted, and children under five are not permitted in the museum. ⊠ *40 Hameyasdim St.* ☎ *04/639–0120* ⊕ *www.nili-museum.org.il* ⊡ *NIS 26* ⊘ *Closed Fri. and Sat.*

Binyamin Pool. The name of this site is a misnomer because it's actually the town's original water tower, built in 1891. Zichron Ya'akov was the first village in Israel to have water piped to its houses; Meir Dizengoff, the first mayor of Tel Aviv, came here to see how it was done. The facade, with its inscription honoring Baron de Rothschild, resembles that of an ancient synagogue. ⊠ *Hameyasdim St.* ✛ *Near Beit Aaronson.*

First Aliya Museum. The museum is dedicated to the lives of the 30,000 immigrants who came to Palestine with the First Aliya (a period of settlement from 1882 until 1904). Life-size model displays of local immigrants (like Zachariya, the seed vendor, and Izer, the cobbler) illustrate life at that time. A film traces the struggles of a family who came from Europe in this difficult period of Israel's modern history. Commissioned by Baron Edmond de Rothschild, the museum's three-floor building is a fine example of late-19th-century Ottoman-style architecture, built of white stone with a central pediment capped by a tile roof. During World War I, the Turks used it as a military hospital. ⊠ *2 Hanadiv St.* ☎ *04/629–4777* ⊡ *NIS 20* ⊘ *Closed weekends.*

Ohel Ya'akov. On a prominent corner stands the old synagogue, Ohel Ya'akov, built by Baron de Rothschild in 1886 to serve immigrants from Romania. It's only occasionally open to visitors, but worth strolling by. ⊠ *Hameyasdim St. and Hanadiv St.*

WHERE TO EAT

$$$
ITALIAN
✕ **Cucina.** Pots of geraniums and rosemary and lavender bushes grace the entrance of this charming, eclectic eatery with a sophisticated Italian and Mediterranean menu. The original settlers peer out sternly from photos on the vanilla-colored walls, and a wood stove in the middle keeps the restored 19th-century space cozy. The chef's lemon-cured salmon with cucumber dressing merits mention, as does the goat-cheese

souffle and roasted eggplant with tomatoes and mint leaves. Each makes a fine introduction to main courses such as seafood pasta in white wine and wild herbs and lemony chicken breast with capers. For dessert, try the phyllo leaves filled with crème anglaise and seasonal fresh fruit. $ *Average main: NIS 76* ⊠ *41 Hameyasdim St.* ☎ *04/629–0249* ⊕ *cucina.rest.co.il/.*

$$$
MEDITERRANEAN

✕ **Kashtunyo Wine Cellar.** This restaurant in a 140-year-old underground wine cellar is an auspicious place to hear about the extensive wine list from owner Amos Meroz, whose hat always rakishly tilts to one side. Eight tables covered with checkered cloths fill a small space defined by curving stone walls. Dishes of olives glisten on a tiny wooden bar in the dimly lit room. Scores of wine bottles line the back wall with vintages from Israel, Italy, Australia, California, France, and South Africa. You can enjoy cheese and stuffed grape leaves or just sit quietly with your glass while French songs fill the air. More substantial lunch and dinner dishes of entrecôte, selections of cold meats, or cheese platters go nicely with a handpicked glass of wine. $ *Average main: NIS 100* ⊠ *56 Hameyasdim St.* ☎ *04/629–1244.*

$$$
MODERN ISRAELI

✕ **Oratorio.** Whether you're at the Elma Arts Complex for a performance or simply for the spectacular views of the Mediterranean, Oratorio satisfies with fine dining in a magnificent setting. The modern dining room provides gallery space for interesting, thought-provoking art from Israel and around the world. Try the oven-roasted sea bass with tomato salsa, or any of the excellent grilled fish or meats; the produce is locally sourced. Pair your meal with excellent wine from area vineyards. $ *Average main: NIS 100* ⊠ *Elma Arts Complex Luxury Hotel, 1 Yair St.* ☎ *04/630–0110* ⊕ *www.elma-hotel.com.*

WHERE TO STAY

$$$
HOTEL
Fodor'sChoice
★

🛏 **Elma Arts Complex Luxury Hotel.** You would be forgiven if you thought this hotel was newly built: with its exposed cement, clean white lines, and natural walnut furnishings, the modern design from 1973 has been renovated into a striking hotel and world-class center for the arts. **Pros:** breathtaking views; historically significant building; world-class art collection. **Cons:** standard rooms are quite small; difficult to reach without a car. $ *Rooms from: $325* ⊠ *1 Yair St.* ☎ *04 /630–0123* ⊕ *elmahotel. co.il* ➲ *95 rooms* ⊗ *Breakfast.*

$
HOTEL

🛏 **Hotel Beit Maimon.** On the western slopes of Zichron Ya'akov, a 10-minute walk from the center of town, this family-run hotel has a spectacular view of the coastal valley and the sea. **Pros:** delicious Israeli breakfast is included; superb views. **Cons:** lots of steps to climb; old-fashioned. $ *Rooms from: $150* ⊠ *4 Zahal St.* ☎ *04/629–0390* ⊕ *www. maimon.com* ➲ *25 rooms* ⊗ *Breakfast.*

BENYAMINA

5 km (3 miles) south of Zichron Ya'akov, 40 km (25 miles) south of Haifa, 55 km (34 miles) north of Tel Aviv.

Picturesque Benyamina, the youngest settlement in the area, was founded in 1922 and has several wineries. It was named after Baron Edmond de Rothschild, the head of the French branch of the famous family, who took a keen interest in the welfare of his fellow Jews in Palestine. (His Hebrew name was Benyamin.)

GETTING HERE AND AROUND

You can easily reach Benyamina by train. If you're driving, take Route 4. Either option makes for a very pretty ride. Once you're here, you need a car to get around because public transport is uneven.

EXPLORING

Binyamina Winery. The large visitor center at the country's fourth-largest winery is housed in a former perfume factory built by Baron de Rothschild in 1925. It hasn't changed as much as you'd think, as cosmetics made from grape seeds are some of the products for sale here. You can also find olive oil, vinegar, and, yes, wine. The production facilities are next door in buildings surrounded by towering palm trees. Reservations are required for the 45-minute tour of the winery and barrel rooms, including a sampling of four or five wines. You can do your tasting while having lunch or dinner in the restaurant, once an orange-packing facility. Or, you can simply drop in for coffee and cake. ⊠ *1 HaYekev St.* ☎ *04/610–7535* ⊕ *www.binyaminawines.com* ✉ *Tour and tasting NIS 25* ⊘ *Closed Sat.*

Tishbi Estate Winery. Set among the hills and valleys of this pastoral area is one of the country's most esteemed wineries and premier labels, Tishbi Estate: the Sauvignon Blanc and Chardonnay are among the best in Israel. The vines were planted here 120 years ago. At the country-style visitor center, you can pair a French Valrhona chocolate with a Tishbi wine, or enjoy breakfast, brunch, or lunch under the grapevines in the courtyard. Apart from wine, you can purchase local cheeses, olive oil, honey, and wine jellies at the shop. Call ahead to arrange a one-hour tour, which includes tastings and a visit to the old alembic distillery, where their prized brandy is made. It's about 3 km (1½ miles) north of Benyamina. ⊠ *Rte. 652, Benyamina Industrial Area* ☎ *04/638–0434* ⊕ *www.tishbi.com* ✉ *Tour and tasting NIS 15* ⊘ *Closed Sat.*

AKKO AND THE FAR NORTHERN COAST

One of the oldest and most entrancing port cities in the world, Akko's rampart-ringed Old City encloses an 18th-century mosque, underground Crusader halls, an extraordinary tunnel, and winding lanes through a bazaar to restaurants at the water's edge. North of Akko, wide beaches, two of them within nature reserves, follow one after the other up the coast. The moshavim and kibbutzim (cooperative agricultural settlements) are unique settings for gourmet restaurants and upscale bed-and-breakfasts. Rosh Hanikra, at the top of the northern coast, has a cable car that carries you down a 210-foot cliff to caves hollowed out by wildly crashing waves.

CLOSE UP

Akko's History

History clings to the stones in the Old City of Akko, which bear the marks of the many civilizations that have inhabited and built it. The city's history began 4,000 years ago, when Akko was first mentioned in Egyptian writings that refer to the mound northeast of its walls. The Old Testament describes in Judges 1 how after the death of Joshua, the tribe of Asher was unable to drive the Canaanites from Akko, so they lived among them.

With its well-protected harbor, fertile hinterland, and strategic position, Akko has always proved worth fighting for. Alexander the Great had such regard for Akko that he set up a mint here. Akko was Phoenician for long periods, but the Hellenistic King Ptolemy II gained control in the 2nd century BC and renamed it Ptolemais.

King Baldwin I led the Crusaders who conquered Akko in 1104, and the port city was the Crusaders' principal link to home. Commerce thrived, and the European maritime powers—Genoa, Pisa, Venice, and Marseilles—developed separate quarters here. After the disastrous defeat of the Crusader armies in 1187, Akko surrendered to Saladin, but Richard the Lionheart soon recaptured the European stronghold. In its Crusader heyday, Akko had about 40 churches and monasteries and a population of 50,000.

In the 13th century, after the conquest of Jerusalem by the Muslims, Akko became the effective capital of a shrunken Latin kingdom; it fell to the Mamluks in 1291 and lay in ruins for centuries. In 1749 Dahr el-Omar, the Bedouin sheikh, moved his capital from Tiberias to Akko and rebuilt the walls of the city.

Napoléon's attempt to conquer the city in 1799 was repulsed, but the British captured it in 1918. With the founding of the State of Israel in 1948, many Arab inhabitants left Akko, though a good number remain. Akko's population now numbers about 46,000, with people living inside the Old City itself and in new developments pushing the city limits to the north.

AKKO

22 km (13½ miles) north of Haifa.

Fodor's Choice ★ The Old City of Akko, a UNESCO World Heritage Site, is an enchanting mix of mosques, markets, and vaulted Crusader ruins (many of them underground). A walk through the cobbled alleys and outdoor market stalls brings you to a small port filled with fishing boats. Views from the surrounding ramparts are some of the country's best. On the way, sample fresh halvah, nougat-filled pralines, whole-wheat pita, or homemade *kibbeh* (a ground lamb and bulgur wheat dish), a specialty of the city's small Greek Orthodox community.

To reach the historic parts of Akko, you'll be driving through a modern city: a bustling metropolis of about 46,000. It's rather plain, so reserve judgment until you've seen the Old City.

GETTING HERE AND AROUND

From Haifa, you can get here via Route 4. A much slower but far prettier inland route takes you north on Route 70, passing through rolling hills and avoiding the drab satellite towns north of Haifa. There are direct buses from Haifa, and trains from Jerusalem and Tel Aviv (you may have to change trains). Once you're here, a car is the best way to get around.

TIMING AND PRECAUTIONS

Plan on spending the better part of a day if you want to see everything, including the excellent presentation in the Turkish bathhouse. Women should exercise caution walking around alone at night.

VISITOR INFORMATION

Contacts Akko Visitor Center. ⊠ *1 Weizmann St.* ⊹ *At town entrance, just inside stone arch* ☎ *04/995–6706* ⊕ *www.akko.org.il/en/.*

EXPLORING AKKO

The walled city of Old Akko is relatively small and the well-marked sights are close to one another, making it easy to tour. You approach the Old City on Weizmann Street (watch for signs that say Old Akko), proceeding through a breach in the walls. If driving, park in the large lot.

OLD CITY

Start your tour at the Akko Visitor Center, just inside the main entrance to the Old City. This is where you purchase tickets. A combination ticket that includes all sights in the Old City is NIS 40. A combination ticket that includes all the sights along with the Turkish bath is NIS 62.

Once you've bought your ticket, take the time to get a map of the area and see the seven-minute film on the history of the region. Before you enter the Old City, you might want to walk along the ramparts and visit the Ethnography Center. To get there, ascend the steps at the opening in the city walls. The Al-Jazzar Mosque, south of the main entrance, also makes a good stop. Deeper in the Old City is the fascinating Hospitaller Fortress, as well as many other sights. You end up at the seaside walls of the Pisan Harbor.

TOP ATTRACTIONS

FAMILY **Al-Basha Turkish Bathhouse.** Built for Pasha al-Jazzar in 1781, Akko's remarkable Turkish bathhouse (*Hamam al-Basha*, in Arabic) was in use until 1947. Don't miss the sound-and-light show called *The Story of the Last Bath Attendant*, set in the beautiful bathhouse itself. You follow the story, with visual and audio effects, from the dressing room decorated with Turkish tiles and topped with a cupola, through the rooms with colored-glass bubbles protruding from the roof domes. The glass bubbles send a filtered green light to the steam rooms below. ⊠ *Al-Jazzar St.* ☎ *04/995–6707* ⊕ *www.akko.org.il* ▤ *Combination ticket NIS 46.*

Fodor's Choice **Al-Jazzar Mosque.** This house of worship, the largest mosque in the country outside of Jerusalem, is also considered one of the most beautiful ★ in Israel. Ahmed al-Jazzar, who succeeded Dahr el-Omar after having him assassinated, ruled Akko from 1775 to 1804. During his reign he built this mosque along with other public structures. His cruelty was so

Akko–Old City

HOSPITALLERS' QUARTER

Mediterranean Sea

Napoleon Bonaparte St.

Weizmann St.

Al-Jazzar Wall

Visitor Center

Moat Garden

Al-Jazzar Wall

Parking

Mausoleum

Salahaddin St.

Majdala Mosque

Al-Jazzar

Shazalia Mosque

Al-Zituneh Mosque

Al-Ramal Mosque

Parchi Sq.

Marco Polo

Yonatan Hachashmonai

TO RIMONIM PALM BEACH CLUB HOTEL

Binyamin Mitudela

St. George's Church

Ramchal Synagogue

Baha'i House

Zalman Hatzoref

Haganah St.

Parking

Maronite Church

Mu'allek Mosque

St. Andrew's Church

Sinan Basha Mosque

Venezia Sq.

Khan A-Shuna

Pisa Sq.

Akko Bay

Akko Port

Church of St. John

Southern Promenade

Lighthouse

Sha'ar Nikanor

0   100 yards

0   100 meters

legendary that he earned the epithet "the Butcher." (He is buried next to his adopted son in a small white building to the right of the mosque.)

Just beyond the entrance is a pedestal engraved with graceful calligraphy; it re-creates the seal of a 19th-century Ottoman sultan. Some of the marble and granite columns in the mosque and courtyard were plundered from the ruins of Caesarea. In front is an ornate fountain used by the faithful for ritual washings of hands and feet before prayer. Inside the mosque, enshrined in the gallery reserved for women, is a reliquary containing a hair believed to be from the beard of the prophet Muhammad; it is removed only once a year, on the 27th day of Ramadan.

The mosque closes five times a day for prayers, so you might have a short wait. On Friday, the prayer duration is longer, as it is the holiest day of the week for Muslims. Although the mosque is open, visitors are advised to plan their trip accordingly. Dress modestly. ⊠ *Off Al-Jazzar St.* ☎ *04/991–3039* ✆ *NIS 10.*

NEED A BREAK

In the plaza outside the Al-Jazzar Mosque are outdoor restaurants, where you can enjoy a falafel, fresh-squeezed orange or pomegranate juice, and coffee while watching the world go by.

Fodor'sChoice ★ **Hospitaller Fortress (Knights' Halls).** This remarkable 12th-century Crusader fortress was once known as the Crypt of St. John—before excavation, it was erroneously thought to have been an underground chamber. The dimensions of the colossal pillars that support the roof (girded with metal bands for extra strength) make this one of Israel's most monumental examples of Crusader architecture. It's also one of the oldest Gothic structures in the world. In the right-hand corner opposite the entrance is a fleur-de-lis carved in stone, the crest of the French house of Bourbon, which has led some scholars to suggest that this was the chamber in which Louis VII convened the knights of the realm.

Just outside this room is an entrance to an extremely narrow subterranean passageway. Cut from stone, this was a secret tunnel that the Crusaders probably used to reach the harbor when besieged by Muslim forces. (Those who are claustrophobic can take an alternate route, which goes back to the entrance of the Turkish bathhouse and continues from there). Emerge in the cavernous vaulted halls of the fortress guard post, with a 13th-century marble Crusader tombstone at the exit.

Here, a series of six barrel-vaulted rooms known as the Knights' Halls has been discovered. Arrows point the way through vast rooms filled with ongoing reconstruction work, huge marble columns, and archaeological pieces from the past. Above this part of the Crusader city stands the Ottoman citadel, which you can glimpse from the courtyard. Built by Dahr el-Omar in the 18th century on the rubble-filled Crusader ruins, the citadel was the highest structure in Akko.

The different factions within Akko's walls probably sowed the seeds of the Crusaders' downfall here. By the mid-13th century, open fighting had broken out between the Venetians and Genoese. When the Mamluks attacked with a vengeance in 1291, the Crusaders' resistance crumbled, and the city's devastation was complete. It remained a subdued place for centuries, and even today Akko retains a medieval cast.

✉ *1 Weizmann St.* ☎ *04/995–6706* ⊕ *www.akko.org.il* 🎫 *Combination ticket NIS 40.*

Pisan Harbor. Climbing the stone steps at the water's edge, you can walk along the sea walls at the Pisan Harbor, so named after an Italian commune here in Crusader times. Start at the café perched on high—a great lookout—and head west in the direction of the 18th-century Church of St. John. You end up at the southwestern extremity of Akko, next to the lighthouse. Head north along Haganah Street, which runs parallel to the crenellated western sea wall. After five minutes you reach the whitewashed, blue-trimmed Baha'i house (not open to the public), where the prophet of the Baha'i religion, Baha'u'llah, spent 12 years of his exile. His burial site is just north of Akko at the Baha'i Founder's Shrine and Gardens. ✉ *Akko* ✛ *At southern tip of Old Akko.*

WORTH NOTING

Khan al-Umdan. In Venezia Square, in front of the port, is the two-tiered Inn of the Pillars. Before you visit this Ottoman *khan*—the largest of the four in Akko—and the Pisan Quarter beyond, take a stroll around the port, with its small flotilla of fishing boats, yachts, and sailboats. Then walk through the khan's gate beneath a square clock tower, built at the turn of the 20th century. The khan served vast numbers of merchants and travelers during Akko's golden age of commerce, in the late 18th century. The 32 pink-and-gray granite pillars that give it its name are compliments of Ahmed al-Jazzar's raids on Roman Caesarea. There was once a market at the center of the colonnaded courtyard. ✉ *Venezia Sq.*

Ramparts. As you enter the Old City, climb the blue-railing stairway on your right for a stroll along the city walls. Walking to the right, you can see the stunted remains of the 12th-century walls built by the Crusaders, under whose brief rule—just less than two centuries—Akko flourished as never before or since. The indelible signs of the Crusaders, who made Akko the main port of their Christian empire, are much more evident inside the Old City.

The wall girding the northern part of the town was built by Ahmed al-Jazzar, the Pasha of Akko, who added these fortifications following his victory over Napoléon's army in 1799. With the help of the British fleet, al-Jazzar turned Napoléon's attempted conquest into a humiliating rout. Napoléon had dreamed of founding a new Eastern empire, thrusting northward from Akko to Turkey and then seizing India from Great Britain. His defeat at Akko hastened his retreat to France, thus changing the course of history. Walk around to the guard towers and up an incline just opposite; there's a view of the moat below and Haifa across the bay. Turn around and let your gaze settle on the exotic skyline of Old Akko, the sea green dome of the great mosque its dominating feature. Walk down the ramp, crossing the rather messy Moat Garden at the base of the walls; straight ahead is the Al-Jazzar Mosque. ✉ *Akko* 🎫 *Free.*

Souk. At this outdoor market, stalls heaped with fresh produce and seafood alternate with specialty stores: a pastry shop with exotic Middle Eastern delicacies; a spice shop filled with Eastern flavors and aromas; a bakery with steaming fresh pita. You often see fishermen sitting on doorsteps, intently repairing their lines and nets to the sounds of Arabic

Now a museum, the 18th-century Turkish bathhouse in Akko is illuminated through a dome with glass bubbles.

music blaring from the open windows above. The loosely defined area twists and turns through the center of the Old City, but Marco Polo Street is a good place to begin your exploration. ⊠ *Akko*.

"Treasures in the Walls" Ethnography Museum. There are two sections to this small but charming museum: one re-creates a 19th-century marketplace, with craftsmen's workshops such as a hatmaker and a blacksmith, filled with every tool needed to make hats and horseshoes; the other room displays a traditional Damascene living room, complete with astounding furniture and accoutrements. To get here once you're up the steps to the Ramparts, keep an eye out for the short flight of stairs heading down to the left. ⊠ *Eastern Wall, 2 Weizmann St.* ☎ *04/991–1004* ✉ *NIS 15.*

NEED A BREAK

✕ **Oudah Brothers.** In the souk, duck into this café and enjoy a coffee, some hummus, or a kebab in the courtyard of the 16th-century Khan al-Faranj, or Franks' Inn. Note the 18th-century Franciscan monastery and tower to your left. ⊠ *Khan Ha-Frankim St.* ☎ *04/991–2013.*

Underground Prisoners Museum. Located at the sea's edge, this museum run by the Ministry of Defense is housed in several wings of the citadel built by Dahr el-Omar and then modified by Ahmed al-Jazzar in 1785. It served as a major prison during the British Mandate. On the way in, you pass the citadel's outer wall; the difference between the large Crusader building stones and the smaller Turkish ones above is easy to spot. The original cells and their meager contents, along with photographs and documents reconstructing the history of the Jewish resistance to British rule in the '30s and '40s, illustrate prison life. During the Mandate, the citadel became a high-security prison whose inmates included

Despite modern boats, the old harbor in Akko retains echoes of past eras.

top members of Jewish resistance organizations, among them Ze'ev Jabotinsky and, later, Moshe Dayan. ✉ *10 Hahagana St.* ☎ *04/991–1375* ✉ *NIS 15* ⊙ *Closed Fri. and Sat.*

NEAR THE CITY

Baha'i Founder's Shrine and Gardens. For the Baha'is, this is the holiest place on earth, the site of the tomb of the faith's prophet and founder, Baha'u'llah. The gardens' west gate is only open to Baha'is, so enter from the north (main) gate. Baha'u'llah lived in the red-tile mansion here after released from jail in Akko and was buried in the small building next door, now the Shrine of Baha'u'llah. It's best to go on weekend mornings (Friday to Monday), when the inner gardens and shrine are open. Going through the black-iron gate, follow a white gravel path in the exquisitely landscaped gardens, with a fern-covered fountain and an observation point along the way, until you reach the shrine. Visitors are asked to dress modestly. The shrine is on Route 4, about 1 km (½ mile) north of the gas station at Akko's northern edge. ✉ *Rte. 4* ☎ *04/835–8845* ⊕ *www.bahaigardens.org.il* ✉ *Free.*

Ghetto Fighters' House Museum (*Beit Lochamei Hageta'ot*). Founded in 1949 by survivors of the German, Polish, and Lithuanian Jewish ghettos set up by the Nazis, kibbutz Lochamei Hageta'ot commemorates their compatriots who perished in the Holocaust at this museum. Exhibits include photographs documenting the Warsaw Ghetto and the uprising, and halls are devoted to different themes, among them Jewish communities before their destruction in the Holocaust; death camps; and deportations at the hands of the Nazis.

The adjacent Yad LaYeled (Children's Memorial) is dedicated to the memory of the 1½ million children who perished in the Holocaust. It's designed for young visitors, who can begin to comprehend the events of the Holocaust through a series of tableaux and images accompanied by recorded voices, allowing them to identify with individual victims without seeing shocking details. There is a small cafeteria on the premises. ⊠ *Kibbutz Lochamei Hageta'ot, Rte. 4* ☎ *04/995–8080* ⊕ *www. gfh.org.il/eng* ⊠ *30 NIS* ⊗ *Closed Fri. and Sat.*

WHERE TO EAT

$$$
SEAFOOD

✕ **Abu Christo.** In the Old City, this popular waterfront fish restaurant stands at one of the original 18th-century gates built by Pasha Ahmed al-Jazzar when he fortified the city after his victory over Napoléon. It's a Greek family business that's been passed from father to son since 1948. The covered patio is an idyllic place to dig into earthy hummus with pine nuts, eggplant salad spiced with sumac, and other salads. Abu Christo serves the daily catch—often grouper, red snapper, or sea bass—prepared simply, either grilled or deep-fried. Shellfish such as jumbo shrimp and crabs, and grilled meats or beef Stroganoff are also available. $ *Average main: NIS 80* ⊠ *Crusader Port, Leofeld HaSheni St.* ☎ *04/991–0065.*

$$$$
SEAFOOD
Fodor'sChoice
★

✕ **Uri Buri.** Justly known far and wide for its excellent fish and seafood, this Akko institution is housed in an old Turkish building near the lighthouse. One room is furnished with sofas, copper dishes, and *nargillas* (water pipes). Everything on the menu is seasonal, and the fresh fish is steamed, baked, or grilled. Allow time to linger here—it's not your everyday fish fry. Two house specialties are gravlax and Thai-style fish; delicious seafood soup is another fixture. Or try the baby calamari with kumquats and pink grapefruit or Creole shrimp with five spices. $ *Average main: NIS 110* ⊠ *11 Ha-haganah St.* ⊹ *On promenade near lighthouse* ☎ *04/955–2212* ⊕ *www.2eat.co.il/uriburi/.*

WHERE TO STAY

$$
HOTEL

⌂ **Akkotel.** This three-story hostelry, a former Turkish police station, is built into the city wall. **Pros:** family run; unusual lodging; warm service. **Cons:** no pool; small rooms. $ *Rooms from: $240* ⊠ *1 Salahaddin St.* ☎ *04/987–7100* ⊕ *www.akkotel.com* ⤳ *18 rooms* ⦿I *Breakfast.*

$$$
HOTEL
Fodor'sChoice
★

⌂ **Efendi Hotel.** Two notable Ottoman-era palaces overlooking the Mediterranean from the Israeli town of Akko have been united to form this uniquely charming boutique hotel. **Pros:** historic palace-home setting; design flair with local flavor; superb staff; perfect Old City location. **Cons:** not a lively nighttime neighborhood. $ *Rooms from: $320* ⊠ *Louis IX St.* ☎ *074/729–9799* ⊕ *www.efendi-hotel.com* ⤳ *12 rooms* ⦿I *Breakfast.*

$
HOTEL
FAMILY

⌂ **Nes Ammim Hotel.** Founded in 1963, this ecumenical Christian settlement between Akko and Nahariya focuses on mutual respect and tolerance; it also runs a hotel. **Pros:** good for families; outdoor swimming pool in summertime. **Cons:** basic rooms; few activities. $ *Rooms from: $115* ⊠ *Rd. 8611, off Rte. 4* ☎ *04/995–0000* ⊕ *www.nesammim.com* ⤳ *48 rooms* ⦿I *Breakfast.*

$ ☷ **Rimonim Palm Beach Hotel.** A private beach with exceptional views and
HOTEL   a country club with state-of-the-art facilities make this hotel a great
FAMILY   deal, especially for families. **Pros:** attentive staff; private beach; tennis
and squash courts. **Cons:** small rooms; away from Old City sights.
⑤ *Rooms from: $175* ✉ *Rte. 4* ☎ *04/987–7777* ⊕ *www.rimonimhotels.
com* ⇘ *125 rooms* ⦿ *Breakfast.*

NAHARIYA

8 km (5 miles) north of Akko.

This seaside recreation spot, Israel's northernmost coastal town, was
built along the banks of a river lined with eucalyptus trees. (The town's
name comes from *nahar*, Hebrew for "river.") Nahariya is popular with
vacationing Israelis who throng the small shops and cafés along the
main street, Haga'aton Boulevard. It's a good place to stop for lunch
if you're traveling along the coast. One of the region's most beautiful
stretches of sand is just at the end of the main street. Achziv Beach, just
4 km (2 ½ miles) north of town, is one of the country's finest.

GETTING HERE AND AROUND

There are direct buses from Haifa. Trains from Tel Aviv travel several
times a day to Nahariya. By car, take Route 4 north of Akko.

EXPLORING

Byzantine Church. This church dedicated to St. Lazarus features an elaborate, 17-color mosaic floor, discovered in 1964, that depicts peacocks,
other birds, hunting scenes, and plants. It was part of what experts
consider one of the largest and most beautiful Byzantine churches in
the Western Galilee, where Christianity spread from the 4th to the 7th
century. ✉ *Bielefeld St.* ▧ *Free.*

BEACHES

FAMILY   **Achziv Beach.** This beautifully maintained stretch of sand in the Achziv
Fodor's Choice   National Park is north of Nahariya, on the road to Rosh Hanikra.
★   Beside the ruins of the ancient settlement of Achziv are two huge
lagoons along the shore, one shallow, the other deep. There are also
watchful lifeguards and playground facilities. In July and August, turtles
lay their eggs on the beach. You can picnic on the grassy slopes or make
use of the restaurant. Enter at the second sign for Achziv Beach, not the
first. For NIS 63 per person, you can camp here overnight. **Amenities:**
food and drink; lifeguards; parking (fee); showers; toilets. **Best for:**
swimming; walking. ✉ *Rte. 2* ☎ *04/982–3263* ▧ *NIS 35.*

Betzet Beach. A bit farther north of Achziv Beach is this nature reserve
with abundant vegetation, shade-giving trees, and the ruins of an
ancient olive press. In season, a lifeguard is on duty on the beach, but
otherwise there are few frills. **Amenities:** food and drink; lifeguard. **Best
for:** solitude, walking. ✉ *Rte. 2* ▧ *Free.*

FAMILY   **Galei Galil Beach.** Nahariya's public bathing facilities at Galei Galil Beach
are ideal for families. Apart from the lovely beach, facilities include an
Olympic-size outdoor pool, heated indoor pool, wading pool, playground for children, and clean changing rooms. The pool area is closed
in winter. In peak season, the beach has exercise classes early in the

At Rosh Hanikra, take a cable car down the cliffs for an up-close look at the sea grottoes.

morning. **Amenities:** food and drink; lifeguards; parking (fee); showers; toilets. **Best for:** swimming. ⊠ *North of Haga'aton Blvd.* 🏖 *Beach free; pool area NIS 45.*

WHERE TO EAT

$$$$
MEDITERRANEAN
Fodor's Choice
★

✕ **Adelina.** When dining at this stellar restaurant, you may wonder how you got so lucky: there's the knockout view of the Mediterranean from the stone terrace, olive-tree-shaded setting, and wonderful Catalonian-accented dishes prepared by Adelina. Cooking is done in the huge silver tabun oven as Spanish music drifts across the dark wooden tables. Try the paella marinara packed with shellfish, roast sirloin with bacon and tarragon, or broccoli cannelloni in a creamy pepper sauce. Move on to *knafe* (a local pastry) with pistachio ice cream. The eatery is about 8 km (5 miles) east of Nahariya. ⑤ *Average main: NIS 110* ⊠ *Kibbutz Kabri, Rte. 89* ☎ *04/952–3707* ⊕ *www.adelina.org.il* ⏱ *Closed Sun.*

$$
MEDITERRANEAN

✕ **BaNahala.** Be prepared for taste-bud overload at this lovely restaurant surrounded by pecan trees. Inside the old building, part of a family estate, wood tables are set with fresh flowers, chairs are made from woven rope, and one wall displays the charming faces of the owners as children. Outside, market umbrellas shade the tables on the huge wood-plank terrace. When kids are finished choosing from their own menu, they can frolic on the lawn. For grown-ups there's everything from lamb kebabs with tahini to sweet red peppers stuffed with tangy cheese and risotto to tuna steak marinated in ginger. The comprehensive list of Israeli wines gives you a chance to sample local vintages.

$ *Average main: NIS 70* ✉ *17 Yitzhak Sadeh, Rasco* ☎ *04/951–2074* ⊕ *www.banahala.co.il* ☾ *Closed Sun.*

$$ ✗**Penguin.** The doors to this legendary institution opened in 1940.
ECLECTIC Three generations of the Oppenheimer family work here, and the
walls carry enlarged photographs of how the place looked when
just a hut. Stop for coffee and cake, or a meal of spinach blintzes
with melted cheese, hamburgers, or Chinese dishes. The management
swears that the schnitzel gets accolades from Viennese visitors. $ *Average main: NIS 70* ✉ *31 Haga'aton Blvd.* ☎ *04/992–8855* ⊕ *www.*
penguin-rest.co.il.

$$ ✗**Portobella.** This tiny but popular place is in a small cottage with
ITALIAN blue window frames and a flower-filled garden. A wood-burning
stove keeps things cozy inside. Locally made goat cheeses from the
Teva Ez dairy next door cram the counter. The menu has nice breakfasts and interesting pastas as well as heartier dishes like baked fish
and lasagna. It's about 3 km (2 miles) east of the city. $ *Average*
main: NIS 55 ✉ *Moshav Ben Ami, HaHoshel St., Rte. 89* ☎ *04/952–*
0299 ☾ *Closed Sat.*

ROSH HANIKRA

7 km (4½ miles) north of Nahariya, 38 km (24 miles) north of Haifa.

Fodor's Choice **GETTING HERE AND AROUND**
  ★ It's a short drive from Nahariya to Rosh Hanikra, the last destination
on the country's northern coast. You need your own car, as there's no
public transportation.

EXPLORING

Rosh Hanikra. The dramatic white cliffs on the coast signal both Israel's
border with Lebanon and the sea grottoes of Rosh Hanikra. Before
you get in line for the steep two-minute ride down on the Austrian-
made cable car, take a moment to absorb the stunning view back
down the coast. Bring binoculars. Still clearly visible is the route of
the railway line, now mostly a dirt road, built by the British through
the hillside in 1943 to extend the Cairo–Tel Aviv–Haifa line to Beirut.
(You are now much closer to Beirut than to Jerusalem.) After the
descent, you can see the 12-minute audiovisual presentation called
The Sea and the Cliff.

The incredible caves beneath the cliff have been carved out by relent-
less waves pounding away at the white chalky rock for millennia.
Footpaths inside the cliff lead from one huge cave to another, while
the sound of waves—and the squealing of fruit bats—echoes off the
water-sprayed walls. Huge bursts of seawater plunge into pools at
your feet (behind protective rails). It's slippery, so hang on to the
children. ✉ *Rosh Hanikra* ✛ *End of Rte. 4* ☎ *073/271–0100* ⊕ *www.*
rosh-hanikra.com ▣ *NIS 45.*

LOWER GALILEE

With Nazareth, Tiberias, and
the Sea of Galilee

WELCOME TO LOWER GALILEE

TOP REASONS TO GO

★ **Sunset on the Sea of Galilee:** The lake at sundown is always evocative, often beautiful, and occasionally spectacular. Walk a beach, sip a drink, or take a sail as dusk slowly settles.

★ **Zippori:** The distant past is palpable at this archaeological site, once a worldly Jewish and Hellenistic city. Set amid woods, it has the loveliest ancient mosaics in the land.

★ **Nazareth:** Tradition and modernity collide in the town where Jesus grew up. Today it's a city of baklava and BMWs, new politics and ancient passions. Talk to a local as you sample Middle Eastern delicacies.

★ **Mount Gilboa:** This little-visited region offers natural beauty and grand views for the independent traveler who has a bit of time and no checklist of must-see famous sites.

★ **A spiritual source:** Tune your ear to the Galilee's spiritual reverberations. Listen as pilgrims chant a Mass at the Mount of Beatitudes or sit meditatively on Tabgha's shore.

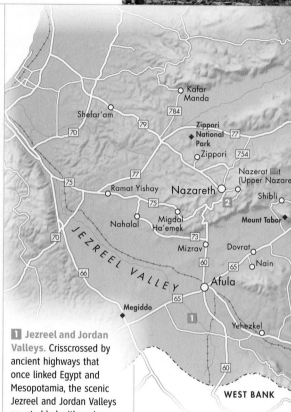

1 **Jezreel and Jordan Valleys.** Crisscrossed by ancient highways that once linked Egypt and Mesopotamia, the scenic Jezreel and Jordan Valleys are studded with major archaeological and historical sites. Megiddo, corrupted in Greek as "Armageddon," is known for a biblical battle and is prophesied to be the site of a future one. Zippori, also called Sepphoris, is a site with Jewish and Christian links. The Roman ruins at Beit She'an evoke the glory of one of the richest cities in the eastern Mediterranean.

2 **Nazareth and the Galilee Hills.** The once-sleepy town of Nazareth, the site of Jesus's boyhood, has boomed in recent decades to become a regional center. The nearby hills, such as Mount Tabor and Mount Gilboa, are both biblical byways and part of the reforested landscape many find so entrancing.

GETTING ORIENTED

The Hebrew word *gal* means "wave," and the Lower Galilee is indeed a hilly country, with deep valleys framed by mountain ridges. Not much more than a creek, the Jordan River cuts through the topography on the eastern border, first draining into the freshwater Sea of Galilee and then flowing south toward the Dead Sea. The Galilee is the storied land where King Saul lost his life fighting the Philistines; where the Romans built cities such as Beit She'an; where Jesus, who grew up in Nazareth, carried out much of his ministry; and where the Crusaders built and lost a kingdom. The lakeside resort city of Tiberias beckons with its hot springs and history.

6

3 Tiberias and the Sea of Galilee. The tranquil Sea of Galilee was the site for much of Jesus's ministry. But you don't have to be a Christian to fall in love with the mystic charm of this harp-shaped lake. A number of historic hotels, inns, ranches, and private villas ring the lake. The hot springs at Tiberias and Hammat Gader have been attracting guests since the time of Augustus Caesar.

Updated by
Shari Helmer

The Lower Galilee is a history-soaked region where scores of events in the Hebrew Bible and the New Testament took place. Blessed with forested hills, fertile valleys, gushing springs, and the Sea of Galilee, it has strong appeal. The graves of Jewish, Christian, Muslim, and Druze holy men attract those seeking spiritual solace, but the region is also the scene of earthly delights, including fine restaurants and spas.

To most Israelis, the Galilee is synonymous with "the North," a land of nature reserves and national parks. In short, they claim, it's a great place to visit but not a place to live: it's provincial and remote. Still, the Lower Galilee has its own quiet beauty and varied landscape. Whatever your agenda is—spiritual, historical, recreational, or restful—savor your time here. Follow a hiking trail above the Sea of Galilee. Wade through fields of irises in the spring. Bathe in a warm mineral spa. Buy some good goat cheese. Nazareth, the region's administrative center, has character and deserves some time.

Farming and tourism form the economic base. The region's kibbutzim and a smaller number of moshavim (Jewish family-farm villages) are concentrated in the Jezreel and Jordan Valleys and around the Sea of Galilee. The rockier hill country is predominantly Arab (*Israeli* Arab; this isn't disputed territory) and Israeli Druze. For the last half century, the communities—Jewish, Druze, and Arab—have been attempting neighborly relations despite the ethnic tensions that swirl around them. By and large, they've succeeded.

Culture and entertainment aren't this region's strong suits. A number of annual festivals and events are the highlights. Tiberias's pubs and restaurants probably come closest to providing lively nightlife, but there are worse ways to spend an evening than sitting by a moonlit lake washing down a good St. Peter's fish or a lamb kebab with an excellent Israeli wine.

LOWER GALILEE PLANNER

WHEN TO GO

The Galilee is prettiest in the spring months of March and April when it's covered with wildflowers, and its hills are draped in green. Summer can be torrid. Avoid the Sea of Galilee during Passover (March and April) and the High Holidays and Sukkot (September and October): although the weather is great at these times, half the country vacations here and rates soar.

Some hotels charge high-season rates during July and August; this is also true the week of Christmas. Weekends in general (Thursday night through Saturday night) are more crowded; some hotels hike rates substantially.

PLANNING YOUR TIME

It's possible to get a feeling for this region in a few days, but you can expand your trip to include some highlights of the Upper Galilee and the Golan including Tzfat (Safed). Tiberias, with its many accommodations, and the Sea of Galilee region are good bases for exploring archaeological sites—Beit She'an is impressive—as well as sites associated with the ministry of Jesus. Nazareth is worth a trip, either from Tiberias or en route to other areas. The Galilee is a low-key area with some lovely national parks and natural sites, including Mount Tabor, if you choose to linger.

Ein Gev, on the eastern shore of the Sea of Galilee, has an Israeli-music festival in the spring. Beit She'an revives its ancient Roman theater for a short series of events in October. In May and December, Jacob's Ladder, the twice-annual folk festival held in Nof Ginosar on the Sea of Galilee, presents traditional folk and country music of the British Isles and North America.

GETTING HERE AND AROUND

BUS TRAVEL

The Egged bus cooperative provides regular service from Jerusalem, Tel Aviv, and Haifa to Nazareth, Beit She'an, Afula, and Tiberias. There's no direct service from Ben Gurion International Airport; change in Tel Aviv or Haifa. There are several buses an hour from Tel Aviv to Afula (2 hours). Egged Bus 825 (*yashir,* or "direct") is quickest. Express bus 821 stops at major stations en route. SuperBus 354 from Afula Central Bus Station to Nazareth (20 minutes) runs once an hour. The Egged 442 and 541 buses leave frequently, every 20 minutes, and continue from Afula to Tiberias (about an hour). The Kavim line 411 and 412 link Afula to Beit She'an (every 30 minutes).

To get from Haifa to Tiberias, take Egged Bus 430 (about an hour), which leaves hourly from Merkazit Hamifratz. From the same Haifa station, the slow SuperBus buses leave two or three times an hour for Afula. Buses from Jerusalem to Beit She'an and Tiberias (Egged Buses 961, 966 to Beit She'an; 961, 962 to Tiberias) depart a few times a day; change in Beit She'an for Afula, where you change again for Nazareth. The ride to Beit She'an is about two hours, to Tiberias another 25 minutes. Nazareth Transport and Tourism runs Bus 431, which connects Nazareth and Tiberias about once every hour.

CAR TRAVEL

Driving is the best way to explore the Lower Galilee. Driving time from Tel Aviv or Jerusalem to Tiberias is two hours. Some newer four-lane highways are excellent, but some secondary roads may be in need of repair.

Signposting is clear (and usually in English), with route numbers clearly marked. Brown signs indicate most sights. The Lower Galilee is served by a number of highways. Route 90, going up the Jordan Valley to Tiberias and on to Metulla on the Lebanese border, is the most convenient road from Jerusalem. Although Route 90 is the quickest route, it traverses occupied territories and you may pass a military checkpoint. Routes 2 and 4, both multilane expressways, lead north from Tel Aviv. Turn east onto Route 65, then north onto Route 60 to get to Nazareth. Stay on Route 65 and turn east on Route 77 to reach Tiberias. While Route 6 is a modern superhighway, it's also an electronic toll road. If driving a rental car, you are charged for using it.

RESTAURANTS

Tiberias in particular and the Sea of Galilee in general have far livelier culinary options than other parts of Lower Galilee. Some places in the countryside are worth going out of your way for. Restaurant attire is casual. The local specialty is the native St. Peter's fish (tilapia), though most restaurants serve the (still excellent) pond-bred variety. Meat dishes tend to be Middle Eastern: *shashlik* and kebabs (ground meat grilled on skewers) accompanied by hummus, pickles, and french fries. Most economical are shawarma (slices of spit-grilled turkey meat served in pita bread) and falafel. The cheapest eats are always at the stands.

HOTELS

Tiberias, the region's tourist center, has hotels for budgets from deluxe to economy. Within a 20- to 30-minute drive are excellent guesthouses, some run by kibbutz residents and some on the Sea of Galilee. Nazareth has a couple of deluxe hotels and several older inexpensive ones that cater primarily to Christian pilgrim groups but also attract individual travelers and Israelis. Also in Nazareth, and to a lesser extent around Tiberias, are hospices run by Christian orders.

Bed-and-breakfasts have sprung up in profusion. Many are in or adjacent to private homes in rural farming communities; others are within kibbutzim. These are a good value, especially for families. Many "guesthouses," as upgraded youth hostels are now called, are suitable for families; these are generally the cheapest deals.

Hotel reviews have been shortened. For more information, visit Fodors.com.

WHAT IT COSTS				
	$	$$	$$$	$$$$
Restaurants	Under NIS 50	NIS 50–NIS 75	NIS 76–NIS 100	over NIS 100
Hotels	Under $200	$200–$300	$301–$400	over $400

Restaurant prices are the average cost of a main course at dinner in NIS (Israeli shekels) or, if dinner isn't served, at lunch. Hotel prices, given in U.S. dollars, are the lowest cost of a standard double room in high season. Non-Israeli citizens paying in foreign currency are exempt from the 17% V.A.T. on hotel rooms.

TOURS

Both Egged Tours and United Tours have one-day tours around the region from Jerusalem and Tel Aviv that take in Nazareth, the Sea of Galilee, and other highlights. Current prices vary, but are in the neighborhood of NIS 335 from Tel Aviv, NIS 355 from Jerusalem.

Contacts Egged Tours. ☎ 03/920-3992 ⊕ www.eggedtours.com. **United Tours.** ☎ 03/617-3315 ⊕ www.unitedtours.co.il.

6

JEZREEL AND JORDAN VALLEYS

"Highways of the world cross Galilee in all directions," wrote the eminent Victorian scholar George Adam Smith in 1898. The great international highway of antiquity, the Via Maris (Way of the Sea), swept up the Mediterranean coast from Egypt and broke inland along three separate passes through the hills to emerge in the Jezreel Valley before continuing northeast to Damascus and Mesopotamia. It made the Jezreel Valley a convenient and frequent battleground. In fact, the Jezreel Valley heard the clash of arms so often that the very name of its most commanding tell—Har Megiddo (Mount Megiddo), or Armageddon—became a New Testament synonym for the final apocalyptic battle of all time. Today, this and other ancient sites such as Beit She'an remain highlights here.

On a topographical map, the Jezreel Valley appears as an equilateral triangle with sides about 40 km (25 miles) long, edged by low mountains and with a narrow extension east to Beit She'an in the Jordan Rift. From there, the Jordan Valley stretches like a ribbon north to the Sea of Galilee. Your first impression is one of lush farmland as far as the eye can see. But as recently as the 1960s, malarial swamps still blighted the area; some pioneering settlements had cemeteries before their first buildings were completed.

With a few exceptions, eating places in this rustic area are confined to roadside cafeterias, lunchtime diners at or near parks, and small restaurants and snack bars in the towns of Afula and Beit She'an.

Abu Sinan

854   864   Zfat   ↑ TO
UPPER GALILEE

91

Shagor   Karmi'el   85   89   90

70

85

Maghar

Sakhnin   65

Migdal   Kibbutz
Ginosar

70   Kafar
Manda   G A L I L E E   Arbel National Park
and Nature Reserve   Tiberias   Sea of
Galilee
(Lake Kinneret)   92

Shefar'am   784   Golani
Junction   Lavi   77

70   Harduf   79   Zippori
National
Park   77   Kfar
Kama   90

75   ← TO
HAIFA   77   Zippori   Cana   65   767   Ma'agan
754   Yavne'el

Ramat Yishay   Nazareth
see detail map   Nazerat Illit
(Upper Nazareth)   Afikim

75   Beit She'arim
National Park   Shibli   Kfar Tavor   90

Nahalal   Migdal
Ha'emek   Mount Tabor   Gesher

73   Mizra   Ein Dor
Kibbutz   10

JEZREEL VALLEY   Dovrat   Shuneh
Shamaliyyeh

66   60   Nain   Belvoir

65   Afula   716   90   65   JORDAN

Tel Megiddo
National Park   65   675   Kfar
Yehezkel   717   Moledet   71

Umm el
Fahm   60   Ma'ayan
Harod   JORDAN VALLEY

596   66   Gan Nit   Hefziba   71
Beit Alfa   Beit She'an
National Park   Beit
She'an
WEST
BANK   Gan Hashlosha
National Park   Park of Springs
Ma'aleh
Gilboa   669   90   Jordan River

Bayt Qad   Mount Gilboa

Jenin   90

60   57   667   65

596   Tubas

0   4 mi

0   4 km

Lower
Galilee

BEIT SHE'ARIM NATIONAL PARK

20 km (12½ miles) southeast of Haifa, 25 km (15½ miles) west of Nazareth.

GETTING HERE AND AROUND

Driving from Tel Aviv, take Route 4 (the old Tel Aviv–Haifa Highway) to Furadis Junction, then turn east on Route 70. Continue to Yokneam Junction, then take Route 722 to Hashomrim Junction. Take the first left, and continue about 10 minutes until you reach the national park.

EXPLORING

Beit She'arim National Park. Chalk slopes are honeycombed with catacombs around this attractively landscaped ancient site. Orthodox Jews pilgrimage here to the early-3rd-century Tomb of Judah ha-Nasi, chief editor and redactor of the Mishnah, the seminal text of rabbinic Judaism, but you don't need to be religious to appreciate the role this vast necropolis has played in the development of modern Judaism. The landscape is soothing, there are pleasant walking paths, and some of the caves have an *Indiana Jones*–style intrigue. Equipped with a flashlight, a free park brochure, and a map, discover ornately carved sarcophagi that attest to the complex intercultural relations in the Roman world.

A Jewish town flourished here after the eclipse of Jerusalem brought about by Titus's legions in AD 70 and its reconstruction as a pagan town by Hadrian in AD 135. For generations, Jews were denied access to their holy city and its venerated burial ground on the Mount of Olives, so the center of Jewish life and religious authority shifted first to Yavne, in the southern coastal plain, and then northward to the Lower Galilee.

By around AD 200 Beit She'arim had become the unofficial Jewish capital, owing its brief preeminence to the enormous stature of a native son. Rabbi Yehuda (or Judah) "ha-Nasi" (the Patriarch: a title conferred on the nominal leader of the Jewish community) was responsible for the city's inner workings and relations with its Roman masters. Alone among his contemporaries, ha-Nasi combined worldly diplomatic skills with scholarly authority and spiritual leadership.

The rabbi eventually moved east to Zippori because of its more salubrious climate, and there gathered the great Jewish sages of his day and compiled the Mishnah, which remains the definitive interpretation of biblical precepts for religious Jews. Nonetheless, it was in his hometown of Beit She'arim that ha-Nasi was laid to rest. If Beit She'arim was a magnet for scholars and petitioners in his lifetime, it became a virtual shrine after his death. With Jerusalem still off-limits, the town became the most prestigious burial site in the Jewish world for almost 150 years.

Two major expeditions in the 1930s and '50s uncovered a series of 20 catacombs. The largest of these is open to the public, with 24 chambers containing more than 200 sarcophagi. A wide range of carved Jewish and Roman symbols and more than 250 funerary inscriptions in Greek, Hebrew, Aramaic, and Palmyrene testify to the great distances people traveled—from Yemen and Mesopotamia, for instance—to be buried here. Without exception, the sarcophagi were plundered over the

6

centuries by grave robbers seeking the possessions with which the dead were often interred. ⊠ *Off Rte. 75 or 722, Beit She'arim National Park* ✛ *Take a left turn at HaShomrim Junction on Rte. 722* ☎ *04/983–1643* ⊕ *www.parks.org.il* ✉ *NIS 22.*

WHERE TO EAT

$ ✕ **Kamah Coffee Shop and Gallery.** You can have a tasty meal and shop
ISRAELI too at this showcase for the creative work produced by members of the local special-needs community. Visiting the coffee shop should include a peek at the workshops based on anthroposophy (a system for nurturing the individual's healthy core), where community members work in the organic vegetable garden and the bakery, as well as in handweaving, ceramics, and paper-products workshops. Feast on a Galilee-style breakfast made with the organic vegetables grown here, and try homemade sweet potato, beet, and cauliflower spreads. Your food is served on exquisite ceramics, produced here and available for purchase. It's about 15 minutes north of Beit She'arim. ⑤ *Average main: NIS 35* ⊠ *Kibbutz Harduf, Off Rte. 7626* ☎ *04/905–9338* ⊕ *www.eng. kamah.org.il.*

TEL MEGIDDO NATIONAL PARK

This ancient city was built on foundations dating back to the biblical era. Today called Tel Megiddo National Park, it's one of the region's most impressive ruins.

GETTING HERE AND AROUND

A car is the best way to get here, as the site is poorly served by public transportation. You can reach the site by taxi from Afula. Taxi-stand published price for trip: NIS 78.

Taxi Contact Yizre'el. ☎ *04/652-3111.*

EXPLORING

Fodor's Choice **Tel Megiddo National Park.** Megiddo's centuries of settlement, from pre-
★ historic times through the Canaanite and early Israelite periods, have left fascinating layers of remains at this UNESCO World Heritage Site. Most people are fascinated by the site's ancient water system. In a masterful stroke, King Ahab's engineers dug a deep shaft and a horizontal tunnel through solid rock to reach the vital subterranean spring outside the city walls. With access secure, the spring's original opening was permanently blocked. There is nothing more than a trickle today, though, the flow perhaps choked by subsequent earthquakes. As you descend 180 steps through the shaft, traverse the 65-yard-long tunnel under the ancient city wall, and climb up 83 steps at the other end, look for the ancient chisel marks and hewn steps. A visit to the water system at noon provides a reprieve from the summer heat.

Apart from the ancient water system, don't miss the partially restored Late Bronze Age gate, perhaps the very one stormed by Egyptian troops circa 1468 BC, as described in the victory stela of Pharaoh Thutmose III. A larger gate farther up the mound was long identified with King Solomon (10th century BC)—Megiddo was one of his regional military centers—but has been redated by some scholars to the time of Ahab, a

The archaeological layers at Megiddo include prehistoric remains and an ingenious biblical-era water system.

half century later. There is consensus, however, on the ruined stables at the summit of the tell: they were certainly built by Ahab, whose large chariot army is recorded in an Assyrian inscription.

Evidence indicates prehistoric habitation here as well, but among the earliest remains of the *city* of Megiddo are a round altar dating from the Early Bronze Age and the outlines of several Early Bronze Age temples, almost 5,000 years old, visible in the trench between the two fine lookout points.

A tiny museum at the site's entrance has good visual aids, including maps, a video, and a model of the tell. A small gift shop alongside the museum sells handsome silver and gold jewelry, some incorporating pieces of ancient Roman glass. There is also a restaurant. ⊠ *Rte. 66* ☎ *04/659–0316* ⊕ *www.parks.org.il* ✉ *NIS 28.*

MOUNT GILBOA

24 km (15 miles) southeast of Tel Megiddo National Park via Rtes. 675 and 667, 10 km (7 miles) southeast of Afula.

Fodor'sChoice Visit Mount Gilboa in February or March, and find yourself surrounded
★ by people enraptured with the delicate purple iris native to these slopes. The views of the valley below and the hills of Galilee beyond are great year-round, but on a clear winter or spring day they're amazing, reaching as far as the snowcapped Mount Hermon, far to the north. Afternoon is the best time to come.

Mount Gilboa—actually a steep mountain range rather than a single peak—is geographically a spur of the far greater Samaria Range (the biblical Mount Ephraim, today the West Bank) to the southwest. Half the mountain has been reforested with evergreens, while the other half has been left in pristine rockiness. Environmentalists prefer the latter, as it protects the wildflowers that splatter the slopes with color every spring. From the gravel parking area off Route 667, easy and well-marked trails wind through the natural habitat of the rare black (actually deep purple) iris, which draws hordes of Israelis every spring.

Three thousand years ago, the Philistines routed the Israelites on Mount Gilboa. Saul, the nation's first king, was wounded and took his own life on the battlefield. The next day, the Bible relates, when the Philistines came to plunder their fallen foes, they discovered the bodies of Saul and his sons. Seeking trophies, "they cut off his head and stripped off his armor, and they fastened his body to the wall of [Beit She'an]" (I Samuel 31). In his eulogy for Saul and his son Jonathan, king-to-be David cursed the battlefield where "thy glory, O Israel" was slain: "Let there be no dew or rain upon you" (II Samuel 1).

GETTING HERE AND AROUND
Driving from Afula, follow Route 71 east, turn right on Route 675, then left on Route 667. There's no reliable public transportation.

EXPLORING
Beit Alfa. In 1928, members of Kibbutz Hefziba were digging an irrigation trench when they discovered this ancient synagogue, now part of Beit Alfa Synagogue National Park. Their tools hit a hard surface, and excavation uncovered a multicolored mosaic floor, almost entirely preserved. The art is somewhat stylized and childlike, but that, too, is part of its charm. An Aramaic inscription dates the building to the reign of Byzantine emperor Justinian in the second quarter of the 6th century AD; a Greek inscription credits the workmanship to one Marianos and his son, Aninas. In keeping with Jewish tradition, the synagogue faces Jerusalem, with an apse at the far end to hold the ark. The building faithfully copies the architecture of the Byzantine basilicas of the day, with a nave and two side aisles, and the doors lead to a small narthex and a onetime outdoor atrium. Stairs indicate there was once an upper story.

Classic Jewish symbols in the top mosaic panel leave no doubt that the building was a synagogue: a holy ark flanked by lions, a menorah, and a *shofar* (ram's horn). The middle panel, however, is the most intriguing: it's filled with human figures depicting the seasons, the zodiac, and—even more incredible for a Jewish house of worship—the Greek sun god, Helios, driving his chariot across the sky. These images indicate more liberal times theologically, when the prohibition against making graven images was perhaps not applied to two-dimensional art. The last panel tells the story of Abraham's near-sacrifice of his son Isaac, captioned in Hebrew. Take time to watch the lighthearted but informative film. Allocate 45 minutes for a visit here. ⊠ *Kibbutz Hefziba, Rte. 669* ☎ *04/653–2004* ⊕ *www.parks.org.il* ✉ *NIS 22.*

FAMILY **Gan Hashlosha National Park.** This beautiful oasis is a national treasure, popular with picnickers and swimmers alike. Lush palm trees and green lawns draw swarms of people who come for the day to relax. The spring water maintains a constant, year-round water temperature of 28°C, or

CLOSE UP

Kibbutz Life Then and Now

Israel's founding fathers and mothers would probably be bewildered by life on a 21st-century kibbutz (a collective settlement, but literally translated as "a gathering"). Many of the country's founders came from Russia in the early 20th century, inspired by Zionist ideals of returning to their ancestral homeland and a work ethic that regarded manual labor as an almost spiritual value. They were socialists who believed "from each according to his ability, to each according to his need."

EARLY DAYS

Degania, the first kibbutz, was founded in 1909 on the shores of the Sea of Galilee, where 10 men and two women began to work the land. The utopian ideology, in which individual desires were subordinated to the needs of the community, was wedded to the need for a close-knit communal structure, in order to cope with forbidding terrain and a hostile neighborhood. Life was arduous, but their numbers grew.

Kibbutzim played a considerable role in molding the fledgling state, absorbing immigrants, and developing agriculture. By 1950, two years after Israel's independence, there were more than 200 kibbutzim. Their egalitarian ethos meant that all shared chores and responsibility—but also ownership of the means of production. The kibbutz movement became the world's largest communitarian movement.

GROWTH AND CHALLENGE

With time, many kibbutzim introduced light industry or tourism enterprises, and some became successful businesses. The standard of living improved, and kibbutzim took advantage of easy bank loans. When Israel's hyperinflation reached 454% during the mid-1980s, many communities found themselves bankrupt. Change became inevitable, and the movement peaked around 1990, when the almost 270 kibbutzim across the country reached 130,000 members. (An individual kibbutz can range from fewer than 100 to more than 1,000 members.)

THE KIBBUTZ TODAY

In today's Israel, many young "kibbutzniks," after compulsory military service or university studies, have found the kibbutz ethos stifling and have opted for the individualism and material attractions of city life. Despite the changes, city folk, volunteers, and tourists are still drawn to this rural environment, which has a slower pace.

Only some 15% of kibbutz members now work in agriculture, though they account for a significant proportion of the national production. Industry, services, and tourism—including kibbutz guesthouses and hotels—are the real sources of income. Differential wage systems have been introduced, and foreign laborers often provide menial labor in fields and factories. All kibbutzim have abandoned children's dormitories, instead allowing parents to raise their children in a family home.

Many members of the older generation have become distressed by what they see as the contamination of pioneering principles. But reality bites hard, and ironically, only those kibbutzim that succeed economically can afford to remain socialist.

6

82°F. As the stream ambles around the property, it has been widened into pools in some areas; there are also some artificial waterfalls. Lifeguards are on duty. Facilities include changing rooms for bathers, two snack bars, and a restaurant. ☒ *Off Rte. 669* ☏ *04/658–6219* ⊕ *www. parks.org.il* ☜ *NIS 39.*

FAMILY **Ma'ayan Harod** (*Spring of Harod*). At the foot of Mount Gilboa is this small national park with huge eucalyptus trees and a big swimming pool fed by a spring. Today it's a bucolic picnic spot, but almost 3,200 years ago, Gideon, the reluctant hero of the biblical book of Judges, organized his troops to fight a Midianite army that had invaded from the desert. At God's command—in order to emphasize the miraculous nature of the coming victory—Gideon dismissed more than two-thirds of the warriors and then, to reduce the force still more, selected only those who lapped water from the spring. Equipped with swords, ram's horns, and flaming torches concealed in clay jars, this tiny army of 300 divided into three companies and surrounded the Midianite camp across the valley in the middle of the night. At a prearranged signal, the attackers shouted, blew their horns, and smashed the jars, revealing the flaming torches, whereupon the Midianites panicked and fled, resulting in an Israelite victory.

The spring has seen other armies in other ages. It was here in 1260 that the Egypt-based Mamluks stopped the invasion of the hitherto invincible Mongols. In the 1930s, the woods above the spring hid Jewish self-defense squads training in defiance of British military law. ☒ *Off Rte. 71* ☏ *04/653–2211* ⊕ *www.parks.org.il* ☜ *NIS 28.*

Park of Springs. Three beautiful springs and a stream are the attractions at this nature park. Electric carts and bicycles are available to rent but not necessary to enjoy a swim or hike. You can also watch the birds of many varieties that make this nature preserve their home and a migration waypoint. ☒ *Rte. 669, at entrance to Gan Hashlosha* ☏ *04/688–1427* ⊕ *www.parkhamaianot.co.il* ☜ *Free.*

NEED A BREAK   ✕ **Barkanit Dairy.** At Michal and Avinoam Barkin's goat farm, you can sample excellent cheeses over wine or coffee in the wooden reception room or enjoy a light meal of salads, toasted sandwiches, or hot stuffed pastries. The farm is open Friday 10–2 and Saturday 10–4. ☒ *Rtes. 71 and 675, 1 km (½ mile) east of Navot Junction, Kfar Yehezkel* ☏ *04/653–1431* ☽ *Closed Sun.–Thurs. No dinner.*

WHERE TO EAT

$$$ ✕ **Herb Farm on Mount Gilboa.** The sweeping panorama from the wooden
MODERN ISRAELI   deck and picture windows is attraction enough at this family restaurant operated by Yossi Mass, his wife Penina, and son Oren. Known for its greens and imaginative salads, it also impresses with homemade bread and tarts of shallot, forest mushroom, and goat cheese, not to mention a colorful pie of beef, lamb, goose, tomatoes, pine nuts, and basil. Desserts make for an agonizing decision, so share. ⑤ *Average main: NIS 100* ☒ *Rte. 667, 3 km (2 miles) off Rte. 675, Gan Nir* ✛ *At entrance to Mount Gilboa* ☏ *04/653–1093* ⊕ *www.herb-farm.co.il* ☽ *Closed Sun.*

WHERE TO STAY

$

B&B/INN

FAMILY

Ein Harod Country Suites and Guest Houses. Set in a lovely landscape, this 95-year-old kibbutz has beautiful cabins and suites to meet every need. **Pros:** serene atmosphere; pretty views; options for both families and couples. **Cons:** luxury suites are pricey on weekends. $ *Rooms from: $150* ✉ *Kibbutz Ein Harod* ☎ *04/648–6083* ⊕ *www.ein-harod. co.il/en* ⤵ *42 units* ⍟ *Breakfast.*

SPORTS AND THE OUTDOORS

Big Walks. Two annual *Tza'adot* (Big Walks) take place in March or April: one along the shore of the Sea of Galilee (2½ km [1½ miles] and 9 km [5½ miles]), the other along the trails of Mount Gilboa (routes range from 6 km [4 miles] to 40 km [25 miles] over two days). These mass rambles attract folks from all over the country and abroad. For information, contact Israeli Sports for All Association. ☎ *03/562–1441* ⊕ *www.isfa.co.il.*

BEIT SHE'AN

6

23 km (14 miles) southeast of Afula, 39 km (24 miles) south of Tiberias.

At the intersection of the Jordan and Jezreel Valleys, the modern town of Beit She'an has little to offer visitors, but the past beckons at a national park nearby. Unlike some archaeological sites that appear to be just piles of rocks, ancient Beit She'an is a gloriously rich ruin, complete with bathhouses, pagan temples, and public theaters.

GETTING HERE AND AROUND

The national park is northeast of modern Beit She'an. From Route 90, turn west on Sha'ul Hamelech Street, and right after Bank Leumi.

EXPLORING

Fodor's Choice

★

Beit She'an National Park. The extensive remains of lavish ancient structures at this archaeological treasure trove make it one of Israel's most notable sites. A Roman theater was excavated in the 1960s, but the rest of Scythopolis, as this Late Roman and Byzantine (2nd–6th centuries AD) city was known, came to light only in more recent excavations. The enormous haul of marble statuary and friezes says much about the opulence in its heyday—especially when you remember that there are no marble quarries in Israel, and all stone was imported from what is today Turkey, Greece, or Italy.

A free site map available at the visitor center gives a good layout. In summer, it's best to arrive early in the morning, as the heat quickly becomes insufferable. Better yet, consider returning in the evening for the engaging sound-and-light spectacle, presented Monday through Thursday at sundown. Reserve tickets in advance and check times.

Scythopolis's downtown area, now exposed, has masterfully engineered, colonnaded main streets converging on a central plaza that once boasted a pagan temple, decorative fountain, and monument. An elaborate Byzantine bathhouse covered more than 1¼ acres. On the main thoroughfare are the remains of Scythopolis's amphitheater, where gladiatorial combats were once the order of the day.

The remains of the wealthy late Roman and Byzantine city of Beit She'an include a large public bathhouse.

The high tell dominating the site to the north was the location of Old Testament Canaanite-Israelite Beit She'an 2,500 to 3,500 years ago. Climb to the top not for the meager archaeological remains, but rather the fine panoramic view of the surrounding valleys and the superb bird's-eye view of the main excavations.

The semicircular Roman theater was built of contrasting black basalt and white limestone blocks around AD 200, when Scythopolis was at its height. Although the upper *cavea*, or tier, has not survived, the theater is the largest and best preserved in Israel, with an estimated original capacity of 7,000 to 10,000 people. The large stage and part of the *scaena frons* (backdrop) behind it have been restored, allowing outdoor sound-and-light performances March to November. ⊠ *Off Sha'ul Hamelech St., Beit Shean* ☎ *04/658–7189* ⊕ *www.parks.org.il* 🖭 *NIS 28; NIS 55 for sound-and-light show.*

WHERE TO EAT

$$$
ISRAELI
✕ **Shipudei HaKikar.** You can't miss the imposing restaurant commanding the corner as you enter Beit She'an. Inside, friendly service in a sparkling clean dining room is a pleasant surprise. Don't fill up on the fresh homemade salads; the grilled meat is delicious, too. 💲 *Average main: NIS 80* ⊠ *35 Sha'ul HaMelech St., Beit Shean* ☎ *04/606–0198* ☾ *No dinner Fri. No lunch Sat.*

WHERE TO STAY

$
HOTEL
🖼 **Beit She'an Hostel.** A cross between a guesthouse and a hostel, this modern limestone and basalt building is wrapped around a courtyard shaded by palm trees. **Pros:** convenient to the national park; pretty pool area. **Cons:** sometimes noisy with teenage groups; no evening entertainment.

⑤ *Rooms from: $117* ✉ *129 Menachem Begin Blvd., Beit Shean* ☎ *02/594–5644* ⊕ *www.iyha.org.il/Eng/* ⤵ *80 rooms* ⑪ *Breakfast.*

NIGHTLIFE AND PERFORMING ARTS

Roman Theater. This marvelous theater hosts concerts, mostly by Israeli artists, every October. ✉ *Sha'ul HaMelech St., Beit Shean* ☎ *04/658–7189.*

BELVOIR

20 km (12½ miles) north of Beit She'an.

The Crusaders chose the site for this fortress well: the Hebrew name *Kochav Hayarden* (the Star of the Jordan) and the Arabic *Kaukab el Hauwa* (the Star of the Wind) underscore Belvoir's splendid isolation. You don't need to be a military historian to marvel at the never-breached concentric walls.

GETTING HERE AND AROUND

Driving north on Route 90 from Beit She'an, turn west on Route 717. While any bus traversing Route 90 lets off at the road, the fortress is high above the valley. It's a long hike of 5 km (3 miles), and don't count on getting a ride. The road from Ein Harod via Moledet is passable in dry weather but in very bad condition in places.

EXPLORING

Belvoir. The Hospitallers (the Knights of St. John) completed the mighty castle in 1173; they called it Belvoir—"beautiful view"—and it was the most invincible fortress in the land. In the summer of 1187, the Arabs under Saladin crushed the Crusader armies at the Horns of Hittin, west of Tiberias, bringing an end to the Latin Kingdom of Jerusalem with one decisive battle. The Crusaders' remnants struggled on to Tyre (in modern Lebanon), but Belvoir alone refused to yield; 18 months of siege got the Muslims no farther than undermining the outer eastern rampart. The Crusaders, for their part, sallied out from time to time to battle the enemy, but their lone resistance had become pointless. They struck a deal with Saladin and surrendered the stronghold in exchange for free passage, flags flying, to Tyre. Today Belvoir is part of Kochav Hayarden National Park.

Don't follow the arrows from the parking lot; instead, take the wide gravel path to the right of the fortress. This brings you to the panoramic view of the Jordan River Valley and southern Sea of Galilee, some 1,800 feet below (the view is best in the afternoon). It's also the best spot from which to appreciate the strength of the stronghold, with its deep, dry moat, massive rock and cut-stone ramparts, and gates. Once inside the main courtyard, you're unexpectedly faced with a fortress within a fortress, a scaled-down replica of the outer defenses. Not much remains of the upper stories; in 1220, the Muslims systematically dismantled Belvoir, fearing another crusade. Once you've explored the modest buildings, exit over the western bridge (once a drawbridge) and spy on the postern gates, the protected and sometimes secret back doors of medieval castles. ✉ *Rte. 717, Belvoir National Park* ⊕ *5 km (3 miles) west of Rte. 90* ☎ *04/658–1766* ⊕ *www.parks.org.il* ⤳ *NIS 22.*

6

NAZARETH AND THE GALILEE HILLS

Remove the modern roads and power lines, and the landscape of this region becomes a biblical illustration. Villages are scattered haphazardly on the hillsides, and small farm-holdings crowd the valleys. Olive groves, the region's ancient resource, are everywhere. Hilltop views and modern pine forests, white-and-red houses, and decorative trees that dab the countryside provide visually arresting moments.

There are several New Testament settings here—Nazareth, where Jesus grew up; the Cana wedding feast; and Mount Tabor, identified with the Transfiguration—but Jewish history resonates strongly, too. Tabor and Yodefat were fortifications in the Great Revolt against the Romans; Shefar'am, Beit She'arim (in a nearby valley), and Zippori were in turn the national centers of Jewish life (2nd–4th centuries AD); and latter-day Jewish pioneers, attracted to the region's untamed scenery, put down roots where their ancestors had farmed.

NAZARETH

25 km (15½ miles) east of Beit She'arim, 56 km (35 miles) east of Haifa, 15 km (9½ miles) north of Afula.

Fodor's Choice The Nazareth where Jesus grew up was an insignificant village in a
★ hollow in the Galilean hills, but today's city of 65,000 pulses with energy. Apart from the occasional donkey plying traffic-clogged Paulus VI Street, there's little that evokes the Bible in contemporary Nazareth, unless you know where to look—and indeed, droves of Christian pilgrims come to pray at the awe-inspiring Basilica of the Annunciation or seek quiet contemplation at one of Nazareth's many smaller churches.

For nonbelievers, Nazareth is a fascinating day or half-day stop; the Christian devout want to spend a full day, if not two. If your goal is to experience Nazareth as Jesus did, plan a tour at Nazareth Village. The calmest days to visit the town are Wednesday, when many businesses close for a midweek sabbatical, and Sunday, the day of rest for the Christians who make up a third of the town. If you're looking for local color (and traffic jams), come on Saturday, when Arab villagers come to the big city to sell produce and buy goods.

GETTING HERE AND AROUND

If you're driving from Beit She'arim or Haifa on Route 75, Route 77 breaks off to the north—to Zippori, the Golani Junction, and Tiberias. Route 75 continues to skirt the north side of the picturesque Jezreel Valley as it climbs into the hills toward Nazareth; at the crest of the hill, Route 60 from Afula joins it. A turn to the left takes you down to Paulus VI, Nazareth's main drag. If you pick up Route 77 from the opposite side, from Tiberias and points north, a left turn onto Route 764 takes you into Nazareth's Paulus VI Street. Nazareth's Central Bus Station is downtown on Paulus VI Street, near the Basilica of the Annunciation.

Nazareth itself is mired in traffic, but the historic and religious sites are all close together, so it's best to park and walk.

Taxi Contacts Abu el-Assal. ☎ *04/655–4745.* **Diana.** ☎ *04/655–5554.*

TOURS

Both Egged Tours and United Tours run one-day tours that take in Nazareth, Capernaum, Tabgha, the Sea of Galilee, Tiberias, and the Jordan River. Current prices are NIS 330 from Tel Aviv, NIS 350 from Jerusalem.

Nazareth is the starting point of two walking trails that trace a path between sites relating to the life of Jesus; both trails are long, but it's possible to walk just a section of either. The **Jesus Trail** (⊕ *jesustrail. com*) is 65 km (40 miles) and goes from Nazareth to Capernaum on the Sea of Galilee. The 60 km (37 miles) of the **Gospel Trail** (⊕ *www. goisrael.com*) go from Nazareth to sites along the Sea of Galilee; it can be done by foot or on bike.

Fauzi Azar Tour. The Old City tour that begins at the Fauzi Azar Inn is unique in that it skips religious sites almost entirely and focuses instead on the sights, sounds, and smells of daily life in Nazareth. You are taken to the souk, where shop owners let you view and taste their wares; unique gift shops far from city center; and various coffee shops, whose managers answer questions about Nazareth life. Tours are offered every day except Sunday at 9:30 am and cost NIS 20 per person (free for inn guests). ⊠ *Fauzi Azar Inn, 2606 St.* ✛ *Off the souk* ☎ *04/602–0469* ⊕ *abrahamhostels.com* ☑ *NIS 20.*

VISITOR INFORMATION

Contacts **Nazareth Tourist Information Office.** ⊠ *Casa Nova St.* ☎ *04/657-0555.*

EXPLORING
TOP ATTRACTIONS

Ancient Bathhouse in Nazareth. In 1993, Elias and Martina Shama-Sostar were renovating their crafts shop when they discovered ancient steam pipes under the store. Further excavation revealed a huge, wonderfully preserved Roman-style bathhouse. Israel's Antiquities Authority has not made any official announcements about the site, but several historians speculate that it might date from the 1st century AD. A one-hour tour takes you to the hot room, heating tunnels, and furnace. Coffee is served in the arched hall where wood and ashes were once kept. ⊠ *Mary's Well Sq.* ☎ *04/657-8539* ⊕ *www.nazarethbathhouse.org* ☑ *NIS 120 for up to 4 visitors* ☼ *Closed Sun.*

Fodor'sChoice ★ **Basilica of the Annunciation.** The Roman Catholic Basilica of the Annunciation, the largest church in the Middle East, was consecrated in 1969; it enshrines a small ancient cave dwelling or grotto, identified by many Catholics as the home of Mary. Here, they believe, the angel Gabriel appeared to her and announced she would conceive and "bear a son" and "call his name Jesus" (Luke 1). Pilgrim devotions suffuse the site throughout the day. Crusader-era walls and some restored Byzantine mosaics near the grotto bear witness to the antiquity of the tradition. The grotto is in the so-called lower church. Look up through the "well," or opening over the grotto, that connects with the upper church to the grand cupola, soaring 195 feet above you.

A spiral staircase leads to the vast upper church, the parish church of Nazareth's Roman Catholic community. Italian ceramic reliefs on the

Nazareth

0 — 200 yards
0 — 200 meters

Church of St. Gabriel
Ancient Bathhouse in Nazareth
Mary's Well
LATIN QUARTER
Namsawi Rd.
Schneller Rd.
Souk
Barclays Bank
EASTERN QUARTER
Basilica of the Annunciation
Central Bus Station
Nazareth Village
Casa Nova
Yom el-Ard
YMCA
El Garage
Shuhada
El Wadd El Jawwani
Paulus VI
El Mastak
Schneller Rd.
Ha-Tsiyonut
WESTERN QUARTER
Khirbat al-Dayr
Haifa Rd.
Derech Ha-Emek

KEY

🛈 Tourist information

huge concrete pillars represent the Stations of the Cross, captioned in the Arabic vernacular. You now have a closer view of the cupola, its ribs representing the petals of an upside-down lily—a symbol of Mary's purity—rooted in heaven.

The large panels on the walls of the upper church, touching on the theme of mother and child, include a vivid offering from the United States, a fine Canadian terra-cotta, and mosaics from England and Australia. Particularly interesting are the gifts from Japan (with gold leaf and pearls), Venezuela (a carved-wood statue), and Cameroon (a stylized painting in black, white, and red).

In the exit courtyard, a glass-enclosed baptistery is built over what is thought to have been an ancient *mikvah*, a Jewish ritual bath. The adjacent small Church of St. Joseph, just past Terra Sancta College, is built over a complex of rock-hewn chambers traditionally identified as the workshop of Joseph the Carpenter. Note that parking is hard to find; try Paulus VI Street or the side streets below it. ✉ *Casa Nova St.* ☎ *04/657-2501* ✉ *Free* ⊘ *Basilica closed for touring Sun. mornings.*

NEED A BREAK

✕ **Mahroum Sweets. Try the unbeatable Arab pastries at this bakeshop.** The place serves wonderful *bourma* (cylindrical pastries filled with whole pistachio nuts), cashew baklava, and great halvah. Don't confuse this spot with Mahroum Bakery: look for the Arab pastries, not gooey Western cakes. ✉ *Casal St., at Paulus VI St.* ☎ *04/655–4470* ⊕ *www.mahroum-baklawa.com.*

Souk. Bathed in the aromas of herbs and spices, this market in the Old City has something for everyone, from coffee sets to antiques to freshly baked pastries. The old lanes are narrow and shops tiny, with goods spilling into the street, but this souk is more orderly than those in many other Israeli cities. When it gets overwhelming, take a coffee break. ✉ *6129 St.* 🏷 *Free* ☉ *Closed Sun.*

WORTH NOTING

Church of St. Gabriel. This Greek Orthodox church is built over Nazareth's only natural water source, a spring dubbed Mary's Well. The Greek Orthodox, citing the noncanonical Gospel of St. James, believe it to be the place where the angel Gabriel appeared to Mary to announce the coming birth of Jesus.

The ornate church was built in 1750 and contains a stunning carved-wood pulpit and iconostasis (chancel screen) with painted New Testament scenes and silver-haloed saints. The walls have frescoes of figures from the Bible and the Greek Orthodox hagiography. A tiny "well" stands over the running water, and an aluminum cup gives a satisfying plop as it drops in. (The water is clean; the cup is more suspect.) The church is open to visitors in the morning. ✉ *6053 St.* ☎ *04/657–6437* 🏷 *Free.*

Mary's Well. This historically important but underwhelming structure marks the place where Mary is reputed to have been told by the angel Gabriel that she would bear a son, an event known as the Annunciation. The current "well" represents a structure that was once in use, but the open-air structure does not contain water anymore. Mary's Well Square is home to several shops and cafés, as well as a Greek Orthodox church. ✉ *Mary's Well Sq., 55 El Bishara St., Old City* 🏷 *Free.*

FAMILY **Nazareth Village.** The shepherds, weavers, and other characters in this reconstructed Jesus-era community delight children and adults alike. Using information gained from archaeological work done in the area, this attraction aims to re-create Jewish rural life as Jesus would have known it more than 2,000 years ago. Workshops, farms, and houses have been built with techniques that would have been used at the time. Interpreters in period costume cook and work at winepresses and looms, giving a sense of daily life. Reservations are required for guided tours, which meet on the second floor of the Nazareth YMCA. ✉ *Nazareth YMCA, 5105 St., 2nd fl.* ☎ *04/645–6042* ⊕ *www.nazarethvillage.com* 🏷 *NIS 50* ☉ *Closed Sun.*

WHERE TO EAT

After a full day of visiting Nazareth's shrines, you can quench your thirst with the locals at one of the little Arab restaurants along Paulus VI Street. Dinner here usually means hummus, shish kebab, baklava, and the like. Decor is incidental, atmosphere a function of the clientele of the moment, and dinnertime early. Needless to say, reservations aren't necessary, and dress is casual. If looking for more upscale dining, several high-end restaurants have opened in the past few years, serving traditional Arab and fusion fare.

$$$
MIDDLE EASTERN

✕**Al-Reda.** In a magnificent 19th-century mansion with a *Thousand and One Nights* atmosphere, this eatery matches its magical setting with excellent Arab cuisine, including interesting salads (eggplant with cheese) and kebabs, as well as dishes with Indian and European influences. Pesto and grilled vegetables stuffed in a chicken breast is a good choice, as are the vegetarian dishes. Don't pass up dessert. $ *Average main: NIS 76* ✉ *23 Al Bishara St.* ✛ *Next to Basilica of the Annunciation* ☎ *04/608–4404.*

$$$$
ECLECTIC
Fodor'sChoice
★

✕**Annai.** In a 200-year-old mansion, this restaurant is perhaps the most elegant in Nazareth—although there's not much competition. There are three choices for seating: an outdoor terrace, a dining room with traditional Middle Eastern accoutrements, and a second indoor area with sleeker, more modern decor. The eclectic menu includes a salad of baby shrimp and calamari in a chili-mayonnaise sauce, appetizers like seasonal vegetables with grilled goat cheese and a date vinaigrette, and the house specialty: chicken cordon bleu with a goose-liver filling. $ *Average main: NIS 101* ✉ *48 Bank Barclay's St., Old City* ☎ *077/789–0064* ☾ *Closed Sun.*

$$$$
MIDDLE EASTERN

✕**Diana.** Ranked among the region's best Arab restaurants, Diana doesn't fail to impress. Owner Duhul Safadi is most famous for his kebabs and lamb chops, but the fish and seafood dishes are all equally wonderful. There's a plant-filled terrace and a sophisticated dining room that would not be out of place in Tel Aviv. $ *Average main: NIS 101* ✉ *51 Paulus VI St.* ☎ *04/657–2919.*

$
CAFÉ

✕**Kahala.** Recharge in an elegant setting in the Old City, sampling delicious pastries and coffee or perhaps a glass of wine. This small café, set in a 200-year old building, is run by local architect Razan Zoubi, whose professional studio is upstairs. Around the corner from Al-Reda restaurant but in the same building, Kahala uses Al-Reda's kitchen to create delicious homemade cookies. Nibble a coffee-pecan or tahini-almond biscuit with a perfect espresso as you browse Razan's beautiful collection of Arab-designed modern and ancient architecture books. $ *Average main: NIS 25* ✉ *23 Al Bishara St.* ☾ *No dinner* ▭ *No credit cards.*

$$
CAFÉ

✕**Mama Salt Room & Cafe.** Leen Shomar Mansour, the "Mama" of the Salt Bar and Cafe, was driving her child 45 minutes to the nearest salt room (a therapy for respiratory ailments) to treat afflictions when she decided to bring the therapy to Nazareth. Opening the café was a natural extension: what would the parents drink while waiting for the child's treatment to finish? Serve only high-quality Italian coffee and homemade desserts, of course. Locals and in-the-know tourists have been flocking here ever since. Great music, always-fresh salads, fruit smoothies, sandwiches, beer, wine, and an undeniable European vibe make this a great destination to break up a touring day in Nazareth. On Thursday and Friday, the café serves dinner. $ *Average main: NIS 55* ✉ *Mary's Well Sq.* ☎ *04/637–7807* ☾ *Closed Sun. No dinner Mon.–Wed., Sat.*

$$
FAST FOOD

✕**Misada Ashraf.** Stop in for a plate of creamy and delicious hummus with various toppings: whole chickpeas, tahini, lamb meat, or pine nuts. Shawarma, schnitzels, and kebabs round out the menu, as do the especially delicious fresh salads. $ *Average main: NIS 60* ✉ *86 HaGalil St.* ☎ *04/655–5579.*

Nazareth's Basilica of the Annunciation has a venerable cave many Catholics believe was the home of Mary.

$$$$
MODERN
EUROPEAN
✕ **Olga's Kitchen and Bar.** Olga was the last headmistress at the school that occupied the 200-year-old space now housing this restaurant. A former student, Samer Milad, opened his restaurant, and with a wink to its origins, created a printed menu to look like a child's school notebook, carrying the theme throughout the elegant dining rooms. But the food is no child's play. Sophisticated fusion meals like beef fillet with caramel sauce, Japanese salad, stuffed mushrooms with goose liver, and lamb rib meat in phyllo do not fail to impress. Ask for a table with a view of the working kitchen or sit outside on the veranda, next to a fragrant herb garden. The bar upstairs turns into a nice place to people-watch in the evenings. ⑤ *Average main: NIS 160* ✉ *6 Al Roum, 6053 St.* ☎ *04/656–7755.*

$$
MIDDLE EASTERN
✕ **Tishreen.** The tile floors, stone walls, and dim lighting at this restaurant and bar named after a month on the Muslim calendar are the perfect setting for the Middle Eastern menu. Known for the wood-burning oven from which fresh breads emerge, this restaurant is big on kebabs and eggplant stuffed with pesto and cheese. Alcohol is served, too. ⑤ *Average main: NIS 75* ✉ *HaBsora St., near Mary's Well St.* ☎ *04/608–4666.*

WHERE TO STAY

$
B&B/INN
🏠 **Fauzi Azar Inn.** A 200-year-old mansion in the heart of the Old City, this inn has rooms with soaring ceilings that are perfect for couples or families, especially after a 2015 renovation in which rooms were enlarged (some are dorm style). **Pros:** historic building; reasonable rates; friendly staff. **Cons:** no elevator; not much parking; hard to find. ⑤ *Rooms from: $100* ✉ *2606 St., Old City* ✛ *Off the souk* ☎ *04/602–0469* ⊕ *abrahamhostels.com* ⇝ *14 rooms* ⦿ *Breakfast.*

$ **Nazareth Plaza Hotel.** The imposing stone facade of the Nazareth Plaza
HOTEL is the first hint that the city has finally acquired an upscale hotel. **Pros:**
sweeping views; pretty swimming pool; air-conditioned rooms. **Cons:**
no evening entertainment; far from Nazareth's shrines. $ *Rooms from:*
$150 ✉ *2 Hermon St., Upper Nazareth* ☎ *04/602-8200* 🛏 *182 rooms*
🍽 *Breakfast.*

$ **Rimonim Hotel Nazareth.** Most of the action here is underground,
HOTEL where the adjoining bar, lounge, and dining room add a bit of buzz.
Pros: convenient to the sights; air-conditioned rooms. **Cons:** street
noise; no evening entertainment. $ *Rooms from: $130* ✉ *1 Paulus VI*
St. ☎ *04/650-0000* ⊕ *www.rimonim.com* 🛏 *226 rooms* 🍽 *Breakfast.*

$ **St. Gabriel.** High on the ridge that overlooks Nazareth, this hotel
HOTEL began life as a convent—hence the charming neo-Gothic church still
in use on the property today. **Pros:** near the shrines; memorable views;
plenty of character. **Cons:** no evening entertainment. $ *Rooms from:*
$110 ✉ *50 Reus El Jibal St.* ☎ *04/657-2133, 04/645-4448* ⊕ *www.*
stgabrielhotel.com 🛏 *60 rooms* 🍽 *Breakfast.*

$ **Villa Nazareth.** A restored schoolhouse, this charming boutique hotel
HOTEL in Mary's Well Square is a perfect place to base your Nazareth visit.
Pros: great location; attentive staff; reliable Wi-Fi. **Cons:** bathrooms a
bit small by American standards. $ *Rooms from: $130* ✉ *Mary's Well*
Sq., 6053 St. ☎ *04/600-0569* ⊕ *www.villa-nazareth.co.il* 🛏 *18 rooms*
🍽 *Breakfast.*

ZIPPORI NATIONAL PARK

Village 5 km (3 miles) northwest of Nazareth off Rte. 79, site 3 km (2
miles) from village via bypass. 47 km (29 miles) east of Haifa.

Lush beauty and fantastic archaeological finds make this place worth
a visit, especially if you have an interest in Roman culture or Talmudic
thought. Like many places during the Roman era, Zippori—known in
the classical world as Sepphoris—was a prosperous city where Jews
and gentiles coexisted fairly peaceably. The ancient city, situated on a
high ridge with commanding views, can be visited in two hours. The
key sites are relatively close together.

GETTING HERE AND AROUND

Driving to this national park from Nazareth, follow Route 79 west and
turn north at the signs. No buses service this route. If you don't have
a car, take a taxi from Nazareth (agree on the price in advance, and
consider asking the driver to wait).

EXPLORING

Fodor'sChoice **Zippori National Park.** The multiple narratives of Zippori, today an
★ impressive, popular archaeological site known for Israel's finest Roman-
era mosaics, begin with a Jewish town that stood here from at least the
1st century BC, and Christian tradition reveres the town as the birthplace of the Virgin Mary. Zippori's refusal to join the Great Revolt of
the Jews against the Romans (AD 66–73) left a serious gap in the rebel
defenses in the Galilee, angering its compatriots but sparing the town
the usual Roman vengeance when the uprising failed. The real significance of Zippori for Jewish tradition, however, is that in the late 2nd or

early 3rd century AD, the legendary sage Rabbi Yehuda ha-Nasi, head of the country's Jewish community at the time, moved here from Beit She'arim, whereupon the Sanhedrin (the Jewish high court) soon followed. Rabbi Yehuda summoned the greatest rabbis in the land to pool their experiences. The result was the encyclopedic work known as the Mishnah. Further commentary was added in later centuries to produce the Talmud, the primary guide to Orthodox Jewish practice to this day.

By the 3rd century AD, Zippori had acquired a mixed population of Jews, pagans, and Christians. The most celebrated find is the mosaic floor of a Roman villa, perhaps the governor's residence, depicting Dionysian drinking scenes. Its most stunning detail is the exquisite face of a woman, which the media dubbed "the Mona Lisa of the Galilee." The restored mosaics are housed in an air-conditioned structure with helpful explanations. In other parts of the park, the so-called Nile Mosaic displays Egyptian motifs, and a mosaic synagogue floor (below the parking lot) is decorated with the signs of the zodiac, like those found in Beit Alfa and Hammat Tiberias.

If the mosaic floors reveal the opulence of Roman Sepphoris, the relatively small Roman theater is evidence of the cultural life the wealth could support. Take a few minutes to climb the watchtower of Dahr el-Omar's 18th-century castle for the panoramic view and the museum of archaeological artifacts. About 1 km (½ mile) east of the main site—near the park entrance—is a huge section of ancient Zippori's water system, once fed by springs north of Nazareth. The ancient aqueduct-reservoir is in fact a deep, man-made plastered canyon, and the effect is extraordinary. ⊠ *Off Rte. 79, Nazareth* ☎ *04/656–8272* ⊕ *www.parks.org.il* 🎟 *NIS 28.*

CANA

8 km (5 miles) north of Nazareth on Rte. 754, 1 km (½ mile) south of junction of Rtes. 77 and 754, 50 km (31 miles) east of Haifa.

Near the large, modern Arab village of Kfar Kanna is the site of the ancient Jewish village of Cana, mentioned in the New Testament. Here Jesus performed his first miracle, turning water into wine at a wedding feast, thereby emerging from his "hidden years" to begin a three-year ministry in the Galilee.

Within the village, red signs lead to rival churches—one Roman Catholic, the other Greek Orthodox—that enshrine the scriptural tradition. (The alley to these churches is just wide enough for cars, and you can sometimes park in the courtyard of a souvenir store. If the street is blocked, park on the main road.)

The plaza of the Greek Orthodox St. George Convent is a peaceful spot. The First Miracle Church, on the grounds, is rarely open to visitors, but you can wander the landscape freely. On a lower plaza is a handsome statue of Jesus (surrounded, perhaps predictably, by souvenir shops).

GETTING HERE AND AROUND

Part of the sprawling suburbs of Nazareth, Kfar Kanna sits astride Route 754, linking Route 77 to the north and Route 79 to the south.

EXPLORING

Cana Wedding Church. This quaint church on a hill was built in 1881 where Catholics believe Jesus performed his first miracle (John 2:1–11). The basement has stones and mosaics that bear witness to the ancient building that once stood on this site. ⊠ *Off Rte. 754* ☎ *04/651–7011* ⚏ *Free* ◷ *Closed Sun.*

Golani Junction Tree Planting Center. Around the Golani Junction are groves of evergreens planted by visitors as part of the Plant a Tree With Your Own Hands project of the Jewish National Fund. Since the early 1900s, more than 250 million trees have been restored to barren hillsides across Israel. At the Golani Junction Tree Planting Center, you can choose a sapling, dedicate it to someone, and plant it yourself; the cost is $18 for adults and $10 for children. Email ahead of time to coordinate your tree planting. ⊠ *Off Rte. 77, Givat Avni* ✛ *East of Golani Junction* ☎ *02/658–3349* ✉ *tovad@kkl.org.il* ⊕ *www.jnf.org* ◷ *Closed Fri. afternoon and Sat.*

MOUNT TABOR

16 km (10 miles) south of the Golani Junction, off Rtes. 65 and 7266, 17 km (10½ miles) northeast of Afula.

Now covered with pine trees, Mount Tabor has a serene look that belies its strategic and historical importance. Here you find the Church of the Transfiguration, which marks the place where tradition says Jesus began to radiate light and was seen conversing with Moses and Elijah. Christian pilgrims have venerated this site for centuries: Napoléon brought 3,000 French soldiers here to battle the Ottomans in 1799. Today Mount Tabor is popular with hang-gliding enthusiasts, and there's a marathon around the mountain in April.

GETTING HERE AND AROUND

If you're driving, take Route 7266 through Shibli, a village of Bedouins who abandoned their nomadic life a few generations ago. A narrow switchback road starts in a clearing between Shibli and the next village, Dabouriya. Nazareth-based taxis often wait at the bottom of the mountain to provide shuttle service to the top. Watch out for them if driving your own car up; they come down in overdrive like the lords of the mountain they almost are.

EXPLORING

TOP ATTRACTIONS

Church of the Transfiguration. As far back as the Byzantine period, Christian tradition identified Mount Tabor as the "high mountain apart" that Jesus ascended with his disciples Peter, James, and John. There, report the Gospels, "he was transfigured before them" (Matthew 17:2) as a radiant white figure, flanked by Moses and Elijah. The altar of the present imposing church, which was consecrated in 1924, represents the tabernacle of Jesus that Peter suggested they build; those of Moses and Elijah appear as small chapels at the back of the church. Step up to the terrace to the right of the church doors for a great view of the Jezreel Valley to the west and south. From a platform on the Byzantine and Crusader ruins to the left of the modern church (watch your step), there is a panorama east and north over the Galilean hills. A nearby

Franciscan pilgrim rest stop has refreshments and restrooms. ⊠ *Off Rte. 7266, Kfar Tavor* ☎ *04/662–0720* ☞ *Free.*

Mount Tabor. The domelike mountain, the region's highest, looms over one of the prettiest stretches of the Lower Galilee. Quilts of farmland kaleidoscope through the seasons as different crops grow, ripen, and are harvested. Modern woods of evergreens cover the hillsides, making this a lovely place for a walk or a hike. To get here from Route 7266, take the narrow switchback road that starts in a clearing between Shibli and the next village, Dabouriya.

Apart from the natural beauty, Mount Tabor and its immediate surroundings have considerable biblical history. About 32 centuries ago, Israelite warriors of the prophetess-judge Deborah and her general, Barak, routed a Canaanite chariot army that had gotten bogged down in the mud. The modern kibbutz of Ein Dor, south of the mountain, is the site of ancient Endor, where King Saul unsuccessfully beseeched the spirit of the prophet Samuel for help before his fateful (and fatal) battle against the Philistines (I Samuel 28:3–25). ⊠ *Rte. 7266, Kfar Tavor* ⊕ *www.parks.org.il* ☞ *Free.*

Tabor Winery. An excellent time-out from historical sights, this winery was founded in 1999, and the quality of its wines has risen steeply since 2005. Chill out with a cheese platter while tasting the winery's finest vintages. Tours are available for groups of more than 10 participants. ⊠ *Kfar Tavor Visitor Center, Keren Kayemet L'Yisrael Ave., Kfar Tavor* ☎ *04/676–0444* ⊕ *www.twc.co.il/en/* ☞ *Free* ☉ *Closed Sat.*

WORTH NOTING

FAMILY **Marzipan Museum.** In the same compound as the Tabor Winery, this charming museum contains explanations about almonds and delectable products made from locally grown almonds. If you have kids in tow, don't think twice about signing up for the fun marzipan-making workshop. (There's also a chocolate workshop.) Best of all, you take your creations home. ⊠ *Kfar Tabor Visitor Center, Keren Kayemet L'Yisrael Ave., Kfar Tavor* ☎ *04/677–2111* ⊕ *www.shakedtavor.co.il* ☞ *Museum free, workshop NIS 64 for children.*

WHERE TO EAT

$$$ ✕ **Al Karma.** A delicious homemade Lebanese meal at this family-run res-
MIDDLE EASTERN taurant in the visitor center of this town near Mount Tabor starts with an array of fresh salads, followed by traditional favorites. Don't miss the meat-and-rice-stuffed zucchini with yogurt sauce, or the catch of the day. End the meal with a sticky and sweet *kanafeh* pastry. $ *Average main: NIS 80* ⊠ *Kfar Tavor Visitor Center, Off Rte. 767, Kfar Tavor.*

EN
ROUTE
If heading to the Sea of Galilee, take Route 767, which breaks off Route 65 at Kfar Tavor. It's a beautiful drive of about 25 minutes. The first village, **Kfar Kama,** is one of two in Israel of the Cherkessi (Circassian) community, Sunni Muslim non-Arabs from Russia's Caucasus Mountains who settled here in 1876. The unusually decorative minaret of the mosque is just one element of the tradition the community vigorously continues to preserve. On the descent to the Sea of Galilee, there's a parking area precisely at sea level. The lake is still more than 700 feet below, and the view is superb, especially in the afternoon. You meet Route 90 at the bottom of the road.

Continued on page 367

Jesus *in the* Galilee

Galilee beckons shyly. As in days of old, there is little of the frenetic pace and charged emotions of Jerusalem. For many Christians, the evocative, soft landscapes breathe new life into old familiar stories, and brush black-and-white scriptures with color. But curious visitors with less religious motivation will be drawn into Galilee's gentle charm. This tour of selected sights will speak to both.

"And passing along by the **Sea of Galilee,** he saw Simon and Andrew the brother of Simon casting a net into the sea, for they were fishermen. And Jesus said to them,

'Follow me and I will make you become fishers of men.'"

(Mark 1: 16–17)

Hills ring the Sea of Galilee, a freshwater lake.

Jesus was born in Bethlehem and died in Jerusalem, but it was in the Galilee that his ministry was forged. Over time, archaeologists and historians have unearthed many sites referred to in the New Testament. Today you can walk the hillsides, sail the Sea of Galilee, explore the ruins, and touch the churches of this beautiful region. Or you can sit under a tree and read scripture in the place where its narrative unfolded. If you have an eye for the contours of the land and an ear for echoes of the past, the experience can be unforgettable.

The activity and teachings of Jesus gain meaning and resonance from the landscape and social setting in which they emerged. Understand their context, and you will enhance your understanding of the events that have so shaped Western civilization.

By Mike Rogoff

RESTLESS SOCIETY, TURBULENT TIMES

Christ in the Storm on the Sea of Galilee by Jan Brueghel the Elder

The Romans came for the weekend in 63 BC and stayed for four centuries. Herod (later "the Great"), scion of a powerful political family, began his brutal reign as King of the Jews, courtesy of Rome, in 37 BC. He died in 4 BC, only a short time after the birth of Jesus (Matt. 2:1).

Herod's kingdom was divided among his three surviving sons: Archelaeus, Herod Antipas (who got Galilee, and Perea beyond the Jordan River), and Philip. It was Herod Antipas who executed John the Baptist (Matt. 14:10), and was in Jerusalem at the time of the crucifixion (Luke 23:7).

RIVAL THEOLOGIES

Jewish society in the land of Israel was anything but unified and placid 2,000 years ago. Two ideological streams dominated: the Sadducees were the establishment, many of them wealthy, led by the priestly class that controlled the Temple-based cult of Yahweh, the One God, in Jerusalem. They took religious texts literally, and rejected the idea of resurrection and an afterlife (Acts 23:6–9).

The Pharisees, on the other hand, drew their strength from the common people, offering a comforting belief in resurrection and an afterlife in a better world.

Their rabbis, or teachers, would interpret biblical law, a practice that laid the groundwork for post-Temple Judaism as practiced until today.

Jesus himself came from the Pharisaic tradition, and "taught in their synagogues" (Luke 4:15). He was critical of the Pharisees' behavior, but not of their theology: They "sit on Moses' seat," he told his followers, "so practice and observe whatever they tell you" (Matt. 23:2).

SECTS AND CATACLYSM

Theological differences and domestic politics gave rise to numerous Jewish sects with strong religious agendas: the followers of Jesus, and of John the Baptist before him, were just two. One of the best known at the time were the Essenes, widely identified today as the monastic Jewish community that wrote the Dead Sea Scrolls.

There were other, less spiritual types like the Zealots—extreme nationalists who spearheaded the Great Revolt against Rome in AD 66. The cataclysm was not long in coming: Jerusalem and the Temple were razed in AD 70, four decades after Jesus's prediction that "there will not be left here one stone upon another" (Matt. 24:2).

Marriage Feast at Cana by Hieronymus Bosch

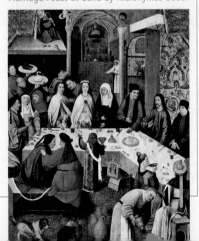

FACT, FAITH, AND TRADITION

The church on the Mount of Beatitudes has sweeping views of the Sea of Galilee.

Finding evidence of events or personalities in the distant past, the New Testament era included, is a kind of treasure hunt; and there is rarely an "X" to mark the spot. But when you do strike gold, through archaeological discoveries or ancient writings, for example, it thrills scholars and laypeople alike.

POPULATING ANCIENT MAPS

There are Galilean towns, like Nazareth and Tiberias, that have survived the centuries and are obviously genuine. Others, like Cana, are still debated. A lot of rocks have been turned over in the last three-quarters of a century, however, and archaeologists have exposed and identified Capernaum, Bethsaida, Chorazin (Korazim), Caesarea Philippi (Banias) in the Upper Galilee, and, to the satisfaction of many, Gennasaret (Ginosar) and Nain as well.

"TRADITIONAL" SITES:
WHERE MEMORIES ENDURE

Other sites have been linked to events over time, though no real evidence exists. Scriptural descriptions don't exactly offer geographical coordinates, and some locations that are still much visited by pilgrims are conjecture that has jelled into tradition. Visitors in the distant past often took local hearsay for hard fact when tour guides and other opportunists pointed out the very rock or glade or spring where this or that happened. It's not surprising that many traditional holy places are found so close to each other. Guides were often paid by the site—why should they journey unnecessary distances?

Events like the Sermon on the Mount, the Transfiguration, the feeding of the multitudes, the "feed my sheep" encounter of John 21, and the swine of the Gadarenes are all in this category. But for the faithful, the personal spiritual experience is more than a search for "the very stone" on which a particular event actually took place. Centuries of prayers and tears will sanctify a site, making it a remembrance place in the region where it all began.

TOURING THE CRADLE OF CHRISTIANITY

An astonishing three-quarters of the activity of Jesus recorded in the New Testament took place on, around, or within sight of the "Sea" of Galilee. The lake provided the largely Jewish towns and villages on its shores with a source of fresh water, a fishing industry, and a means of transportation.

Base yourself in Tiberias and head north, or clockwise, around the lake. The sights are close enough to see in a day. To visit Nazareth, Cana, and Mount Tabor, 25 miles west of Tiberias, allot another day or be selective. Below are key places associated with Jesus, and scriptural references to them.

❶ TIBERIAS *"…boats from Tiberias came near the place…"* (John 6:23). Herod Antipas, son of Herod the Great, built the city as the capital of the Galilee in AD 20. The town never lost its importance, and is today the region's urban center.

❷ GINOSAR/GENNESARET Eight kms (5 miles) north of Tiberias, modern Ginosar is a kibbutz, with a museum that houses the extraordinary 1st-century-AD wooden boat found nearby. *"…they came to land at Gennesaret…immediately the people recognized him…and as many as touched [the fringe of his garment] were made well"* (Mark 6:53–56).

❸ MOUNT OF BEATITUDES *"Seeing the crowds, he went up on the mountain, and when he sat down his disciples came to him…'Blessed are the poor in spirit…'"* (Matt. 5–7). The traditional site of Jesus's Sermon on the Mount is set in hilltop gardens, with a church and a superb view of the lake.

❹ TABGHA Two events in the life of Jesus are recalled in two churches here. The Multiplication was one: a famous 5th-century mosaic records the event. Crowds followed Jesus and evening came. What about food? *"You give them something to eat'…'We have only five loaves here and two fish'…'Bring them…' He looked up to heaven, and blessed…And they all ate and were satisfied…about 5,000 men, besides women and children"* (Matt. 14: 15–21).

The primacy of Peter is another. The beach and an attractively simple chapel recall the appearance of Jesus on the shore: *"'Have you any fish?'…'No'…'Cast the net'…'It is the Lord!'…'Simon [Peter]… Do you love me?…Feed my sheep'"* (John 21:1–19).

❺ CAPERNAUM Jesus made this thriving Jewish town, now an archaeological site, the center of his ministry: *"He went and dwelt in Capernaum…"* (Matt. 4:13). Here he preached— *"…and immediately on the sabbath he entered the synagogue and taught"* (Mark 1:21).

Greek Orthodox church, Cana

Basilica of the Annunciation, Nazareth

Golani Junction

Lavi

❾ Cana

65

Zippori

754

79

Kfar Kama

Nazerat Illit (Upper Nazareth)

Nazareth ❿

Kfar Tavor

Migdal Ha'emek

Shibli

Mount Tabor

❶❶

Mount Tabor

716

6 BETHSAIDA This was the hometown of the disciples Philip, Andrew, and Peter (John 1:44), and the place where Jesus cured a blind man (Mark 8:22–25). The town was left stranded when its lagoon dried out, and eluded identification until recently. It's in th Jordan River Park.

7 KURSI Jesus cured two madmen on the Golan Heights slopes, *"the country of the Gadarenes": "…a herd of swine was feeding… [the demons] came out [of the demoniacs] and went into the swine…"* (Matt. 8:28–34).

Synagogue at Capernaum

8 JORDAN RIVER Today people come to be baptized in the Jordan at Yardenitin this northern region, but the New Testament story almost certainly refers to the river's southern reaches, near Jericho: *"Then Jesus came from the Galilee to the Jordan to John, to be baptized by him"* (Matt. 3:13).

9 CANA When the wine ran out at a wedding feast, Jesus (after some persuasion) turned six stone jars-full of water into superior wine. *"This, the first of his signs, Jesus did in Cana of Galilee…"* (John 2:1–11).

Mount of Beatitudes **3** **5** Capernaum **6** Bethsaida
4 Tabgha
87 92

2 Ginosar

Kursi **7**

Sea of Galilee (Lake Kinneret)

1 Tiberias
90

Ein Gev

Byzantine church at Kursi

Ancient boat at Ginosar

Kinneret

767
Yavne'el
Jordan River
Degania Alef **8**

0 —— 4 mi
0 —— 4 km

10 NAZARETH Here, the New Testament relates, an angel appeared to Mary to announce the coming birth of Jesus (Luke 1:26–38). It was here he grew up (his so-called "hidden years") and to Nazareth he returned as a teacher: *"…he went to the synagogue… on the sabbath… he stood up to read… the prophet Isaiah…"*(Luke 4:16–30).

11 MOUNT TABOR In the event called "the Transfiguration," Jesus took three of his disciples *"up a high mountain apart,"* where they had a vision of him as a radiant white figure flanked by Moses and Elijah (Mark 9:2–8). Mount Tabor has long been identified as the place, though some prefer Mount Hermon in the far north.

Baptism in the Jordan River

6
IN FOCUS JESUS IN THE GALILEE

TIPS FOR EXPLORING THE GALILEE

Greek Orthodox church at Capernaum

GETTING AROUND

Buses may be the cheapest way to see Israel, but they are not time-effective in the Galilee. Nazareth and Tiberias are easy to get to (and are 45 minutes apart), and a few less-frequent lines stop at Cana, Ginosar, and near Tabgha. Other Christian sites in the area are a fair hike from the highway or only doable by car.

HOLIDAYS, SERVICES, AND MORE

The Christmas and Easter celebrations that are so much part of the culture in many places are absent in Israel, where only 2% of its citizens are Christian. In the Galilee, the exception is

Nazareth, with its lights and Christmas trees, and a traditional procession downtown at 3 pm on Christmas Eve. Many denominations are represented here, but Nazareth has no scheduled services in English.

In Tiberias, English-speakers can attend Catholic mass in St. Peter's Church (daily at 6:30 pm Sundays at 8:30 am) and occasional Protestant services at YMCA Penuel (just north of town) and St. Andrew's (opposite the Scots Hotel).

VISITING SUGGESTIONS

Christian sites demand respectful behavior and conservative dress (no shorts, short skirts, or sleeveless tops). Photography is usually permitted, but professionals may require prior permission. Pay attention to advertised opening times and allow time for unexpected delays in getting there.

HIKING THE LANDSCAPE

Hikers can consider the Jesus Trail (www.jesustrail.com). Its primary route is 65 kms (40 miles) long from Nazareth to Capernum, but you can select sections for a shorter hike.

You can also walk or cycle along the footpaths of the 60-km (37-mile) Gospel Trail (www.go-israel.com), which traces the path that Jesus took along the Sea of Galilee.

CREATING SPECIAL MOMENTS IN THE GALILEE

■ Carry a Bible and a good map.

■ In fine weather, the Mount of Beatitudes is best in the afternoon, when the light is gentler on the lake and the hills.

■ If you are unencumbered by luggage, and don't have a car to retrieve, stroll the easy trail from Mount of Beatitudes down to Tabgha (cross the highway with care), visit the two sites there, and then walk the 2-mile

promenade that follows the highway east to Capernaum.

■ The little beach of volcanic pebbles at Tabgha (the Primacy site) can be magical.

■ Bethsaida in Jordan River Park is evocative—pure 1st century: no Byzantine, Crusader, or modern structures. It's never crowded, and offers a great place to sit with a view of the lake and read your favorite verses.

TIBERIAS AND THE SEA OF GALILEE

The Sea of Galilee is, in fact, a freshwater lake, measuring 21 km (13 miles) from north to south and 11 km (7 miles) east to west. Almost completely ringed by cliffs and steep hills, the lake lies in a hollow about 700 feet below sea level, which accounts for its warm climate and subtropical vegetation. This is Israel's Riviera-on-a-lake, replete with beaches and outdoor recreation facilities. Its shores are also dotted with sites hallowed by Christian tradition (note that several of these sites demand modest dress) as well as some important ancient synagogues. Tiberias itself is one of Judaism's four holy cities, along with Jerusalem, Hebron, and Tzfat.

The city of Tiberias is the logical starting base for exploration. One sightseeing strategy is to circle the Sea of Galilee clockwise from Tiberias (via Routes 90, 87, 92, and 98).

TIBERIAS

38 km (23½ miles) north of Beit She'an, 36 km (23 miles) east of Nazareth, 70 km (43 miles) east of Haifa.

As the only city on the Sea of Galilee, Tiberias, with a population of 40,000, has become the region's hub. The city spreads up a steep hillside, from 700 feet below sea level at the lake, to about 80 feet above sea level in its highest neighborhoods—a differential big enough to create significant variations in comfort levels during midsummer.

The splendid panoramic views of both the lake and the Golan Heights on the far shore deserved a better sort of development. Tiberias has little beauty and less charm, and although almost 2,000 years old, it still has the atmosphere of a place neglected for decades, if not centuries. It's at once brash and sleepy, with a reputation as a resort town based more on its location than its attractions. Travelers tend to see little of the town itself, sticking to the restaurants and hotels along the lake, and the boardwalk, which comes alive at night with vendors hawking clothes, jewelry, and knickknacks. Those traveling by car often skip the town altogether, opting for the numerous bed-and-breakfasts that dot the region.

GETTING HERE AND AROUND
The city sits astride the junction of Routes 90 and 77. Egged buses regularly serve Tiberias from Haifa, Nazareth, Tel Aviv, and Jerusalem. Haifa is one hour away, while Tel Aviv and Jerusalem are both two hours distant. Tiberias is small enough to walk to most locations, though given the punishing summer heat you may wish to have a taxi take you for even short jaunts.

Taxi Contacts **HaEmek.** ☎ *04/604–4888.* **Udi Taxi.** ☎ *072/221–4701.*

VISITOR INFORMATION
Contacts **Tiberias Tourist Office.** ✉ *9 Habanim St.* ☎ *04/672–5666.*

EXPLORING

Hammat Tiberias National Park. This is where Israel's hottest spring gushes from the earth at 60°C (140°F) due to cracks in the earth's crust along the Syrian-African Rift. Alas, this is an archaeological site known for its superb mosaics, so you don't get to dip you toes into the waters here. (You can do that at the more impressive hot springs at Hammat Gader.)

By the end of the Second Temple period (the 1st century AD), when settlement in the Sea of Galilee region was at its height, a Jewish town called Hammat (Hot Springs) stood here. With time, Hammat was overshadowed by its newer neighbor, Tiberias. The benefits of the mineral hot springs were already legendary: a coin minted in Tiberias during the rule of Emperor Trajan, around AD 100, shows Hygeia, the goddess of health, sitting on a rock with a spring gushing out beneath it.

Parts of ancient Hammat have been uncovered, bringing to light a number of ruined synagogues. The most dramatic dates from the 4th century AD, with an elaborate mosaic floor that uses motifs almost identical to those at Beit Alfa: classical Jewish symbols, human figures representing the four seasons and the signs of the zodiac, and the Greek god Helios at the center. They are among the finest ever found in Israel.

CLOSE UP

Tiberias Through Time

Herod Antipas, son of Herod the Great, founded Tiberias in AD 18 and dedicated the town to Tiberius, then emperor of Rome. The Tiberians had little stomach for the Jewish war against Rome that broke out in AD 66. They soon surrendered, preventing the vengeful destruction visited on other Galilean towns.

With Jerusalem laid waste in AD 70, the center of Jewish life gravitated to the Galilee. By the 4th century, the Jewish high court, the Sanhedrin, had settled in Tiberias. Here Jewish oral law was compiled into what became known as the Jerusalem Talmud, and Tiberias's status as one of Judaism's holy cities was assured.

Tiberias knew hard times under the Byzantines, and further declined under the hostile Crusaders in the Middle Ages. Starting in the 1700s, newcomers from Turkey and Eastern Europe swelled the Jewish population, but an 1837 earthquake left Tiberias in ruins.

Relations between Jews and Arabs were generally cordial until the Arab riots of 1936, when some 30 Jews were massacred. During the 1948 War of Independence, an attack by local Arabs brought a counterattack from Jewish forces, and the Arabs abandoned the town. Today the citizenry is entirely Jewish, and abandoned mosques stand as silent monuments.

6

As for how the spring was created, legend says that Solomon, the great king of Israel, wanted a hot bath and used his awesome authority to force some young devils below ground to heat the water. Seeing that the springs brought great happiness to his subjects, Solomon worried about what would happen when he died and the devils stopped their labors. Solomon made the hapless devils deaf, so to this day they continue to heat the water for fear of his wrath. ⊠ *Rechov HaMerchatzaot, Rte. 90* ⊹ *2 km (1 mile) south of Tiberias* ☎ *04/672–5287* ⊕ *www.parks. org.il* ☜ *NIS 14.*

Promenade. A promenade ideal for walking or running follows the lakeshore for about 5 km (3 miles) south of Tiberias, with nice views of the lake and Golan Heights. As you leave the hotels behind, you appreciate the Sea of Galilee's mystic beauty. The path is lighted. ⊠ *Tiberias* ☜ *Free.*

Tiberias Hot Springs. In addition to sophisticated therapeutic services and facilities, this modern spa has a large, warm indoor mineral pool (35°C [95°F]) and a small outdoor one right near the lake's edge. A restaurant serves lunch. ⊠ *Eliezer Kaplan Blvd. (Rte. 90)* ☎ *04/612–3600* ☜ *NIS 88.*

Tomb of Moses Maimonides. Foremost among Tiberias's many venerated resting places is this tomb. Born in Córdoba, Spain, Moses Maimonides (1135–1204)—widely known by his Hebrew acronym, the "Rambam" (for Rabbi Moshe Ben Maimon)—was the greatest Jewish scholar and spiritual authority of the Middle Ages. To his profound knowledge of the Talmud, Maimonides brought an incisive intellect honed by his study of Aristotelian philosophy and the physical sciences. The result was a rationalism unusual in Jewish scholarship and a lucidity of analysis and style admired by Jewish and non-Jewish scholars alike.

Maimonides never lived in Tiberias, but after his death in Egypt, his remains were brought to this Jewish holy city for interment. His white-washed tomb, topped by a soaring spire of red steel girders, has become a shrine, dripping with candle wax and tears. ⊠ *Ben Zakkai St.* 📧 *Free* 🕓 *Closed Sat.*

WHERE TO EAT

At a right angle to the waterside promenade, the *midrachov* (pedestrian mall) has a wide range of affordable dining options. If you're into local color, look for the tiny, modest restaurants (where English really *is* a foreign language) on Hagalil Street and in the little streets that connect it to Habanim Street, like the pedestrian-only Kishon Street.

Use the coordinates at the end of each listing (✛ A1) to locate a site on the corresponding map.

$$
BRITISH
FAMILY
✕ **Big Ben Pub** (*Big Ben BBQ Restaurant*). You can't miss Big Ben, just at the top of the boardwalk; this casual spot is practically a landmark. An outdoor terrace with seating overlooks the promenade, and inside, a beautiful antique wooden bar features eight beers on tap. There are more tables indoors, too. The menu covers all the bases: pastas, fish and meat on the grill, chicken schnitzel and fries for the kids. The friendly vibe at this large place is what draws people back: the food is not always the best. 💲 *Average main: NIS 70* ⊠ *Tiberias Promenade* ✛ *On waterfront near Caesar Hotel* 📞 *53/944–0764* 🌐 *bigben.rest.co.il* 🚫 *No credit cards* ✛ *D2.*

$$$
MODERN ISRAELI
✕ **Decks.** Built on a pier extending into the Sea of Galilee, this family-run restaurant has breathtaking views from seats indoors and outside. This airy, casual spot with wooden tables and metal chairs is some-thing of an institution, and locals keep coming back for the delicious meats—sizzling steaks, succulent goose liver, or long skewers of veal and vegetables, grilled slowly over hickory wood. The bluefin tuna carpaccio, caught by the manager's brother, is a delicacy. Save room for dessert, as all dishes are homemade. 💲 *Average main: NIS 100* ⊠ *11 HaGdud Barak St.* 📞 *04/671–0800* 🌐 *www.lido.co.il* 🕓 *No dinner Fri. No lunch Sat.* ✛ *D2.*

$
MIDDLE EASTERN
✕ **Guy.** Stuffed vegetables are the calling card at this kosher eatery, whose name means "ravine" in Hebrew. The cook-matriarch Geula comes from a Tiberias family, but her Moroccan ancestry shines through in delicious dishes like eggplant stuffed with seasoned ground beef. There are good, if more conventional, Middle Eastern options, but go for the excellent soups, and try some *kibbeh* (a Kurdish-Iraqi specialty of seasoned ground meat and bulgur). Ask your waiter to recommend the tastiest treats, such as apricots or dates stuffed with rice. The restaurant faces the lake and is slightly set back from the sidewalk; keep your eyes open or you'll miss it. It gets busy at lunchtime but is quieter at dinner. 💲 *Average main: NIS 48* ⊠ *52 Hagalil St.* 📞 *04/672–3036* 🚫 *No credit cards* 🕓 *Closed Sat. No dinner Fri.* ✛ *D3.*

$$
ASIAN
✕ **Pagoda.** This faux-Chinese temple has an outdoor patio overlooking the lake, and across the road is a maze of more intimate rooms entered through a garden. The kosher menu of various Asian cuisines and some international favorites is identical at both places, so pick your favorite and try the Thai soups (such as the tasty hot-and-sour soup), the lamb

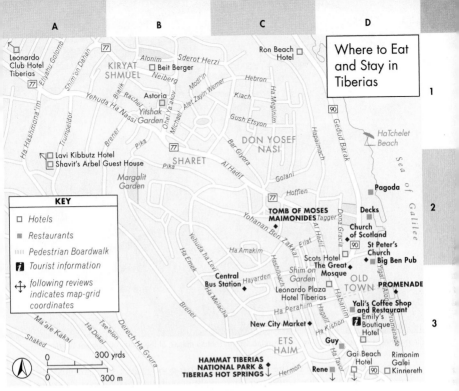

Where to Eat and Stay in Tiberias

KEY

☐ Hotels
■ Restaurants
▥ Pedestrian Boardwalk
🛈 Tourist information
⊕ following reviews indicates map-grid coordinates

spareribs, or strips of beef with peanut sauce. There's a sushi bar, too. Note that Pagoda is closed for the Sabbath. ⑤ *Average main: NIS 75* ⊠ *Gedud Barak St.* ☎ *04/671–0800* ☾ *Closed Sat. No dinner Fri.* ⊕ *D2.*

$$
CAFÉ
✕ **Rene.** An impressive brick building and a terrace with lovely views of the Sea of Galilee are great draws. The dairy and salad menu of this bistro, bar, and café has a fine selection of breakfast dishes, salads, pasta, calzones, sandwiches, quiche, and desserts. Locals rave about the cheese blintzes with sweet cheese and raisins. There is music most evenings, plus air-conditioning and a full bar. ⑤ *Average main: NIS 70* ⊠ *Eliezar Kaplan Blvd.* ⊕ *Across from Tiberias Hot Springs* ☎ *04/646–2323* ⊕ *renebistrobarcafe.co.il* ☾ *Closed Fri. No lunch Sat.* ⊕ *D3.*

$$
ISRAELI
✕ **Yali's Coffee Shop and Restaurant.** This quiet, modern café is a good place for a meal anytime. The menu features pasta, pizza, and salads as well as breakfast items. There is outdoor seating, but ask for a table inside near the window to enjoy the Wi-Fi, air-conditioning, and people-watching. ⑤ *Average main: NIS 60* ⊠ *16 HaBanim St.* ☎ *04/999–7996* ☾ *Closed Fri. afternoon, Sat.* ▭ *No credit cards* ⊕ *D3.*

WHERE TO STAY
Use the coordinates at the end of each listing (⊕ A1) to locate a site on the corresponding map.

$
HOTEL
▨ **Astoria.** One of Tiberias's better moderately priced hotels, the Astoria is set away from the lake, but don't worry; there are still views

The god Helios occupies the center of a spectacular 4th-century mosaic of the zodiac at Hammat Tiberias.

from some of the guest rooms. **Pros:** good value; some rooms with water views. **Cons:** too far to walk downtown; basic decor. ⑤ *Rooms from: $160* ⊠ *13 Bruria St.* ☎ *04/672–2351* ⊕ *www.astoria.co.il* ⤙ *100 rooms* ⍥ *Breakfast* ✛ *B1.*

$
HOTEL

☷ **Beit Berger.** This family-run hotel has spacious rooms, most with balconies. **Pros:** reasonable rates; hillside views; handy kitchens. **Cons:** too far to walk downtown; no swimming pool. ⑤ *Rooms from: $120* ⊠ *27 Neiberg St.* ☎ *04/671–5151* ⊕ *www.bergerhotel.co.il* ⤙ *43 rooms* ⍥ *Breakfast* ✛ *B1.*

$$
HOTEL
Fodor'sChoice
★

☷ **Emily's Boutique Hotel.** On-site parking and a central location attracts young and budget-watching tourists to this small, family-owned boutique hotel, one of Tiberias's newer hotels. **Pros:** friendly staff; reasonably priced; easy access to attractions. **Cons:** on main road. ⑤ *Rooms from: $220* ⊠ *66 HaGalil St.* ☎ *04/664–7500* ⊕ *emilys_hotel.xwx.co.il* ⤙ *48 rooms* ⍥ *Breakfast* ✛ *D3.*

$$$
RESORT
FAMILY

☷ **Gai Beach Hotel.** The rare lakeshore location is a big plus, and for some, so is the distance from the noisy downtown promenade. **Pros:** on the lake; gorgeous spa; far from the hubbub. **Cons:** a bit isolated; crowded on weekends. ⑤ *Rooms from: $400* ⊠ *Rte. 90* ☎ *04/670–0700* ⊕ *www.gaibeachhotel.com* ⤙ *198 rooms* ⍥ *Breakfast* ✛ *D3.*

$$
HOTEL

☷ **Lavi Kibbutz Hotel.** The peaceful rural atmosphere has much to recommend it. **Pros:** opportunity to experience kibbutz life; central location; good children's programs. **Cons:** no evening entertainment; the kibbutz is religious so no checking in or out Friday evening and Saturday. ⑤ *Rooms from: $250* ⊠ *Rte. 77, Lavi* ✛ *11 km (7 miles) west of Tiberias* ☎ *04/679–9450* ⊕ *hotel.lavi.co.il* ⤙ *184 rooms* ⍥ *Breakfast* ✛ *A1.*

$$ **Leonardo Club Hotel Tiberias.** Cascading down a hillside, this all-
HOTEL   inclusive, all-suites hotel boasts an unimpeded view of the lake. **Pros:**
FAMILY   spectacular views; spacious rooms; resort feel. **Cons:** crowded on
weekends; away from downtown. $ *Rooms from: $300* ⊠ *HaBanim
St.* ☎ *04/671–4444* ⊕ *www.leonardo-hotels.com* 400 rooms ⦿ *All-
inclusive* ✛ *A1.*

$$$ **Leonardo Plaza Hotel Tiberias.** With lake views, comfortable rooms,
HOTEL   relaxing common areas, and a variety of spa services, the Leonardo
Plaza is a welcoming spot. **Pros:** convenient to Tiberias; lake views from
most rooms. **Cons:** no beach. $ *Rooms from: $310* ⊠ *1 Habanim St.*
☎ *04/671–3333* ⊕ *www.leonardo-hotels.com* 262 rooms ⦿ *Breakfast* ✛ *D3.*

$$$ **Rimonim Galei Kinnereth.** It's easy to understand why this resort was a
HOTEL   personal favorite of Israel's founding prime minister, David Ben-Gurion:
its location on the lake with its own private beach is unbeatable. **Pros:**
convenient to Tiberias; lakeside swimming pool; quiet atmosphere.
Cons: can be crowded on weekends and in summer. $ *Rooms from:
$350* ⊠ *1 Eliezer Kaplan St.* ☎ *04/672–8888* ⊕ *www.rimonim.com*
120 rooms ⦿ *Some meals* ✛ *D3.*

$$ **Ron Beach Hotel.** The family-run establishment is the northernmost
HOTEL   hotel in Tiberias and has rare private lake frontage, though no beach.
Pros: lakeside location; pretty pool. **Cons:** too far to walk to downtown;
no beach. $ *Rooms from: $244* ⊠ *Gedud Barak St.* ☎ *04/679–1350*
⊕ *www.ronbeachhotel.com* 127 rooms ⦿ *Breakfast* ✛ *C1.*

$$$$ **Scots Hotel.** This upscale hotel, with a contemporary structure link-
HOTEL   ing two older, superbly refurbished Ottoman-style ones, has a pleas-
Fodor'sChoice   ingly asymmetrical design filled with pleasant surprises, such as a roof
★   terrace, where you can enjoy a drink or light meal. **Pros:** boutique-
hotel feel; historic setting; private beach. **Cons:** no
nightly entertainment. $ *Rooms from: $450* ⊠ *1 Gedud Barak St., at
Hayarden St.* ☎ *04/671–0710* ⊕ *www.scotshotels.co.il* 69 rooms
⦿ *Breakfast* ✛ *D2.*

$$ **Shavit's Arbel Guest House.** Israel and Sarah Shavit make congenial
B&B/INN   hosts, with the added bonus that he's a licensed tour guide and chef.
Pros: warm hospitality; delicious food; pretty grounds. **Cons:** far
from downtown Tiberias. $ *Rooms from: $200* ⊠ *Rte. 7717, off
Rte. 77, Arbel Village* ☎ *04/679–4919* ⊕ *www.4shavit.com* 5 suites
⦿ *Breakfast* ✛ *A2.*

NIGHTLIFE AND PERFORMING ARTS

Much of the entertainment, especially in the larger hotels in Tiberias, is
of the live lounge-music variety: piano bars, one-man dance bands, and
crooners. Generally speaking, the younger set wouldn't be caught dead
here, preferring to hang out at one of the few pubs, where the recorded
rock music is good and loud and the beer is on tap.

Bet Gabriel. This cultural center is located on the southern shore of
the Sea of Galilee, a 10-minute drive from Tiberias. Its fine architec-
ture, beautiful garden setting, movie theater, galleries for changing art
exhibits, and concert facilities have established its popularity in the
area. ⊠ *Rte. 92* ✛ *East of Tzemach Junction* ☎ *04/675–1175* ⊕ *www.
betgabriel.co.il.*

SHOPPING

Tiberias relies heavily on tourism yet has little particularly interesting in the way of shopping. The exception is jewelry. There are a few jewelry stores near the intersection of Habanim and Hayarden Streets and in some of the better hotels.

Big Center Tiberias. Take a break from the hot, sticky weather in the city's newest mall, just five minutes on foot from the Central Bus Station. Home to 150 stores, restaurants, and coffee shops, this is where the locals go for a shawarma or slice of pizza and to escape the punishing heat. ⊠ *1 Yehuda HaLevi St.* ☎ *072/360–0477* ⊕ *www.bigcenters.co.il* ☾ *Closed Fri. evening and Sat.*

SPORTS AND THE OUTDOORS

BEACHES

The Sea of Galilee—a freshwater lake—is a refreshing but rocky place for a swim. You can recline on pleasant commercial beaches with amenities ranging from cafeterias to water parks, or on free beaches with minimal facilities. Note that after several years of drought conditions in the region, the water level remains low.

September's Kinneret Swim, a tradition since 1953, has amateur (3½ km [2 miles] and 1½ km [1 mile]) categories.

Gai Beach. Open May to October, Gai Beach has a private bathing beach and one of the country's most attractive water parks. **Amenities:** food and drink; lifeguards; parking (fee); showers; toilets; water sports. **Best for:** swimming. ⊠ *Rte. 90* ☎ *04/670–0713* ☒ *NIS 90.*

HaTchelet Beach. Near the northern entrance to Tiberias, this well-kept private beach is open May to October. Picnic areas and raft rentals are available. **Amenities:** food and drink; lifeguards; parking (fee); showers; toilets; water sports. **Best for:** swimming. ⊠ *Rte. 90* ☎ *04/672–0105* ☒ *NIS 50.*

WATER SPORTS

At several locations around the Sea of Galilee, you can hire pedal boats, rowboats, and motorboats and arrange to water-ski. Serious kayakers convene for an annual international competition in March.

Holyland Sailing. This company has seven wooden boats that are replicas of those in use during the time of Jesus. The 45-minute cruises include historical commentary and concerts of traditional music. Sunset cruises are especially popular. Groups of 20 people can order a cruise for $150, while smaller groups can take sunset sails or call ahead and see if they can join an existing group for $15 per person. Private charters are available too. ⊠ *Tiberias Marina* ☎ *04/672–3006* ⊕ *www.jesusboats.com.*

ARBEL NATIONAL PARK AND NATURE RESERVE

8 km (5 miles) northwest of Tiberias.

Jesus is said to have preached and performed miracles at the foot of Mount Arbel, which is now a popular nature reserve. The reserve has few trees, but, depending on the season, there are flowers and small fauna.

GETTING HERE AND AROUND

To get here from the Tiberias-Golani junction road (Route 77), turn at the Kfar Hittim junction to Route 7717. Turn right at the turnoff for Moshav Arbel, then turn left.

EXPLORING

Arbel National Park and Nature Reserve. This 2,600-acre park sits on a plateau that slopes from the Arbel Valley to a towering cliff at the top of Mount Arbel, with panoramic views of the Sea of Galilee, the Golan Heights, and Mount Hermon beyond. Ancient texts indicate that the Seleucid Greeks conquered the Biblical-era Jews of Arbel while making their way to Jerusalem. Roman historian Flavius Josephus describes a battle here in 37 BC between the Jews and Marc Antony, who had been sent to suppress the Jewish rebellion. According to Josephus, the Jews were "lurking in caves...opening up onto mountain precipices that were inaccessible from any quarter except by torturous and narrow paths." Antony eventually crushed the rebels by lowering his soldiers into the caves from above. Today, hikers can take trails to that fortress of natural caves, and see other evidence of ancient settlements, including the ruins of an ancient synagogue. ⊠ *Rte. 7717, Tiberias* ☎ *04/673–2904* ⊕ *www.parks.org.il* ✆ *NIS 22.*

6

KIBBUTZ GINOSAR

10 km (6 miles) north of Tiberias.

Many Israelis know Ginosar, a kibbutz founded in 1937, as the home of the late Yigal Allon (1918–80), commander of the crack Palmach battalions in the War of Independence and deputy prime minister of Israel in the 1970s under Golda Meir and Yitzhak Rabin. Travelers, however, come here to see the ancient fishing boat.

GETTING HERE AND AROUND

Egged buses frequently make the short trip here from the Tiberias Central Bus Station. Ask the driver to tell you where to get off.

EXPLORING

Yigal Alon Museum. Kibbutz Ginosar's premier tourist attraction is a wooden fishing boat from the 1st century AD, found on the shore by two amateur archaeologists in 1986. Today it is beautifully exhibited in all its modest but evocative glory in a specially built pavilion in the Yigal Alon Museum: a short video tells the story. Three years of drought had lowered the level of Lake Kinneret and exposed bits of the ancient wood in the mud. Excavated in a frenetic 11 days, the 28-foot-long boat became an instant media sensation. Given the frequency of New Testament references to Jesus and his disciples boating on the Sea of Galilee—including coming ashore at Gennesaret, perhaps today's Ginosar—the press immediately dubbed it the "Jesus Boat."

On the other hand, the vivid relic might have been a victim of the Roman naval victory over the rebellious Jewish townspeople of nearby Magdala in AD 67, as described by the historian Flavius Josephus. Whatever its unknown history, it is the most complete boat this old ever found in an inland waterway anywhere in the world. ⊠ *Nof Ginosar, Off Rte. 90* ☎ *04/672–7700* ⊕ *bet-alon.co.il* ✆ *NIS 20.*

WHERE TO EAT

$$$$ ✕ **Magdalena Chef Restaurant.** Located in the "holy triangle," an area
INTERNATIONAL north of the Sea of Galilee considered to be one of the most important
Fodor's Choice pilgrimage sites in the world, Magdalena upgrades Galilee-style Ara-
★ bic food into contemporary gourmet. Using mostly local ingredients,
Magdelena's menu includes Christian-Arab cuisine with influences of
Lebanese and Mediterranean traditions. Fish gets the spotlight, but
creative dishes of lamb, beef, and seasonal vegetables fill out the menu.
The views of hillsides and the lake knock you out. ⑤ *Average main: NIS*
150 ✉ *Migdal Junction compound, Rte. 90, Migdal* ☎ *04/673–0064*
⊕ *www.magdalena.co.il.*

$$$ ✕ **Tanureen Authentic Lebanese Restaurant.** No fewer than 20 fresh salads
LEBANESE of seasonal produce and traditional recipes arrive at your table in this
large and efficient dining room. Catering to busloads of tourists, the
dining room is surprisingly quiet, and small groups do not feel outnum-
bered. Fish is the star, but traditional favorites like grilled beef and lamb
are also exceptional. ⑤ *Average main: NIS 85* ✉ *Sonol Gas Station, Rte.*
90, Tiberias-Migdal Rd., Migdal ☎ *053/809–6629* ⊕ *tanureen.rest.co.il.*

WHERE TO STAY

$$ 🛏 **Ginosar Village.** Its grand location—with a private beach right on the
B&B/INN Sea of Galilee—makes this kibbutz guesthouse near Tiberias especially
popular. **Pros:** convenient location; opportunity to experience kibbutz
life; beautiful gardens. **Cons:** too far to walk to town; no evening entertainment. ⑤ *Rooms from: $275* ✉ *Rte. 90* ☎ *04/670–0300* ⊕ *www.*
ginosar.co.il ⬦ *243 rooms* 🍽 *Breakfast.*

TABGHA

4 km (2½ miles) north of Ginosar, 14 km (8 miles) north of Tiberias,
at Capernaum Junction (Rtes. 90 and 87).

With a name that's an Arabic corruption of the Greek *Heptaegon*
(Seven Springs), Tabgha is a cluster of serene holy places associated
with Jesus's ministry in the Galilee. A promenade and hiking trails
connect the shrines.

GETTING HERE AND AROUND

Tabgha is located off Route 87, a few hundred meters from the junction
with Route 90. A promenade connects the Church of the Multiplication with the Church of the Primacy of St. Peter. A trail leads up to the
Mount of Beatitudes, but the hike is best enjoyed going downhill, with
the glorious views of the lake in front of you.

EXPLORING

Church of the Multiplication. The German Benedictines dedicated this large,
orange-roofed Roman Catholic church in 1936 on the scanty remains
of earlier shrines. The site has long been venerated as the "deserted
place" (Mark 6:30–6:34) where Jesus miraculously multiplied two
fishes and five loaves of bread to feed the crowds. The present airy
limestone building with the wooden-truss ceiling was built in the style of
a Byzantine basilica to give a fitting context to the beautifully wrought
5th-century mosaic floor depicting the loaves and fishes in front of

the altar. The nave is covered with geometric designs, but the front of the aisles is filled with flora and birds and, curiously, a nilometer, a graded column once used to measure the flood level of the Nile for the purpose of assessing that year's collectible taxes. ✉ *Rte. 87, Ginosar* ☎ *04/667–8100* ✆ *Free.*

Church of the Primacy of St. Peter. The austere, black basalt church, just east of the Church of the Multiplication, is built on the water's edge, over a flat rock known as *Mensa Christi* (the Table of Christ). After his resurrection, the New Testament relates, Jesus appeared to his disciples by the Sea of Galilee and presented them a miraculous catch of fish. Three times Jesus asked his disciple Peter if he loved him, and after his reply of "You know that I love you," Jesus commanded him to "feed my sheep" (John 21:17). Some scholars see this affirmation as Peter's atonement for having thrice denied Jesus in Jerusalem. The episode is seen as establishing Peter's "primacy."✉ *Rte. 87, Ginosar* ☎ *04/672–4767* ✆ *Free.*

> **KIBBUTZ MUSIC**
>
> Nof Ginosar hosts the twice-annual **Jacob's Ladder Festival** (⊕ *www.jlfestival.com*), a perennial favorite for folk-music fans. The music is eclectic, with international artists performing anything from Celtic to country classics. The crowd is equally diverse, coming from the United States, Canada, Britain, and around the world.

MOUNT OF BEATITUDES

8 km (5 miles) north of Ginosar, 3 km (2 miles) north of Capernaum Junction.

Fodor's Choice ★ Tradition identifies this tranquil hillside as the site of Jesus's most comprehensive teaching, recorded in the New Testament as the Sermon on the Mount: "And seeing the multitudes, he went up into a mountain; and when he was set, his disciples came unto him. And he opened his mouth, and taught them, saying: 'Blessed are the poor in spirit, for theirs is the kingdom of Heaven'" (Matthew 5:3).

GETTING HERE AND AROUND

It's best to drive here. Lots of tourist buses make the journey, but there's no public transportation. It's on a spur road off the main lake road, atop a hill.

EXPLORING

Church of the Beatitudes. This domed Roman Catholic church, run by the Franciscan Sisters, was designed by the famous architect and monk Antonio Barluzzi. Commissioned by Fascist leader Benito Mussolini while he was dictator of Italy, the church was completed in 1937. The windows are inscribed with the opening words of the Sermon on the Mount. The terrace surrounding the church has a superb view of the Sea of Galilee, best enjoyed in the afternoon when the diffused western sun softens the light and heightens colors. Keep in mind this is a pilgrimage site, so dress modestly and respect the silence. The gardens on the Mount of Beatitudes and the church open daily at 8 am, but they close from noon until 2:30 pm. ✉ *Rte. 8177, off Rte. 90, Ginosar* ☎ *04/672–6712* ✆ *NIS 10 per vehicle.*

Churches are among the sights along the peaceful shores of the Sea of Galilee.

KORAZIM

Rte. 8277 at Rte. 90, 6 km (4 miles) north of Capernaum Junction.

Built on a basalt bluff a few miles north of the Sea of Galilee, the town of Korazim has long been renowned for its high-quality wheat. It's famous as the home of Korazim National Park.

GETTING HERE AND AROUND

Scenic Route 8277 has some breathtaking views of the Sea of Galilee far below, but you need a car to enjoy them. There's no public transit to Korazim. Consider saddling up a horse from the stables at Vered Hagalil and riding here.

EXPLORING

Korazim National Park. These extensive and often remarkable ruins, dating from the 4th or 5th century AD, are on the site of the ancient Jewish village that Jesus condemned for rejecting him (Matthew 11:21). The monumental basalt synagogue is decorated with the stone carvings of plants and animals. One remarkable artifact, a decorated and inscribed stone "armchair" dubbed the Throne of Moses, is thought to have been used by the worthies of the community during the reading of the Torah. The views of the Sea of Galilee are also impressive. ⊠ *Rte. 8277* ☎ *04/693–4982* ⊕ *www.parks.org.il* ☎ *NIS 22.*

WHERE TO STAY

$
B&B/INN

The Frenkels Bed-and-Breakfast. Americans Etha and Irwin Frenkel retired to this rustic village on the border between the Lower and Upper Galilee and have made gracious hospitality a second career. **Pros:** convenient to national parks; charming rooms; pleasant hosts. **Cons:** no evening entertainment; no telephones in rooms. ⑤ *Rooms from: $160* ✉ *Rte. 8277* ☎ *04/680–1686* ⊕ *www.thefrenkels.com* ⊟ No credit cards ↩ *3 suites* ��❘ *Breakfast.*

$$
RESORT
🛏 **Vered Hagalil Guest Farm.** Yehuda Avni and his Jerusalem-born wife Yonah have created something special in Israel: a ranch where guests can ride horses during the day and retire to cozy rooms at night. **Pros:** best stables in the area; convenient to national parks; panoramic views. **Cons:** no evening entertainment. ⑤ *Rooms from: $220* ✉ *Rtes. 8277 and 90* ☎ *04/693–5785* ⊕ *www.veredhagalil.co.il* ↩ *30 rooms* ⓒ❘ *Breakfast.*

CAPERNAUM

3 km (2 miles) east of Tabgha and the Capernaum Junction, 17 km (10½ miles) northeast of Tiberias.

A must-see destination for many Christian travelers, Capernaum is one of the places most often associated with Jesus. Many of the sites mentioned in the Gospels are found in and around Capernaum National Park.

Anyone raised on spirituals extolling the Jordan River's width and depth will be surprised to find how small a stream it really is. The Jordan enters the Sea of Galilee near Capernaum.

GETTING HERE AND AROUND
Capernaum is on Route 87, east of the intersection with Route 90. Since buses leave you a few miles from the site, it's best to drive.

EXPLORING

Fodor's Choice
★
Capernaum National Park. For Christians, this park is among the most moving places in Israel, because it's where Jesus established his base for three years and recruited some of his disciples ("Follow me, and I will make you fishers of men" [Matthew 4:19]). It is also the site of the House of St. Peter, the ruins of an actual home where Jesus is believed to have lodged. Astride the ruins is an ultramodern Franciscan church, looking a bit like a spaceship.

Capernaum is also a site of interest to Jews, and the prosperity of the ancient Jewish community (it is *Kfar Nahum* in Hebrew) is immediately apparent from the remains of its synagogue, which dominates the complex. Once thought to date to the 2nd or 3rd century AD, the synagogue is now regarded by many scholars as belonging to the later Byzantine period (4th–5th centuries AD).

Limestone reliefs on the synagogue exterior represent a typical range of Jewish artistic motifs: the native fruits of the land, the biblical Ark of the Covenant, a seven-branched menorah, a shofar, and an incense shovel (to preserve the memory of the Temple in Jerusalem, where they were used prior to the city's destruction in 70 AD). A small 1st-century mosaic from Magdala shows a contemporary boat, complete with oars and sails—a dramatic illustration of the many New Testament and Jewish references to fishing on the lake.

Jesus eventually cursed the people of Capernaum for failing to heed his message, saying "And you, Capernaum, will you be lifted up to the skies? No, you will go down to the depths" (Matthew 11:23–24).

6

When visiting Capernaum, dress appropriately: you aren't allowed in shorts or a sleeveless shirt. ⊠ *Rte. 87* ☎ *04/679–3865* ⊕ *www.parks. org.il* ☑ *Free.*

Jordan River Park. This park north of the Sea of Galilee contains typical riverside vegetation as well as some ancient sites. In the southeast section, archaeologists have partially excavated an ancient fishing village, identified as the likely site of the Bethsaida of the Second Temple period. It includes the remains (now rubble) of several homes that provide an idea of how communal life once occurred here. Now, as then, the village has a view of the Sea of Galilee (though the shoreline moved drastically in an earthquake in AD 363). A shaded and serene sitting area includes arrows pointing to other Christian sites around the lake. Other than the sitting area, shade is limited here, so bring a hat and plenty of water. Several well-marked hiking trails lead to sites of historical and religious importance. Jordan River Park is 9 km (5½ miles) northeast of Capernaum. ⊠ *Rte. 888, Bethsaida* ☎ *04/692–3422* ⊕ *www.kkl-jnf. org* ☑ *NIS 60 per car.*

SPORTS AND THE OUTDOORS

Abukayak. Northeast of Capernaum, this outfitter's so-called kayaks are really inflated rubber canoes, used for serene one-hour paddles down the lower Jordan River; a truck picks you up at the end. Life jackets are provided, and the trip is appropriate for young children. ⊠ *Jordan River Park, Rte. 888, Bethsaida* ☎ *04/692–1078* ⊕ *www.abukayak.co.il* ☑ *NIS 90* ⟳ *Closed Sat. and Dec.–Feb.*

KURSI NATIONAL PARK

Kursi is 17 km (10½ miles) southeast of Capernaum on Rte. 92, 5 km (3 miles) north of Ein Gev.

Kursi, where Jesus healed two men possessed by demons (Matthew 8:28–32), is today a park incorporating the ruins of a Byzantine monastery. The eastern shore of the Sea of Galilee is far less developed, retaining more of its relatively rural character than the western and northern sides.

GETTING HERE AND AROUND

Route 92 follows the eastern shore of the Sea of Galilee, while Route 87 circles to the north of the lake. You can reach Kursi either by driving north or south from Tiberias. Whether you circle the lake clockwise or counterclockwise, the views are often breathtaking.

EXPLORING

Kursi National Park. Huddling under the imposing cliffs of Golan Heights, where Route 789 climbs away from 92, this place is linked with the New Testament story of a man possessed by demons. Jesus exorcised the spirits, causing them to enter a herd of swine grazing nearby, which then "rushed down the steep bank into the lake, and perished in the waters" (Matthew 8:32). Fifth-century Byzantine Christians identified the event with this spot and built a monastery. It was an era in which earnest pilgrims inundated the holy places, and the monastery prospered from their gifts. The partly restored ruins of a fine Byzantine church are

Capernaum was the base of Jesus's Galilean ministry, but the synagogue remains date from a later era.

a classic example of the basilica style common at the time; the ruined monastery is higher up the hillside. ✉ *Rte. 92, Kursi* ☎ *04/673–1983* ⊕ *www.parks.org.il* 🖃 *NIS 14.*

WHERE TO EAT

$$$
MIDDLE EASTERN
✗ **Ein Gev Fish Restaurant.** At lunchtime this popular establishment on the eastern shore bustles with tour groups, but it's a fine dinner option, too. Famous for St. Peter's fish, it has added sea bream, trout, and gray mullet to the menu, as well as entrées such as quiche, pizza, pasta, and salads. In fine weather, sit on the large outdoor terrace, and take in the view across the lake to Tiberias. Watch for the signs for "Kibbutz Inn Ein Gev." ⑤ *Average main: NIS 80* ✉ *Kibbutz Ein Gev, Rte. 92, Ein Gev* ☎ *053/944–4101* ⊕ *www.eingev.co.il.*

$$$$
BARBECUE
✗ **Marinado.** Marinado started as a cattle ranch and is still a butcher and gourmet food shop. It is the only restaurant in Israel that produces its own meat, wine, and olive oil. The restaurant specializes in beef and has a large indoor seating area and breezy outdoor dining with lovely views of the Kinneret. The restaurant also has several branches in and near Tel Aviv, although this is its flagship location. ⑤ *Average main: NIS 150* ✉ *Kibbutz Ein Gev, Off Rte. 92, Ein Gev* ☎ *04/665–8555* ⊕ *marinado.rest.co.il.*

WHERE TO STAY

$
RESORT
FAMILY
🏨 **Ein Gev Holiday Resort.** Located on the palm-shaded eastern shore of the Sea of Galilee, this complex has everything from waterfront units with sunset-watching patios to spacious apartments with room for the whole family. **Pros:** private beach; convenient to national parks. **Cons:** no evening entertainment. ⑤ *Rooms from: $180* ✉ *Rte. 92, Ein*

Gev ✛ 12 km (7½ miles) north of Tzemach Junction ☎04/665–9800 ⊕ www.eingev.com ⊃ 178 rooms ⦿ Breakfast.

NIGHTLIFE AND THE ARTS
Ein Gev Spring Festival. This festival's focus is Israeli vocal music, from traditional to contemporary. It is held on Kibbutz Ein Gev during Passover each spring. ⊠ *Kibbutz Ein Gev, Off Rte. 92, Ein Gev ☎04/675–1195.*

SPORTS AND THE OUTDOORS
The shoreline of the Sea of Galilee has receded somewhat with the low level of the water, and the bottom now drops precipitously. Keep a close eye on children.

BEACHES
Golan Beach. The best-known beach on the lake's northeastern shore has powerboat, rowboat, kayak, and pedal-boat rentals, as well as water-skiing and other water sports. **Amenities:** food and drink; lifeguards; parking (fee); showers; toilets; water sports. **Best for:** swimming. ⊠ *Rte. 92, Kursi ✛ 7 km (4½ miles) north of Ein Gev ☎04/667–8010 ⌁ NIS 6 for 3 hrs of parking.*

Kursi–Lavnun–Halukim Beach. Each of the three beaches has its own personality: the Lavnun (named after an indigenous fish) and Halukim ("pebbles") beaches have vast lawns with abundant shade. You must wear shoes on Halukim Beach, because it is, indeed, filled with pebbles. Young people with grills and music find Kursi (named after the nearby Byzantine Church) and Lavnun more attractive, while families and those seeking a quieter experience find the Halukim Beach more to their liking. **Amenities:** food and drink; lifeguards; parking (fee); showers; toilets. **Best for:** swimming. ⊠ *Rte. 92, located 3 km (2 miles) north of Ein Gev, Kursi ⌁ NIS6 for 3 hrs of parking.*

HAMMAT GADER

10 km (6 miles) east of Tzemach Junction on Rte. 98, 22 km (14 miles) southeast of Tiberias, 36 km (22½ miles) northeast of Beit She'an.

Built around three hot springs, the impressive complex of baths and pools at Hammat Gader attests to its opulence during the time of the Romans. The large number of ancient clay oil lamps found in one small pool is proof of nighttime bathing.

GETTING HERE AND AROUND
Whether you're driving via Tiberias (Route 90) or the Golan Heights (Route 98), this highway is one of the most captivating in Israel, with expansive views across the Yarmuk River into Jordan. Don't leave the roadway. The minefield signs mean exactly what they say.

EXPLORING
FAMILY **Hammat Gader.** Popular with Israelis—who come for the freshwater and mineral pools, giant waterslide, alligator farm, performing parrots, petting zoo, and restaurants—this place has history, too: in its heyday, it was the second-largest spa in the Roman Empire (after Baiae, near Naples). There's a hotel, a spa, and restaurants here, too. ⊠ *Rte. 98 ☎ 04/665–9999 ⊕ www.hamat-gader.com ⌁ NIS 105.*

DEGANIA, KINNERET, AND YARDENIT

Degania Alef: 10 km (6 miles) south of Tiberias; Kinneret: 2 km (1 mile) northwest of Degania Alef.

Degania and Kinneret, two historic kibbutzim founded in the early 20th century, contain museums and historic graveyards worth a visit. Also nearby is Yardenit, a baptism site for Christians.

GETTING HERE AND AROUND

Both Degania Alef and Kinneret are south of Tiberias along Route 90. If you take a bus, ask the driver in advance about stopping.

EXPLORING

Kibbutz Degania Alef. The first kibbutz, the collective village of Degania Alef was founded by Jewish pioneers from Eastern Europe in 1909 (Alef is the *A* of the Hebrew alphabet). Near the entrance is a small Syrian tank of World War II vintage. On May 15, 1948, the day after Israel declared its independence, Arab armies invaded it from all sides. Syrian forces came down the Yarmuk Valley from the east, overran two other kibbutz complexes en route, and were only stopped here, at the gates of Degania. A teenager with a Molotov cocktail set alight the lead tank. On the grounds is the museum of Beit Gordon, named for the spiritual mentor of the early pioneers. It houses two collections: one devoted to the region's natural history, the other examining the history and archaeology of human settlement in the surrounding valleys. ⊠ *Near Rte. 90, Degania Aleph* ☎ *04/675–0040* ⊕ *www.beitgordon.co.il* 🖾 *Museum NIS 20* ⊗ *Closed Fri. afternoon and Sat.*

FAMILY **Galita Chocolate Farm.** At Kibbutz Degania Bet, a short drive from Degania Alef, you can smell the chocolate long before you get to the farm. In addition to the "bar" serving hot and cold chocolate drinks, and a tempting gift shop, Galita has eight different chocolate-making workshops. Reservations can be made on the website; there are workshops in English. ⊠ *Kibbutz Degania Bet, Off Rte. 90, Degania Aleph* ☎ *04/675–5608* ⊕ *www.galita.co.il* 🖾 *Free; workshops NIS 55–75.*

Kibbutz Kinneret. Across the Jordan River from Degania, Kinneret was founded in 1911 as the country's second kibbutz, taking its name from the Hebrew word for the Sea of Galilee. The serene Kibbutz Kinneret Cemetery includes the grave of Rachel Bluwstein, better known as Rachel HaMeshoreret (Rachel the Poetess), a secular shrine for many Israelis. The pebbles left on her grave by visitors (a token of respect in the Jewish tradition) are a tribute to her renown and the romantic hold she has on the national imagination. Born in Russia in 1890, she became a poet of national stature in the Hebrew language; she died in 1931. The cemetery has a superb view of the lake, Golan Heights, and majestic Mount Hermon. ⊠ *Off Rte. 90, Degania Aleph* ✛ *South of junction with Rte. 767* ☎ *04/675–9500.*

Yardenit. On a picturesque bend of the Jordan River, where huge eucalyptus trees droop into the quiet water, this spot was developed as a baptism site by Kibbutz Kinneret for Christian pilgrims. The baptism of Jesus by John the Baptist (John 1:28) is traditionally identified with the southern reaches of the Jordan River, near Jericho. But when the area became a hostile frontier between Israel and Jordan, pilgrims began to seek out accessible spots beyond the conflict zone. You often see groups of pilgrims being immersed in the river amid prayers and hymns and expressions of joy. The white robes required to enter the water become transparent when wet, so bring a bathing suit or large towel. Snacks and souvenirs are available. ⊠ *Off Rte. 90, Degania Aleph* ☎ *04/675–9111* ⊕ *www.yardenit.com* ✉ *Free.*

WHERE TO STAY

$$

RESORT

FAMILY

🏨 **Ma'agan Holiday Village.** At the southern tip of the Sea of Galilee, this kibbutz has arguably the most enchanting view of all the properties around the lake. **Pros:** pretty beach; gorgeous lake views; convenient location. **Cons:** no evening entertainment. ⑤ *Rooms from: $250* ⊠ *Rte. 92, 1 km (½ mile) east of Tzemach Junction, Ma'agan* ☎ *04/665–4411* ⊕ *www.maagan.co.il* ⇗ *148 rooms* ⦿ *Breakfast.*

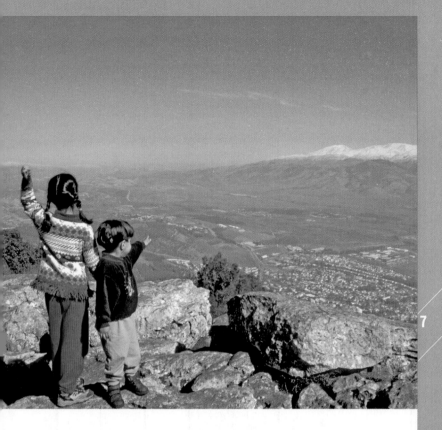

UPPER GALILEE AND THE GOLAN

with Tzfat (Safed)

WELCOME TO UPPER GALILEE AND THE GOLAN

TOP REASONS TO GO

★ **Old City of Tzfat:** While the tiny historic synagogues offer a rare taste of Jewish houses of worship from bygone days, the galleries are saturated with contemporary colors and shapes.

★ **Kayaking on the Jordan River:** A cool ride downriver can be a strenuous adventure or a tame family float; either way, it adds an interesting accent to a trip to the northern Galilee.

★ **Hula Lake Nature Reserve:** The Hula reserve provides shelter for birds, some 500 million of which fly over the Hula Valley twice a year on migrations between Europe and Africa.

★ **Hermon Stream Nature Reserve:** Hike to the Banias Waterfall and the Crusader ruins, and pick up a freshly baked pita from the Druze mill along the way.

★ **Gamla Nature Reserve:** This is the site of the Jews' heroic last stand following a siege by the Romans in AD 67. It also offers a challenging hike or an easy amble, all with glimpses of wildlife.

1 **Tzfat (Safed) and Environs.** At 3,000 feet above sea level, Tzfat is Israel's highest city, known for being the center of Kabbalah, or Jewish mysticism. This city north of the Sea of Galilee has a spiritual dimension found nowhere else in the country. Its ancient twisting passageways caught the attention of artists, who make this one of the country's most unique destinations every spring and summer.

2 **Upper Hula Valley.** Situated between the Golan Heights, Naftali Ridge, and the Beqaa Valley, the Upper Hula Valley is best known for the Tel Dan Nature Reserve. Spread out over 800 acres, it's a prime spot for hiking, cycling, or picnicking. Kiryat Shmona and sleepy Metulla are the region's largest communities.

3 **Golan Heights.** This region's main geographic feature is the Sea of Galilee, the country's primary water reservoir. This is the northernmost part of the country, and from Mount Hermon you can gaze out over Lebanon and Syria. The Golan Heights draws visitors to its relaxing countryside, inventive restaurants, and leading wineries.

Mount
Hermon

Hermon Stream
Nature Reserve/
Banias Waterfall

Majdal
Shams

Beit
Ussishkin

Neve Ativ

Tel Dan
Nature Reserve

2

Ein
Kuniya

HULA VALLEY

Jordan River

978

918

Kibbutz
El-Rom

Khan
Arnabehi

98

959

Hula Lake
Nature
Reserve

959

Merom
Golan

Mount
Bental

UNDOF Zone
(U.N. Disengagement
Observer Force)

Quneitra

978

918

98

Alonei
Habashan

SYRIA

91

Khushniya

Katzrin

888

GOLAN
HEIGHTS

3

Al Ashsheh

87

Gamla
Nature Reserve

808

869

98

92

Sea of
Galilee
(Lake Kinneret)

Moshav Ramot

Kursi

Ramal
Magshimim

Ein Gev

789

98

0   4 mi

0   4 km

GETTING ORIENTED

The undulating hills of Western Galilee push upward into sharp limestone and basalt formations, bordered on the north by Lebanon and on the east by the volcanic, mountainous Golan Heights, beyond which lies Syria. The major cities—Tzfat in the rugged Galilee mountains and Katzrin in the Golan Heights—are a study in contrasts. The former is immersed in Jewish mysticism, and the latter is the result of a hardheaded determination to secure Israel's border with Syria by establishing a modern town in what was once a battlefield.

7

Updated by
Inbal Baum

"Israel's Little Tuscany" has long been a nickname for the Upper Galilee. The green countryside, the growing numbers of both large-scale and boutique wineries, and the laid-back atmosphere have attracted urbanites on weekend jaunts as well as adventurous travelers.

The mountain air is redolent with the fragrance of spice plants; visitors can hike, cycle, or ride horses along trails that range from easy to challenging; and opportunities for kayaking, bird-watching, and other outdoor pursuits abound. These are the best vacation treats, all in a fascinating historical setting.

The main geographical feature of this region is towering Mount Hermon, known as Israel's "sponge." Huge volumes of water from winter snow and rainfall soak into its limestone, emerging at the base of the mountain in an abundance of springs that feed the Jordan River and its tributaries and provide a significant amount of Israel's water supply. The water also sustains lush vegetation that thrives year-round and is home to wildcats, hyraxes, gazelles, and hundreds of species of birds.

This water and the strategic vantage points of the Galilee mountaintops and the Golan Heights have made the region a source of political contention since time immemorial. Over the centuries, Egyptians, Canaanites, Israelites, Romans, Byzantines, Muslims, Crusaders, and Ottomans locked horns here; in the 20th century alone, the borders have been changed by Britain, France, and, of course, Israel, Lebanon, and Syria.

Borders aren't the only things that have shifted here. A geological fault line, the Syrian–African Rift, cuts straight through the 30-km (19-mile) Hula Valley; in 1837 an earthquake razed Tzfat and Tiberias, though no significant rumbles have been heard since. Extinct volcanic cones give the Golan its unusual topographic profile.

With all this water and fertile soil, the region has long been an agricultural center and is today studded with apple and cherry orchards, fishponds, and vineyards. The pastoral beauty and variety of outdoor activities attract visitors from elsewhere in Israel and the world, supplying the region's other main industry: tourism.

Proximity to Lebanon and Syria doesn't ordinarily deter people from visiting the Upper Galilee and the Golan. On the contrary, the combination of an exciting past with a gorgeous natural setting is precisely the draw here.

Over the last century, both Jews and non-Jews have faced hardships and hurdles in this region. Yet the tenacious Galileans will say there's no better place to live. Although the area is only a three-hour drive from Tel Aviv and Jerusalem, visitors find this is a world away in personality.

UPPER GALILEE AND THE GOLAN PLANNER

WHEN TO GO

Unlike other parts of the country, there's no best time of the year to tour the Upper Galilee and the Golan. The range of colors is wonderful in spring, when hillsides are covered with wildflowers. Summer brings families traveling with children, as well as music and culinary festivals. Days can be hot, but the low humidity makes summer manageable. Nights can be cold year-round. Wine fans appreciate the area in autumn during harvest time at the vineyards. In winter, more precipitation means gushing streams and gray skies, and a bit of skiing for a few weeks of the year.

PLANNING YOUR TIME

A day trip to the Golan Heights from Tiberias is doable, but there's something about the lush foliage and the mountain air that makes you want to linger. Three or four days is ideal to explore the region, including visiting Tzfat, doing some wine tasting, hiking a piece of wilderness, kayaking, or just kicking back in a room with a stunning view. The ideal way to see this area is by car, though local buses will get you almost anywhere you want to go if you have time.

GETTING HERE AND AROUND

Only one airline flies from Tel Aviv to the small airport of Mahanayim, near Rosh Pina. Ayit operates two 35-minute flights each day.

There's no transportation at the airport except for taxis. Nevertheless, you can arrange for a rental car to be waiting at the airport. From the airport, it's 10 km (6 miles) to Tzfat and 30 km (19 miles) to Kiryat Shmona.

BUS TRAVEL

Local Egged buses stop at all major sights in this region (there's always a kibbutz or some other residential settlement nearby). Avoid buses if you're on a tight schedule, as they tend to be infrequent.

Contacts Egged. ☎ *2800 ⊕ www.egged.co.il.

CAR TRAVEL

The Upper Galilee and the Golan are a 1½-hour, 60-km (37-mile) drive from both Akko and Nahariya; a three-hour, 180-km (112-mile) drive from Tel Aviv; and three hours from Jerusalem, which is 200 km (124 miles) to the south.

There are a few different ways to get here. From Tiberias and the Sea of Galilee, Route 90 runs north between the Hula Valley, on the east, and the hills of Naftali, on the west. The more rugged Route 98 runs from the eastern side of the Sea of Galilee up through the Golan Heights to Mount Hermon. Near the top of Route 98 you can pick up Route 91, which heads west into the Upper Galilee.

From the Mediterranean coast there are several options, but the main one is Route 85 from Akko. Route 89 runs parallel to Route 85 a little farther north, from Nahariya, and has some gorgeous scenery.

From Haifa, take Route 75 to Route 77, turning onto Route 90 at Tiberias, or Route 70 north onto Route 85 east. If you're starting from Tel Aviv, drive north on Route 4 or 2 to Hadera; from there you'll head northwest on Route 65, exiting onto Route 85 east.

The state of Israel's roads is generally fair to good, but in the Upper Galilee some roads are still two-lane. Drive cautiously. Try to avoid driving during peak hours (usually late Thursday and Saturday afternoons), when city folk crowd the roads back to Jerusalem and Tel Aviv after a day out in the country.

HOTELS

There are few grand hotels here; instead, the area has an ample selection of guesthouses and inns ranging from ranch to home-style. As the tourist industry has developed, luxury-level bed-and-breakfasts are often the most enjoyable options, and for budget-minded travelers many kibbutzim and moshavim have added hotels (or guest wings attached to homes); some also arrange tours, from rafting to Jeep excursions. Rooms in kibbutz guesthouses can be reserved directly or through the Israel Kibbutz Hotels chain (⊕ *en.kibbutz.co.il*), a central reservation service based in Tel Aviv, although not all the kibbutzim are represented. *Hotel reviews have been shortened. For more information, visit Fodors.com.*

RESTAURANTS

The Upper Galilee and the Golan's crisp, appetite-whetting air is an exquisite backdrop for some excellent restaurants. Fresh grilled Dan River trout, Middle Eastern fare prepared by Druze villagers, or home-style Jewish cooking in Tzfat are all regional treats. Excellent wines enhance any meal—be sure to ask for local boutique wines, as most restaurants carry at least a handful. In a few places (such as Tzfat), it can be hard to find a restaurant open on Shabbat (sundown Friday to sundown Saturday).

WHAT IT COSTS				
	$	$$	$$$	$$$$
Restaurants	Under NIS 50	NIS 50–NIS 75	NIS 76–NIS 100	over NIS 100
Hotels	Under $200	$200–$300	$301–$400	over $400

Restaurant prices are the average cost of a main course at dinner in NIS (Israeli shekels) or, if dinner isn't served, at lunch. Hotel prices, given in U.S. dollars, are the lowest cost of a standard double room in high season. Non-Israeli citizens paying in foreign currency are exempt from the 17% V.A.T. on hotel rooms.

VISITOR INFORMATION

Beit Ussishkin Nature Museum near Tel Dan Nature Reserve has information about area nature reserves, natural history, and bird-watching. The Israel Nature and Parks Authority website (⊕ *www. parks.org.il*) has detailed information about national parks in this area and around the country; you can also buy money-saving multi-park tickets. The Tourist Information Center–Upper Galilee can also provide information.

Contacts Tourist Information Center–Upper Galilee. ✉ *Gome Junction, Rte. 90 and Rte. 977, Kiryat Shmona* ☎ *04/681–7152* ⊕ *www.gogalilee.org.*

TZFAT (SAFED) AND WESTERN GALILEE

In the southern part of the Upper Galilee, attractions range from the narrow streets and historic synagogues of Tzfat to the wilderness of the Hula Nature Reserve. Other sites, like Mount Meron, pair scenic appeal with spiritual importance. In Rosh Pina, you can shop and dine where the Galilee's first Zionist pioneers labored, or you can just relax at one of the many family-run B&Bs and enjoy the fresh air.

TZFAT

33 km (20 miles) north of Tiberias, 72 km (45 miles) northeast of Haifa.

Fodor'sChoice This magical town on a hill attracts artists searching for inspiration, ★ travelers charmed by its cobblestone alleys, and religious people in search of meaning—a rare example of harmony between the secular and the spiritual. The city is known for its spiritual, even sacred, vibe and its breathtaking views.

It doesn't take long to walk all of Tzfat's Old City, but allow plenty of time to poke around the little stone passages, remnants of the Crusader and Ottoman eras, that seem to lead nowhere. You can linger over some minute architectural detail on a building from another time, or browse through shops filled to overflowing with locally made art. It's almost impossible to get lost; Yerushalayim (Jerusalem) Street is a good orientation point—it runs through the heart of the Old City, encircles the Citadel, and from there, steps lead down to the two main areas of interest, the Old Jewish Quarter and the adjacent Artists' Colony. There's no way to avoid the hilly topography, so remember to wear comfortable walking shoes. As the town is largely Jewish Orthodox, modest dress is recommended when visiting synagogues. For women, this means a below-the-knee skirt or long pants and at least a short-sleeve top; for men, long pants are appropriate. In the hot summer days, dress lightly and carry around a shawl or cover up for visiting holy places.

Tzfat hibernates from October through June, when the city's artists move to their galleries in warmer parts of the country. This doesn't mean you should leave Tzfat out of your itinerary during those months; there's enough to occupy the curious wanderer for at least a few hours, and much of it is free. In summer, especially during July and August,

Tzfat (Safed)

← TO MOUNT MERON

Central Bus Station

OLD JEWISH QUARTER

Kikar Hameginim

Gur'e Ha'ari

OLD CITY

1 The Citadel

4
3
6 **5**
9
8
7 New Cemetery
10
2
11

Hatem Sofer

Ma'alot Moshe

Yerushalayim St.

Ma'alot Olei Hagardom

Montefiore

Pedestrian Mall

ARTISTS' COLONY

Kikar Hama'ayan Haradum

Zvi Levanon

Kikar David Gilboa

Merzer

Alwail

Zahal

Keren Hayesod

Hakeren Hakayemet

0   1/8 mile
0   1/8 kilometer

KEY
Pedestrian stairway

What Is Kabbalah?

Kabbalah, which means "receiving," is an ancient study of Jewish mysticism that gained popularity in the 13th century. Tzfat has been the main center for Kabbalah scholarship since the 16th century, making it one of Judaism's four holiest cities (along with Jerusalem, Tiberias, and Hebron).

Kabbalah, as opposed to formal rabbinical Judaism, is about reading between, behind, and all around the lines. Each letter and accent of every word in the holy books has a numerical value with particular significance, offering added meaning to the literal word. One of the most popular Kabbalistic concepts is that of *tikkun olam,* or "fixing the world." According to Jewish mystics, the universe was "broken" by God in order to make room for the physical realm. Thus the quest of humankind is to repair the universe through good works and service to God.

Although classical Kabbalah studies are intertwined with those of the Bible and the Talmud, not all religious Jews study Kabbalah. In fact, tradition holds that a person studying Kabbalah must be at least 40 years old and have a thorough knowledge of other Jewish texts. Outside of Hasidic Judaism, which has incorporated some Kabbalah into its worldview, many mainstream Orthodox Jews don't study Kabbalah at all, preferring to focus on matters of the perceivable world.

7

Tzfat is abuzz with activity: galleries and shops stay open late, *klezmer* music (Eastern European Jewish "soul music") dances around corners, and the city extends a warm welcome to everyone.

GETTING HERE AND AROUND

If you're driving to Tzfat from Jerusalem, take Route 6 north. If you're starting in Tel Aviv, head north on Route 2. Either way, you'll want to turn east on Route 65, then north on Route 90, then west on Route 89 to Tzfat. If your journey starts in Haifa, head north on Route 4, then east on Route 89 to Tzfat. Egged runs at least two buses daily to Tzfat from Tel Aviv, at least seven from Jerusalem, and at least 30 from Haifa.

Both of Israel's major bus companies, Egged Tours and United Tours, offer one- and two-day guided tours of the region, departing from Tel Aviv and Jerusalem. In Tzfat, the private company Nateev Express runs 13 local routes. Buses from Tzfat's central station, at the entrance to the city, head to most towns in the region.

Within the Old City, the many streets closed to traffic make it difficult to drive. You may have to drive around the perimeter of the city rather than through it. The best way to get around is on foot.

Bus Contacts Nateev Express. ☎ *3553 ⊕ www.nateevexpress.com.*

VISITOR INFORMATION

Contacts Tzfat Visitors Center. ✉ *17 Alkabets St.* ☎ *04/692–4427* ⊕ *www.livnot.org/about-livnot/tzfat-visitors-center.*

TOP ATTRACTIONS

Abuhav Synagogue. This spacious Sephardic synagogue is named for a 14th-century Spanish scribe whose Torah scrolls found their way here with the Spanish Jewish exiles 200 years later. A look around reveals several differences between this synagogue and its Ashkenazi counterparts: for example, the walls are painted the lively blue typical of Sephardic tradition, and the benches run along the walls instead of in rows (so that no man turns his back on his neighbor).

Every detail is loaded with significance. There are three arks—for the three forefathers, Abraham, Isaac, and Jacob (the one on the right is said to be the Abuhav original)—and 10 windows in the dome, referring to the Commandments. The charmingly naive illustrations on the squinches (supports) include a depiction of the Dome of the Rock (referring to the destruction of the Second Temple) and pomegranate trees, whose seed-filled fruit symbolizes the 613 Torah Commandments. The original building was destroyed in the 1837 earthquake, but locals swear that the southern wall—in which the Abuhav Torah scroll is set—was spared. ✉ *Abuhav St.* ☎ *04/692–3885* 💲 *Free* 🌑 *Closed Sat. to visitors.*

Artists' Colony. Set in the city's old Arab Quarter, the Artists' Colony was established in 1951 by six Israeli artists who saw the promise hidden in Tzfat's war-torn condition. For them, the old buildings, the fertile landscape, and the cool mountain air fused into the magic ingredients of creativity. Others soon followed until, at its peak, the colony was home to more than 50 artists, some of whom exhibit internationally. Many galleries host workshops as well as exhibits, and many are open only in the spring and summer, from about 10 am to 6 pm. ✉ *Old City* 💲 *Free.*

Caro Synagogue. Tucked among art galleries, the charming Caro Synagogue appears quite run-down, but it is considered one of the Old City's most interesting destinations by those who feel a deep spiritual connection to the great scholar who lent it his name. Rabbi Yosef Caro arrived in Tzfat in 1535 and led its Jewish community for many years. He is the author of Shulchan Aruch, the code of law that remains a foundation of Jewish religious interpretation to the present day, and this synagogue is said to have been his private study hall. It was destroyed in the great earthquake of 1837 and rebuilt in the mid-19th century. If you ask, the attendant might open the ark containing the Torah scrolls, one of which is at least 400 years old. A glass-faced cabinet at the back of the synagogue is the *geniza,* where damaged scrolls or prayer books are stored (because they carry the name of God, they cannot be destroyed). The turquoise paint here—considered the "color of heaven"—is believed to help keep away the evil eye. ✉ *Alkabets St.* ☎ *04/692–3284* 💲 *Free* 🌑 *Closed Sat. to visitors.*

General Exhibition. An important stop in a tour of the Artists' Colony, the works inside this large space are a representative sample of the work of Tzfat's artists, ranging from oils and watercolors to silkscreens and sculptures, in traditional and avant-garde styles. The permission of the Muslim authorities was required to organize the exhibition, as it is housed in the old mosque, easily identified from afar by its minaret. The Artists' Colony has recognized the growing presence of artists from the former Soviet Union, and the adjacent building holds the **Immigrant Artists' Exhibition.** In either facility, if any works catch your fancy, just ask directions to the artist's gallery for a more in-depth look at his or her work. ⊠ *Leon Isakov and Zvi Levanon Sts.* ☎ *04/692–0087* ☞ *Free.*

Ha'Ari Synagogue. This Ashkenazi synagogue has associations going back to the 16th century. It's named for a rabbi who left an indelible mark on Judaism: Isaac Luria, known to all as the Ari, Hebrew for "lion" and an acronym for Adoneinu Rabbeinu Itzhak ("our master and teacher Isaac"). In his mere three years in Tzfat, he evolved his own system of the Kabbalah, which drew a huge following that would influence Jewish teaching the world over. Even more astounding is that he died in his thirties; it is generally said that one should not even consider study of the Kabbalah before the age of 40, when one reaches the requisite level of intellectual and emotional maturity.

The pale colors of this tiny Ashkenazi synagogue contrast sharply with its olive-wood Holy Ark, a dazzlingly carved tour de force with two tiers of spiral columns and vibrant plant reliefs. The Sephardic Ari Synagogue, where the rabbi prayed, is farther down the quarter, by the cemetery. The oldest of Tzfat's synagogues, this 16th-century structure has especially fine carved wooden doors. ⊠ *Najara St.* ☞ *Free* ☉ *Closed Sat. to visitors.*

Hameiri House. This centuries-old three-story stone building, at the northern end of Keren Ha'yesod Street, houses a historical museum that offers great insight into the daily life of Jews in Tzfat over the past 200 years. Textiles, tableware, and Judaica-like ornate menorahs are displayed with notations in Hebrew and English. Guided tours are available by appointment. ⊠ *158 Keren Ha'yesod St.* ☎ *04/697–1307* ☞ *NIS 20* ☉ *Closed Sat.*

WORTH NOTING

Citadel Park. In Talmudic times, hilltop bonfires here served as a beacon to surrounding communities, heralding the beginning of the lunar month, the basis for the Jewish calendar. In the 12th century, the Crusaders grasped the strategic value of this setting and built the Citadel. The Muslim sultan Baybars conquered it in 1266, leaving only the scattered pieces you see today.

The Jewish settlement outside the Citadel's walls grew and prospered during and after the Crusader era, becoming a center of Kabbalah studies. When the departing British Mandate forces left the town's strategic positions to the Arab forces, the remains of the Citadel again became a battleground between Jews and Arabs. ⊠ *Derech Hativat Yiftach* ☞ *Free.*

Kikar Hameginim. In the Old Jewish Quarter, "Defenders' Square" was once its social and economic heart. A sign points to a two-story house that served as the command post of the neighborhood's defense in 1948—hence the plaza's name. ⊠ *Bar Yochai St., at Ma'alot Gore Ha'Ari* ☞ *Free.*

Tzfat is an artsy village in the northern Galilee known for being a historic center of Kabbalah (Jewish mysticism).

Ma'alot Olei Hagardom. Part of Tzfat's charm is its setting, on the slope of a hill. This *ma'alot,* or stairway, which extends from Yerushalayim Street to Keren HaYesod Street, forms the boundary between the Old Jewish Quarter and the Artists' Colony. It is named for Tzfat freedom fighters executed by the British during the Mandate. ⊠ *Off Yerushalayim St.* 🎫 *Free.*

Memorial Museum of Hungarian-Speaking Jewry. The founders of this museum are Tzfat residents and Holocaust survivors Hava and Yosef Lustig. The exhibits in the museum's three small rooms, including letters, children's books, drawings, items of clothing, and more, tell of the everyday life of communities and individuals in the Hungarian-speaking Jewish pre-Holocaust world. The computer database has information about 1,700 Jewish communities in Hungary, Transylvania, Slovakia, and other countries. Guided tours can be arranged in advance. ⊠ *Old Ottoman Government Center, Independence Sq.* ☎ *04/692–5881* ⊕ *www.hjm.org.il* 🎫 *NIS 15* ☉ *Closed Sat.*

Old Jewish Cemetery. Old and new cemeteries are set into the hillside below the Old Jewish Quarter. The old plots resonate with the names and fame of the Kabbalists of yore, as their graves are identifiable by sky-blue markers. It is said that if the legs of the devout suddenly get tired here, it is because they are walking over hidden graves. The new cemetery holds the graves of members of the pre-State underground Stern Gang and Irgun forces, who were executed by the British in Akko's prison. In a separate plot, bordered by cypresses, lie the 21 Tzfat teenagers killed by terrorists in 1974—they were taken hostage while on a field trip in the northern Galilee town of Ma'alot. ⊠ *Below Keren Hayesod St.* 🎫 *Free.*

WHERE TO EAT

$$$
ISRAELI
FAMILY
Fodor's Choice
★

✕ **Ein Camonim.** The Galilee Hills make a perfect pasture for livestock—in this case, goats—and here you can taste the fresh output of Ein Camonim's dairy, one of the best in Israel. The all-you-can-eat menu includes a platter of about three dozen goat cheeses, a selection of home-baked breads, a variety of fresh salads, and house wine. There's a half-price menu for kids. The specialty shop next door sells the dairy's cheeses, olives, and other homemade products. The eatery is 20 km (12½ miles) southwest of Tzfat, 5 km (3 miles) west of Kadarim Junction. $ *Average main: NIS 88* ⊠ *Rte. 85* ☎ *04/698–9894* ⊕ *www.ein-camonim.rest-e.co.il.*

$$
ECLECTIC

✕ **Gan Eden.** The setting, a charming stone house with both indoor and outdoor seating, lends great atmosphere to this family-run eatery set above the Old City and taking in the view of Mount Meron (the restaurant's name means "paradise"). Gan Eden is best known for its fish, especially fillets of sea bass and sea bream. What they call calzones are actually dumplings stuffed with salty Tzfat cheese and served with a delicious salad of lettuce, cranberries, and walnuts. The place is kosher for dairy, meaning no meat is served. $ *Average main: NIS 70* ⊠ *Mount Canaan Promenade, 33 HaGedud Hashlishi St.* ☎ *04/697–2434* ⊗ *Closed Sat.*

$
MIDDLE EASTERN

✕ **Lachuch Original.** This popular Old City eatery's upstairs dining room has benches and tables inlaid with Middle Eastern designs, walls painted the soft shade of blue found inside local synagogues, and colorful carpets from all over the region. The strikingly dressed owner and chef, Ronen Jarufi, makes each meal to order. Choose from a variety of Yemenite breads—*lachuch, malawa,* or *jachnun* are all good picks—and he'll top it with homemade cheese and his own hot sauce. The place also stocks books on Kabbalah and CDs of evocative Jewish music. $ *Average main: NIS 40* ⊠ *18 Alkabets St.* ☎ *050/225–4148* ⊗ *Closed Sat. No dinner Fri.*

WHERE TO STAY

$$$
HOTEL

▦ **Canaan Spa.** The focus of this hotel on the outskirts of Tzfat is on the spa treatments, including aromatic massages with olive oil and honey or hot-stone treatments using warmed pieces of basalt. **Pros:** pool; brunch and dinner included. **Cons:** remote location; outdated room furnishings; not for families with young kids. $ *Rooms from: $396* ⊠ *Mount Canaan Promenade, Gdud Hashlishi St.* ☎ *04/699–3000* ⊕ *www.canaan-spa.com* ⊃ *124 rooms* ⦿ *Some meals.*

$
B&B/INN
FAMILY

▦ **Joseph's Well Country Inn.** Each room at this friendly kibbutz lodging is like a cozy studio apartment, with pine furnishings and chintz curtains. **Pros:** informal vibe; terrific for families; a peek into kibbutz life. **Cons:** plain decor; basic breakfast. $ *Rooms from: $199* ⊠ *Kibbutz Amiad, Off Rte. 90* ✛ *10 km (6 miles) south of Tzfat* ☎ *073/759–9747* ⊕ *www.amiad-inn.com* ⊃ *27 rooms* ⦿ *Breakfast.*

$$
HOTEL

▦ **Ruth Rimonim.** Built 200 years ago for a Turkish sultan, this spectacular castle has been transformed into a hotel with a reputation for charming rooms. **Pros:** romantic retreat; nice pool; central location. **Cons:** some older rooms are on the small side. $ *Rooms from: $273*

✉ *45 HaNasi St., off Tet Zayin St.* ☎ *04/699–4666* ⊕ *www.rimonim. com* ⟿ *77 rooms* ⎮○⎮ *Breakfast.*

$ 🛏 **Safed Inn.** On the outskirts of Tzfat, the budget-minded Safed Inn
B&B/INN caters especially well to families. **Pros:** very good value; family-friendly atmosphere. **Cons:** owner can be a bit brusque; no kids in deluxe rooms; breakfast not included. ⑤ *Rooms from: $87* ✉ *Mount Canaan Promenade, Off HaGdud Hashlishi St.* ☎ *04/697–1007* ⊕ *www.safedinn. com* ⟿ *20 rooms* ⎮○⎮ *No meals.*

NIGHTLIFE AND PERFORMING ARTS

Klezmer Festival. Every July or August Tzfat hosts the Klezmer Festival, and there could be no better setting for three days of "Jewish soul music" than this mystical community. Many events are street performances and therefore free. Tzfat practically bursts at the seams at this time, with revelers both religious and secular. ✉ *Tzfat* ☎ *04/697–4403* ⊕ *klezmerim.info.*

SPORTS AND THE OUTDOORS

FAMILY   **Bat Ya'ar Ranch.** In the Birya Forest near Tzfat, Bat Ya'ar Ranch offers outdoor fun for the whole family including pony rides through the fields, rope bridges swinging between the trees, and outdoor bowling with wooden lanes and balls. The wooded-mountaintop setting enhances the timbered restaurant's delicious food. A meaty bowl of bean stew, eaten by the fireplace, is a pleasure any time of year. Bat Ya'ar is 5 km (3 miles) north of Tzfat. It's best to call for directions. ✉ *Off Rte. 90, Amuka* ☎ *04/692–1788* ⊕ *www.batyaar.co.il.*

SHOPPING

Safed Candles. This place has grown from a one-room workshop to a huge space filled with the pleasant aroma of beeswax and the bright colors of hand-decorated Sabbath, Havdalah, and Hanukkah candles. ✉ *62 HaAri St.* ☎ *04/682–2068.*

Safed Craft Pottery. Creative stoneware, porcelain, and ceramics can be found in Daniel Flatauer's studio and shop in the Old City. His salt-fire glazes are especially worth noting. The artist, who came to Tzfat from England, is welcoming and helpful. ✉ *63 Yud Alef St.* ☎ *04/697–4970* .

Sheva Haya Glassblowing Gallery. Colorado-born Sheva Haya's blown-glass sculptures and vibrant watercolors are meant to evoke the beauty of the land and its people. The artist offers demonstrations of her work and explains how it relates to Kabbalah, but you can also just poke around her studio. ✉ *7 Tet Vav St.* ☎ *050/430–5107* ⊕ *www. shevachaya.com.*

MOUNT MERON

29 km (18 miles) northwest of Tzfat.

For many centuries, Mount Meron has drawn thousands upon thousands of Orthodox Jews to pay homage to the great rabbis of the Roman era who are buried at the eastern foot of the mount. It's also a nature reserve. Around the area are a number of other sights.

GETTING HERE AND AROUND

From Tzfat, take Route 89 west, following signs to "Tomb of Rashbi," which is an abbreviation for the Tomb of Rabbi Shimon Bar Yochai.

EXPLORING

Erez Komarovsky. Chef Erez Komarovsky's cooking workshops are held in his home in Matat, which is surrounded by gardens of fresh herbs and vegetables. An unforgettable day of fine food, great wine, and breathtaking views will give you plenty of inspiration as you can learn recipes to bring home with you. The dishes are all seasonal and focus on local ingredients: think red snapper tartare with avocado, fish steamed in banana leaves, lamb stuffed with pistachios, and fennel sautéed in saffron-infused clarified butter. At lunch you enjoy everything you've prepared, along with slabs of crusty bread. Matat is 14 km (9 miles) west of Mount Meron. ⊠ *North of Rte. 89, off Rte. 899, Matat* ☎ *03/977–2929* ⊕ *www.erez-komarovsky.co.il* ☎ *NIS 260* ⌂ *Reservations essential.*

Fodor'sChoice **Lotem Winery.** Come for the wine, stay for the delicious tapas, and find ★ yourself hours later still at Lotem for the good company, live music, and valley views. At this organic winery (one of Israel's two of this kind), a tour and tasting includes learning about organic grapes in Israel and about why the winery plays music to the barrels and bottles 24/7.

The winemaker, Jonathan, can also whip up some of the region's tastiest ceviche, fish kebabs, and salads to balance the elegant red blends. The restaurant is open on the weekends and tasting tours are possible throughout the week with advance reservations. The winery is 45 minutes by car south of Mount Meron. ⊠ *Kibbutz Lotem, Off Rte. 804, Amirim* ✛ *Go south on Rte. 804 from Rte. 85 and enter through kibbutz gate, following winery signs* ☎ *054/791–5868* ⊕ *lotemwinery.co.il* 🖭 *35 NIS for tasting and tour.*

Mount Meron. The most important site on lovely Mount Meron—and one of the holiest places in Israel—is the **Tomb of Rabbi Shimon Bar Yochai,** survivor of the Bar Kochba Revolt of almost 2,000 years ago. The simple building that houses the tomb is a place for quiet reflection and prayer, though you may encounter a bar mitzvah or other festive event in the courtyard outside. Women and men have separate prayer areas, and all are expected to dress modestly (coverups are available for those who don't have them). ■TIP➜ **Signs point to the Tomb of Rashbi, which is the Hebrew acronym of the rabbi's name.**

Bar Yochai is said to have fled from the Romans with his son Elazar after the fall of Jerusalem to a cave at Peki'in, not far from here, where he remained for 13 years. The faithful, beginning with the 16th-century mystics who settled in Tzfat, believe that from his cave-hideout Bar Yochai penned the *Zohar* (*The Book of Splendor*), his commentary on the first five books of the Hebrew Bible. Others claim that the Zohar dates from 13th-century Spain. Nevertheless, the constant flow of visitors is evidence of the pilgrims' devotion to the great rabbi and rebel.

The pilgrimage is still celebrated en masse on Lag Ba'Omer, the festive 33rd day of the seven solemn weeks that begin with Passover. At this time Mount Meron comes alive as a grand procession arrives on foot from Tzfat, with many participants carrying Torah scrolls and singing fervently. Bonfires are lighted, with celebrations lasting days.

Mount Meron is the highest peak in Israel after Mount Hermon, and parts of it are a nature reserve (⊕ *www.parks.org.il*) with hiking trails. ⊠ *Off Rte. 89* 🖭 *Free* ⊗ *Closed Sat.*

WHERE TO EAT

$$$$
MODERN ISRAELI

✕**Aluma Bistro.** The town of Maalot-Tarshisha is home to Jewish, Christian, and Muslim families, and they rub elbows at Aluma Bistro. Decorated with artifacts from Provence, the burgundy-toned dining room buzzes with locals in search of an extraordinary meal. Young Arab chef Alaa Sweetat weaves seasonal French and traditional Galilean styles into a tapestry of taste. Inquire about the daily specials, which may include seasonally foraged vegetables and a fresh catch of the day. $ *Average main: NIS 116* ⊠ *Tarshisha Rd., Maalot-Tarshisha* ✛ *21 km (13 miles) west of Mount Meron via Rte. 89* ⊕ *www.alumabistro.co.il.*

$
BAKERY

✕**Bread and Cake** (*Lehem V'Uga*). Fresh-baked sourdough breads, oil- and preservative-free pastries, and healthy whole wheat challah are the cornerstone of Gal Levi's kosher bakery in the rural heart of the Galilee. Grab a seat on Friday morning in the backyard outdoor garden with the locals to taste stone-oven-baked Turkish-style cheese *burekas,* artichoke carpaccio with olives and sun-dried tomatoes, or a light dish of homemade granola and locally produced yogurt. ⑤ *Average main: NIS 40 ⊠ Kibbutz Moran, HaZayit St. ✣ South of Rte. 85 ☎ 04/698–8992 ⊕ www.bread-cake.co.il ⊘ Closed Sat. No dinner.*

$$
CAFÉ
FAMILY

✕**Maarag.** This kosher restaurant's colorful dishes highlight Galilean delicacies. The Israeli breakfast is a rich way to enjoy the flavors of homemade jams or grilled baby eggplant with tahini. For a light lunch try the plentiful salads, especially the halloumi cheese and sautéed mushrooms served over romaine lettuce. The sun-filled gallery inside the café fills the walls with color and showcases the works by artists from the local special needs community (who also receive part of the café's profits). ⑤ *Average main: NIS 58 ⊠ 1 Meron Rd., Kfar Vradim ✣ Kfar Vradim is south of Maalot-Tarshisha, 21 km (13 miles) west of Mount Meron ⊕ www.maarag.org.il ⊘ No dinner.*

WHERE TO STAY

$$
HOTEL
FAMILY

🏨**Hacienda Forest View.** Families with active kids will enjoy the enclosed green grounds of this hotel surrounded by forest. **Pros:** kosher meals, including Friday night traditional dinner; kid-friendly activities; various meal plans available. **Cons:** grounds are dated. ⑤ *Rooms from: $250 ⊠ Yafeh Nof, Maalot-Tarshisha ✣ 21 km (13 miles) west of Mount Meron ☎ 04/957–9000 ⊕ www.c-hotels.co.il/en/ ➟ 142 rooms* ⑩ *Some meals.*

$$$
B&B/INN

🏨**Tamar v'Gefen.** In the Western Galilee, Tamar and Yaron Cohen created three lovely suites off their home, where they focus on their love of wine. **Pros:** hot tub in a stunning garden; complimentary use of bikes; delicious breakfast. **Cons:** away from the usual tourist attractions. ⑤ *Rooms from: $320 ⊠ Off Rte. 89, Mitzpe Hila ✣ 25 km (15 miles) west of Mount Meron ☎ 050/997–8911 ⊕ www.tamar-gefen. co.il ➟ 3 rooms* ⑩ *Breakfast.*

BAR'AM NATIONAL PARK

15 km (9 miles) northwest of Meron, 22 km (14 miles) northwest of Tzfat.

In an otherwise deserted spot lie the ruins of Bar'am, one of the best-preserved ancient synagogues anywhere. Like most other synagogues uncovered in this area, this structure dating from the 3rd century faces south toward Jerusalem; unlike any other, however, this one has lavish architectural elements, such as an entrance with a segmental pediment and freestanding columns in front.

GETTING HERE AND AROUND

From Mount Meron or Tzfat, head west on Route 89, then north on Route 899. After 2 km (1 mile), turn right onto a dirt road. There's no bus service to Bar'am. Near the park, you can check out one of the area's wineries as well as an ice-cream factory.

EXPLORING

Bar'am National Park. The interior of this ancient house of worship, which resembles that of other Galilean synagogues of the Talmudic period (3rd to 8th centuries AD), is less well preserved than the impressive exterior. Rows of pillars in the prayer hall apparently served as supports for the ceiling, and the building may have had a second story. A section of the facade's lintel, now in the Louvre in Paris, contains the Hebrew inscription "May there be peace in this place, and in all the places of Israel. This lintel was made by Jose the Levite. Blessings upon his works. Shalom." Allow at least an hour to wander around or bring a picnic and enjoy it on one of the tables. ⊠ *Off Rt. 899, 3 km (2 miles) east of Khiram Junction, Tzivon* ☎ *04/698–9301* ⊕ *www.parks. org.il* ⊠ *NIS 15.*

FAMILY **Buza Ice Cream Factory.** Artisanal ice-cream-making workshops are offered at the factory of the budding Buza Ice Cream chain. During the hour-long session, participants earn about the ice-cream-making process and taste the results of their hard work. Although the workshop is geared toward kids, adults can participate; everyone can savor tastings from the adjacent shop, including cardamom- or chocolate-flavored specialty cones filled with seasonal sorbets and ice creams. Reservations are required for the workshop. ⊠ *Kibbutz Sasa, Off Rte. 89* ✛ *Enter kibbutz and follow signs to right toward Buza* ☎ *04/691–8880* ⊕ *buzaisrael.co.il* ⊠ *Workshop NIS 50.*

Galil Mountain Winery. Producing more than 15 blends and varietals in a yearly production of 1 million bottles, this is one of Israel's largest wineries. The tour in the modern, well-designed visitor center begins with an overview map of the six Upper Galilee vineyards, continues with a look at the modern press and stainless-steel storage tanks, and then moves to the tasting room for a sampling of whites, a rosé, and reds. End the tour on the balcony with its panoramic view of vineyards and hills. ⊠ *Kibbutz Yiron, Off Rte. 899* ✛ *Enter through kibbutz gate and follow signs to winery* ☎ *04/686–8748* ⊕ *www.galilmountain.co.il* ⊠ *Tour NIS 20* ☾ *Closed Sat.*

ROSH PINA

31 km (19 miles) east of Bar'am National Park, 10 km (6 miles) east of Tzfat, 25 km (15½ miles) north of Tiberias.

Fodor's Choice
★

The restored village of Rosh Pina is a gift-shop-and-gallery-browser's delight, and the dilapidated wooden doors and stonework of some still-abandoned premises are part of the charm.

Rosh Pina—literally "cornerstone"—gets its name from Psalm 118:22: "The stone that the builders rejected has become the chief cornerstone." This verse inspired the Galilee's first Zionist pioneers, who came from Romania in 1882, determined to build a village in the malaria-infested area. They bought this land, at the foot of the mountain ridge east of Tzfat, from the neighboring Arab villagers of Ja'uni.

The pioneers, who had little experience in agriculture, struggled to survive until Jewish philanthropist Baron Edmond de Rothschild bought the land. He provided them with tools, workers, and a new industry: the production of silk by silkworms. By the turn of the 20th century, Rosh Pina had grown into the country's fourth-largest Jewish farming community. Today it's a vacation destination and a year-round residence for 2,500 people.

GETTING HERE AND AROUND

From Tel Aviv, you can fly into the small airport of Mahanayim, near Rosh Pina. There are also daily buses from Tzfat, Tiberias, and Haifa. The most practical way is driving. If arriving from Tzfat, head east on Route 89, then north on Route 90.

Taxi Contacts Meir Taxi. ☎ *04/693–5735.*

EXPLORING

HaBaron Garden. Unveiled in 1886, this public park was created at the request of philanthropist Baron Edmond de Rothschild. Olive and almond trees and fragrant herbs like rosemary are planted in terraces on the hillside so that you can enjoy shade and a tree-framed view of the valley below. ⊠ *HaChalutzim St.* 🎟 *Free.*

Professor Mer House. This office and house belonged to Professor Gideon Mer, a leading expert on malaria in the 1930s. Legend has it that Mer used to inject his wife and children with experimental remedies in his efforts to combat malaria in this region. (Happily, all survived.) The British were so impressed with Mer's work that they sent him to Burma to fight malaria epidemics there. Implements and household items from the early days of Rosh Pina are on display. Next door, a colorful audio-visual presentation showcases the founding of this pioneering community. ⊠ *HaRishonim St.* ☎ *04/693–6603* 🎟 *NIS 15.*

Synagogue. The old synagogue's interior remains pretty much as it was when it was built in the mid-1880s. The dark pews, made of the timber brought from Romania, have aged gracefully. The painted ceiling has depictions of palm trees and biblical motifs. The building is usually locked, but ask around and you might find someone to open it for you. ⊠ *HaRishonim St.*

WHERE TO EAT

$$$$
EUROPEAN
Fodor'sChoice
★

✕ **Auberge Shulamit.** This charming inn takes its name from the original Hotel Shulamit, where the 1948 Armistice Treaty was signed. The home-smoked meats and fish are unique and worth trying, as are the seasonal soups, seafood dishes, and the elegant array of desserts. If you can't bear to leave, the inn has three French country–style guest rooms. ⑤ *Average main: NIS 160* ⊠ *34 David Shuv St.* ☎ *04/693–1485* ⊕ *www.shulamit.co.il.*

$$$$
ARGENTINE

✕ **Babayit Shel Rafa.** The sizzling steaks of his native Argentina figure prominently on Rafa's menu. The best starters are the pickled tongue and the meat or corn empanadas. Entrées include roast beef and a sausage and lamb casserole with rice and green beans. Vegetarians shouldn't despair, as the rich vegetable, mozzarella, prune, and almond stew is delicious. Business lunches, served daily from noon to 5 pm, are tasty and economical. ⑤ *Average main: NIS 120* ⊠ *HaChalutzim St., next to Old Rosh Pina Office* ☎ *04/693–6192.*

$$
CAFÉ
FAMILY

✕ **Chocolata.** The original arched stone basement of the old synagogue is the setting of this chocolate shop and café. True to its name, the kitchen serves a host of chocolate delights (drinks, cakes, and more), including 37 different kinds of pralines made by the house chocolatier. Delightful chocolate-making workshops are offered occasionally. ⑤ *Average main:*

Visit Rosh Pina for its charming streets, shops, and galleries.

NIS 60 ⊠ HaRishonim St., lower entrance to synagogue ☎ 04/686–0219 ⊕ www.chocolatte.co.il.

$$$
ECLECTIC
✕ **Ja'uni.** Named after the Palestinian village that stood on this spot until 1948, this hippie-chic bistro serves salads, pasta, fish, and meat dishes with Italian flair. While the food may not be the most sophisticated, the atmosphere defines the relaxed, casual vibe of Rosh Pina. During the day, this is a perfect spot for a coffee break or a light lunch. The outdoor seating is pleasant, especially when there's live music on summer evenings. ⑤ *Average main: NIS 80* ⊠ *30 David Shuv St.* ☎ 04/693–1881.

$$$$
STEAKHOUSE
✕ **Meat-balim.** Go easy on the appetizers here, as you'll want to save room for this sleek, modern kosher eatery's savory meat dishes. Those in the know recommend the generous veal entrecôte and the lamb chops in a flavorful sauce of caramel, oranges, mint, and ginger. Avoid the creamy desserts, which don't contain real dairy. The extensive wine list is a pleasure, however. ⑤ *Average main: NIS 130* ⊠ *Hagalil St.* ☎ 04/686–0107 ⊘ *Apr.–Sept., no dinner Fri., no lunch Sat.; Oct.–Mar., closed Fri. and Sat.*

WHERE TO STAY

Rosh Pina is a budding center of tourism for this region, and many residents are now opening their homes as B&Bs, some of whose breakfasts alone are worth the stay.

$$$
B&B/INN
▣ **Ahuzat Hameiri.** This stunning mansion has been in the Hameiri family since it was built in the late 1880s. **Pros:** breathtaking views; nice grounds; family-friendly atmosphere. **Cons:** no pool; many steps to rooms. ⑤ *Rooms from: $325* ⊠ *1 HaChalutzim St.* ☎ 04/693–8707 ⊕ *www.hrp.co.il* ⤴ *9 rooms* ⏝ *Breakfast.*

$$$$
HOTEL
Fodor's Choice
★
⊞ **Mizpe Hayamim.** With a splendid view of the Sea of Galilee, this colonial-style hotel south of Rosh Pina specializes in pampering its clients. **Pros:** great food and variety of meal plans; enchanting walking paths; pretty pool. **Cons:** need a car to get around; not a place for kids. ⑤ *Rooms from: $580 ⊠ Off Rte. 8900 ☎ 04/699–4555 ⊕ www.mizpe-hayamim.com ↬ 100 rooms* ⦿ *Some meals.*

$$$
B&B/INN
Fodor's Choice
★
⊞ **Pina BaLev.** Each of these distinctively designed suites offers all of the amenities you could want in a Rosh Pina retreat. **Pros:** welcoming owner; soothing spa treatments; luxurious amenities. **Cons:** limited number of suites. ⑤ *Rooms from: $395 ⊠ 31 HaChalutzim St. ☎ 04/693–0970 ⊕ www.pinabalev.com ↬ 5 suites* ⦿ *Breakfast.*

$$
HOTEL
⊞ **Pina Barosh.** The stained-glass windows, wood furniture, and hand-woven rugs make it hard to guess that this charming small boutique hotel used to house livestock. **Pros:** romantic restaurant; relaxing atmosphere; great place for couples. **Cons:** no view from rooms; not for families. ⑤ *Rooms from: $210 ⊠ 8 HaChalutzim St. ☎ 04/693–6582 ⊕ www.pinabarosh.com ↬ 7 rooms* ⦿ *Breakfast.*

$$
B&B/INN
FAMILY
⊞ **Villa Tehila.** Amichai and Tehila Yisraeli bought this 19th-century farm and converted the former stables, storehouse, and dairy into a charming guesthouse. **Pros:** family-friendly vibe; convivial owners; pool open year-round. **Cons:** some rooms very small; courtyard dimly lit at night. ⑤ *Rooms from: $220 ⊠ 7 HaChalutzim St. ☎ 04/693–7788 ⊕ www.villa-tehila.co.il ↬ 11 rooms* ⦿ *Breakfast.*

NIGHTLIFE

Shiri's Bistro. A must for wine lovers, this pleasant spot is not only a good place to sample local varietals but also a great source of information about the wine industry. The bar stocks local wines from both well-known and up-and-coming vineyards, all at reasonable prices. Enjoy the wine alongside creative smaller plates like the sweet potato and onion fritters, or more substantial homemade pasta dishes. ⊠ *8 Ha Chalutzim St. ☎ 04/693–6582 ⊕ www.pinabarosh.com/engBistro.htm.*

SHOPPING

The Well. Sigal Eshet-Shafat and her husband, Inbar, used to sell typical handicrafts, but it turned out that their jams, sauces, and liqueurs were what attracted customers. The on-site shop lets you sample the store's many unique delights. The onion jam is a favorite for both dairy and meat dishes. ⊠ *HaRishonim St. ☎ 04/693–0020.*

TEL HATZOR NATIONAL PARK

8 km (5 miles) north of Rosh Pina, 14 km (9 miles) east of Tzfat.

On the Via Maris—the major trade route linking Egypt and Mesopotamia—Hatzor is referred to several times in documents from ancient archives in both lands, and scholars believe a huge archive may someday be found here.

GETTING HERE AND AROUND

From Rosh Pina, head north on Route 90; from Tzfat, head east on Route 89, then north on Route 90.

EXPLORING

Tel Hatzor National Park. This site on the Via Maris, an ancient trade route, is a good stop for archaeology buffs—its massive mound is made up of the remnants of 21 cities. The excavation and restoration of some of these antiquities have produced fascinating results.

The book of Joshua (11:13) notes that Joshua destroyed Canaanite Hatzor in the 13th century BC, and Israelites resettled it. Its next heyday came three centuries later, when King Solomon decided it would serve him well as a regional military and administrative center, like Megiddo and Gezer. In 732 BC, Hatzor met its end when invading Assyrian king Tiglath Pileser III conquered the Galilee and forced its Israelite inhabitants off the land in chains and into exile.

The huge site is divided into two areas: the **Upper City,** where you can explore the remains of some ancient settlements, and the **Lower City,** first settled in the 18th century BC. Only the Upper City, covering less than a fifth of the total excavation site, is open to the public. The **Hatzor Museum** (on the grounds of Kibbutz Ayelet Hashachar, across the highway) houses figurines, weapons, stone pots, and other artifacts unearthed in the two areas; others are at the Israel Museum in Jerusalem. It's open by appointment: check ahead. ⊠ *Rte. 90, Yesod Hama'ala* ☎ *04/693–7290* ⊕ *www.parks.org.il* ☜ *NIS 18.*

HULA LAKE NATURE RESERVE

14 km (8½ miles) north of Tel Hatzor, 35 km (22 miles) northeast of Tzfat.

These wetlands were drained during the 1950s after a malaria outbreak, which drove away the unique wildlife. In recent years, the lake was reflooded and birds, especially cranes, once again make it their winter home. About a half-million birds pass through each year.

GETTING HERE AND AROUND
From Tzfat, head east on Route 89 and north on Route 90.

EXPLORING

Ahuzat Dobrovin. For a bit of history head to Ahuzat Dobrovin, near the entrance to the Hula Lake Nature Reserve. The Dobrovin family, Russian immigrants who moved here in 1909, once owned this reconstructed farmhouse. The property was eventually donated to the Jewish National Fund and opened to the public in 1986. An exhibit in the former family home highlights the old days of the Hula Valley, and a short video provides context. A pleasant garden surrounds the property. ⊠ *East of Rte. 90, Yesod Hama'ala* ☎ *04/693–7371* ☜ *NIS 10* ☉ *Closed Sat.*

Hula Lake Nature Reserve. More than 390 avian species flock to the Hula Lake during the migration season (fall and spring), and some remain here for the winter or to nest, which makes this nature preserve a prime spot for bird-watching. The park offers an 8.5-km (5.2-mile) trail with bird-watching huts along the way. Bicycles and golf carts are available for rent. Sunrise and night tours are available for 85 shekels, as are private guides for 350 shekels. Note that this is different from the Hula

Nature Reserve (⊕ *www.parks.org.il*). ⊠ *Off Rte. 90, Yesod Hama'ala* ☎ *04/681–7137* ⊕ *www.agamon-hula.co.il* ☎ *NIS 5.*

WHERE TO STAY

$$$ ⬚ **Hotel Galilion.** At the entrance to the Hula Lake Nature Reserve, the
HOTEL Hotel Galilion is a luxurious haven for bird-watchers. **Pros:** convenient
location for exploring the north; scenic views; variety of meal plan
options. **Cons:** pool area may be noisy if there is a conference or event.
⑤ *Rooms from: $301* ⊠ *Rte. 90, Yesod Hama'ala* ✢ *Near entrance to
Hula Lake Nature Reserve* ☎ *04/697–8008* ⊕ *www.galilion.co.il/en/*
⤴ *120 rooms* ⍾ *Some meals.*

UPPER HULA VALLEY

The sights that hug the border with Lebanon show contrasting sides
of Israel. The bustling town of Kiryat Shmona and sleepy Metulla bear
eloquent witness to the varying fortunes of Israel's relationships with
its Arab neighbors. Tel Dan Nature Reserve, on the other hand, draws
visitors with its antiquities, surging river, and lush, wild beauty.

KIRYAT SHMONA

55 km (34 miles) north of Tiberias, 42 km (26 miles) north of Tzfat.

The major urban center in the Upper Hula Valley, Kiryat Shmona is
known for the scenic cable car up Manara Cliff and as a practical base
for exploring the most northern sections of the country. Adventure seek-
ers and families can enjoy kayaking and sports in the many surround-
ing nature parks. For years, the instability in neighboring Lebanon
profoundly affected life in the town, and by 1982 the spate of terrorist
attacks had reached such proportions that Israel responded by invading
Lebanon, the first stage of what would become the First Lebanon War.
In 2006, Hezbollah again lobbed rockets into northern Israel, sparking
the Second Lebanon War.

GETTING HERE AND AROUND

From Tzfat, head east on Route 89, then north on Route 90; from
Tiberias, head north on Route 90. There are at least 20 buses daily from
Tel Aviv, at least 19 from Haifa, and three from Jerusalem.

Taxi Contacts Hatzafon Taxi. ☎ *04/694–2333.*

EXPLORING

FAMILY **Manara Cliff.** The Kiryat Shmona–Kibbutz Manara cable car at Manara
Cliff gives you a bird's-eye view of the Hula Valley. It has one station
midway on the 1,890-yard trip, where the adventurous can step out
and do some rappelling and dry sliding (a roller-coaster-like activity) or
try the climbing wall. Another option is to ride a mountain bike down
or experience the thrill of a 600-foot zip line. If you opt to remain in
the cable car, the trip takes eight minutes each way, overlooking cliffs
and green hills. At the bottom are a trampoline and other attractions
for kids. There is wheelchair access to the cable car and upper station.
⊠ *Kibbutz Manara, Rte. 90* ☎ *04/690–5830* ⊕ *www.cliff.co.il* ☎ *NIS
59 weekdays; NIS 69 weekends.*

Upper Hula Valley and the Golan Heights

LEBANON

SYRIA

Mount Hermon

Hermon Stream (Banias) Nature Reserve

Majdal Shams

Metulla

Tel Dan Nature Reserve

Kfer Yuval

Banias Falls

Neve Ativ

Nimrod's Fortress National Park

Ayun Stream Nature Reserve

Kfar Gilad

Dan

Ein Kuniya

Mas'ada

Tel Hai

She'ar Yashuv

Hagoshrim

Golani Lookout

Odem Mountain Winery

Kiryat Shmona

Golan Lookout

Kibbutz El-Rom

Khan Arnabeh

LEBANON

NAFTALI HILLS

HULA VALLEY

GOLAN

UNDOF Zone (U.N. Disengagement Observer Force)

Kfar Blum

Yiftah

Merom Golan

Quneitra

Mount Bental

Ein Zivan

Sede Eliezer

Alonei Habashan

Jish

Meron

Hazor HaGelilit

Golan Archaeological Museum

Khushniya

Mount Meron

Tzfat (Safed)

Rosh Pina

Ancient Katzrin Park

Katzrin

Golan Heights Winery

GOLAN HEIGHTS

Korazim

Had Nes

Gamla Nature Reserve

GALILEE

Maghar

Capernaum

SYRIA

Tabgha

Moshav Ramot

Ramat Magshimim

Eilabun

Sea of Galilee (Lake Kinneret)

Tiberias

Lavi

Golani Junction

Ein Gev

Kafr Kamma

Kinneret

Yavne'el

Degania Alef

Jordan River

JORDAN

Kelar Tavor

Afikim

Um Qais

Adasiyyeh

0   4 mi

0   4 km

Tel Hai. Perched on the northern edge of Kiryat Shmona is Tel Hai, meaning "Hill of Life," a site that played an important role in Israel's history. In the aftermath of World War I, while Britain and France bickered over control of the Upper Hula Valley, bands of Arabs often harassed the Jewish farms, and finally overran Tel Hai in 1920. Only Kibbutz Kfar Giladi was successful in defending itself.

Following this incident, Tel Hai resident Josef Trumpeldor and seven comrades were called on to protect the place. Trumpeldor already had a reputation as a leader in the czar's army in his native Russia. Fired by Zionist ideals, he had moved to Palestine in 1912 at the age of 32. During the final battle in 1920, Trumpeldor and his comrades were killed, and it is for them that Kiryat Shmona—City of the Eight—is named. It is said that Trumpeldor's last words were: "It is good to die for our country." He is buried up the road from the Tel Hai Courtyard Museum, beneath the statue of a lion.

The heroic last stand at Tel Hai was important not only because it was the first modern instance of Jewish armed self-defense, but also because the survival of at least two of the Jewish settlements meant that when the final borders were drawn by the League of Nations in 1922, these settlements were included in the British-mandated territory of Palestine and thus, after 1948, in the State of Israel. ⊠ *Off Rte. 90, Kfar Giladi.*

Tel Hai Courtyard Museum. This museum displays agricultural tools used in the early 20th century when Josef Trumpeldor lived here. A moving audiovisual show highlights the history of the place. Call ahead for reservations. ⊠ *Off Rte. 886, Kfar Giladi* ☎ *04/695–1333.*

WHERE TO EAT

$$
BURGER

✕ **Arburger.** This eatery's cozy interior offers a nice break after a long drive or hike, and the menu is varied enough to suit most tastes. Arburger offers 12-ounce burgers, sizzling steaks, and fresh seafood, as well as some vegetarian options. Unlike many local restaurants, this Western-inspired burger joint is open on weekends. ⑤ *Average main: NIS 55* ⊠ *Gome Junction, Off Rte. 90, behind the gas station* ☎ *057/ 944 –3587.*

$$$$
SEAFOOD

✕ **Dag al Hadan.** This forested area beside the gurgling Dan River draws enthusiastic crowds, especially on the weekends. This was the first restaurant in the region to specialize in the abundant fish from the river; you can also take a look at the trout ponds in a small installation on the grounds. The slightly outdated restaurant, opposite Kibbutz Hagoshrim, is tucked away behind the main road, but it's large and well signposted. The same management also runs a café next door serving vegetarian fare. ⑤ *Average main: NIS 101* ⊠ *Off Rte. 99, Hagoshrim* ☎ *04/695–0225* ⊕ *www.dagaldan.co.il.*

$$
ECLECTIC

✕ **Focaccia Bar.** Ask any local about their favorite place to eat and they will direct you toward this family restaurant tucked into a small shopping center. The menu has a hearty selection of pastas, pizzas, seafood, and meat dishes, all with a contemporary Middle Eastern touch. It sits opposite Kibbutz Ma'ayan Baruch. Reservations are highly recommended, especially on weekends when the place is packed with locals, and for good reason. ⑤ *Average main: NIS 75* ⊠ *Gan Hatzfon, Off Rte. 99, Hagoshrim* ☎ *04/690–4474* ⊕ *www.foccacia.co.il.*

WHERE TO STAY

$$$
B&B/INN
🏨 **Grand Vista Boutique Hotel.** Orchards surround this small hotel, so the heady aromas of the peaches and nectarines will bring you closer to nature as soon as you arrive. **Pros:** excellent baked goods; cozy environment; whirlpool tub in each room. **Cons:** in a residential neighborhood; decor is a bit outdated. ⑤ *Rooms from: $375* ⊠ *31 Kfar Yuval, Kfar Yuval* ☎ *052/638–8783* ⊕ *www.grandvista.co.il* 🛏 *5 rooms* ⑩ *Breakfast.*

$$$
HOTEL
🏨 **Hagoshrim Kibbutz and Resort Hotel.** The waters of the Hermon Stream flow through a glass-covered channel in the lobby of this laid-back lodging. **Pros:** wide selection of activities; kid-friendly vibe; good selection of tours. **Cons:** basic decor; can get loud in summer. ⑤ *Rooms from: $309* ⊠ *Rte. 99, Hagoshrim* ☎ *04/681–6000* ⊕ *www.hagoshrim-hotel. co.il* 🛏 *164 rooms* ⑩ *Breakfast.*

$$
HOTEL
🏨 **Kfar Giladi Hotel.** Atop a hill behind Tel Hai is one of the country's oldest and largest kibbutz hotels; it's run very efficiently, but retains a homey atmosphere. **Pros:** good value; indoor and outdoor swimming pools; good place for souvenirs. **Cons:** basic decor; uninspired food. ⑤ *Rooms from: $250* ⊠ *Rte. 90, Kfar Giladi* ☎ *04/690–0000* ⊕ *www. kfar-giladi.co.il* 🛏 *170 rooms* ⑩ *Breakfast.*

$
HOTEL
FAMILY
🏨 **Pastoral Kfar Blum Hotel.** Part of Kibbutz Kfar Blum, this hotel in the Upper Hula Valley has spacious and elegantly appointed rooms. **Pros:** excellent amenities; lovely spa; variety of programs for children. **Cons:** not all rooms are close to the amenities. ⑤ *Rooms from: $154* ⊠ *Off Rte. 90, Kfar Blum* ☎ *04/683–6611* ⊕ *www.kfarblum-hotel.co.il* 🛏 *120 rooms* ⑩ *Breakfast.*

PERFORMING ARTS

Chamber Music Days. Each year in late July and early August, the Upper Galilee Regional Council hosts Chamber Music Days, a nationally renowned festival of chamber music in a pastoral setting. ⊠ *Off Rte. 90, Kfar Blum* ☎ *04/681–6640.*

SPORTS AND THE OUTDOORS

A plethora of outfits organize water-sports trips in this region, and almost all hotels can make reservations for you. The minimum age for kayaks and other water "vehicles" is usually six.

KAYAKING

Hagoshrim Kayaks. This outfit offers a 5-km (3-mile) family course that takes about 90 minutes and a 6-km (4-mile) "stormy" course that lasts almost two hours. ⊠ *Off Rte. 99, Hagoshrim* ☎ *077/271–7500* ⊕ *www. kayak.co.il* 🎫 *From NIS 89.*

OFF-ROAD VEHICLES

Easy Track. Based in the northern Hula Valley, Easy Track offers wind-in-your-hair ways to explore the countryside, including self-drive dune buggies and 1½-hour guided Jeep trips. ⊠ *Near Rte. 99, She'ar Yashuv* ☎ *04/690–4440* ⊕ *www.mbez.co.il* 🎫 *NIS 150 per family for 1½-hr guided Jeep trip.*

In the Upper Hula Valley, you'll find the Tel Dan Nature Reserve and the Hermon Stream (Banias) Nature Reserve.

Royi Rimon Jeep Tours. Set your alarm clock to the crack of dawn and head out with expert guide Royi Rimon for a sunrise Jeep tour through the wilderness, usually including part of the Golan Heights and a ride by a river. He'll drive you up through terrain you would not otherwise be able to visit without a 4x4 vehicle, stopping along the way to explain the surroundings and to brew coffee and tea. Daytime and sunset rides are also fun options. ✉ *Off Rte. 99, Kfar Blum* ☎ *052/297–6312* 💲 *From $190.*

METULLA

9 km (6 miles) north of Kiryat Shmona, 50 km (31 miles) north of Tzfat.

Israel's northernmost town, Metulla, is so picturesque that it's hard to believe this tranquil spot is just a stone's throw from a contentious border. The tensions of the Middle East dissipate here in the charm of the European-style limestone buildings that line Metulla's quaint main street, and the city itself seems to have changed little since its founding as a farming settlement in 1896. The signs offering *zimmer* (German for "room") for rent enhance the Continental atmosphere. Even the weather is un-Mediterranean, with refreshingly cool mountain breezes carrying whiffs of cypress and spice plants in summer, and snow in winter.

GETTING HERE AND AROUND
From Tzfat, head east on Route 89, then north on Route 90.

EXPLORING

Ayun Stream Nature Reserve. In summer, the stream that gives this nature reserve its name slows to a trickle because the water is channeled away to irrigate crops. In winter, though, the water gushes, becoming a beautiful backdrop for hiking trips. Two trails meander through the reserve; the shorter one, taking about half an hour, begins and ends in the lower parking lot and goes to Tanur (Oven) Falls, the most famous of the reserve's four waterfalls. The longer one, taking 1½ hours, begins in the upper parking lot and leads downstream. ⊠ *East of Rte. 90* ☎ *04/695–1519* ⊕ *www.parks.org.il* ⊠ *NIS 29.*

WHERE TO EAT

$$$$
STEAKHOUSE

✕ **HaTachana.** This ranch-style restaurant, whose name means "The Mill," uses only the best beef from local cattle for its T-bones. The kitchen also grills up tasty sausages, lamb chops, and hamburgers. Each entrée comes with grilled vegetables and either fries or baked potatoes, so you won't go away hungry. The place gets crowded, so reservations are a good idea. ⑤ *Average main: NIS 140* ⊠ *1 Harishonim St.* ☎ *04/694–4810.*

TEL DAN NATURE RESERVE

15 km (9½ miles) southeast of Metulla, 10 km (6 miles) northeast of Kiryat Shmona, 50 km (31 miles) northeast of Tzfat.

Full of biblical-era ruins, the nature sanctuary of Tel Dan has three trails running through about 120 protected acres dotted with laurel trees.

GETTING HERE AND AROUND

From Tzfat, head east on Route 89, then turn north on Route 90. Once you pass Kiryat Shmona, turn east on Route 99. The reserve is near Kibbutz Dan.

EXPLORING

FAMILY

Beit Ussishkin Museum. Adjacent to the Tel Dan Nature Reserve, the Beit Ussishkin Museum has interesting exhibits about the flora, fauna, and geology of the Hula Valley, the Golan Heights, and the Jordan River. The audiovisual presentations are concise and informative. The museum is open daily, but you must make an appointment to visit on Friday and Saturday ⊠ *Off Rte. 99, Dan* ☎ *04/694–1704* ⊠ *NIS 18.*

Fodor'sChoice
★

Tel Dan Nature Reserve. This wildlife sanctuary is hard to beat for sheer natural beauty, and it also contains Tel Dan, an important archaeological site; allow an hour or two for a visit. A river, the Dan Stream, surges through it, and lacy trees provide shade. A host of small mammals lives here—many partial to water, such as the otter and the mongoose—as well as the biblical coney, also known as the hyrax. Tel Dan is home to Israel's largest rodent, the nocturnal Indian crested porcupine, and its smallest predator, the marbled polecat. The reserve has several hiking trails, and a raised wooden walkway is wheelchair accessible.

Dan was a majestic city in biblical times. According to Genesis, Abraham came here to rescue his nephew Lot and, five centuries later, Joshua led the Israelites through the area to victory. Fine ruins from several epochs lie here. Among them are the 9th-century BC city gate and the cultic site where King Jeroboam set up a golden calf to rival the Jerusalem Temple. Just inside the city gate is the platform for a throne, where the city's king pronounced judgment. One of the site's most extraordinary finds is an arched gateway dating from the 18th-century BC Canaanite period, more than a millennium earlier than scholars had previously thought. ⊠ *North of Rte. 99, Dan* ☎ *04/695–1579* ⊕ *www. parks.org.il* ☜ *NIS 29.*

WHERE TO STAY

$$ ⊞ **Pausa Inn.** Leaders in Israel's Slow Food movement own this beautiful
B&B/INN boutique hotel, and their minimalist taste is reflected in the lovely and warm setting. **Pros:** unforgettable meals; lovely decor; outdoor hot tub. **Cons:** remote location; small rooms; no pool. ⑤ *Rooms from: $205* ⊠ *Rte. 99, She'ar Yashuv* ☎ *054/690–4434* ⊕ *www.pausa-inn.co.il* ↩ *8 rooms* ⦿ *Breakfast.*

GOLAN HEIGHTS

Considered the most fertile land in Israel, the Golan Heights is known for its many fine wineries. As you drive through these verdant hills, covered with wildflowers in the spring, you'll also see abundant olive groves and apple and cherry orchards. Fruit picking is a popular tourist activity: cherries from mid-May through June and figs in August and September. You can explore the area by joining a guided tour, perhaps galloping away on a horse or zipping by in a four-wheel-drive vehicle.

The region was once volcanic, and many symmetrical volcanic cones and pronounced reliefs dominate the landscape, particularly in the Upper Golan. The gentle terrain and climate of the rest of the region have historically attracted far more settlement than the less hospitable northern Upper Galilee. Today it's home to Jewish, Druze, and Alawite communities.

For many years the Golan Heights was a source of regional conflict. In 1967 during the Six-Day War, Israel captured the Golan Heights from Syria, which led to the United Nations establishment of a ceasefire line between Israel and Syria, known as the Purple Line. In 1973 Syria attempted unsuccessfully to recapture the Golan Heights during the Yom Kippur War. Israel officially annexed the western two-thirds of the Golan Heights in 1981, although the United Nations condemned the move; Syria controls the eastern third of the area.

HERMON STREAM (BANIAS) NATURE RESERVE

20 km (12½ miles) east of Kiryat Shmona, 50 km (31 miles) northeast of Tzfat.

The country's most impressive waterfall is fed from the spring at the foot of Mount Hermon, which flows powerfully through a canyon before cascading over the rocks.

GETTING HERE AND AROUND

From Tzfat, head east on Route 89, then turn north on Route 90. Once you pass Kiryat Shmona, go east on Route 99.

EXPLORING

Fodor's Choice ★ **Hermon Stream (Banias) Nature Reserve.** One of the most stunning parts of Israel, this reserve contains gushing waterfalls, dense foliage along riverbanks, and the remains of a temple dedicated to the god Pan. There are two entrances, each with a parking lot: the sign for the first reads "Banias Waterfall," and the other is 1 km (½ mile) farther along the same road and is marked "Banias."

The **Banias Spring** emerges at the foot of mostly limestone Mount Hermon, just where it meets the basalt layers of the Golan Heights. The most popular short route in the reserve is up to the **Banias Cave,** via the path that crosses the spring. Excavations have revealed the five niches hewed out of the rock to the right of the cave; these are what remain of Hellenistic and Roman temples, depicted in interesting artist renderings. Three of the niches bear inscriptions in Greek, mentioning Pan, the lover of tunes, Echo, the mountain nymph, and Galerius, one of Pan's priests. All early references to the cave identify it as the source of the spring, but earthquakes over the years have changed the landscape, and the water now emerges at the foot of the cave rather than from within it.

The reserve offers three interconnected hiking trails—ask for the English-language trail map and advice at the cashier's booth. One, which passes a Crusader gate, walls, and moat, takes about 45 minutes. The second, also about 45 minutes, explores the magnificent 1,613-square-foot palace complex dating to the 1st century AD and the reign of Herod's grandson, Agrippa II, on top of which are the ruins of what is thought to have been the marketplace of the day: a string of single chambers along a well-preserved section of wall might well have been shops. The third is a 90-minute trail leading past the **Officers' Pool,** built by the Syrians, and a water-operated flour mill, to the thundering 33-meter-high **Banias Waterfall.** The trails are spiced with the pungent aroma of mint and figs, and studded with blackberry bushes. If time is short, you may prefer to take a brief walk to the falls, return to your car, then drive on to the second entrance to see the caves and the spring where the Hermon Stream originates. The cost of admission covers entry to both sites.

If you're ready for a real hiking challenge and can have a car waiting at the other end, a long, very steep trail leads from the parking lot at the Banias Nature Reserve through the oak and thorny broom forest up to Nimrod's Fortress, a 40- to 60-minute climb. ✉ *Off- Rte. 99, Snir* ☎ *04/695–0272, 04/690–2577* ⊕ *www.parks.org.il* ✉ *NIS 29.*

▌**QUICK BITES**   **Druze Pita Stand.** A few minutes' walk along the trail leading to the Banias Waterfall is the ancient flour mill and a stall where Druze villagers make their traditional pita bread (bigger and flatter than the commercial version). It's not only baked on the premises but also milled here. Pull up a rock, and for a few shekels you'll be served a large rolled-up pita with *labaneh* (yogurt cheese) and Turkish coffee. ✉ *Hermon Stream (Banias) Nature Preserve, Off Rte. 99, Snir.*

Banias, the City of Pan

The name *Banias* is an Arabic corruption of the Greek *Panias* (Arabic has no *p*), the original name given to the area that, in the early 4th century BC, was dedicated to the colorful Greek god Pan, the half-goat, half-human deity of herdsmen, music, and wild nature—and of homosexuals and nymphs. The Banias Nature Reserve encompasses the ruins of this ancient city.

Herod the Great ruled the city in the 1st century BC; his son Philip inherited it and changed the city's name to Caesarea Philippi, to distinguish it from the Caesarea his father had founded on the Mediterranean coast. The city continued to flourish until after the Muslim conquest in the

7th century AD, when it declined into little more than a village. In the 10th century AD, Muslim immigration brought renewed settlement and Jews also came to Banias (as it became known sometime during the 7th century).

In the early 12th century, Crusaders held Banias, who saw it as a natural border between their kingdom and the neighboring Muslim realm, whose center was Damascus. The Muslims recaptured Banias in 1132, but the city declined in importance and was taken over by Bedouin chieftains. It became a small village, which it remained until the Israel Defense Forces (IDF) conquered the area in the 1967 Six-Day War.

OFF THE BEATEN PATH

Golani Lookout. The large number of monuments to fallen soldiers in the Golan is a reminder of the region's strategic importance—and the price paid to secure it. Among the easily accessible sites, where pre-1967 Syrian bunkers give a gunner's-eye view of the valley below, is the Golani Lookout, known in Arabic as Tel Faher, in the northern Golan. Here you can explore the trenches and bunkers that now stand silent. ⊠ *Off Rte. 99, Snir.*

NIMROD'S FORTRESS NATIONAL PARK

5 km (3 miles) east of Hermon Stream (Banias) Nature Reserve, 58 km (36 miles) northeast of Tzfat.

Don't pass up a chance to explore the medieval castle called Nimrod's Fortress, which sits near Mount Hermon. Set in a strategic spot, it was sought after by both Christians and Muslims for centuries.

GETTING HERE AND AROUND

From Tzfat, head east on Route 89, then turn north on Route 90. Once you pass Kiryat Shmona, go east on Route 99. Once you pass the Hermon Stream Nature Reserve, turn north on Route 989. The fortress is on the left.

EXPLORING

FAMILY

Fodor'sChoice ★

Nimrod's Fortress National Park. The dramatic views of this towering, burly 13th-century fortress, appearing and disappearing behind each curve of the narrow road that leads to it, are part of the treat of a visit to Nimrod's Fortress (Kal'at Namrud), the largest surviving Middle Ages fortress in Israel. Once you're there, the fortress commands superb vistas of the

Golan and the Upper Galilee, especially through the frames of its arched windows and the narrow archers' slits in its walls. Nimrod's Fortress is a highlight for kids, with a ladder down to a vaulted cistern, a shadowy spiral staircase, and unexpected nooks and crannies. A path leads up to the fortress's central tower, or keep, where the feudal lord would have lived.

In 1218, the Mamluk warlord al-Malik al-Aziz Othman built this fortress to guard the vital route against a possible Crusader reconquest after their 1187 defeat. It changed hands between Muslims and Christians in the succeeding centuries, as both vied for control of the region. ⊠ *Rte. 989, Mount Hermon* ☎ *04/694–9277* ⊕ *www.parks.org.il* ☙ *NIS 22.*

MOUNT HERMON

16 km (10 miles) north of Nimrod's Fortress National Park, 25 km (15½ miles) northeast of Kiryat Shmona, 66 km (41 miles) northeast of Tzfat.

Israel's highest point is not to be missed for the pleasures the mountain provides, including flower-lined hiking trails in the summer and ski slopes that open with the winter's snow.

GETTING HERE AND AROUND

From Tzfat, head east on Route 89, then turn north on Route 90. Once you pass Kiryat Shmona, go east on Route 99. At Mahanayim Junction turn east on Route 91, then north on Route 98.

EXPLORING

Mount Hermon. The summit of Mount Hermon—famous as Israel's highest mountain, at 9,230 feet above sea level—is actually in Syrian territory. Its lower slopes attract winter visitors to the country's only ski resort, though summer is arguably the most interesting time on the Hermon. After the winter snows melt, hikers can discover chasms and hidden valleys here, the long-term result of extremes in temperature. A powerful array of colors and scents emerges from the earth as the summer sun draws out cockscomb, chamomile, and scores of other flowers and wild herbs. Approaching from Nimrod's Fortress, you'll pass **Moshav Neve Ativ,** designed to look like a little piece of the Alps in the Middle East, complete with A-frame chalet-style houses, a handful of which have guest rooms. A detour through the old Druze village of **Majdal Shams** offers a number of good eateries. **Ein Kiniya**, another Druze village, appears across a valley on your left as you head east into the Golan on Route 99, is the most picturesque in the area. The houses are built from the black basalt typical of the Golan. ⊠ *Rte. 98.*

MAJDAL SHAMS

25 km (15½ miles) east of Kiryat Shmona, 35 km (22 miles) north of Katzrin.

Majdal Shams may not look like much, but the Druze town is a hub for skiers in the winter and berry pickers in the fall. It's also a year-round destination for wine lovers because of the local vineyards, and for foodies, as Druze cuisine is renowned in the region.

Unlike their counterparts in the Galilee, the Druze of the Golan Heights do not, for the most part, consider themselves Israeli citizens. They do, however, consider themselves an important part of the country's cultural landscape.

GETTING HERE AND AROUND

From Kiryat Shmona, head east on Route 99, then turn north at Mas'ada onto Route 98, which will take you into Majdal Shams. The streets aren't signed in English, so call ahead for directions to your hotel.

EXPLORING

Bahat Winery. This winery sells 5,000 bottles of its kosher wine, made using traditional methods, each year. The grapes—mostly Cabernet Sauvignon, Pinot Noir, and Chardonnay—are grown in basalt soil 3,280 feet above sea level. The wines' distinctive flavor comes from being aged in French oak barrels. Owner Ofer Bahat is happy to divulge information and offer tastings. ⊠ *Off Rte. 91, Ein Zivan* ☎ *050/877–1770* ⊕ *bahatwinery.co.il* ⊗ *Closed Sat.*

De Karina Chocolate Boutique. Selling treats for the young and young at heart, De Karina was founded by a third-generation chocolatier from Argentina. Try the Mount Hermon—milk-chocolate cones topped by white-chocolate "snow." Call in advance for factory tours and chocolate-making workshops. ⊠ *Off Rte. 91, Ein Zivan* ☎ *04/699–3622* ⊕ *www.de-karina.co.il* ☎ *Tour NIS 22, workshop NIS 65* ⊗ *Closed Sat.*

Odem Mountain Winery. This family-owned boutique kosher winery, located between Majdal Shams and Merom Golan, produces 80,000 bottles a year, mostly dry reds nurtured by the area's volcanic soil, but also a crisp Chardonnay. There are lovely fortified wines and cherry wines as well. Drop in for an impromptu tasting, where local cheeses are also for sale. Half-hour tours of the vineyards are available by appointment. ⊠ *Moshav Odem, Off Rte. 978* ☎ *04/687–1122* ⊕ *www. harodem.co.il* ☎ *Free* ⊗ *Closed Sat.*

Fodor'sChoice ★
Pelter Winery. An Australian-trained winemaker named Tal Pelter aspired to bring his modern oenology training and methodology to the Israeli market. Starting with a yearly release of 4,000 bottles and rapidly increasing production to more than 100,000 bottles, Pelter is now one of Israel's most beloved wineries. In addition Pelter makes cognac, which he offers as part of the intimate winery tours; both wine and cognac pair nicely with his wife's homemade goat cheese—also available for purchase. ⊠ *Off Rte. 91, Ein Zivan* ☎ *052/866–6384* ⊕ *pelter.co.il/ en* ☎ *NIS 50 for tour and wine tasting.*

WHERE TO EAT

$ ✕ **Abu Zaid.** The main street in Majdal Shams is speckled with pita
MIDDLE EASTERN stands where the popular street wrap is served warm and filled with tangy yogurt cheese. For dessert, stop by Abu Zaid, which sells a type of orange-hued pastry called *knafeh*. Similar to baklava, it has delicious layers of gooey goat cheese covered in a flaky crust and peppered with pistachios. Ask for a slice from the large tray—one serving could be easily enjoyed by two. The to-go delicacy loses its charm when it cools down, so eat it while it's warm. ⑤ *Average main: NIS 10* ⊠ *Northern end of main street* ☎ *052/698 –3190* ▭ *No credit cards.*

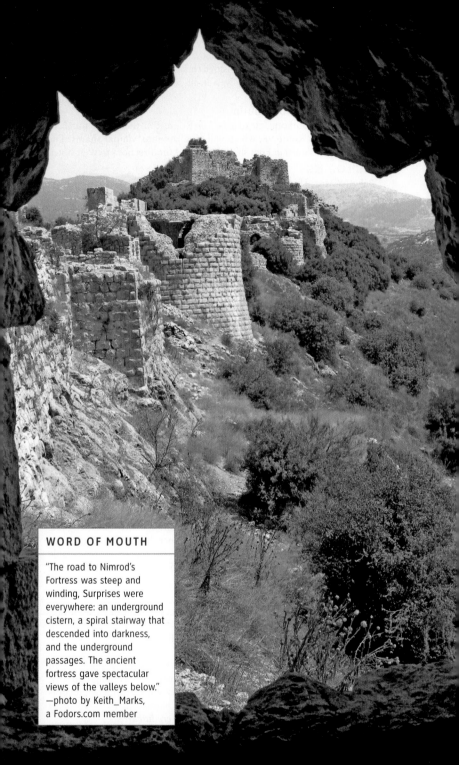

$$$$ ✕ **The Witch's Cauldron and the Milkman.** Located in Nimrod, a short drive
ECLECTIC   south of Majdal Shams, this whimsical restaurant is decorated with
smiling witch dolls and boasts a magnificent view of volcanic lakes and
cherry fields. The staff is attentive and friendly, and the food is hearty.
The chef specializes in casseroles, such as salmon cooked with coconut
milk, ginger, and oranges. Another tasty dish is the lamb simmered in
white wine and served with root vegetables. $ *Average main: NIS 125*
✉ *Off Rte. 98, Nimrod* ☎ *04/687–0049* ⊕ *www.the-witch.co.il.*

MEROM GOLAN

*20 km (12½ miles) south of Mount Hermon, 46 km (28 miles) north-
east of Tzfat.*

Kibbutz Merom Golan was the first settlement built in the Golan after
the Six-Day War. Its fields and orchards are typical of local kibbutzim.
Apples and cherries are especially good in these parts. Another popular
attraction is the nearby Mount Bental lookout.

GETTING HERE AND AROUND
From Tzfat, head east on Route 89, then north on Route 90. At Mah-
anayim Junction, turn east on Route 91, then north on Route 98.
Merom Golan is on the left.

EXPLORING
Mount Bental. From the top of this volcanic cone, at an open-air lookout
that was once a military outpost, you can see Mount Hermon rising
majestically to the north and the Syrian side of the Golan stretching
eastward. Opposite is the ruined town of Kuneitra, captured by Israel in
1967, lost and regained in the 1973 Yom Kippur War, and returned to
Syria in the subsequent disengagement agreement—it is now a demili-
tarized zone. Modern Kuneitra is in the distance. The cluster of white
buildings south of old Kuneitra houses the United Nations Disengagement Observer Force. A pine-cabin shop serving coffees, herbal teas,
and a nice selection of snacks is the perfect place to get out of the wind
that often sweeps this peak. The lookout is near Kibbutz Merom Golan;
signs along the rural roads point the way. It's open all the time. ✉ *Off
Rte. 98 and Rte. 959, Mount Bental* 🖼 *Free.*

7

WHERE TO EAT
$$$$ ✕ **Cowboys' Restaurant.** This is the best corral this side of the Israel-Syria
STEAKHOUSE   disengagement zone. Saddle-shaped stools at the bar and cattle hides
on the walls contribute to the frontier atmosphere. But it's the grub—
specifically the hearty steaks and the house specialty, chicken breast
stuffed with smoked meat—that packs 'em in at this place, known
locally as HaBokrim. Advance reservations are required for the Friday night kosher buffet. $ *Average main: NIS 125* ✉ *Off Rte. 959*
☎ *04/696–0206.*

KATZRIN

20 km (12½ miles) south of Merom Golan, 38 km (23½ miles) north-east of Tiberias, 35 km (22 miles) northeast of Tzfat.

Katzrin, founded in 1977 near the site of a 3rd-century town of the same name, has a suburban feel, despite its strategic location. The water here, which comes straight from the basalt bedrock, is delicious and makes your skin feel like silk.

GETTING HERE AND AROUND

From Tzfat, head east on Route 89, then north on Route 90. At Mahanayim Junction turn east on Route 91, then south on Route 9088.

EXPLORING

FAMILY **Ancient Katzrin Park.** About 2 km (1 mile) east of downtown Katzrin, this attraction is a partially restored 3rd-century Jewish village. The Katzrin synagogue has decorative architectural details, such as a wreath of pomegranates and amphorae in relief on the lintel above the entrance. The complexity of its ornamentation reflects the importance of the city. Built of basalt, the synagogue was used for 400 years until it was partly destroyed, possibly by an earthquake, in AD 749. Two reconstructed buildings, the so-called House of Uzi and House of Rabbi Abun, are attractively decorated with rope baskets, weavings, baking vessels, and pottery (based on remnants of the originals), and lighted with little clay oil lamps. ✉ *Rte. 87* ☎ *04/696–2412* 💲 *NIS 28, includes Golan Archaeological Museum.*

Assaf Winery. A family business in every sense, father and son work together harvesting grapes at the Assaf Winery. The wines feature seven varieties that are harvested separately—and by hand—to maintain strict control over every cluster. A visit to the family's "wine village" can also include lunch at daughter Adi's adjacent restaurant. Call to make a reservation to visit. ✉ *Off Rte. 91* ☎ *054/391–5552* ⊕ *www.assafwinery. com* 💲 *NIS 30 for tour and wine tasting* ⊙ *Closed Sun.*

Golan Archaeological Museum. This museum has a fascinating collection of animal bones, stones, and artifacts that put the region into historical and geographical perspective. Among the exhibits is a Bronze Age dwelling reconstructed from materials excavated nearby. Don't miss the moving film on the last stand at Gamla, the "Masada of the North," during the Jews' Great Revolt against Rome in AD 66. The museum reveals how it was rediscovered by archaeologists 1,900 years later. ✉ *Near corner of Sion and Daliyot Sts.* ☎ *04/696–1350* 💲 *NIS 28, includes Ancient Katzrin Park* ⊙ *Closed Sat.*

Golan Heights Winery. This winery caught the world's attention with its award-winning Yarden, Gamla, and Golan labels. The area's volcanic soil, cold winters, and cool summers, together with state-of-the-art wine making, have proven a recipe for success. The shop sells the full line of wines, including the Katzrin Chardonnay, the Yarden Gewürztraminer, and the Yarden Cabernet Sauvignon, as well as sophisticated accessories for the oenophile. Call in advance about a tour of the winery and a tasting; the winery offers a number of options ✉ *Derekh-ha-Yayin St., near southern entrance to town* ☎ *04/696–8435* ⊕ *www.golanwines. co.il* 💲 *NIS 20 1-hr tour and tasting* ⊙ *Closed Sat.*

WHERE TO EAT

The commercial center of Katzrin, the "capital" of the Golan Heights, has a number of falafel stands, a couple of restaurants, and a pizzeria, making it a convenient midday stop for travelers.

$ ✕ **Hummus'illa.** Hilla Ben Yosef, the second generation in the family to

ISRAELI run this tiny and unassuming eatery, offers fresh hummus and other home-style dishes. Dishes arrive with fluffy pitas and crushed garlic—not for the faint of heart. Middle Eastern salads and other local favorites are also on offer. $ *Average main: NIS 30* ⊠ *Off Derech Hahermon and Daliyot Sts.* ☎ *04/696–2120* ▭ *No credit cards* ⊘ *Closed Fri. and Sat. No dinner Sun.–Wed.*

GAMLA NATURE RESERVE

20 km (12 miles) southeast of Katzrin.

Aside from the inspiring history of the "Masada of the North," the beauty of Gamla's rugged terrain, softened in spring by greenery and wildflowers, is truly breathtaking. Griffon vultures soar above, and you can often see gazelles bounding through the grasses.

GETTING HERE AND AROUND

From Tzfat, head east on Route 89, then south on Route 90. Turn east on Route 87, then south on Route 808. Watch for the Gamla signpost.

EXPLORING

FAMILY **Gamla Nature Reserve.** The main story of the camel-shaped Gamla (the name comes from *gamal,* the Hebrew word for "camel") goes back to the year AD 67, when at the beginning of the Great Revolt, Vespasian launched a bloody attack here that ended seven months later, when the 9,000 surviving Jews flung themselves to their deaths in the abyss below the town. The vivid descriptions of the battle, as written by Flavius Josephus in *The Jewish War,* are engraved in stones along the trail site: "Built against the almost vertical flank, the town seemed to be hung in the air"—exactly the impression visitors still have as they approach the site.

Because Gamla was never rebuilt, the relics of the battlefield still eerily match the ancient sources, among them the fortifications, 2,000 "missile stones," and a large number of arrowheads. From a much earlier period (probably the 2nd millennium BC), there are about 200 **dolmens** scattered in the area—strange basalt structures shaped like the Greek letter *pi,* probably used for burial. There is an excellent film on the story of Gamla at the Golan Archaeological Museum in Katzrin. The raptor observation station adds a fun touch for kids. Also in the reserve are Israel's tallest waterfall, picturesque streams for nature walks, and varied wildlife. ⊠ *Off Rte. 869, Gamla* ☎ *04/682–2282* ⊕ *www.parks. org.il* ▭ *NIS 29.*

WHERE TO EAT

$$ ✕ **HaBikta.** With a name that literally means "the cabin," HaBikta

ISRAELI evokes the smoked meats for which it's best known. The chicken and steaks, smoked over cherrywood and grapevines, come with access to the generous salad buffet. Try the whole chickpeas coated in cumin and green onions, or the coriander tossed with slivered almonds and lentils. ⑤ *Average main: NIS 75* ⊠ *East of Rte.92* ✛ *Follow directions (there are no street names in the area) when you get to Moshav Ramot* ☎ *04/679–4016* ⊕ *www.ha-bikta.co.il* ⊘ *Closed Sat. No dinner Fri.*

$$$$

STEAKHOUSE

✕ **Moshbutz.** The local spirit at play in this restaurant's name—a combination of moshav and kibbutz, two types of Israeli agricultural communities—also shapes the menu at Moshbutz. This eatery's farm-fresh philosophy is integral, as the chef sources all of the ingredients from Golan Heights. The abundant wine and beer menu offer a chance to taste options from the surrounding vineyards and microbreweries. Choose the rump carpaccio and liver pâté for starters, but save room for the aged beef and lamb. Sit in the nicely converted cow shed and enjoy a glass of Muscat dessert wine or port from a nearby vineyard while the enjoying a spectacular sunset over the Sea of Galilee. ⑤ *Average main: NIS 130* ⊠ *Nof Kinneret St.* ☎ *04/679–5095* ⊕ *mushbutz. rest-e.co.il* ⊘ *No lunch.*

WHERE TO STAY

$$

B&B/INN
FAMILY

▦ **Beit Ram Sheraf.** The four suites owned by Judit Sheraf and Avi Ram are the perfect place for a family weekend: each cottage has a double bedroom, living room that sleeps three, kitchenette, heated outdoor Jacuzzi, and very large private yard with grill and hammock or swing set. **Pros:** heated pool; child-friendly atmosphere. **Cons:** relatively expensive. ⑤ *Rooms from: $250* ⊠ *32 Zevitan St.* ☎ *052/284–4013* ⊕ *www.beit-ram.co.il* ⇗ *5 cottages* ❙⊘❙ *No meals.*

$$$

B&B/INN
Fodor'sChoice
★

▦ **Cnaan Village.** If relaxation is what you're after, look no further than this homey getaway in the Golan Heights. **Pros:** unique pool; extraordinary breakfast; lovely owner. **Cons:** signage is hard to see. ⑤ *Rooms from: $345* ⊠ *Had Nes 13, Had Nes* ☎ *04/682–2128* ⊕ *www.cnaan-village.co.il* ⇗ *5 rooms* ❙⊘❙ *Breakfast.*

$$

HOTEL

▦ **Ramot Resort Hotel.** High in the foothills of Golan Heights, this hotel is only a few minutes from good beaches and a water park. **Pros:** convenient to national parks; cooler temperatures than at the lake; beautiful vistas. **Cons:** no evening entertainment. ⑤ *Rooms from: $221* ⊠ *East of Rte. 92* ☎ *04/673–2636* ⊕ *www.ramot-nofesh.co.il* ⇗ *123 rooms* ❙⊘❙ *Breakfast.*

EILAT AND
THE NEGEV

WELCOME TO EILAT AND THE NEGEV

TOP REASONS TO GO

★ **Coral Beach Nature Reserve:** Put on a snorkel and marvel at the brilliantly colored fish and entrancing corals at one of the world's finest protected coral reefs.

★ **Hiking the Negev:** Explore the splendid scenery, deep wadis, rugged heights, and steep cliff faces of the Negev. The mountains of Eilat and the desert craters offer spectacular hikes.

★ **Makhtesh Ramon:** This giant crater is an utterly unique geological phenomenon, with hundreds of rock formations and multihue cliffs.

★ **Timna Park:** A half-hour from Eilat, trek across the lunarlike landscape, making sure to see this desert park's famous red-hue Solomon's Pillars and its 20-foot mushroom-shape rock formation.

★ **Yotvata Hai-Bar Nature Reserve:** Come face-to-face with fearsome birds of prey in the Predator Center of this thrilling nature preserve north of Eilat.

1 **Eilat and Southern Israel.** Sun-drenched Eilat, a resort town on the shores of the Red Sea, brims with hotels, restaurants, duty-free shopping, and the lion's share of the Negev's nightlife. It's just south of Timna Park, which isn't to be missed.

2 **The Heart of the Negev.** In the very center of the upside-down triangle that makes up the Negev, you'll find several of the region's top sites, including the Ramon Crater and Ben-Gurion's desert home and grave, as well as the remains of the ancient Nabatean city of Avdat.

3 **Beersheva.** Israel's fourth-largest city, Beersheva makes a great jumping-off point for trips around the Negev. Tel Beersheva, with the remains of a biblical-era city, is a World Heritage Site.

GETTING ORIENTED

Three basic areas in the inverted triangle of the Negev, Israel's southern desert, make up the southern part of the country. The first, and farthest south, is carefree Eilat, with the Underwater Observatory Marine Park at Coral Beach, and Timna Park. Next is the Negev's heart, with sites such as Ben-Gurion's desert home and grave, the ancient Nabatean-Roman-Byzantine ruins at Avdat, and the amazing Makhtesh Ramon (Ramon Crater). The third, in the north, includes the regional capital city of Beersheva.

8

Updated by
Shari Helmer

With its stark mountains, dramatic wadis, archaeological treasures, colorful Bedouin encampments, and the spectacular Ramon Crater, the Negev—a word meaning "dry" in Hebrew—is much more than simply "a desert." The Negev contains Israel's most dramatic natural scenery, with its rugged highlands, as well as Eilat, a resort town set on the Red Sea, with luxury hotels, good restaurants and bars, and duty-free shopping. There's even a growing winery scene here that will intrigue oenophiles.

The region can satisfy both history buffs and adventure lovers. You can visit the kibbutz home and grave of Israel's founding father and first prime minister—David Ben-Gurion, the man who first dreamed of settling the desert—and on the same day, you can tour the millennia-old ruins at Tel Beersheva, visited by the biblical patriarch Abraham. For those seeking adventure, the Negev is the place to take camel treks and Jeep tours, spend the afternoon hiking, or scuba dive in the Red Sea.

The Negev makes up about half the country's land area, yet is home to only about 8% of its population. The ancient Israelites had fortifications here, as did the merchant Nabateans and the Romans after them. The region's first kibbutzim were established in the early 1940s, with new immigrants sent south after the War of Independence, in 1948. Two years later, people started trickling into Eilat, which was nothing but a few rickety huts. The desert itself was made to bloom, and the semiarid areas between Tel Aviv and Beersheva became fertile farmland. Today, agricultural settlements throughout the Negev make use of advanced irrigation to raise tomatoes, melons, olives, and dates that are exported to winter markets in Europe.

EILAT AND THE NEGEV PLANNER

WHEN TO GO

October through May is the best time to explore the Negev. In early March, scarlet, bright yellow, and hot pink desert flowers burst out against the brown desert earth; March is also when Eilat's International Bird-watchers' Festival takes place. In January and February, it's dry and cold, especially at night. Scorching-hot conditions prevail in the summer, from June through September, though it's very dry, and locals claim this is the "sleeper season" to be here: no humidity, cool nights, fewer crowds, and easier availability at desirable hotels, restaurants, and venues.

DESERT PRECAUTIONS

To remain comfortable and safe, respect certain rules of the desert. Drink 2 quarts of water a day in winter and 1 quart per hour in summer. Keep a jerrican (which holds 5 gallons) of water in your car, plus extra bottles. Water fountains along the way don't always work. Flash floods pose an occasional danger from September through March, especially after rainfall farther north. If even a small amount of water is flowing across the road, wait for it to stop (it can take a while); it can be a sign of imminent flooding. Driving at night isn't recommended; plan to reach your destination by 5 pm in winter and by 8 pm in summer. Make sure to have a car charger for your cell phone; service is spotty, and phones seeking available networks eat up battery life.

PLANNING YOUR TIME

The main attraction in Israel's south is the resort town of Eilat, the country's beach playground. Its attractions are sand, sun, and surf, and it's the place for a few days of scuba, snorkeling, and sunbathing. Some desert excursions like Timna Park are nearby, and it's also easy to arrange a day trip to Petra, in Jordan, from Eilat.

However, if you don't care for the beach, or if you love the desert landscape, consider a couple of days in Mitzpe Ramon instead. About an hour's drive south of Beersheva, and perched on the edge of a vast crater 40 km (25 miles) long, Mitzpe Ramon offers abundant outdoor activities. Ecotours, mountain biking, and Jeep trekking, as well as guide-led hiking to take in the history and science of the area, are among the options. You can explore nearby sites including Sde Boker, the desert home of David Ben-Gurion, Israel's first prime minister, and the remains of the ancient Nabatean city of Avdat, a UNESCO World Heritage Site. Israel's wine industry has put down some roots in the Negev, and you can visit wineries such as Carmey Avdat.

Most Negev sites open at 8:30 am and close by 4 pm in winter and 5 pm in summer. Keep in mind that outside Eilat, restaurants close early on Friday for the Jewish Sabbath, and since the main meal of the day is served at noon in the desert, lunch may be history if you arrive after 1:30; roadside diners close at around 1:30 pm.

8

GETTING HERE AND AROUND

AIR TRAVEL

Flights to Eilat take off from Ben Gurion Airport (about halfway between Jerusalem and Tel Aviv), Sde Dov Airport in north Tel Aviv, and Haifa Airport. Two domestic airlines serve Eilat: Arkia and Israir. Fares vary wildly, often cheapest for crack-of-dawn flights or off-hours. Eilat Airport, close to the middle of the city, is a short cab ride from the hotels and the resort action; however, a larger regional and international airport, **Ramon Airport** (⊕ *www.ramon-airport.com*), is scheduled to open during 2017. The new airport is 18 km (11 miles) north of Eilat; shuttles will take travelers to Eilat until a rail link opens. The existing airport will close when Ramon opens.

BUS TRAVEL

Egged, the national bus company, runs frequent service to Beersheva from Tel Aviv and Jerusalem; each takes about 1½ hours. Buses to Eilat from the same cities take 4½ to 5 hours. You can reserve tickets up to two weeks in advance, which is recommended for weekend travel. Within Eilat, Bus 15 starts at the Central Bus Station (near the entrance to town) and runs through the hotel area before heading south to the Taba border with Egypt. Bus 16 follows the same route, only in reverse.

CAR TRAVEL

The only way to see the Negev Desert is to drive (air-conditioning is a must, especially in the summer). Beersheva is 113 km (70 miles) southeast of Tel Aviv and 83 km (52 miles) south of Jerusalem. To get to Eilat from Tel Aviv, the most direct way is Route 40 south to Beersheva, which takes about five hours.

TRAIN TRAVEL

Israel Railways runs between Tel Aviv and Beersheva. There's frequent service (except on Saturday, when there are only two trains, both late in the evening). High-speed trains have shaved a lot of time off the trip, allowing you to get from Tel Aviv to Beersheva in 50 minutes.

HOTELS

Hotels in sunny Eilat run from family-style inns to huge, lush, and luxurious lodgings. Luxurious spas with a wide range of treatments can be found at every large hotel. Even many of the smaller hotels have installed spas to catch the attention of travelers in search of pampering. In Eilat, a few hotels operate on an all-inclusive basis. Rooms are hardest to come by, and most expensive, around Hanukkah and Christmas, Passover and Easter, and July and August. Eilat is Israel's number one destination for families, so expect lots of kids at the pool.

Hotel reviews have been shortened. For more information, visit Fodors.com.

RESTAURANTS

Although Eilat is nestled at the southern tip of a desert, there are all sorts of cuisines to choose from when you're dining out: Italian, Indian, French, Argentinean, Yemenite, and Thai among them. There's excellent fish, including delicacies such as *denis* (sea bream). In the past few years, Beersheva has added a host of tasty options to its dining scene. In the rest of the Negev, meals often reflect the cook's ethnic heritage. Visitors who keep kosher should note that while most hotels serve kosher meals, few of the restaurants in Eilat are kosher, including chains with kosher branches elsewhere.

WHAT IT COSTS				
	$	$$	$$$	$$$$
Restaurants	Under NIS 50	NIS 50–NIS 75	NIS 76–NIS 100	over NIS 100
Hotels	Under $200	$200–$300	$301–$400	over $400

Restaurant prices are the average cost of a main course at dinner in NIS (Israeli shekels) or, if dinner isn't served, at lunch. Hotel prices, given in U.S. dollars, are the lowest cost of a standard double room in high season. Non-Israeli citizens paying in foreign currency are exempt from the 17% V.A.T. on hotel rooms.

EILAT AND SOUTHERN ISRAEL

The Arava Plain comes to an abrupt end where it meets the Bay of Eilat, home to Israel's southernmost town: the sun-drenched resort of Eilat. The Gulf of Eilat gives way to the Red Sea, which lies between the Sinai Mountains to the west and Jordan's Edom Mountains to the east. The Jordanian port of Aqaba is directly across the bay, so close you can see the distinctive flag flapping on its pole.

Most travelers fly down to Eilat to flop down on its beaches and snorkel or scuba dive among its tropical reefs. But if you have time, explore the vast desert landscape to the north of Eilat. You'll find cliffs, canyons, and unique geological formations at Timna Park and indigenous animals at Yotvata Hai-Bar Nature Reserve. Both make good side trips from Eilat.

EILAT

307 km (190 miles) south of Jerusalem, 356 km (221 miles) south of Tel Aviv.

A legend says that after the Creation, the angels painted the earth and when they got tired, they spilled their paints: the blue became the waters of Eilat, and the other colors became its fish and coral. Combine Eilat's year-round warm weather, its superb natural surroundings of sculptural red-orange mountains, and its prime location on the sparkling Red Sea—whose coral reefs attract divers from all over the world—and you've got a first-rate resort.

Eilat, a city of about 50,000, is now Israel's prototypical "sun-and-fun" destination. But its strategic location as a crossroads between Asia and Africa has long given it a place in history. Because of its position on a main trade and travel route, Eilat was conquered by every major power: the Romans, Byzantines, Arabs, Crusaders, Mamluks, Ottoman Turks, and, most recently, the British, whose isolated police station, called Umm Rash Rash (headquarters of their camel corps), was the first building in modern-day Eilat.

Most travelers agree that Eilat's natural assets more than make up for its undistinguished architecture and overdevelopment. For wherever you are in Eilat, a glance eastward presents you with the dramatic sight of the granite mountain range of Edom, whose shades of red intensify toward evening, culminating in a crimson sunset blaze over the Red Sea.

GETTING HERE AND AROUND

The most direct way to Eilat from both Tel Aviv and Jerusalem is via Beersheva. By car, the trip takes about five hours. For bus travel between Eilat, Tel Aviv, Jerusalem, and points in between, the national bus company, Egged, provides widespread service.

In Eilat, the preferred way of hopping from one place to another is by taxi. Rides don't usually cost much more than NIS 35, and you can hail a cab on the street.

Contacts **Eilat Central Bus Station.** ⊠ *12 Ha-Tmarim Blvd., next to Shalom Mall.*

VISITOR INFORMATION

The Eilat Tourist Information Office packs lots of information into a tiny space. Inside, you'll find a wall of helpful flyers about attractions and cultural events. Accommodating employees will happily connect you with guides and outfitters, writing down numbers and even making calls when they can.

Contacts Eilat Tourist Information Office. ⊠ *8 Beit HaGesher St.* ☎ *08/630–9111* ⊕ *eilat.city/en.*

EXPLORING

TOP ATTRACTIONS

Fodor's Choice
★

Coral Beach Nature Reserve. Less than 1 km (½ mile) south of Eilat, this is one of the finest and most densely populated coral reefs in the world. Close to the shoreline, the reef is 1¼ km (¾ mile) long and is zealously guarded by the Israel Nature and Parks Authority. The northernmost reef in the world, it contains over 100 types of coral and 650 species of fish. In the lagoon, divers and snorkelers take two bridges or a trail marked by buoys to get to the reef wall. Stunning multicolored fish and soft and hard corals are your rich reward. There are hot showers, a snack bar, and snorkel rentals. Kids should be at least five to snorkel. ⊠ *Rte. 90 (Eilat–Taba Rd.), opposite Eilat Field School* ☎ *08/632–6422* ⊕ *www.parks.org.il* ☎ *NIS 35.*

> ### THE RED SEA
>
> This incongruous name for a body of water that's brilliantly turquoise along the shore is the result of a 17th-century typographical error by an English printer: in setting the type for an English translation of a Latin version of the Bible, the printer left out an *e* and thus *Reed Sea* became *Red Sea*. The name was easily accepted because of the sea's red appearance at sunset.

Promenade. Start at the quieter, northernmost end of Eilat's waterfront *tayelet*, or promenade, which begins near the Jordanian border. The 3-km (2-mile) stretch is also known as the Peace Walk, because it is hoped that one day it will continue to Aqaba, Jordan. As you head south, purple and pink bougainvillea pour down from the Royal Beach Hotel's terrace above. Add to your enjoyment by stopping for an ice cream from one of the stands. If you're here at sunset, savor the show-stopping view of the Red Sea turning deeper and deeper shades of red against the backdrop of the Edom Mountains to the east and the rugged Eilat Mountains to the west. On a clear day, you can see as far as Saudi Arabia and Egypt.

A stroll past swanky hotels on one side and palm-lined beaches on the other brings you to the Dutch Bridge, which opens for tall-masted vessels. The lagoon is where yachts are anchored and various small craft are for hire; on the other side is the marina, where cruise boats of all types wait to sally forth. The promenade winds past more beaches covered with sunbathers. The scene includes artists doing quick portraits, vendors selling all sorts of knickknacks, and meandering street performers.

At the roundabout at Durban and Arava Streets you can continue along the waterfront—with the Mul Yam shopping mall on your right—until you reach a small palm-filled plaza with a tiny, cement-block-shaped building with a statue of four fighters raising a comrade aloft. This is Umm Rash Rash, where the Israelis first took control of the Gulf of Eilat in March 1949, as determined by the United Nations' partition plan. The small building—the only one that existed at that point—is a far cry from today's luxury resorts. The promenade effectively ends right before U Suites hotel. ⊠ *Eilat* ☎ *Free.*

8

NEED A BREAK

On the promenade underneath the Royal Beach hotel sits Aldo, one of Israel's better ice-cream chains. Queue up for a luscious cup or cone topped with a generous lashing of halvah or seasonal fruit.

Fodor's Choice
★

The Relaxation Pools at Dolphin Reef. A planked walkway leads to a hideaway consisting of a warren of open spaces designed for pure relaxation. Blink and you might miss it—and trust us, you won't want to. This place offers a true one-of-a-kind experience. Three pools—a deep seawater pool, a soft rainwater pool, and a saltwater pool that'll have you floating Dead Sea–style—offer hours of rest and relaxation. Before you change and shower, help yourself to a glass of wine or the delicious selection of cookies and dried fruits, or slice and squeeze your own fresh orange juice from a juicer set up on a rustic tree stump. Admission to the pools is strictly capped, ensuring a lack of overcrowding; you must reserve in advance by booking online or by phone. During the day, the pools offer stunning views of the water through tented-plastic windows; at night, candles and heaters enhance the atmosphere. For an additional fee, an instructor will float you around the pool in a 30-minute "relaxation technique," a series of undulating exercises that further enhance the experience. Once you're done floating, you can spend the rest of the day walking along the boardwalk to look at the dolphins or ordering drinks from the small bar in the front room. For the price of admission, you get to stay as long as you want. ✉ *Rte. 90 (Eilat–Taba Rd.)* ☎ *08/630–0111* ⊕ *dolphinreef.co.il* ✉ *Weekdays NIS 170, weekends and holidays NIS 200.*

FAMILY
Fodor's Choice
★

Underwater Observatory Marine Park. One of Eilat's star attractions can be recognized by its tall, space-needle-like structure punctuating the waves just offshore. A short drive from Eilat, this is the largest aquarium complex in the Middle East. Plan to spend several hours here (there's a cafeteria for lunch on the premises). The **Aquarium's** 12 windows provide views of rare fish so magnificent and so Day-Glo colorful that it's hard to believe they're real; there's an unlighted room where phosphorescent fish and other sea creatures glow in the dark. And there are turtle and stingray pools, too. Don't miss feeding time (11 am daily) in the 650,000-liter **Shark Pool.** The anaconda snakes, poisonous frogs, and piranha are fed in the **Amazonas** exhibit at 3 pm. Captain Jaws takes you on a sea journey during an audiovisual show presented in a simulated-motion theater with moving seats at the **Oceanarium.**

A 300-foot wooden bridge leads to the **Underwater Observatory.** Head down the spiral staircase and into the sea—you are now 15 feet underwater, where two round, glass-windowed halls, connected by a tunnel, offer stunning views of the surrounding coral reef, home to exotic tropical fish. The **Observatory Tower**—reached by stairs—gives coastal views of Israel's neighboring countries. There's a café up here. You can also take a ride on the *Coral 200* glass-bottom boat. Bus 16 runs to, and Bus 15 runs from, downtown Eilat every half hour. ✉ *Rte. 90 (Eilat–Taba Rd.)* ✛ *8 km (5 miles) south of Eilat* ☎ *08/636–4200* ⊕ *www.coralworld.com/eilat* ✉ *NIS 99; Oceanarium NIS 10, glass-bottom boat NIS 35.*

The Red Sea, just off the coast of Eilat, offers spectacular snorkeling and scuba diving.

WORTH NOTING

FAMILY **Botanical Garden of Eilat.** This former military base is now home to plants from all over the world, as well as some grown from seeds thousands of years old. The small, family-friendly park is a green oasis in the middle of the desert. An easy walk takes you to a waterfall and an artificial rain forest that mists every few minutes. You can explore the whole garden in under an hour. The refreshment area serves coffee and ice cream. ✉ *HaCarmel St.* ✛ *Behind gas station* ☎ *08/631–8788* ⊕ *www. botanicgarden.co.il* ✆ *NIS 25.*

FAMILY **Dolphin Reef.** Very popular with families, this observation point has a high admission charge, but the perks make it worthwhile. The highlight is the opportunity to walk on wooden paths extending into the water. You may see a dolphin leaping, but more likely you'll see groups snorkeling with dolphins. If you feel like trying it yourself, it costs about NIS 290 per person. In addition to a spacious sandy beach punctuated with billowing palms and bright tropical flowers, chairs and umbrellas are available (but get there early to avoid crowds.) There's an indoor café-bar to escape the sun, a great gift shop, and even a video you can watch to learn about dolphins. ✉ *Rte. 90 (Eilat–Taba Rd.), South Beach* ☎ *08/630–0111* ⊕ *dolphinreef.co.il* ✆ *NIS 67.*

Mount Yoash. This lookout point along the border road with Egypt is an easy trip from Eilat. Head west along Route 12 into the Eilat Mountains Nature Reserve. After 12 km (7½ miles), turn left at the orange sign for Mount Yoash and continue 1 km (½ mile) up a rough and winding stone road. Park and take in knockout views of the alternating light and dark ridges of the Eilat Mountains, the mountains of Edom rising behind the Jordanian city of Aqaba, and the Nahal Geshron gorge emptying into the Red Sea at Taba, in Egypt. A beautiful two-hour hiking trail begins in the parking lot. The Jordanian army operated a strategic post here until 1949, when Israeli forces took it during the last campaign of the War of Independence. The raising of a makeshift Israeli flag here marked the end of the war. ⊠ *Rte. 12.*

WHERE TO EAT

Eilat has so many restaurants that you can easily dine on a different cuisine each night over a long holiday. Savor fine local seafood and fresh fish, charcoal-grilled meats of every kind, or Chinese, Indian, Yemenite, and Italian cuisine that represent Israel's many waves of immigration. Many restaurants offer outdoor seating, often amid pots of pink bougainvillea or within sight of the sea. Outdoor cafés serve *hafuch* (strong coffee with a frothy, hot-milk topping) and light meals.

Use the coordinates (✛ A1) at the end of each listing to locate a site on the corresponding map.

$$
BURGER
FAMILY
✕ **Agadir.** The Eilat offshoot of the Tel Aviv chain is known for juicy burgers and a copious selection of beers on tap. In a small complex of bars and restaurants, Agadir's slightly off-the-beaten-track locale makes it feel more intimate than your average burger joint. The restaurant draws a lively nighttime crowd seeking solid food and drink, the main draw being good-quality beef (or veggie) patties topped with condiments ranging from goose breast to a sunny-side-up egg and caramelized onions. Appetizers include juicy merguez sausage and meat-filled Moroccan "cigars" that are made on the premises. You can also opt for Moroccan fish or meaty sirloin sandwiches. $ *Average main: NIS 55* ⊠ *10 Kamen St.* ☏ *08/633–3777* ⊕ *www.agadir.co.il* ✛ *C3.*

$$
ASIAN
✕ **Ginger Asian Kitchen and Bar.** A duo of Thai chefs presents Asian-fusion and sushi cuisine of delicate spiciness at this spiffy New York look-alike. Recessed lighting contributes to the chic vibe, as do off-white walls and black leather chairs. It's small, but the menu is huge. Start with plump *gyoza* dumplings stuffed with chicken, goose, and vegetables, or shrimp tempura on avocado with miso sauce. For a main dish there's the Jakarta (chicken or beef with eggplant and zucchini served with an Indonesian sweet sauce) or the Exotica (chicken or seafood dressed with coconut milk and chili paste and scattered with basil leaves). Finish off with a light-as-air pavlova topped with berries and whipped cream. $ *Average main: NIS 65* ⊠ *3 Yotam St.* ☏ *08/637–2517* ⊕ *www.gingereilat.com* ✛ *A3.*

$
MOROCCAN
✕ **Lalo.** A longtime favorite in Eilat, this kosher lunch place is a top-drawer example of Moroccan-Israeli cooking, all of it by an accomplished mother-and-son team. When you arrive, five different salads (including cauliflower, tahini, eggplant, and hot peppers) are quickly placed on your table. The menu rewards any adventuresome choices you make. Consider such delicacies as beef cooked with hummus (a house specialty), calves' brains served with Moroccan spices, or succulent couscous with vegetables, chickpeas, and tender chicken. No fancy pitas here—just plain bread. Dessert is specially prepared fruit, such as oranges or plums cooked until thick and soft, accompanied by fresh mint tea. $ *Average main: NIS 40* ⊠ *259 Horev St.* ☏ *08/633–0578* ☉ *Closed Fri. and Sat. No dinner* ✛ *A3.*

$$$ ✕ **Last Refuge.** Locals hold this fish and seafood restaurant (known in
SEAFOOD Hebrew as Hamiflat Ha'acharon) in high regard and take their guests
from "up north" here as a real treat. The dining room, with dark paneling
and nautical motifs like ships' wheels, spills out onto a spacious balcony
where diners eat beside the water, looking at Jordan across the way.
Presented with a flourish are fish or crab soups, freshly caught charcoal-
grilled Red Sea fish, and creamed seafood served in a seashell. A specialty
here is stir-fried sea crabs, prepared with a bit of spice in olive oil and
garlic. Weekends tend to be extra busy, so it's smart to reserve several
days ahead (and to ask for balcony seating). $ *Average main: NIS 85*
⊠ *Rte. 90 ⊕ Across from Isrotel Yam Suf Hotel* ☎ *08/637–3627 ⊕ A6.*

$$$ ✕ **Les Sardines.** This chic bar and upscale fish restaurant overlooks the
SEAFOOD harbor at the Eilat promenade, offering white-tablecloth dining indoors
and out. Recommended starters are gravlax and seafood carpaccio.
Steaks are a choice entrée, but innovative, attractive fish presentations
are the star of the show; portions are generous. The friendly, attentive
staff can recommend a nice pairing from the extensive wine and beer
menu. $ *Average main: NIS 90* ⊠ *3 HaMayim St. ⊕ Under Laguna
Hotel* ☎ *08/676–7488 ⊕ les-sardines.net ⊕ C3.*

$$$ ✕ **Olla.** One of the best tapas bars in Eilat, Olla has a relaxing atmo-
TAPAS sphere, thanks to leather-backed booths and tastefully subdued lighting.
Fodor'sChoice The bar, quite lively on weekends, offers some of the most accomplished
★ bartenders in the city. As for the tapas, you can't go wrong with the
goose liver and pears on brioche. You can also choose between your
favorite cuts of meat, or opt for the locally raised lamb ribs or the foie
gras marinated in a red wine sauce. $ *Average main: NIS 95* ⊠ *Bell
Hotel, 7 Tarshish St.* ☎ *08/632–5566 ⊕ www.olla-tapas.co.il* ⊘ *No din-
ner Fri. No lunch Sat. ⊕ C3.*

$$$ ✕ **Pago Pago Restaurant.** This longtime crowd-pleaser began serving
SEAFOOD in 1986 from its present location on a boat in the marina, but today
Pago Pago occupies a striking, nautical-looking building (it resembles a
ship) with walls of windows overlooking the water. The fusion of South
American, Asian, and Mediterranean influences creates interesting menu
options. Seafood soup or seaweed salad makes a good starter, and seafood
main courses include Brazilian *moqueca*, a fish stew made with coconut
milk, and shrimp and calamari gratin with artichokes and garlic. Steak
and sushi lovers have good options, too. Pair your meal with a bottle
from the impressive list of regional wines. $ *Average main: NIS 100* ⊠ *99
HaMayim Rd.* ☎ *08/637–6660 ⊕ pagopagorest.com/index_en.php ⊕ C3.*

$$$$ ✕ **Ranch House.** Accessed directly from the Promenade, this kosher steak
STEAKHOUSE house distinguishes itself from the pack with service as solicitous as its
steaks are juicy. Wooden tables and comfy chairs set the stage for a
meal that will have you begging for a doggy bag. Appetizers are named
after American states: "Texas" is a serving of crispy, honey-barbecued
chicken wings. Steaks, including a copious rib eye, are cooked to order
and arrive with a tangle of crispy fried onions and a side of spinach
that isn't quite creamed, but is delicious nonetheless. The wine list is
diverse and offers several reasonably priced selections. $ *Average main:
NIS 110* ⊠ *Royal Beach Hotel, 3 Shvil Hayam* ☎ *08/636–8989 ⊕ www.
ranchhouse.co.il* ⊘ *No lunch. No dinner Fri. ⊕ C4.*

Kids in the Negev

Think of the Negev as a huge sandbox for kids. There's lots to do and enjoy: beaches, alpaca rides, camel trips, Jeep excursions, snorkeling, and boat rides on the Red Sea. And children like the kind of food prevalent in the Negev, such as french fries, schnitzel (fried, breaded chicken cutlets), and ice cream. Even fancy restaurants have these on their menus to please the young ones, and it's not unusual to see baby strollers parked beside candlelit tables. Many hotels in Eilat go out of their way to cater to kids, trying to outdo one another with their children's programs and playrooms. These are separate facilities on the hotel grounds, filled with every imaginable distraction, from toys and crafts to PlayStations, and qualified supervisors are on hand. Many hotels employ staff trained to keep kids entertained, allowing parents some much-needed R&R.

$$$$
SEAFOOD

✕**Whale.** The husband-and-wife chef-owners of Whale ran their previous restaurant in Eilat's industrial area for years, drawing foodies from all over the country. In late 2015 they relaunched in the tourist area, and Whale quickly became one of Israel's top seafood restaurants. Browse the cookbooks on the shelves while you wait for your order. Salt-baked beetroot salad or zucchini blossoms makes a nice starter, and for a main course, try the shrimpburger, the only menu item that migrated from the former restaurant. For dessert, don't miss the salted caramel tart with ice cream. ⑤ *Average main: NIS 105* ⊠ *Herods Hotel, 6 HaYam St., North Beach* ☎ *08/920–9393* ⊘ *No lunch* ✛ *D4.*

WHERE TO STAY

Use the coordinates (✛ A1) at the end of each listing to locate a site on the corresponding map.

$$$
RESORT
FAMILY
Fodor'sChoice
★

Dan Eilat Hotel. The design of the glitzy Dan Eilat, by internationally acclaimed Israeli architect Adam Tihani, effectively combines high style with creature comforts. **Pros:** great location on the beach; excellent breakfasts. **Cons:** sometimes noisy; crowded dining room. ⑤ *Rooms from: $325* ⊠ *North Beach Promenade* ☎ *08/636–2222* ⊕ *www.dan-hotels.com* ⟿ *423 rooms* ⎟⦾⎟ *Breakfast* ✛ *D4.*

$$$$
HOTEL

Herods Palace Hotel. Designed with the legendary king in mind, this massive hotel is all about over-the-top opulence and Vegas-style pizzazz. **Pros:** on the quietest beach in Eilat; wide choice of accommodations; largest hotel in the area. **Cons:** public areas could use a refresh; furniture worn in some rooms. ⑤ *Rooms from: $405* ⊠ *North Beach, 6 Hayam St.* ☎ *08/638–0000* ⊕ *www.herods-hotels.com* ⟿ *297 rooms* ⎟⦾⎟ *Breakfast* ✛ *D4.*

$$$$
HOTEL

Hilton Eilat Queen of Sheba. The palatial entrance of this grand hotel is certainly fit for a queen, capped with a pillared dome rising between two turrets. **Pros:** elegant rooms; prime location near the waterfront; stunning views of the Eilat Bay. **Cons:** late-night music can be heard on lower floors; lines for the dining room at dinner are sometimes long.

8

$ *Rooms from: $405* ✉ *8 Antib Rd.* ☎ *08/630–6666* ⊕ *www3.hilton.com* ⬄ *501 rooms* ⫶◉⫶ *Breakfast* ✛ *C4.*

$$
HOTEL
⬚ **Isrotel Agamim.** The name means "lakes," so it's no surprise that this cluster of four-floor buildings is set amid palm trees, emerald grass, and tropical plants, around a lagoon-shaped pool with hammocks and swing chairs. **Pros:** laid-back atmosphere; great pool area; excellent breakfast buffet. **Cons:** a 10- to 15-minute walk to the beach. $ *Rooms from: $295* ✉ *Campne St., North Beach* ☎ *08/630–0300* ⊕ *www.isrotel.co.il* ⬄ *288 rooms* ⫶◉⫶ *Breakfast* ✛ *D2.*

$$$$
HOTEL
FAMILY
⬚ **Isrotel King Solomon.** Solomon's entire court could easily have been accommodated at this huge and comfortably furnished family hotel. **Pros:** Eilat's most child-friendly hotel; lots of activities for the whole family; rooftop lounge with free Internet access. **Cons:** not on beach; food is uninspired. $ *Rooms from: $415* ✉ *Piestany St., North Beach* ☎ *08/636–3444* ⊕ *www.isrotel.com* ⬄ *419 rooms* ⫶◉⫶ *Breakfast* ✛ *C3.*

$$$
HOTEL
⬚ **Isrotel Yam Suf.** Across from Coral Beach, this charming property has a six-story wing where most of the rooms have balconies facing the sea, as well as a couple of three-story buildings set amid private gardens. **Pros:** great beach for snorkeling; daily activities for kids; close to the aquarium. **Cons:** bland food; not within walking distance of downtown. $ *Rooms from: $350* ✉ *Rte. 90 (Eilat–Taba Rd.), South Beach* ☎ *08/638–2222* ⊕ *www.isrotel.com* ⬄ *261 rooms* ⫶◉⫶ *Breakfast* ✛ *A6.*

$$$
HOTEL
⬚ **Leonardo Plaza Hotel Eilat.** Sitting along the Promenade, this hotel near the beach and the marina puts everything within walking distance. **Pros:** excellent beachfront location, in the middle of the action; extensive children's activities. **Cons:** within earshot of the beachfront discos; expensive online access. $ *Rooms from: $350* ✉ *North Beach Promenade* ☎ *08/636–1111* ⊕ *www.leonardo-hotels.com* ⬄ *308 rooms* ⫶◉⫶ *Breakfast; Some meals* ✛ *C4.*

$$$
RESORT
FAMILY
Fodor's Choice
★
⬚ **Orchid Reef Hotel.** This boutique beachcombing property is one of South Beach's favorites because it's one of the few with direct ocean access. **Pros:** lots of complimentary amenities; great beach proximity; free Internet access. **Cons:** limited dining options; not close to downtown. $ *Rooms from: $315* ✉ *Rte. 90 (Eilat–Taba Rd.), Almog Beach* ☎ *08/636–4444* ⊕ *www.orchidhotels.co.il* ⬄ *79 rooms* ⫶◉⫶ *Breakfast* ✛ *A6.*

$$$$
HOTEL
⬚ **Royal Beach Eilat.** One of the most sprawling hotels on the Red Sea, this hotel, part of the Isrotel chain, blends comfort, glamour, and sophistication. **Pros:** pleasant pool area graced by waterfalls; excellent seaside location; lots of dining options nearby. **Cons:** standard rooms can be small; some in-room fixtures could use a refresh. $ *Rooms from: $650* ✉ *North Beach Promenade* ☎ *08/636–8888* ⊕ *www.isrotel.com* ⬄ *383 rooms* ⫶◉⫶ *Breakfast* ✛ *D4.*

$$$
HOTEL
FAMILY
⬚ **U Suites Eilat.** The first thing you'll see when you enter this hotel is its breathtaking view of the shimmering sea and the mountains beyond. **Pros:** lovely views; short walk from shopping area; feels separated from the boardwalk hubbub. **Cons:** pool can be cold in winter months; late-night music may disturb some guests; not much of a beachfront. $ *Rooms from: $320* ✉ *Arava Rd.* ☎ *08/638–3333* ⊕ *www.fattal-hotels.com* ⬄ *246 suites* ⫶◉⫶ *Breakfast* ✛ *B4.*

After a day at the beach, secure a seat with a waterside view at one of Eilat's many restaurants.

NIGHTLIFE AND PERFORMING ARTS

Most hotels in Eilat have a bar, and many have dance clubs. Other nightlife options include beach parties, where bronzed bodies groove all night to recorded music (often local favorites like trance or house). Keep an eye out in town for English-language posters listing times and places. Admission is free.

For an overview of local events, pick up a copy of the detailed leaflet "Events and Places of Interest" at the tourist information office. Check out Friday's *Jerusalem Post* magazine, or the *Herald Tribune*'s *Haaretz Guide,* both of which carry listings for Eilat.

NIGHTLIFE

Fifth Avenue. If you're looking to avoid the more touristy spots, this restaurant and bar in the park is the closest you'll get in Eilat. This New York–style joint has tables lit with flickering candles, a wide-ranging menu, and a dance floor where locals venture late at night. Low ceilings make this a louder-than-necessary experience, particularly on Friday when the DJs spin electronic music. It's closed Sunday. ⊠ *Shofron St.* ☎ *08/633–3303.*

Mike's Place. The newest in the Mike's Place chain, this lively sports bar and live-music destination offers a friendly oasis with an American vibe. Families as well as nightlife seekers will feel equally at home with the menu of more than 70 sandwiches and salads, burgers, and burritos. ⊠ *King Solomon Promenade ✢ Facing harbor at King Solomon Promenade* ☎ *08/864–9550* ⊕ *www.mikesplacebars.com.*

Paddy's Irish Pub. Looking for all the world like an American sports bar, Paddy's Irish Pub stocks more than 50 kinds of international beers, including 16 on draft. Everything here is big: the food menu, wooden patio, and the bar, said to be the largest in Eilat. On game nights you have your choice of nine different screens, or you can pass the time upstairs on one of the four pool tables. Bands play twice a week on summer nights. ⊠ *Derekh Yotam St.* ☎ *08/637–0921* ⊕ *paddys.co.il/en/.*

Three Monkeys Pub. Live music is the claim to fame at this very popular pub, where the shows kick off most nights at around 10:30 pm. The crowd includes people of all ages, and they hang out around the bar or dance until last call. ⊠ *Royal Beach Promenade* ☎ *08/636–8888.*

PERFORMING ARTS

Fodor's Choice ★ **Red Sea Jazz Festival.** Many Israelis and foreign visitors plan their trips to coincide with this twice-a-year, three-day event, which draws top-notch musicians from all over the world. The main festival is typically held the third week in August and generally attracts Israeli, European, and American artists. The winter festival, usually held in February, highlights Israeli talent. Now that the festival is sponsored by Isrotel, many of the winter performances take place at one of the hotels in the chain. Summer concerts are held in large outdoor stage areas at the port created with shipping containers ⊠ *Eilat* ⊕ *redseajazz.co.il.*

FAMILY **WOW.** This 90-minute circus-style show combines magic, juggling, and gravity-defying acrobatics—all in a 3–D video-art setting. New shows, produced by a top Israeli choreographer, debut every year or two. Call ahead to reserve tickets. There are no shows on Sunday. ⊠ *Isrotel Royal Garden, Antibes St, North Beach* ☎ *08/638–6701* ⊠ *NIS 130.*

SHOPPING

Eilat is a duty-free zone, meaning that shoppers from all over Israel make the journey here to take advantage of tax-free shopping. You'll find that most of the prices are lower here than the rest of the country.

Along the beachside Promenade, on the ground level of each hotel, you'll pass one designer boutique after another. If you'd rather hit the beach during the day, you'll still have plenty of time to shop after dark—these places are open until 9 pm or later every night except Friday.

ART AND CRAFTS

Cardo. This intriguing series of shops carries unusual paintings, sculptures, Judaica, old-style objets d'art, Moroccan furnishings, painted and inlaid mirrors, boxes and frames, gifts, and wall hangings. ⊠ *Herods Vitalis Hotel, North Beach Promenade, North Beach* ☎ *08/638–0000.*

BEAUTY

Laline. Israeli-made soaps, shampoos, and candles are the specialty of this chain. The salt scrubs, infused with mineral oils, are especially luxurious, and the verbena-coconut body lotion is a perfect salve for sunburned skin. ⊠ *North Beach Promenade* ✛ *Near Hilton Eilat Queen of Sheba* ☎ *054/334–5024* ⊕ *www.laline.co.il.*

CLOTHING

Designer Gallery. A cluster of boutiques offers an excellent variety of high-end Israeli designer women's clothing and accessories. Some of the most internationally renowned Israeli designers—including Ronen

Chen, Daniela Lehavi, Naama Bezalel—display their airy knit dresses, classy leather bags, and sassy shoes in adjacent showrooms, which make for a great local shopping experience that's a far cry from the ubiquitous large shopping malls found in Eilat. Once or twice a year, the shops put on a fashion show on the promenade out front. ⊠ *King Solomon Promenade, North Beach.*

JEWELRY AND ACCESSORIES

H. Stern. With two locations in Eilat, this shop has an excellent reputation for high-quality gold and diamond pieces. The location at the Royal Beach Hotel has an especially good selection. ⊠ *Royal Beach Hotel, North Beach Promenade* ☎ *08/633–0674* ⊕ *www.hstern.net.*

Padani. Look for Breitling and Cartier timepieces at this shop, considered one of Israel's premier sources for watches. Both locations are at the Royal Beach—one inside the hotel and one on the promenade below. ⊠ *Royal Beach Hotel, North Beach Promenade* ☎ *08/631–5038* ⊕ *padani.co.il.*

MALLS AND SHOPPING CENTERS

Adom Mall and Shalom Plaza. The two sections of this shopping center are connected by a passage filled with cafés where you can stop and take stock of all the bargains you've found. On a smaller scale than Mul HaYam Mall, it nevertheless has a wide variety of stores. There's a notable absence of tacky souvenir shops. ⊠ *2 HaTamarim St.* ✛ *Near entrance to Eilat Airport.*

Mull HaYam Mall. One of Eilat's prime shopping destinations, Mull HaYam Mall is noted for its made-in-Israel products. Here you can stroll along with the chattering crowd, pick up a lottery ticket, or enjoy a glass of freshly squeezed orange or carrot juice. Then check out such stores as **Intima** for soft and sexy lingerie, **Gottex** for famous swimwear, **Honigman** for women's casual wear, and **Fox** for cheeky clothing for adults and children. The more than 90 stores also include a bookstore and drugstore, and there are several coffee shops. ⊠ *Arava Rd. and Yotam St.*

SPORTS AND THE OUTDOORS

At its heart, Eilat is one long oceanfront resort, and the town takes pride in its beaches. It's not unusual to hear locals bragging about the clarity of the water and the quality of the snorkeling, scuba diving, and other water sports. Beach managers ensure the cleanliness of their sections, which everyone refers to as North and South Beaches. Look for beaches with large white signs indicating that swimming is authorized. Here you'll find lifeguards that are usually on duty until 4 or 5 in the afternoon. Many beaches turn into clubs after sunset, with plenty of music and dancing.

Many outdoor activities can be arranged through your hotel. Several tour operators maintain desks in the lobbies of larger hotels.

BEACHES

Families and luxury travelers favor North Beach, which fronts most of Eilat's high-end hotels and generally has a sleeker, more organized look and feel. Young people tend to hang out at the southernmost beaches, near the dive centers (south of the port, along the Eilat–Taba road). In recent years Eilat has made a number of beaches wheelchair accessible. The best is opposite the Neptune Hotel, where a wheelchair path leads from the promenade to the water's edge.

Fodor'sChoice
★

North Beach. Running northeast from the intersection of Durban and Arava Streets, North Beach is what comes to mind when most people think about Eilat. This part of the beach is convenient if food and drink are on your agenda. Here you'll find kiosks selling drinks, ice cream, and other snacks, and along the Promenade are many more options for fuller meals. Adventurous types can go paragliding or rent a paddleboat. Across the bridge—opposite the Queen of Sheba, Royal Beach, Dan, and Herods hotels—lies a beautifully landscaped series of beaches.

Walking south, you'll pass several mellow beaches, including Kochav Hayam and HaZahav, before you come to Royal Beach, where white-shirted attendants rent space on private platforms. Very expensive drinks can be ordered from the nearby Royal Beach Hotel and vendors sell popsicles and sodas. Head past the marina, where you can enjoy a ride in a glass-bottom boat, and you'll encounter family-friendly beaches with names like Tarshish, Leonardo, Rimonim, and HaPnina, where hard-core sunbathers oil themselves for maximum exposure. North Beach comes to a natural end by Le Meridien Hotel, whose beach is the only private one. **Amenities:** food and drink; lifeguards; showers; water sports. **Best for:** partiers; sunset; swimming; walking.

South Beach. Attracting a younger crowd, South Beach retains a bit of a funky vibe. Stretching for 11 km (7 miles), South Beach is actually much longer than North Beach, but Eilat Port (look for the gaudy gambling boats moored there) cuts it in two pieces. North of the port sits Dekel Beach, with a shaded Bedouin tent, tanning raft, snorkeling station, and beach bar. It's great for families during the day, and often hosts private parties in the evening. Past Dolphin Reef sits Almog Beach, a relaxation haven with a full bar and restaurant, low-slung tables, and ample parking. Farther down the shore, Aquasport Beach is a standout; local scuba divers and water-sports enthusiasts know this is the laid-back alternative to better-trodden coves, and the vibe is free-spirited and decidedly chilled-out. There's a scuba school suitable for all levels of skill and experience. **Amenities:** food and drink; showers; water sports. **Best for:** swimming, snorkeling. ✉ *Off Rte. 90 (Eilat–Taba Rd.).*

BIRD-WATCHING

International Birding and Research Center of Eilat. More than a billion birds migrate annually through these skies between Africa and Eurasia, and bird-watching enthusiasts increasingly come for the spectacle between late February and mid-May and early September to late November. Spring is by far the larger of the two migrations. This nonprofit birding center seeks to create a safe haven for the species whose natural habitats in and around Eilat have degraded due to pollution, overdevelopment, and other environmental factors. The center offers guided tours of the sanctuary where birds like imperial eagles, desert eagle owls, and long-legged buzzards can be seen in a majestically preserved habitat. Tours must be arranged in advance. Binoculars are provided. ✉ *Rte. 90 ✛ 10 km (6 miles) north of center of Eilat* ☎ *050/767–1290* ⊕ *www.birds.org.il* ✉ *Free.*

DESERT TOURS

FAMILY **Camel Ranch Eilat.** A 10-minute drive from Eilat, this family-friendly venue lets kids get up close and personal with camels. You can explore the surrounding hills on a 90-minute trek, a half-day excursion, or a sunset tour. Longer trips end in Bedouin style with food and drink. There are plenty of other activities, including a ropes course designed for climbers of all ages. Reserve the camel excursions in advance. ⊠ *Nahal Shlomo St., South Beach* ☎ *08/637–0022* ⊕ *www.camel-ranch.co.il/ en/* ⊠ *Free; rides start at NIS 150.*

Glitch. This multisport company, which specializes in desert tourism, runs customized Jeep tours and rappelling (known in Israel as snappelling) trips for both novices and more seasoned adventurers. It also offers desert archery courses. Call ahead to reserve. ⊠ *Eilat* ☎ *053/739–9557* ⊕ *www.glitch.co.il.*

SNORKELING AND DIVING

Snorkeling and scuba diving are extremely popular activities in Eilat, and no wonder: Eilat Bay is located at the northern tip of a coral reef that extends from the equator. Here you'll find everything from beginner's courses to expert certification courses.

Fodor'sChoice **Aqua-Sport.** For more than 50 years, this dive center has been operating
★ PADI-certified diving courses in Eilat, as well as snorkeling and diving trips to the most magnificent sections of the reef. There are special Bubblemaker introductory courses for kids and courses ranging from a few hours to several days to help you get accreditation. Prices vary according to courses, excursions, and your experience level. ⊠ *Coral Beach, Rte. 90 (Eilat–Taba Rd.), South Beach* ☎ *08/633–4404* ⊕ *www. aqua-sport.com.*

Fodor'sChoice **Manta Diving Center.** Known for its incredibly supportive staff, Manta
★ offers the full range of equipment and courses for scuba divers and snorkelers of all levels. Courses are available in English for groups or four and more. ⊠ *Isrotel Yam Suf Hotel, Rte. 90 (Eilat–Taba Rd.), South Beach* ☎ *08/633–3666* ⊕ *www.divemanta.com* ⊠ *1-hr snorkeling from $60–$75 for up to 3 people.*

Red Sea Lucky Divers. In business for decades, Eilat's only PADI Gold Palm five-star diving center offers all manner of dive courses, from two-hour introductory dives to a five-day, open-water certification course (NIS 890). ⊠ *Rte. 90 (Eilat–Taba Rd.), Coral Beach* ⊹ *Near Orchid Reef Hotel* ☎ *08/632–3466* ⊕ *www.luckydivers.com.*

FAMILY **Snuba Eilat.** Kids ages eight and older have fun exploring Caves Reef, one of the most popular diving spots in the Coral Beach Nature Reserve. Snuba, a snorkeling-diving hybrid, lets you breathe through tubes connected to tanks carried in an inflatable raft on the surface. The price includes instruction, a practice session, and a guided underwater tour that goes no deeper than 20 feet. Snorkels and wet suits are also available for rental. Reserve in advance. ⊠ *Rte. 90 (Eilat–Taba Rd.), South Beach* ⊹ *Between Underwater Observatory and Princess Hotel* ☎ *08/637–2722* ⊕ *www.snuba.co.il* ⊠ *NIS 20.*

8

One of many unique rock formations in Timna Pane.

TIMNA PARK

25 km (15 miles) north of Eilat, 15 km (9 miles) south of Yotvata Hai-Bar Nature Reserve.

A lunarlike desert landscape interspersed with amazing geological shapes and ancient archaeological sites, Timna Park is surrounded by beautiful cliffs ranging from sandy beige to rich red and dusky black.

GETTING HERE AND AROUND

From Route 90 (Dead Sea–Eilat Road), turn left at the sign for Timna Park and Timna Lake. A 3-km (2-mile) access road (which passes Kibbutz Elifaz) leads to the entrance booth.

EXPLORING

Fodor's Choice ★ **Timna Park.** The granite Timna Mountains (whose highest peak is 2,550 feet) are just the beginning of this park's spectacular collection of rock formations and canyons. Millions of years of erosion have sculpted shapes of amazing beauty, such as the red-hue Solomon's Pillars (sandstone columns created by rare patterns of erosion, not by the biblical king) and the 20-foot-high freestanding Mushroom. Late afternoon provides the best light for spectators and photographers alike.

People have also left their mark here. South of the pillars are the remains of a small **temple** built in white sandstone by Egyptians who worked the mines 3,400 years ago, during the Egyptian New Kingdom (the time of Moses). The temple was dedicated to the cow-eared goddess Hathor. This "Lady of the Rock" was the patroness of miners, as you can discover at the multimedia presentation called *Mines of Time*. Inside the temple, archaeologists have discovered a snake made of copper (*nehushtan* in Hebrew)—according to Numbers 21:4–9, Moses made a serpent in the wilderness to heal people suffering from snake bites, and the snake remains a symbol of healing to this day. Near the temple, a path and stairway lead up to the observation platform overlooking the valley. Above the platform is a rock-cut inscription whose hieroglyph you can see clearly with the aid of a telescope. It shows Ramses III offering a sacrifice to Hathor. You can also explore a life-size replica of the biblical tabernacle the Israelites carried through the desert.

When you arrive, ask for the explanatory pamphlet, which shows the driving route in red. The park measure 60 square km (23 square miles), so we suggest driving from sight to sight and exploring each on foot. A small building just inside the entrance screens a multimedia video (with a revolving stage and 360-degree screen) detailing humanity's 6,000-year-old relationship with the Timna area. Wall panels explain the valley's fascinating geological makeup.

Experienced hikers can pick up a map detailing various serious hikes that take from 7 to 10 hours to complete. They're best done in winter, as summer daytime temperatures exceed 100 degrees. Watch out for old mine shafts, take adequate water, and be sure to let the staff at the gate know you are going and when you plan to return. You can also rent bikes and paddleboats near the small lake, where you'll find a restaurant serving charred bread cooked in a *taboon* (traditional oven), along with goodies and refreshing drinks. ⊠ *Rte. 90 (Dead Sea–Eilat Rd.), Yotvata* ☎ *08/631–6756* ⊕ *www.parktimna.co.il* ✉ *NIS 49; night entrance for concerts and special events NIS 59.*

NEED A BREAK

✕**Yotvata Inn.** If you're looking for fantastic kibbutz-made ice cream (try the one flavored with *tmarim*, or dates), stop by this inn, an Israeli institution next to a gas station on Route 90 between the Yotvata Hai-Bar Nature Reserve and Timna Park, 40 km (25 miles) north of Eilat. The kibbutz of the same name is across the way, and its dairy products are much loved by locals. Hot chicken or beef dishes are available as well. It's open 24 hours (though closed Saturday night), but the late-night food menu is more limited. ⊠ *Rte. 90 (Dead Sea–Eilat Rd.), Yotvata* ☎ *08/635-7449.*

YOTVATA HAI-BAR NATURE RESERVE

35 km (21½ miles) north of Eilat on Rte. 90, between Kibbutz Yotvata and Kibbutz Samar, 15 km (9 miles) north of Timna Park.

In the southern Arava Valley, this nature preserve makes a good day trip from Eilat and can be combined with a visit to the Timna Park. It was created not only as a refuge for animals that were almost extinct in the region, but also as a breeding ground for animals that will be set free in the Negev.

GETTING HERE AND AROUND

The reserve is located on Route 90 (Dead Sea–Eilat Road), between Kibbutzim Yotvata and Samar. Look for the sign for Yotvata Hai-Bar Nature Reserve, opposite the entrance to Kibbutz Samar. Drive 1½ km (1 mile) to the entrance. The reserve is also accessible via Egged Bus 390 from Tel Aviv, Bus 397 from Beersheva, or Bus 444 from Jerusalem.

EXPLORING

FAMILY
Fodor's Choice
★

Yotvata Hai-Bar Nature Reserve. This popular nature preserve is a natural habitat for biblical-era animals and birds. Roaming around are stripe-legged Africa wild asses, Dorcas gazelles, Arabian oryx, and other desert herbivores. Try to be here in the morning, when animals are most active. You need a car in order to enter the safari-like nature reserve, and a CD player (available for rent) if you want a 45-minute "guided tour." A second section, the Desert Night Exhibition Hall, is a darkened room where you can observe the habits of nocturnal animals such as bats and barn owls. An upgraded ticket allows you into the Predator Center, where feeding time is a highlight. Carnivores, including feral wolves, foxes, leopards, jackals, birds of prey, and striped hyenas are kept in enclosures. ⊠ *Rte. 90 (Dead Sea–Eilat Rd.), Yotvata* ☎ *08/637–6018* ⊕ *www.parks.org.il* ⊠ *NIS 29; combination ticket including Predator Center NIS 46.*

THE HEART OF THE NEGEV

The Negev Highlands offers a wide range of sights: David Ben-Gurion's kibbutz home and grave site; an icy desert pool at Ein Avdat; the remains of the 2,000-year-old Nabatean hilltop stronghold of Avdat; and the immense Makhtesh Ramon (Ramon Crater). You'll also have the opportunity to meet the Negev's indigenous people, the Bedouin.

MITZPE RAMON AND MAKHTESH RAMON

21 km (13 miles) south of Avdat National Park, 80 km (50 miles) south of Beersheva, 150 km (93 miles) north of Eilat.

Israel's most spectacular natural sight, and one of the largest craters in the world, the Makhtesh Ramon (Ramon Crater) in the heart of the Negev is a place of unparalleled serenity and breathtaking views. The crater's walls are made from layers of different-color rock beds containing fossils of shells, plants, and trees. Once under the sea, the makhtesh floor is today covered with heaps of black basalt, the peaks of ancient volcanoes, jagged chunks of quartzite, natural prism rock, and beds of multicolor clays.

Mitzpe Ramon, a town of 5,500 people on the northern edge of the crater, makes a great base for exploring the area. Slowly but surely, commerce and culture are beginning to catch up with the area's unparalleled scenic and adventure offerings. A promenade winds along the edge of the crater, and a huge sculpture park sits on its rim. Outdoors enthusiasts will enjoy exploring the stunning scenery by foot, mountain bike, or four-wheel-drive vehicle. The winter weather here is cool and pleasant.

The Heart
of the Negev

GETTING HERE AND AROUND

On Route 40, Mitzpe Ramon sits between Beersheva and Eilat. Egged Buses 392, 382, and 395, as well as Metropoline Bus 160, run about once an hour until 5 pm from Beersheva (a 1¾-hour drive); there are no direct buses from Jerusalem. There are no gas stations between Mitzpe Ramon and Yotvata, near Eilat, a distance of more than 100 km (62 miles).

EXPLORING

FAMILY **Alpaca Farm.** Just west of Mitzpe Ramon you'll find this farm and its herd of 200 sweet-faced alpacas and llamas. Young and old get a kick out of feeding the animals, even if they receive the occasional spit in the face from these long-lashed creatures. Children weighing less than about 55 pounds can take a llama ride, and grown-ups can enjoy horseback rides. You can also weave wool on a loom, purchase items at the local factory, and enjoy a picnic on the grounds. The shearing festival, which takes place around Passover, is worth catching if you're here. ✉ *Extension of Ben Gurion Blvd., 4 km (2 miles) west of downtown, Mitzpe Ramon* ⊕ *Turn off main road onto Ben Gurion Blvd., opposite gas station at the town's main roundabout* ☎ *08/658–8047* ⊕ *www. alpaca.co.il* ✉ *NIS 30.*

Fodor's Choice ★ **Makhtesh Ramon** (*Ramon Crater*). Words simply cannot do this natural wonder justice. This immense depression is 40 km (25 miles) long, 10 km (6 miles) wide, and at its deepest, it measures 2,400 feet. Because it's a phenomenon known only in this country (there are two others in the Negev), the Hebrew term *makhtesh* is now accepted usage. By definition, a makhtesh is an erosion valley walled with steep cliffs on all sides and drained by a single watercourse.

You can take a 1-km (½-mile) walk along the Albert Promenade, which winds westward along the edge of the crater from the Mitzpe Ramon Visitor Center to a cantilevered observation platform hanging over the rim. This is not the time to forget the camera—the view is overwhelming. The promenade is fashioned from local stone, as is the huge sculpture by Israel Hadani, the back of which faces the town and represents the crater's geological layers.

With the crater as a magnificent backdrop, the Desert Sculpture Park exhibits a collection of 19 huge contemporary sculptures. The park took shape in 1962 with the work of a group of prominent national and international sculptors under the direction of Negev artist Ezra Orion. Their idea was to add to the natural stone formations with geometric sculptures of similar design. Ibex often wander through the area. To get to the sculpture park, turn off the main road (Route 40) near the gas station at the sign marked Ma'ale Noah.

For a look at one of Makhtesh Ramon's geological wonders, drive down into the crater to see the Carpentry Shop, a hill of black rocks that appears to have neatly sawed edges. Long ago, the sandstone was warmed by volcanic steam and split into the shapes seen today. A wooden walkway protects this fascinating area from travelers' feet.

Another of nature's works is the Ammonite Wall, on the right as you finish the descent into the crater. The rock face, actually part of the crater wall, contains hundreds of ammonite fossils, which look like spiraled rams' horns. From here there's a 5-km (3-mile) hiking trail, suitable for more experienced hikers. ⊠ *Rte. 40, Mitzpe Ramon* ⊕ *parks.org. il* ⊠ *Free.*

Mitzpe Ramon Visitor Center. This visitor center—dedicated to Israeli astronaut Ilan Ramon, who perished in the 2003 Space Shuttle *Columbia* disaster—is perched at the very edge of the crater. Interesting 3–D models and other information about the history and formation of the crater makes it a good place to start your journey. The museum's panoramic view of the crater is breathtaking. There is also a restaurant and a branch of the popular Faran beauty products store. ⊠ *1 Maale Ben Tor, Mitzpe Ramon* ☎ *08/658–8691, 08/658–8698* ⊕ *www.goisrael. com* ⊠ *NIS 28.*

WHERE TO EAT

$$ VEGETARIAN ✕ **Hadasaar.** The brainchild of Hadas and Sa'ar Badash, this inviting eatery and store-cum–community center is bringing new life to the moribund Spice Quarter. The large space features an area selling hard-to-find organic ingredients, a funky secondhand shop, and several cases of fetching jewelry. Best of all is the sweet little café that sells coffee made with house-roasted beans. There's also an expansive vegetarian menu

Makhtesh Ramon (Ramon Crater), shown in the valley below, is one of the Negev's top sites.

that includes organic gazpacho, freshly baked bread layered with local cheeses, and some of the best tahini cookies in Israel. A half hour spent in the sunny garden or browsing among the local products will leave you wanting more. ⑤ *Average main: NIS 50* ✉ *6 Har Boker St., Spice Quarter* 🕾 *08/940–8473.*

$$ ✕ **HaHavit.** At this pub-restaurant frequented by everyone from
BURGER teenagers to octogenarians, you can choose juicy homemade burgers, tasty onion soup, and stuffed mushrooms, among other dishes. What's unusual is the copious selection of Israeli beers, which reflects the explosion of the microbrews throughout the country. ⑤ *Average main: NIS 50* ✉ *Chachmov Center, 10 Nakhal Tsikhor, Mitzpe Ramon* 🕾 *08/658–8226.*

WHERE TO STAY

$$$$ 🏨 **Beresheet Hotel.** For sheer natural magnificence, few venues can top
RESORT the splendor of the most luxurious lodging in Mitzpe Ramon. **Pros:**
Fodor'sChoice unmatched setting; access to natural wonders; gorgeous pools. **Cons:**
★ extremely pricey; amenities could be spiffier for a five-star hotel. ⑤ *Rooms from: $450* ✉ *1 Derech Beresheet, Mitzpe Ramon* 🕾 *08/638–7797* ⊕ *www.isrotel.com* ⇌ *111 rooms* ⦿ *Breakfast.*

$$ 🏨 **Desert Home.** Here's a little piece of heaven on the outskirts of
B&B/INN Mitzpe Ramon: a laid-back lodging with five lovely guest rooms with covered terraces facing the surrounding desert hills. **Pros:** lots of privacy; well-stocked kitchenette. **Cons:** remote location; not for families with kids. ⑤ *Rooms from: $225* ✉ *70 Ein Shaviv St., Mitzpe Ramon* 🕾 *052/322–9496* ⊕ *www.baitbamidbar.com* ▭ *No credit cards* ⇌ *5 rooms* ⦿ *Breakfast.*

$$
HOTEL

🍴 **InnSense.** Set in the slowly developing industrial zone, this unpretentious boutique restaurant-hotel has half a dozen high-ceilinged suites outfitted with modern furnishings, local beauty products, and cozy fireplaces—some even have private jetted tubs. **Pros:** ideal for couples looking for privacy. **Cons:** no views; no bathtubs; can feel a bit remote. ⑤ *Rooms from: $250* ⊠ *8 Har Hardon St., Spice Quarter* ☎ *08/653–9595* ⊕ *www.innsense.co.il* ⌁ *6 suites* ⍩ *Breakfast.*

$$
HOTEL

🍴 **Isrotel Ramon Inn.** There's nothing rugged about a stay at this charming desert hotel, which has an open fireplace in the lobby for chilly winter nights. **Pros:** ideal for mountain bikers looking to take advantage of nearby trails; tasty meals; private feel. **Cons:** no elevator; not much to do nearby at night. ⑤ *Rooms from: $230* ⊠ *1 Ein Akev St., Mitzpe Ramon* ☎ *08/658–8822* ⊕ *www.isrotel.com* ⌁ *96 rooms* ⍩ *Breakfast.*

$
B&B/INN

🍴 **Succah in the Desert.** Down an unpaved road, this out-of-the-ordinary cluster of stone-and-wood huts sits on a rocky hillside; for the rugged traveler seeking the starkness and purity of the desert, it's an appealing example of ecotourism. **Pros:** homemade vegetarian breakfasts included in price; great for stargazing; dinner may be included in price on weekends. **Cons:** can be cold at nights; difficult to reach without a car; shared bathrooms. ⑤ *Rooms from: $130* ⊠ *Off Rte. 171, Mitzpe Ramon* ✛ *7 km (4½ miles) west of Mitzpe Ramon* ☎ *08/658–6280* ⊕ *www.succah.co.il* ⌁ *9 rooms* ⍩ *Breakfast.*

SHOPPING

Faran. For all-natural, deliciously scented cosmetics, soaps, and skin-care products, visit this shop. The products use local herbs and goat and camel milk, making them great souvenirs of the region. Faran is closed Saturday. ⊠ *12 Har Ardon St., Spice Quarter* ☎ *08/653–9333* ⊕ *www.faran-cosmetic.com.*

SPORTS AND THE OUTDOORS

ARCHERY

Desert Archery. This outfit offers excursions where you hike through a desert course while shooting arrows at targets—a kind of cross between archery and golf. The company works with groups, and you need to call ahead to arrange an activity. ⊠ *Derech Mitzpe Kohavim, Mitzpe Ramon* ☎ *050/534–4598* ⊕ *www.desertarchery.co.il.*

HIKING

Adam Sela Tours. Camel-supported hikes, four-wheel-vehicle excursions, and mountain-bike trips are run by Adam Sela Tours, which also offers ecological tours and visits to Bedouin villages. ⊠ *Mitzpe Ramon* ☎ *050/530–8272* ⊕ *www.adamsela.com* 💰 *$200 for up to 8 people for 2-hr guided Jeep tour.*

Fodor'sChoice
★

Negev Jeep. If you're in search of a guide company in Mitzpe Ramon, look no further than Negev Jeep. Though the name refers to the wonderful Jeep tours—you'll get a firsthand education on the flora, fauna, animal life, and anthropological history of the region—there's so much more. Owner Haim Berger, a longtime area resident and excellent English speaker, is a behavioral scientist by training but also an expert in everything about Mitzpe Ramon and the environs. He and his friendly staff can coordinate many activities, from tours highlighting prehistoric rock art to hikes to the top of Mount Karkom, which some believe to be biblical Mount Sinai. ⊠ *Mitzpe Ramon* ☎ *054/534–3797* ⊕ *negevjeep. co.il* ✉ *$200 for up to 8 people for 2-hr guided Jeep tour.*

STARGAZING

Fodor's Choice
★
Astronomy Israel. Mitzpe Ramon turns pitch-black at night—one of the factors Astronomy Israel guide Ira Machefsky claims makes the city a stargazer's paradise. American transplant Machefsky will either pick you up from your hotel or lead you in a two-car caravan to a secret desert plateau where his telescopes have been expertly situated for maximum viewing pleasure (if you've never seen the surface of the Moon up close, you're in for a treat). Machefsky's easygoing charm allows him to impart his vast knowledge in terms even inexperienced stargazers can understand, from pointing out constellations to explaining the basic science behind astronomy. What's more, to counteract Mitzpe Ramon's chilly nights, he supplies blankets, hot-water bottles, and a double dose of good cheer. ⊠ *Mitzpe Ramon* ☎ *052/544–9789* ⊕ *www. astronomyisrael.com* ✉ *NIS 150.*

AVDAT NATIONAL PARK

21 km (13 miles) north of Mitzpe Ramon, 101 km (63 miles) south of Beersheva.

The name Avdat is the Hebrew version of Oboda (30 BC–9 BC), a deified Nabatean king who may have been buried here. The prominent local dynasty intermarried with the family of Herod the Great, and in AD 106 the Romans finally abolished the Nabatean kingdom. The Nabatean temple on Avdat's acropolis left almost no remains, but its magnificence can be imagined from its restored gateway.

GETTING HERE AND AROUND

On Route 40 (Beersheva–Mitzpe Ramon Road), Avdat is a 15-minute drive south of Sde Boker.

EXPLORING

Fodor's Choice
★
Avdat National Park. The remains of the Nabatean city of Avdat loom on a hilltop over part of the old Incense Route between Petra and Gaza, a reminder of how valuable incense, spices, and perfumes from Arabia were in ancient times. The Nabateans were seminomadic people who came here from northern Arabia in the 3rd century BC. With their prosperous caravan routes connecting the desert hinterland to the port city of Gaza, they soon rose to glory with a vast kingdom whose capital was Petra, in present-day Jordan. Strongholds to protect the caravans were established along these routes, usually a day's journey apart. Most of the remains on the acropolis date from the 3rd, 4th, and 5th centuries—the Christian Byzantine period. The city continued to flourish until it was sacked by the Persians in AD 620; it was rediscovered only in the 20th century.

Start at the **visitor center,** where you can learn about the Nabateans in a 10-minute video, see examples of what these ancient traders actually transported across the desert, and examine archaeological artifacts

These ruins in the ancient Nabatean city of Avdat are perched more than 2,000 feet above sea level.

found in the excavations. Drive up the road (save your energy for walking around the site), stopping first at the sign for the **Roman burial cave**, which is well worth a quick peek. The 21 double catacombs cut into the rock date from the 3rd century BC.

Back in your car, drive up to the lookout point at the restored Roman building (note the watchtower with an inscription dating to the late 3rd century). The cultivated fields below were re-created in 1959 in order to see if the ancient Nabatean and Byzantine methods of conserving the meager rainfall would still work. The proof is in the lush greenery before you.

Using the Israel Nature and Parks Authority's excellent map, you can trace the lifestyle of the original inhabitants at sites that include a reconstructed three-story Roman tower, a rare Nabatean pottery workshop, a Byzantine-era winepress, two Byzantine churches, and a large baptismal font built to accommodate the converted. Near the baptismal font, you can walk down the steps to see 6th-century Byzantine dwellings, each consisting of a cave (possibly used as a wine cellar) behind a stone house. At the bottom of the hill, north of the gas station, is a Byzantine bathhouse. There is a rest area with food and drinks near the visitor center. ✉ *Rte. 40, Avdat* ☎ *08/655–1511* ⊕ *www.parks.org.il* 🎫 *NIS 28.*

EIN AVDAT NATIONAL PARK AND VICINITY

14 km (9 miles) north of Avdat National Park on Rte. 40.

Ein Avdat (Avdat Spring) lies at the foot of the narrow canyon dividing the plateau between the ancient Nabatean city of Avdat and Kibbutz Sde Boker, in Ein Avdat National Park. This oasis is a lovely place to explore. Also worth visiting is Sde Boker, where David Ben-Gurion, Israel's first prime minister and a man dedicated to the dream of making the Negev flourish, lived and is now buried. Nearby are other attractions including goat farms.

GETTING HERE AND AROUND

Ein Avdat National Park is located off the Beersheva–Mitzpe Ramon road (Route 40). To get to the lower entrance, head down the curving road from Ben-Gurion's grave. The upper entrance is about 5 km (3 miles) to the south.

Ben-Gurion's home and grave are also along Route 40; driving north, you'll see the sign for Ben-Gurion's home directing you to turn right immediately after Kibbutz Sde (pronounced *se-day*) Boker. Egged Bus 392 runs to Sde Boker from Beersheva five times a day, and Metropoline Bus 60 runs seven times a day (a 45-minute ride).

EXPLORING

TOP ATTRACTIONS

Ben-Gurion's Desert Home. Thousands of people make their way to this pilgrimage site every year. David Ben-Gurion (1886–1973), Israel's first prime minister, was one of the 20th-century's great statesmen. He regarded the Negev as Israel's frontier and hoped that tens of thousands would settle there. When Ben-Gurion resigned from government in 1953 (later to return), he and his wife, Paula, moved to Kibbutz Sde Boker to provide an example for others. "Neither money nor propaganda builds a country," he announced. "Only the man who lives and creates in the country can build it." And so, the George Washington of Israel took up his new role in the kibbutz sheepfold. In February 1955, he became prime minister once more, but he returned here to live when he retired in 1963.

Set amid the waving eucalyptus trees is Paula and David Ben-Gurion's simple dwelling, a testament to their typically Israeli brand of modesty and frugality. Ben-Gurion's small Negev home is commonly known as "the hut," owing to its humble appearance. It's a one-story wooden home with a small kitchen, an eating corner with a table and two chairs, and simple furniture throughout. Visitors such as United Nations Secretary-General Dag Hammarskjöld drank tea with Ben-Gurion in the modest living room. Ben-Gurion's library shelves contain 5,000 books (there are 20,000 more in his Tel Aviv home, on Ben Gurion Boulevard). His bedroom, with its single picture of Mahatma Gandhi, holds the iron cot on which he slept (often only three hours a night) and his slippers on the floor beside it. The house is exactly as he left it.

Next door, in three adjacent painted-wood buildings, are exhibitions with original documents whose themes are the story of Ben-Gurion's extraordinary life in Sde Boker, his youth, leadership, and army service,

8

and the leader's vision for the Negev. A film showing the footage of kibbutz members actually voting on his acceptance into their community is shown in the **visitor center**; the shop here sells gifts, jewelry, and books about the "Old Man," as he was known locally. ⊠ *Off Rte. 40, Sde Boker* 🕾 *08/656–0469* ⊕ *www.bgh.org.il* ✏ *NIS 20* ⟟ *Last admission 1 hr before closing.*

Ben-Gurion's Grave. The revered prime minister's grave, just 3 km (2 miles) south of his desert home in Kibbutz Sde Boker, is often visited at the same time. Walk through the beautiful garden until you reach the quiet, windswept plaza; in the center are the simple raised stone slabs marking the graves of David and Paula Ben-Gurion (she died five years before her husband). The couple's final resting place commands a view of Zin Valley's geological finery: a vast, undulating drape of stone that changes hue as the daylight shifts. The cluster of greenery and palm trees to the right on the valley floor marks Ein Avdat (Avdat Spring). ⊠ *Off Rte. 40, Sde Boker* 🕾 *08/655–5684* ✏ *Free.*

NEED A BREAK

✕ **Menta.** Just off Route 40 at a gas station, south of the entrance to Ben-Gurion's Desert Home in Kibbutz Sde Boker, is a small café called Menta. It's conveniently open around the clock and offers tasty cappuccino, espresso, muffins, and sandwiches. ⊠ *Rte. 40, Sde Boker* 🕾 *08/657–9938.*

Fodor's Choice ★ **Carmey Avdat Farm Winery.** Set on an ancient riverbed and vineyard, this winery–guesthouse–gift shop complex is the labor of love of Hannah and Eyal Israel, who moved here in 1998. Pick up a handy map of the property, which includes ancient stone terraces and rock drawings, a small olive grove, and assorted fruit trees and herb bushes. Then ask Eyal to show you around the winery, where he'll share the story of how he came to plant new vines on an ancient terrace with a 1,500-year legacy. You can sample the delicious kosher wines and learn about Eyal's fascinating journey to wine making—even create your own customized wine label (NIS 90). At the farm store you can buy wines, local fruit, and local pottery. You need to call ahead for scheduling and pricing information. ⊠ *Rte. 40, south of Tziporim Junction, Midreshet Ben Gurion* 🕾 *08/653–5177* ⊕ *www.carmeyavdat.com* ✏ *NIS 30.*

FAMILY **Ein Avdat National Park.** Water flowing from Ein Avdat (Avdat Spring) has cut a beautiful, narrow canyon through the area's soft white chalk, forming a marvelous oasis that offers the ideal respite from your desert travels. Walk toward the thickets of rushes and look for ibex tracks, made with pointed hoofs that enable these agile creatures to climb sheer rock faces. It's not easy to spot an ibex—their coats have striped markings that resemble the rock's strata. Rock pigeons, sooty falcons, and Egyptian vultures (black-and-white feathers, bright yellow beak, and long, pinkish legs) nest in the natural holes in the soft rock and in cliff ledges.

The big surprise at Ein Avdat is the Ein Marif pools of ice-cold, spring-fed water, complete with a splashing waterfall. To reach this cool oasis, shaded by the surrounding cliffs, walk carefully along the spring and across the dam toward the waterfall. Swimming and drinking the water are not allowed (you'll not be *sorely* tempted, though—the water is swarming with tadpoles), but enjoying the sight and sound of water in the arid Negev certainly is. The trail leads through stands of Euphrates poplars, and by caves inhabited by monks during Byzantine days, and then continues up the cliff side (using ladders and stone steps), but you can't follow it unless your party has two cars and leaves one at the destination. The easier and more common option is to walk along the streambed from the lower entrance to the Ein Marif pools at the foot of the waterfall and then return along the same path. Ask for the explanatory leaflet when you pay. Lock your car, taking valuables with you. ⌧ *Rte. 40, Avdat* ☎ *08/655–5684* ⊕ *www.parks. org.il* ⌦ *NIS 28.*

WORTH NOTING

Kornmehl Goat Cheese Farm. This farm lets you watch adorable goats being fed and milked daily. You also have the opportunity to buy cheese or to sample the dairy's superb (and often quite pungent) cheeses at the charming restaurant. Perched on a beautiful desert hillside, the wooden restaurant offers indoor or outdoor seating and a menu that includes goat-cheese pizza, bruschetta, and calzones—there's even a tender goat-cheese cheesecake lavished in fruit sauce. ⌧ *Rte. 40, Mashabbe Sade* ⊕ *www.kornmehl.co.il* ⌦ *Free* ⊘ *Closed Mon.*

Na'ot Goat Farm. Make sure to sample the local goat cheeses that have become cult favorites around the country. At this farm, Gadi and Lea Nachimov craft soft and hard cheeses, yogurt, and other products from a herd of 150 goats who clamber over their land. Sign up for 45-minute tours of the facility. ⌧ *Rte. 40, Mashabbe Sade* ⊕ *www.naotfarm.co.il* ⌦ *NIS 22.*

WHERE TO EAT

$ ✕ **Pola's Café.** This café and gift shop is a pleasant, clean place for a
CAFÉ break before or after a tour of the Ben-Gurion Desert Home complex. It's convenient for coffee and pastries or a soft drink and a slice of pizza. The shop features wine and olive oil from the Sde Boker Winery and also sells locally produced skin-care items and cosmetics from Faran, made with minerals from the Ramon Crater area. If you have time, ask to see a screening of the short documentary *Dreaming—A Love Story,* about the establishment of Kibbutz Sde Boker. ⑤ *Average main: NIS 35* ⌧ *Ben-Gurion Desert Home Complex, Sde Boker* ☎ *08/656–0479.*

WHERE TO STAY

$$ 🏠 **Carmey Avdat Farm.** These six cabins are designed for anyone craving
B&B/INN an authentic Negev experience. **Pros:** unique experience; quiet setting; private feel. **Cons:** two-night minimum stay on weekends and holidays; paths to rooms could be better lit. ⑤ *Rooms from: $220* ⌧ *Rte. 40, south of Tziporim Junction, Midreshet Ben Gurion* ☎ *08/653–5177* ⊕ *www.carmeyavdat.com* ⇴ *6 rooms* ⍩ *Breakfast.*

8

BEERSHEVA

Although Beersheva has often been overlooked by visitors, in recent years Israel's fourth-largest city (population 200,000) has managed to raise its profile by introducing or renewing public spaces, museums, and attractions and encouraging investment in infrastructure and the arts. Beersheva houses a major university, named after David Ben-Gurion, a sparkling performance hall, and a regional hospital serving Bedouin shepherds, kibbutzniks, and other desert dwellers.

The Old City, anchored by Smilansky Street and dotted with handsome stone structures and the lion's share of Beersheva's better restaurants, continues to evolve. The Ottomans had controlled the Beersheva area since the 16th century, but it wasn't until the early 1900s that they quarried stone from a nearby canyon to build the distinctive buildings that form the nucleus of the Old City. These historic buildings are gradually being repurposed as restaurant, gallery, and nightlife spaces, pumping fresh, much-needed energy into the area. The famed Bedouin market, once a source of some of Israel's best ethnic handicrafts, has been hit hard by modern times (especially the competition of cheap imports from the Far East), and isn't what it used to be. But it now has a permanent location, and you might still find something authentic. Most intriguing are the Bedouin themselves, sitting cross-legged with their goods spread out on the ground.

Tel Beersheva, just outside the city, is the site of biblical Beersheva and could easily be the site of Abraham's well. An expression from the book of Judges, "from Dan to Beersheva," once indicated the northern and southern boundaries of the land of Israel. UNESCO declared Tel Beersheva a World Heritage Site in 2005.

Today this unpretentious city serves as a northern jumping-off point for Negev travel—main roads branch out from here; buses serving the Negev depart from here; and trains from the north end up in Beersheva. If your schedule permits, stay overnight in Beersheva for a glimpse of a growing desert city with an interesting citizenry and a gentrifying population.

GETTING HERE AND AROUND

Beersheva is 113 km (70 miles) southeast of Tel Aviv and 120 km (75 miles) southwest of Jerusalem. The drive from either Tel Aviv or Jerusalem takes about 1½ hours. To get to Beersheva from Tel Aviv, take Route 2 (the Ayalon Highway) south until the turnoff marked "Beersheva–Ashdod." After this you'll be on Route 41, which runs into Route 40 after 6 km (4 miles). Continue on Route 40 to Beersheva; there are clear signs all the way.

To reach Beersheva from Jerusalem, take Route 1 west to the Route 6 turnoff. Follow Route 6 southbound; after Kiryat Gat it turns into Route 40 south, which leads into Beersheva.

The Israel Air Force Museum is 7 km (4½ miles) west of Beersheva on a narrow desert road that pushes past the city's drab outskirts.

EXPLORING

TOP ATTRACTIONS

FAMILY **Israel Air Force Museum.** For plane lovers, this is a field of dreams. Housed on the Hatzerim Air Force Base, this open-air museum has more than a hundred airplanes and helicopters parked in rows. The fighter, transport, and training (plus a few enemy) aircraft tell the story of Israel's aeronautic history, from the Messerschmitt—obtained in 1948 from Czechoslovakia, and one of four such planes to help halt the Egyptian advance in the War of Independence—to the Kfir, the first fighter plane built in Israel. Young Air Force personnel lead tours (included in the price) that take about 90 minutes and include a movie shown in an air-conditioned Boeing 707 used in the 1977 rescue of Israeli passengers held hostage in a hijacked Air France plane in Entebbe, Uganda. Another attention-getting display is a shiny, black Supermarine Spitfire with a red lightning bolt on its side, flown by Ezer Weizmann, the IAF's first pilot and later president of Israel. The museum also houses an antiaircraft exhibit and a rare collection of historical and instructive films. Tours are available in English, French, and Russian. ⊠ *Hatzerim Air Force Base, Rte. 2357 ✛ 7 km (4½ miles) west of Beersheva on a desert road* ☎ *08/990–6888* ⊕ *iaf.co.il/5915-en/IAF.aspx* ☜ *NIS 30* ☻ *Closed Fri. and Sat.*

FAMILY
Fodor'sChoice
★

Museum of Bedouin Culture. This one-of-a-kind museum focuses on the Bedouin people, who have long populated the Negev and whose traditional way of life is changing in the 21st century. The study center (marked with an orange sign) is named for the late Colonel Joe Alon, a pilot who took a great interest in this area and its people. Housed in a circular building designed by Israeli architect Tzvi Lissar, the museum tells the story of the Bedouin's rapid change from a nomadic to a modern lifestyle through tableaux of life-size mannequins. They are grouped by subject: wool spinning and carpet weaving, bread baking, wedding finery (including a camel elaborately decorated for the event), donkeys and camels at work, and toys made from found objects such as pieces of wire and wood. The tools and artifacts—most handmade, and many already out of use in modern Bedouin life—form an outstanding collection. Another wing of the museum explores the Bar Kochba revolt of the Jews against Romans in the 2nd century AD. Admission includes a cup of thick coffee in a real Bedouin tent, where the sheikh performs the coffee ceremony over an open fire. ⊠ *Rte. 325 ✛ Next to Kibbutz Lahav* ☎ *08/991–3322* ⊕ *www.joealon.org.il* ☜ *NIS 25* ☻ *Closed Fri. and Sat.*

Tel Beersheva National Park. Traditionally associated with the biblical patriarch Abraham, Tel Beersheva is a mound of ruins created by nine successive settlements. Archaeologists have uncovered two-thirds of a city dating from the early Israelite period (10th century BC). Because of the site's significance for the study of biblical-period urban planning, UNESCO has recognized Tel Beersheva as a World Heritage Site. At the top of the tell is the only planned Israelite city uncovered in its entirety; the site includes sophisticated waterworks and a fascinating reconstructed horned altar. A fine example of a circular layout typical of the Iron Age, the city is believed to have been destroyed around 706

BC by Sennacherib of Assyria. At the northeastern end, outside the 3,000-year-old city gate, is a huge well (the deepest in Israel), which apparently once reached groundwater 90 feet below. This ancient well served the city from its earliest times, and scholars speculate that it could be the well that is documented in the Bible as Abraham's Well (Genesis 21:22–32). The observation tower is rather ugly, but it does afford beautiful views. ⊠ *Off Rte. 60* ☎ *08/646–7286* ⊕ *www.parks. org.il* ✉ *NIS 14.*

WORTH NOTING

Negev Museum of Art. This handsomely renovated structure—once home to a Ottoman Mandate–era governor—houses a rotating exhibit of classic and modern Israeli art. Located in Beersheva's Old City, the museum displays art from national and international artists. During the summer it hosts live concerts in its sculpture-laden courtyard. In the same area is the Museum of Islamic and Near Eastern Cultures, in a 1906 mosque. ⊠ *60 HaAtzma'ut St.* ☎ *08/699–3535* ⊕ *www.negev-museum.org.il* ✉ *Free* ☉ *Closed Sun.*

Rota Winery. One of the pioneers of the Negev wine-making scene, Erez Rota lives and works on a secluded ranch that's worth a stop. Since Rota began to make wines over a decade ago, his vintages have gained recognition for their complexity and sophistication—and they're all

CLOSE UP

Bedouin Culture

Bedu, the Arabic word from which the name Bedouin derives, simply means "inhabitant of the desert." Some 160,000 Bedouin, seminomadic Arab tribespeople and full citizens of Israel, live in the Negev. The present-day Bedouin of the Negev (and the Sinai) trace their origins to nomads of the Arabian Peninsula who wandered west 400 to 600 years ago. The exceptions are members of the Jebeliya tribe, descendants of East European slaves sent by Emperor Justinian to serve Greek monks at St. Catherine's Monastery at Mount Sinai. The slaves slowly adopted the Bedouin way of life, and they still serve the monks from their desert nearby.

Since Israel gained independence in 1948, the Bedouin's urbanization and integration into Israeli society has been difficult. The Negev's Bedouin men have loyally served in the Israeli army, and some have lost their lives doing so. Starting in the late 1960s, however, the Israeli government built seven Bedouin towns, the largest of which is Rahat (a settlement of over 40,000 residents, 10 minutes north of Beersheva), and encouraged resettlement. Their simple, nomadic way of life becomes more difficult to maintain each year as they resist these policies.

EARNING A LIVING
The Bedouin's main livelihood is the raising of livestock, camels, and black goats in particular. The animals supply milk, meat, hair for weaving, and dung for burning as fuel. The wanderings of the Bedouin are driven by the unending search for grazing land and water for their flocks. Marriages are arranged, taking family interests into account. It is not uncommon today for a man to have two wives, the first

wife and a younger one to help her. The Bedouin boast one of the highest birth rates in the world.

The family is structured as a business. Men, who work as herders, make decisions about buying and selling livestock as well as finding new pastures. Women and children do the cooking, weaving, searching for firewood, and often caring for the flocks.

HOSPITALITY AND HERITAGE
A Bedouin proverb says, "He who shares my bread and salt is not my enemy." Bedouin are known for their warm hospitality. It is not only a pleasure to extend hospitality; the Bedouin see it as a duty. A Bedouin host would never fail to invite a stranger into his tent. And refusing a Bedouin's invitation would be unthinkable because it would deny the host an opportunity to display his kindness. Having the honor of being invited by a Bedouin host to drink sweet tea or coffee, made over an open fire in his tent, is an unforgettable experience. A Bedouin tent is customarily divided into two sections by a woven curtain known as a *ma'nad.* Having been welcomed into a tent, guests are honored, respected, and nourished, frequently with cardamom-spiced coffee, and with music played on a traditional instrument called the *rababa*, a one-string violin.

A rich heritage of poetry has been passed down through the generations by word of mouth. Only in the past few years have these words been recorded, written in their original Arabic, and preserved by scholars who recognize that the Bedouin way of life is rapidly slipping away.

8

made in an incredibly rustic, mildly hippie-dippie setting. Call in advance to arrange a tasting (try the Yael, a nuanced Cabernet-Merlot fusion) accompanied by a selection of local Negev cheeses. An accomplished artist, Rota has created a free-form sculpture garden around the property, punctuated by his metal creations. He'll tour you around the property and tell you the story of how a Tel Aviv artist became one of the Negev's winemakers to watch. ⊠ *Rte. 222, Revivim* ✛ *40 km (25 miles) south of Beersheva* ☎ *054/496–8703* ⊕ *www. rotawinery.co.il* ⌧ *NIS 35 with minimum group of 10* ⊙ *Closed Fri. and Sat.*

WHERE TO EAT

$$
MOROCCAN
FAMILY

✕ **Authentic.** The decor is rather basic, but this is the place locals dine at for a full range of delicious Moroccan and North African specialties. Try a starter of Moroccan cigars (ground beef wrapped in phyllo dough) with a bowl of lentil soup. Follow it with *ferakh maamer,* delicious spring chicken stuffed with sweetened couscous and simmered in a honey sauce, or with merguez, a spicy lamb sausage. End your meal with a glass of hot mint tea and perhaps a bite of homemade dessert. There's a nice wine menu. $ *Average main: NIS 58* ⊠ *Rasco Shopping Area, 18 Rager Ave.* ☎ *073/782–8177* ⊙ *No table service Fri., just takeout.*

$
MODERN ISRAELI
Fodor's Choice
★

✕ **Cafe Lola.** This whimsically decorated café in the Old City is a breath of fresh air in every respect. Eclectic, funky decor with wooden tables and splashes of color are the backdrop for a menu serving tasty dishes at breakfast, lunch, and dinner. There's a smashing Israeli breakfast for two featuring house-made bread, smoked salmon, and fresh-squeezed juices. Lunch is equally fetching, with a delicious *haloumi* (a firm Greek cheese) salad as a star choice. At night the vibe changes, and the small bar mixes up basic cocktails with flair to go with tapas-style dishes like bruschetta with juicy, thinly sliced steak and preserved lemon. Try one of the thick shakes, like an indulgent combination of dates, candied pecans, and coconut milk. There are nice choices for vegan diners as well, and you can hear live music Monday and Tuesday evenings. $ *Average main: NIS 45* ⊠ *13 Smilansky St., Old City* ☎ *08/628–8937.*

$$
EUROPEAN

✕ **Kapara.** On a tree-lined stretch with old-fashioned streetlights, this is the perfect place for a laid-back meal. Located in a renovated Ottoman-era building in Beersheva's Old City, the rustic restaurant and tapas bar has high ceilings, arabesque tilework, an inner courtyard for alfresco dining, and an atmospheric balcony. Candles flicker from boxes on the walls, and padded chairs and beautifully set tables give the place a serene elegance. There's a separate dining room for families with kids, as well as a bar area. The chef and owner, Yariv Eitani, apprenticed in Provence before returning to his hometown. His creatively prepared tapas-style dishes don't disappoint: wild mushroom risotto, sirloin carpaccio, and seared fresh fish are among the standouts. $ *Average main: NIS 50* ⊠ *23 Smilansky St., Old City* ☎ *08/665–4854* ⊕ *www. rol.co.il/sites/kapara.*

$ ✗**Saba Gepetto.** If you need a break from traditional Middle Eastern
MODERN ISRAELI food, head to Grandpa Gepetto, tucked into an alleyway off a small
shopping mall. The dark, cavelike room features gourmet sandwiches
served on fresh focaccia bread, with fillings ranging from stir-fried
goose breast to chicken breast with pesto. All of them have whimsical names like Mad Cow and Chicken Little. The restaurant offers
English-language menus and an excellent beer selection. For an after-
dinner drink, ask the hostess about Bar Basaba (Grandpa's Bar). She'll
take you around the corner, unlock an unmarked door, and lead you
into the coolest bar in Beersheva, hidden in the courtyard between
office buildings. There you'll find local Negev beers on tap and, for
the homesick, select American beers in bottles. $ *Average main: NIS
45* ✉ *109 Rasco St., near Leonardo Hotel Negev* ☎ *08/627–2829*
⊙ *No lunch Sat.*

$$$$ ✗**Yakota.** On a sleepy corner in the Old City sits this classic Moroccan
MOROCCAN restaurant, run by the same family since the 1960s. Though Yakota—
decorated sumptuously in Moroccan textiles, hammered metal, and
ornate tilework—often seems empty, the food is exceedingly fresh,
creative, and delicious. Just say the word and chef Bebe will order for
you, starting with a course of delicious house-made salads featuring
seasonal ingredients like fennel, dates, and candied oranges, followed by
simmering *tagines* of tender meat and vegetables (even local specialties
like *kmehin*, a tuberlike desert root). For dessert, a local baker prepares
a host of delicate petits fours, delivered to the table on a tiered metal
tower alongside steaming mint tea. $ *Average main: NIS 120* ✉ *27
Mordai Hagettaíot St., Old City* ☎ *08/623–2689* ⊙ *No lunch Sat.*

8

WHERE TO STAY

$$ ⛺**Leonardo Hotel Negev.** The biggest and most well-known chain hotel
HOTEL in town, the Leonardo is a business-oriented hotel that has some ame-
nities with appeal for many travelers. **Pros:** decent rates for what you
get; well-equipped gym; convenient city-center location. **Cons:** listless
service; Internet costs extra. $ *Rooms from: $245* ✉ *4 Henrietta Szold
St., near City Hall* ☎ *08/640–5444* ⊕ *www.leonardo-hotels.com* ⤳ *300
rooms* ⊚ *Breakfast.*

$ ⛺**Trumpeldor Ba'Atika.** The Ottoman Empire's expansion plans in the
B&B/INN early 20th century envisaged Beersheva as a regional capital, and the
Turks built handsome stone structures in what is now the Old City;
this special boutique lodging occupies what could have been an office
complex surrounding a central courtyard. **Pros:** historic and charm-
ing setting; close to restaurants. **Cons:** can be loud, so ask for room
far from main street; some challenges for those with mobility issues;
breakfast not included in price. $ *Rooms from: $140* ✉ *21 Trumpel-
dor St., Old City* ☎ *54/761–1933 for reservations, ask for Oshrat* ⤳ *4
rooms* ⊚ *No meals.*

NIGHTLIFE AND PERFORMING ARTS

BARS

Atica Beersheva Bar. You can choose from 15 beers on tap and five local brews in bottles at this bar in a finely preserved former home with much of its original tilework. This laid-back spot attracts a more mature crowd in the evening. Old-timers may remember a similarly named Attica, but don't be put off; this is a different place. ⊠ *28 Histadrut St., corner of Smilansky St., Old City* ☎ *54/558–7202.*

Coca Bar. Join Ben-Gurion University students for a beer, pizza, and burgers at Coca Bar, behind the student dorms. ⊠ *50 Arlozorov St.* ☎ *050/773–7772.*

MUSIC

Israel Sinfonietta Beer Sheva. This well-regarded symphony orchestra was founded in 1973 as an outlet for immigrant musicians; the concert season includes classical music from around the world as well as some family-focused performances. The orchestra's concert hall seats more than 400 and has state-of-the-art acoustics. ⊠ *Center for Performing Arts, 41 Rager Blvd.* ☎ *08/626–6422* ⊕ *english.isb7.co.il.*

SHOPPING

Bedouin Market. Although the Negev is still home to the Bedouin people, many of today's Bedouin women are less inclined to stay home weaving. But if you have an eagle eye and a saint's patience, Beersheva's Bedouin Market might yield goods made by elder generations. The market starts at daybreak each Thursday and lasts until early afternoon, but it's best to get there early. Walk to the back, passing coffee and tea sellers. For sale, if you can find them, are embroidered dresses, woven camel bags, bales of wool, coin headbands (used as dowry gifts), and *finjans* (Bedouin coffeepots). ⊠ *Derech Eilat and Derech Hevron Sts.*

Wine Aficionado. State-of-the-art design, a stock of imported and local wines, and a knowledgeable staff (including owner Oded Arnat) distinguish this well-established shop. It also sells a well-curated selection of chocolates, olive oils, and coffees. ⊠ *117 Trumpeldor St.* ✢ *Across street from Muslim Cemetery* ☎ *08/628–9444.*

PETRA

Updated by
Shari Helmer

Poet Dean Burgon called Petra, the ancient city of dazzling facades tucked into the mountains of southern Jordan, the "rose red city, half as old as time." Situated between the Red Sea and the Dead Sea, Petra is about two hours north of Eilat and four hours south of the Jordanian capital Amman. Its boulevards, temples, and splendid tombs (800 in all), secreted among the high cliffs, evoke incomparable mystery and grandeur. Once inaccessible to all but an intrepid few, this fabulous archaeological site is now easier to reach and has become an increasingly popular destination.

Petra (called Rekem in the Dead Sea Scrolls) lies in the biblical region of Edom. According to Genesis, the Edomites were descendants of Esau, Jacob's brother and rival. Edom's fertile land was a magnet that desert dwellers couldn't ignore, but the Edomites were careful to keep it exclusive. When Moses led the Israelites to the Promised Land and asked to pass through Edom, he was denied.

By the 7th century BC, a new group had swept in from Arabia: the Nabateans. The spectacular tombs and carved monuments of these intrepid traders draw travelers to Petra today. With a wealthy empire that at its height reached from Damascus to the Sinai, the Nabateans controlled the region's trade routes, their caravans bearing frankincense and myrrh, Indian silks, and African ivory.

Most of Petra's famous tombs—which fuse Greco-Roman, Egyptian, and Mesopotamian styles—were carved during the 1st century AD, before the Nabatean kingdom was subsumed into the Roman Empire. Although the combination of a necropolis and a capital city may seem strange today, this custom was common among ancient peoples, who established cemeteries at the entrances to many of their capitals. The presence of tombs of the rich and powerful near the city's major monuments was perhaps part of a cult of the dead. When travelers came to the city, they would leave offerings at the tombs to honor the success of their journeys.

Gradually, Christianity replaced the old religion, and churches were built in Petra. Around the same time, the rise of sea trade began to precipitate Petra's decline, as ancient traders learned that they could use prevailing winds to hasten ships across the sea. Some Arabian goods began to come to Egypt and its Mediterranean ports via the Red Sea. It didn't help that a series of earthquakes left a ruinous mark on the city.

After Petra's takeover by the Muslims in 633, alliances and crossroads changed and the rest of the world lost interest in the area. The Crusaders built fortifications among the ruins in the 11th century, but after their 1189 surrender to the Muslim warrior Saladin, the city sank into oblivion. Only the local Bedouin knew its treasures. It wasn't until 1812 that Swiss explorer Johann Ludwig Burckhardt rediscovered Petra, providing the Western world with its first contemporary description of the marvels of this Nabatean caravan-city. It's now justly recognized as a UNESCO World Heritage Site.

PETRA PLANNER

WHEN TO GO

Summer temperatures hit 100 degrees, but it can get chilly and rainy in January and February. In all seasons, sturdy shoes are essential for negotiating the rocky, uneven terrain. If traveling during the Muslim holy month of Ramadan, be aware that some services may not be operating or operating at reduced hours; however, all tourist sites and services are open for regular business. Check with your hotel or the tourist office ahead of time.

PLANNING YOUR TIME

An overnight trip to Petra is optimal. Be prepared for a lot of walking: it's about 3 km (2 miles) from the entrance to the Basin restaurant.

Begin at the Horse Square and walk through the narrow, mysterious Siq to the Treasury, Petra's most magnificent facade. From there, continue along what was once the city's main street, lined with monuments from Petra's glory days. Walk along the colonnaded street to the Basin for lunch. The route back is the same, but the sun striking the rocks at different angles reveals new dimensions of the site's beauty; note that the way back is uphill. The horse-drawn carriages you'll see are meant only for the infirm, but they can be hired, gypsy-cab style, by tired pedestrians.

Expect to pay JD 50 for a day pass from the entrance to the Treasury if you are spending the night in Jordan (those who do not stay overnight in Jordan pay JD 90 for entrance). Multiday passes are also available for JD 55 (two days) or JD 60 (three days). In the evening, enjoy the sunset from a hotel balcony or rooftop terrace. Check at the visitor center to see if the Petra by Night tour is on.

Petra

KEY
- ━━━ Main Roads
- ═══ Unpaved Roads
- ∷∷ Steps
- ⋯⋯ Paths

Bab a-Siq **5**
Broken Pediment Tomb .. **13**
Byzantine Church **22**
Colonnaded Street **23**
Corinthian Tomb **17**
Djinn Blocks **2**
Great Temple **21**

High Place of Sacrifice **8**
Horse Square **1**
Lion Monument **10**
Monastery **26**
Nymphaeum **20**
Obelisk Tomb **4**
Obelisks **9**

Palace Tomb **18**
Qasr al-Bint **25**
Renaissance Tomb **12**
Roman Soldier's Tomb .. **11**
Silk Tomb **16**
Siq **6**
Snake Tomb **3**

Temple of the
Winged Lions **24**
Theater **14**
Tomb of Sextius
Florentinus **19**
Treasury **7**
Urn Tomb **15**

On the second day, you can return to the Treasury and explore other sites, perhaps making the climb up to the Monastery. There are lots of well-stocked souvenir shops near the visitor center if you're looking for something to take home.

GETTING HERE AND AROUND

AIR TRAVEL

El Al and Royal Jordanian Airlines both fly to Amman, Jordan's capital, from Tel Aviv's Ben Gurion Airport. This option has limited appeal, as you must be at the airport two hours before flight time for the 15-minute flight, then drive three hours from Amman to Petra.

Many people use Eilat, the resort city at the southern tip of Israel, as a base for exploring Petra. There are frequent flights to Eilat from Tel Aviv and Haifa. Two domestic airlines serve Eilat: Arkia and Israir. A new international airport is under construction there and expected to open sometime in 2017. (*See Eilat and the Negev for more information.*)

CAR TRAVEL

Israeli rental cars can't be taken into Jordan, so if you want your own wheels you'll have to arrange for one in Amman or Aqaba. Shared taxis at the Israel-Jordan border can take you into Aqaba, where you can rent a car. A shared taxi to Aqaba costs about JD 10, which is divided among the passengers.

TAXI TRAVEL

Taxis from the Israel-Jordan border to Aqaba cost JD 10. If your time is limited, consider taking a private taxi all the way to Petra, which will run you JD 45 to JD 50. Be prepared to negotiate.

CROSSING THE BORDER

The closest border crossing to Petra is just north of Eilat at what's called the Arava Crossing. Cross the border early in the morning to avoid waiting in line behind large tour groups and so that you can be in Petra before noon. It's about a two-hour ride to Petra. Expect to pay NIS 109 to exit Israel. When crossing back from Jordan to Israel, bring JD 10 for the Jordanian exit tax.

Americans need a visa to enter Jordan. It can be bought on the spot at Arava Crossing for about JD 40.

Two other border crossings might be convenient if you don't plan to visit Eilat, but both of these options require you to arrange for a visa in advance. The Allenby Bridge Crossing (known in Jordan as the King Hussein Crossing) is about 45 minutes from Jerusalem. From the border it's a four-hour drive to Petra. The northern Beit She'an Crossing is approximately 40 minutes from Tiberias. Once you're across it's a five-hour drive to Petra. Note that you cannot get a visa at these borders, so arrange one in advance at the Jordanian consulate. The exit tax to leave from these crossings is NIS 176.

Regardless of where or how you cross the border, the rules can change, often without any advance notice. We strongly advise anyone planning a trip to Petra to use a knowledgeable and experienced tour operator.

MONEY MATTERS

The Jordanian unit of currency is the dinar, abbreviated JD. The exchange rate at this writing was approximately JD 0.71 to the U.S. dollar. You can change money at the Mövenpick Resort Petra, next to the entrance to Petra.

WHAT IT COSTS			
$	**$$**	**$$$**	**$$$$**
Restaurants Under JD 9	JD 9–JD 12	JD 13–JD 17	over JD 17
Hotels Under $75	$75–$129	$130–$200	over $200

Restaurant prices, in Jordanian dinar, are the average cost of a main course at dinner or, if dinner is not served, at lunch. Hotel prices, in U.S. dollars, are the lowest cost of a standard double room in high season.

TOURS

A number of operators run tours to Petra that you can reserve in advance from Eilat. They're an excellent option to see the highlights without worrying about what can be rather complex logistics.

Arkia. Several times a week, Arkia Israeli Airlines offers one-day guided tours in which you fly from Tel Aviv to Eilat, then drive to Petra in an air-conditioned bus. You return the same evening. ☎ *03/690–2255* ⊕ *www.arkia.com/petra-day-tours-c182* ✉ *From $375 for 1-day tour to Petra from Tel Aviv.*

Fodor'sChoice **Desert Eco Tours.** Consistently friendly and professional service is why
★ Desert Eco Tours is a popular choice for travelers who want a tour. In addition to Petra, the company can arrange other tours in Jordan, as well as more extensive travel to Egypt and the Sinai Desert. ✉ *Eilat* ☎ *08/632–6477* ⊕ *desertecotours.com* ✉ *From $249 (excluding $125 for visa, taxes, and tips) for 1-day tour to Petra from Eilat.*

VISITOR INFORMATION

Petra Visitor Center. The visitor center, next to the main entrance, is stocked with maps and brochures and can help you arrange local guides for a basic two-hour Petra tour for a flat fee of JD 15. If the weather is particularly hot, or if you're simply interested in the long and fascinating history of the place, check out the museumlike exhibition. It's a compact overview of Petra and will not take more than 15 minutes, but the site miniatures are helpful in getting your bearings before your visit. A one-day pass costs JD 50, a two-day pass JD 55. If you don't stay overnight in Jordan, a one-day pass costs JD 90. ✉ *Petra* ☎ *03/215–6029 Israel phone number* ⊕ *visitpetra.jo.*

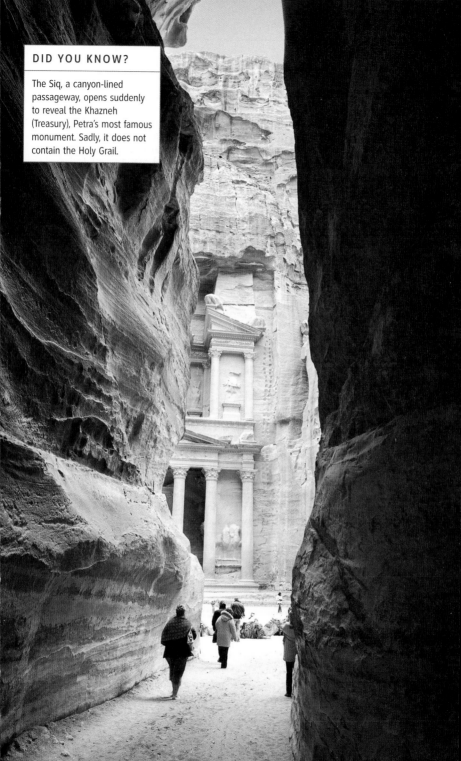

EXPLORING PETRA

TOP ATTRACTIONS

Colonnaded Street. The Romans built the main street of Petra in the early 1st century BC. In typical Roman style, it became the city's major thoroughfare, suitable for both commerce and grand ceremonial processions. After the Roman annexation of the Nabatean kingdom, the street was restored, as noted in an inscription dated AD 114, and dedicated to Emperor Trajan. The original marble paving stones as well as remains of statues of deities still stand, including those depicting Hermes (messenger of the gods) and Tyche (goddess of fortune). In AD 363 an earthquake devastated Petra and the surrounding region, and the street never returned to its former glory. ⊠ *Petra* ⊕ *visitpetra.jo.*

Great Temple. No one can say for sure which god was worshipped at this temple, or whether it was the seat of the city's government. But the dozens of columns that adorn its courtyards, beautifully restored by archaeologists from Brown University, attest to its ancient grandeur. The building even boasted its own theater, which some scholars believe may have been a meeting hall for Petra's rulers. ⊠ *Petra* ⊕ *visitpetra.jo.*

Fodor'sChoice

★ **Monastery** (*Al-Deir*). Second only to the Treasury in its magnificence, the Monastery is reached at the end of a winding uphill 4-km (2½-mile) trail. It's larger than the Treasury (it stands 170 feet wide), but less impressively ornate. An inscription was discovered nearby referring to "the symposium of Obodas the God." From this inscription, archeologists deduced that the Monastery was built 2,000 years ago as a meeting place for members of the cult of Obodas. Either tomb or temple, it holds a spacious chamber cut deep into the mountainside, and offers sweeping views of the adjacent gorges. ⊠ *Petra* ⊕ *visitpetra.jo.*

Qasr al-Bint. This structure's full name, which translates as the "Palace of the Daughter of Pharaoh," derives from a legend that the pharaoh's daughter promised she would marry the man who could channel water to the city where she lived. When she had to choose between two winners, she asked each how he had managed his appointed task. The one whose answer she preferred won her hand. In fact, the structure was the most important temple in Petra, built in the early 1st century AD. As in the Temple of the Winged Lions, the identity of the deity worshipped here isn't known, but a statue depicting him or her—perhaps Dushara, the greatest deity of the Nabatean pantheon—stood in the temple's inner sanctum. A giant marble hand, part of a colossal statue, was discovered here in 1959. ⊠ *Petra* ⊕ *visitpetra.jo.*

Siq. The main entrance to Petra, in ancient times as well as today, winds through the Siq (meaning "cleft"), a long, narrow canyon between towering walls of astonishing red and purple-hued stone. Bands of Nabatean paving stones are still visible along the way. Votive niches, some of which contain inscriptions dating from the 2nd and 3rd centuries AD, show that this road served as much as a ceremonial path as a passageway. Your first glimpse of the magnificent Treasury,

after you've walked a hundred meters or so through the Siq, will take your breath away. Film buffs may recall Harrison Ford galloping through this area in *Indiana Jones and the Last Crusade*. ⊠ *Petra* ⊕ *visitpetra.jo.*

Temple of the Winged Lions. This impressive building overlooking the Colonnaded Street takes its name from the sculptures that serve as capitals for its columns. The identity of the deity worshipped within is unknown, but votive figurines suggest that it may have been Isis, Egyptian goddess of the heavens and patroness of fertility. An inscription dates the construction of the temple to around AD 27, during the reign of Aretas IV. ⊠ *Petra* ⊕ *visitpetra.jo.*

Theater. This semicircular amphitheater is a clear sign of the extent to which the Nabateans, like most other peoples of this region, had adopted Roman culture. The Nabateans apparently had no qualms about building a theater in a cemetery; their stonemasons even cut into some of the existing tombs (the remains of which you can see at the back of the rock-cut theater) to do so. The capacity of the theater has been estimated at 7,000. ⊠ *Petra* ⊕ *visitpetra.jo.*

Fodor'sChoice
★
Treasury (*Khazneh*). The Siq opens suddenly onto Petra's most famous monument, known locally as the Khazneh. This 130-foot-tall structure displays a splendid frontage graced by a number of mythological figures adopted by the Nabateans from Greek and Roman worship. Castor and Pollux (who after their deaths became the two brightest stars in the constellation Gemini), Amazons, Gorgons, eagles, and other creatures march across the Khazneh's rosy facade. Between the columns of the *tholos* (the rounded section above the tympanum) are the remains of a female deity holding a cornucopia; she is believed to be al-Uzza, the patroness of Petra and the Nabatean version of Aphrodite, goddess of love.

The full Arabic name for this monument is Khazneh Fara'un, or Pharaoh's Treasury. It was assumed by archaeologists to be a royal tomb, and legends of treasures allegedly secreted within have drawn grave robbers to this place for centuries. The urn carved at the top of the tholos was thought to be the hiding place for the hoard. The Bedouin have been taking potshots at it for generations in the hopes of dislodging its contents, a practice whose results are still visible. ⊠ *Petra* ⊕ *visitpetra.jo.*

WORTH NOTING

Bab a-Siq. The Gate of the Cleft opens onto the Siq, the canyon-lined passageway leading to Petra's main sights. From here you can spot the remains of a Nabatean tunnel, built to divert flood waters from coursing through the narrow cleft and flooding the necropolis. A dam, constructed for the same purpose in the second half of the 1st century AD, was restored by the Jordanians in 1963 and again in 1991. ⊠ *Petra* ⊕ *visitpetra.jo.*

Broken Pediment Tomb. One of a series of facades carved into the western face of Jabal Madhbah, or the Mount of the Altar, this tomb is characterized by the broken-off gable of its roof, supported by four pilasters topped with Nabatean capitals. ⊠ *Petra* ⊕ *visitpetra.jo.*

Byzantine Church. Richly decorated with mosaics in the characteristic style of the period, this church (discovered by the American archaeologist Kenneth Russell, and excavated in the 1990s) appears to have been destroyed by fire soon after its construction, perhaps in the severe earthquake of AD 551. The remains, including a spectacular mosaic floor, have undergone only partial conservation; 140 papyrus scrolls were found here. ⊠ *Petra* ⊕ *visitpetra.jo.*

Corinthian Tomb. Set among some of Petra's finest tombs is one named for its large number of Corinthian capitals, now badly deteriorated, that once decorated its facade. ⊠ *Petra* ⊕ *visitpetra.jo.*

Djinn Blocks. The function of these three large structures is unclear; they may have been connected to Nabatean worship, perhaps symbolizing one of their deities. In Arabic, *djinn* refers to malevolent spirits, a common theme in Arab folklore. You may recognize them by their anglicized name, "genies."⊠ *Petra* ⊕ *visitpetra.jo.*

High Place of Sacrifice. An ancient flight of stairs cut into the rock—and restored by the Jordanian Department of Antiquities—leads to the summit of Jabal Madhbah, or the Mount of the Altar. Its peak, besides offering spectacular views of Petra below, contains a rectangular court surrounded on three sides by benches in the triclinium style of the Roman dining room. In the center of the court is a raised block of stone, upon which the priest may have stood. To the west are two altars accessed by steps, as well as a channel into which the blood of sacrificial animals drained. ⊠ *Petra* ⊕ *visitpetra.jo.*

Horse Square. Horses used to be the conveyance of choice for the approximately 1-km (½-mile) trip to Petra's main buildings. The admission price entitles you to a horseback ride along the first 800 yards of the path to the Siq. Offer a tip of about JD 5. ⊠ *Petra* ⊕ *visitpetra.jo.*

Lion Monument. Surface runoff fed this fountain along the path to the High Place of Sacrifice via a channel leading to the lion's mouth. ⊠ *Petra* ⊕ *visitpetra.jo.*

Nymphaeum. Dedicated to water nymphs, this fountain was used for both refreshment and worship. The fountains of the two-story structure were fed by a channel that continued along the city's main street. ⊠ *Petra* ⊕ *visitpetra.jo.*

Obelisk Tomb. This upper story of a two-story tomb is named for the four freestanding obelisks that decorate its facade. The lower story, the Triclinium Tomb, was so named because three walls of the empty room are lined with *triclinia*, a Latin word for this kind of bench. Sacred memorial feasts to honor the dead were held here. ⊠ *Petra* ⊕ *visitpetra.jo.*

Obelisks. On a terrace stand two obelisks hewed from the bedrock, examples of a common method of representing deities in the ancient Near East. Some scholars believe them to be representations of Dushara and al-Uzza; others believe they are simply the remains of quarries. ⊠ *Petra* ⊕ *visitpetra.jo.*

Palace Tomb. This unfinished tomb is one of the few in Petra not carved entirely out of solid rock. Many of the tomb's constructed segments

9

have fallen away, so it's hard to ascertain its original dimensions. At the base of the Palace Tomb are the remains of the northern city wall, built after the 1st century BC. ⊠ *Petra* ⊕ *visitpetra.jo.*

Renaissance Tomb. This tomb, bearing a pediment with three urns, bears a close resemblance to the Tomb of Sextius Florentinus in the main part of the city. It may have been created around the same time, the first third of the 1st century AD. ⊠ *Petra* ⊕ *visitpetra.jo.*

Roman Soldier's Tomb. The headless figure in the niche of this unusual tomb's facade is dressed in typical Roman military garb, while the friezes and floral capitals appear more typical of Nabatean architecture before the Roman annexation. Directly opposite the Roman Soldier's Tomb is a triclinium; the rubble in between was probably once a colonnaded courtyard connecting the two edifices. ⊠ *Petra* ⊕ *visitpetra.jo.*

Silk Tomb. The striations of natural color in the Silk Tomb's rock make it one of Petra's finest (and certainly one of the easiest to spot). The ribbons of rock flow across the facade like a multicolored silk scarf blowing in the wind. ⊠ *Petra* ⊕ *visitpetra.jo.*

Snake Tomb. No outward decoration marks this tomb, but 12 burial niches are carved into the floor inside. The name comes from a rough wall relief that shows two snakes attacking what may be a dog. Notice also the horse-and-rider relief above it. ⊠ *Petra* ⊕ *visitpetra.jo.*

Tomb of Sextius Florentinus. This is one of the few Petra monuments that can be dated with certainty: the name of this Roman governor of Arabia who died in office in AD 128 appears in the Latin inscription over the tomb's doorway. ⊠ *Petra* ⊕ *visitpetra.jo.*

Urn Tomb. Named for the vaselike decoration at the top of its pediment, this is the largest of Petra's royal tombs. It is supported by a series of vaults at its lower level, dubbed *al makhamah* (the law court) by the locals for some long-lost reason; the upper level was called *a-sijn* (the prison). Although originally carved around AD 70, according to an inscription within, Petra's Byzantine Christians turned the Urn Tomb into a church in AD 446. ⊠ *Petra* ⊕ *visitpetra.jo.*

WHERE TO EAT

Dining in the town closest to the antiquities site of Petra—Wadi Musa—ranges from simple, inexpensive fare to the elegant and pricey, with little in between. Both dining experiences, however, have one thing in common: courteous service and a welcoming spirit. Don't be put off by the plainness of center-village eateries. The locals enjoying their meal at the next table will remind you that the best fare is often to be had at such unostentatious restaurants.

$

MIDDLE EASTERN

✕ **Al-Arabi.** This simple but bright eatery is a reliable place for a quick, inexpensive lunch. You can expect a substantial meal, including hummus, shawarma, and a tasty mixed grill (the house specialty). Look for the red sign on the left as you walk uphill. ⑤ *Average main: JD8* ⊠ *Main St.* ☎ *03/215–7661.*

$$$ · ✕ **The Basin.** The only eatery inside the archaeological site, this restau-

MIDDLE EASTERN · rant at the end of the Colonnaded Street serves a buffet lunch with a variety of offerings. Run by the Crowne Plaza hotel chain, the bright dining room caters to large tour groups and is ready for a crowd. The air-conditioning and restroom facilities are a welcome break after a dusty day of hiking. $ *Average main: JD17* ✉ *Colonnaded St.* ☎ *03/215–6266.*

$$$$ · ✕ **Petra Kitchen.** If you're in town for more than the day and are looking

MIDDLE EASTERN · for a different kind of experience, Petra Kitchen is an enticing choice. You meet other visitors as you chop, slice, and cook your meal, learning how to make and present Jordanian specialties like *maqluba*, a layered meat-and-vegetable dish, and *fattoush*, a moistened bread salad. Then you sample what you've made. Dinners usually begin around 6:30 pm and run for three hours. Market tours can be arranged with advance notice. $ *Average main: JD35* ✉ *Main St.* ☎ *03/215–5900* ⊕ *www. petrakitchen.com.*

WHERE TO STAY

Petra has many lodging options. You can choose from luxurious to money-saving accommodations; both can be found adjacent to or near the site. The hotels closest to the site obviously provide the most convenient access to Petra and save you taxi money. A short car drive away in Wadi Musa are several good hotels, with some on the ridge above Wadi Musa. Taybet Zaman, in the village of Taybeh 9 km (5½ miles) from Petra, is the farthest from the site, but its uniquely authentic flavor is worth the ride.

$$$$ · ⬚ **Mövenpick Resort Petra.** Just steps from the entrance to Petra, this

HOTEL · Swiss-run hotel blends Middle Eastern style and Western amenities.

Fodor'sChoice · **Pros:** wonderful restaurant; excellent breakfast buffet; quiet setting.

★ · **Cons:** slow Internet. $ *Rooms from: US$250* ✉ *Tourism St.* ☎ *03/215– 7111* ⊕ *www.movenpick.com* ⤳ *183 rooms* ⦿| *Breakfast.*

$$$$ · ⬚ **Petra Marriott Hotel.** This excellent three-story hotel sits on the

HOTEL · ridge above Petra, so most rooms offer spectacular views of the valley below. **Pros:** stunning sunset views; Petra's best Italian restaurant, L'Affresco. **Cons:** 15-minute drive to Petra entrance; does not change Israeli currency. $ *Rooms from: US$210* ✉ *Queen Rania Al Abdallah St.* ☎ *03/215–6407* ⊕ *www.marriott.com* ⤳ *100 rooms* ⦿| *No meals.*

$$ · ⬚ **Petra Moon Hotel.** This perfectly located hotel, 300 feet from the main

HOTEL · entrance to Petra, has rapidly become a favorite with visitors to the site.

Fodor'sChoice · **Pros:** convenient location; great service. **Cons:** expensive restaurant.

★ · $ *Rooms from: US$115* ✉ *Tourism St.* ☎ *03/215–6220* ⊕ *www.petra- moonhotel.com* ⤳ *52 rooms* ⦿| *Breakfast.*

$$$ · ⬚ **Taybet Zaman Hotel.** On the outskirts of the town of Taybeh, 9 km

HOTEL · (5½ miles) from Petra, this charming lodging was an abandoned Bed-

FAMILY · ouin village before it was revamped into a serene hotel that has every modern amenity. **Pros:** on a ridge high above Petra; lovely garden terrace; excellent service. **Cons:** not within walking distance of Petra. $ *Rooms from: US$190* ✉ *Queen Rania St.* ☎ *03/215–0111* ⤳ *110 rooms* ⦿| *Breakfast.*

9

NIGHTLIFE AND PERFORMING ARTS

Petra by Night. Strolling through the Siq by candlelight as shadows play on the canyon walls allows you to appreciate another side of the magnificent carved city. During this two-hour event offered on Monday, Wednesday, and Thursday starting at 8:30 pm, music is played on traditional instruments such as the *rababa*. If you arrive in the evening, it's a good introduction to the ancient city. Keep in mind that the walk through the Siq to the Treasury is about 1 km (½ mile)—downhill on the way in, uphill on the way back; it begins at the visitor center. There are no carriages at night. ⊠ *Petra* ☎ *03/215–6029* ⊕ *www.visitpetra. jo* ☜ *JD 17.*

SHOPPING

Petra's handicraft specialty is the work of its "sand artists"—artisans who fill bottles with sand in a variety of hues and complex designs. They mine the various colored sands from the area. Artists can customize the purchase by writing a name or other text in the sand; they work and sell their unique wares in shops in Wadi Musa, as well as in the Siq.

Petra Sand Castle. The largest souvenir shop of all is the Petra Sand Castle, a four-room maze with everything from inlaid backgammon boards to handwoven rugs to flowing scarfs. Ask to visit the back room to see what the owners call their personal Ali Baba Cave filled with antique Bedouin silver and other crafts. This is one place to get a sand bottle. ⊠ *Main St.* ⊕ *www.petrasandcastle.com.*

UNDERSTANDING ISRAEL

HEBREW VOCABULARY

Many people in Israel speak at least one other language, in addition to Hebrew, and most can get by in English. So the chances of getting too lost for words are slim. At the same time, your traveling experience can be enriched by having at least a few words to share in conversation or to use while touring and shopping, even at the local grocery store. Here are some basic words and expressions that may be of use during your stay. Please note that the letters "kh" in this glossary are pronounced like the "ch" in chanuka or the Scottish loch.

ENGLISH	HEBREW TRANSLITERATION	PRONUNCIATION

GREETINGS AND BASICS

ENGLISH	HEBREW TRANSLITERATION	PRONUNCIATION
Hello/good-bye/peace	Shalom	shah-**lohm**
Nice to meet you	Na'im me'od	nah-**eem** meh-**ohd**
Good morning	Boker tov	boh-ker **tohv**
Good evening	Erev tov	eh-rev **tohv**
Good night	Layla tov	lahy-lah tohv
How are you?	Ma shlomekh?	mah shloh-**maykh**
How are you? (to a man)	Ma shlomkha?	mah shlohm-**khah**
How are you?	Ma nishma?	mah-nee-**shmah**
Fine	Beseder	beh-**say-dehr**
Everything is fine	Hakol beseder	hah-kohl beh-**say-dehr**
Is everything okay?	Hakol beseder?	hah-kohl beh-**say-dehr**
Very well	Tov me'od	tohv-meh-**ohd**
Excellent/terrific	Metzuyan	meh-tzoo-**yahn**
Send regards!	Timsor dash!	teem-sohr **dahsh**
Thank you	Toda	toh-**dah**
Thank you very much	Toda raba	toh-dah rah-**bah**
See you again	Lehitra'ot	leh-heet-rah-**oht**
Yes	Ken	kehn
No	Lo	lo
Maybe	Oolai	**oo**-ligh
Excuse me/Sorry	Slicha	slee-**khah**
Again/Could you repeat that?	Od pa'am	ohd pah-**ahm**

ENGLISH	HEBREW TRANSLITERATION	PRONUNCIATION

DAYS

Today	Hayom	hah-**yohm**
Tomorrow	Machar	mah-**khahr**
Yesterday	Etmol	eht-**mohl**
Sunday	Yom Rishon	yohm ree-**shohn**
Monday	Yom Sheni	yohm sheh-**nee**
Tuesday	Yom Shlishi	yohm sh-**leeshee**
Wednesday	Yom Revi'i	yohm reh-**vee**
Thursday	Yom Chamishi	yohm kha-mee-**shee**
Friday	Yom Shishi	yohm shee-**shee**
Saturday, Sabbath	Shabbat	yohm shah-**bat**

NUMBERS

1	Echad	eh-**khad**
2	Shtayim	shtah-**yeem**
3	Shalosh	shah-**lohsh**
4	Arba	ah-**rbah**
5	Chamesh	chah-**maysh**
6	Shesh	shehsh
7	Sheva	**sheh**-vah
8	Shmoneh	**shmoh**-neh
9	Teisha	**tay**-shah
10	Esser	**eh**-sehr
11	Achad esreh	ah-**chahd** eh-**sreh**
12	Shteim esreh	sht**aym** eh-**sreh**
20	Esrim	eh-**sreem**
50	Chamishim	khah-mee-**sheem**
100	Me'a	may-**ah**
200	Ma'tayim	mah-**tah**-yeem

ENGLISH	HEBREW TRANSLITERATION	PRONUNCIATION

USEFUL PHRASES

ENGLISH	HEBREW TRANSLITERATION	PRONUNCIATION
Do you speak English?	Ata medaber anglit?	ah-ta meh-dah-ber ahng-**leet**
I don't understand (man)	Ani lo mevin	a-**nee** loh meh-**veen**
I don't understand (woman)	Ani lo m'vina	a-**nee** m'veena
I don't know (man)	Ani lo yodea	a-nee loh yoh-**day**-ah
I don't know (woman)	Ani lo yodaat	a-nee loh yoh-**dah**-aht
I am lost (man)	Ani avud	a-nee ah-**vood**
I am lost (woman)	Ani avuda	a-nee ahvoo-**dah**
I am American	Ani Amerika'i	ah-nee ah-mer-ee-**kah**-ee
I am British	Ani Briti	ah-**nee bree**-tee
I am Canadian	Ani Canadi	ah-**nee** kah-**nah**-dee
What is the time?	Ma hasha'a?	mah hah-shah-**ah**
Just a minute	Rak rega	rahk **reh**-gah
Minute, moment	Rega	**reh**-gah
Now	Achshav	ahkh-**shahv**
Not yet	Od lo	ohd loh
Later	Achar kach	ah-**khahr** kahkh
I would like	Hayiti mevakesh	hah-**yee**-tee m-vah-**kehsh**
Where is..?	Eifo..?	**ay**foh
The central bus station	Hatachana hamerkazit	hah-tah-khah-**nah** hah-mehr-kah-**zeet**
The bus stop	Tachanat ha'autobus	tah-khah-**naht** hah-oh-toh-**boos**
The train station	Tachanat harakevet	tah-khah-**naht** hah-rah-**keh-veht**
The city center	Merkaz ha'ir	mehr kahz hah-**eer**
The post office	Hado'ar	hah-**doh**-ahr
A pharmacy	Beit mirkachat	bayt meer-**kah**-khaht

ENGLISH	HEBREW TRANSLITERATION	PRONUNCIATION
A public telephone	Telefon tziburi	teh-leh-**fohn** tzee-boo-**ree**
A good restaurant	Mis'ada tova	mee-sah-**dah toh-vah**
The rest rooms	Hasherutim	hah-shay-roo-**teem**
Right	Yemina	yeh-**mee**-nah
Left	Smola	s-**moh**-lah
Straight ahead	Yashar	yah-**shar**
Here	Kan	kahn
There	Sham	shahm
Do you have a (vacant) room?	Yesh lachem cheder (panui)?	yehsh lah-**chehm khed**-ehr (pah-**nooy**)
Is it possible to order a taxi?	Efshar lehazmin monit?	ehf-**shahr** leh-hahz-**meen** moh-**neet**
Taxi	Monit	moh-**neet**
A little	k'tzat	keh-**tzaht**
A lot	harbe	hahr-**beh**
Enough	maspik	Mah-**speek**
I have a problem	Yesh li ba'aya	yehsh lee bah-**yah**
I don't feel well (man)	Ani lo margish tov	ah-**nee** loh mahr-**geesh** tohv
I don't feel well (woman)	Ani lo margisha tov	ah-**nee** loh mahr-**gee-shah** tohv
I need a doctor (man)	Ani tzarich rofe	ah-**nee** tzah-**reech** roh-**feh**
I need a doctor (woman)	Ani tzricha rofe	ah-**nee** tzree-**khah** roh-**feh**
Help	Ezra	Eh-**zrah**
Fire	Dleika	duh-leh-**kah**

DINING

I would like	Hayiti mevakesh	hah-**yee**-tee m-vah-**kehsh**
Some water, please	Mayim, bevakasha	mah-**yeem** beh-vah-kah-**shah**
Bread	Lechem	**leh**-khehm

ENGLISH	HEBREW TRANSLITERATION	PRONUNCIATION
Soup	Marak	mah-**rahk**
Meat	Bassar	bah-**ssahr**
Chicken	Off	ohf
Vegetables	Yerakot	yeh-rah-**koht**
Dessert	Kinuach	kee-**noo**-ahkh
Cake	Ooga	**oo**-gah
Fruit	Perot	peh-**roht**
Coffee	Cafe	kah-**feh**
Tea	Te	teh
Fork	Mazleg	mahz-**lehg**
Spoon	Kapit	kah-**peet**
Knife	Sakin	sah-**keen**
Plate	Tzalachat	tzah-**lah**-chaht
Napkin	Mapit	mah-**peet**
Food	Ochel	**oh**-khehl
Meal	Arucha	ah-roo-**khah**
Breakfast	Aruchat boker	ah-roo-**khaht boh**-ker
Lunch	Aruchat tzaharayim	ah-roo-khaht tzah-hah-**rah**-yeem
Dinner	Aruchat erev	Ahroo-**khaht eh**-rehv
Do you have a menu in English?	Yesh tafrit be'anglit?	yehsh tahf-**reet** beh- ahng-**leet**
A pita filled with falafel	Manat felafel	mah-naht feh-**lah**-fehl
Without hot sauce	Bli charif	blee khah-**reef**
It's tasty, delicious	Zeh ta'im	zeh tah-**eem**
I don't like the taste	Zeh lo ta'im li	zeh loh tah-**eem** lee
The check, please	Cheshbon, bevakasha	Khehsh-bohn beh-vah-kah-**shah**

ENGLISH	HEBREW TRANSLITERATION	PRONUNCIATION

SHOPPING

ENGLISH	HEBREW TRANSLITERATION	PRONUNCIATION
Do you have..?	Yesh lecha..?	yesh leh-khah
Milk	Chalav	khah-**lahv**
(Orange) Juice	Mitz (tapuzim)	meetz (tah-poo-**zeem**)
Butter	Chem'a	khem-**ah**
Cream cheese	Gevina levana	geh-vee-**nah** leh-vah-**nah**
Hard cheese	Gevina tzehuba	gevee-**nah** tzeh-**hoo**-bah
Sausage	Naknik	Nahk-**neek**
Jelly	Riba	**ree**-bah
Sugar	Sukar	**soo**-kahr
Ice cream	Glida	**glee**-da
Map	Mapa	**mah**-pa
Cigarettes	Sigariyot	see-gahr-ee-**yoht**
Telephone card (for public phones)	Telecart	teh-leh-**kahrt**
That one, please	Et zeh, bevakasha	eht zeh, beh-vah-kah-**shah**
May I see it?	Efshar lir'ot?	ehf-**shahr** leer-**oht**
How much does it cost?	Kama zeh oleh?	**kah**-ma zeh **ohleh**
That's expensive!	Yakar!	yah-**kahr**
No, it's too expensive	Lo, zeh yakar midai	loh, zeh yah-**kahr** meed-**igh**
Too big	Gadol midai	gah-dohl meed-**igh**
Too small	Katan midai	kah-tan meed-**igh**
Perhaps there's a discount ?	Yesh hanacha oolai	Yehsh hah-na-**khah** oo-ligh oo-**ligh**
I'll take it	Ani ekach et zeh	ah-nee eh-**kakh** eht zeh

PALESTINIAN ARABIC VOCABULARY

Arabic is spoken by all Arab citizens of Israel (about 20% of the Israeli population) and in the West Bank and Gaza. The areas where you're most likely to hear Arabic are East Jerusalem, Jaffa, and Nazareth, and in the popular sites of the West Bank, Bethlehem, and Jericho (when these are open to travelers). Many people in these areas speak some English, but a little Arabic will come in handy with some vendors and taxi drivers or when you're in more rural areas and villages. It helps to have a written address for a taxi ride as well. You may run into small differences in dialect and accent between villages and cities, but for the most part Palestinians' dialects are similar.

Some letters in Arabic don't have English equivalents. This glossary tries to approximate Arabic sounds. The letter 'r' is always rolled. When you see 'gh' at the start of a word, pronounce it like a French 'r', lightly gargled at the back of the throat. Any double letters should be extended: 'aa' is pronounced as an extended 'ah'; 'hh' is an extended 'h' sound; 'ss' is an extended hiss.

ENGLISH	ARABIC TRANSLITERATION	PRONUNCIATION
GREETINGS AND BASICS		
Hello/ peace be upon you	salamou alaikom	sah-**lah**-moo aah-**lay**-kom
(reply) Hello/ and peace be upon you	wa aalaikom essalaam	wah aah-**lay**-kom **ehss**-sah-**ahm**
Good-bye	maa issalameh	**maah** is-**ah-lah**-meh
Mr./ Sir	sayyed	**sigh**-yed
Mrs./ Madam	sayyida	**sigh**-yee-dah
Miss	anisseh	**ah**-niss-say
How are you? (man speaking)	keif hhalak	kayf **hah**-luck
How are you? (woman speaking)	keif hhalik	kayf **hah**-lik
Fine, thank you	bi kheir elhhamdilla	bee **khayr** el-**ham**-dihl-lah
Pleased to meet you	tsharrafna	tshahr-**ruhf**-nah
Please (man)	min fadlak	min **fahd**-lahk
Please (woman)	min fadlik	min **fahd**-lik
Thank you	shokran	shohk-rahn
God willing	Inshallah	ihn-**shahl-lah**
Yes	aah or naam	aah or naahm
No	la	lah

ENGLISH	ARABIC TRANSLITERATION	PRONUNCIATION
I'm Sorry (man)	mit assif	miht **ass**-sef
I'm Sorry (woman)	mit assfeh	miht **ass**-feh

DAYS

Today	eliom	el-**yohm**
Tomorrow	bokra	bok-rah
Yesterday	embarehh	ehm-**bah**-rehh
Sunday	il ahhad	**il ah**-had
Monday	Ittinein	it-tee-**nayn**
Tuesday	ittalata	it-tah-**lah**-tah
Wednesday	il 'arbaa	il **ahr**-bah-**aah**
Thursday	il khamees	il khah-**mees**
Friday	iljumaa	il zhum-**aah**
Saturday	issabet	**iss-sah**-bet

NUMBERS

1	wahed	**wah**-hed
2	tinein	tee-**nayn**
3	talati	tah-**lah**-tee
4	arbaa	**ahr**-bah-aah
5	khamseh	**khahm**-seh
6	sitteh	**sit**-teh
7	sabaa	sub-**aah**
8	tamanyeh	tah-**mah**-nee-**yeh**
9	tisaa	**tiss**-aah
10	aashara	**aah**-shah-rah
11	ihhdaaesh	ihh-**dah**-ehsh
12	itnaaesh	it-**nah**-ehsh
20	ishreen	iish-**reen**
50	khamseen	khahm-**seen**
100	meyyeh	**may**-yeh
200	mitein	**mee**-tain

ENGLISH	ARABIC TRANSLITERATION	PRONUNCIATION
USEFUL PHRASES		
Do you speak English?	btihki inglizi?	btih-**kee** in-**glee**-zee?
I don't understand (man)	mish fahem	mish **fah**-him
I don't understand (woman)	mish fahmi	mish **fah**-meh
I don't know (man)	mish aarif	mish **aah**-ref
I don't know (woman)	mish aarfi	mish **aahr**-fee
I'm lost (man)	ana dayih	ah-nah **dah**-yeh
I'm lost (woman)	ana dayaa	ah-nah **dah**-ye-aah
I am American (man)	ana amriki	ah-nah ahm-**ree**-kee
I am American (woman)	ana amrikiyya	ah-nah ahm-**ree-key**-yah
I am British (man)	ana baritani	ah-nah bah-**ree-tah**-nee
I am British (woman)	ana baritaniya	ah-nah bah-**ree-tah-nay**-yah
What is this?	eish hada?	aysh **hah**-dah?
What time is it?	Addeish el wa'ed?	Ahd-**daysh**-el **wah**-ed
Where is?	wein?	wayn?
The train station	mahattit iltrain	mah-huht-**tit il-train**
The bus station	mahattit el buss	mah-**huht**-tit el **buhss**
The intracity bus station	mahattit el bus eddakheli	mah-huht-**tit el** buhss **ed-dah-khe-lee**
The taxi station	mujammaa el takasi	moo-**jam**-maah el tah-**kah**-see
The airport	el matar	el mah-**tahr**
The hotel	el oteil	el **ooh**-tayl
The cafe	el ahwi	el ah-**weh**
The restaurant	el mataam	el **matt-aahm**
The telephone	el tiliphon	el tih-lih-**fohn**
The hospital	el mostashfa	el moos-**tash**-fah
The post office	el bareed	el bah-**reed**

ENGLISH	ARABIC TRANSLITERATION	PRONUNCIATION
The rest room	el hammam	el huhm-**mahm**
The pharmacy	el saydaleyyeh	el sigh-dah-**lay-yeh**
The bank	el bank	el bahnk
The embassy	el safara	el sah-fah-**rah**
Right	yameen	yah-meen
Left	shmal	shmahl
Straight ahead	doughri	doo-ghree
I would like a room	beddi ghorfi	bed-dee **ghor-fih**
A little	shway or aleel	shway or ah-leel
A lot	kteer	kteer
Enough	bikaffi	bee-kaf-fee
I have a problem	aandi moshkili	aahn-dee **moosh**-keh-lee
I am ill	ana mareed	ah-nah mah-reed
I need a doctor	beddi daktor	bed-**dee** dac-**tor**
Help	saadoonee	**saah-doo**-nee
Fire	naar or harika	naahr or hah-**ree**-kah
Caution/ look out	entebeh or owaa	in-teh-beh or ohw-**aah**

DINING

ENGLISH	ARABIC TRANSLITERATION	PRONUNCIATION
I would like	beddi	behd-dee
Water	mayy	muhyy
Bread	khobez	kho-bihz
Vegetables	khodra	khod-rah
Meat	lahhmi	**lahh**-meh
Fruits	fawakeh	fah-**wah**-keh
Cakes/ Sweets	helou/ halaweyyat	**heh**-loo/ hah-lah-**way-yaht**
Tea	shay	shahy
Coffee	ahwi	ah-weh
A fork	shokeh	show-keh
A spoon	maala a	**maah**-lah ah

ENGLISH	ARABIC TRANSLITERATION	PRONUNCIATION
A knife	sikkeen	sick-**keen**
A plate	sahin	sah-hin

SHOPPING

I would like to buy	beddi ashtri	bed-**dee** ahsh-tree
Cigarettes	sagayer or dokhkhan	sah-**gah**-yer or dokh-**khahn**
A city map	khareeta lal madeeni	khah-**ree**-tah lahl mah-**dee**-nee
A road map	khareeta lal tareek	khah-**ree**-tah lahl tah-**reek**
How much is it?	addaish ha o	**ad**-daysh **ha** oh
It's expensive	ghali	**ghah**-lee

TRAVEL SMART
ISRAEL

GETTING HERE AND AROUND

■ AIR TRAVEL

The least expensive airfares to Israel are often priced for round-trip travel and must be purchased well in advance. Airlines generally allow you to change your return date for a fee; most low-fare tickets, however, are nonrefundable.

Flights to Israel tend to be least expensive from November through March, except for the holiday season at the end of December. Prices are higher during the Jewish High Holiday period (usually in September or October) and Passover (usually in April).

Flying time from New York to Israel is approximately 11 hours; from Los Angeles or San Francisco, it's about 14 hours nonstop, or 18 to 19 hours with the usual stopover in Europe or New York. International passengers are asked to arrive at the airport three hours prior to their flight time in order to allow for security checks.

From North America, the New York City area international airports have the highest number of nonstop flights, with El Al Airlines, United, and Delta providing nonstop service. Direct flights are also available on El Al from Los Angeles, Boston, and Toronto, and on United from San Francisco. Major European carriers—including Aeroflot, Air France, Alitalia, Austrian Airways, British Airways, Brussels Airlines, Czech Airlines, Iberia, KLM, Lot, Lufthansa, Swissair, Turkish Airways, and Virgin Atlantic—have daily flights from the United States and on to Israel with stopovers in their domestic hub airports.

Because Israel is only slightly larger than New Jersey, it's more efficient to drive within the country than fly. The exception is the resort city of Eilat, which is about 360 km (224 miles) south of Tel Aviv on the Gulf of Aqaba. There are flights several times a day from Tel Aviv and Haifa.

Reconfirmation obligations differ from airline to airline (and change from time to time); be certain to check with your carrier for all legs of your journey.

Airline Security Issues Transportation Security Administration. ⊕ *www.tsa.gov.*

AIRPORTS

Israel's main airport, Ben Gurion International Airport (TLV), is a few miles southeast of Tel Aviv. The airport has towering interior walls of Jerusalem stone adorned with 5th- and 6th-century Byzantine mosaics discovered throughout Israel. A soothing fountain is in the center of the departure hall, which has plenty of comfortable seating and cafés. Free Wi-Fi means you can stay connected while waiting for your flight. The spacious food court serves Middle Eastern cuisine and fast-food favorites. From Sde Dov Airport (SDV), about 4 km (2½ miles) north of Tel Aviv's center, domestic airlines fly to Eilat in the south and Haifa or Rosh Pina in the north.

From October to April, there are charter flights to the Red Sea resort town of Eilat from Moscow, St. Petersburg, Amsterdam, Copenhagen, Helsinki, and Tallinn. There are also charter flights to Eilat from Paris and London during the Jewish holiday months of September and October. Eilat will close its current airport and open a new international airport in 2017. Ramon Airport (⊕ *www.iaa.gov.il*) will be 19 km (12 miles) north of the current one in the city center. All international charters to Eilat land at Ovda Airport (VDA), about 60 km (37 miles) north of Eilat; Ovda may close for civilian flights when the new Ramon Airport opens.

Airport Information Ben Gurion International Airport. ☏ *03/975–5555* ⊕ *www.iaa. gov.il/rashat/en-US/airports/bengurion.* **Eilat Airport.** ✉ *42 Eilat St., Eilat* ☏ *700/705–022* ⊕ *www.iaa.gov.il.* **Ovda Airport.** ☏ *700/705– 022* ⊕ *www.iaa.gov.il.* **Sde Dov Airport.** ☏ *03/698–4500* ⊕ *www.iaa.gov.il/rashat/ en-US/airports/sdedov.*

GROUND TRANSPORTATION

The quickest and most convenient way to get to and from Ben Gurion International Airport is by taxi. Taxis are always available outside the arrivals hall and charge fixed prices. Fares are NIS 155 to Tel Aviv and NIS 288 to Jerusalem, plus NIS 4.50 per piece of luggage. Between 9 pm and 5:30 am, prices are NIS 175 to Tel Aviv and NIS 345 to Jerusalem.

From the airport, trains depart for Tel Aviv every half hour. They take you to the city in 15 minutes for NIS 13.50. Trains continue on to Herzliya, Netanya, Haifa, Akko, and Nahariya. For Jerusalem, change at Haganah Station in Tel Aviv, and expect a two-hour commute.

The Nesher shuttle service takes you to Jerusalem for NIS 64. The 10-passenger *sherut* taxis (minibuses) depart whenever they fill up. The main disadvantage is that there's no telling if you'll be the last passenger to be dropped off, so it can take an hour while the driver lets off the other passengers. To get to Ben Gurion International Airport from Jerusalem the same way, call Nesher a day in advance. Otherwise order a private cab from any taxi company, called a "special" taxi, for the fixed price of NIS 290, or NIS 340 after 9 pm nightly and on Saturday and holidays.

If you depart for the airport from central Tel Aviv by car or taxi at rush hour (7 to 9 am, 5 to 7 pm), note that the roads can get clogged. Allow 45 minutes for a trip that would otherwise take only about 20 minutes.

Taking the bus from Ben Gurion International Airport to Jerusalem is tedious. Board the Egged local shuttle (line 5, NIS 5.80) for the 10-minute ride to the El Al Junction, and wait there for a Jerusalem-bound bus (line 425 or 947, NIS 25). It runs to Jerusalem's Central Bus Station about every 30 minutes during the day, less frequently in the evening.

Contacts Egged. ☎ 03/694–8888 ⊕ www.egged.co.il. **Nesher.** ☎ 02/625–7227 ⊕ www.neshertours.co.il.

FLIGHTS

The national carrier, El Al Israel Airlines, is known for maintaining some of the world's strictest security standards. It's not necessarily the cheapest carrier, especially from the United States. United and Delta often have cheaper nonstop fares, and some European airlines have better prices if you don't mind a stopover in their hub cities. Within Israel, Arkia Israeli Airlines and Israir Airlines have flights from Tel Aviv to Eilat and Haifa. If you plan to travel in Jordan, Royal Jordanian is an option; it has flights from Ben Gurion International Airport.

To Israel Delta Airlines. ☎ 800/221–1212 for reservations for U.S., 800/241–4141 for international reservations ⊕ www.delta.com. **El Al Israel Airlines.** ☎ 800/223–6700 in U.S., 03/977–1111 in Israel ⊕ www.elal.co.il. **Royal Jordanian Airlines.** ☎ 212/949–0050 ⊕ www.rj.com. **United Airlines.** ☎ 800/241–6522 ⊕ www.united.com.

Within Israel Arkia Israeli Airlines. ☎ 03/690–2210 local number in Israel ⊕ www.arkia.com. **Israir Airlines.** ☎ 03/510–9589 local number in Israel ⊕ www.israirairlines.com.

▮ BIKE TRAVEL

Biking has taken off in Israel, with tens of thousands of avid cyclists hitting the trails every year. With mountains, deserts, and wooded hills, this small country is ideal for two-wheel adventures. Off-road tours take you to remote archaeological sites and other places not reachable by car. The Keren Kayemet LeIsrael (Jewish National Fund) has information about trails through some beautiful areas. Keep in mind that the going can get rough due to the summer's extreme heat, and there are winding and hilly roads with aggressive drivers. The weather is best from September to June.

Urban biking is also becoming popular. Tel Aviv has 120 km (75 miles) of designated bike lanes and a bike rental system.

Look for the green Tel-O-Fun pay stations throughout the city. Use a credit card to pay the daily fee of NIS 17 (NIS 23 on Saturday and holidays) or weekly fee of NIS 70. If you need help, dial *6070 to talk to the call center.

In Jerusalem, there are a number of bicycle paths to ride, including the landscaped 5-km (3-mile) pedestrian and bike path that goes along the old train tracks, starting at the First Station, where you can rent bicycles. A new circular bike trail opened in Jerusalem's Metropolitan Park, and there are plans to expand it in coming years.

Bikes are welcome on intercity buses with luggage holds. Trains accept bikes Sunday through Thursday during nonpeak hours (between 9 and 3 and after 7) and anytime on Friday. Folding bicycles stored in carrying bags are always allowed.

Bike maps in English can be hard to find, but Israel Bike Trails has comprehensive trail information listing elevations and level of difficulty on its website.

Bike Contacts Israel Bike Trails. ⊕ www.israelbiketrails.com. **Israel Cycling.** ☎ 054/333–9543 local phone in Israel ⊕ www.israelcycling.com. **Keren Kayemeth LeIsrael.** ⊕ www.kkl-jnf.org.il. **Sovoo Jerusalem Bike Rental.** ✉ First Station, 4 David Remez St., Jerusalem ☎ 02/648–0334 ⊕ smart-tour.co.il/eng/sovoo-bike-rentals/. **Tel-O-Fun.** ⊕ www.tel-o-fun.co.il/en.

▌ BOAT TRAVEL

Many large cruise companies, including Costa, Holland America, Regent Seven Seas, and Seabourn have Mediterranean itineraries that include stops at the Israeli ports of Ashdod and Haifa. In addition, the Israeli company Mano sails from Haifa to many points in the Mediterranean between April and November.

Cruise Lines Mano Maritime. ☎ 03/517–7888 local number in Israel ⊕ www.mano.co.il/cruises/eng.

▌ BUS TRAVEL

Buses can take you almost anywhere in Israel. Most in Jerusalem are run by Egged and most buses in Tel Aviv are serviced by Dan, though other city bus companies also operate. Buses in Israel are clean, comfortable, air-conditioned, and some have Wi-Fi. Intercity bus fares vary according to distance traveled. During weekday rush hours, allow time for long lines at the obligatory security checks to enter most bus stations. Buses are often overcrowded on Saturday night as people return home after Shabbat and always packed on Sunday morning when it looks like the entire Israeli army is returning to base after a weekend at home.

The Central Bus Station in Tel Aviv resembles an M.C. Escher drawing: a jumble of staircases and escalators appearing to lead nowhere. The stark concrete building has multiple entrances and exits on several levels, endless corridors, and a dizzying array of platforms. It's all topped off by dozens of kiosks selling fast food and cheap merchandise, plus Asian minimarkets serving the local community of foreign workers. By contrast, Jerusalem's Central Bus Station is clean, well-organized, and easy to navigate. There's a pleasant enough food court, ATMs, information desk, and branches of some of the country's best-known stores.

Although buses resemble those in most other countries, there are a few quirks. When you're in Jerusalem, lines 1 and 3 primarily service ultra-Orthodox Jewish neighborhoods and end at the Western Wall area. On bus lines like these, it's generally accepted that women sit separately, in the back of the bus, and men in the front half. Although gender segregation is not compulsory by law, in ultra-Orthodox society it is the norm. If you're a woman and sit in an empty seat next to an ultra-Orthodox man, you shouldn't be surprised if he would rather stand than sit beside you. (In case you're wondering, ultra-Orthodox women generally accept this arrangement.)

Frequent bus service is available between Jerusalem and Tel Aviv. Egged Bus 405 runs from the Tel Aviv Central Bus Station every 15–20 minutes, and Bus 480 from the Arlozorov Street terminal (near the Savidor train station in Tel Aviv) leaves a bit more frequently, depending on the time of day (NIS 16 for each). There's a similar service to Jerusalem from most major cities, terminating at the Central Bus Station. The three small bus stations in East Jerusalem are for Palestinian-operated bus lines, with daily service to West Bank towns such as Bethlehem and Ramallah. The main bus depot is next to Damascus Gate light-rail stop.

FARES

For both local and long-distance travel, drivers accept payment in shekels. Drivers on long-distance buses grumble when they have to make change for a bill over NIS 100, so make sure to have smaller denominations. Unless you are running to catch a bus, it's almost always faster to buy your ticket at the office in the bus station. On city buses you don't need exact change. Children under age five ride free whether or not they occupy their own seat.

If you need a round-trip bus ticket, you have to buy an electronic Rav Kav card from the bus driver. It costs NIS 5 but you can load money on the card and use it for all tickets on all Israeli buses, trains, and Jerusalem's city tram.

The fare on most central city routes is NIS 5.90. If taking another bus within 90 minutes, ask for a free *ma'avar*, or transfer ticket.

Intercity fares are based on distance traveled. The one-hour trip between Tel Aviv and Jerusalem cost NIS 16, while the 2½-hour journey between Tel Aviv and Tiberias runs NIS 37.50. There are no advance reservations except to Eilat or the Dead Sea area.

SCHEDULES

Most major bus lines are available Sunday to Thursday from about 6 am to midnight. Keep in mind that public transportation in all cities except Haifa ceases to run on Jewish holidays and Shabbat, which lasts from sundown Friday afternoon to an hour after sundown Saturday evening. Be sure to give yourself extra time if traveling just before Shabbat.

Every large bus station has an information booth with schedule and platform information in English. The Egged website has an easy-to-use trip planner that includes timetables, routes, and fares.

Bus Information Dan. ☎ *03/639–4444* ⊕ *www.dan.co.il/Eng/.* **East Jerusalem Bus Station.** ✉ *Sultan Suleiman St., opposite Damascus Gate, East Jerusalem* ☎ *02/627–2881.* **Egged.** ☎ *03/694–8888* ⊕ *www.egged. co.il/eng.* **Jerusalem Central Bus Station.** ✉ *224 Jaffa Rd., Romema* ☎ *03/914–2237* ⊕ *egged.co.il/eng.* **National Bus Hotline.** ☎ **8787* ⊕ *www.bus.co.il.*

▌CAR TRAVEL

The Hebrew word for a native-born Israeli is *sabra*, which is the name of a prickly cactus that's sweet inside. You meet sweet Israelis if you get lost or have automotive difficulties—helping hands are quick to arrive—but behind the wheel, Israelis are aggressive and honk their horns far more than their Western counterparts.

Some travelers feel more comfortable hiring a driver, and there are plenty of ways to find someone reliable. Ask for recommendations at your hotel. Every hotel has taxi drivers who serve their guests, and most are familiar with all parts of the country and happy to quote you a daily rate.

Israel's highways are numbered, but most people still know them simply by the towns they connect: the Tiberias–Nazareth Road, for example. Intersections and turnoffs are similarly indicated, as in "the Tiberias Junction." Brown signs indicate tourist sites.

ADDRESSES

In Israel, streets are generally named after famous people or events, meaning that almost every community has a Herzl Street and a Ben Gurion Street. Don't worry about the "boulevard" or "alley" attached to many street names—Israelis just use the proper name. You don't find a Jabotinsky Street and a Jabotinsky Alley in the same city. What you likely encounter is a street that changes names after a couple of blocks. Street numbers follow the standard format, with odd numbers on one side and even numbers on the other.

If you know history, you'll have an easier time finding your way around Jerusalem's neighborhoods. In Baka a block of streets are named after biblical tribes, in Rehavia they're medieval Jewish scholars, and in Old Katamon, the brigades who fought in Israel's War of Independence.

Towns in Israel that have functioning Old Cities, some dating back to biblical times, include Jerusalem, Jaffa, Akko, and Tzfat. Streets and alleys in these areas have names, but sometimes it's hard to find numbers.

GASOLINE

Gas stations are found at regular intervals along the country's major highways, except in the Negev. On highways they're generally always open, while those in the city tend to close at midnight. Prices are standardized, so it doesn't matter which station you choose (though gas tends to be cheaper in Eilat). Most offer both full- and self-service pumps. If you go the full-service route, ask for a *kabbalah* (receipt). Attendants don't expect to be tipped. Most rental cars take unleaded gas, which at the time of this writing costs NIS 6.15 per liter. Most stations accept international credit cards.

PARKING

In Tel Aviv, Jerusalem, and Haifa, parking laws are stringently enforced. Expect a ticket of NIS 100 on your windshield if you've overstayed your welcome at a paid parking spot. Cars are towed if parked in a no-parking zone. Pay attention to the curb, as parking is forbidden where it's painted red. In downtown areas, parking is permitted only where there are blue and white stripes on the curb, meters, or pay stations.

Parking in Jerusalem costs NIS 5.70 per hour, and in central areas, pay stations print out small parking tickets to wedge at the top of the car window on the curb side. Parking in Tel Aviv costs NIS 6.20 an hour and you can only pay with a cell phone payment service like Pango. Read the signs carefully: in some areas free evening parking begins at 6, in others at 7 or 8.

Sound complicated? Stick to parking lots. Covered and open parking lots are plentiful in the major cities and can cost around NIS 15 per hour or NIS 70 per day.

RENTAL CARS

If you plan on heading north to the Golan or Upper Galilee, a rental car is a significant time-saver. If sticking to cities, a rental car is often more bother than boon. In Jerusalem, a combination of walking and taking cabs and the city tram is your best bet.

Familiar American car-rental companies operate in Israel, as do local ones such as Eldan. Rental rates in Israel start at around US$35 per day and US$200 per week for an economy car. Minivans and four-wheel-drive vehicles are very popular and should be reserved well in advance, especially during high season. Allow plenty of time to pick up and drop off your vehicle if renting from a city office.

Drivers must be at least 21. Your driver's license is acceptable in Israel.

RENTAL CARS IN THE WEST BANK

There are no restrictions on driving Israeli rental cars into West Bank areas under full Israeli control (known as Area C). However, your rental-car insurance coverage doesn't extend to West Bank areas under Palestinian control. If you rent from companies at the airport, in Tel Aviv, or in West Jerusalem, you are unable to drive the car to Bethlehem, Jericho, and other towns under the Palestinian Authority. If you plan on visiting these areas by car, use Dallah or one of the other Palestinian-operated car-rental companies in East Jerusalem. Have your passport with you to show Israeli guards at West Bank checkpoints if asked.

Even if you're using GPS, it's always a good idea to discuss possible routes with your car-rental company if you plan on passing through the West Bank.

Local Rental Agencies Best. ☎ *8883 ⊕ www.best-car.co.il/English. **Dallah Rent A Car.** ✉ American Colony Hotel, 1 Louis Vincent St., East Jerusalem ☎ 02/627–9725 ⊕ www.dallahrentacar.com. **Eldan.** ☎ 03/977–3400 ⊕ rent.eldan.co.il/en. **Green Peace Car Rental.** ✉ Mount of Olives Hotel, 53 Mount of Olives Rd., East Jerusalem ☎ 02/585–9756 ⊕ www.greenpeace.co.il.

ROAD CONDITIONS

Israel's highway system is very modern and has signs in English as well as Hebrew and Arabic. Route 6, the main north–south toll road, can save significant time on longer journeys. The highway starts at the Maahaz Junction, south of Kiryat Gat (south of Tel Aviv), and ends about 138 km (85 miles) north at the Ein Tut Junction near Yokneam (in the Lower Galilee). Electronic sensors read your license plate number and transmit the bill to your rental-car company. Car rental companies set their own rates for driving on Route 6, so be sure to ask what they charge. Expect to pay around NIS 60 to drive the length of the highway.

Route 1 is the chief route to Jerusalem from both the west (Tel Aviv, Ben Gurion International Airport, Mediterranean coast) and the east (Galilee via Jordan Valley, Dead Sea area, Eilat). The road from Tel Aviv is a divided highway that presents no problems except at morning rush hour (7 am to 9:30 am), when traffic backs up at the entrance to the city. For this reason, some drivers prefer Route 443—via Modi'in—which leaves Route 1 just east of the Ben Gurion Airport, and enters Jerusalem from the north (most convenient for East Jerusalem locations). Route 1, which enters Jerusalem under the Bridge of Strings, is more convenient for Givat Ram, West Jerusalem, and downtown.

Jerusalem, Haifa, and Tel Aviv are all clogged with traffic during the workday. In Jerusalem, the Old City and Jaffa Road are closed to private vehicles, with traffic routed around the periphery. Don't consider driving in Jerusalem if not comfortable negotiating narrow spaces or parking in tight spots.

If driving through the Negev, watch out for camels that can come loping out of the desert and onto the road. In the winter rainy season, sudden flash floods sometimes cascade through the desert *wadis* (streambeds that are usually dry) with little warning, washing out roads and posing danger to motorists. It's best to postpone your desert trip if there's heavy rain in the forecast.

The desert can be unbelievably hot, sometimes even in the winter. It's a good idea to carry extra water—both for yourself and your car—while driving at any time of year.

ROADSIDE EMERGENCIES

In case of an accident or roadside emergency, call the police. Should anything happen to your rental car, call your rental company for roadside repair or replacement of the vehicle.

Emergency Services Police. ☎ 100 ⊕ www.police.gov.il.

RULES OF THE ROAD

By law, drivers and all passengers must wear seat belts at all times. Police crack down on drunk driving; the legal blood-alcohol limit is 0.05%. It's against the law to use a cell phone while driving.

Speed limits vary little across Israel: motorways (represented with blue signs) have speed limits of 110 kph (68 mph). Highways with green signs have speed limits of 80 or 90 kph (50 or 56 mph). Urban roads are 50 kph (31 mph).

Headlights must be turned on in daylight when driving on intercity roads from November 1 through March 31. A flashing green traffic light indicates that the red stoplight is about three seconds away and you should come to a halt.

Children under eight must be seated in age-appropriate car seats, and children under 13 aren't allowed in the front seat.

■ TAXI TRAVEL

Taxis are the most convenient way to get around cities. They're not cheap, but if you need to get somewhere fast or are unfamiliar with the area, a taxi (*monit* in Hebrew) is your best bet. Hail one on the street or order by phone. Taxis are white sedans with a yellow sign on the roof. On the whole, drivers are knowledgeable, talkative, and like to practice their English with tourists. But be warned: some try to take advantage of tourists, charge hefty prices, or run up the meter.

According to law, taxi drivers must use the meter. Be firm when you request this (*moneh* is meter in Hebrew) and make sure the meter is running at the beginning of the ride. The exception is if you hire a driver for the day or a trip out of town, for which there are set rates. In those cases, agree on the price before you begin the journey and assume that the driver has built in a tip. In the event of a serious problem with the driver, report his cab number (on the illuminated plastic sign on the roof) or license plate number to the Ministry of Tourism or the Ministry of Transport. It is not customary to tip drivers.

Certain shared taxis or minivans have fixed rates and run set routes, such as from Tel Aviv to Haifa or from the airport to Jerusalem or Haifa; such a taxi is called a sherut (as opposed to a "special," the term used for a private cab). Some sheruts can be booked in advance.

Sheruts are an option if traveling between Jerusalem and Tel Aviv. They operate from the (grungy) side street alongside Tel Aviv's Central Bus Station seven days a week, departing when they fill up (NIS 24 on weekdays; NIS 35 on Saturday). They end their journey with stops near the Jerusalem Central Bus Station and 31 Haneviim Street, about a block from Zion Square. From Jerusalem, the sherut leaves from 31 Haneviim Street. A "special" cab on this route costs NIS 320, or about NIS 350 after 9 pm and on Saturday and holidays.

Jerusalem Taxi Contacts Hapalmach. ☎ *02/679–3333.* **Hapisgah.** ☎ *02/642–1111.* **Rehavia.** ☎ *02/625–4444.* **Smadar.** ☎ *02/566–4444.*

Eilat Taxi Contacts Hacohanim. ☎ *08/631–6007.* **Taba.** ☎ *08/633–3333.*

■ TRAIN TRAVEL

Train travel between Jerusalem and Tel Aviv is more a pleasant and scenic excursion than an efficient way to travel. The journey currently takes nearly an hour and a half, compared to an hour by bus. It's a comfortable ride, and many just do it for the attractive scenery. The train, which departs every one to two hours, runs nonstop between Jerusalem's Malcha Station and Tel Aviv's Savidor Station. There are connections to Haifa and other destinations to the north. Service ends midafternoon on Friday and resumes about two hours after dark on Saturday. The fare to or from Tel Aviv is NIS 20 one way and NIS 32 round-trip.

Other cities—including Ashkelon, Beersheva, Beit Shemesh, Haifa, Herzliya, Akko, and Nahariya—are easily reachable by train from Tel Aviv. There are no different classes of service. All carriages are clean, spacious, and comfortable with well-upholstered seats. They're often crowded, however.

All train stations post up-to-date schedules in English. Complete schedules are also available on the website of the Israel Railway Authority. Tickets may be purchased at the ticket office in the station.

Reserved seats are available Sunday to Thursday and may be bought up to a week in advance at the ticket office. Reserved seating is not available for the Jerusalem–Tel Aviv line and other short rides in metropolitan areas.

Jerusalem has a light-rail train, the country's first. It's a much more comfortable way to traverse the city than the bumpy roller-coaster rides on the city's buses. There's only one tram line, but it hits many points of interest. For information, see ⊕ *www.citypass.co.il/English*.

Information Israel Railways. ☎ *08/683–1222* ⊕ *www.rail.co.il/EN.*

ESSENTIALS

■ ACCOMMODATIONS

In Israel you can find every possible type of lodging, including luxury spa resorts, chic boutique hotels, country inns, and rural bed-and-breakfasts. There are also some more specialized offerings, including Christian guesthouses and kibbutz hotels (lodgings on the grounds of collective communities).

Some are utilitarian, but some recent trends are a rise in distinctive boutique hotels and in luxury properties, whether in the cities or the countryside. In contrast, options such as kibbutz hotels and bed-and-breakfasts (known as *zimmers* in Israel) offer a glimpse into local life and a more leisurely experience.

Israel has a one- to five-star ranking system for hotels similar to that used in many places in Europe, though only a limited number of hotels participate in the system. The Ministry of Tourism has already rated the country's 9,000 B&Bs. They're ranked A, B, or C, based on size and the facilities offered.

Non-Israeli citizens paying in foreign currency are exempt from the 17% V.A.T. on hotel rooms.

Throughout Israel, lodging prices often include breakfast. Prices in the reviews are the lowest cost of a standard double room in high season.

APARTMENT AND HOUSE RENTALS

Short-term rentals are popular, especially in Jerusalem and Tel Aviv and particularly for families who would otherwise be taking two or three hotel rooms. Options range from basic studios to mansions, and most are privately owned.

Contacts Good Morning Jerusalem.
☎ 02/623–3459 ⊕ www.accommodation.co.il. **Israel Holiday Apartments.** ☎ 09/772–7163 ⊕ www.holidayapartments.co.il. **Vacation Rental By Owner.** ⊕ www.vrbo.com.

BED-AND-BREAKFASTS

Since 2005, thousands of zimmers have sprung up, especially in the Galilee and the Golan. These are intimate cabins, usually featuring one or two bedrooms, a kitchenette, a hot tub, and an outdoor lounging area. Prices aren't necessarily lower than hotels, but if it's peace and quiet you're after, these may be just the thing.

Many zimmers are located in moshavim— semicommunal rural communities. Private-home owners are also increasingly opening their doors to guests.

Contacts Home Accommodation Association of Jerusalem. ⊕ www.bnb.co.il. **Rural Tourism in Israel.** ⊕ www.zimmeril.com.

CHRISTIAN HOSPICES

Lodgings called Christian hospices (meaning hotels) provide accommodations and sometimes meals; these are mainly in and around Jerusalem and the Galilee. Some hospices are real bargains, while others are merely reasonable; facilities range from spare to luxurious. Those in rural settings are often tranquil retreats. Most give preference to pilgrimage groups, but many will accept individual travelers when space is available.

Contacts Travelujah. ☎ 052/744–4033 *Israel phone number* ⊕ www.travelujah.com/groups/category/Christian-Guest-Houses.

KIBBUTZ HOTELS

Around the country, kibbutz hotels offer a variety of accommodations in what are often lovely settings. Some kibbutz hotels are luxurious, while others are more basic. Most have large lawns, swimming pools, and athletic facilities. Some offer lectures about the history of kibbutzim and tours of the settlements and the surrounding areas. These kibbutz hotels are popular with tour groups.

Contacts Kibbutz Hotels Chain. ☎ *03/560–8118* ⊕ *en.kibbutz.co.il.*

▌COMMUNICATIONS

INTERNET

Most hotels in Israel have connections for laptops, and most have wireless access. Ask about the price, as some charge for the privilege. You can also find Internet access in most cafés. Tel Aviv has free public Wi-Fi, and Jerusalem has free Wi-Fi in the downtown area, in the German Colony, and Safra Square. Ben Gurion and Eilat airports also have free Wi-Fi.

PHONES

Israel's landline phone numbers have seven digits, beginning with a two-digit area code, and mobile phone numbers have 10 digits, beginning with a three-digit prefix. Toll-free numbers in Israel begin with 177, 1800, 1700, or 1888. Many toll-free customer service numbers begin with an asterisk followed by four digits. When calling an out-of-town number within Israel, be sure to dial the zero that begins every area code.

The country code for Israel is 972. When dialing an Israeli number from abroad, drop the initial 0 from the local area code. The country code for Jordan is 962. When dialing from Israel, dial 00962 and the area code 3 before landline numbers in Petra; for Amman, use 00962 and the area code 6. When dialing within Jordan, include the initial 0 from the area code.

CALLING WITHIN ISRAEL

Making a local call in Israel is quite simple. All public telephones use phone cards that may be purchased at newspaper kiosks and post offices. Pick up the receiver, insert the card in the slot, dial the number when you hear the tone, and the number of units remaining on the card appears on the screen. One unit equals about two minutes. From 7 pm to 7 am, calls are much cheaper.

The area codes for dialing between cities within Israel are Jerusalem (02); Tel Aviv (03); Netanya and Herzliya (09); Haifa, Galilee, Tiberias, Tzfat, and Nazareth (04); Eilat and the Negev (08).

Dial 144 for directory or operator assistance. Operators all speak English. Dial 188 for an international operator.

CALLING OUTSIDE ISRAEL

When calling internationally direct from Israel, first dial 00 then the country code. The country code for the United States and Canada is 1.

You can make international calls using a telecard from a public phone. A call from Israel to the United States costs 2.5 units a minute, or about 40¢ per minute.

MOBILE PHONES

If you have a multiband phone and your service provider uses the world-standard GSM network (like T-Mobile, AT&T, and Verizon), you can probably use your phone abroad. Roaming fees can be steep, however: 99¢ a minute is considered reasonable. Overseas you normally pay the toll charges for incoming calls. It's almost always cheaper to send a text message than to make a call.

If you just want to make local calls, consider buying a new SIM card (note that your provider may have to unlock your phone to allow a different SIM card) and a prepaid service plan in the destination. You then have a local number and can make local calls at local rates.

■**TIP➜** If you travel internationally frequently, save one of your old mobile phones or buy a cheap one on the Internet; ask your cell-phone company to unlock it for you, and take it with you as a travel phone, buying a new SIM card with pay-as-you-go service in each destination.

Depending on your cell phone provider's global roaming rates, it could be cheaper to rent a cell phone at Ben Gurion International Airport or order a rental phone to arrive at your address before leaving for Israel. Rental booths are in the airport arrivals hall.

Contacts ATS. ☎ 718/838–1511 from U.S., 052/482–6681 from Israel ⊕ www.atsisrael. com. **Cellular Abroad.** ☎ 800/287–5072 in U.S. ⊕ www.cellularabroad.com. **Mobal.** ☎ 888/888–9162 in U.S. ⊕ www.mobalrental. com. **Planet Fone.** ☎ 888/988–4777 in U.S. ⊕ www.planetfone.com.

■ CUSTOMS AND DUTIES

For visitors with nothing to declare, clearing customs at Ben Gurion International Airport requires simply following the clearly marked green line to the baggage claims hall. There are generally no lines and customs inspectors rarely examine luggage. The red line for those with items to declare is next to the green line. Those over 17 may import into Israel duty-free: 250 grams of tobacco products; 2 liters of wine and 1 liter of spirits; ¼ liter of eau de cologne or perfume; and gifts totaling no more than US$200 in value. You may also import up to 3 kg of food products, but no fresh meat.

You may bring a pet if you bring a general health certificate in English issued by a government veterinary officer in your country of origin issued within 10 days prior to travel. The certificate must state that you've owned the pet for more than 90 days and that the animal has been vaccinated against rabies not more than a year and not less than one month prior to travel. Dogs and cats less than four

months old won't be admitted. As soon as you receive the health certificate, but no less than 48 hours prior to arrival, pet owners must fax or email the veterinary department at Ben Gurion International Airport, including the name of the owner, veterinary health certificate, animal species, age, date of birth, breed, sex, identification number of electronic chip (for dogs), flight number, approximate arrival time, and your contact information.

Contacts U.S. Customs and Border Protection. ☎ 877/227–5511 ⊕ www.cbp.gov.

■ EATING OUT

Israeli restaurants are sophisticated and varied, as one would expect from a country with immigrants from dozens of countries and a well-traveled population. Be sure to sample the culinary traditions of the Middle East at neighborhood restaurants. Here you fill up on dishes such as hummus and warmed pita bread accompanied by a variety of skewered grilled meats, bowls of falafel, and an astonishing array of fresh salads and mezze. Unlike the street version, pita is served on the side to tear into pieces and dip into mezzes, and portions tend to be very generous. Restaurants in Eilat, Haifa, and Tel Aviv take advantage of their seaside location to serve the best in seafood dishes, and in the major cities it's not difficult to find authentic Italian, Georgian, Latin American, French, Japanese, and American food.

While "kosher" once meant "boring," the number of inventive and sophisticated kosher restaurants is growing. Restaurants certified as kosher by the local rabbinate in every city are required to display a dated and signed Hebrew certificate. All the major hotels throughout the country are kosher and their restaurants and cafés welcome nonguests. The website eLuna is a good source for listings, reviews, and discount coupons for kosher eateries.

Kosher Restaurants eLuna. ⊕ www.eluna.com.

MEALS AND MEALTIMES

Hotels serve a huge, buffet-style breakfast called *arukhat boker,* comprising a variety of breads and rolls, eggs, cereal, excellent yogurt, local cheeses, olives, vegetables, fish salads, and such American-style breakfast foods as pancakes and granola. (It's generally included in hotel rates.) You can find the same spread at many cafés. Outdoor coffee shops serving salads, sandwiches, cakes, and delicious coffee abound. Every city and small town has modestly priced restaurants that open midmorning and serve soup, salad, and grilled meats.

Many restaurants have business lunch specials or fixed-price menus, but à la carte menus are most common. A service charge (*sherut*) of 10% to 15% is sometimes levied and should be noted separately on your bill.

Because Friday isn't a workday for most Israelis, Thursday night is the big night out at the start of the weekend, when cafés and restaurants fill up quickly. Friday mornings at Israeli cafés are the equivalent of the U.S.–style Sunday brunch.

PAYING

Credit cards are widely accepted in restaurants, but always check first. Tips between 12% and 15% can usually only be paid in cash, but sometimes restaurants can add the tip to your credit card if you ask. If you're dining in a smaller town or village, make sure you have sufficient cash with you, as credit cards are sometimes not accepted.

RESERVATIONS AND DRESS

Dress in all but the most expensive Israeli restaurants is generally casual. Except for some restaurants in five-star hotels, men don't need a jacket and tie. Israeli restaurants in the larger cities fill up in the evening. Unless you're dining early—before 7 pm—reservations are advised for all except the smallest neighborhood restaurants.

WINES, BEER, AND SPIRITS

Wine has deep roots in Israeli culture. Israel is one of the earliest wine-producing areas in the world, and the symbol of Israel's Ministry of Tourism is a large cluster of grapes borne on a pole by two men—straight from the Bible story of the spies sent to fetch fruit from the Promised Land. Wineries built during the 19th century are still producing wine today, and a plethora of boutique wineries have sprung up in the past decade. Dalton, Domaine du Castel, Tishbi, Yarden, and Carmel are good bets and on many Israeli wine lists. As for spirits, those with a taste for Greek ouzo may enjoy the comparable local arak. Sabra is a locally produced chocolate- and orange-flavored liqueur.

The commercially produced beers in Israel are Maccabee and Goldstar (lagers), and Carlsberg, Heineken, and Tuborg are popular imports. Beer is most commonly available by the bottle, though most bars serve it on draft. In recent years, the microbrew trend has hit Israel, with more than 20 boutique breweries producing craft beers and some winning awards in international competitions. Ask for Dancing Camel or Malka, if you're adventurous. The Palestinian beer Taybeh is very popular and often available in Israeli bars.

▌ELECTRICITY

The electrical current in Israel is 220 volts, 50 cycles alternating current (AC); wall outlets generally have three round holes, but most of these will also take continental-type plugs with two round prongs. Some outlets require plugs with three flat prongs in a Y shape.

If your appliances are dual-voltage, you need only a small adapter plug. Most large hotels provide 110-volt outlets marked for shavers, but don't use those outlets for high-wattage appliances such as blow-dryers. Most laptops operate equally well on 110 and 220 volts and so require only an adapter.

▌ EMERGENCIES

Israel has an extremely sophisticated emergency response system and a high percentage of citizens who are trained medics. If you find yourself in any kind of medical or security emergency in a public place, the professional and citizen response is likely to be instantaneous.

To obtain police assistance at any time, dial 100. For emergency ambulance service, run by Magen David Adom, dial 101. To report a fire, dial 102. Emergency calls are free at public phones.

MEDICAL CENTERS

Emergency rooms in major hospitals are on duty 24 hours a day. Be sure to take your passport with you. There is a fee.

EILAT AND THE NEGEV

Three hospitals serve the Negev: Soroka in Beersheva, Barzilai in Ashkelon, and Yoseftal in Eilat. All have English speakers on staff and 24-hour emergency rooms (bring your insurance documents). At this writing, Yoseftal faced possible closure at the end of 2017.

JERUSALEM

The privately run Terem Emergency Care Center in Jerusalem provides first aid and full medical attention, 24 hours a day, at its Romema and Bikur Holim clinics, and more limited hours at its third Jerusalem location.

The major hospitals in Jerusalem are Hadassah Ein Kerem, Shaare Zedek near Mount Herzl, and Hadassah Mount Scopus.

TEL AVIV

Tel Aviv Sourasky Medical Center (also known as Ichilov Hospital) is in north Tel Aviv, about a 10-minute drive (depending on traffic) from downtown. There's a 24-hour emergency room. Be sure to bring your passport with you. You are provided with all records in English for your insurance providers at home.

▌ GAY AND LESBIAN TRAVEL

Israel has earned a reputation as a popular destination for gay and lesbian travelers. The country recognizes same-sex marriages performed abroad, bans discrimination based on sexual orientation, and has long allowed gays to serve openly in the military. Most gays gravitate toward Tel Aviv, one of the most gay-friendly cities in the world. The city has a gay beach, a vibrant gay nightclub scene, an annual gay film festival, and a gay pride parade that attracts 100,000 participants every June. The Red Sea resort of Eilat is renowned for its pride festival in May.

Information Tel Aviv Gay Vibe. ⊕ *telavivgayvibe.atraf.com.*

▌ HEALTH

No vaccinations are required to visit Israel. The country has one of the world's most advanced health-care systems. Most doctors at emergency clinics and hospitals in Israel speak English. Emergency and trauma care is among the best in the world.

It's safe to drink tap water and eat fresh produce after it's been washed as well as food from outdoor stands. Heat stroke and dehydration are real dangers if you're going to be outdoors for any length of time. A sun hat and sunblock are musts, as is plenty of bottled water (available even in the most remote places) to guard against dehydration. Take at least one liter per person for every hour you plan to be outside. Use sunscreen with SPF 30 or higher. Most supermarkets and pharmacies carry sunscreen in a range of SPFs, but it's much more expensive than in the United States.

U.S. brands of mosquito repellent with DEET are available in pharmacies and supermarkets. Wear light, long-sleeved clothing and long pants particularly at dusk, when mosquitoes are most likely to attack.

Yad Sarah is a nationwide voluntary organization that lends medical equipment and accessories such as wheelchairs, crutches, and canes. There's no charge, but a contribution is expected. In Jerusalem, it's open Sunday to Thursday 8:30 to 6:45 and Friday 8:30 to 11:45. Equipment can be returned elsewhere in the country.

OVER-THE-COUNTER REMEDIES

At the pharmacy (*beit mirkachat*), it's easy to find many of the same over-the-counter remedies as at home. Imodium (Rekamide) and Pepto-Bismol (the local version is Kal Beten) are available over the counter at every pharmacy. Everyday pain relievers such as Tylenol (called Acamol) and Advil are also widely available. You need a prescription for antibiotics. Medication can be obtained from pharmacies, which are plentiful. English is spoken in the majority of pharmacies. Locally produced medication is fairly inexpensive, but expect to pay more for drugs that are imported.

The municipal website of every city lists the pharmacies on duty at night, on Saturday, and holidays. This information is also available from Magen David Adom. In Jerusalem, Super-Pharm on the pedestrian mall is open Sunday to Thursday 8 am to 2 am, Friday 8:30 am to 4:30 pm, and Saturday one hour after the Sabbath ends until 2 am.

In Eilat, Michlin Pharmacy delivers to your hotel and is open Sunday to Thursday 8 am to 9 pm and Friday 8 to 3. Super-Pharm Mul Hayam is open Sunday to Thursday 9 am to 1 am, Friday 8:30 to midnight, and Saturday 9 am–1 am. There are also pharmacies in this region in Arad, Beersheva, and Mitzpe Ramon.

HOURS OF OPERATION

Sunday is a regular workday in Israel. All government offices and most private offices and travel agencies are closed on Friday, Saturday, and all Jewish religious holidays. Businesses are generally open by 8:30 am.

Although hours can differ among banks, almost all open by 8:30 Sunday to Thursday. Most close around 12:30 and then reopen from 4 to 7 pm some evenings. Banks are closed on Saturdays and Jewish religious holidays and have limited hours on Friday. In Muslim areas, banks are closed Friday. In Christian areas they're closed Sunday.

Museums don't have a fixed closing day, so although they are usually open 10 to 6 and on Saturday mornings, confirm the schedule before you go.

Most local pharmacies close at 7 pm. Large chain stores, such as Super-Pharm and NewPharm, are usually open until at least 10 pm. In most cities a few drugstores are open all night, on a rotating basis. Shops generally open at 9 or 9:30; neighborhood grocery stores usually open around 7. A few shops still close for a two- or three-hour siesta between 1 and 4. Most stores don't close before 7 pm; supermarkets are often open later, and in large cities, there are all-night supermarkets. Arab-owned stores usually open at 8 am and close in late afternoon. Mall hours are generally 9:30–9:30 Sunday to Thursday. In Jerusalem, malls shut down about two hours before sundown on Friday and reopen two hours after sunset on Saturday evening. Outside Jerusalem, some malls keep regular hours on Saturday, while others stay closed.

MAIL

The post office does it all: handles regular and express letters, sends and receives faxes, accepts bill payments, sells phone cards and parking cards, handles money transfers, and offers quick-delivery service. Nearly every neighborhood has a post office, identified by a white racing deer on a red background. English is almost always spoken. The main branches are usually open from 8 until 6 or 7, and small offices are usually open Sunday to Tuesday and Thursday 8 to 12:30 and 3:30 to 6, Wednesday 8 to 1:30, and

Friday 8 to noon. In Muslim areas the post office is closed Friday, and in Christian areas it's closed Sunday.

It takes 7 to 12 days for mail to reach the United States from Israel. Mail delivery from Israel is mostly reliable.

Israel changed from using postal codes with five digits to seven in 2013. In mailing addresses, the abbreviation M. P. stands for Mobile Post (M. P. Gilboa, for example). You see this as part of the address in more rural areas. Tourists who want to receive mail at a local post office should have it addressed to "Poste Restante" along with the name of the town. Such mail is held for pickup free of charge for up to one month.

SHIPPING PACKAGES

Most stores offer shipping to international destinations. If you choose to send your purchases home yourself, all the supplies you need are at any local post office, but be prepared to wait in a long line. Bring picture ID with you. To Canada and the United States, packages take approximately two weeks by air. Quicker, more expensive alternatives are FedEx and UPS.

Express Services EMS Service.
☎ 076/887–0007 ⊕ www.israelpost.co.il.
FedEx. ☎ 700/700–339 ⊕ www.fedex.com.
UPS. ☎ 800/834–834 ⊕ www.ups.com.

▍ MONEY

Israel is a country similarly priced to Western Europe for visitors, but more expensive than many of its Mediterranean neighbors. Prices tend to be cheaper in smaller towns. To save money, try the excellent prepared food from supermarkets, take public transportation, eat your main meal at lunch, eat inexpensive local foods such as falafel, and stay at hotels with kitchen facilities and guesthouses. Airfares are lowest November through March, except for the holiday season at the end of December.

Sample prices: cup of coffee, NIS 12; falafel, NIS 12; beer at a bar, NIS 25–30; canned soft drink, NIS 14; hamburger at a fast-food restaurant, NIS 30; short taxi ride, about NIS 35 to NIS 45; museum admission, NIS 50; movie, NIS 38.

Prices throughout this guide are given for adults. Substantially reduced fees are almost always available for children, students, and senior citizens.

■ TIP➔ **Banks never have every foreign currency on hand, and it may take as long as a week to order. If planning to exchange funds before leaving home, don't wait until the last minute.**

Currency Conversion Google.
⊕ www.google.com. **Oanda.com.**
⊕ www.oanda.com. **XE.com.** ⊕ www.xe.com.

ATMS AND BANKS

ATMs—called *kaspomats* in Hebrew—are ubiquitous all over Israel. Look for machines that have stickers stating that they accept foreign credit cards or PLUS, NYCE, or CIRRUS signs. All have instructions in English. Almost all ATMs now have protective shields around the keypad to prevent anyone seeing your PIN.

With a debit card, the ATM gives you the desired amount of shekels and your home account is debited at the current exchange rate. Note that there may be a limit on how much money you are allowed to withdraw each day and that service charges are usually applied. Make sure you have enough cash in rural areas, villages, and small towns where ATMs may be harder to find.

The main branches of all the banks—Hapoalim, Leumi, Discount—are in Jerusalem's downtown area but are arguably the last resort for changing money. Several times a week they have morning hours only (different banks, different days) and give relatively low rates of exchange. It usually involves waiting in line and having the clerk fill out paperwork.

Your own bank probably charges a fee for using ATMs abroad, but some apply no foreign transaction fees. The foreign bank you use may also charge a fee. Nevertheless, you usually get a better rate of exchange at an ATM than in a bank. Extracting funds as you need is a safer option than carrying around a large amount of cash.

■TIP➔ PIN codes with more than four digits aren't recognized at ATMs in Israel. If yours has five or more, remember to change it before you leave.

CREDIT CARDS

It's a good idea to inform your credit-card company before you travel, especially if you're going abroad and don't travel internationally often. Otherwise, the credit-card company might put a hold on your card owing to unusual activity. Keep all your credit-card numbers and phone numbers to call if your cards are lost or stolen in a safe place. Both MasterCard and Visa have general numbers you can call (collect if you're abroad) if your card is lost.

All hotels, restaurants, and shops accept major credit cards. Plastic is also accepted at banks for cash advances. Visa and MasterCard are widely accepted.

Most credit cards offer additional services, such as emergency assistance and insurance. Call and find out what additional coverage you have.

Reporting Lost Cards American Express. ☎ *800/992–3404 in U.S., 336/393–1111 collect from abroad* ⊕ *www.americanexpress. com.* **Diners Club.** ☎ *800/234–6377 in U.S., 514/877–1577 collect from abroad* ⊕ *www. dinersclub.com.* **MasterCard.** ☎ *800/627–8372 in U.S., 180/941–8873 in Israel* ⊕ *www.mastercard.com.* **Visa.** ☎ *800/847–2911 in U.S., 180/941–1605 in Israel* ⊕ *www.usa.visa.com.*

CURRENCY AND EXCHANGE

Israel's monetary unit is the new Israeli shekel, abbreviated NIS. There are 100 agorot to the shekel. The silver 1-shekel coin is the size and shape of an American dime, but thicker. Smaller-value bronze coins are the half-shekel (50 agorot) and the 10-agorot coin (both of which are larger than the shekel). There's also a 2-shekel round coin (silver), a 5-shekel coin with 12 edges (silver), and a similar-size 10-shekel coin (bronze center, silver rim). Paper bills come in 20-, 50-, 100-, and 200-shekel denominations.

Dollars are widely accepted at hotels and shops, less so at restaurants. As of this writing, the exchange rate is about 3.80 shekels to the U.S. dollar.

In Israel, the best rates are at ATMs or at the myriad of currency-exchange shops (typically marked "Change") in and around the central areas of the large cities. In Jerusalem, these are around Zion Square, the Ben Yehuda Street pedestrian mall, and a few strategic locations elsewhere in the city (Jerusalem Mall, German Colony neighborhood, Jewish Quarter).

▌PACKING

Israel is a very casual country, and comfort comes first. For touring in the hot summer months, wear cool, easy-care clothing and sensible shoes for walking. If coming between May and September, you don't need a coat, but you should bring a sun hat that completely shades your face and neck. Take one light sweater for cool nights, particularly in hilly areas (including in and around Jerusalem) and the desert. Also take long pants to protect your legs and a spare pair of walking shoes for adventure travel or hiking shoes for more serious hiking. A raincoat with a zip-out lining is ideal for October to April, when the weather can get cold enough for snow (and is as likely to be warm enough in the south for outdoor swimming). Rain boots may also be a useful accessory in winter. Pack a bathing suit for all seasons.

Note that many religious sites forbid shorts and sleeveless shirts for both sexes, so a light scarf comes in handy to throw over the shoulders. Women should bring modest dress for general touring in religious neighborhoods.

Along with a sun hat, take sunscreen, insect repellent, and sunglasses in summer. Essentials such as contact-lens solution and feminine hygiene supplies are available everywhere but are more costly than in North America.

▌ PASSPORTS AND VISAS

Israel issues three-month tourist visas free of charge at the point of entry when a valid passport is presented. Make sure your passport is valid for at least six months after your travel date or you won't be permitted entry. No health certificate or inoculations are required. Many Arab and Muslim countries in the Middle East, except Egypt and Jordan, have long refused to admit travelers whose passports carry any indication of having visited Israel. But that shouldn't be a problem now for tourists: Israel doesn't stamp passports anymore, only issues entry and exit permits on small slips of paper. Keep your entry permit paper in your passport during your visit.

Embassies U.S. Embassy. ⊠ *71 Hayarkon St., Tel Aviv* ☎ *03/519–7575* ⊕ *israel.usembassy. gov.*

▌ RESTROOMS

Public restrooms are plentiful in Israel and similar in facilities and cleanliness to those in the United States. At gas stations and some parks, toilet paper is sometimes in short supply, so you might want to carry some with you. Few public sinks, except those at hotels, have hot water, but most dispense liquid soap. Occasionally you may be asked to pay 1 shekel at some facilities.

▌ SAFETY

For the latest governmental travel advisories regarding travel to and within Israel, check with the U.S. State Department. The Israel Ministry of Tourism includes a section on its website with a nonalarmist perspective on visiting Israel during periods of unrest. For the latest local news, check the English-language papers *Haaretz,* the *Jerusalem Post,* or the *Times of Israel,* available online.

General Information and Warnings Israel Ministry of Tourism. ⊕ *www.goisrael.com.* **U.S. Department of State.** ⊕ *travel.state.gov/ content/passports/english/alertswarnings/ israel-travel-warning.html.*

Online News Haaretz. ⊕ *www.haaretz.com.* **Jerusalem Post.** ⊕ *www.jpost.com.* **Times of Israel.** ⊕ *timesofisrael.com.*

▌ TAXES

A value-added tax (V.A.T.) of 17% is charged on all purchases and transactions except tourists' hotel bills and car rentals paid in foreign currency (cash, traveler's checks, or foreign credit cards). Upon departure, you're entitled to a refund of tax on purchases made in foreign currency of more than NIS 400 (about US$100) on one invoice; but the refund isn't mandatory, and not all stores provide V.A.T. return forms. Stores so organized display "tax refund for tourists" stickers, or you can inquire. Make sure you fill out the tax refund form.

Keep your receipts and the tax refund form, and ask for a cash refund at Ben Gurion Airport. Change Place Ltd. has a special desk for this purpose in the departures hall in Terminal 3. You also need to present the items you purchased.

▌ TIME

Israel is two hours ahead of Greenwich Mean Time, or three hours ahead during Daylight Saving Time, known in Israel as Israel Daylight Time (IDT). Normally, New York and Montreal are seven hours behind Israeli local time; California is 10 behind. From late March until late October, Israel operates on Daylight Saving Time. When the Daylight Saving Times don't match, the time difference is reduced by one hour.

Time Zones timeanddate.com. ⊕ *www.timeanddate.com/worldclock.*

▊ TIPPING

There are no hard-and-fast rules for tipping in Israel. Locals do not tip taxi drivers. In other situations, a gratuity for good service is in order. If you've negotiated a price, assume the tip has been built in. If a restaurant bill doesn't include service, locals tend to tip 12% to 15%—round up if the service was particularly good, down if it was dismal. Hotel bellboys should be tipped a lump sum of NIS 10 to NIS 20, not per bag. Tipping is customary for tour guides, tour-bus drivers, and chauffeurs. Bus groups normally tip their guide NIS 30 to NIS 40 per person per day, and half that for the driver. Private guides normally get tipped NIS 100 to NIS 120 a day from the whole party. Both the person who washes your hair and the stylist expect a small tip—except if one of them owns the salon. Leave NIS 10 per day for your hotel's housekeeping staff, and the same for spa personnel.

TIPPING GUIDELINES FOR ISRAEL	
Bartender	10%–15% per round, depending on the number of drinks.
Bellhop	NIS 10–20, not per bag.
Hotel Concierge	NIS 20 or more, if he or she performs a special service for you.
Hotel Doorman	NIS 10 if he helps you get a cab, but not necessary.
Hotel Maid	NIS 10 per day.
Hotel Room-Service Waiter	If service isn't already added to the bill, tip 10%–15%.
Taxi Driver	No tip expected.
Tour Guide	NIS 30–NIS 40 per day.
Waiter	If service isn't already added to the bill, tip 12%–15%. Tips in cash only, or ask if you can include in bill if paying by credit card.
Other	No tip expected.

▊ TOURS

Although Israel is a very small country, its wealth of different terrains, climate zones, and historical periods can make it overwhelming to tackle on your own. Should you join an organized tour? That depends on whether this is your first visit to Israel, if you have friends or family in the country, and how much local color you want to take in.

If it's your first time in the Middle East and you're looking for a general overview of the main historic, religious, and natural sites, an escorted tour can be both efficient and cost effective. These trips are led by licensed tour guides and usually include visits to Jerusalem, Tel Aviv, Masada, and the Dead Sea. It's not difficult to find itineraries tailored to your religious affiliation or areas of interest.

If an organized trip isn't for you, a private tour with a licensed guide is another option. However, all tours aren't equal, so be sure to check out the itinerary to make sure it matches your pace and whether the accommodations and restaurants are up to snuff.

SIGHTSEEING GUIDES

Licensed tour guides must undergo a rigorous two-year training program with annual continuing education required to maintain their credentials. Licensed guides can put together a complete customized itinerary for your group or take you on a private multiday tour. Many are native English speakers and have fascinating backgrounds they're happy to share with you.

Freelance guides may approach unaccompanied travelers near the Jaffa Gate in the Old City of Jerusalem and other places on the beaten path. Some of these guides aren't licensed, so it's impossible to know whether the tour they're offering is worthwhile or if they're planning on taking you to their best friend's souvenir stall. It's best to ignore them and walk on.

Modern, air-conditioned limousines and minibuses driven by expert, licensed guides are a great way to see the country for anyone whose budget can bear it. At this writing, the cost was US$500 to US$600 per day; add another US$100 for bigger vans. An additional US$150 to US$200 per night is charged for the driver's expenses if he or she sleeps away from home. Half-day tours are also available, and you may hire a guide without a car.

Abboud Tours. Haifa-based Abboud Tours, run by Israeli Christian Abboud Maroun, specializes in private minibus tours of Jerusalem and the Dead Sea, Nazareth and the Galilee, and the fascinating walled city of Akko. ☎ *04/852–5077* ⊕ *www. abboudtours.com* ✉ *From $80 to $150 per person for day trip from Haifa to Jerusalem and the Dead Sea; price depends on size of group.*

Consolidated Tour Operation. This experienced tour agency was founded by Moshe Eshed, a former president of the International Association of Tour Managers. The company arranges everything from day trips to Nazareth and the Galilee to a few days in Petra. ✉ *Tel Aviv* ☎ *03/522–5253* ⊕ *www.highlightstoursofisrael.com* ✉ *From $71 to $89 dollars for a day tour of Jerusalem from Jerusalem or Tel Aviv.*

Superb Limousine Services. Getting around Israel can be daunting, so leave the driving to this experienced company. The company also arranges private tours for special interests such as archaeology or hiking, so prices vary widely. ☎ *03/973–1780* ⊕ *www.superb.co.il/eng/.*

GENERAL-INTEREST TOURS

Several major international tour companies run all-inclusive one-to-two-week trips geared to the general traveler. On a smaller scale, two Israeli-based companies—Egged Tours and United Tours—offer shorter excursions. Prices start at around US$50 for half-day tours, US$100 per person for one-day tours, and US$300 per person for two-day tours. These tours

are good options for solo travelers or people who don't want to be part of a tour for their entire trip.

Egged Tours. This well-regarded local company runs half- , one- , and two-day bus tours to many parts of Israel and the West Bank. There are also four-day tours that take you farther afield. ☎ *03/694–8888* ⊕ *www.eggedtours.com* ✉ *From $88 for day trip to Nazareth from Tel Aviv.*

Israel Discovery Tours. Perfect for first-time visitors to Israel, this company has tours that give you a general overview of the country. Tours last from 7 to 12 days and often include seldom-visited sights. ☎ *800/362–8882* ⊕ *israeldiscoverytours. com.*

United Tours. If you want to explore mostly on your own, United Tours has great half- and full-day tours that give you the lay of the land. Several trips cover just Jerusalem, while others take you to Masada and the Dead Sea or the Roman ruins at Caesarea. ☎ *03/617–3333* ⊕ *www.unit-edtours.co.il* ✉ *From $104 for a one-day trip including Caesarea, Haifa, Akko, and Rosh Hanikra.*

SPECIAL-INTEREST TOURS

ART

Israel My Way. Haifa-based Israel My Way has exciting six-day "Art Lover" tours that include curator-guided tours of the latest exhibits at the country's top museums, studio visits with local artists, and a dinner in a chef's private home. They also offer other private tours tailored to your interests, such as architecture, diving, Israeli lifestyle, and other themes. ☎ *77/300–5717* ⊕ *www.israelmyway.co.il.*

BIKING

Tourist Israel. For a few half-day bike tours (or a bike-and-hike combination) throughout Israel, try Tourist Israel. ☎ *058/713–5678 Israel phone* ⊕ *www. touristisrael.com* ✉ *From $55 for a half-day bike tour in Tel Aviv.*

BIRD-WATCHING

Carmel Birding Tours. The highly regarded Carmel Birding Tours is run by Dr. Carmel Zitronblat, an experienced birder whose single- and multiday tours for small groups include well-known birding destinations in the Beit She'an and Hula Valleys. ☎ *054/800–1212* ⊕ *www.carmelbirdingtours.com.*

Kibbutz Lotan Center for Birdwatching. The center arranges bird-watching tours for small groups during the winter and spring around Eilat and Lotan. ☎ *08/635–6888* ⊕ *www.kibbutzlotan.com.*

HIKING

Israel Extreme. This company can create custom hiking itineraries for you in the Galilee and Golan, the Judean Desert, or around Eilat. You can also book kayaking tours and biking excursions. ☎ *052/647–8474* ⊕ *www.israel-extreme.com.*

Israel National Trail. Try a segment or two of the nearly 1,000-km (620-mile) Israel National Trail if you want to experience the diversity of the landscape. Note that this is a trail; it's not a hiking tour. ☎ *03/638–8719* ⊕ *natureisrael.org/INT* ✉ *Trail is free.*

Jesus Trail. For hiking the Galilee, the 65-km (36-mile) Jesus Trail combines rugged scenery with historic and religious sites. You can do the trail on your own, and the creators of the trail also offer tour packages of different lengths. ⊕ *www.jesustrail.com.*

Society for the Protection of Nature in Israel. The Society for the Protection of Nature in Israel runs "field schools" across the country and conducts city walks and nature hikes with commentary in Hebrew. ☎ *03/638–8683* ⊕ *www.natureisrael.org.*

JEWISH EDUCATIONAL TOURS

Da'at Educational Expeditions. Providing in-depth explorations of the country and its history, Da'at Educational Expeditions is staffed by an experienced team of Jewish educators and guides. Another option is a tour with a private guide. The company offers Jewish-themed trips around the world. ☎ *888/811–2812* ⊕ *www.daattravel.com.*

Keshet. Offering customized guided tours, Keshet focuses on Judaism and Jewish history. ☎ *646/843–6221* ⊕ *www.keshetisrael.co.il.*

▌TRIP INSURANCE

Comprehensive trip insurance is valuable if booking a very expensive or complicated trip (particularly to an isolated region) or booking far in advance. Comprehensive policies typically cover trip cancellation and interruption, letting you cancel or cut your trip short because of illness, or, in some cases, acts of terrorism. Such policies cover evacuation and medical care. Some also cover you for trip delays because of bad weather or mechanical problems as well as for lost or delayed luggage.

Another type of coverage to consider is financial default—that is, when your trip is disrupted because a tour operator, airline, or cruise line goes out of business. Generally you must buy this when you book your trip or shortly thereafter, and it's available to you only if your operator isn't on a list of excluded companies.

Always read the fine print of your policy to make sure you're covered for the risks that most concern you. Compare several policies to be sure you're getting the best price and range of coverage available.

Comprehensive Insurers AIG Travel Guard. ☎ *800/826–4919* ⊕ *www.travelguard.com.* **Allianz Global Assistance.** ☎ *866/884–3556* ⊕ *www.allianztravelinsurance.com.* **CSA Travel Protection.** ☎ *877/243–4135* ⊕ *www.csatravelprotection.com.* **Travel Insured International.** ☎ *800/243–3174* ⊕ *www.travelinsured.com.* **Travelex Insurance.** ☎ *888/228–9792* ⊕ *www.travelexinsurance.com.*

Insurance Comparison Information Insure My Trip. ☎ *800/487–4722* ⊕ *www.insuremytrip.com.* **Square Mouth.** ☎ *800/240–0369* ⊕ *www.squaremouth.com.*

▮ VISITOR INFORMATION

The Israel Ministry of Tourism has an information-packed website.

Contacts Israel Government Tourist Office. ☎ *888/774–7723 in U.S.* ⊕ *www.goisrael.com.*

ONLINE TRAVEL TOOLS

The Israel Nature and Parks Authority has extensive information on its website about the country's outdoor attractions as well as the historical and archaeological sites it oversees. It also sells discounted admission cards.

Contacts Israel Nature and Parks Authority. ⊕ *www.parks.org.il.*

INDEX

NOTES

NOTES

NOTES

NOTES

NOTES

ABOUT OUR WRITERS

Inbal Baum, who updated the Tel Aviv and Upper Galilee chapters, founded Delicious Israel, a culinary tour company that reveals local and insider aspects of Israel. Passionate about lifestyle and culture, Inbal left her career as an attorney and immigrated to Israel in 2009. Based in Tel Aviv, she spends her free time as an amateur chef and yoga instructor. Contact Inbal at www.deliciousisrael.com and inbal@deliciousisrael.com.

Shari Giddens Helmer is a Tel Aviv–based writer and Israel enthusiast. A native Chicagoan, she has made Israel her home for more than a decade. Shari updated the Haifa and the Northern Coast, Lower Galilee, Eilat and the Negev, Travel Smart, and Experience Israel chapters. Contact her at shari.helmer@gmail.com.

Mike Rogoff, a professional tour guide and writer, has been exploring the byways of Israel with visitors of all persuasions since the early 1970s. South African–born and Jerusalem-based, Mike is a recipient of the Israel government's Guide of the Year award, and has contributed to Fodor's Israel since 1985. He updated the Jerusalem Exploring section. Contact Mike at rogoff@netvision.net.il.

Shira Rubin, a Tel Aviv–based journalist, is a lover of travel and living abroad. She has called Israel home since 2006. Shira updated the Jerusalem chapter (except Exploring) as well as the Around Jerusalem and the Dead Sea chapter. Contact her at shirarrubin@gmail.com.